THE NATIONAL INSTITUTE OF ECONOMIC AND
SOCIAL RESEARCH

Economic and Social Studies
XXII

THE MANAGEMENT OF THE

BRITISH ECONOMY

1945-60

THE NATIONAL INSTITUTE OF ECONOMIC AND SOCIAL RESEARCH

OFFICERS OF THE INSTITUTE

PRESIDENT

THE RT. HON. LORD FRANKS, G.C.M.G., K.C.B., K.B.E., F.B.A.

COUNCIL OF MANAGEMENT

SIR ROBERT HALL* (CHAIRMAN)

DIRECTOR
G. D. N. WORSWICK

EXECUTIVE SECRETARY
MRS A. K. JACKSON

2 DEAN TRENCH STREET, SMITH SQUARE
LONDON, S.W.1

The National Institute of Economic and Social Research is an independent, non-profit-making body, founded in 1938. It has as its aim the promotion of realistic research, particularly in the field of economics. It conducts research by its own research staff and in co-operation with the universities and other academic bodies. The results of the work done under the Institute's auspices are published in several series, and a list of its publications up to the present time will be found at the end of this volume.

THE

MANAGEMENT OF THE

BRITISH ECONOMY

1945-60

BY
J. C. R. DOW

WITH A FOREWORD BY
SIR ROBERT HALL

CAMBRIDGE
AT THE UNIVERSITY PRESS
1965

PUBLISHED BY

THE SYNDICS OF THE CAMBRIDGE UNIVERSITY PRESS

Bentley House, 200 Euston Road, London, N.W.1
American Branch: 32 East 57th Street, New York 22, N.Y.

©

First published 1964
Reprinted 1965

Printed in Great Britain by Metcalfe and Cooper Ltd., London, E.C.2

CONTENTS

PART III

THE GENERAL BEHAVIOUR
OF THE ECONOMY

PART IV

CONCLUSIONS

  * *The argument in these chapters is of a more technical or theoretical nature
than in other chapters. Readers more interested in the conclusions than the
reasoning are referred to the final section of each of these chapters.*

LIST OF TABLES

LIST OF FIGURES

NOTE ON REFERENCES AND ABBREVIATIONS

Articles and books are referred to by title once only in each chapter, any subsequent reference being by author and year. Full references are given in the bibliography at the end.

The abbreviations used for economic and statistical journals follow the UNESCO *World List of Social Science Periodicals*.

Account. Res.	Accounting Research
Amer. econ. R.	American Economic Review
Banca naz. Lav. R.	Banca Nazionale del Lavoro Quarterly Review
Bank England quart. B.	Bank of England Quarterly Bulletin
Banker	Banker (The)
Bankers' Mag.	Bankers' Magazine (The)
B. Banque nat. Belgique	Bulletin d'Information et de Documentation de la Banque Nationale de Belgique
B. Oxford Inst. Statist.	Bulletin of the Oxford University Institute of Statistics
Econometrica	
Econ. int.	Economia internazionale
Econ. J.	Economic Journal (The)
Econ. Rec.	Economic Record (The)
Economica	
Ekon. Ts.	Ekonomisk Tidskrift
Harvard Business R.	Harvard Business Review
Int. Aff.	International Affairs
Int. econ. Pap.	International Economic Papers
J. industr. Econ.	Journal of Industrial Economics
J. polit. Econ.	Journal of Political Economy (The)
J. roy. statist. Soc.	Journal of the Royal Statistical Society
Lloyds Bank R.	Lloyds Bank Review
London Cambridge econ. B.	London and Cambridge Economic Bulletin
Manchester Sch.	Manchester School of Economic and Social Studies (The)
Nat.-økon. Tss.	Nationaløkonomisk Tidsskrift
Nat. Inst. econ. R.	National Institute Economic Review
Oxford econ. Pap.	Oxford Economic Papers
Productivity Meas. R.	Productivity Measurement Review
Pub. Finance	Public Finance
Quart. J. Econ.	Quarterly Journal of Economics
R. econ. Stud.	Review of Economic Studies (The)
R. Econ. Statist.	Review of Economics and Statistics (The)
Scott. J. polit. Econ.	Scottish Journal of Political Economy
Westminster Bank R.	Westminster Bank Review
Yorkshire B.	Yorkshire Bulletin of Economic and Social Research

References to parliamentary debates are by date and column number in the official report: thus for the House of Commons, *H.C. Deb.*, 12 April 1945, 1234 (or for House of Lords, *H.L. Deb.*).

The *Report of the Committee on the Working of the Monetary System* (Cmnd. 827) is referred to as the *Radcliffe Report*; its Minutes of Evidence as *Radcliffe, Minutes*, **Q** 1234 (indicating the number of the question and answer); and its Memoranda of Evidence as

Radcliffe, Memoranda, X. 12 (indicating Part of the memoranda and its number). The *Report of the Tribunal appointed to inquire into Allegations of Improper Disclosure of Information relating to the Raising of the Bank Rate* (Cmnd. 350) is referred to as the *Bank Rate Tribunal Report;* and its Proceedings as *Bank Rate Tribunal, Evidence,* (Q 1234 indicating the number of question and answer).

The following abbreviations are used for international and other organizations:

ECE	United Nations Economic Commission for Europe
EPU	European Payments Union
IARIW	International Association for Research in Income and Wealth
IMF	International Monetary Fund
NATO	North Atlantic Treaty Organization
NEDC	National Economic Development Council
NIESR	National Institute of Economic and Social Research (London)
NBER	National Bureau of Economic Research (New York)
OEEC	Organisation for European Economic Co-operation, and OECD its successor, the Organisation for Economic Co-operation and Development
UNESCO	United Nations Educational, Scientific and Cultural Organization

Official statistical sources are denoted as:

AAS [1945]	Annual Abstract of Statistics (year)
BPWP [April 1945]	White Paper, United Kingdom Balance of Payments (half-year)
UKBP [1959]	United Kingdom Balance of Payments, 1946–1957 (1959)
NI & E [1955]	'Blue Book', National Income and Expenditure (year)
NIWP [1945]	White Paper, National Income and Expenditure, or Preliminary Estimates of National Income and Expenditure (year)
MDS	Monthly Digest of Statistics
Econ. Trends	Economic Trends
Fin. Statist.	Financial Statistics
M. of L. Gaz.	Ministry of Labour Gazette
Statist. Inc. & Prices	Statistics on Incomes, Prices, Employment and Production
OEEC (OECD) Gen. Statist.	OEEC (OECD) Statistical Bulletin: General Statistics
UN Statist. Bull.	United Nations Monthly Bulletin of Statistics

SYMBOLS USED IN THE TABLES

..   not available

—   nil or less than half the unit stated

FOREWORD

Mr Dow's book on *The Management of the British Economy 1945-60* is a distinguished contribution to a subject of great practical importance. Nowadays it is almost completely taken for granted in Britain, as in many other countries and in international discussions, that governments of countries which rely mainly on market forces for the guidance of their economies, should nevertheless be responsible for the levels of activity and employment. So much is this so, that we tend to forget how very recent, from a historical point of view, is this state of affairs. Yet before 1951, it was a matter of constant concern to the Labour Government whether they could maintain full employment at all: and it was not generally recognized for several years after the Conservative Government came to power, that they would and could follow their predecessors in this respect.

Although the general form of the techniques that would have to be employed had been understood by most economists in the period which followed the appearance of Keynes's *Treatise on Money*, the practical application of them— the 'know-how' as the Americans say—was completely uncharted. The broad rule—to stimulate demand when it is deficient and to restrain it when excessive—is simple enough. But the actual performance will be good or bad according to the skill with which adjustments are timed and according to the strength and direction of the forces employed. The timing requires a complex statistical apparatus and the ability to interpret it, while the correct application of economic force requires both an understanding of the system and a good deal of empirical work. In 1945 very little was known about any of this. As Mr Dow says, we know more about the behaviour of the economy than we did a decade ago, though as he himself makes very clear, we have still much to learn.

In the event, full employment turned out to be much more easy to achieve than most people had expected—and the achievement has transformed the social existence of the countries who have attained it. This was not so much because of increased knowledge about the exact way in which the economy behaved, as because it was generally evident at least that movement should be one way or the other, so that stimuli or checks could be applied until it could be seen that they had worked. It was, however, at all times difficult to know how much to attribute to this or that force, partly because of differing views among economists, and partly because all measures in the economic field damage or benefit someone and hence all have a political aspect. Governments had to do what they thought to be practicable, and it was usually impossible (as is clear from the Treasury evidence to the Radcliffe Committee) to distinguish the constituents of what was always a 'package deal'. This is one of the reasons for which there is still so much controversy about the nature of monetary measures.

Meantime, it became increasingly evident that full employment brought with it difficulties connected with the price level and the balance of payments. A good deal was known about the characteristics of open inflation, but very little about the border regions between this condition and that of high employment, and practically nothing about how the associated difficulties could be avoided or at any rate mitigated.

As Mr Dow makes clear throughout his book, much still remains to be done—the reader who is 'hot for certainty' will find some of the answers rather dusty. But he himself has done a good deal of pioneering work, and it is his hope that this book will encourage others to continue the investigations; the National Institute of Economic and Social Research intends to do so.

R. L. HALL

August 1963

PREFACE

It is often said—by economists—that economic history should be written by economists not historians. Having finished this book, it seems to me a miracle that history gets written at all. The object, I take it, is to learn from the past; for the full effects of their actions are generally obscure to the chief actors. But the answer on any important issue does not become clearer with the mere passage of time, and remains to some extent a matter of opinion. Hence it requires to be argued out; and it seems useless to embalm the puzzles of time in a smooth, uninterrupted narrative. The present book, though about history, may appear more an essay in applied economics, with digressions into economic theory.

I was a member of the Economic Section of the Cabinet Office and latterly the Treasury from 1946 to 1954. Experience of working on policy matters led me, in common with other colleagues, to believe that many questions underlying modern fiscal and monetary policy had been inadequately studied, and that economics was not as good a guide to policy as it should be. In 1954 I was awarded a Fellowship for two years by the Leverhulme Trustees, under their Leverhulme Research Awards, to make a study of the behaviour of the British economy and the impact on it of post-war policy. It is only now, eight years later, that something like that study has been completed.

Two sorts of difficulty, which should no doubt have been obvious from the beginning, seemed to prevent my getting down to this task straightaway. First, the subject is very large: to specify the effects of policy in a particular period one needs not merely an account of particular acts of policy, but a general knowledge of how different sectors of the economy respond to outside stimuli and to changes in other sectors. Second, it is not only economists who have opinions on such matters. To be useful as a guide to policy, a study of such matters has to carry weight with the general body of informed opinion.

On two basic, underlying questions, opinion has been deeply divided: namely, on the question of why prices rise, and whether or not the sole cause is a high level of demand; and on the role of monetary factors. It seemed to me therefore that progress had to be made indirectly, by spending time first on the study of these underlying matters. In the interval since 1954 these two basic questions have been studied by many others also; and the *Report of the Committee* (presided over by Lord Radcliffe) *on the Working of the Monetary System* has been written, published and discussed. It is therefore a much better time now than earlier to attempt to formulate a view. Work on the present book has taken the best part of 1958–62.

This study has throughout been undertaken at the National Institute of Economic and Social Research; and the conditions and circumstances could in no way have been more favourable.   In 1954, the Institute initiated a general programme of research into the post-war experience of the United Kingdom; and, particularly with the institution of its *Economic Review* in 1959, its work has been increasingly concentrated in this field.   The present study was originally conceived as a first survey, mapping out the field of study, which would be followed by more intensive studies of particular aspects.   In the event, the order has been the reverse: various detailed studies have been completed before mine, which I have been able to draw on.   More generally, since the work of the Institute is closely related, I have benefited much from the advice and assistance of various members of the staff.

Economics is increasingly specialized, so that it is impossible to go far without nearing the frontiers of one's competence.   But there is need from time to time for studies that try to cover the whole of a wide field, and relate the parts to the whole.   On the practical conclusions, I can claim only to have presented a reasoned case, not to have settled issues.   From the beginning of this programme of research, it was recognized 'that at the end of the study there will remain many points in the argument where a view has been taken on the basis of impressions.   In the present state of information and analytical technique this has to be accepted, and does not necessarily make it useless to attempt as good an assessment of past experience as we can'[1].   Any work inevitably remains to some extent personal.   I know, for instance, that some of my colleagues at the Institute, with whom I often agree, take somewhat different views on some matters discussed.

Though I served in the civil service up to 1954 and thus saw some events, as it were, from the inside, this book has been written entirely from published sources.   Access to confidential papers might at times have saved labour, but would not have greatly facilitated work on this study.   For its centre of interest is the economic consequences, necessarily public, of public policy.   It does not aim—as did, for instance, Professor Sayers's volume in the Official War Histories, *Financial Policy, 1939–45*—at describing the evolution of policy and events as seen by the Treasury.   It was completed before my return to the Treasury in October 1962.

Foremost among my acknowledgements I must express my gratitude to the Executive Committee of the National Institute, and Mr W. A. B. Hopkin and Mr C. T. Saunders who were successively its Director, for continuing to believe that time spent would eventually be justified by results, and for encouraging me, though Deputy Director, to devote the greater part of my time to this study. As already explained, I was awarded a Research Fellowship by the Leverhulme Trustees for the first two years of study that led to this book.   Its remaining

---

[1]   NIESR *Annual Report, 1954*, p. 13.

expense was met out of grants by the Rockefeller Foundation to the National Institute in support of its research programme. Some of the material (as noted in the text where relevant) has previously been published, but appears in this book in considerably revised form.

Many people were good enough to act as critics to the whole or parts of this study, and I have learnt much from their comments. Professor R. S. Sayers, Professor E. Lundberg of Stockholm University, and Mr C. T. Saunders read the whole in draft; and at a later stage Sir Robert Hall. Others who read parts were Mr D. H. Aldcroft (chapter VI); Mr W. Beckerman (XV and XVI); Mr L. A. Dicks-Mireaux (XI); Mr R. R. Neild (XV and XVI); Professor A. Peacock (VIII); Mr C. R. Ross (XII); Mr D. A. Rowe (XI); Professor B. Tew (II, III, IX and XII); and Mr R. Turvey (XII).

Mr David Friedman acted during the last two and a half years as my part-time assistant, and has prepared under my direction most of the tables and the data for the charts. Without his tireless help the work would hardly have been possible: chapter VI, in particular, embodies so much of his work that, had it been published as a separate article on the extent of post-war controls, he would properly have figured as joint author. For their great care and patience I must thank my secretary, Miss Dorothy Tharp, who typed most of the text; her two predecessors, Miss Ruth Clarke (now Mrs J. Rummins) and Mrs Maureen Potter; Mrs G. Ray, who drew the charts; and Miss Jane Harington, who saw the book through the press.

From one light, this book is a study of the interrelation between theory and practice: modern economic policy is based on Keynesian theory; and study of practice should in turn suggest improvements to theory. I hope it will interest various sorts of reader. But—since the twentieth-century economy cannot be run well without good economists—I would like to dedicate this book primarily to the next generation of economists, in the hope that they do better than we.

J.C.R.D.

NATIONAL INSTITUTE OF ECONOMIC
  AND SOCIAL RESEARCH

September 1962

CHAPTER I

INTRODUCTION:

THE 'MANAGEMENT' OF THE ECONOMY

The concern of the government with the management of the economy dates from its formal acceptance, in 1944, of responsibility for maintaining a 'high and stable' level of employment[1]—which led to it being responsible for much more; or, before that, from Kingsley Wood's 'stabilization' budget of 1941— which was a fairly direct application of the Keynesian remedy for wartime inflation[2]. Since then, one of the main aims of economic policy has been to maintain a high, but avoid an excessive, level of demand. Since the level of demand affects not only the level of employment, but also the course of prices and the balance of payments, and possibly also the rate of economic growth, the government has become involved in the general 'management' of the economy.

It is this post-war attempt to manage the economy which is the subject of this book. The chief instruments used by the government have been fiscal policy, which in practice has meant the adjustment of tax rates; and monetary policy. Changes in tax rates directly impinge chiefly on consumers' demand. Changes in hire-purchase regulations have clearly affected consumers' demand for durables. What other effects monetary policy has is debateable, and will require to be discussed at length; but whatever they are, the effects must be achieved, like those of fiscal policy, through their effect on the level of demand. The level of demand, in turn, affects prices, the balance of payments, and possibly the pace of growth. Thus the power of fiscal and monetary policy to affect these things is indirect, not direct.

Total demand has been significantly affected also by changes in public invest-ment and in government current expenditure. But these have chiefly been determined by prevailing political views as to the need for such expenditures: neither can in practice be rapidly varied much merely for the sake of their effect on the rest of the economy. For many years after the war, direct controls were retained over a host of commodities which continued in short supply. The impact of each control was local and particular. But taken together they had also, while they remained extensive, an effect on total demand, as they had had during the war itself. Direct controls must therefore be included too,

---

[1]'The Government accept as one of their primary aims and responsibilities the main-tenance of a high and stable level of employment after the war': the first sentence of the 1944 White Paper on *Employment Policy* (Cmd. 6527).

[2]See R. S. Sayers [1956], *Financial Policy, 1939–45*, chapter III; and also chapter VII.1 below.

though such use is probably exceptional, as ways of dealing with very high demand.

None of the terms usually used to describe this area of economic policy are quite satisfactory. It originated as an attempt to eliminate the pre-war trade cycle. 'Trade-cycle policy' therefore exactly conveys the type of policy, but not the problem with which it is now faced—for, largely as a result of policy, we are no longer faced with a trade cycle of the pre-war type. 'Stabilization policy' is a better term—and one which will be used in this book. But it gives a negative impression, and does not convey that what has to be maintained is the stability of a growing economy. Both the main instruments of policy (i.e. changes in tax rates or credit regulations) and the things policy is intended to affect (i.e. employment, output, prices and the balance of payments) can be expressed in quantitative terms. What Professor Tinbergen means by 'quantitative economic policy' happens, therefore, to cover the same field[1]. But while this may be a good definition, it is not a good description of the policies involved. The policies in question are concerned essentially with large-scale effects on the main economic magnitudes: employment, the general price level, and the aggregates which figure in national income accounts. The term 'macro-economic policy', or 'macro-economic control', is therefore, perhaps, as good a description as there is. But no one likes such neologisms; and vaguer terms, like 'the management of the economy' or 'the control of the economy', will here be used to mean the same thing.

Three further points only need be made by way of definition. First, it should perhaps be said once that the kind of economic management here discussed, which operates largely by affecting the total level of demand, and thus the general climate in which business operates, is different from full-scale economic planning of a socialist character, that is when government organs make the major decisions about the price and volume of industrial output.

The kind of economic management here discussed must leave a place for some types of policy which, though potentially important, happen to have been of subordinate importance in the first fifteen years after the war—the period formally covered by this study. A change in exchange rates can affect the whole problem. But the external value of sterling was changed only once; and so does not require to be discussed continuously[2]. During this period, the management of the economy has depended chiefly on fiscal and credit policy. Since 1960 there have been new developments in wages policy; and also in economic planning—in the more recent sense of a voluntary co-ordination of the long-term expansion plans of public enterprises and private firms. It will be one of the conclusions of this study that policies of this sort can greatly help in 'managing' economic development.

[1] J. Tinbergen ([1956], *Economic Policy: Principles and Design*, chapter I.
[2] See Chapter II.2 and, for the general issue, chapter XVI.2.

. Finally (as hardly needs saying), the short-term management of the economy is not the whole of economic policy. This study, for instance, does not consider agricultural policy, nor policy relating to the distribution of industry. Nor does it consider many other important areas of policy: for instance, tariff changes, international payments arrangements, legislation against restrictive practices, or the improvement of education. Though these sorts of policy have not quick precise results, but long-term and general effects, they are mostly intended in one way or another to foster economic development. They may therefore become more closely associated with stabilization policy in future than in the past, as emphasis on economic growth increases.

The issues to be discussed require a more discursive treatment than might be expected in a historical work; and it may be as well to say why, since this will explain the arrangements of the parts of the book. The problem with which the government is faced in trying to control the behaviour of the economy is in some ways like that of operating a control which governs the behaviour of a machine. How the control should be operated depends on the kind of fluctuations to which the machine's behaviour is subject, and on how it responds to the control. To say how post-war government policy has affected the economy requires, then, not merely a description of government measures, but also some account of how the economy behaves—how it responds to outside stimuli, and how the behaviour of different sectors of the economy is interrelated.

This book is therefore as much concerned with the behaviour of the economy as with government policy. Many questions relating to the behaviour of the economy are at present the subject of dispute. These include very broad questions—such as the causes making for rising prices or how monetary trends affect the economy—which are widely disputed, not only among economists, but among a larger public also. There are also other less basic, but still important, questions on which a firm view is as yet impossible—how hire-purchase controls affect spending; whether the income-tax depreciation allowances affect investment; or how stock fluctuations may be expected to proceed.

Remaining uncertainties notwithstanding, we know more about the behaviour of the economy than a decade ago. It therefore seems worthwhile attempting a statement of present knowledge. It is both the difficulty, and the justification, of such an attempt that it involves reference to a wide range of theoretical economic discussion and empirical research. To get anywhere at all, it is necessary to stick to the broad questions. At the present stage of the debate it hardly seems possible to do more than give reasons for selecting certain lines of causal interconnections as the main ones of importance; and to indicate, where possible, the probable magnitude of the responses[1]. This however suffices for drawing broad conclusions about the impact of policy.

[1]Those who believe in macro-economic models will find this disappointing. The evidence of econometric studies seems to me valuable (as will be clear from later chapters).

These considerations have determined the general structure of the book. Part I gives a chronological narrative of the main events with which successive Chancellors of the Exchequer were confronted, and describes in rapid summary the setting in which the fiscal and monetary policies of the post-war years evolved. Part II then analyses different aspects of policy in detail—the most important chapters being those dealing with fiscal policy (VII) and monetary policy (IX). Other chapters deal with the results and effects of official forecasting (V); the effects of direct controls (VI); and the use, limited as it was, of variations in public investment as a means to stabilize the economy (VIII). Part III then turns to discuss general questions about the behaviour of the economy. One chapter (XI) gives a summary of recent research regarding the factors influencing different categories of demand. A second (XII) attempts to deal with a wide range of theoretical questions underlying monetary policy. A third chapter (XIII), partly theoretical, partly empirical, discusses inflation and the factors causing prices to rise. Those more interested in the conclusions themselves than the reasons for them could omit much of part III without losing the thread of the argument[1].

The results are applied in part IV, which tries to assess the impact of post-war policy on the economy. Though a high level of employment has been maintained throughout the post-war years, the economy has not been immune from fluctuations: there have been phases when demand and output grew rapidly followed by phases of little or no growth of demand. Chapter XV is chiefly concerned with analysing the role which policy played in the genesis and correction of such fluctuations. Even if policy had been more successful in avoiding such fluctuations, the performance of the economy would however probably still have left a good deal to be desired: in particular, a stable growth of demand might by itself have done little to promote a more rapid growth of productive capacity. It is suggested in chapter XVI that the promotion of more rapid growth requires something more than the fiscal and monetary measures which have been chiefly used hitherto to manage the economy—and with which this study is therefore chiefly concerned. If a more rapid growth of capacity could be achieved, it is also argued, this would greatly ease the problem of managing the economy.

Looking back on events, it is only too easy, even for those closely involved at the time, to forget what things were like. A schematic and analytical treatment of history, such as outlined above, does not bring back the reality to mind.

But before they can be called in evidence, there seem to me prior questions to be discussed. To explain a complex reality, complex hypotheses have to be used; and considerable theoretical discussion is needed merely to justify such constructions and be clear as to the implications of alternative hypotheses. Until the *form* of an equation has been properly considered, it is premature to estimate the parameters. See further chapter X below.

[1]For the convenience chiefly of such readers, I have indicated with an asterisk (*) those chapters (chapters XI to XIII) where the argument is of a more technical or theoretical nature than in other chapters: conclusions are summarized in the final section of each.

'These departures from chronological order'—says Professor Sayers, in the preface to his account of wartime financial policy[1]—'essential for ease of exposition, cause the reader to lose sight of one very important fact: that all the problems discussed in this book were being handled by very much the same small handful of men all the time. The Chancellor's immediate advisers, especially those within the Treasury itself, would be dealing in any week with budget policy, lend-lease, financial relations with India and the Dominions, foreign exchange control, and a host of other questions'. The same applies, *mutatis mutandis*, to the post-war years.

The main object of part I is to give an impression of this interconnectedness, and of the pressure and unexpectedness of events. In order to do so, it is necessary not to write too much with the benefit of later wisdom. Analysis of cause and effect is therefore restricted to the more obvious interconnections, such as might have been surmised by a well-informed observer at the time, or one looking back on events when the facts first became available. Later chapters analyse the historical experience more rigorously and abstractly, and carry the analysis of cause and effect to a deeper level. At times this calls for modification or amplification of the judgements implied in the historical narrative of part I.

[1]R. S. Sayers [1956], *op. cit.*, p. xiv.

PART I

HISTORICAL NARRATIVE

CHAPTER II

THE LABOUR CHANCELLORS, 1945–51

This chapter covers the first six post-war years, the period of Labour government: the next chapter, the succeeding eight years of Conservative government. The emphasis is not intended to be political. This study is concerned not with social policy, which by its nature is political, but with economic policy; and with that, only in so far as it relates to the general financial 'management' of the economy. Such policy has been determined more by the facts of the case than by political philosophies. Given the large measure of agreement about its aims, in particular about the importance of full employment, the facts of the post-war economic situation left little space for manoeuvre. The struggle to face the facts nevertheless put different strains on the two parties, according to their respective starting points.

The Labour Government of 1945 took over an economy mobilized for war; and its problems were at first an extrapolation of the problem of war. Whichever party had formed the government, its attitude to economic policy would have been largely determined by the thinking about the problems of the post-war transition which had gone on inside the government during the war years of coalition. Neither party therefore questioned that extensive controls would have to be continued for several years after the war. The Labour Party's attitude was also coloured by its disposition towards *dirigisme*; and controls, though not originally instituted for this purpose, tended to be regarded as instruments for a new departure in economic planning. Both strands of thought (as argued in §1) affected the attitude towards budgetary and monetary policy.

The following narrative deals with budgetary and monetary policy along with many other matters; and at this stage of the argument, judgements expressed are inevitably brief. Some questions will be discussed at much greater length later on. The narrative is conveniently divided according to successive Chancellors' tenure of the Exchequer. This is convenient not so much because policy was personal, as because the succession of a new Chancellor usually marked a reorientation of policy to a new stage in the country's economic evolution. Dr Dalton was Chancellor of the Exchequer for the two and a half years up to the end of 1947. Policy in these years was dominated by the ideas of demobilization and reconversion; inflationary pressure tended to be dismissed as temporary, inevitable and tolerable (§2). Sir Stafford Cripps's three years at the Exchequer, up to the end of 1950, were remarkable equally for his attempt to implement redeployment by government precept, and for his long-drawn attempt at disinflation: budgetary (though not monetary) policy had therefore a positive role (§3).   Mr Gaitskell was Chancellor of the Exchequer for the further year up to the general election of October 1951.   His budget in April of that year attempted to deal with the complex repercussions of the Korean war— among them the major increase in British defence expenditure (§4).

1. THE CLIMATE OF ECONOMIC AND SOCIALIST IDEAS IN 1945

During the latter years of the war, the government was consuming three fifths of the national product, while taxation took over a third of the national income; and in addition to this massive financial intervention, the flow of most goods and services was governed at all important stages by direct controls.   A third of consumers' expenditure was subject to rationing; and all imports and most building were subject to licence.   Controls over materials and labour governed what could be produced.   Economic policy in the first post-war years continued the wartime system of controlling the economy[1].

In war, financial considerations take second place.   Financial policy, and in particular budgetary policy, nevertheless had played an important role—a role which by virtue of Keynes's influence had been unprecedentedly explicit. Keynes had set out his ideas on how to pay for the war in 1939[2].   The huge rise in government spending, he argued, would create more demand than the economy could meet, unless private spending were to be sufficiently curtailed by taxation; if it were not so curtailed, the gap would be closed by inflation.

In Mr Kingsley Wood's 'stabilization' budget of 1941, this doctrine was adopted as official orthodoxy.   From then on, government financial arrangements ceased to be framed with an eye merely to the government's financial needs, and aimed at securing a balance of total demand.   This change (as Professor Sayers[3] remarks) 'incidentally implied the transformation of the budget speech into a comprehensive survey of the national economy'—a tradition which endured.

But whatever may have been the theoretical ideal, financial policy was not in practice called on to do the whole job of controlling demand.   The system of consumer rationing, price controls and material allocations had grown up piecemeal, to meet particular shortages.   When fully developed however, it must have been sufficiently extensive to be an effective brake on total demand. From the economic discussions of the war years, it is clear that considerable

[1]See chapter VI below.

[2]Keynes's three articles in *The Times* in November 1939 were revised and reprinted as *How to Pay for the War* [1940].   This is the chief source of the theory underlying post-war budgetary practice: see chapter VII.1.

[3]R. S. Sayers [1956], *Financial Policy, 1939–45*, p. 59.   For a fuller description of wartime financial policy, see his chapters III and V.

reliance was placed on direct controls to hold back demand; and that budgetary policy was devised after making allowance for this effect[1]. Such implicit reliance on controls probably increased as the war went on.   Once this effect is accepted, it is clearly difficult to know how much it can be properly counted on to do; and early post-war discussion seemed indeed, at times, to assume that since controls were there, no budgetary measures were necessary.

Two other features of wartime practice were also important as precedents. First, monetary policy had practically no *economic* role during the war.   Monetary policy was dominated by the government's desire to borrow as cheaply as possible.   The effect of low interest rates on investment demand may still be doubtful; but during the war it was certainly quite unimportant, for controls and scarcities compelled the virtual cessation of most forms of fixed investment. This practice of ignoring the economic effect of monetary policy was however carried on unquestioned into the discussions of the first post-war years.

Second, notwithstanding the intellectual emphasis on demand inflation, practical justice was done to the importance of cost inflation[2].   To prevent a wage-price spiral, cost of living subsidies were formally introduced in 1941,

---

[1]The calculations in *How to Pay for the War* aimed at eliminating the inflationary gap. By 1941, personal savings had grown considerably, *partly because direct controls prevented spending*.   The official calculations of the inflationary gap (as described by Sayers, pp. 70–2) assumed that savings would increase, thus implicitly taking credit for the effect of controls. The 1941 budget speech, indeed, explicitly counted on new limitations on the supply of consumer goods to increase savings (*H. C. Deb.* 7 April 1941, 1326).   The speech included also a more general acknowledgement of this reliance on direct controls:

'The huge sums which the Government is expending at home on the conduct of the war have generated a corresponding amount of purchasing power in the hands of the public to which we cannot be indifferent.   If it were all to be used to purchase whatever goods are obtainable in the shops, it would overcome and sweep away all the obstacles set up and the precautions taken against a rise in prices, just as a torrent will sweep away a dam if it develops sufficient force . . .   To avert that menace, it is vital for us to possess a stout and well-constructed dam.   That is the object of our system of food and industrial controls, of our systems of price control, rationing and the like.   But we also have to abate the force of the torrent.   That is the function of finance.'   (*H. C. Deb.* 7 April 1941, 1302.)

[2]The Chancellor in 1941, after discussing the size of the inflationary gap, went on:

' . . . there is another very important matter . . . relevant to any consideration of the question of inflation.   The higher cost of imports and other increased costs unavoidable in time of war exercised a strong tendency from the very outset of the war to raise the prices of essential foodstuffs quite apart from any effect of higher wages.   For some time past it has been our policy to check any excessive rise in prices due to such higher costs by means of the centralised purchasing of imported foodstuffs through the Ministry of Food and the control of the margins of selling prices of distributors, but after a time it became apparent that these measures by themselves would not be sufficient to prevent food prices from rising . . .   It was, therefore, decided to allow the Ministry of Food to incur substantial trading losses which we have carried upon the Exchequer . . . a considerable and increasing burden, now ranging at about £100,000,000 a year . . .   There is this prospect of a continuing further rise in the cost of living unless the Exchequer is prepared to undertake a much greater burden.   If this rise were to occur, it might lead to further rises in wages and other repercussions.'   (*H. C. Deb.* 7 April 1941, 1322–3.)

with the proximate object of keeping the cost of living index within a range of 125–130 in terms of the pre-war level, and with the more remote hope of enabling 'the wages situation to be held about where it now is'[1]. Though the cost of the subsidies doubled[2], this policy was continued unchanged during the war years. In later years the policy came to be modified, but this was done very gradually. Economics was late to take full cognizance of cost inflation; but even when unhelped by economic theorists, politicians have not been able to ignore the fact of trade union power.

Even while the war was still being fought, post-war economic policy had been the subject of intensive discussion inside the government[3]. Post-war policy would have been much the poorer without these 'reconstruction' preparations. But inevitably the post-war world was not exactly as envisaged while the guns were still firing; and some presuppositions, being on good authority though they turned out false, undoubtedly misled policy in the first years of peace.

The main problems of turning over the economy from war to peace had long been foreseen[4]. Most critical was the balance of payments aspect. The loss of overseas income and the shift in the terms of trade meant that exports would have to be much higher than before the war. During the war exports had been reduced to a fraction of their pre-war volume. It was expected that the war against Japan would continue for some years longer than the war in Europe, during which the economy could be partially demobilized, and exports expanded. Beyond this, continued American financial assistance was counted on. Both expectations were to be falsified almost immediately after the end of the war.

Official thought about internal policy was dominated by the memory of the post-1918 boom and slump. This had several consequences. First, there was general determination that an open inflation should not recur, both because it was itself disorderly, and because it was believed that this would intensify the subsequent slump that was anyhow thought likely. To avoid an open inflation, it was generally agreed that wartime controls should be retained while shortages persisted. This phase, however, was not expected to last long. In this country, as in America, high demand was expected to persist only for one or two or perhaps three years[5]. The need to take active steps to reduce the

---

[1] *H. C. Deb*. 7 April 1941, 1324.

[2] In 1941/42 the cost was £125m. (*H. C. Deb*. 14 April 1942, 105); by the end of the war it was running at a rate of £250m. (*H. C. Deb*. 23 Oct. 1945, 1880).

[3] This discussion had started as early as 1940: see W. K. Hancock and M. M. Gowing [1949], *British War Economy*, chapter XIX.

[4] See for instance the summary of the official study prepared in 1942 in Hancock and Gowing [1949], pp. 535–6.

[5] Two quotations from the White Paper on *Employment Policy* (Cmd. 6527, 1944) indicate the sort of expectations which were held:

    'There will, however, be no problem of general unemployment in the years immediately after the end of the war in Europe.' (Forward to the White Paper.)

    'It is not yet possible to forecast the length of the transition period during which the prevailing tendency will be for demand to outrun supply. . . [But] the recuperative

pressure of demand during this interim period seems, consequently, not to have been considered[1].   Still less was it foreseen that the control of inflation was going to prove a continuous, major problem.   The White Paper on *Employment Policy* is its own evidence of how seriously the likelihood of deflation was taken. In view of pre-war history, the White Paper was of understandable importance as a symbol; but it was not to prove an immediately applicable guide to policy.

The proposals regarding international trade and payments, debated in wartime London and the subject of long international negotiation, were intended, also, for application only after the post-war transition was over. The final products of these discussions were the International Monetary Fund, the International Bank for Reconstruction and Development, and the scheme for an International Trade Organization[2].   They amounted, as Keynes could claim, to 'a more or less complete outline for the re-ordering of commercial and currency policies'[3].   This however was a long-term ideal: restrictions for balance of payments reasons on trade and on payments were to be permitted for a transitional period of five years[4].   International trade in fact took twice as long to get back into fair balance; and during this time many interim international arrangements had to be devised, for which the wartime blue-prints

powers of modern productive technique are very strong.   Under favourable external conditions, it may not be very long before production becomes adequate to meet the various calls upon it.' (para. 19.)

An unofficial forecast by Kalecki made in 1944 was strikingly more accurate.   His calculation was based on the volume of durable goods which consumers had had to forgo, and the volume of investment which business had been unable to undertake, during the war.   He concluded that 'the transition period during which man power will be scarce is unlikely to be below five or above eight years'.   (M. Kalecki [1944], 'Employment in the United Kingdom during and after the Transition Period', *B. Oxford Inst. Statist.*, 4 December 1944, p. 277.)

[1]The *Employment Policy* White Paper emphasized (para. 16) that during the transition from war to peace rationing, price control, and investment control would have to continue; but made no explicit mention of the level of taxation.   Interest rates were to be kept low.

[2]The agreements relating to the IMF and the IBRD were negotiated in July 1944 (*United Nations Monetary and Financial Conference, held at Bretton Woods*, Cmd. 6546, 1944).   *Proposals for Consideration by an International Conference on Trade and Employment* (Cmd. 6709) was published on the authority of the United States Government in December 1945, and accepted as a basis for international discussion by the United Kingdom Government, which was 'in full agreement on all important points'.

[3]In his last speech in defence of the Loan Agreement in the House of Lords (*H.L. Deb.* 18 Dec. 1945, 778).

[4]Restriction on the convertibility of currencies applying to current transactions might be retained for a transitional period of five years from the date on which the Fund began operations (in the event, April 1953): their further retention was to be permitted after consultation with the Fund (Articles VIII (2a), XIV (2) and XIV (4) of the IMF Agreement).   *Trade* restrictions for balance of payments reasons were to be permitted during a transitional period defined as in the IMF Agreement (chapter III, section C2 of the Trade Proposals).

Under the United States Loan Agreement the United Kingdom had later to accept for herself the restoration of convertibility at a much earlier date (see §2 below).

provided little guide.   The uncertainty of the British balance of payments
has to this day been an ever-present limitation on internal policy.   The constant
need, when framing budgetary policy, to watch the balance of payments, was
however something not stressed in wartime discussion of employment policy.
If this discussion, in consequence, now seems unrealistic, this is at bottom due
to its having been framed not with inflation but with deflation in mind.

The role of budgetary policy in the post-war years grew gradually as controls
were removed: only then was the full importance of the 'Keynesian revolution'
revealed.   In the meanwhile, an extensive battery of direct controls seemed to
run happily with the strong Labour predilection for a highly interventionist
type of economic policy.   'Economic planning' meant various things to various
people; but many of the ideas about it were pre-Keynesian in origin.   The
philosophy of *dirigisme* may not in fact have meant that controls were retained
unnecessarily long.   But it certainly made it more difficult to sort out what were
the essential, and what the less important, economic functions of the state in
the post-war world.

The Labour Party came to power in 1945 committed to planning—or
re-planning—the whole economy.   The election manifesto had declared that it
would 'plan from the ground up, giving an appropriate place to constructive
enterprise and private endeavour in the national plan . . .' and promising 'a
firm constructive hand on our whole productive machinery'[1].   Labour was in
effect declaring that it would make better use of the opportunities of peace than
had Conservative governments in the inter-war years[2]; and all its ideas on
economic policy stemmed from determination to remedy the social miseries of
that time.

The poverty, unemployment and insecurity of the 'thirties had brought a
great change in socialist thinking: 'capitalism' was attacked, not as formerly for
being unjust, but for being inefficient[3].   The socialist literature of those days
was therefore essentially economic.   Much of it written by those who later
became ministers, it was certainly an influence still active on the policy of the
Labour Government of 1945.   All lines of thought started with exasperation at
the 'paradox' of poverty in the midst of potential plenty.   But there were two
chief ways in which the further argument was developed.   The older, more
popular line of argument was neo-Marxist: capitalism had 'broken down';
no attempts at patching could make it work, booms and slumps being an
essential part of the system; the only solution therefore was that 'production

---

[1] *Let us Face the Future* (Labour Party election manifesto, 1945, p. 4).

[2] 'This election was a challenge not to the Government of the last 5 years . . . it was the
total record of all the governments of the twenty years between the wars that was at stake.'
(R. B. McCallum and A. Readman [1947], *The British General Election of 1945*, p. 44.)

[3] As was pointed out at the time by Barbara (now Lady) Wootton.   Taking G. D. H. Cole
as typifying the socialist attitude, she said: 'today he writes . . . not so much of wrongs
as of muddles' (B. Wootton [1934], *Plan or No Plan*, p. 104).

for profit' should be superseded by a more or less complete government direction of production, 'to meet human needs'[1].

The other line of argument, more to the fore somewhat later, endeavoured to come to terms with Keynesian ideas: its chief propounders were indeed academic economists. It was in consequence much more discriminating: the evils of pre-war capitalism could be tackled one at a time. Unemployment could be cured by the management of total demand, inequality by redistributive taxation, and monopolistic restrictions by selective nationalization; while a control over investment would ensure effective influence over the pace and direction of economic growth. If all this was done, there would be no need to go in for complete government planning, nor to supersede the price system: consumers' choice was indeed a positive good to be preserved. Interventions could be made piecemeal, wherever particular interventions seemed required[2].

This more sophisticated version of socialism was in fact to prove a reasonable philosophic basis for the conduct of a Labour government. But it is not surprising that in 1945 the more primitive faith survived, more fervid and fundamentalist, of hostility to capitalism and all its ways. Allied with the wartime habit of getting things done by direct action, not by financial means, it was one element in the relative neglect of budgetary and still more of monetary policy in the first post-war years. It certainly ran dead against any idea of drastic

---

[1]This line of argument was perhaps expounded most forcefully by Sir Stafford Cripps in his [1934] short book *Why This Socialism?* In view of his energetic use of power when later a minister, two quotations may be worthwhile to show his directness of approach in 1934. 'There is no real problem', he said: 'a body of competent engineers could solve it in a few months at the most, if once we could tell them what we want' (p. 82). 'The allocation of commodities [under the heads of consumption, investment, government expenditure, etc.] is a matter for the community to decide, always bearing in mind that the more we allocate to one head the less there will be for others' (p. 88).

Complete socialist planning was also espoused by G. D. H. Cole in his later books: for instance, [1935] *Principles of Economic Planning.* Dr Hugh Dalton, in his [1935] *Practical Socialism for Britain* also appeared to advocate the supersession of the pricing system (and was criticized for so doing by Durbin in his review of the book). But the greater part of the book was devoted to the practical, political and parliamentary arrangements that a Labour Government would require: those he proposed hardly provided a machinery for comprehensive planning.

Barbara Wootton's [1934] *Plan or No Plan* was one of the more thoughtful attempts to justify planning; but after her clear exposé of the rationale of the pricing system, her demonstration of the need for planning is surprisingly slight. Appearing before Keynes's *General Theory*, her book was least adequate on employment theory.

[2]This line of argument was best set out by Douglas Jay [1938] in *The Socialist Case*— which Mr Attlee recommended in his foreword to the second [1947] edition as setting out the 'basic philosophic arguments for collective management of our economic resources' —adding 'I believe myself these arguments are unanswerable'.

On this kind of approach, the idea of 'planning' became somewhat general. 'It is a mistake', said Mr Jay, 'to suppose we must either plan wholly or not at all' (p. 272). 'The case for socialism and planning in a free society is, therefore, nothing more than a plea for the application of reason and intelligence to the job of producing and distributing the good things of life' (p. 279). The previous writings of E. F. M. Durbin (collected in his [1949] *Problems of Economic Planning*) had given much of this basic argument.

action to eliminate inflation at the close of the war, as the 'monetary reforms' in many continental countries attempted to do. Such an approach was indeed not in tune with the age. Very likely it would have been foolish: it is still remarkable that it should have been so little discussed[1].

2. ECONOMIC DEMOBILIZATION, 1945–7

The first two years after the war saw an enormous redirection of economic effort, formerly engrossed by war production, towards the satisfaction of long-deferred civilian needs. As time went on, the questions on which decisions were most crucial changed; wartime methods of controlling the economy became outdated; and new methods of both economic policy itself, and of administering it, had to be evolved.

The main decisions during the war centred on the allocation of specific scarce resources—manpower, materials and also shipping. Financial decisions, though important, had been secondary. The administrative machinery for economic co-ordination had grown up outside the Treasury. The Treasury, indeed, had in the early part of the war lost much of its departmental pre-eminence; and was not fully to recover it until 1947[2]. The machinery was essentially interdepartmental. But the Lord President, as chairman of the main committees, played a role somewhere between overlord and senior co-ordinator. In this he was served by the Cabinet secretariat, with the Economic Section in effect part of his staff.

This system was retained under the Labour government[3]. Dr Dalton became Chancellor of the Exchequer; Mr Morrison, Lord President of the Council with general responsibility, among other heavy duties[4], for economic co-ordination—

[1]A comment of Professor Robbins, head of the Economic Section of the Cabinet Office till shortly after the end of the war, perhaps indicates something of the official attitude:

'In recent months, Mr Hawtrey has been recommending a surgical operation, in the Belgian manner, whereby a proportion of outstanding currency and credit would be sterilized. This could undoubtedly be effective, though the administrative complications are formidable. But it is extremely drastic treatment and . . . I do not favour it here and now' (L. Robbins [1947], *The Economic Problem in Peace and War*, p. 62).

[2]See D. N. Chester [1951], 'The Central Machinery for Economic Policy' in *Lessons of the British War Economy*, edited by D. N. Chester [1951]. He remarks that 'the Treasury was under a cloud and not very powerful' during the early part of the war, and did not fully retrieve its old position until Sir Stafford Cripps became Chancellor of the Exchequer in November 1947 (pp. 5 and 17).

[3]See D. N. Chester [1952], 'Machinery of Government and Planning' in *The British Economy, 1945–1950*, edited by G. D. N. Worswick and P. H. Ady [1952]. The chief development was in the arrangements for interdepartmental co-ordination at the official level.

[4]The range of Mr Morrison's duties is described in his book [1954], *Government and Parliament*. 'The Lord President's Committee had assigned to it questions of domestic policy not assigned to other Committees, including in the earlier period internal economic policy and the supervision of the general development of the nation's economy' (p. 20).

in which Sir Stafford Cripps at the Board of Trade was to become also increasingly interested.   There was therefore a division of responsibility for economic policy, financial and budgetary policy being the responsibility of the Treasury, while 'physical' planning was for the most part outside it.   This was a system which had worked well during the war: for peacetime it had defects, which became more evident as time went on[1].

The disposition of the economy at the end of the war is summarized in table 2.1.   When the war ended, a quarter of the country's manpower was in the armed forces.   The government was spending over half the national product.   Civilian output was heavily curtailed.   Gross investment was negligible.   Consumers' expenditure, though higher than at the worst period during the war, was still only 90 per cent of its pre-war level, being restricted both by high taxation, and even more severely by rationing and shortages.   Since 1942, the balance of payments deficit had been met by lend-lease.   To further the war effort, exports had been reduced in the middle years of the war to a third of their pre-war volume.   Reconsideration of this policy had led to some later recovery; but in 1945 the volume of exports was still less than half pre-war.   Invisible earnings too had been greatly reduced by the disposal of British assets overseas to pay for the war.   Notwithstanding the low level of imports, the foreign deficit in 1945 amounted therefore to about ten per cent of the national product.

When the war ended, there was pressing need to 'demobilize this war structure and to set the civilian economy moving'[2].   To pay for food and raw materials, imported from abroad, exports had to be expanded.   Capital equipment had to be renovated : 'our houses and buildings had been heavily battered from the

Mr Morrison was also Leader of the House of Commons, and, as Lord President, chairman of the Future Legislation Committee and the Committee on the Socialization of Industries (p. 22).   He therefore bore much of the burden of planning, preparing and carrying through the heavy legislative programme of the Labour Government that he could claim to be 'the most extensive and significant legislative programme of our great Parliament' (p. 241).

[1]'Until economic planning was absorbed into the Treasury organisation it was a matter of some doubt how far the Treasury was subject to the machinery of economic co-ordination' (Morrison [1954], p. 308).   Though responsibility for most physical controls lay outside the Treasury, it continued to be responsible for the import programme, which became of increased importance as finance rather than shipping became the limiting consideration.

It was incidental to the general divorce of physical from financial planning that government economists were outside the Treasury and thus more closely in touch with the former than with budgetary and monetary policy.   Professor (later Sir Dennis) Robertson and Sir Hubert Henderson had served in the Treasury during the war, but both left before it ended; while Lord Keynes, till his death in April 1946, was preoccupied with the loan negotiations.   The fact that the economists in the Economic Section remained part of the Cabinet Office did not imply that their advice was not sought on Treasury policy; but till the two aspects of policy were united under Sir Stafford Cripps, they were inevitably at a little distance from financial matters.

[2]The needs of the case were often recited: this paragraph follows the *Economic Survey for 1947* (Cmd. 7046), paras. 30, 42 and 47.

Table 2.1. *The British economy, 1945–8*

	1938		*1945*	*1946*	*1947*	*1948*
Percentage distribution of manpower[a]						
Armed forces	*2*		24	10	6	4
Civil employment	*89*		76	85	92	94
Not employed[b]	*9*		½	5	2	2
Industrial production[c]	*100*		..	102	108	117
Percentage allocation of national product[de]						
Consumers' expenditure	*75*		(55)	69	72	69
Government expenditure	*15*		(50)	26	18	17
Gross domestic investment	*12*		(5)	9	16	15
Net investment abroad	*−2*		(−10)	−4	−5	—
Personal income and expenditure						
Percentage of personal income[e]						
Taxed	*8½*		18	14½	13½	13½
Saved	*5*		11	4	2	1½
Volume of personal consumption[f]	*100*		91	100	103	103
Foreign trade						
Volume of exports[g]	*100*		46	99	109	138
Volume of imports[g]	*100*		62	68	78	81
Balance of payments (£m.)[h]	*−70*		..	−300	−450	—

[a]Ministry of Labour (old series) figures for June in each year: for details and definitions see e.g. *AAS* [1952], table 120.

[b]Post-war figures include ex-servicemen on release leave.

[c]From Lomax, *J. roy. Statist. Soc. A* [1959].

[d]Percentages of GNP at factor cost.

[e]Years 1938 and 1948 are from *NI & E* [1958]; 1946 and 1947 from *NI & E* [1956]; 1945, unrevised estimates (shown rounded) from *NIWP* [1948].

[f]Expenditure revalued at 1938 prices: from *NIWP* [1949], but year 1945 from *NIWP* [1948].

[g]Board of Trade estimates, 1938 = 100: 1948 obtained by linking to 1947-based series: see *ASS* [1952], table 217.

[h]From *UKBP* [1959]: year 1938 from *NI & E* [1958]: rounded to nearest £25m.

For key to abbreviations see introductory note, p. xiii above.

air', and industrial equipment had been 'worked at great pressure throughout the war, with entirely insufficient maintenance'. The private consumer's needs were hardly less urgent: 'food supplies during the war had been 'nutritionally adequate, but no better than that. In the six years of the war the people had received less than four years' normal supply of clothing and less than three years' supply of household goods'.

Which needs were to be met first depended very largely on the decisions of the government. It alone decided how quickly war contracts should be cancelled, and men returned from the forces.   Imports were completely controlled; and decisions here largely determined the size of the food ration.   How much went to consumption as a whole, or to investment, was again very largely influenced—if not very accurately controlled—by rations, allocations and licences.

The effectiveness of controls as an instrument of planning was however far smaller than was suggested by the plethora of legal powers possessed by the government.   With the coming of peace, the economic powers of the state had in fact become negative, not positive as in war.   War planning had centred on the direction of labour: this ceased to be practicable; and manpower budgeting, though continued, dwindled to little more than arithmetical wish-fulfilment. Even had the direction of labour remained, it would have been a difficult power to wield.   The economy was in a state of very rapid change; and the purpose of economic activity, formerly monolithic, became multifarious as the consumer re-emerged as sovereign.   As was not always admitted, what was now required was the kind of 'fine adjustments in the economic structure' which 'controls cannot by themselves bring about'[1].

Controls were not adaptable to detailed planning: nor was it easy to use them for broader purposes of policy.   It was possible to use import controls in favour of investment by importing timber rather than food.   Exports could be favoured by prohibiting the sales of some kinds of goods at home, and sometimes also by giving bonuses in the allocation of materials for good export performance: the mere existence of allocation schemes was indeed a sanction which gave the government a great influence with industry[2].   Nevertheless what existed was a congeries of many separate controls, each, unless deflected from above, sharing out scarce supplies on its own principles of compromise or 'fair shares'.   Controls were far more effective in sharing out what supplies were available, than in altering the quantities that were to be shared.   Since

---

[1]The quotation is from the *Economic Survey for 1947* (para. 27).   The *Survey* itself drew the conclusion that 'the people' must 'accept the objectives and then work together to achieve the end', a Crippsian ideal discussed further in §3 below.

Important contributions to the 'great debate' on the use of controls were made at this time by various economists.   Sir Hubert Henderson and Professor Meade both advocated, for the transition, the retention of controls, and an attempt to use the pricing system at the same time (H. Henderson [1947], 'The Uses and Abuses of Economic Planning' reprinted in [1955] *The Inter-War Years*; and J. E. Meade [1948], *Planning and the Price Mechanism*.   Professor Robbins [1947] (*The Economic Problem in Peace and War*) pointed out the radical difference between planning in war and peace: 'Total war is a matter of death or victory . . .   In such circumstances the major problem of allocation, the allocation of resources between private and public consumption, undergoes a most drastic simplification.   For the time being private consumption, which normally is an end in itself, becomes something which is purely instrumental' (p. 47).

Professor Jewkes ([1948] *Ordeal by Planning*) and Sir Oliver Franks ([1947] *Central Planning and Control in War and Peace*) represented more extreme—and opposing— viewpoints.

[2]The most important example was the informal understanding with the manufacturers about the proportion of engineering goods and vehicles which should be sold abroad.

the 'apparatus of Government controls' existed, it was right that an attempt should be made to use it 'to guide the economy'[1] in the desired direction. But in practice, to quote Mr Morrison, 'it is fair . . . to say that what happened was that the *ad hoc* use of economic and financial controls came first', and on top of this 'a limited amount of economic planning' was superimposed[2]. The government's wide legal powers to regulate the economy in detail did not and could not mean that the government had power to direct it in detail—though they were apt to give that impression. As in the war controls were justified primarily as a way of dealing with shortages, and as a way of preventing the consumer from taking too large a share of resources[3].

Government policy was directed to closing the yawning gap in the balance of payments as quickly as might be: equally, it was entirely dependent on finding some way of financing the gap while it remained. The new government was brought starkly face to face with this problem as soon as it had assumed office. That there was to be a problem had long been foreseen[4]. But the unexpectedly quick end of the war with Japan removed the year or two's breathing space which it had been hoped would allow some rebuilding of our export trade. The abrupt ending of lend-lease, that equally unexpectedly followed, removed the assistance which we had come to count on almost as a moral right[5].

There seemed no alternative but to seek a loan from the United States. Till exports could be increased a balance of payments deficit was inevitable. The war had left us abnormally dependent on American supplies; hence the deficit was bound to be chiefly a dollar deficit. Only the United States, moreover, was in a position to lend us money. But 'three months of very intricate discussions and some very hard bargaining'[6] showed that a loan could only be had

[1] *Economic Survey for 1947*, para. 26.
[2] Morrison [1954], p. 299.
[3] See further chapter VI below.
[4] See §1 above.
[5] Mr. Truman 'was still somewhat new to his high office of President'; and the sudden cessation of lend-lease was partly due to the speed of events and to the accident of the advice he received: see R. F. Harrod [1951], *The Life of John Maynard Keynes*, p. 595.
[6] Dr Dalton's defence of the agreement: *H.C. Deb.* 12 Dec. 1945, 427. Later in his memoirs Dr Dalton said that 'as the talks went on,' we had 'retreated, slowly and with bad grace and with increasing irritation, from a free gift to an interest-free loan, and from this again to a loan bearing interest; from a larger to a smaller total of aid; and from the prospect of loose strings, some of which would be only general declarations of intention, to the most unwilling acceptance of strings so tight that they might strangle our trade and, indeed, our whole economic life'. (H. Dalton [1962], *High Tide and After*, pp. 74–5). It seems clearly to have been the view of Keynes (who was chiefly responsible for the negotiations in Washington) that the provisions of the agreement were workable (Harrod [1951], chapter XIV), though Dr Dalton himself appears to have had private reservations (Dalton [1962], p. 89).

For an account of the negotiations, see also R. N. Gardner [1956], *Sterling-Dollar Diplomacy*, chapters XI and XII. The advent of a Labour Government in Britain was probably one of the minor factors underlying the American attitude. As Keynes said (in a letter quoted in Dalton [1962], p. 77): 'There is no way out remotely compatible with

at a price; and the price aroused the deepest misgiving.   Misgiving was due less to the financial terms of the loan[1], than to the other conditions attached.   It was a condition, first, that the United Kingdom should accept the Bretton Woods proposals for the International Monetary Fund and the International Bank.   These would undoubtedly have been accepted in any case, though far less abruptly.   The Bretton Woods proposals had not been debated in the House while the negotiations were in progress, on the understanding that till reasonable consideration could be given them this country remained uncommitted.   The coupling of the Loan Agreement with the acceptance of the proposals meant that the House could be given only five days in which to study the complex documents relating both to the loan and to the Fund and Bank[2].

Even more onerous was the required undertaking to restore convertibility almost immediately.   In the Bretton Woods negotiations the United Kingdom had insisted on remaining free to maintain exchange controls on current transactions for a transition period of five years; and this had been accepted as a general provision of the agreements.   But under the Loan Agreement, she had to agree to restore the convertibility of sterling within one year of the agreement coming into operation.   Neither the government, nor probably the opposition had it been in power, would have accepted this condition except under duress[3]. The debate in the House was therefore a scene of gloom and disillusion:

> 'We are sitting here today as the representatives of a victorious people, discussing the economic consequences of victory', said Mr Stanley.   'If a visitor were to come . . . from Mars . . . he might well be pardoned for thinking that he was listening to the representatives of a vanquished people discussing the economic penalties of defeat'[4].

The Chancellor's defence of the agreements was bleak but compelling. 'They fall short of what we should have desired, and of what we strove for through long negotiations.'   But—his blunt question to critics—'What is your alternative?'   Together with the further credit subsequently granted by Canada, the financial assistance amounted to some £1,250 million.   This, on the expectations of the time, seemed enough—but only barely enough—to cover deficits foreseen on the balance of payments for the next three years[5].

the present domestic policy of the Government except on the basis of substantial American aid.   Indeed, the fact that some Americans are becoming aware of this is one of the hidden, unmentioned snags in our path'.

[1] A interest-free loan had been hoped for.   Nevertheless, considered as a commercial loan, the terms were generous.   The loan was for $3,750 million: in addition, $650 million was granted in final settlement of lend-lease.   Interest was at 2 per cent.   Repayment was to be over 50 years.   But neither repayment nor interest was to start till the end of 1951; and interest could be cancelled in any year in which exports, visible and invisible, were insufficient to pay for the pre-war volume of imports (Cmd. 6708, 1945).   Canada subsequently granted a credit of $1,250 million on similar terms.

[2] *H.C. Deb.* 13 Dec. 1945, 653.

[3] 'We came nearest to breaking the negotiations on this point': Dalton [1962], p. 82.

[4] *H.C. Deb.* 13 December 1945, 652–3.

[5] The loans together added up to the overall deficits foreseen for the years 1946–8 (£750

Dr Dalton's budgetary and monetary policy was dictated by considerations which seemed far less pressing. Despite Keynesian principles, the war had been largely financed by borrowing: we emerged from the war with a deficit on government current account of some £2,500 million[1]. During the war controls had been relied on to contain what remained of inflation after high taxation had done what it could[2]—a policy which had had some success. It was hardly in question that, for the first year or two of peace, it should be continued.

Dr Dalton did not fully follow the tradition, begun in the war and later developed, of relating budget proposals to a detailed survey of the economy. Exact calculations of the inflationary gap would hardly have been relevant in the circumstances. The economy was in a state of rapid transition: three million men were demobilized in the first year of peace. Beyond the immediate transition period, the danger foreseen was not inflation but deflation. As Dr Dalton put it on taking office, 'the risk of inflation now is less than the risk of deflation later'[3]. In 1946 it seemed not at all impossible that a serious unemployment problem would emerge by 1948[4].

That the Chancellor reduced taxes in 1946 did not imply that he neglected inflation meanwhile. Demand was certainly high; but not higher than in the war—and wartime controls were still in force[5]. As war expenditure tailed off, and civilian production revived, the pressure must already have been ebbing: the system—it could have been argued—could tolerate some cut in taxes. Moreover some relief from wartime rates would be an incentive: in the long run, 'the only counter to inflation' was 'to produce more goods'[6]. The 1945–6 budgets thus had to balance very broad considerations: on the one hand, 'the need to stimulate more production, and the need on the other to hold back purchasing power from too precipitate and premature a release'[6].

---

million, £250 million and £250 million respectively: see *Statistical Material presented during the Washington Negotiations* [1945], Cmd. 6707). In the event, taking the three years together, the deficit was only £750 million. But the scale of assistance made no provision for the extra strain of convertibility nor for financing any of the deficit of the overseas sterling area; nor was there provision for unforeseen contingencies. For all these reasons, there was considerable doubt whether the assistance was large enough: see Gardner [1956], pp. 202–3 and 211.

[1] *NIWP* [1948]: average for years 1944 and 1945, central government only.

[2] See §1 above.

[3] Dalton [1962], p. 165. See further §1 above. Kalecki's forecast, already quoted, suggests that official expectations ought not to have been so unrealistic.

[4] For instance, in considering how soon to release post-war credits Dr Dalton said 'we may well need this mass of reserve purchasing power in the next year or two, as an anti-deflationary corrective, should there be any worsening in the prospects of trade and employment' (*H.C. Deb.* 9 April 1946, 1833).

[5] Reliance on direct controls was an explicit assumption throughout Dr Dalton's budgeting.

'So far, our price controls, our financial and physical controls, our production and our saving have held the inflation reasonably well in check' (*H.C. Deb.* 15 April 1947, 54).

[6] *H.C. Deb.* 9 April 1946, 1825.

In the special budget introduced in October 1945, Dr Dalton—in his own judgement—went 'slow in tax remissions . . . quite deliberately, because there is an inflationary risk in any reduction of taxation'[1]. Taxes were reduced by about £400 million, most of the reductions being in income tax[2]. The war-time excess profits tax was also reduced from 100 to 60 per cent: the war damage contributions had already ceased in August[3]. Both these levies were soon to go into reverse, and provide a stream of refunds through the next five years to finance the re-equipment of industry and the repair of war damage.

None of the tax remissions, except for the minor cut in purchase tax, was to take effect till the following April—by which time 'we shall all see the picture much more clearly than any of us can see it now'[4]. When April came, the Chancellor felt able to announce a further 'series of modest proposals' which yet fell 'within the bounds of prudence'[5]. Consumers' purchasing power was increased by a further £95 million, again mainly in the form of income tax reliefs[6]. Death duties were raised[7]; and excess profits tax abolished completely.

As a former authority on public finance[8], Dr Dalton took pride in being liberated from the old orthodoxy of balanced budgets. It is nevertheless only in a broad sense that his approach was Keynesian. For him the budget should still be balanced over a period of years—a compromise which had also found its way into the White Paper on *Employment Policy*[9]. After this 'transitional and exceptional period' he said, we should deliberately plan 'surpluses when trade is firmly good', and 'deficits when trade is bad . . . but balancing over a period, surpluses against deficits'[10].

By 1947, the budget, on the traditional arrangement of the accounts, had reached this mid-point of balance. But this was only accomplished by taking into revenue some abnormal 'miscellaneous receipts'. The 1946 budget had already begun to include substantial receipts from the sale of war stores: the 1947 budget included also receipts of some £150 million or so which represented no more than the 'clawing back' into the Exchequer of sums voted in previous years but not actually spent. These seemed indeed, as the Chancellor said, a 'litter of rabbits . . . out of my Departmental hat': hardly something—as he

---

[1]*H.C. Deb*. 23 Oct. 1945, 1902.

[2]Effect on tax yields in a full year: of this some £300 million must have gone to consumers, the rest to companies.

[3]Amounting to some £40 million a year. *H.C. Deb*. 23 Oct. 1945, 1887.

[4]*H.C. Deb*. 23 Oct. 1945, 1902.

[5]*H.C. Deb*. 9 April 1946, 1825.

[6]Full year rate, omitting the extra revenue from death duties (£22 million). The abolition of EPT was estimated to cost a further £75 million.

[7]Dr Dalton used H. G. Wells as his authority: 'No energetic, directive, people can be deeply in love with inheritance. It is a fatty degeneration of property' (*H.C. Deb*. 9 April 1946, 1839). Nevertheless he increased the yield of death duties by no more than a quarter.

[8]The first edition of his *Public Finance* was published in 1922.

[9]See Cmd. 6527, para. 77.

[10]*H.C. Deb*. 23 Oct. 1945, 1886.

went on to claim—that would 'help us on our way'[1]. The episode showed the traditional accounts in a curious light, and led to much later discussion of their adequacy as a guide for policy[2].

Dr Dalton was to be much vilified for his monetary policy. But by the end of the war, cheap money was an unquestioned, and bipartisan, orthodoxy. Recent policy had been dominated by the need to finance the war cheaply. What it should be after the war had been set out in the 1944 White Paper on *Employment Policy*. The economic functions of the rate of interest had not been ignored completely—as they were, perhaps, by Dr Dalton. Nevertheless the White Paper had firmly announced the Government's determination 'to avoid dear money' for 'urgent reconstruction needs'[3]. The Chancellor at first aroused no opposition when he spoke of 'cheaper money and lower interest rates'—explaining that he had in mind the possibility of reducing not only the debt charge in the budget, but also the cost of borrowing by industry and by public bodies. 'There is no sense', he said, 'or so it seems to me—I hope no high authority will differ from me—in paying more than we must for the loan of money'[4].

He began at the short end of the Debt. After discussion with the Bank and the banks, the rate on Treasury bills was reduced in October 1945, from about 1 to about $\frac{1}{2}$ per cent[5]. After this 'hopeful beginning'[5] he turned to longer-term rates and for the next two years was to be occupied in trying to drive the long-term rate down from 3 to $2\frac{1}{2}$ per cent. Both steps had the full support of the Opposition[6]. Even in April two years later, Dr Dalton was to be criticized by Sir John Anderson—his predecessor as Chancellor—not for trying 'to get down to the $2\frac{1}{2}$ per cent basis', but for being 'in too great a hurry' to get there[7].

But by the autumn of 1946 the cheap money policy was running into mounting criticism, not so much in Parliament as in financial circles outside[8]. The breakdown of the policy was perhaps due at bottom to a general belief that $2\frac{1}{2}$ per cent was 'unsound', and therefore untenable. There may also have been some loss of nerve by the authorities in face of the successive crises of 1947 —crises which public opinion tended to blame on an over-inflationary government policy. Nevertheless it must remain doubtful whether cheap money was seriously harmful. Investment demand—high in any case, and subject moreover to direct controls—cannot have been greatly stimulated by a half per cent

---

[1] *H.C. Deb.* 15 April 1947, 51.
[2] See further chapter VII.1 below on the theory of budgetary policy.
[3] Cmd. 6527, para. 16. See further chapter IX.1 below, where the cheap money policy is discussed more extensively.
[4] *H.C. Deb.* 23 Oct. 1945, 1881.
[5] *H.C. Deb.* 23 Oct. 1945, 1882: the rate on Treasury deposit receipts was reduced, also by $\frac{1}{2}$ per cent, to $\frac{5}{8}$ per cent.
[6] For fuller references see chapter IX.1.
[7] *H.C. Deb.* 16 April 1947, 203.
[8] For various references, see chapter IX.1 below.

interest-rate incentive[1]. Nor was home demand a main cause of the two particular crises of 1947.

Nevertheless, by 1947, the mood had changed; and the earlier air of unquestioning assurance[2] had considerably thinned. Difficulties were growing. Fuel was short. The balance of payments deficit (which in 1946 had been smaller than expected)[3] was mounting again—almost all of it a dollar deficit. It was in the spirit of taking 'the people frankly into its confidence' about these difficulties, that the Government produced the first of what was to be the annual series of *Economic Surveys*[4]. By the time it appeared in February, the fuel crisis had supervened. Coal stocks had got dangerously low in the autumn. Bad weather further reduced them; and the power stations ran short. Not till the eleventh hour would the Minister of Fuel admit a crisis[5]: late on a Friday (7 February) Mr Shinwell announced that from Monday industrial consumers in London, the south-east, the midlands and north-west would get no electricity, and that domestic use would be severely curtailed. Unemployment rose temporarily to over two million; and among other irritating casualties, the weekly press was stopped for two weeks. It was later estimated that the disruption of production cost £200 million in exports[6].

By March the dollar position, which was causing anxiety in the autumn, was moving towards crisis. Not till August was the Government forced to act[7]. After a fairly steady gold and dollar deficit[8], of little over $50 million a month, during the first three quarters of 1946, it rose in the last quarter of the year to $135 million. In February it was over $200 million; and from then on grew steadily. By July it had risen to over $500 million a month—or $6·5 billion a year; by August, to over $600 million a month—or $7·5 billion a year. Convertibility had been substantially introduced before 15 July, the date agreed under the Loan Agreement. In the last full week before its retraction on 20 August, we paid out $237 million, as much as the total deficit for 1946. By then $3·6 billion of the $5 billion credits granted by the United States and Canada

---

[1]For fuller discussion see chapter XII below.

[2]In the previous February Mr Morrison in answer to a question about economic planning had replied: 'I am happy to say that the machinery of economic coordination and administration has undoubtedly improved enormously during recent years' (*H.C. Deb.* 28 Feb. 1946, 2136).

[3]The deficit in 1946 was estimated at £400 million; £750 million had been forecast.

[4]Mr Attlee's foreword to the *Economic Survey for 1947*. On this occasion the economic debate on the *Survey* preceded the budget (*H.C. Deb.* 10–12 March 1947). The *Survey* had been long announced (*H.C. Deb.* 20 Nov. 1946, 889).

[5]According to Chester [1952], p. 343, some Ministers, particularly Sir Stafford Cripps, are known to have 'been worried about the increasingly strong possibility of such a crisis for some months previously but could do little or nothing against the entrenched and determined autonomy of the Minister of Fuel and Power'.

[6]An estimate given by Dr Dalton (*H.C. Deb.* 7 Aug. 1947, 1662).

[7]The following account is partly based on an unpublished study by Mr M. FG. Scott.

[8]Reduction of United Kingdom reserves plus drawing on American and Canadian lines of credit drawing rights in IMF and South African gold loan.

had been exhausted. The Loan, upon which all other plans depended, negotiated with difficulty and intended to last three years or so, in fact lasted only one year and a half[1].

The Government came out badly from this disaster. It had miscalculated policy; delayed action till very late; and gave subsequently no adequate explanation of what had happened. At the time of the negotiations for the Loan it had been hoped that it would be possible to persuade some of the countries holding sterling balances to agree to their being partly cancelled as war debts; and that apart from limited amounts they would agree to them being blocked[2]. In fact only Australia and New Zealand agreed to their balances being scaled down. Starting with negotiations with Argentina in October 1946, the Government made a series of agreements with the main non-sterling countries, intended to give them convertibility for currently earned sterling but not for accumulated balances. But it appeared that only half the total of the balances was blocked in this way. Even those countries with whom agreements were made retained access to considerable 'working balances'. With the main sterling countries, no formal agreements were thought necessary; and the countries of Western Europe also held large unblocked balances. The only safeguard was the self-restraint of the holders[3].

The Government nevertheless appeared entirely confident about these arrangements. Convertibility had been introduced piecemeal over the last nine months: in July Dr Dalton assured the House that 'in large measure, 15th July has already been discounted and the additional burden of assuming these new obligations . . . will be noticeably less than many people may suppose'[4]. The Government was equally complacent about the trend in the balance of payments. In June it announced a new import programme. By then it had to be admitted that (chiefly because of the February fuel crisis) exports would not increase as fast as foreshadowed by the *Survey*; while the rapid rise in import prices was likely to raise the import bill by well over £200 million. The Government refused drastic cuts: after some minor cuts the programmed volume of

---

[1]Drawings on the credits started in July 1946. After August 1947 the dollar drain slackened immediately. By the end of the year it was down to $200 million a month; and in the second half of 1948 was to be further reduced to little more than $100 million a month. (Figures for 1946 and 1948 are from Cmd. 8976; for 1947 first half from *H.C. Deb.* 7 Aug. 1947, 1670; and for 1947 second half from Cmd. 7324.)

[2]This was set out in the Loan Agreement (Cmd. 6708, article 10). See also R. N. Gardner [1956], pp. 204–6.

[3]Gardner [1956], pp. 327–8. Convertibility was not granted by 15 July to France, Denmark, the U.S.S.R. and eleven other countries with whom agreements had not been concluded.

[4]*H.C. Deb.* 8 July 1947, 2158. Dr Dalton also argued that convertibility was inevitable: 'all these countries', he said 'are running very short of dollars, and are increasingly demanding from us sterling convertible at once into dollars, quite apart from any obligations of the American agreement' (*H.C. Deb.* 7 Aug, 1947, 1673). Events were to show the inconsistency of these two arguments.

imports remained higher than in the previous twelve months[1]. Critics later argued that the Loan had been frittered away on luxuries. Even more cogently it was argued that current transactions alone could not possibly account for much, and that only a capital outflow could explain the rapid loss of dollars[2]. All these charges were indignantly repudiated by Dr Dalton, even in October. 'I repeat that there is no evidence whatever to substantiate the loosely formulated charges that have been made by highly educated men that large quantities of this sum of dollars were wasted, and dissipated, and have leaked away or disappeared through some miracle or failure of control by those who work for me, whether at the Bank of England or the Treasury. I repulse these allegations'[3].

The facts may not have been clear at the time[4]: they now leave little doubt. The United Kingdom's current deficit[5] can account for only three fifths of the £1,250 million loss of gold and dollars in 1946 and 1947—the years when the Loan was used up. The current deficit worsened between 1946 and 1947; but this can explain only one-fifth of the worsening of the dollar outflow in that year[6]. The rest must have been due almost entirely to capital movements of one sort or another. The capital flight can be blamed in part on the looseness of the arrangements that had been made to tie up the sterling balances. But such an explanation does not go deep: in the conditions of the time no arrangements could be expected to stand the strain of convertibility. As Dr Dalton was to argue in announcing its suspension, there was a world-wide shortage of dollars: 'sterling, alone of all the other currencies of the European belligerents, was freely convertible': the 'burden of the desperate dollar shortage of so many

---

[1]*H.C. Deb.* 30 June 1947, 961. Under the Loan Agreement (article 9) the Government had also agreed not to discriminate against dollar imports. Given its refusal to cut imports, the Government may have been right in claiming (*H.C. Deb.* 6 Aug. 1947, 1500) that since supplies could only be obtained from the western hemisphere, this provision of the Agreement had 'hardly been operative at all'. This would not have been true if the Government had tried to cut imports as drastically as it had to later.

[2]For instance by Professor (now Lord) Robbins, who till 1945 was Director of the Economic Section of the Cabinet Office (see 'Inquest on the Crisis', *Lloyds Bank Review*, Oct. 1947).

[3]*H.C. Deb.* 24 Oct. 1947, 410.

[4]The statistics section of the Overseas Finance division of the Treasury was set up after the crisis.

[5]This included substantial government outgoings for supplies to Germany and relief to other parts of Europe.

[6]The best summary of the position is given by the following figures:

	£ million 1946	£ million 1947	Total 1946 plus 1947	Worsening 1946 to 1947
1. Deficit on current account	−295	−442	−737	−147
(of which with dollar area)	(−299)	(−506)		
2. Gold and dollar deficit	−225	−1,024	−1,249	−794
2−1 All other capital movements	+70	−582	−512	−652

Item 1 from *UKBP* [1959]: item 2 from *BPWP* [1953]

other countries was simply shifted to our shoulders'[1]. What is surprising is that, despite forebodings in 1945 the government did not suspect that convertibility would lead to trouble[2]; and was slow to believe the mistake would have to be undone[3]. Its advisers can hardly escape all blame[4].

[1] Broadcast of 20 Aug. 1947: quoted Gardner [1956], p. 315. Dr Dalton's diagnosis then, though late, is irrefutable. It is hardly possible to accept Gardner's conclusion that 'the obligation to make sterling convertible . . . was not itself a major cause of the economic crisis' (p. 318).

[2] As already made clear, the British government had fought hard against a rigid commitment to the early resumption of convertibility. Even after the negotiations, Dr Dalton noted in his diary the 'secret reflection' that 'even in the next year or two, circumstances may require a large revision' of the conditions (Dalton [1962], p. 89).

Looking back on these events later, Dr Dalton remarked, 'my colleagues and I had, from the beginning, very serious fears of the consequences of this premature commitment, as it had always seemed to us. Nor, looking at the trend of our external trade since we undertook this commitment, was there any rational ground for being less fearful now. But there had gradually grown up, even in some most knowledgeable circles, a mood of optimism, which we can now see to have been quite irrational.

'I was gravely informed by some that "convertibility has now been discounted", and "when it comes it will make very little difference". I am still surprised, looking back, by this profound error of practical judgement. It is quite clear now that we had no chance at all of holding this degree of convertibility in mid-1947.'

The suspension of convertibility, 'seemed to me at the time a personal humiliation and a bad setback for the Government. But, on a rational view, it should have been obvious for some while that this retreat would be inevitable' (Dalton [1962], pp. 257 and 262).

The Bank of England, as on so many later occasions, appears to have thought of the problem purely in terms of 'confidence' effects. 'Many and careful arrangements were made before 15th July', said the Governor in October. 'Confidence was returning: sterling balances were being more and more freely held in London as in the days before the war, and there was a possibility that convertibility of sterling on current account might be feasible. . . And it might have succeeded had it not been that confidence became undermined by the balance of payments crisis in this country and, indeed, all over the world. Suddenly, everybody wanted dollars . . .' (Lord Catto at Mansion House dinner, October 1947, quoted in Gardner [1956], p. 319).

[3] The Loan Agreement contained a clause permitting the postponement of convertibility after consultation (in article 7: see Cmd. 6708). This clause was not invoked. For the Government believed that the United States Government would have rejected any earlier request for the suspension of convertibility—a belief that was probably correct (see Gardner [1956], pp. 320–1). Even had the United States Government been complaisant, it could have done nothing without congressional approval; and 'of congressional debate on our affairs', said Dr Dalton later 'we had had enough in 1946 when the Loan Agreement was under discussion . . . Many congressmen had deployed lengthy, ill-informed, unfriendly and even spiteful criticism of Britain. We did not want a repetition of this; which would have been damaging to our credit and to Anglo-American co-operation generally' (Dalton [1962], p. 255).

[4] There were a few outside critics, notably in Oxford. Sir Hubert Henderson early on made a strong, though temperately-worded, attack on the 'non-discrimination' and the 'convertibility' provisions of the Loan Agreement:

'Thus any country can call upon us, within little more than a year from now, to supply it with dollars to an amount represented by its favourable balance of payments with us . . . together with that part of the accumulated balances that we agree to release. Since the world is hungry for goods, most of which can be obtained most easily from the United States, we must expect to be called on to supply dollars to virtually the full extent of this twofold liability . . . Clearly, under these arrange-

Convertibility was suspended on 20 August.   There followed a hurried series of import cuts in the late summer and early autumn.   The imports of many commodities from North America were virtually eliminated: to have spent $200 million on American fruit, vegetables and dried eggs, as we did in 1947, would in later years have appeared unthinkable.   The sterling countries, at the Commonwealth conference summoned for September, agreed to cut their dollar imports also.

Though the dollar drain was thus reduced to more manageable proportions it was clear that the financial reserves remaining at the end of 1947 were no longer adequate.   By then, the problem had been recognized as a world problem.   The Government was wide open to the attack of appearing to have no policy but to wait for yet further American assistance.   But it was probably true, as Sir Stafford Cripps said, that 'separate nations cannot deal individually with this situation'[1].   In June Mr Marshall in his speech at Harvard, had sowed the seed which was rapidly to blossom into Marshall Aid.   The conception of the Marshall Plan was however as much Mr Bevin's as Mr Marshall's.   The American Secretary of State, in the course of his speech, had thrown out the suggestion that further American aid for European countries should depend on their organizing themselves for recovery[2].   It was on this pretext that

ments, we must expect to lose dollars on a large scale unless we can succeed in re-adjusting our balance of payments quickly' (H. Henderson [1946], 'The Anglo-American Financial Agreement', *B. Oxford Inst. Statist*, Jan. 1946, p. 7).
    Dr Balogh also strongly criticized the 'non-discrimination' and the 'convertibility' provisions of the Loan Agreement: see T. Balogh [1947], 'The Problem of the British Balance of Payments', *B. Oxford Inst. Statist.*, July 1947; and also letters by Sir Hubert Henderson and Dr Balogh to *The Times*, 12 December 1945.
[1] *H.C. Deb.* 7 Aug. 1947, 1763.
[2]   'Europe's requirements for the next three or four years of foreign food and other essential products—principally from America—are so much greater than her present ability to pay that she must have substantial additional help or face economic, social and political deterioration of a very grave character . . .   Before, however, the United States can proceed much further . . . there must be some agreement among the countries of Europe as to the requirements of the situation and the part these countries themselves will take.   It would be neither fitting nor efficacious for this Government to undertake to draw up unilaterally a programme designed to place Europe on its feet . . .   The initiative . . . must come from Europe.   The role of this country should consist of friendly aid in the drafting of a European programme and of later support of such a programme, so far as it may be practical for us to do so. The programme should be a joint one agreed to by a number, if not all, European nations.'
Extract from Mr Marshall's speech at Harvard in June 1947 (quoted in *General Report* of Committee of European Economic Co-operation [1947], p. 5.)   The offer was originally intended to apply to all European nations, including Russia and the satellite countries. Though he walked out after a week, Mr Molotov attended the first Paris discussions.
    Mr Bevin read the report of the speech (in *The Daily Herald*) on the morning of 7 June. That day the British Ambassador in Washington was instructed to thank the Secretary of State for his offer and inform him that Mr Bevin was immediately consulting with the French foreign minister as to how best to implement his offer.   Nearly three weeks later Mr Snyder, Secretary to the Treasury, was saying that all Mr Marshall had done was 'to

Mr Bevin took the initiative in calling the European nations into conference. The British and French foreign ministers met in Paris three weeks later at the end of June; and from July to September, the *ad hoc* Committee of European Economic Co-operation—to lead later to the Organisation for European Economic Co-operation—was already in session in Paris.

The fuel crisis and the convertibility crises were both cases where a specific problem had been mismanaged: neither need have been. Their close succession, however, provoked doubt about the whole of the Government's policy. In this reappraisal, Sir Stafford Cripps, then President of the Board of Trade, was able to play a steadily increasing role. When Mr Morrison was laid low by thrombosis in the early part of 1947, Sir Stafford had taken over the Lord President's economic responsibilities. It thus fell to him to introduce the debate on the first *Economic Survey* in March, and too, to announce the decision to institute a 'central economic planning staff'. Sir Edwin Plowden was appointed Chief Planning Officer in May. At the end of September Sir Stafford Cripps moved from the Board of Trade to the new post of Minister for Economic Affairs: inheriting the economic responsibilities of the Lord President, he was to give 'undivided attention to our economic problems at home and abroad'[1]. There was little time to test this new arrangement. When Dr Dalton resigned after his autumn budget, a month and a half later, Sir Stafford Cripps succeeded him as Chancellor of the Exchequer.

By the autumn the Government had accepted the view that inflationary pressure was excessive, and that it was no longer possible to stand by and wait till it cured itself. Conversion to this view had in fact been gradual. Dr Dalton had in April laid some stress on the need for surplus budgeting: the immediate danger, he argued, far from being deflation, was 'of an inflation going beyond bounds, and breaking through the various controls'[2]. In his April budget the Chancellor had therefore increased taxes a little. The consumers' gain from the cut of £85 million in income tax was about offset by higher taxes on tobacco and heating appliances, imposed to save dollars and fuel. Death duties were also increased again. Stamp duties were raised—partly by the new but economically irrelevant tax on 'bonus issues'. Profits tax was also raised—being for the first time made into a tax discriminating against the distribution of

---

invite European countries to see what their problem is. He didn't say anything about letting the United States know how much is wanted'. (Francis Williams [1952], *Ernest Bevin*, pp. 264–5.)

It has been claimed that Mr Marshall's Harvard speech 'was no hasty improvisation'. It is true that in the years since 1946 there had been other American advocates of economic aid to Europe; and that Dean Acheson had set forth the essentials of a European recovery programme in a speech in May (see E. M. Earle [1951], 'The American Stake in Europe', *Int. Aff.*, Oct. 1951, p. 428).

[1] Official announcement: for details of the administrative changes, see Chester [1952], pp. 344–8.

[2] He added that this had not happened yet. 'There has been inflationary pressure . . . but there has been no inflationary break-through the dams' (*H.C. Deb.* 15 April 1947, 54).

dividends[1]. The wartime policy of stabilizing the cost of living index was—with the introduction of a new index—now modified[2].

By the autumn the need to contain inflation seemed altogether more pressing. It dictated the investment cuts, announced in October, and intended to amount to £200 million.   It dictated also, 'for the second time in three years', the introduction of an autumn budget. 'My reason today' said Dr Dalton, 'is that we must strengthen still further, and without delay, our budgetary defences against inflation. This need arises from the decisions . . . taken . . . to increase exports and reduce imports, in order to narrow, as swifty as we can, the very wide and dangerous gap in our overseas balance of payments . . . The effect of these decisions must be, if taken alone and unsupported by other measures, to increase the inflationary pressure by reducing the supply of goods . . . without, at the same time, reducing the total of purchasing power'[3]. Dr Dalton refused any elaborate justification of what he did[4]. He merely resolved to raise £200 million in as simple a way as possible—some £50 million by doubling the profits tax, the rest by higher duties on drink and by an all-round rise in the various rates of purchase tax[5].

The autumn budget of 1947 set the pattern for the next three years; and it is unjust to Dr Dalton that so little of the credit properly given to his successor has been meted out to him[6]. It was he who first directed budgetary policy towards disinflation: while Sir Stafford Cripps was to show inflexible deter-mination in not relaxing taxation, it was Dr Dalton who accepted the heavy political onus of *increasing* it. The day after budget day Dr Dalton tendered his resignation as Chancellor of the Exchequer. He had always, as he once said, tried to keep his relations with the financial press 'very bright and good'[7]. On this occasion he confided something of his budget proposals to a Lobby

[1]Though total tax revenue was raised by £50 million in a full year, none of these latter three provisions was likely to affect consumers' spending much.   The tax on distributed profits was raised to 12½ per cent from 5 per cent, which rate continued to apply to retained profits.

[2]The policy of allowing subsidies to increase as demanded by the previous policy of stabilizing the index was abandoned.   No limit was however placed on the subsidy bill, as it was later to be by Sir Stafford Cripps.   The old policy had in fact been something of a cheat, for being based on 1914 weights the index had become very unrepresentative. The budgetary burden of subsidies had been kept down by concentrating subsidies on those items most overweighted in the index.   When the new index was introduced, no link was provided with the previous series.

[3]*H.C. Deb.* 12 Nov. 1947, 393.

[4]He remained robustly sceptical of 'inflationary gap' calculations: 'Nobody, not even the most skilful statistician, can measure this inflationary pressure, whether new or old, with any close precision' (same deb. 395).

[5]The new rates of profits tax became 10 per cent on retained profits and 25 per cent on distributed profits.   This was not likely to reduce expenditure proportionately: the effect of the budget was therefore less disinflationary than appeared.   (See further chapter VII.3.)

[6]As I. M. D. Little has pointed out: see his [1952] chapter on 'Fiscal Policy' in *The British Economy, 1945–1950*, p. 172.

[7]*H.C. Deb.* 15 April 1947, 51.

correspondent, and *The Star* was on sale with the news half an hour before he spoke[1].   Dr Dalton had been under heavy fire for all aspects of his policy: not only for his late change of front on budgetary policy, but for the recent débâcle over convertibility, and for cheap money as well[2].   Going out at this time, he inevitably went under a cloud.

Just or not, Dr Dalton's departure marked the end of a phase.   It opened the way to a reorientation of policy which two and a half years from the end of the war was overdue.   Alarms and crises notwithstanding, the conversion of the economy from a war to a peace footing had been accomplished fairly smoothly in those two and a half years (table 1.1).   Demobilization was all but over. Industrial production was well above pre-war, and rising rapidly.   The recovery of exports, now also well above the pre-war level, had been even more rapid. The worst of the balance of payments problem was therefore on the way to being met: the deficit was in fact eliminated in 1948.   Largely because of the still severe restraint on consumption, a good start had been made with investment; which—though the need was admittedly for more—had at least reclaimed its pre-war share of resources.

3. ECONOMIC RECOVERY AND ECONOMIC CRISES, 1948–51

By 1948, truer measure had been taken of what the war had done.   The next three years were to see unexpectedly rapid, and fairly complete, recovery. Sir Stafford Cripps was Chancellor of the Exchequer from the end of 1947 till his resignation in October 1950.   The new austerity of policy during those years has become closely associated with his name.   But other nations had much the same road to tread: 1948 marked a new era not only for this country but for all the countries of Western Europe; and the financial assistance we received from America, upon which our recovery depended, was given as part of a joint effort at European recovery.   In 1948 Western Europe faced economic crisis; but behind this lay fear of the gradually recognized, new power of Russia. The initiative lay largely not with the Chancellor, but with Mr Bevin as Foreign Secretary, the main motive of whose policy was to rebuild an area of security in the vacuum left by the war; and its culmination, not only the inauguration of the Organisation for European Economic Co-operation in April 1948, but the North Atlantic Treaty of April 1949.

By the end of 1947, Europe had run through all the special assistance originally provided for its recovery from the war.   Without the means to finance a bare

---

[1] *Economist*, 22 Nov. 1947, p. 831; *H.C. Deb.* 17 Nov. 1947, 825; and Dalton [1962], pp. 276–86.

[2] 'A number of my friends told me afterwards', said Dr Dalton ' . . . that month by month they saw a growing change in me . . . more and more, I seemed strained and ill, and it was clear to many that a break might come.   One of my friends recalls that I said to him that to watch the continued loss of our reserves was "like watching a child bleed to death" and being unable to stop it' (Dalton [1962], p. 5).

minimum of the imports on which it depended, as near as countries can do, it faced bankruptcy[1].   But not only the economic hopes nurtured in 1945 had gone awry: even more serious, the political hope of an Anglo-American-Soviet effort to rebuild a democratic Europe was falling apart.   Communist parties were strengthening their grip on one after another of the countries occupied by the Russian armies[2].   Confidence in Soviet intentions could no longer be taken for granted.   With large communist minorities in both France and Italy, the division of Europe, daily deepening, unmasked new dangers.   To those surveying this scene, Mr Marshall's 'momentous offer' of aid appeared like 'new hope'[3]; and since the offer applied also to Russia, it was also a decisive test of her policy.   Should the Russians refuse, there was still the opportunity to rebuild the prosperity of Western Europe: 'the second chance that so rarely comes, and'—said Mr Eden—'when it does come, has the nature of a miracle'[4].   In the event the discussions on economic co-operation were almost from the start confined to Western Europe[5]; and the *ad hoc* Committee of European Economic Co-operation represented the sixteen nations later to join together in the permanent organization of OEEC[6].   The agreed report produced in September 1947, after surveying the economic problem of these countries and of Western Germany, outlined a recovery programme which, the countries hoped, would 'help to solve the economic problems which today face a large part of the European continent'[7].   Recovery from the worst

[1]'To the outside world, the most spectacular manifestation of this bankruptcy lay in the staggering $9 billion of foreign disinvestment, borrowings, and grants absorbed by Europe in 1947 in a desperate effort to maintain minimum levels of output, consumption and investment' (R. Triffin [1957], *Europe and the Money Muddle*, p. 31).

[2]   'We have to fact this fact, that ratification of the peace treaties with which the right hon. Gentleman [Mr Bevin] struggled for so long a period, is taking place in conditions of considerable cynicism, and the concessions for which he fought hardest . . . with their safeguards of such very simple things as the right of free speech, are being flouted in many lands before the ink on the document is dry . . . for those of us who do really want to see Anglo-American-Soviet friendship, it would be hypocritical to pretend that confidences are unshaken, or that good relations are unimpaired'.   Mr Eden: *H.C. Deb.* 19 June 1947, 2253.

    'When you . . . get down to the masses, what do they want?' said Mr Bevin in his reply to the debate.   'I find no differences in the hopes of the fathers or the loves of the mothers for their children . . . they have the same kind of dreams and aspirations.   Why not let them live?   Why set them at each other's throats?   That is the basis of my approach to the problems of a war-scarred Europe and world'.   (Same deb. 2359.)

[3]'New hope to Europe and the world': Mr Eden, same deb. 2254.

[4]Same deb. 2256.

[5]After Mr Molotov walked out of the first ministerial discussion, Czechoslovakian delegates continued for a short while to attend the official conference.   The communist *coup d'état* in Czechoslovakia did not occur till June 1948.

[6]The sixteen nations were Austria, Belgium, Denmark, France, Greece, Iceland, Ireland, Italy, Luxembourg, the Netherlands, Norway, Portugal, Sweden, Switzerland, Turkey and the United Kingdom.   Western Germany became officially a member in October 1949; Spain in July 1959.

[7]*General Report* of CEEC [1947], p. ix: prefatory 'Letter Addressed to Mr Marshall'.

dislocations of the war had been remarkably rapid.   Nevertheless in 1947 output
in Western Europe as a whole was still well below pre-war; and Europe's external
deficit with the rest of the world amounted to six or seven per cent of its collective
national product[1].   Gold reserves were being rapidly depleted: by the autumn
it was reported that many countries were already being forced to 'restrict their
imports of the fuel and raw materials which are indispensable for industrial
and agricultural production and to cut their imports of food to a point at which
industrial efforts can no longer be sustained . . . '[2]   The long-term solution
proposed was a 'strong production effort' by each country, directed particularly
at the modernization of its equipment and at the expansion of exports, especially
of exports to the American continent[2].   A large deficit meanwhile, declining
over the next three or four years, would be not only difficult to avoid, but indeed
desirable.   This was the case for Marshall Aid[3].

The need for a continuing organization to progress the recovery programme,
distribute aid, and foster co-operation led in April 1948 to the institution of the
Organisation for European Economic Co-operation—an organization which in
the years to come was to provide a region of increasing and effective liberalism
in a world not yet ready for the fully multilateral ideals of Bretton Woods.   To
the Organisation each country had to explain how it would so manage its affairs
that it could do without 'extraordinary external assistance' by the end of Marshall
Aid in four years' time.

The 'long-term plan' submitted by the United Kingdom claimed to be 'no
more and no less than a statement of economic strategy'.   The strategy, however, dominated policy during the next few years; and the document made the
strategy quite unusually explicit[4].   It was estimated in 1948 that over the next
four years 'physical' output might be increased to a third above its pre-war level[5].
This could be no more than a hope.   Desirable though high investment might
be to attain it, there were limits to how much was possible: both timber and steel

---

[1]See subsequent estimates in *A Decade of Co-operation* [Ninth annual report of OEEC:
1958], tables 1 and 3.   *Per capita* output was estimated at 75 per cent of 1938.

[2]*General Report* of CEEC, p. 6.

[3]The original estimate was that the deficit would be $8 billion in 1948 (*General Report*
of CEEC, p. 28): aid granted for this year was however $4·8 billion.   By 1950 it had
been reduced to $2·6 and by 1952 to $0·5 billion.   The deficit was in fact about $4·1 billion
in 1948, and by 1949 was already to be reduced to $1·3 billion (Triffin [1957], p. 314).

[4]The Long-Term Programme of the United Kingdom was submitted to the OEEC
in October 1948 and it seems to have been the original intention not to publish it.   It was,
however, published as a White Paper in December (along with 'The 1949–50 Programme')
under a title which somewhat disguised its importance: *European Co-operation: Memoranda
submitted to the Organisation for European Economic Co-operation relating to Economic
Affairs in the period 1949 to 1953* (Cmd. 7572).

[5]Long-Term Programme, para. 219.   This was not in fact an ambitious aim.   By 1947
industrial *plus* agricultural output was above the 1938 level.   Though the full figures
were not then available, output rose markedly in 1948.   By 1948/49 it must have been
15–20 per cent above pre-war, leaving only another 10–15 per cent expansion to be achieved
in the next four years.

were short; and, equally important, room had to be found for increased exports[1]. It was hoped to expand exports almost forty per cent above the 1947 level—to about 50 per cent above pre-war[2]. Imports were to continue to be severely curtailed—practically no increase in their volume being allowed for[3]. Though food rationing would have to be continued, there seemed room for a distinct increase both in food consumption, and in consumption in general—at that date (on a *per capita* basis) still well below pre-war.

It was a general assumption, here as in other countries, that considerable government intervention would be required to achieve these aims. A rigorous fiscal policy would be needed to restrain consumption, and thus free resources for exports and investment. But something more positive seemed needed than mere financial restraint. The scale on which resources would have to be redirected seemed more like the wartime problem—though now, as the White Paper recognized, wartime controls were only partly applicable[4]. 'A large measure of control will have to be retained over imports, over the total amount of home consumption, and over the scale and composition of investment'. But a great deal would still depend on persuasion and 'the willing co-operation and understanding of the general public'[5]. Policy was in fact to be an intimate mixture of cajolery and compulsion[6].

---

[1]Fixed investment was expected to increase by only 13 per cent between 1947 and 1952/53 (*LTP*, para. 156). Investment in 1948 was already in fact considerably higher than in 1947, but this was not then known.

[2]*LTP*, para. 23. This was again a very modest aim: exports in 1948 were already 27 per cent higher than in 1947.

[3]*LTP*, para. 23: they were still to be 'significantly less than pre-war'.

[4]'In present conditions, the quasi-automatic operation of economic forces could not produce the right results or produce them without immense social upheaval' (*LTP*, para. 2). But 'no economic planning body can be aware (or indeed ever could be aware) of more than the very general trends of future economic developments' (*LTP*, para. 3).

[5]*LTP*, para. 6.

[6]The White Paper gave two illustrations of the Government's very various powers of influence.

'A number of domestic policies are directed to ensuring that, wherever possible, ample supplies are available for export. The Government has established the practice of laying down each year, in consultation with each industry, a series of export targets, and has appealed to industry, with very considerable success, to co-operate in reaching them as a matter of national endeavour. Supporting this voluntary effort, general fiscal measures help to prevent the pressure of home demand from restricting export supplies and to secure that production for export is at least as profitable as production for the home market. So long as physical controls over raw materials and production are available, they provide a further means of seeing that production for export is kept at the highest possible level.' (para. 57.)

'There is a wide range of controls in force to ensure that investment resources are canalised in the desired direction. In addition to the control of capital issues on the capital market these also include the licensing or authorisation of all building work above small fixed limits, statutory distribution schemes for steel and timber and arrangements, statutory or voluntary, with the various sections of the engineering industries about the division of the output of plant and machinery between the home and export markets. In the case of the nationalised industries the Boards are required

Ambitious economic policy requires strong direction; and, as it happened, Sir Stafford Cripps's elevation to Chancellor of the Exchequer had brought a major concentration of the powers of economic control. As Chancellor he continued to exercise the functions of Minister of Economic Affairs[1], which he had just taken over from Mr Morrison as Lord President. The newly created economic planning staff was transferred to the Treasury, and acquired a more central role as the context of economic policy developed[2]. The appointment of an Economic Planning Board[3] and the Economic Information Unit[4] were marginal additions whose inception owed much to the Crippsian philosophy of government by persuasion. With its increased responsibility, the Treasury gained a new junior minister. Mr Douglas Jay was appointed to the newly created post of Economic Secretary in December 1947. Sir Stafford Cripps's old post as President of the Board of Trade had been filled by Mr Harold Wilson, then young to senior office; and partly because of this, the Treasury exercised a special degree of influence over the affairs of this large department.

It is probably the case that no minister before or since, even during the war years, had as great power to direct the economy as Sir Stafford Cripps. Such

by statute when framing programmes of reorganisation or development involving substantial outlay on capital account to act on lines settled from time to time by the responsible Minister.' (para. 160.)

[1] This was made clear in the official announcement of his appointment in November 1947: see Chester [1952], p. 348.

[2] The allocation of a declining number of materials by a separate central committee continued throughout the Labour Government's term. But as time went on the two major allocation tasks came to be investment and import programming (Morrison [1954], p. 301). Responsibility for organizing interdepartmental consultation on the allocation of imports, and framing recommendations thereon, continued to be the function of an established division of the Treasury, that of Overseas Finance. The Planning Staff's main tasks were investment programming; and general 'co-ordination', particularly where this required interdepartmental co-operation (see Sir Edward (now Lord) Bridges's [1950] Stamp Memorial Lecture, *Treasury Control*). The Economic Section remained formally under the Cabinet Office; but economic decisions were now made by the Chancellor not the Lord President, and when the Section was transferred to the Treasury in 1953 it had for five years been part of it in all but name.

These developments in the 'machinery of government' were no doubt important; but too much can be made of them. The development of the official machine during and after the war was little more than the development of a way of working, through various committees, interdepartmental or otherwise. The number of the 'administrative' grade in the post-war Treasury was hardly more than twice pre-war (Bridges [1950], p. 25). The Economic Planning Staff consisted of 25-30 people, mostly in the upper level of the 'administrative' class; the Economic Section, of never more than 15 people graded as economists; and the Central Statistical Office of as many statisticians. (Chester [1952], p. 353.)

[3] The Economic Planning Board had been appointed in July 1947 'to advise His Majesty's Government on the best use of resources' (*H.C. Deb.* 27 March 1947, 1414-5 and 7 July 1947, 1810-4). It consisted of permanent secretaries of various Ministries, together with representatives of the Federation of British Industries, the British Employers' Confederation and the Trades Union Congress: the chairman was the Chief Planning Officer, Sir Edwin Plowden.

[4] Later renamed the Information Division of the Treasury.

D

responsibilities, with his temperament, inevitably bore heavily; and within eighteen months of his appointment as Chancellor he was in very poor health[1]. Mr Gaitskell, then Minister of Fuel and Power in succession to Mr Shinwell, came to play an increasing part in economic policy, a fact recognized by his appointment as Minister of State for Economic Affairs[2] in February 1950.

Economic policy tends to be relatively impersonal, but that of Sir Stafford Cripps cannot be separated entirely from his ideals. The idea of 'democratic planning', which dominated the first *Economic Survey* and ran through all his major speeches, though liberal as to method, was essentially *dirigiste* in aim. It was the part of government 'to assess our national resources', 'to formulate the national needs', and to state how resources could 'best' be used 'in the national interest'[3]. Some controls, physical and financial, were acceptable to public opinion: and as far as they went, these should be utilized to implement the plan. But complete direction from the centre being impossible in a democracy, the direction of the economy must in great part be accomplished by 'agreement, persuasion, consultation and other free democratic methods'[4]. To Cripps himself, the 'first call' was 'to put into practice in our industrial life those basic principles of honesty and honour which we have so long declared to be the foundation of our spiritual life' and 'to submerge all thought of personal gain and personal ambition in the greater and deeper desire to give our all to secure the future prosperity and happiness of our people'[5]. To him, at the same time both lawyer and a Christian, moral imperatives were as binding and also as clear as the law; and he felt able confidently to call for the voluntary co-operation of the nation in the tasks appointed by the government. It is not surprising that, as he once said, 'it has always been difficult to explain, especially to those who did not wish to understand, the real object and the limitations of democratic planning'[6].

He himself had a straightforward grasp of the needs of the case; and his speeches at times an almost Cromwellian directness.

'You will see, then, that as long as we are in this impoverished state, the result of our tremendous efforts in two world wars, our own consumption requirements have to be the last in the list of priorities. First are

---

[1] In 1949, unable to sleep and suffering from indigestion, he had to retire to a Swiss clinic for six weeks, from mid-July to the beginning of September (Colin Cooke [1957], *The Life of Richard Stafford Cripps*, p. 389).

[2] This was a new Treasury post which replaced the more junior post of Economic Secretary.

[3] *Economic Survey for 1947*, para. 12: similar statements occur in many of Cripps's speeches.

[4] *H.C. Deb.* 18 April 1950, 39.

[5] Speech to Norwich, Lowestoft and Great Yarmouth Chamber of Commerce, 19 March 1947 (quoted in Cooke [1957], p. 355).

[6] In his last budget speech: *H.C. Deb.* 18 April 1950, 38.

exports ... ; second is capital investment in industry; and last are the needs, comforts and amenities of the family'[1].

If by then the issues of post-war policy began to seem much clearer, this is partly because the new Chancellor brought to economic policy an altogether new sense of drive and direction; and because the result of his own spirit was to get done many things that would not otherwise have been done. His most striking success, perhaps, was the impetus he gave to the export drive. Between 1947 and 1948 exports rose 25 per cent; and it is difficult not to believe that this was due in large part to the system of export targets, which had been agreed in considerable detail with all the main industries while Sir Stafford Cripps was still at the Board of Trade[2].

Almost equally impressive are the many restraints, backed by no legal sanction, which were in fact observed. Voluntary dividend restraint must partly account for the very small increase in dividends between 1947 and 1950[3]. Industry also agreed to a voluntary restraint of advertising[4]. Wage restraint dates from February 1948[5]: in the next two and a half years (while retail prices rose 8 per cent) wages rates rose only 5 per cent. Another manifestation of Cripps's policy was the appointment of 'working parties' to study the problems of particular industries[6]; and the less successful attempt to furnish each with a 'development council'.

[1]In a speech at Workington, January 1949 (quoted *Economist*, 22 Jan. 1949, p. 130).

[2]In September 1947 Cripps had announced targets for 153 classes of exports, which had been agreed both for the middle and the end of 1948: Cooke [1957], p. 361. In the next few months, they were 'exhaustively reviewed and revised' (*H.C. Deb.* 6 Apr. 1948, 40).

[3]By agreement with the Chancellor, the Federation of British Industries recommended a relatively rigid code of behaviour to its members (see *Economist*, 20 March 1948, p. 466). Companies themselves were doubtless anxious to plough back large profits. But dividend payments had hardly increased since 1938 (they were only a quarter of company profits compared with almost half in 1938); and without 'restraint', would almost certainly have increased.

[4]Dr Dalton had proposed to disallow one half of expenditure on advertising as a tax-free expense (*H.C. Deb.* 12 Nov. 1947, 403). Instead, a voluntary scheme to limit advertising expenditure was worked out by the Federation of British Industries.

[5]The *Statement on Personal Incomes, Costs and Prices* (Cmd. 7321) was much more forthright than previous appeals for restraint. It proposed that, with some exceptions, increases in costs due to higher wages should be disallowed for purposes of price control. But the effectiveness of the policy was due less to this sanction, which did not prove easy to enforce, than to its acceptance by the trade unions. After a period of increasing restiveness, the unions abandoned such restraint about October 1950. Mr Deakin had been its strongest supporter: in October the Transport and General Workers' Union decided officially to take up the wage claims of its member groups (*Economist*, 21 Oct. 1950, p. 620). The partial success of wage restraint should not make one forget that the White Paper included an equally confident appeal to entrepreneurs to reduce prices, which had no discernible effect.

[6]This too had been started by Cripps when President of the Board of Trade: seventeen were eventually appointed. Their reports led to the Industrial Organisation and Development Act, under which development councils might be appointed. Only four were. (See P. D. Henderson [1952] 'Development Councils: an Industrial Experiment', in *The British Economy, 1945–1950*.)

The impressiveness of Sir Stafford Cripps's budgets depended less on the rigour of his measures, than on the uncompromising principles on which they were based and the tenacity with which he held to them.   At times, he almost appeared to regard budgetary action as no more than the background to planning proper: too high a level of demand drew off resources to 'inessential' uses, and made 'all planning a matter of extreme difficulty'[1].   But budgetary policy had in truth a more positive role to play.   The existing inflationary pressure meant that 'the economic system cannot work smoothly'[1].   Since inflationary pressure would be increased as investment and exports expanded, consumption had to be limited to what was left after these prior 'claims' had been met[2].   'Disinflation' however, proved in the event to be an unexpectedly slow process[3].

Sir Stafford Cripps was now not only Chancellor of the Exchequer but 'economic overlord', and one consequence of his approach was fully to rein-state the general economic survey in the budget speech.   The *Economic Survey for 1948*, issued in March as background to the budget debate, was a much more precise and detailed document than its predecessor.   It included national income forecasts for the year ahead; and on this occasion was preceded by a separate White Paper on the capital investment programme[4].   The 1948 budget speech fully reflected this range of reference.   A good third was taken up with actual tax proposals.   The greater part of the rest was taken up with the balance of payments and import and export policy; the European recovery plan: inflation, manpower targets, and forecast claims on resources; and, finally, price and wage restraint.   Little time was spent on recital of 'the year's out-turn' and other details of narrowly financial nature.

After the disasters of 1947 it was inevitable that the dominant theme of the 1948 *Survey* and speech should be the need for exports.   Exports had not risen

---

[1]*H.C. Deb.* 6 April 1948, 44.

[2]The Chancellor himself relied not only on taxation, but on the 'voluntary withholding of spending', to produce disinflation: 'Inflationary pressure cannot be removed entirely by Government action unless we envisage a degree of economic control which is too rigid to be operated in a democracy' (*H.C. Deb.* 6 April 1948, 47).

[3]Use of the term 'disinflation' attracted some ridicule.   As Mr Churchill said

'The Chancellor of the Exchequer is very delicate in his language.   One must not say "deflation" but only "disinflation".   In a similar manner, one must not say "devaluation", but only "revaluation", and, finally, there is the farce of saying there must be no increase in personal incomes when what is meant is no increase in wages. . . I suppose that presently when "disinflation" also wins its bade name, the Chancellor will call it "nonundisinflation" and will start again' (*H.C. Deb.* 27 Oct. 1949, 1628).

Cripps had however already given a neat example of what he meant by disinflation:

'If I may take the simple analogy of a motor tyre, if it is pumped up too hard you disinflate it to the right level, but when you get a puncture you deflate it altogether. We want to disinflate our economy and not to puncture or deflate it' (*H.C. Deb.* 5 July 1948, 46).

[4]*Capital Investment in 1948* (Cmd. 7268, December 1947).

as hoped; and though imports were only three quarters the pre-war volume, the external deficit had been nearly £700 million, and we had lost £1,000 million in reserves.   Marshall Aid had given us time, but only limited time. 'Time', said the Chancellor, 'is the scarcest commodity of all today, and we cannot afford to waste a moment of it'[1].   The stages of the argument from this starting point, to the Chancellor's final proposals, were, however, not made explicit.   His conclusion that he should aim at a 'true overall surplus' of about £300 million came in his speech very much as an article of faith.   This was what would result if no changes in tax were made, and 'in my view' said Sir Stafford, 'it is just about adequate'[2].   The *Survey* put the matter more plainly. Government expenditure was falling, while tax revenue was naturally rising; the autumn investment cuts were expected to be effective.   Despite much smaller borrowing abroad, a considerable disinflation therefore seemed quite possible, even with a 'no change' budget[3].

The centre piece of the 1948 budget was the 'special contribution'—'a special once-for-all levy . . . largely payable out of capital'[4].   Some £50 million of the contribution was expected within the year: including this, budget tax increases about matched the reductions.   'It is undoubtedly right', said the Chancellor 'that those who possess large capital assets should make some contribution to help the country in this emergency'.   Being largely a tax on capital, however, it was unlikely to affect spending much.   In effect, then, the tax changes went in the inflationary direction, to the tune of £50 million.   Indirect taxes were raised by some £55 million, while income tax was reduced by £100 million—concentrated on personal earned incomes at the lower end of the scale[5].

The 'degree of inflationary pressure' seemed at the time impossible to measure with any confidence[6]; and the knife-edge between inflation and deflation was doubtless greatly exaggerated.   To 'watch the situation carefully, and be ready

[1]*H.C. Deb*. 6 April 1948, 44.

[2]Same deb. 59–60.   In spite of the loose form of his justification, the Chancellor was much concerned with criticism that the traditional budget accounts did not measure the economic impact of the budget; this criticism had arisen through Dr Dalton's treatment of 'unspent balances' the previous April (§2 above).   Sir Stafford met it by including an experimental 'alternative classification' of the budget accounts in the *Financial Statement*. The 'true overall surplus' was the overall surplus on this new definition.   (See further chapter VII.1 below.)

[3]*Economic Survey for 1948* (Cmd. 7344), tables XXIV–XXVI.

[4]*H.C. Deb*. 6 April 1948, 71.   It was based on the previous year's income from investment, as assessed to income tax.   Compared with most capital levies, it was thus easy to assess. The full yield was estimated at £105 million.

[5]Effects in a 'full year'.   Taxes on drink and tobacco and betting were increased somewhat; and there was a major readjustment of the structure of purchase tax, which involved a net loss of revenue.   The income tax reductions were by way of earned income relief, and reduction of the 'reduced rates' of tax applying to the first 'tranches' of taxable income. (See further chapter VII.3.)

[6]'It is not possible to give any accurate answer to the question: "How much inflation is there?" ' (*H.C. Deb*. 6 April 1948, 47).

to detect the moment when the inflationary pressure vanishes and gives place to deflationary tendencies' seemed a real need; and a 'rapid readjustment' of policies, something that might quite well be called for[1]. Nothing like this occurred. All that the Chancellor could claim at his next budget was that 'a comfortable and not excessive degree of disinflation' had been brought about[2]. In most ways, however, as the next *Economic Survey* claimed, 1948 was 'a year of great and steady progress'[3]. Production rose rapidly; exports rose even more spectacularly; and the balance of payments appeared at last to be swinging into surplus (table 2.2).

It is not surprising, then, that the mood at the beginning of 1949, was to repeat the mixture as before. The forecasts in the *Survey* provide a good idea of what was expected. With policy running on the same lines, great difficulties seemed unlikely. Resources would still have to be diverted from consumption to export. Investment, strangely enough, despite its unplanned increase in the previous year[4], was not expected to show a further rise. Indeed, all developments were expected to be less dynamic. The implication seemed to be a 'no-change' budget[5]; and this is indeed what the Chancellor decided. There were some small changes in indirect taxes, which in effect cancelled out. The duty on beer was reduced by £20 million, but the rise in the tax on football pools and matches, and in post office charges, added up to the same amount. At the same time, death duties were slightly increased and, more important, the 'initial' depreciation allowances were doubled[6]. Neither of these was likely to affect consumption. But it seems clear that in the mind of the Chancellor, who

---

[1] *H.C. Deb.* 6 April 1948, 49.

[2] He pointed to the fall in unfilled vacancies—still, however, in excess of the number unemployed; to the derationing of bread, jam, confectionery and clothing; and to the slow rise in wage rates (*H.C. Deb.* 6 April 1949, 2078–9). The budget speech was rather more complacent than the *Survey*, which after reciting the same evidence, added 'But disinflation has not gone very far' (para. 108).

[3] *Economic Survey for 1949*, para. 3.

[4] Instead of declining as originally planned, the volume of fixed investment rose £200 million between 1947 and 1948. This was explained as being in part due to a revision of policy 'once Marshall Aid had become an established fact'. But it seems likely that most was due to the unexpectedly large rise in the output both of steel, and of plant, machinery and vehicles (see *H.C. Deb.* 6 April 1949, 2075).

[5] This was the general import of the *Survey's* discussion of the national income forecasts and their implications for the budget: see paras. 113–5.

[6]   'All plant and machinery, of course, receives in wear and tear allowance 100 per cent of its cost over the agreed life of the plant, so that the initial allowance of 20 per cent makes no difference to the total result in the long-run. But the immediate result is important, for early relief in Income Tax and Profits Tax on the larger sum is afforded, and thus more money becomes available for re-equipment at an earlier date. Owing to the further rise in prices, it is now urged that this help is not enough, and current depreciation allowances on machinery, bought at prices much lower than those now ruling, are not sufficient to allow replacement at existing prices.

'I have therefore decided to double the existing initial allowance in respect of plant and machinery purchased on or after 6th April 1949, making it 40 per cent of the new cost'. (*H.C. Deb.* 6 April 1949, 2105.)

Table 2.2. *The British economy, 1948–51*

	1946	1947	1948	1949	1950	1951
Changes in final expenditure[a] (£m., 1948 prices[b])						
Consumer durables[c]	..	75	25	50	50	−25
Other consumption	..	200	−75	75	150	−25
Government current expenditure	..	−825	—	150	—	150
Fixed investment	..	250	125	125	75	—
Investment in stocks[d]	..	400	−175	−100	−250	600
Exports, goods and services	..	100	425	250	325	125
TOTAL	..	200	325	550	350	825
of which imports	..	150	−25	175	25	375
Gross domestic product[e] (% change[f])	..	1	3½	4½	3½	3½
Industrial production (% change[f])	..	6	8	6½	6½	3½
Labour market						
Percentage unemployment	1·8	1·6[g]	1·5	1·5	1·5	1·2
Index of excess demand[h]	2·0	2·0	1·4	0·8	0·5	1·4
Prices and wages (% change in year[i])						
Retail prices	0·2[j]	2·4[j]	5·9	3·3	3·0	11·8
Wage rates	8·2	4·1	4·2	1·9	3·4	10·7
Foreign trade[k] (1947=100)						
Volume of exports	91	100	127	140	162	167
Volume of imports	88	100	105	114	114	132
Terms of trade	93	100	102	101	108	123
Balance of payments[l] (£m.[b])						
Exports	925	1,150	1,600	1,850	2,250	2,750
Imports	1,075	1,550	1,800	1,975	2,400	3,500
Invisibles	−125	−25	200	175	425	325
Current balance	−300	−450	—	50	300	−425
Special receipts, from USA and Canada[l] (£m.)	279	812	251	334	259	77
Change in reserves (£m.)	54	−152	−55	−3[m]	575	−344

[a]From *NI & E* [1957] at market prices.
[b]Rounded to nearest £25m.
[c]Household durables *plus* motor vehicles.
[d]Table shows *change* in investment in stocks: investment in stocks (£m.) was

1946	1947	1948	1949	1950	1951
60	360	170	60	190	400

[e]Average of changes shown by production and expenditure series: from *NI & E* [1957].
[f]Change of year's average over previous year.
[g]Adjusted to remove effects of fuel crisis.
[h]Roughly twice the difference between % vacancies and % unemployment; the amplitude of the index is thus twice that originally presented in Dow and Dicks-Mireaux [1958], *Oxford econ. Pap.* (see chapter XIII.2 below).
[i]Change during year, measured between successive fourth quarters.
[j]Official index understates rise in consumers' prices.
[k]Board of Trade estimates: *AAS* [1952], tables 208 and 330.
[l]From *UKBP* [1959], tables 1 and 15.
[m]Excludes sterling revaluation of the reserves on 18 Sept.
For key to abbreviations see introductory note, p. xiii above.

still justified what he did in the somewhat mystical terms of a 'required' overall budget surplus, they were an integral part of his budget arithmetic[1].

To defend his budget behind a 'right' surplus did not save the Chancellor all further trouble. To keep taxes high and expenditure down for such a purpose seemed only too much like austerity for its own sake. Sir Stafford Cripps was not the Chancellor to fly this reputation. The main impact of his 1949 budget came not from what he did, but from the warnings—intended for his own party —on the social services. No one wanted to cut them he said, for 'we all know their immense value'. Equally, however, we must 'recognise the unpleasant fact that these services must be paid for, and they must be paid for by taxation . . .' But redistributive taxation had reached its limit. Any extension of social services must therefore be narrowly limited: 'ability to pay for them' would only increase with national income[2]. He was equally stern about the food subsidies. In the previous April it had been hoped to keep them down to £400 million; to help wage restraint they had in fact been allowed to rise to £485 million. In the coming year, if the price stabilization policy were continued, they were likely to mount to £570 million. The Chancellor proposed for the future a ceiling of £465 million[3]. All this does not, in retrospect, seem particularly austere. But it was evidently austere compared with what his party had been expecting[4].

As in 1948, the Chancellor again emphasized the need to remain 'alert' and ready to change policy should 'disinflation . . . widen into . . . deflation'[5].

---

[1]   'On the whole, therefore, in view of the world tendencies which I have mentioned [i.e. a world disinflationary trend], and the check on the growth of inflationary pressure which we have manifestly secured during the past year, and which has probably not yet entirely worked itself out, it seems that we should follow the same general policy as last year for our Budget, though not with so sharp an accent upon the urgent need to check inflation. We shall certainly need an over-all balance on the right side, though not so large an over-all balance as we realised last year. Similarly we should aim at a true revenue surplus which, while in itself very substantial, need not be so large as that realised last year' (*H.C. Deb.* 6 April 1949, 2085–6).
The Chancellor's audience can hardly have understood the argument, and it is difficult to believe that they were intended to.

[2]Same deb. 2091–2.

[3]Same deb. 2093. 'We must call a halt', he said, 'or else we shall find ourselves in the ridiculous position of having to refuse to import much needed food, because we cannot afford to pay the subsidy out of our Budget'.

[4]'I very much wish' said the Chancellor in the conclusion to his speech, 'that the facts of the situation had enabled me to present a more attractive picture. . . But we have to face our . . . problems with realism, and must not allow ourselves to be carried away by the quite understandable desire to court electoral popularity' (*H.C. Deb.* 6 April 1949, 2107). *The Economist* commented: 'Sir Stafford Cripps's Budget caused an internal eruption in the Labour Party which was only with difficulty brought under control.' Labour lost seats at the London and other county elections next day. 'There is no doubt that the defeats that local labour parties have suffered have come as a shock to the national party, and it will be all too easy to reason that the "austerity" Budget and the local election losses were simple cause and effect.' (*The Economist*, 16 April 1949, p. 689.)

[5]*H.C. Deb.* 6 Apr. 1949, 2086.

His concern was chiefly with developments abroad, particularly in the United States, then entering the first of her post-war recessions. These developments were in fact to have major repercussions on the United Kingdom during 1949. But it was the gold reserve, not the pressure of demand, that was affected; and exchange policy, not budget policy, that had to adapt.

Had sterling been devalued in April, it would have been as a considered move, not as a crisis measure. As had later to be admitted, there were good arguments for some devaluation of sterling—as of many other currencies—though not necessarily by the whole of the eventual thirty per cent. The dollar gap was a persistent disequilibrium. Devaluation would not only tend to correct direct trade between the United Kingdom and the United States. Equally important, it would favour British as against American exports in third markets.

When however finally made, the decision had the air of bowing to overwhelming inevitability. There were two main reasons for the exchange crisis in the summer of 1949. First, the trade position of the outer sterling area had weakened, partly because of the recession in the United States in the first half of the year. Sterling exports to the United States fell moderately—at a time when imports from the United States had been allowed to increase[1]. Second, there was strong speculative pressure due to the world-wide expectation that sterling would in fact have to be devalued. This speculation appears to have gone beyond the unassisted expectations of the market. Though the United States authorities appear to have put no direct pressure on the British government, they had long been known to favour the devaluation of sterling; and under their leadership, there appears to have been something of a campaign by the International Monetary Fund[2]. By June, *The Banker* was reporting the almost universal belief in the City that devaluation was inevitable ; and, even at this date, there were many in the City and in Basle who were talking of 'floating rates'[3]. Many economists had come by then to the conclusion that devaluation though not inevitable, would be advantageous[4].

---

[1]See ECE survey, *Economic Survey of Europe in 1949*, particularly pp. 121–2.

[2]The Chancellor said specifically that 'the question had not in fact been discussed with our American or Canadian friends' (*H.C. Deb.* 27 Sept. 1949, 8); and later evidently indicated dissent when Mr Churchill referred to a statement that the 'United States authorities have pressed us to devaluate' (same deb. 28 Sept. 163). In February, however, Mr Snyder, giving evidence to the Senate Foreign Relations Committee, said that devaluation should be 'explored' with countries receiving Marshall Aid: in previous similar remarks he appears to have gone out of his way to exclude sterling from the currencies that might be devalued (*Economist*, 26 Feb. 1949, p. 384). Triffin remarks that the British had in September been 'irked by a previous American-led Fund campaign in favour of sterling devaluation' (Triffin [1957], p. 119). In mid-September, immediately before the devaluation, the annual report of the IMF came out in public favour of 'exchange adjustments' for countries with dollar difficulties.

[3]*Banker*, June 1949, p. 71 and Sept. 1949, p. 159. For 1952–5 discussion of floating rates see chapter III.3 below.

[4]The ECE *Survey*, in May, surveying export prices, concluded that 'European currencies in general are over-valued in relation to the dollar' (*Economic Survey of Europe in 1948*,

To all these pressures, Sir Stafford Cripps returned a sequence of determined denials that devaluation was either necessary or intended[1]. The Government's reaction was to take all alternative lines of defence. The tide began to be apparent in the early summer. After a steady improvement for eighteen months, the dollar deficit began to worsen. In the second quarter of 1949 it doubled, and we lost £160 million of gold[2]. In June and July the Government imposed dollar import cuts[3]. The deterioration in sterling trade that was then apparent led it in July to raise this country's 'bid for aid'—which created a 'considerable furore' among the other claimants for aid at OEEC[4]—and to convene the finance ministers of the Commonwealth to meet in London in July. At this conference the other sterling countries agreed to cut dollar imports as the United Kingdom was doing. In due course this had considerable effect in amending the sterling area's dollar account[5]. But it could not be immediate; it did not stop the speculative pressure; and the dollar drain continued.

p. 106). *The Economist's* leading article of 7 May was entitled 'Rigidities'. 'Sir Stafford Cripps', it said 'has performed more miracles in making the unworkable work than would have been believed possible. But it cannot go on for ever at full stretch. Something must be relaxed somewhere—or something will give way somewhere' (*Economist*, 7 May 1949, p. 826). Later in the same issue (p. 851) it discussed exchange rates more explicitly.

[1] One of the 'most categorical' of these rebuttals was made by the Chancellor when visiting Italy at the beginning of May. As *The Economist* then commented, his rejection of devaluation appeared to be in danger of becoming 'a rigid and eternal dogma' (*Economist*, 7 May 1949, p. 851). The explanation may be that financial manipulation of this sort appeared to him too easy to be effective. In the middle of 1947, during an early bout of devaluation rumours, he had said: 'When you are at the limit of exports and already rigidly control your imports, you do not get any better control by monkeying about with your currency' (see Cooke [1957], p. 369).

[2] The deterioration was moderate rather than spectacular. The dollar deficit in the four quarters of 1948 was £147 million, £107 million, £76 million, and £93 million respectively. For the first two quarters of 1949 the figures were £82 million and £157 million (*H.C. Deb*. 27 Sept. 1949, 10). In the next two and a half months to 18 Sept. (devaluation), the deficit must have been about as large as in the second quarter; in the succeeding 3½ months, there was a small surplus. A good part of these fluctuations can be explained in terms of the dollar deficit of the overseas sterling area, and of the United Kingdom import cuts which began to take effect in the fourth quarter. This suggests that speculation was of secondary importance in the crisis.

[3] Before mid-June purchasing departments had been instructed to postpone all new dollar purchases (*H.C. Deb*. 6 July 1949, 2161). On 14 July it was announced that dollar imports in the OEEC (American fiscal) year 1949/50 would be cut by 25 per cent or £100 million (*H.C. Deb*. 14 July 1949, 690).

[4] The 'bid' was raised from $940 million to $1,114 million: $962 million was eventually allotted (*Economist*, 30 July 1949, p. 258 and 3 Sept. 1949, p. 488).

[5] Speaking of the change in the trade position of the overseas sterling area, the next ECE *Survey* said:

'In the second half of the year, the decline in exports was accentuated (although recovering somewhat towards the end of the year), but was more than offset by the drastic fall in imports from the United States, resulting in large part from the import restrictions agreed upon between the United Kingdom and other sterling area countries in July . . .' (*Economic Survey of Europe in 1949*, p. 122).

At this juncture Sir Stafford Cripps fell ill. He had worked incessantly[1]; and to recover, retired to a clinic in Switzerland for six weeks. Sir Stafford did not return till the second part of August; and the decision to devalue may well have owed something to those who had been concerned with policy in his absence[2]. The announcement was delayed till Sunday 18 September, during the Chancellor's attendance at the IMF meeting in Washington; and took effect next day.

As expected, this provoked a major realignment of other currencies[3]. The main reason for delaying the announcement was, indeed, so that other countries might have an interval, though inevitably brief, in which to consider how they would react[4]. The need to do so must have added greatly to the anxieties of the operation: as the Chancellor said, 'it is really remarkable that with all these widespread notifications there was not any leakage of this information'[5]. Since many finance ministers would anyhow be coming together in Washington, for the meeting of the Fund, it no doubt seemed a convenient occasion for the announcement, besides making it simple to arrange a special meeting of the Fund formally to approve the change[6].

The extent of the devaluation was greater than expected, and has been

---

[1]Sir Stafford Cripps's own day 'began somewhere about 5 a.m., with several hours of drafts in his own hand on the papers he had with him'. (Cooke [1957], pp. 382 and 402.)

[2]Sir Stafford Cripps in his statement on devaluation:

' . . . I did not return to take any part in affairs until 19th August. As soon as I then arrived back I reviewed the situation with those of my colleagues who had been particularly concerned with those matters during my absence, and with my advisers. The adverse tendencies which had already been noticeable in July . . . were in fact persisting.'

'In these changed circumstances . . . we changed our intentions, and decided that we must take action but that it would not be wise or practicable for us to act until after our visit to Washington . . .' (*H.C. Deb.* 27 Sept. 1949, 8–9).

Mr Gaitskell, then Minister of Fuel and Power, had evidently been concerned with the general economic situation since July (see *Economist*, 9 July 1949, p. 57).

[3]Many countries, including many of the sterling countries as well as the Scandinavians, followed Britain down by the full 30·5 per cent. Some others, including Canada, France, Germany and Belgium, went half way. Many others, including Brazil, Japan, Pakistan and Switzerland, retained their old dollar parity.

[4]Commonwealth Governments, and the French, were informed on the Friday. Other members of the OEEC, and 'other Governments particularly concerned' were notified on the Saturday. A special meeting of the Fund was called at the United Kingdom's suggestion for the Saturday to approve 'our own and other proposed changes in exchange rates'. (*H.C. Deb.* 27 Sept. 1949, 9–10.)

[5]Same deb. 10.

[6]'The Fund's Agreement provided that the Fund would have seventy-two hours to declare its attitude when a proposed change in par value did not exceed 20 per cent. The British request left the Fund less than twenty-four hours to agree or disagree with a 30·5 per cent devaluation, deemed unquestionably excessive by most Fund members. The Board agreed, in fact, the very same Saturday afternoon.' (Triffin [1957], pp. 119–20.) It is doubtful how far full consultation is in fact practicable. In the 'fifties, the expectation that major changes of exchange policy would be announced at the September meeting of the IMF caused this to become one of the major destabilizing dates in the financial calendar.

argued then and since to have been excessive. Sir Stafford Cripps's account of the reasons for going so far is of interest, not least for showing that the idea of floating rates, later to be so much in prominence[1], had powerful sponsors even at that date. 'Our first consideration' said the Chancellor 'was whether to adopt a fixed or, as it is called, a floating rate'[2]. The latter had been rejected as being unsettling, and probably, destabilizing in the face of the speculative pressures to which sterling was subject. The large devaluation of thirty per cent, to the new fixed rate of 2.80 dollars to the pound, had been decided for a number of reasons. To place British exporters 'in a fairly competitive position in the North American markets' it seemed necessary to go 'at very least as low as three dollars to the pound'. Some 'cheap sterling' transactions were already at below three dollars. 'Finally, it was necessary to make it absolutely plain that this was not a tentative first step but . . . that we had without doubt gone far enough'[3].

Devaluation called in turn for an adjustment of internal policy. The 'first and most obvious' repercussion, as the Chancellor said, was on prices—which, however, looked like being very limited. 'It may be', he said 'that by the end of the year . . . the index will have gone up by a point or so'. This probably was in fact a fair measure of the immediate impact[4]. The 'second danger' arose through the contraction of supplies at home if, as intended, devaluation stimulated exports. To meet this, the Government envisaged cuts in investment and government spending[5], announced in detail a month later.

Sir Stafford Cripps now saw devaluation as the only alternative to 'severe deflation', and a renewed opportunity to achieve equitable prosperity. 'I am still', he declared at the close of his devaluation speech, 'and shall remain, a

---

[1]See further chapter III.3 below.

[2]This had apparently been advocated as an accompaniment to convertibility, but in this form rejected at the outset:

'If by a "floating rate" its sponsors mean to imply that all our exchange and import controls should be taken off and the pound allowed to find its own level, we could not possibly think of such a course . . . The only question we considered was whether the pound should be left to find its own level within the limited range of transactions which are at present permitted over the exchanges.' (*H.C. Deb.* 27 Sept. 1949, 12.)

[3]Same deb. 14. The Chancellor added

'The general adjustment of exchange rates that followed our own change is . . . roughly in accordance with our expectations. We never had any intention of starting a general competitive lowering of exchange rates, and we therefore welcome the adjustments that have taken place as being a general contribution towards the attainment of equilibrium . . .'

[4]Since many countries followed us down, the average extent of our devaluation, allowing for the fact that many countries had devalued with us, was about 15 per cent (OEEC report [1950] on *Internal Financial Stability*, table 3). Since the import content of final output is about one sixth, the *direct* impact on the price level (after six months or so) may have been about $2\frac{1}{2}$ per cent. This in turn undoubtedly stimulated the rise in home costs (see further chapter XIII.4).

[5]Same deb. 27–30: an increase from 25 to 30 per cent in the profits tax on distributed profits was made straightaway.

persistent believer in the good of humanity'[1].   To the Opposition, this seemed somewhat jaunty.   The Chancellor, said Mr Eden, spoke in the tone of a conjuror who has brought off a 'clever trick and expects everyone to join rapturously in the applause'[2].   Party politics apart[3], the Government was, indeed, open to criticism.   The charge that, though necessary now, it was past government policies that had made it so, was perhaps off the mark: a post-war adjustment of the dollar parity—both of sterling and other currencies—would probably have had to be made sometime.   Nevertheless it would have been in every way better if measures of disinflation had been taken before, not after the devaluation; for among other reasons the need for more exports—which was one of the main grounds on which the emergency measures were justified—was not new.   After repeated specific government denials that it was going to be necessary, the act of devaluation inevitably appeared more a forced measure than wise statesmanship.   It was delayed till a late stage in the crisis; and cost a heavy, even if temporary, drain on the reserves.   This in turn probably led to a devaluation larger than necessary[4].

Measures to cut home demand were announced in detail by the Prime Minister at the end of October.   Fixed investment had been expected to rise by £100 million from 1949 to 1950.   Cuts were now to be made in the 'capital expenditure of the fuel and power industries, the expanding education programme, new housing, and the large field of miscellaneous investment'.   In total the cuts were intended to amount to £140 million—to become effective, however, only by the 'the second half' of the next year[5].   Government expenditure was to be cut by almost as much, though again with an inevitable delay: in total the

[1]Same deb. 32.   Earlier he had appealed 'that nothing—and I mean literally nothing—should be done to increase personal incomes arising out of profits, wages and salaries at least until we can see how far policy has succeeded . . .' (same deb. 25).

[2]*H.C. Deb.* 29 Sept. 1949, 429: Mr Eden was referring to the Chancellor's broadcast on devaluation.

[3]The imminence of a general election gave particular edge to the Opposition's attack, Mr Churchill going so far as to question the Chancellor's 'political honesty'.

'Ordinary people', he said, 'find it difficult to understand how a Minister, with all his knowledge and reputation for integrity, should have felt it right to turn completely round . . . and do what he repeatedly said he would never do . . . I am surprised, I must say, that the Chancellor's own self-respect did not make him feel that, however honest and necessary was his change of view, his was not the hand that should carry forward the opposite policy.   Certainly he stands woefully weakened in reputation, first by his lack of foresight, and secondly, by having had completely to reverse the reasoned convictions with which he has made us familiar.   Of course we know that changes in currency cannot be announced beforehand.   The secret had to be kept . . . we congratulate the Chancellor . . . and the Foreign Secretary on the high art which they displayed in the necessary process of deception.'   (Same deb. 28 Sept., 167–8.)

[4]The criticism, also made in the debate of 27–29 Sept., that other countries were given too little notice, seems less substantial.

[5]*H.C. Deb.* 24 Oct. 1949, 1018–9.   Investment was to be £140 million *less than originally intended*: this implied a much smaller fall as compared with the existing level (see *Economic Survey for 1950*, table 20).

saving was intended to be 'well over £100 million' for the financial year 1950/51. Apart from an unspecified cut in defence expenditure, most of the saving came from a highly miscellaneous list affecting most of the civil departments: a penny on school meals, and reduced transport facilities for pupils; smaller potato-acreage subsidies and 'the slowing down of proposed acquisition of farm land'; reduction of the strength of the Royal Ordnance factories; curtailment of local Food Offices; a cut for the British Council; the deferment of parts of the Legal Aid Scheme; cuts in the subsidies on food for the consumer, and on feeding stuffs for animals; and a shilling on National Health prescriptions. These piecemeal measures drew scathing Opposition attack: 'scratched together in the last fortnight', still 'sketchy and indefinite', 'only effective in the distant future' and out of all 'relation . . . to the needs of the hour' said Mr Eden; and Mr Thorneycroft: 'a make-shift arrangement got together by . . . harassed men . . . overtaken by the march of events'[1]. Neither investment nor government expenditure have ever been easy to control; and it is dubious how far the cuts were effectively enforced[2].

The next budget followed the election of February 1950. Though the Labour Government was returned, its majority was so greatly reduced as to make it doubtful how long it could carry on[3]. Though the new Parliament in fact lasted eighteen months, it was always under the shadow of a further election. In Mr Attlee's reconstituted administration, Sir Stafford Cripps was again Chancellor of the Exchequer; but he remained so for six months only, and failing health forced his retirement in October. Till then, Mr Gaitskell, as Minister of State for Economic Affairs, acted as a kind of deputy Chancellor.

By the spring the alarms of devaluation seemed a thing of the past. There had been spectacular improvement in the external situation. Three fifths of the loss of reserves during the summer had been recovered by the end of 1949; and at the beginning of April, the Chancellor was able to announce that the rest had

---

[1]*H.C. Deb.* 26 Oct. 1949, 1356, 1360 and 1394.

[2]It is always difficult to conduct a *post mortem* on cuts which are announced as cuts on a 'programme'; or to gauge what the actual figure would have been had the cuts not been made. Total fixed investment in 1950 was not, as intended, lower than in 1949, but higher by £100 million. It showed however no rise in volume between 1950 and 1951; and this may have been, in part, a delayed result of the cuts (as was suggested in the *Economic Survey for 1951*, para. 77: see further chapter VII). Investment in transport and communications— which was supposed to be affected—fell in both years. The same is true of housing; but here the cuts were revoked in early 1950 (*H.C. Deb.* 18 April 1950, 51).

At least one of the October economies in government account was also revoked—the shilling charge for National Health prescriptions (same deb. 60). Those enforced must have had much the effect that was intended. They were in part offset by supplementary estimates; but these (at £67 million in 1950/51) were much less than they had been (£310 million in 1948/49 and £170 million in 1949/50).

[3]'The tiny working majority was clearly going to make parliamentary life extremely difficult. Sick M.P.s were brought to the Commons at much risk, even on stretchers. The Inner Lobby was not a pleasing sight' (Mr Morrison, *Sunday Times*, 3 April 1960, p. 14).

been regained[1]. Many factors had contributed to this improvement. Of these—even though there had been a recovery in British dollar exports, and also a reversal of speculation—the effects of the devaluation were probably the least. The United States, now recovering from recession, was buying more wool, cocoa and other sterling commodities; and as a result of dollar import cuts, both in this[2] and the other sterling countries, the sterling area was buying less from the United States. At the beginning of 1950, balance of payments prospects looked generally favourable: at that date, the British balance was expected to improve by something like £100 million[3].

Sir Stafford Cripps's last budget in 1950 introduced few changes, and was by intent uncontroversial. The *Economic Survey* had concluded that—though the post-war, internal pressure of demand was at last 'beginning to ease'—demand in 1949 had been 'at an excessively high level'[4]. The Chancellor's budget speech seemed to put a more optimistic gloss on the interpretation: 'our internal situation' he said 'is on the whole less inflationary than at any time since the war': and 'having reached that condition', it was necessary only 'to take the necessary measures to maintain that balance which is in constant danger of being upset'[5]. As at other times, Sir Stafford Cripps was not prepared to shift the balance of the economy far; and was, if anything, ever too much aware of that 'narrow and difficult path between inflation . . . and deflation'[6].

On this occasion the need for 'necessary measures' arose chiefly out of the hoped-for 'favourable change in our foreign balance' which 'must be a first charge on our extra production in 1950'[7]. From this argument, the Chancellor slid—as before, by sleight of hand rather than by economic reasoning—to the conclusion that he needed an 'overall' balance in the budget. The estimates suggested that he had this already, the 'ordinary' account being in substantial surplus. This he was under heavy political pressure to reduce[8]—a consideration which may make it understandable that he should again aim no higher than a 'no-change' budget. The tax on petrol was increased to save dollars: petrol

[1] The figures (in $ million) were: end-March 1948 (immediately prior to Marshall Aid), *2,241*; end-March 1949, *1,912*; 17 Sept. 1949, *1,340*; end-Dec. 1949, *1,688*; end-March 1950, *1,984* (*Economic Survey for 1950*, paras. 13–16 and *H.C. Deb.* 4 April 1950, 1018–21).

[2] As a result of the gradual shift away from dollar imports, United Kingdom dollar imports had fallen, and non-dollar imports had risen, by one third in volume between 1947 and 1949.

[3] This figure was assumed for purposes of budget arithmetic. In fact the improvement was two and a half times as great (table 2.2).

[4] *Survey*, para. 27.

[5] *H.C. Deb.* 18 Apr. 1950, 66.

[6] Same deb. 52.

[7] Same deb. 67.

[8] The Chancellor went out of his way to give a lecture on 'the function of the Budget surplus'. 'There is one fallacy which seems to crop up almost every year. There is a belief amongst some people that a Budget surplus is like the declared profits of a company, and represents a fund available by way of remission of taxation. It is of course nothing of the kind' (same deb. 61–3).

in this country had previously been cheaper than in almost any other country in Europe. Income tax on the lower range of incomes, on the other hand, was reduced (by lowering the 'reduced rates' of income tax). These two changes more or less offset each other, resulting only in a redistribution of taxation[1]. Unlike his previous budget, this appears to have been accepted by his party without demur[2].

The reasoning behind this and other of Sir Stafford Cripps's budgets—at least as publicly presented—was open to technical objection. As *The Economist* pointed out—and as indeed the Chancellor had admitted in his experiment with the 'alternative classification' of the government accounts[3]—'the size of the below-line account' was quite irrelevant in deciding 'how large a surplus is needed to prevent inflation'[4]. The Chancellor, moreover, had hardly abided by the reasoning in the *Economic Survey*, 'strict adherence' to which would have compelled him to 'increase his "true" budget surplus by at least £100 million'[4].

Cripps's measure of austerity was however proving a test for the country's endurance. 'This year's budget', *The Economist* also said, 'will be taken as the final illustration of the fixed and rigid mould into which the British economy, and with it the British fiscal system, has been forced'[5]. Taxes had been kept high in the interest of disinflation; for this they barely sufficed; and except in supreme crisis could barely be raised higher. The most stern Chancellor it would be reasonable to expect seemed to have found the political limit to functional finance. 'Do not let us', he said in the peroration to his last budget speech, 'risk losing the advantages we have built up with such difficulty over these post-war years, just because we are unwilling to acknowledge the need to continue for a while longer stern measures . . .'[6] A little confused in theory, a little cautious in action, Sir Stafford Cripps's achievement was to have managed to have continued disinflationary budgeting for three years.

Sir Stafford Cripps's active budgetary policy accompanied an almost total disregard of monetary policy. The use of interest rates played no part in Sir Stafford Cripps's conception of democratic planning. He had for long resisted a change in the exchange rate as irrelevant under a system which relied on other more direct controls; and investment being controlled, interest rate changes

[1]The 'full year' effects were: petrol etc., plus £73 million; and income tax, minus £82 million. An extra £13 million was also expected from purchase tax on commercial vehicles (see further chapter VII.3).
[2]*Economist*, 22 April 1950, p. 871.
[3]See discussion above of the 1948 budget.
[4]*Economist*, 22 April 1950, p. 900.
[5]*Economist*, 22 April 1950, p. 865.
[6]'If we were now to relax our restraint and seeked to distribute our hardly earned and essential surplus' he continued—in a metaphor which became rather confused as it went on—'we should be like those bees, which seeing their honey stored in their hive for the winter, gave up their work and indulged themselves upon their apparent but much needed surplus, with fatal results in the ensuing cold weather' (*H.C. Deb.* 18 April 1950, 79).

seemed unimportant for much the same reasons[1]. Dr Dalton's monetary policy had been no more than a development—even though extreme—of a long tradition of official and economic thinking. Its collapse, therefore, left the authorities with no articulate policy.

Despite the epithet of 'neutral money' that has been applied to monetary policy during this period, government finance could hardly avoid some monetary impact. Though short-term rates hardly changed, long-term rates of interest crept up by about one percentage point during these three years. This was probably due to a mixture of reasons. It may have reflected a revision of market expectations in face of repeated balance of payments crises—and in face of the failure of the long heralded post-war slump to appear. It may also have reflected a degree of restraint in monetary policy. Though the growth of bank deposits continued, it grew less rapidly than the value of national output; and such relative restraint, acting on the public's liquidity preferences, may have helped to raise interest rates. Though hardly intended, it can well be argued that in an era of high investment demand this adjustment was appropriate. Sir Stafford Cripps, as other Chancellors of the Exchequer, can be criticized for lacking a well-conceived monetary policy. What actually happened under his aegis may however not be so far from what a well-conceived policy would have dictated[2].

Even if demand was still in some sense excessive in 1950, inflationary pressure was by then much lower than in the first post-war years. This can be regarded as no more than a natural development. As output expanded it was to be expected that it would increase the supply of goods and services more than the demand for them. This would however not have happened if tax rates had not been kept high. An indirect indication of the falling pressure of demand is provided by the statistics of the labour market. The change in unemployment, and the inverse change in unfilled vacancies may seem small (table 2.2); but these are probably sensitive indicators of economic balance[3]. They, however, understate the progress made; for, as shortages disappeared, the 'dam' of direct controls was also being dismantled without ill effect.

The dismantlement of controls acquired momentum only three years after the end of the war; and there were to be six more years before the last important control, the building licensing system, was abolished in 1954. The process, essentially continuous, was dramatized by Mr Wilson in the so-called 'bonfire' of Board of Trade controls in November 1948. Many minor controls, by then serving no economic function, were eliminated—a recognition of shortages already passed. Equally important was the easing of clothes and furniture

[1]See chapter IX.1 and IX.2 for quotations from Sir Stafford Cripps's 1947 defence of cheap money, and for the other details of monetary policy during this period.

[2]Both the reasons for the rise in interest rates, and the proper objects of interest policy, are complicated questions which must be much more fully discussed later: see chapter XII below.

[3]See further chapter XIII.2 below.

E

rationing about the same time, and their complete decontrol in the spring of 1949. There was a second stage of decontrol about 1950. Many price controls (which chiefly applied to consumer goods) had been suspended by the beginning of the year. The 'points' scheme (which rationed 'inessential' foods) was abolished in May, as was petrol rationing. In 1948 most industrial materials had been subject to allocation. Though allocations were later to be reimposed during the Korean war, by 1950 they applied to only half the materials consumed by industry[1].

Import controls remained extensive: even by 1950 most imports were still subject to control by the government[2]. In the first post-war years some two thirds of imports had been bought directly on public account. By 1950 this had been reduced to under half. The greater part of private imports was still restricted in 1950: only for sterling imports had there been an important removal of restriction. Progress with further relaxations was held up by the tangle of trade and payments arrangements that persisted in Europe till the European Payments Union was instituted in 1950. On British initiative[3]—and, it may be surmised, with full American blessing—the OEEC countries agreed in the middle of 1949 to cut away quota restrictions on trade between them. This— the first of the 'liberalization' pledges—was given quantitative form; and, as far as it went, was successful. By the end of 1949 most OEEC countries, including Britain, had removed restrictions from half of their imports from each other. But it soon became clear that further progress required a basic reform of intra-European payments[4].

'In the immediate post-war period', said an OEEC retrospect[5], 'quantitative restrictions were so widespread that for some time customs tariffs were of secondary importance. The extensive use of such restrictions by practically all countries was self-defeating . . . The innumerable bilateral agreements regulating international trade were similar to primitive forms of barter'. The effort to make bilateral trade 'balance within narrow limits and over rather short periods' led both to severe limitation, and severe distortion, of trade. The tangle was made still more complex by the grafting on of 'drawing rights', by which a portion of Marshall Aid was allotted against anticipated bilateral deficits. Intended to inject an element of multilateralism, the system was in fact—according to one close observer—'as unpredictable and haphazard as that of the better known Monte Carlo roulette'[6].

---

[1]For details, see chapter VI.
[2]A detailed review is given by Hemming, Miles and Ray [1959]: see chapter VI.4 below.
[3]*Economist*, 11 June 1949, p. 1100.
[4]After the EPU was set up, it took only 6 months for countries to free three quarters of their imports from each other. For a summary of the successive 'liberalization' agreements, see OEEC [1958] *A Decade of Co-operation*, pp. 54–9.
[5]*Ibid.*, p. 53.
[6]Triffin [1957], *Europe and the Money Muddle*, p. 153: see also Tew [1952], *International Monetary Co-operation, 1945–52*, chap. VIII.

The European Payments Union of 1950 effected a major revolution.   To the American officials attached to the Economic Cooperation Administration in Paris should go a major share of credit, both for the initial conception of the scheme, and for the preservation of its essentials through months of negotiations, intricate and protracted as those that had preceded the International Monetary Fund five years earlier[1].   There were two main features of the new arrangements. The first 'lay in making authorised payments among the member countries of the OEEC and their associated monetary areas fully multilateral'.   Only the *net balance* of each country with all its partners in the Union remained to be settled[2].   The second lay in settling the net balance—up to an agreed 'quota'— partly in gold, partly in credit extended by member countries to each other on prearranged principles.   To an agreed limit, countries could rely on 'automatic' credit[3].

In the negotiations, the United Kingdom played for a time a highly reluctant role, her ambivalent attitude being due to unresolved conflicts in her own policy.   The failure of convertibility in 1947 had induced a 'frightened, defensive attitude'[4]; and bred a reliance on direct controls, which attuned well with the *dirigiste* bias of Labour policy.   When it came to the point, the Government hesitated to limit its right to control trade.   Its attitude was further complicated by concern over 'the special position' of sterling 'as an international currency transferable and widely used in payments between non-sterling countries'[5].   Negotiations were abruptly halted in February 1950 by the memorandum submitted to the OEEC Council by Sir Stafford Cripps, which

[1]Triffin [1957], pp. 162–8.   The origin of the scheme in fact went back to studies made by the IMF in 1948–9.   It was only later that the Fund withdrew into 'increasing reserve and hardly veiled hostility' to the EPU (p. 136).

[2]*A Decade of Co-operation*, p. 79.   The offsetting operations prior to the striking of the net balance in fact 'sufficed to cancel almost half of the gross surpluses and deficits incurred, without recourse to either gold or credit'.

[3]*Ibid.*, p. 80.   For debtors, the 'gold portion rose gradually from zero to 100 per cent . . . so as to put more and more pressure on them to correct persistent disequilibria in their payments'.   For a creditor, the gold portion rose abruptly from zero to 50 per cent when its cumulative surplus reached 20 per cent of the country's quota; the settlement of surpluses above the quota was left for *ad hoc* negotiation.   All settlements were based on the country's *cumulative* position in the Union i.e. the sum of their surpluses and deficits since the inception of the Union.

[4]Triffin [1957], p. 160.

[5]This was rationalized as a calculation of monetary loss.   'What the British experts chiefly fear is that accumulations of sterling, which at present carry no gold payment clause, might through the operation of the European Payments Union be converted into EPU credits on which . . . gold payments would have to be made' (*Economist*, 4 March 1950, p. 495).   Underlying this fear, however, there was a reluctance to see the emergence of a system which would be a substitute for the use of sterling as an international currency, and which seemed to entail a reduction of the 'transferability' of sterling—which the Bank of England would have preferred on the contrary to extend.   'The British view has been that the transferability of currencies with Europe will not be served by abolishing a mechanism which already serves that purpose so well' (*Economist*, 18 March 1950, p. 607).

flatly rejected the principles which had been generally agreed a month before[1]. A further memorandum in March proposed in effect that sterling should contract out of the Union, which should apply only to the other OEEC countries' transactions with one another[2]. But by May British opinion—'far less unanimous on the issue than appeared on the surface'[3]—had changed. It was Mr Gaitskell[4], not Sir Stafford Cripps, who attended the final negotiations in June. The agreement was formally signed in September, with retrospective effect to mid-year.

The European Payments Union should rank as one of the major achievements of post-war European economic co-operation. The first, but transitional task of the OEEC had been to distribute American aid, which had been extremely important in the early years[5]. In its more enduring role of fostering co-operative policies between its members, the EPU—always intended as a temporary scheme, and lasting till the general resumption of convertibility in 1958— played a key role. 'It loosened overnight the stranglehold of bilateralism on intra-European trade and payments'[6]. The EPU moreover was a managed system, considerable powers of judgement being assigned to its Managing Board; and the trade code, rather than being a set of rigid obligations, operated also as a managed system integrated with it. This gave point and weight to all major consultations in the Organisation. The OEEC has probably been the most successful international organization to date; and the European Payments Union was the centre of its work and the main reason for its success[7].

In October 1950, Sir Stafford Cripps, after further illness for which he had

---

[1]The memorandum stated that the United Kingdom 'could never accept the multilateral clearing system', and argued that all countries 'should retain the right to use quantitative controls'—even 'discriminatory restrictions'. (Triffin [1957], p. 164.)

[2]'All sterling claims and debts would continue, in principle, to be financed under bilateral agreements, and automatic compensations would apply only to the continental countries' surpluses and deficits with one another'—to which general principle there were to be complicated exceptions. The proposals, says Triffin (p. 165) 'were ingeniously presented' and 'many people tended at first to regard them as a great British concession'.

[3]Triffin [1957], p. 166.

[4]*Economist*, 3 June 1950, p. 1231.

[5]American aid paid for one fourth of Western Europe's total imports of goods and services in the period 1947–50, or almost two thirds of its merchandise imports from the dollar area. (*A Decade of Co-operation*, p. 33.)

[6]Triffin [1957], p. 208.

[7]Much was also due to the 'admirable negotiating machinery' which had already been brought into existence for the allocation of Marshall Aid—to which indeed Triffin (p. 162) attributes part credit for the successful negotiation of the EPU. It is doubtful however whether this would have survived Marshall Aid but for the EPU; and since its demise, OEEC has certainly exerted much less integrative force.

As Triffin (p. 208) says, the EPU 'paved the way toward the resumption of multilateral trade and the resumption of currency convertibility'. But it also provided an object lesson in consultative procedures, which the wider organizations to which its functions have partly been ceded have not been and may never be able to match. (See Triffin, pp. 137–8 and 256–66.)

again to retreat to Switzerland for some months, felt forced to retire from politics; and accordingly surrendered his office. As Chancellor of the Exchequer inflexibility had perhaps been both his weakness and his strength[1]. By 1950, much of the task he had set himself had in fact been accomplished. The British economy, it may be judged, had by then completed its recovery from the effects of the war; and in December the British Government announced the termination of Marshall Aid to this country. During the three years of Sir Stafford Cripps's tenure of the Exchequer, national output had risen almost four per cent a year[2]. Of this increase, consumption, though increasing considerably[3], took hardly more than a third. Almost as much of the rise in output had gone to fixed investment. Merchandise exports had risen by sixty per cent —to a level one and two thirds as high as before the war. Despite a moderate rise of imports (of some fourteen per cent) the balance of payments had improved from a deficit of some hundreds of £ million to a surplus of like size[4]. Sir Stafford Cripps's time happened, too, to be a period of relative quiescence in the process of price inflation (table 2.2): at this date it might even have been hoped that price inflation was not to prove a serious problem. This was partly a matter of luck, in that import prices did not rise much till war broke out in Korea in the middle of 1950; but it was partly also because of the moral authority with which the Chancellor had invested his appeal for wage restraint.

The general development of the economy during these years proved to be remarkably close to the long-term aims with which the government had gone on record in the early days of Sir Stafford Cripps's chancellorship[5]. But this

---

[1]'The soul of honour' Mr Churchill was to say on his death in April 1952: 'There are few hon. members in any part of the House who have not differed violently from him at this time or that, and yet there is none who did not regard him with respect and admiration, not only for his abilities but for his character.' (*H.C. Deb.* 22 Apr. 1952, 219.)

[2]All comparisons here are between 1947 and 1950 levels and are in terms of volume (see table 2.2.).

[3]The volume of consumption rose by 5 per cent in total, or by 3 per cent per head.

[4]The development of the external balance being erratic, comparison between two single years fails to show the improving trend. In 1946 and 1947 the deficits were nearly £300 million and nearly £450 million respectively. In 1950 the surplus was £300 million after being £40 million in 1949. Next year, largely because of the Korean war, it swung back into even heavier deficit. The United Kingdom deficit with the dollar area was reduced from £500 million in 1947 to under £100 million in 1950.

[5]The 'Long Term Programme' (published in Cmd. 7572) related to the four-year period, mid-1949 to mid-1953. Comparison of the forecasts with the actual out-turn has to allow for numerous changes in statistical definition. A detailed study by Miss Joan Mitchell shows that the aims of the Programme were 'undoubtedly achieved by 1952-53', both 'in broad outline and in considerable detail', (Joan Mitchell [1955], *Economic Planning and the Long-Term Programme*: unpublished thesis, University of Nottingham, p. 209). Industrial production 'was about one third above pre-war, as the Programme had supposed' (p. 212). The allocation of output was also much as set forth in the Programme. Investment increased more than expected—particularly however in housing, rather than in 'productive' investment (pp. 192–3). By 1952/53 the volume of exports in fact reached the Programme figures of 50 per cent above 1938 (pp. 58 and 212). The balance of payments, if revalued at 'programmed prices' (so eliminating the worsening in the terms of trade

was to some extent an accident.   Under the influence of the disasters of 1947, the 'Long Term Programme' had taken a cautious view about the possible expansion of output and exports.   Most of the aims which the government then set itself were in fact achieved as early as 1950.   By 1952—the end of the period to which the programme nominally related—the onset of the war in Korea, and the rearmament programme, made conditions very different from those originally envisaged.   Moreover the achievement of the plan rested primarily on the rapid growth of output; and over this the government had little control.   Granted the increase in output, however, government policy went far to determine its broad allocation.   It is perhaps fair to conclude that, very broadly and roughly, the government in its long-term programming in 1948 had taken the measure of the problem with which economic policy was faced.

The policy followed was essentially that originally proposed in the 'reconstruction' plans of the war days: that of sitting on the post-war boom till it blew itself out.   This took far longer, and required immensely more determination, than all but a few had then foreseen.   The government's handling of many important, but in the last resort subsidiary, issues, is certainly debateable: but on the broadest questions of economic policy there is much less room for doubt.   Only greater austerity could have greatly shortened the period of disinflation and control; and for the policy itself it is difficult to imagine a sensible alternative[1].

4. THE 'KOREAN' INFLATION, 1950-1

In October 1950, Mr Gaitskell, young to high office, was appointed Chancellor of the Exchequer in succession to Sir Stafford Cripps[2].   Europe had hardly congratulated itself on its 'remarkably successful attack' on the problems left over from the 1939-45 war[3], when the outbreak of war in Korea imposed a wholly new set of strains.   In a world already heading for a boom, this caused

that in fact occurred), showed at least as great an improvement as had been programmed. Both the increase in dollar earnings and the fall in dollar expenditure (again if revalued at 'programmed prices') were also close to that foreshadowed in the programme (pp. 30–6).

[1]This study is not primarily concerned with external economic policy.   But here too a similar assessment seems valid.   It was part of the 'reconstruction' assumptions that sterling should be inconvertible during the post-war 'transition'.   As in domestic policy the transition period lasted much longer than foreseen.   The handling of the external crises of 1947 and 1949 can be called clumsy.   But crises are essentially temporary and undo later much of their first damage; and in the last resort tactical mistakes must be judged to have mattered less than that, after 1947, non-convertibility was maintained while the dollar shortage lasted.   Similarly, doubts about the extent of devaluation matter less than the fact that devaluation was carried through at this stage.

[2]Elected to Parliament in 1945, Mr Gaitskell became Parliamentary Secretary to the Ministry of Fuel and Power in 1946 and Minister of Fuel and Power in 1947, and had for eight months been Minister of State for Economic Affairs under Sir Stafford Cripps. When he became Chancellor, Mr Edwards became Economic Secretary to the Treasury.

[3]Third report of OEEC [1951], *Economic Progress and Problems of Western Europe*, p. 19.

the sharpest burst of inflation in the post-war period, and world-wide shortage of materials.   To the United Kingdom it brought rising prices; a major increase in defence spending; and within a year, balance of payments crisis.

The remaining year of the Labour Government's term of office was pre-occupied with the complex series of adjustments that this entailed for the British economy.   The inflationary strain was, however, to prove as short-lived as it had been rapid.   The years 1950–1 saw a temporary and partial return to a war economics of shortages and controls.   But, paradoxically, they also mark another transition.   By the end of 1951, the economy had arrived at a state where under-employment was a possibility never far below the surface, and inflation no longer, year in year out, the sole problem.

The world boom of 1950–1 was not primarily due to the impact of the Korean war, though this added fuel to the fire.   Between 1949 and 1950, world industrial production rose by thirteen per cent—almost a record, certainly a post-war one[1].   This was partly due to the recovery, till then hesitant, of Western Germany, where industrial production rose more than a fourth; and, even more, to the rebound of the United States from the 1949 recession. Industrial expansion far outstripped the supplies of materials, which increased very little: for textile materials supplies contracted; and a shortage of metallic ores and of sulphur developed also[2].   These shortages alone would have driven up commodity prices.   In this they were greatly reinforced by the United States Government's precautionary stockpiling of strategic materials; and by speculative demand for commodities in all countries, engendered by expectations of rising prices and of shortages.   These fears were founded, at this date 'more on anticipated than actual increases in military expenditure'.   Even in the United States, actual military expenditure did not begin to rise steeply till the end of 1950: in Europe, it was still more gradual[3].

Commodity prices rose astronomically.   By December 1950, the price of rubber had risen to three and a half times its price a year earlier; that of wool and cotton to double; and those of other raw materials by something ranging round 50 per cent.   Food prices rose distinctly less[4].   As a result, the price of British imports rose 25 per cent in the course of 1950—and were to rise another 25 per

[1]The only comparable peacetime jump appears to have been between 1935 and 1936: see ECE [1951] *Economic Survey of Europe in 1950*, especially chap. 1, on which the above account is based.

[2]ECE estimates suggest there was no increase in the production of the twelve major raw materials.   Textile supplies *fell*, because of restrictions on United States cotton planting, and the exhaustion of the wartime stocks of wool.   Supplies of metal 'warscrap' had also been worked through.   (*Economic Survey of Europe in 1950*, pp. 5–6.)

[3]United States military expenditure had been declining till the fourth quarter of 1950. In the first half of 1951 it was planned to rise to double, and by the end of 1951 to three times, the 1950 rate (ECE, *Economic Survey of Europe in 1950*, p. 22).   Notwithstanding plans for a more rapid acceleration (*ibid.* table 66), European military expenditure rose 50 per cent only between 1950 and 1952 (OEEC [1958], *A Decade of Co-operation*, table 1).

[4]*Economic Survey of Europe in 1950*, chart 2.

cent before the inflationary wave reached top, in the middle months of 1951[1]. This caused a drastic reversal of the favourable trend in the British balance of payments. It gave, too, violent new impetus to the mechanics of the internal price and wage inflation, till then tending to peter out, whose subsequent reiteration was to last several years[2].

The adjustment required of the British economy by these international developments would in any case have been extensive. It was further complicated by the rapid increase in our own outlay on defence. The fighting in Korea altered the look of strategy in Europe; and led the United States both to increase her own commitments in Europe, and to urge on European governments an increase in their own contribution to the collective defence of Western Europe. Though this was in line with Mr Bevin's previous foreign policy, it was with reluctance that the British government appeared to be persuaded that it too should give a lead to Europe[3]. In the summer and autumn of 1950, defence plans were revised three times[4]. The new defence estimates, when they appeared, provided for expenditure of £1,300 million in 1951/52 as compared with £830 million in 1950/51. Though the build-up was to prove somewhat less rapid than this, defence expenditure, which had been reduced to about 7 per cent of national product since 1948, was to increase to 8½ per cent in 1951, and 10½ per cent in 1952.

This radically altered the economic problem: the execution of the rearmament programme was, indeed, now declared to have 'become the first objective' of

---

[1]Some of the rise in import prices was due to the devaluation in the previous September. But the *average* degree of devaluation was about 15 per cent (see discussion, §3 above); and much of the effect on import prices had already appeared by the beginning of 1950. Export prices rose also, but only about half as rapidly.

Price indices	1949		1950		1951
(Dec. 1949=100)	Sept.	Dec.	June	Dec.	June
Import prices	91	100	109	126	159
of which					
food, drink and tobacco		100	109	110	125
raw materials, etc.		100	115	151	215
Export prices	99	100	105	111	126

[2]For detailed analysis see chapter XIII below.
[3]In the rest of Western Europe, defence expenditure was relatively lower than in the United Kingdom; in the United Kingdom it took 7 per cent and in other OEEC countries on average about 5 per cent of gross national product in 1950 (OEEC *General Statisics*).
[4]An increase in defence expenditure of £100 million was announced in July; in December Mr Gaitskell was referring to a Treasury estimate of the extra cost as about £300 million; by February, the estimate had become £500 million (*Economist*, 29 July 1950, p. 201 and 2 Dec. 1950, p. 926; *H.C. Deb.* 15 Feb. 1951, 646). Shonfield [1958] (*British Economic Policy since the War*, pp. 91–2) implies that American influence was behind these revisions. When the programme was undertaken, though we never insisted, as Mr Gaitskell made clear (*H.C. Deb.* 7 Nov. 1951, 217–9), that our defence programme was 'dependent on specific promises of American aid', there was an understanding 'that the burdens would be fairly shared' between the members of NATO. It was not till 1952 that we received sizeable sums in 'defence aid' (£120 million in 1952 and progressively less in later years).

economic policy[1]. The increase in defence spending was rather greater than the increase in output that could be hoped for. It was moreover heavily concentrated on aircraft, motor vehicles, ships and radio and radar equipment; and this in turn called for heavy expenditure on new machine tools and re-tooling existing plant[2].

Partial reversion to a war economy meant partial reversion to direct controls. Though the wartime system of 'priorities' for defence production was not reinstated, firms were expected to obtain departmental 'guidance' when defence and other orders were in conflict; and the employment exchanges operated an informal system of 'labour preferences' to guide workers to key jobs[3]. The scarcest materials were sulphur, zinc and copper, for which detailed allocation schemes had to be reintroduced by the beginning of the year. Steel—only recently freed from allocation—aluminium, nickel, cotton, wool and softwood were also short. At the time, these shortages seemed likely to be deep-seated and persistent[4].

A 'strict fiscal and monetary policy'—though 'not enough by itself'—was also necessary to back up direct controls and to 'restrain civilian expenditure'[5]. There seemed however a strict limit to how far it could be pushed. Defence expenditure bore heavily on the engineering and building industries. No policy therefore could prevent its impact falling, not on consumption, but on exports and investment. The strain on the balance of payments, inevitable anyhow, was further increased by the purchase of machine tools abroad, and by the heavy stockpiling of strategic materials. In a year when the terms of trade were running heavily against us, this clearly involved a large deterioration in the balance of payments. In 1950 there had been a surplus of £300 million or so: in 1951 the Government expected this to be turned into a small deficit. That was deliberately accepted as one of the costs of rearmament[6].

Budgetary measures, it was argued, could not do much to mitigate these

---

[1]*Economic Survey for 1951*, para. 7.

[2]Three fifths of the increase was to consist of engineering products. Something like another fifth was to consist of defence building works. The cost of machine tools and re-tooling was estimated at £100 million in 1951/52 (*Survey*, table 1 and para. 68).

[3]*H.C. Deb.* 15 Feb. 1951, 651 and *Economic Survey*, para. 35. Compulsory use of employment exchanges was not reimposed till February 1952.

[4]At the beginning of 1951 the shortage of raw materials appeared not 'merely as a transitory problem associated with rearmament'; but likely to last 'for many years to come' (*Economic Survey for 1951*, para. 56). Shortages were in any case a world-wide problem. In December 1950 the United States, the United Kingdom and France joined in establishing the International Materials Conference in Washington. International allocation was however not achieved till the third quarter of 1951.

[5]'not enough by itself' to ensure 'that the particular resources are released which are needed for defence and exports' (Mr Gaitskell, *H.C. Deb.* 15 Feb. 1951, 653).

[6]The surplus in 1950 was then put at £370 million (since revised to £300 million). In 1951 it was hoped that the deficit would be no greater than the purchase of imports for strategic stockpiling, of about £100 million (*Economic Survey*, paras. 89–93 and table 24; *H.C. Deb.* 15 Feb. 1951, 658–9). The deterioration turned out to be, not £500 million. but £700 million,

developments. 'Without doubt it would be far better for our economy' said the Chancellor, that 'we should meet the greater part by reducing consumption . . . But with the best will in the world'—because defence spending was concentrated on industries on which the consumer made little claim—'there is a limit to the extent to which we can put this principle into practice'[1]. The limit to exports, 'particularly of consumer goods', was set not by 'our ability to supply' but by 'the capacity of overseas markets to absorb'. 'Thus a too severe Budget might give us losses, unemployment and austerity at home without any substantial benefit to our external situation'[2]. The problem was, in fact, no longer that of general excess demand.

Nor, it seemed, could the budget do much to prevent prices rising: 'at the moment it is a costs inflation which is affecting us. Higher prices for imported raw materials . . are pushing up our cost of living more and more. A tough Budget can only give limited help here . . . it can, and should, ensure that excessive demand does not add its influence to that of high costs. But it cannot directly reduce a generally high level of costs to any material extent . . .'[3] The rising cost of imports was expected to be passed on with some delay. As a result, the cost of living was expected to rise about as rapidly as consumers' incomes, so that—unlike previous years—real purchasing power was expected to increase very little. 'As a result' the *Survey*[4] remarked, 'the problem of maintaining a balance between the purchasing power of consumers and the reduced volume of goods and services available' was not 'so great as at first sight might appear'.

These complex adjustments were analysed in the *Economic Survey for 1951* with a sophistication unsurpassed in exercises of this kind. There is little doubt that its analysis—'though in detail . . . bound to be falsified by events' —did correctly 'illustrate the main lines of the problems with which we are faced'[5]. The general argument was summarized by Mr Gaitskell in a budget speech as complex and compressed as any we are likely to see. Examination shows too that his argument, though as closely fenced with arithmetic as Sir Stafford Cripps's had been, was far more reputably Keynesian than that of his predecessor—whose 'spirit' he invoked as mantle for his own integrity[6].

[1]*H.C. Deb.* 15 Feb. 1951, 648.
[2]*H.C. Deb.* 10 April 1951, 828.
[3]Same deb. 829.
[4]Para. 123.
[5]As the *Survey* claimed: para. 118. As an exercise in forecasting, the 1951 *Survey* was a technical advance in several ways. The forecasts were published in far more detail than previously; the main national income projections were expressed both in terms of constant and of predicted current prices; and some predicted 'sector balance sheets' were published. (See further chapter V below.)
[6]"Upon how the Chancellor of the Exchequer of the day makes up his mind . . . very important consequences to the nation will always depend. It is, therefore, enormously important that he should do so honestly and objectively and . . . should stick to it and not be moved by pressure of any kind, however insidious or well-intentioned . . . I have no doubt . . . that the decisions of my predecessor were made in this spirit, and . . .

Mr Gaitskell's conclusion, as Chancellor, was that taxes affecting consumers would have to be raised substantially (by £150 million), but by much less than the increase in defence expenditure (some £700 million)[1]. It followed that much of the burden would have to fall on investment, and that investment too should be discouraged.   To restrict consumption both direct and indirect taxes were raised.   Income tax was raised by sixpence, the 'standard rate' thus again becoming 9s. 6d. in the £; and taxes on petrol and entertainments were increased. To discourage dividends, the tax on distributed profits was raised from thirty to fifty per cent; to discourage spending on goods which competed with defence needs, purchase tax on cars, wireless and domestic electrical equipment was doubled.   Various changes in social expenditure were part of the same scheme. To keep the ever-mounting cost of the health service down to £400 million a year, adult patients were to be charged half the cost of dentures and spectacles (at a saving of £25 million a year).   To avoid the severe hardship rising prices would have inflicted on old age pensioners, pensions were increased by about a sixth.   Lastly, and equally important, notice was given that the 'initial' depreciation allowances on new plant, machinery and industrial building were to be entirely suspended[2].

Mr Gaitskell also took considerably more account than had Sir Stafford Cripps of monetary policy.   He recognized that bank credit had 'an important bearing' on investment.   The increased cost of stocks made some increase in

---

because of that . . . were able to play a vital part in protecting us from inflation and cherishing our economic recovery.   I can only say that I have tried to follow the same course this year'   (*H.C. Deb*. 10 April 1951, 840).

Mr Gaitskell's argument, however, was no longer in terms of the 'overall surplus' by which Sir Stafford Cripps had defended his austerity.   It ran:

'I estimate that the total of private savings, both company and personal, will increase by about £170 million.   Having regard to the fall of £15 million in the surplus of other public authorities, the total savings from sources other than the Central Government increase by £155 million.   We have to deduct this from the £305 million which we have arrived at, and we get about £150 million as the short-fall in savings necessary which must be made good by the Government' (844).   He remarked after this—the half-way point in his speech—'I realize that the Committee may be finding this rather tough going'.

Earlier, Mr Churchill had risen in his seat to say: 'I only venture to assure the right hon. Gentleman that, if he wants more time, it will be gladly accorded by the House, but if he would speak a little slower, it would be for the convenience of everybody in understanding these complicated matters' (831).

[1] Including civil defence, strategic stockpiling, and government assistance for the expansion of industrial capacity for defence production, defence expenditure in 1951/52 was estimated at £1,490 million, as against £800 million in the previous year (836).

[2] Financial methods were adopted in deliberate preference to the reintroduction of the war system of machinery licensing (841).   The suspension of the initial allowances from April 1952 was estimated to deprive firms of some £170 million in a full year.   The other tax changes—primarily affecting consumers—were expected to bring in an extra £140 million in 1951/52, or £220 million in a full year: though the increase in profits tax would hardly affect the revenue till 1951/52, the Chancellor's reckoning (856) allowed for the probability that it would have immediate effect in discouraging dividends.   For further details see chapter VII.3 below.

bank advances seem 'inevitable', but the banks were under request to keep it moderate[1]. Credit restraint was not enforced without friction. The banks appear to have been increasingly restive under the régime of repeated informal 'requests'; and to have argued that it would be better to rely on the 'market mechanism' of raising short-term rates. This proposal was not accepted by the Government[2]—in effect it meant that the banks would have been paid more to hold Treasury bills; and in July Mr Gaitskell repeated 'with emphasis' his request to the banks for credit restraint[3]. He had however, in his budget speech, welcomed the further rise in *long-term* rates, since these were likely to 'exercise some check on investment'[4]. Monetary policy was thus allotted some role: if it remained nevertheless a distinctly subsidiary one, it is not clear that this was ill-advised.

However intelligently designed, no policy of rearmament and of renewed austerity could be expected to be popular. The budget itself appears to have been accepted without enthusiasm, but with relief that it was not worse[5]. At the end of April however Mr Bevan brought his disagreement with Mr Gaitskell into the open and resigned as Minister of Health—partly in opposition to the health service charges made in the budget a fortnight earlier, partly in opposition to the scale of the defence programme he had supported in the previous January[6]. Mr Wilson's resignation as President of the Board of Trade followed.

---

[1] Same deb. 841–2. New guidance had been given to the Capital Issues Committee about the types of lending not to be allowed, and the banks were expected to comply with these very general instructions.

[2] Mr Gaitskell, *H.C. Deb*. 7 Nov. 1951, 227.

[3] *H.C. Deb*. 26 July 1951, 2343: see further chapter IX.3 below.

H.C. Deb. 10 April 1951, p. 842.

[5] 'relief among the Labour Party that the burdens on consumers were not heavier, and among the Opposition that none of the hints of capital levies or capital gains taxes had materialized' (*Economist*, 14 April 1951, p. 846).

[6] Mr Bevan chiefly attacked the scale of *American* rearmament, on the grounds that it would make such demands on 'the world's precious raw materials that the civilian economy of the Western world outside America will be undermined. We shall have mass unemployment . . . the foundations of political liberty and Parliamentary democracy will not be able to sustain the shock'. Because of shortages, the British rearmament programme was 'unrealisable'. Mr Bevan went on to attack the prospective rise in the cost of living—which it 'is clear from the Budget that the Chancellor of the Exchequer has abandoned any hope of restraining'. His objection to the health service charges was made as a subsidiary point. 'The Chancellor of the Exchequer . . has taken £13 million out of the Budget total of £4,000 million', 'that is the arithmetic of Bedlam. He cannot say that his arithmetic is so precise that he must have the £13 million, when last year the Treasury were £247 million out.'

In his new position of 'comparative freedom', Mr Bevan went on to give this advice: 'Take economic planning away from the Treasury. They know nothing about it . . . they think they move men about when they move pieces of paper about . . . It has been perfectly obvious on several occasions that there are too many economists advising the Treasury, and now we have the added misfortune of having an economist in the Chancellor of the Exchequer himself.' (*H.C. Deb*. 23 April 1951, 34–43.) Mr Wilson next day gave much the same grounds for his resignation. 'It is not a matter of teeth and spectacles.' He was 'strongly in support of an effective defence programme'. But Mr Gaitskell's

The policy of relying on 'disinflation through rising prices' never made sense to the man in the street, and as time went on became increasingly unpopular[1]. To meet this feeling, price controls were reviewed or reimposed in July. This was somewhat belated, since the peak of the commodity boom was already passed; and it was recognized that price controls could in any case do no more than delay the appearance of cost increases already working their way through[2]. As a further sop to popular feeling, the Chancellor also promised a control of dividends. In spite of the budget change in profits tax, dividends were still increasing 'on a scale far greater than the general increase in money incomes'. 'This kind of thing' he said 'inevitably acts as a continual irritant on the great majority of the population . . . They are a body blow to moderation in claims for higher personal incomes by wage and salary earners'[3]. In general no increase in dividends was to be permitted over the average of the last two years. The bill promised for the autumn was overtaken by the general election; but the announcement of the scheme had some immediate effect[4]. As Dr Dalton said, 'My friend Gaitskell's speech, whatever else it has done, has thrown the Stock Exchange into complete disorder, and that is good fun anyway'[5].

The last months of the Labour Government were overshadowed by the developing external crisis. Already in July it was clear that the situation was worse than expected. Our imports were costing more, and invisible earnings were less, than had been hoped. Though the reserves rose $100 million in the second quarter, the sterling area dollar surplus had fallen off drastically—by $300 million since the first quarter; and, partly for reasons which seemed at the time exceptional, it seemed possible that in the third quarter it would be in 'quite substantial' deficit[6]. Mr Gaitskell, maybe by policy, sounded no note of alarm; but admitted nevertheless that 'the changed outlook does call for some corrective action'. Dollar imports were 'reviewed'; and to concert sterling area

budget was based on estimates 'which included a re-armament programme which I do not believe to be physically practicable with the raw materials available to us' (*H.C. Deb.* 24 April 1951, 228–31).

[1] In July Mr Gaitskell was having to explain away the impression 'that the Government have deliberately allowed prices to rise so as somehow or other to pay for re-armament' (*H.C. Deb.* 26 July 1951, 2335). An increase in the cost of living subsidies had been rejected in April as being too costly. It is arguable that this would have been justified to prevent a *temporary* peak in the index, because it would have prevented much of the subsequent cost inflation. To prevent the consequent effect on demand inflation would however have required further stiff tax increases.

[2] Many Board of Trade price controls had been abandoned in the post-war years, but remained on 'utility' and various other goods. Controls were reimposed on a long list of goods—ranging from saucepans to toilet paper—in July (same deb. 2341–2). But this did not really amount to much: see chapter VI.2 below.

[3] *H.C. Deb.* 26 July 1951, 2346–7.

[4] Short details of the proposed bill were set out in a special White Paper on Control of Dividends (Cmd. 8318) issued in July.

[5] Reported in *Economist*, 4 Aug. 1951, p. 297.

[6] Dollar imports were expected to be $100 million 'more than in a normal quarter', and the deficit with EPU was expected to be seasonal (*H.C. Deb.* 26 July 1951, 2328).

policy, steps were taken to arrange a meeting of Commonwealth finance ministers as soon as possible[1].

Already in July outside commentators smelt 'the beginning of a new period of economic stringency'; but the news in September and October was worse than anyone had foreseen[2].   In September, the sterling area dollar deficit in the third quarter was put at $500 million.   By October the estimate had risen to $640 million.   In the month of October—as was known later—the drain accelerated again, and was $320 million in that month alone[3].   The United Kingdom position worsened as spectacularly.   The last public occasion on which Mr Gaitskell reviewed the situation as Chancellor of the Exchequer was to be his speech at the Mansion House dinner on 3 October.   It then appeared that the balance of payments deficit, in place of £100 million which had originally been assumed for 1952, was going to be £450 million or £500 million[4].

As on past and future occasions, part of the drain was due to rumours of devaluation[5].   Mr Gaitskell was not disposed to be 'panicked by this movement of funds'[6].   Imports would have to be cut, not only by Britain but by the other sterling countries; and with reserves at $3,670 million there was, he argued, time for them to meet and agree what should be done[7].   Immediate preparations were made to cut British imports.   It is doubtful whether time would have allowed them to be imposed before the general election, by then fixed for 25 October.   The new Government imposed them immediately after it: though blaming its predecessors for the necessity[8], its policy was much what theirs would probably have been.

---

[1]Same deb. 2329: though 'at the end of the year, or . . . shortly afterwards' seemed the earliest possible, Mr Gaitskell originally hoped for September (Gaitskell [1952], 'The Sterling Area', *Int. Aff.*, April 1952, p. 176).

[2]*Economist*, 7 July 1951, p. 2 and 6 Oct. 1951, p. 815.

[3]Mr Butler, *H.C. Deb.* 7 Nov. 1951, 191.

[4]Mr Gaitskell quoted his earlier estimate in November (*H.C. Deb.* 7 Nov. 1951, 212). By then Mr Butler put the figure even higher, at 'between £500 million and £600 million' (192).   The latest estimate is about £420 million.

[5]*Economist*, 6 Oct. 1951, p. 815.

[6]To judge by his advice to Mr Butler in November (same deb. 213).

[7]*Economist*, 6 Oct. 1951, pp. 815–7.

[8]To have to seek re-election at this juncture was no more fortunate for Labour, than it was for the Conservatives to have an emergency on their hands immediately they took office.   Members of the new Government charged it against their predecessors that they had concealed the gravity of the situation; and that they had in effect absconded from their responsibility by advising a dissolution in October.   'We realised', said Mr Churchill, that the position 'was very bad, but we did not realise how bad it was until we saw the reports, on which no doubt the right hon. Gentleman determined the date of the Election' (*H.C. Deb.* 31 Jan. 1952, 382).

Mr Butler admitted in November that his predecessor's speech at the Mansion House had been based on 'the best information then available to him' (*H.C. Deb.* 7 Nov. 1951, 192).   To Mr Boyd Carpenter's assertion that the Labour Party's reaction to the emergency had been 'to abandon their responsibilities' Mr Attlee asked 'does the hon. Gentleman think, then, that when a Prime Minister goes to the country he is evading responsibility or seeking responsibility?' (*H.C. Deb.* 31 Jan. 1952, 387–8.)

Despite party heat, the next *Economic Survey*'s account of the causes of the crisis was praiseworthily objective. For 'the swing which took place during 1951 in the balance of payments of the sterling area', it commented, 'the United Kingdom and the overseas sterling area each accounted in roughly equal measure[1]. The United Kingdom balance had swung by over £700 million— from a healthy surplus of some £300 million in 1950 to an even larger deficit of over £400 million in 1951[2]. The rise in import prices alone[3] was more than enough to account for the whole of this deterioration. But almost all of this had been predicted when the plans had been drawn up at the beginning of the year; and it was not for this reason that the deficit was very considerably worse than anyone had foreseen. For this there were two main reasons[4]. Invisible earnings fell £150 million—partly because of the Persian seizure of the Abadan oil refineries in March. Second, the volume of imports rose even more than expected, accounting for another £150 million. This no doubt was due to many causes: low stockbuilding in 1950; and speculative stockbuilding in 1951; unexpectedly high production; increased consumption of food, and perhaps also the domestic pressure of demand which built up in 1951. But Mr Gaitskell was undoubtedly right in claiming that what had happened was not due (as one banker was apparently to assert) to our having lived in a 'quagmire of inflation'[5].

The deterioration in the position of the other sterling countries was of equal importance in bringing on the crisis. This had not been foreseen. The *Survey* for 1951 had said: 'The very large earnings from sales of raw materials by the rest of the Sterling Area can be expected to continue'[6]. In fact however, as the next *Survey* said[7],

> 'These conditions did not last. Indeed, to some extent they contained the seeds of their own destruction because the big sales of raw materials generated large incomes in the overseas sterling area, and these, when they came to be spent, were bound to result in an increase in expenditure on imports . . . in the second half of the year the overseas sterling area was importing from North America at double the 1950 rate. Meanwhile there had been a break in prices of sterling area raw materials . . . due partly to a cut in stockpiling purchases, partly to measures taken in the United States and other countries to check inflation . . . partly also [to] the natural

---

[1] *Economic Survey for 1952*, para. 10.

[2] Table 2.2. On contemporary estimates the deficit looked even larger: it was then put at £520 million.

[3] The volume of exports also rose somewhat less, and the terms of trade worsened somewhat more, than had been forecast. The statements in round terms in the text above are true whether one compares the forecasts with the 1952 estimates, or with the most recent estimates (see chapter V.2 below).

[4] See ECE *Economic Survey of Europe in 1951*, p. 82.

[5] *H.C. Deb.* 30 Jan. 1952, 213.

[6] *Economic Survey for 1951*, para. 107.

[7] *Economic Survey for 1952*, para. 11. An essentially similar account is given in the ECE *Economic Survey of Europe in 1951*, pp. 10–3.

reaction from the excessive buying . . . As a result, between the first and second six months of 1951 the dollar earnings of the overseas sterling area fell by nearly 50 per cent.'

In large part, then, as in 1949, the crisis was due to the tendency for large swings in the exports and imports of the overseas sterling area to come exactly out of phase. Once started, the crisis was quickly worsened by speculation or (as Mr Butler[1] was to say) by a cumulative 'weakening of confidence in sterling throughout the world'.

The crisis must, in any obvious sense, be blamed on international fluctuations of a scale and rapidity not likely to be paralleled. If, in part, British policy is to be blamed, it must be for errors of judgement on matters which can never be more than matters of opinion. The 1951 *Survey* was undoubtedly an intelligent analysis of a highly complex situation. To direct attention to the right questions, may be half-way to getting the right answers; but it is only half-way. Forecasts are always uncertain and can mislead; and it is difficult not to feel that, on this occasion, insufficient allowance was made for the full range of possibilities, both more and less favourable than the official forecasts implied[2]. It can be argued on these grounds that rearmament was too rapid: for the defence programme contributed to the balance of payments strain, and it was calculated to be about the limit of what the balance of payments could bear, if all went as expected. But the main disadvantage of the defence programme was undoubtedly the burden it was to impose on the economy over the next decade; and this was to become only gradually apparent[3].

The crisis revealed how much more closely co-ordinated the sterling area system would have to have been in order to react rapidly to the strain thrown on it. It can therefore be argued, either that so much strain should not have been risked; or, as Mr Gaitskell later suggested, that a more effective co-ordination should have been attempted[4]. The crisis was inherently temporary: neither the confidence factors that exacerbated the crisis, nor in this case the trade factors that underlay it, could be expected to last. Had the reserves been

[1]*H.C. Deb.* 7 Nov. 1951, 192.

[2]Mr Gaitskell later, after remarking that the *Survey* had been 'very prescient' about much of what was to happen, added: 'the trouble is that it is not possible to be very precise in estimates' (Gaitskell [1952], *Int. Aff.*, April 1952, p. 174). But see chapter V.3 below.

[3]The diversion of effort to the defence programme was probably to contribute to the weakening of our competitive position, particularly *vis-à-vis* other European countries who were less burdened. Opinion may differ as to whether the government was right to accept this burden: but it is a decision which subsequent governments substantially accepted. Both Mr Bevan and Mr Wilson at the time criticized the speed of rearmament. But (as already noted) they were objecting more to the speed of American than British rearming; and the balance of payments cost was not their chief concern. Balance-of-payments-wise, our strategic stockpiling must have been as costly as defence production proper.

[4]Later in diagnosing the causes of the crisis Mr Gaitskell pointed to the lowness of the sterling area's gold reserves; and added: 'what is needed in the sterling area is really a tighter, more continuous arrangement for consultation and taking decisions . . . I accept that while we were in power maybe more should have been done' (*H.C. Deb.* 30 Jan. 1952, 218 .

higher, therefore, there might not have been a crisis. It could well be argued that when embarking on the defence programme (in addition to an understanding about sharing the cost of defence), we should have sought an advance undertaking from the United States of temporary support, should the strain on sterling prove too great[1].

But the last word should not lie with such criticisms, since criticisms can always be made. There is no doubt that, whatever his mistakes, Mr Gaitskell, himself an economist, had as sure a grasp of economic policy as Chancellors who preceded or followed him. It is mostly by accident that for most of the time most Chancellors have been successful. Mr Gaitskell had one year at the Exchequer, and 1951 was an unlucky one to choose.

[1]This never seems to have been envisaged. Mr Gaitskell was later to suggest that the 'burden-sharing' discussions in NATO ought to take into account the deterioration in the British balance of payments position since the defence programme was agreed on (*H.C. Deb.* 7 Nov. 1951, 217).

F

CHAPTER III

CONSERVATIVE CHANCELLORS, 1952-60

The election of October 1951 gave the Conservatives a large majority. In the nine years up to the resignation of Mr Heathcoat Amory in July 1960, four successive Chancellors held office at the Exchequer: Mr Butler for four years, until the end of 1955; Mr Macmillan and Mr Thorneycroft in turn for almost exactly a year each; and then, for two and a half years, Mr Heathcoat Amory.

These nine years saw a major transformation of the country's economic position. After the recovery from the 1951 crisis, the external environment was kinder to the United Kingdom and balance of payments crises were less frequent. Production continued to expand; and as shortages disappeared, controls were one by one removed. Economic policy thus became markedly less interventionist. Even greater weight, accordingly, reposed on budgetary policy as a means of controlling the economy; and greater use was made of monetary policy —with debateable success. As the first post-war pressure of demand became less intense, something of the old trade-cycle problem re-emerged. The economy showed a distinct tendency to swing between phases of mild recession and of rapid growth and boom. The problem of diagnosing, and acting in time to moderate, this cycle emerged as one of the main problems of policy. By the end of the period, the slow average rate of growth of the British economy began to appear as another, perhaps more fundamental, cause of dissatisfaction with economic policy.

Mr Butler's four years at the Exchequer saw the recovery from the 1953 recession and then the failure to moderate the build-up of the boom of 1955 (§2). Though policy showed no abrupt break, the Conservative Government was open to the influence of ideas which had little weight with the previous administration (§1). This produced some conflict of policy, half hidden from the public eye, which came to an issue over convertibility—a major issue, half outside the scope of this study, which yet impinged on internal policy (§3). In the two years after 1955, the main aim of policy was to get the expansionary pressure under control (§4). Only in the course of 1958 did policy again become expansionary: yet by the end of 1960, the need for restraint was—most disappointingly—again becoming evident (§5).

1. THE CLIMATE OF IDEAS IN 1951

In the process of criticizing the policies of the Labour Government, the Conservatives had built up something like an alternative philosophy of economic government. Much of what their parliamentary spokesmen had to say was echoed by the financial press; and, in more extreme form by the City. The

Conservative Government that took office in 1951 had therefore some broad preconceptions of what it thought economic policy should be, as had the Labour Government in 1945[1]. But, being much less dependent on preparatory studies in Whitehall—being rather strands of opinion from different quarters—it is less easy to summarize.

Conservative arguments during the 1951 budget debate[2] provide a convenient cross-section of opinion. By then an early election had come to be expected; and Conservative speakers had made the occasion one for criticizing not only the 1951 budget, but the whole course of Labour's financial administration. Several interconnected points were repeatedly made. First, government expenditure was too high—perhaps much too high[3]. Second, high taxation was no remedy for the inflationary effects of high spending—the sheer size of the budget was thus 'itself an inflationary force'[4]. Third, the rise of prices was, then, largely a result of 'imprudent financial administration[5]'. Fourth, the way to avoid inflation was by 'keeping money sound through a credit and monetary policy'[6]: references to the 'discipline' provided by the rate of interest[6], and the need to submit a soft economy to a 'tough expansionist policy'[7], almost suggested that monetary policy had a moral superiority. There was some undercurrent of dislike for the general idea of Keynesian budgeting[8]; and this included dislike for national income forecasts[9]. Another line of Conservative attack, criticism of state trading and of government controls, was on this occasion less to the fore.

These views were to some extent echoed by—or echoed—one school of thought among economists, of which it is perhaps not unfair to single out Professor Robbins's Stamp Memorial Lecture (delivered in November 1951) as particularly forceful and influential[10]. His major premise was that balance of payments equilibrium should be regarded as the sole test of financial policy—

[1]See chapter II.1.
[2]References are to *H.C. Deb.* 10–16 April 1951.
[3]Mr Lyttelton, who opened for the Opposition, thought £50 million could be saved in administrative economies (1049); Mr Eccles (1131) and Mr Spearman (1573) thought the social services would have to be cut; and Captain Waterhouse (1261–79) and Mr Assheton (1307–9) listed possible economies in detail.
[4]Mr Eccles (1131): also Sir Edward Boyle in his maiden speech (1514).
[5]Mr Lyttelton (1054).
[6]Mr Assheton (1304) and (1302); see also Mr Maudling (1122) and Mr Butler (1580–1).
[7]Mr Eccles (1139).
[8]'pure "hooey" ': Viscount Hinchingbrooke (1105–6).
[9]Mr Lyttelton (1046).
[10]Lionel Robbins [1951], *The Balance of Payments.* Though it must always be invidious to discuss an author's ideas, not in their own right, but as an historical influence, the following parallel may appear an amusing instance of their dissemination. Professor Robbins's rather learned remark (p. 18)—'The supply of money and credit has been almost completely passive to the so-called needs of business. The shades of Tooke and Fullarton have reigned triumphant in Great George Street' came after, not before, Mr Eccles's very similar quip—'the ghosts of Tooke and Fullarton reign supreme in the Bank's parlour today'— in the budget debate of the previous April (*H.C. Deb.* 11 April 1951 1136).

a test by which past policy failed. The premise was admittedly qualified: import controls were legitimate as emergency measures; and even if a country was a model of rectitude, its balance of payments could be affected by outside events. Nevertheless it could and should adjust to its changed environment by financial policy: 'the persistence of external disequilibrium can always be attributed to a failure of financial policy'[1]. There was a minor premise to this line of argument, which was equally important: Professor Robbins assumed that a country could adapt itself quickly, provided only that monetary policy was restored to its rightful place. Budgetary measures, he argued, were a 'clumsy and inadequate' way of adapting to conditions that were continually changing[2]. Direct controls, too, were always imposed too late, when a crisis was already on the way. Hence, he said, 'the vulgar spectacular nature of this side of economic life nowadays, with its big men flying about wildly in aeroplanes, its grandiose conferences, its last-minute compromises, and its penumbra of high politics even over consignments of canned meat and sardines'. The old monetary policy was more flexible: 'we have thrown overboard, as oldfashioned scrap, all the delicate mechanism of financial control which the experience of ages was gradually fashioning.' The obvious course was to revive a monetary policy conducted with full regard to the external balance. 'When in surplus expand, when in deficit contract . . . that is a rule which we must adopt ourselves, if the pound is not to drop still further.'

Similar sentiments were expressed in the financial press. A leader in *The Banker*, for instance, entitled 'Free Enterprise on Trial'[3] started with the axiom:

'The British economy cannot at present meet all the demands now being made upon it, therefore it is running heavily into debt abroad.' It went on, 'The way to minimize the range of controls is not to try to scrap them overnight, but first to cut down the excess of demand and the pressure set up by unnatural prices that the controls try to hold in place. This is the way of free enterprise, the distinctive way that not only combats inflation, but simultaneously clears the road for bigger output.' Again, 'with the problem of incentives, the most crucial step must be to attack inflation by the methods of financial retrenchment and of freeing the price system, to allow mobile prices to do their natural work of bringing demand and supply into equilibrium.' *The Banker* was prepared to face the logic of this deflationary argument: 'the Government must not be unduly inhibited by promises that may be deemed to have been given during the election. It will quickly find . . . that a sufficient disinflation will not be attainable merely by marginal and mainly painless prunings of administrative

[1]Robbins, *op. cit.*, p. 13.
[2]This and following quotations are from pp. 20, 25, 21 and 27 respectively.
[3]*The Banker*, November 1951, pp. 272–5.

expenditure.' But real economy would hardly be possible before the next budget; and 'the world must not be left to wait until then for a clear sign.' 'Therefore there is the greater need to enlist the monetary instruments of discipline, for these can be used without delay.'

A re-emphasis on monetary policy, and on the external situation as the test for internal policy, implied a shift back in the institutional distribution of influence from the Treasury towards the Bank of England[1]. Institutions, however—themselves, in one aspect, no more than fossilized ideas—in turn impose their own flavour on thought. Under the Labour administration, with monetary policy in abeyance, the Bank had played a minor role; since the convertibility débâcle in 1947, it had indeed hardly been more than the government's agent in the operation of exchange control, and in the issue of government stock. But though nationalized in 1946 it remained essentially as Lord Norman had created it[2]. In his conception, the Bank was a power alongside—though, in the last resort, subordinate to—the government[3]. The tradition of independence certainly survived Lord Norman's resignation in 1944. In theory, though to a decreasing extent in practice, contact between the Bank and the Treasury remained at the highest level[4]; and it is fair to say that Bank officials did not regard their role merely as that of civil servants facilitating the decisions of ministers[5].

[1]Sir Henry Clay remarked on a similar shift in power that accompanied the return to the gold standard in 1925: see Sir Henry Clay [1957], *Lord Norman*, p. 293.

[2]When 'Norman came to the governorship it was still a somewhat old-fashioned, semi-private institution, run to an extraordinary extent by part-timers. When he left it, it was a fully developed public office with a permanent staff of superb expert quality' (Professor Robbins, *The Listener*, 6 June 1957).

[3]'Norman' says Sir Henry Clay, 'was well aware of the limit within which Central Banks could expect to enjoy "independence" ' and illustrates this with Norman's views on the position of the Reichsbank in 1921:

> 'A Central Bank which is so much dominated by its own Government as to have no independence and initiative, and even no right of protest, is not in a fair position . . .'
> ' . . . No one wishes to give an independent Reichsbank the power of veto over the "entire financial and economic programme" of the German Government. I think that what we all have in mind is . . . to make unsound finance and dangerous methods difficult though, as the State is Sovereign, not impossible' (p.290).

[4]This was the old tradition. In 1932, for instance, an internal committee on the organization of the Bank confirmed tradition by recommending that 'relations between the Bank and Whitehall should be "intimate and cordial", but, to avoid misunderstandings, all communications should be through the Governors' (Clay [1957], p. 315).

[5]Changes in Bank rate being a symbol of monetary policy, the question of whether Bank or government is responsible for changing Bank rate has become a symbolic indication of the degree of independence of the Bank. In Lord Norman's day, the Bank appears to have asserted its right to change the rate without prior agreement or even prior consultation (Clay [1957], pp. 293–4). The Bank maintained before the Radcliffe Committee that the Bank of England Act of 1946 had not altered the constitutional position (*Radcliffe Report*, paras. 762–5). But in practice, as Mr Amory could assure the House in 1959, 'for very many years no change in the Bank Rate has been made without the approval of the Chancellor' (*H.C. Deb.* 26 Nov. 1959, 579). For the recent formal recognition of this position, see §5 below.

Though it would seem likely that, with the change in government, the Bank sought a greater say in economic policy, its actual influence can only be surmized. The new government would probably have been willing enough to lean more on monetary policy, even without urging from the Bank; but it must be supposed that the Bank was closely concerned with the form of monetary measures adopted. No government since the war has been in a position to disregard the external situation, as a constraint on policy. But the Bank, looking less at the balance of payments than at the reserves, has its own way of looking abroad; and a new official stress on the psychological factors underlying foreign confidence in sterling is apparent after 1951. The early adoption of convertibility, perhaps especially if coupled with a floating exchange rate, would have compelled a much greater emphasis on external conditions as the touchstone of policy. Both these policies, it is clear, were unsuccessfully pressed by the Bank.

What was most talked about was, however, by no means the same as what mattered most in practice; and a description of Conservative economic philosophy in terms of these pressures does less than justice to the less vocal, middle-of-the-road tradition that in fact generally carried the day. Conservative governments, no less clearly than Labour governments before them, in fact put full employment first as the main object of policy. When doctrinal pressures came up against this aim, the result was less to deflect policy than to create an ambiguity in the intentions of the government. Conflict of this sort over convertibility was a continued undercurrent to the actual course of policy, described below, under Mr Butler; and re-emerged for a brief spell under Mr Thorneycroft in 1957.

2. RECESSION, RECOVERY AND BOOM, 1952-5

The new administration under Mr Churchill took office in November 1951. Mr Butler was Chancellor of the Exchequer, remaining at this post till he moved to the Home Office in December 1955. It thus fell to him to introduce the four normal budgets of 1952, 1953, 1954 and 1955 and the autumn budget of 1955. Sir Arthur Salter was both Secretary of State for Economic Affairs, and in effect in charge of the new (and, as it proved, temporary) Ministry of Materials. He was replaced by Mr Maudling in November 1952, who was Economic Secretary till April 1955, when he was succeeded by Sir Edward Boyle.

Though some shift in the emphasis of economic policy was apparent, there was probably less change in deeds than in the doctrines by which they were justified. References to the 'strength of sterling' appeared in government statements, where there were none before; but much the same sort of measures were taken. Import restrictions, though regarded as regrettable, still seemed necessary. A role was found for Bank rate and credit restrictions; but, except for the unfortunate instance of 1955, it was on budgetary policy that main reliance continued to be placed. The *Economic Survey* ceased to provide forecasts. But, as Mr Butler made clear, unpublished forecasts continued to be made, and budgets to be based on them[1]. The 'economic justification' continued to be the centre piece of budget speeches, though it was never again as precise as Mr Gaitskell's. This was no doubt partly a matter of temperament. Mr Butler never sought to rival his predecessor's display of economic erudition; and was averse neither to the broad statements acceptable to the plain man, nor to the metaphorical language frequently employed for the discussion of monetary policy[2].

The first concern of the new Government was necessarily with the payments crisis, at its height when it took office. The crisis had been mainly due to a failure to foresee in full the consequences of the outbreak of the Korean war in 1950: that overseas sterling countries would swing from heavy surplus to heavy deficit was not foreseen; nor was the effect of heavy stockbuilding in the United Kingdom[3]. The swing in the United Kingdom balance was the most sudden on record—from £300 million surplus in 1950 to over £400 million deficit in 1951, mostly concentrated in the second half of the year, and all of it with the non-sterling world. The overseas sterling area's position with the non-sterling world also worsened, and by about as much. The crisis was necessarily accompanied and aggravated by speculation—itself probably aggravated by doubts about British exchange policy, in fact under discussion at the time[4]. In the second half of 1951 we lost almost as much gold as we had gained in 1950, and by the end of the year the reserves were down to £834 million.

The main action taken was a series of drastic import cuts, designed to save £600 million on the import bill: the first, announced directly the new Government took office in November, was followed by further cuts in January and March. The cuts, which took effect with varying delays, affected food, timber and many other imports; the tourist allowance was also reduced to a minimal £25. This policy involved a major retreat from the 'liberalization' programme introduced

---

[1]In his concluding speech to the debate on his first budget, the Chancellor gave an assurance to Mr Gaitskell and other critics 'that my conclusions were reached after making full use of the whole machinery of economic forecasting that is available to any Chancellor of the Exchequer, and was, indeed, available to my predecessors when they were in office' (*H.C. Deb.* 17 March 1952, 2050).

[2]Mr Gaitskell commented as follows on his successor's turns of speech:
  'We all know that the Chancellor of the Exchequer uses metaphors very freely. We used to be travelling in a ship through a storm. We are accustomed to climbing mountains with him. We are sometimes undergoing operations in hospital. Sometimes we are convalescing . . . '
He added:
  'I must confess that we had a certain amount of amusement from these metaphors, but I am beginning to think they really do harm. When we tell people that "the roses have to be pruned", they do not think of themselves as the rose . . . ' (*H.C. Deb.* 27 Oct. 1955, 399).

[3]See chapter II.4.

[4]See §3 below.

only a short time before in OEEC, largely under British leadership[1]. At the Commonwealth finance ministers' conference—already arranged to take place in January—the other sterling countries agreed to parallel reductions in their imports, intended to get the sterling area back into balance by the second half of the year.

All this was little different from what a Labour government might have done, and indeed action on these lines had already been set in train by the outgoing Government. It was a new—and to many, a puzzling—note for the Commonwealth conference to give great stress to convertibility as an aim: but no direct action followed[2]. This line of thought may however have had one immediate effect. The desire for convertibility went along with distaste for discrimination; and the conference played down the previous policy whereby sterling countries had cut only non-sterling imports. Shortly afterwards Australia— one tenth of our export market—imposed heavy cuts on British imports[3].

It was novel too for the Commonwealth conference to accept the *simpliste* diagnosis that the sterling area's difficulties were largely due to its own sins, and to proclaim accordingly that 'all possible measures' must be taken 'to combat inflation'[4]. There was a series of restrictive measures to implement this country's share in that resolution. The rise in Bank rate in November 1951 from 2 to $2\frac{1}{2}$ per cent was at the time hailed as 'the most significant change in monetary policy since the beginning of the war'[5]. In the light of monetary history since then (reviewed as a whole more fully in chapter IX below) the rise seems modest enough; and was in fact dwarfed by the further rise to 4 per cent made at the budget in March. As on so many later occasions, hire-purchase restrictions were also introduced (in January—on cars, radios and other electrical goods); and various steps, going somewhat short of direct control, were taken to curtail fixed investment[6].

The simple diagnosis of 'too much demand' could not however, on close

---

[1]The 'deliberalization' of imports from OEEC countries represented only about a quarter of the total saving expected, the rest being cuts in government purchases (not covered by the OEEC agreement) or in other non-sterling imports. The total figure of £600 million was a cut on a 'programme': compared *with the previous year* the volume of visible imports (in the budget year 1951/52) was expected to fall by £300 million or so (*Economic Survey for 1952*, para. 115).

[2]See §3 below.

[3]Mr Butler shared 'the regret expressed by the Prime Minister of Australia' that Australia felt it necessary to restrict British imports (*H.C. Deb.* 11 March 1952, 1276). But the agreement had apparently not been couched in terms of non-sterling imports, but rather 'that each sterling country should seek to live within its means' i.e. achieve overall balance (Mr Thorneycroft, *H.C. Deb.* 13 March 1952, 1594).

[4]*Economist*, 26 Jan. 1952, p. 225.

[5]*Economic Survey for 1952*, para. 104.

[6]By the suspension (in the March budget) of 'initial' depreciation allowances, and by 'voluntary arrangements' with 'the manufacturers of capital goods . . . about the proportion of production which should be devoted to export' (*Economic Survey for 1952*, para. 117).

inspection, be pressed very far.   Restrictions on investment could be justified by the high demand for 'metal goods', due in the main to the defence programme.   But consumer industries faced, not high, but slack demand; and the Australian import cuts made this worse.   To add to their difficulties, 'by depressing home demand even further', would, as Mr Butler said, 'result not in still higher exports, but in a further reduction of activity and employment'[1].

Budget day had been advanced to 11 March as an emergency measure; but there was in fact little the budget could do to help with the crisis.   A demand recession was in fact already under way.   This was not in fact foreseen[2]: nevertheless, the budget at least, did not make matters worse.   Consumers benefited by the cut in income tax; but lost by the rise in petrol duty, and by the cut in food subsidies[3].   The mildness of the budget appears to have taken opinion by surprise.   The needs of the case in fact pulled in opposite ways. Economic logic, calling for leniency, was in fact followed: the appearance of toughness required to convince 'overseas opinion that Britain means business in its drive for external solvency'[4] was provided, perhaps, by the rise in Bank rate.

Actual developments during 1952 (table 3.1) were dominated by two factors. Import prices now fell again—by about half as much as they had risen in the previous phase.   At home, for the first time since the war, an inventory recession caused a fall in output.   Both factors must have helped to reverse the previous heavy accumulation of stocks of materials.   Thus the balance of payments gained on three counts: less imports were used, less imports were stocked, and the terms of trade improved.   Notwithstanding a ten per cent fall in export volume, the balance of payments was in surplus by about £300 million—a turn-round from the previous year of almost £700 million.   The rest of the sterling area also restored its accounts to surplus in the second half of the year, a result of import cuts and also of a recovery in the price of wool and other commodities.   By the fourth quarter of the year the reserves were rising again.

It would have been less than human if the Government had not claimed credit for this transformation; but part only was due to its own actions.   Nearly

---

[1]Budget speech: *H.C. Deb.* 11 March 1952, 1286.

[2]It was clear at the time of the budget that production had ceased to expand; but the government hoped that output would rise in the rest of the year (*Economic Survey*, para. 115).   See further chapter V below.

[3]The budget speech was in more general terms than in previous years, and the intended impact of the budget is less easy to follow.   Food subsidies, running at the rate of about £450 million a year, were to be reduced to £250 million.   It appears from the next year's *Economic Survey* that 'that part of the rise in retail prices which was due to the reduction in food subsidies and to the increases in indirect taxes was roughly matched by the effects on personal incomes after tax of the income tax concessions and the increases in national insurance and other transfer payments, for which the Budget also provided.   Thus the net effect of the Budget changes was to leave consumers' real purchasing power virtually unchanged' (*Economic Survey for 1953*, para. 38).   The new excess profits levy, introduced as a temporary measure in view of high profit in the armaments industries, affected next year's revenue only; and of course hardly affected consumers.

[4]*Economist*, 15 March 1952, p. 656.

Table 3.1. *The British economy, 1952–5*

	1951	1952	1953	1954	1955
Changes in final expenditure[a] (£m., 1954 prices[b])					
Consumer durables	—	—25	150	150	100
Other consumption	—150	—25	325	400	350
Government current expenditure	200	300	100	—	—75
Fixed investment	—	—	225	200	125
of which manufacturing and distribution	25	—25	—	75	150
Investment in stocks[c]	800	—525	100	—75	225
Exports, goods and services	—50	—75	75	200	250
TOTAL	800	—350	975	875	975
of which imports[d]	300	—300	250	125	450
Gross domestic product[e] (% change[f])	2½	—	4	4	3
Industrial production (% change[f])	3½	—3	6	7	5
Labour market					
Percentage unemployment	1·2	2·0	1·6	1·3	1·1
Index of excess demand[g]	1·4	—0·5	—0·1	0·6	1·5
Prices and wages (% change in year[h])					
Retail prices	11·9	6·7	1·4	3·4	5·9
Wage rates	10·7	6·7	3·2	4·7	7·0
Balance of payments[i] (£m.[b])					
Exports	2,725	2,775	2,675	2,775	3,075
Imports	—3,500	—3,075	—2,950	—3,000	—3,475
Invisibles	375	450	400	375	225
Current balance	—400	150	125	150	—175
Change in reserves (£m.)	—344	—175	240	87	—229

[a]From *NI & E* [1961] at market prices.

[b]Rounded to nearest £25 m.

[c]Table shows *change* in investment in stocks. Investment in stocks (£m.) was

1951	1952	1953	1954	1955
565	40	130	50	315

[d]At factor cost.

[e]Average of changes in production and expenditure series, which often diverge appreciably: from *NI & E* [1960].

[f]Change of year's average over previous year.

[g]Roughly twice the difference between % vacancies and % unemployment: the amplitude of the index is thus twice that originally presented in Dow and Dicks-Mireaux [1958], *Oxford econ. Pap.* (see chapter XIII.2 below).

[h]Change *during* year, measured between successive fourth quarters.

[i]For the sake of continuity, taken from *NI & E* [1961]—not from *BPWP*. Because of subsequent revisions, figures for 1951 do not tally exactly with those shown in table 2.2.

For key to abbreviations see introductory note, p. xiii above.

half the improvement in the balance of payments was due to the terms of trade[1]. The recession had not been foreseen and, undetected, was already in train when the new Government took office: a stock cycle is essentially the delayed reaction to a pause in the growth of demand, and both exports and consumption had ceased to rise by the end of 1951. If it had an effect, the new monetary policy must have worsened the recession—an effect neither useful nor claimed as such[2]. The 'stop-gap' restrictions on imports, however, were undoubtedly both requisite and reasonably effective. It is true that imports would have fallen without the cuts, partly because some of their effect was in the event overtaken by the unforeseen fall in demand. It is also true that a good part of their impact was to reduce stocks, a temporary palliative only. Looking back, it seems likely that even without restrictions the external account would have returned, though not to surplus, at least to something like balance. Even had this been known, the low state of confidence would have been enough to justify the cuts. In the light of what was known at the time, it would have been brave indeed not to have imposed them[3].

By the beginning of 1953 the successive repercussions of the 'Korean' boom had largely worked through. 'The international barometer' said Mr Butler[4], 'still stands at "changeable weather" ' but 'we may hope to see it climb to "fair" '. Renewed expansion of world trade, and hence of exports, seemed likely. Falling import prices had greatly slowed down the rise in retail prices[5]; and production had nearly recovered to its pre-recession level. But little further expansion seemed in sight[6]. Productive capacity seemed in danger of being under-employed; and were this to go uncorrected, industrial investment, which had started to fall during the recession, seemed unlikely to pick up. These considerations underlay the expansionary tone of the 1953 budget. To encourage investment the 'initial' allowances were restored. To stimulate consumption, sixpence came off income tax, and purchase tax was cut by about a sixth—all told, an increase in consumers' incomes of some £150 million.

In the event, 1953 was a year of rapid expansion. National output rose four per cent, chiefly because of rising consumption—but, among other reasons,

---

[1]*Economic Survey for 1953*, para. 14.

[2]Mounting unemployment in Lancashire led the Government in March to accelerate defence orders for textiles by some £20 million.

[3]This view is based on the detailed analysis given by W. M. Corden [1958], 'The Control of Imports: A Case Study—The United Kingdom Import Restrictions of 1951–52' (*Manchester Sch.*, Sept. 1958) and for the main accepts his assessment: see further chapter VI.4 below.

[4]Budget speech: *H.C. Deb.* 14 April 1953, 49.

[5]'Retail food prices', the *Survey* noted, had been increased, 'mainly in the first half of the year, as a result of the Budget decision to reduce food subsidies; but other retail prices were on average only about 2 per cent higher in December 1952 than a year earlier' (*Economic Survey for 1953*, para. 44).

[6]'my estimate—and the best I can give the Committee—is that we are unlikely to do much more than make good the decline in output last year' (budget speech, *H.C. Deb.* 14 April 1953, 49).

partly also because of the vigorous expansion of house-building under Mr Macmillan's housing 'drive'[1]. Industrial investment, however, still showed little increase—perhaps, as the next *Survey* commented, because the budget measures had not yet had time to have their full effect[2]. Expansion had raised the volume of imports; but prices were lower and the balance of payments surplus was more or less repeated. The continued growth in the reserves was however chiefly due to low imports by the rest of the sterling area; and it seemed unlikely to persist. Recession in the United States was alarming the world; and, as ever, the sterling area appeared particularly vulnerable. It was this prospect which dominated the 1954 budget:

> 'So far production in the U.S.A. has fallen about as far as it did during the recession of 1948-49; and we do not know whether it will fall further before it recovers. The sterling area could be affected in two ways. It might suffer some direct loss of dollar income; or, if a fall in activity in the United States were to lead to a reduction in commodity prices, a decline in prices and incomes might result in a general fall in trade and activity[3].

This made it far from clear what the budget should aim at. If all went well, expansion looked likely to continue. If not, and world recession hit our exports, there might be a need to support home activity. But the weakening balance of payments would make this all the more difficult. Mr Butler in fact decided to wait and see. It was almost a 'no-change' budget. The only expansionary measure was the investment allowance, whose effect on investment, though likely to be potent, would take time[4].

Budgetary policy thus still trod its perpetual compromise, between the desire for more expansion and the fear of too much. The narrow constraint imposed by the balance of payments left indeed little choice. To some there

---

[1]Mr Macmillan's aim was to build 300,000 houses a year, which he achieved.
[2]*Economic Survey, 1954*, para. 67.
[3]Budget speech: *H.C. Deb.* 2 April 1954, 214–5. The prospect had made the latest of the series of Commonwealth conferences avert its eyes somewhat from convertibility. The Chancellor's speech continued:
> 'At Sydney, in January, the Commonwealth Finance Ministers were unanimous that we should try to ride the inevitable fluctuations of world trade without a return to restrictions on trade and payments. We also agreed that if all played their part in endeavouring to maintain a high level of trade, activity and employment . . . a moderate decline of activity in the United States could be prevented from having serious repercussions elsewhere.'

It was not made clear whether *dollar* import cuts were envisaged. Since world trade could hardly have been maintained without discrimination, it may be as well that good intentions were not put to the test.
[4]In place of the previous 'initial' allowance, which, being an accelerated depreciation allowance, merely postponed liability for tax, the new allowance exempted from tax 20 per cent of expenditure on plant and machinery and 10 per cent of expenditure on industrial or agricultural buildings. Since income tax plus profits tax took 47½ per cent of undistributed profits, this was for most firms in effect a subsidy on investment of about 10 per cent and 5 per cent respectively.

seemed so little difference between Mr Butler's and Mr Gaitskell's policy, that the term 'Butskellism' was invented to cover both[1]. Unemployment had remained almost as low as under the Labour Government. Though the food subsidies had been halved, the social services had not been sacrificed to the pressure for lower social expenditure. Only steel and road transport were in process of being denationalized. Discussion of convertibility had (as described in the next section) continued all this while: but, if ominous, it also seemed end-less, and any major step continued to be postponed.

The Government followed a Fabian policy also towards controls. They were removed only gradually[2]. Many raw material controls—which had been greatly extended during 1951—were removed during 1953, the general steel allocation ending in May. The crisis restrictions on OEEC imports were also largely removed during 1953; and during 1952 and 1953 the Government progressively returned the importing of materials to private trade. Sterling imports of course remained free: by the end of 1953 the relaxations left half non-sterling imports unrestricted. Food rationing, though much reduced, did not end till July 1954. When rationing went, most of what remained of price control—which had once covered one half of consumers' expenditure— also went. Building controls, too, though greatly eased, were not to be finally abolished till November 1954. By that time 'the main body of controls over the home economy' had been removed[3].

Things thus far had gone very happily for Mr Butler's conduct of affairs. Each year seemed better than the one before, as if by some golden law of progress. Even the perturbations about the American recession had proved groundless. The old world had stepped in to redress the new: output in Western Europe, as it happened, had increased rapidly just as the United States went into recession. This was probably the main reason why commodity prices did not fall, as had been feared; and why world trade, far from falling, continued to expand[4]. Continued immunity could not but breed growing confidence in continuing prosperity—a feeling dramatized by Mr Butler by his question: 'why should we not aim to double the standard of living in the next twenty years?'[5]

---

[1]'Mr Butskell' said *The Economist*, 'is already a well-known figure in dinner table con-versation' (13 Feb. 1954, p. 440).

[2]See further chapter VI.

[3]*Economic Survey, 1955*, para. 69.

[4]*See Economic Survey, 1955*, paras. 1–5: some other factors are mentioned in the ECE *Economic Survey of Europe in 1954*, pp. 33–6.

[5]This motif appeared first in Mr Butler's address to the National Joint Production Advisory Committee on Industry in May 1954. In his address, this followed a comment on the United States recession:

'Between July 1953 and April 1954, United States industrial production fell 10 per cent. Between the same two dates sterling area gold and dollar reserves rose 19 per cent. If anyone in the middle of last year had forecast this combination of percentages he would have been written of as an optimist or an ignoramus—possibly

In fact however expansion was soon to get badly out of hand.   Total real expenditure had risen five per cent between 1953 and 1954; and it was to increase again by as much in 1955—stock accumulation as a driving force being added to the earlier consumption boom (table 3.1).   By 1955 the boom drew in a very sizeable increase in imports, and the balance of payments was back in deficit. Excess demand returned; and the rise in prices and wages accelerated.   In the early months of the year, even before the budget, there were clear signs of what was to come[1].   The action taken by the Government, on the other hand, proved neither consistent nor timely.

Some corrective measures were taken in February.   Bank rate, which had stood at 3 per cent since the previous May, and had just been raised to $3\frac{1}{2}$ per cent in January, was raised again to $4\frac{1}{2}$ per cent; hire-purchase restrictions, abolished in July, were also reintroduced[2].   The pound had come under strain: as both cause and result, rumours of exchange moves were again in the air.   The Government was, in fact, again under pressure to undertake convertibility, to which it partly acceded by allowing the Bank to support the rate on 'transferable' sterling[3].

By the time the budget came in April Mr Butler claimed that these measures to 'moderate the growth of imports and to encourage exports' had already been effective.   It seems clear however that he was relying not on the evidence of the trade accounts, but on the strengthening of sterling[4]—particularly uncertain evidence at this juncture[5].   Arguing that he could continue to rely on the 'resources of a flexible monetary policy' and that there was now room for expansion[6], he reduced income tax by sixpence—the tax reductions amounting in all to £150 million[7].

This faith in credit control soon proved misplaced.   'By the summer' as the

both.   Yet there it is' (*Economist*, 5 June 1954, p. 821).
In Mr Butler's later references to this theme, as in his 'invest in success' speech to the Conservative Party Conference in October, 'twenty' became 'twenty-five' years (*Economist*, 16 Oct. 1954, p. 191).
[1]The *Survey*, speaking of the change which came over the balance of payments in the second half of 1954, said :
'Late in 1954 and early in 1955 . . . imports were rising sharply in value . . . with the result that the trade gap was widening, particularly on the non-sterling side. The gold and dollar reserves did not rise in January, and in February they fell by £29 million . . .   Meanwhile, at home the demand for labour was still rising at a time when unemployment was already very low . . .   At the same time the general atmosphere in the economy was hardly favourable to reductions in costs and prices' (*Economic Survey, 1955*, paras. 71–2).
[2]Though not mentioned at the time in the *Survey* or in the budget speech, it would seem also that some restriction of credit was expected of the banks: see below and chapter IX.3.
[3]See further §3 below.
[4]*H.C. Deb.* 19 April 1955, 39.
[5]The abatement of speculation must partly have been due to the fact that the exchange rate had not, as half expected, been allowed to fall: see § 3 below.
[6]*H.C. Deb.* 19 April 1955, 55–6.
[7]Almost all falling on personal incomes: £135 million in 1955/56, £155 million in a full year.

next *Survey* said, it became evident 'that the pressure of demand persisted and that monetary policy was not operating as rapidly as had been expected'[1]. In July the banks were called on sharply to reduce advances; and local authority and nationalized industry investment was 'pruned'. This too proved insufficient to restrain home demand. Moreover renewed rumours about convertibility policy—described more fully in §3 below—led to a new run on the pound. Without this, the supplementary budget in October might never have been necessary. Credit and hire-purchase restrictions had been greatly strengthened in July. In the autumn budget, purchase tax was raised by a fifth, so reversing about half the leniency of April[2].

Charges were freely made that the April tax reductions were only made because of the general election which followed in May. The autumn budget was implicit admission that it had been a mistake to cut taxation; but various considerations made the question somewhat less clear-cut at the time. First, Mr Butler appears to have relied on monetary control, exercised with his right hand, to balance the budget concessions given by his left. To a cold eye it may seem that he was relying on monetary policy to work wonders[3]. Nevertheless, though there was little evidence to justify it, such faith in monetary policy had become widely held[4]; and the general success of the past four years had allowed it to persist uncontroverted as one strand in official thought.

Errors in diagnosis would seem to have been equally important. The kind of analysis provided by the *Economic Survey* showed clearly that demand pressure was mounting; by April 1955, it was, indeed, probably already too late to stop the boom. But the evidence was not all one way: at the time of the budget, there seemed, for some reason, to be a temporary lull in the growth of output[5]. Nor was this the only kind of evidence thought important. It was

---

[1]*Economic Survey, 1956*, para. 68.

[2]Purchase tax was expected to increase revenue (in a full year) by £75 million. The increased tax on distributed profits (£38 million) may possibly also have had a small impact on consumers' incomes.

[3]Monetary policy was constantly spoken of as providing an essential 'discipline' without being restrictive or impeding expansion—phrases echoed by Mr Butler at the April budget (*H.C. Deb.* 19 April 1955, 39).

[4]For instance, *The Economist* commented that Mr Butler, coming into office 'at a time of grave economic crisis, used the one weapon' that had previously been 'shunned for political reasons—the weapon of Bank rate—and found that it worked even more effectively than he, his civil servants or (let us admit it) even critics of previous policy'—such presumably as *The Economist*—'had ever expected. Partly as a result of this . . . he was able to introduce a mild first budget and a very popular second one' (*Economist*, 13 Feb. 1954, p. 440).

[5]As Mr Gaitskell pointed out: 'the *Economic Survey* foresees an appreciable increase for 1955 . . . So far this does not seem to be happening . . . according to the Treasury's own index, and allowing for seasonal variations, there has been virtually no increase in production for the past five months, and I am a little surprised that the Chancellor made no comment about this'. The figures Mr Gaitskell quoted were 131 (1948=100) for the fourth quarter of 1954, and the same figure for January and February 1955 (*H.C. Deb.* 20 April 1955, 186).

part of the mystique both of monetary policy and of convertibility to lay great stress on week-to-week fluctuations of the reserves; and, indeed, to judge policy in general according to the confidence it inspired abroad—an unreliable guide, particularly at this juncture. There were indeed very different approaches to policy, which did not necessarily cancel out to produce the *via media*; and the vacillations of policy in 1955 can in the last analysis be ascribed very largely to irresolution between them.

3. THE CONVERTIBILITY 'PLAN'

It was only towards the end of Mr Butler's period as Chancellor of the Exchequer that the non-convertibility of sterling was relaxed; and then the step was no more than half-way[1]. But throughout this period, the possibility of an earlier and more radical move to convertibility was in the air. If this had happened, internal policy would in all probability have had to be profoundly modified: even as it was, the uncertainty had, as already argued, repercussions on budgetary and monetary policy. The dispute on convertibility was largely conducted behind closed doors. The discussion within the Treasury and the Bank of England, and with other governments, and the rumours to which this gave rise, made it clear that something was in the wind. But, in spite of numerous conferences to discuss them, the details of successive proposals remained veiled in official secrecy. Like the cavorting of an elephant under a dust-sheet the Government's intentions remained wrapped in a species of obscurity. Sufficient was however plain for the main elements to be now discernible[2].

Convertibility was put publicly on the agenda in the first months of the new Government. The Commonwealth conference that met in London in January 1952, had been originally convened to deal with the payments crisis. But it also discussed convertibility. The communiqué indeed treated the achievement of convertibility as a main aim of policy[3]—words which seemed 'strangely

---

[1]In February 1955 the Bank of England was permitted to support the rate for 'transferable' sterling: see further below.

[2]This account is based chiefly on articles in *The Economist* and on what emerged in the parliamentary debates.

An account of the proposals from the point of view of Lord Cherwell has also recently been given in Lord Birkenhead's [1961] *The Prof in Two Worlds*, chapter X. For two years till October 1953 Lord Cherwell was Paymaster-General; and, 'spending almost every other weekend' at Chequers, played something of the same role of personal adviser to the Prime Minister as he had during the war. With Mr G. D. A. (now Sir Donald) MacDougall as his assistant, he was chiefly concerned with economic issues. He was a strong opponent of the convertibility proposals; and countered them with a proposal of his own for an 'Atlantic Payments Union'.

[3]Two study groups were set up 'to put into practice some of the ideas . . . discussed and to study their implications'. One was concerned with 'the steps to be taken towards the convertibility of sterling'; the other, with 'development' (*H.C. Deb.* 29 Jan. 1952, 42).

brave'[1] after the silence which had reigned since the convertibility fiasco five years before. All this could be taken to imply no more than that convertibility was an ultimate goal. But if so, why such emphasis, when sterling was so weak?

Strong rumours were indeed circulating that, at an early date, the pound was to be made convertible and that the rate was to be let free—even it seems, that this step was to be taken on budget day[2]. These rumours inevitably further weakened the reserves. The budget was in fact advanced from April to 11 March, for a reason not explained[3]. The fact of the rumours, and the question of the policy, were referred to by many speakers in the debate, Mr Assheton being bolder than most in voicing what many in the City thought. He welcomed the Chancellor's 'intention to make the £ convertible as soon as possible'; and claimed that the lowness of the reserves was no reason for delay—if they fell still lower, the authorities, he said, would be forced to acquiesce in convertibility: 'this is a problem about which the Chancellor must be thinking a great deal. I hope he will be bold'[4].

By July there were again strong rumours of an imminent move to convertibility. It also came to be widely believed that about this time detailed proposals had again been under consideration, and that the Cabinet had been

---

[1] *Economist*, 26 Jan. 1952, p. 225.

[2]　　'Between the late summer of last year and March 11, a considerable short position in sterling was built up over the greater part of the world . . . Rumours were rife that sterling was due for another plunge, either by a further devaluation or by letting the rate of the pound float in a more or less free market (*The Banker*, April 1952, p. 200).

It appears that the Cabinet had rejected such a proposal in February (Birkenhead [1961], p. 288).

[3] Mr Butler said that the main function of the budget was to 'restore confidence in the pound' (*H.C. Deb.* 11 March 1952, 1290).

Contrary to expectations, however, the budget changes were not deflationary (§2 above). Mr Gaitskell commented:

'If the only change to be made in the Budget is a change in the distribution of existing burdens, and if, in fact, the change has no relationship to the crisis, why did we have an early Budget at all? Perhaps there may have been some other reason. We should certainly be interested to know how this extraordinary discrepancy can be explained' (*H.C. Deb.* 12 March 1952, 1392).

Mr Butler in his summing-up to the debate reported that the budget had had a good reception and that 'markets overseas have shown increased confidence in sterling' (*H.C. Deb.* 17 March 1952, 2048). This may well have been not because of the measures that were taken, but because of the fact that sterling had *not* then been made convertible or the rate set free, as speculators seem to have expected.

[4] 'We cannot survive without an honest currency. Therefore, we were all glad to hear, after the Chancellor's meeting with the Commonwealth Finance Ministers, that it was his intention to make the £ convertible as soon as possible.'

'The point is, how soon it can be done? There are always people who say: "This is not the time. We must build up our reserves more . . ." Believe me there may come a much worse time. Suppose the drain on our gold and dollar reserves goes on . . . What shall we have to do then? We shall have to let the currency run free, or to devalue it, without having a reserve at all' (*H.C. Deb.* 12 March 1952, 1423–4).

G

deeply divided[1]. For the debate at the end of July an announcement had originally been promised by the Prime Minister of 'very serious measures . . . in all fields'[2]. Again however, the rumours were falsified. When it came the debate turned out to be innocuous[3]; and the only announcement was that a new Commonwealth conference would be held in November at which 'the whole position of the sterling area' would be 'searchingly reviewed'. At the conference, not the Chancellor of the Exchequer, but the Prime Minister was to preside; and, not the Chancellor, but the Foreign Secretary was to be in charge of the preparations for it[4].

The conference in November was to be the first in a long series of conferences and diplomatic exchanges in furtherance of what was designated 'the collective approach' to convertibility. This therefore is a convenient point to summarize the convertibility plan in its various stages, fairly full accounts of which had by the middle of the year appeared in the press[5].

The proposals were at the time the subject of great argument; and it is impossible to describe either their nature or their subsequent fate without taking sides in the argument. In my view the 1952 proposals were misguided; and the delay of convertibility for many years was in fact the only wise course. The objection to any of the proposals was, on this view, basic and insurmountable. If the world was short of dollars, and we allowed foreign holders of sterling to convert it into dollars at their request, they would rush to do so. Inconvertibility was the financial sanction to trade discriminations against dollar imports. Its removal would allow other countries to import dollar goods at our expense; it would also invite restrictions on our exports by other countries as a way of paying for greater imports from America. A general preference for holding reserves in dollars was thus only one reason for expecting a rush on the reserves. The position might admittedly have been held by restricting activity at home:

[1]In the debate in November, Mr Gaitskell was to say:
    ' . . . there have been very substantial rumours that the Government were intending to adopt a policy of convertibility. These were mentioned in the Press, particularly last July . . . '
    'I have heard an interesting rumour . . . that the Cabinet very nearly reached a decision that there should be a return to convertibility, but that . . . the noble Lord, Lord Cherwell, intervened very effectively, having as we all know, the ear of the Prime Minister, and managed to get this policy stopped . . . He has really done us a very good service if his relationship to the Prime Minister has enabled him to stop such a disastrous turn in our policy' (*H.C. Deb.* 11 Nov. 1952, 797–8).
    It appears in fact that the scheme had been revived, and again rejected, in June (Birkenhead [1961], p. 289).
[2]*H.C. Deb.* 16 July 1952, 2149. Mr Churchill—'never at ease in such matters'—clearly wavered about convertibility (see Birkenhead [1961], pp. 280 and 288).
[3]The Government motion for debate merely 'welcomed the Government's determination to improve 'the balance of payments and to take such further measures as may be necessary' (*H.C. Deb.* 29 July 1952, 1276).
[4]*H.C. Deb.* 30 July 1952, 1498–9.
[5]In particular *The Economist* leader for 26 July, 'Set Sterling Free?' (26 July 1952, pp. 205–8).

but deflation and unemployment would, on this view, have been the price of premature convertibility.

Such consequences, it is to be supposed, were not envisaged by the advocates of convertibility. In a sense this was because a different view was taken of the extent of the world dollar shortage[1]. In a more profound sense it was because the argument, being couched in terms of 'confidence', avoided such questions[2]. That there were risks in convertibility was nevertheless obvious. The successive phases of the convertibility plan were attempts to mitigate them.

The expedient first proposed was to allow the exchange rate to 'float'. 'The new factor that has emerged in recent months is that the City is, for the first time, willing to accept a fluctuating exchange rate for sterling as the price that has to be paid for this step towards convertibility'[3]. The 'floating rate' appears indeed to have been the main feature of the scheme as it existed in the early months of 1952—the idea being that this would 'take the strain' of going convertible 'off the reserves and put it on to the rate of exchange'[4].

At this date the United Kingdom was severely restricting imports. Strange as it may seem, it appears that 'the earliest drafts laid store on the maintenance of import restrictions in order to limit the amount of convertible sterling that would come into the hands of non-resident holders'[5]. As a matter of practical politics, however, such restrictions could hardly have been retained without retaliation by other countries. Even apart from this, convertibility would (as already noted) have provided an incentive to other countries to restrict imports from us. The Board of Trade, in particular, cannot have been blind to such considerations[6].

The 'collective approach' was therefore a further attempt to reduce the risks[7].

---

[1]This is suggested by the short-lived experiment in commodity arbitrage in August 1952: see below.

[2]Sir Dennis Robertson's comment was justified:

'Inter-convertibility of currencies is not an end in itself, but a means to the promotion of a steady and abundant flow of international trade . . . This might seem too obvious to be worth saying; but I think that, in forming a judgement on practical issues, it is sometimes necessary to be on the look-out for a certain tendency on the part of those engaged in administering a currency to be a little too much swayed by considerations of prestige—of the ability of their own idol to "look" the other idols "in the face" ' (*Optima*, March 1954).

[3]*Economist*, 26 July 1952, p. 206.

[4]This scheme bore the dramatic title of 'Operation Robot': even this code name was supposed to be secret. See Birkenhead [1961], p. 284, and Shonfield [1958], *British Economic Policy Since the War*, pp. 216–7.

[5]*Economist*, 27 Sept. 1958, p. 1043.

[6]Mr Thorneycroft, to whom as President of the Board of Trade these considerations must have come home, appeared in January cautious about convertibility: ' . . . none of us, in any part of the House, is oblivious to the dangers of precipitate convertibility before the necessary stability, confidence and financial reserves have been built up' (*H.C. Deb.* 30 Jan. 1952, 235).

[7]This set of proposals emerged during August 'after much hard and bitter argument

As its name implies, all major currencies were—if the Governments concerned could be persuaded—to undertake convertibility simultaneously. Equally important they were to forswear the use of import restrictions against each other. To protect the reserves, a 'support fund' was to be sought, while exchange rates were still to be allowed to vary.

The proposals took something like a fixed form at the Commonwealth conference in December 1952, which accepted them at least in broad principle. The communiqué reaffirmed 'the achievement of convertibility' as the aim; and stated three requisite conditions (later to be much quoted): the curbing of inflation, the general adoption of unrestrictive trade practices, and the availability of adequate international credit[1]. None of these conditions, however, was clear-cut; and different interpretations were possible. The fact of an agreement suggested on the one hand that something might be done soon to implement it[2]. On the other hand, insistence on pre-conditions could be read as a triumph for gradualism.

Policy therefore remained in a considerable state of irresolution. Since the real difficulties about convertibility had not been faced, there always seemed a danger that they would be ignored, and the pound be declared convertible despite them. It was evident from the beginning that the Bank of England strongly advocated speedy convertibility; and it was almost as much a matter of public knowledge that many Treasury officials took much the same view[3]. Mr Butler, while remaining cautious in practice, evidently continued to hanker after the principle of convertibility. The result was not deeds but words.

Overt action towards making sterling convertible was, till 1955, minimal. At the very beginning of the episode, one step was taken which attracted little attention, but may have had some importance. In December 1951, the Bank of England ceased to support the forward rate. This step, perhaps undertaken to

and manoeuvring between officials of various Departments, the meetings often lasting till 3 a.m.' (Birkenhead [1961], p. 290).

[1] Cmd. 8717: the conference also discussed development and commodity policy.

[2] The Prime Minister of Australia appears to have come away with this impression. He was reported as saying that 'the first move towards the convertibility of sterling and freer world trade would follow discussions soon to be held with Western Europe and the United States' (Mr Menzies quoted by Mr Gaitskell: *H.C. Deb.* 3 Feb. 1953, 1706).

[3] *The Economist*, 22 Nov. 1952, p. 580, remarked that 'a surprising number of leading bankers and public servants . . . looking out upon the sorry mess of post-war exchange controls, have become converted to the philosophy of Rupert Brooke's fish:

    "This life cannot be All," they swear,
    "For how unpleasant, if it were!" '

Shonfield [1958], p. 227, gives the names of Treasury officials who with the Governor of the Bank were supposed to have advocated the 'Robot' scheme. It was believed that there was later an important difference of emphasis between the Treasury and the Bank. Thus in July 1955 *The Financial Times* spoke of the 'two voices' on convertibility; and Mr Gaitskell asked whether it was not true that, while 'the Treasury speaks of convertibility as something remote which we are not going to reach for a very long time and about which we must be very cautious', the Bank spoke of it 'as something that is just round the corner and which we have very nearly approached already' (*H.C. Deb.* 26 July 1955, 1004).

prepare the way for a floating spot rate, may be judged to have increased the sensitivity of sterling to speculation; and thus to have exposed the economy more fully to 'confidence' factors, in a way entirely consistent with the convertibility approach[1]. In August 1952, there was an ill-starred experiment in commodity arbitrage, which amounted to convertibility by a side door. European countries were permitted to buy dollar commodities in London; but the rush was so great that this freedom had to be hurriedly withdrawn[2]. A much more cautious process of reopening commodity markets began in 1954, with careful delimitation of permitted arbitrage on dollar commodities[3]. This was certainly a new freedom; but it had little essential connection with convertibility. In March 1954 there was, too, a great simplification of exchange control, practically all non-sterling countries outside the dollar area from then on being treated alike. But though the 'transferable account' area was thus greatly enlarged it was still separated from the 'dollar account' area.

The most important step taken was undoubtedly that made in February 1955, when the Bank of England was permitted to support the 'transferable' rate. The step is worth discussion in order to show the fragile foundation on which the structure of exchange control reposed, and the difficulty of gauging the implications of changes in the controls. Transferable sterling was supposed not to be convertible into dollars. There was however a market in transferable sterling, on which such sterling had hitherto been traded at a discount. It thus paid those who wished to buy sterling-area exports to buy them with such cheap sterling. The sale of transferable sterling was not in any strict sense 'illegal', since those who sold it were not usually subject to British law. Nor— though it might involve deceiving the customs officials at some sterling-area port—was it illegal to use it for commodity shunting[4]. Even more than with domestic controls, the powers of coercion underpinning the non-convertibility of sterling were thus, at best, frail[5].

---

[1] It can be argued that to cease to support the forward rate is in effect to remove a guarantee that sterling will not be devalued. For subsequent discussion of the complex issues involved, see in particular the *Radcliffe Report*, paras. 703–7 and the memoranda of evidence submitted by Sir Donald MacDougall and Mr J. Spraos (*Radcliffe, Memoranda*, XIII. 25 and 37).

[2] The United Kingdom was then 'beyond the quota' in EPU so that additional receipts of European currencies reduced a debt that would otherwise have had to be repaid in gold: i.e. we got dollars for the dollars we lost. But if large enough, such additional receipts would take us inside the quota, i.e. into a region where debt had to be repaid only partly in gold. Since traders were wiser than the Bank in believing that this could be a temporary concession only, this quickly happened.

[3] For details see *Economist*, 16 Jan. 1954, pp. 181–2.

[4] If the deceit was detected, the shipper might in due course be placed on a black list. But he was breaking no law: indeed, from his point of view, black listing by the sterling-area customs might seem an arbitrary interference with his right to dispose of his goods as he wished.

[5] It is fair to say that all direct controls rest as much on consent as on compulsion (see chapter VI below). In this case the control rested very largely on the consent of foreigners.

The support of the transferable rate at the beginning of 1955 involved no formal change in the exchange control.   But from now on any excess supply of transferable sterling was, in practice, to be met by official support.   Dollars could therefore always now be obtained for transferable sterling at the official rate.   It was in fact very nearly *de facto* convertibility.   Such support of the rate was bound to cause some drain on the reserves.   As against this, commodity shunting had also lost us dollars (since sterling was sold cheap).   Doubtful though it seems, it was the official argument that the latter drain (now saved) was less than the former (now incurred): it was, said Mr Butler, 'a case of putting in the troops to save sterling from being sold at too great a discount'[1].

At the time the move was represented to be a largely technical step[2].   In fact however the transferable rate was held close to parity; and this had two important consequences.   First, since shunting operations were no longer profitable, there was no need to enforce regulations against them; and this meant that the possibility of reimposing effective regulations became increasingly remote.   Second, once the markets had got used to a stable, transferable rate, any fall would have been liable to weaken confidence in sterling.   In time, therefore, the back-stairs convertibility of February 1955, came to appear irreversible[3].   But the apparatus of control was not completely dismantled, and must have had some effect in reducing the strain; and while it stayed, a retreat to the former position remained not too difficult[4].

[1] *H.C. Deb.* 19 April 1955, 40.   This argument had long been in circulation: see *Economist*, 26 July 1952, p. 206.   The support of the transferable rate was in practice analogous to the removal of a means of rationing sterling purchases of dollars.   It appears to me that the removal of such a means of rationing, however defective it was, could never *reduce* the volume of purchases; and, as long as the control had had any restrictive effect at all, its removal was bound to permit some increase, and thus cost dollars.

[2] It was announced in the course of a statement by the Chancellor to the House, on which there was little discussion (*H.C. Deb.* 24 Feb. 1955, 1457–63).   Subsequently at question time Mr Gaitskell asked whether the Chancellor realized that it meant in effect 'convertibility of the £ by the back door'.   Mr Butler replied: 'No, Sir . . . the position is that this practice does not alter or increase the rights of a foreign holder of sterling.   The authorities will refrain or intervene as they think fit, but I do not think we have quite reached the situation which the right hon. Gentleman has described.'   (*H.C. Deb.* 1 March 1955, 1870.)

[3] Mr Heathcoat Amory, defending the initiation of *de jure* convertibility four years later, was to say: 'Some have argued, I know, that . . . we had freedom to allow the discount to widen in times of strain. . . but, in practice, that freedom has simply not been there.   This is not only because a widening of the discount would have restored the profitability of commodity shunting; it is also because falls in the transferable rate—and this is very important—would have advertised a weakness in sterling (*H.C. Deb.* 28 Jan. 1959, 1083).

But arguments from inevitability generally go a shade too far: see further §4 below for the introduction of *de jure* convertibility in 1958.

[4] I myself do not fully accept the 'irreversibility' argument.   Whether controls are feasible is a political question, and depends on whether it is possible to persuade people to work them.   If there had been real and pressing need to restore full control, I do not see why one should assume that it would have been impossible any more than it had been when the controls had been operative.

Thus convertibility, first bruited in the winter of 1951–2, was to be approached half-way in 1955, and only fully achieved in 1958.   Meanwhile the Commonwealth meeting in December 1952 was followed by a long series of conferences and diplomatic expeditions, spread over the next two years, in pursuit of the 'collective approach'.   Mr Eden and Mr Butler went together to Washington in March 1953 to put the case to the Americans : they showed less than enthusiasm.   The Republican administration had taken office in January, and study of foreign economic policy was entrusted to the Randall Commission, who did not report till January 1954.   Meanwhile European governments were increasingly resentful at not having been let into the secret.   Convertibility clearly threatened the end of EPU; and failure to consult the other countries who would be involved naturally rewoke suspicions that Britain was ready to back out of European co-operation.   The 'collective approach' however envisaged that European countries, too, should embrace convertibility.   Having visited Washington, Mr Eden and Mr Butler went to Paris to explain to the member countries of OEEC their part in the plan.   This seems not to have been a complete success, for the visit was followed in April by a series of bilateral talks in London with the finance ministers of France, Germany and other countries.   In January 1954 the Commonwealth conference in Sydney discussed 'progress with the plans for moving towards a system of freer trade and payments'[1].   In July there was a conference of West European finance ministers in London, who were by then at least sufficiently converted to agree that OEEC should study the impact of convertibility and what should replace the EPU.

This long series of discussions had some useful results.   The American government may well have been influenced towards greater liberality, both as regards stand-by credits and as regards 'good creditor' policies generally; and it was no doubt wise for OEEC to give some forethought to convertibility.   But the constant emphasis, year in and year out, on convertibility as an aim, so far in advance of its being undertaken, quickly appeared absurd.   Moreover constant discussion necessarily bred widespread rumours that a move was imminent, which frequently resulted in speculation against the pound[2].   Those accompanying the internal discussions in 1952 have already been mentioned. Later rumours, too, frequently had a circumstantial air.   Thus in 1954, after one lot of rumours in July[3], there was further talk of 'C Day' being declared when

[1]This conference met during the downswing in the United States and (as noted in §2) the danger of the recession spreading took much of the conference's time.

[2]Speculation must have been greatly increased by the fact that convertibility was expected to be accompanied by a floating rate.   The rumours generally came at a time of crisis, when the rate consequently was expected to deteriorate, so causing speculation against the pound.

[3]On the occasion of the European finance ministers' meeting in London.   The pound was then strong, so that on this occasion the speculation strengthened sterling further (*Economist*, 8 May 1954, p. 470 and 12 June 1954, p. 869).

Commonwealth finance ministers met in Washington in September for the annual meeting of the Bank and the Fund[1]. There again seems to have been talk of early convertibility in the speculative crisis early in 1955[2], which led to the 'little budget' of 14 February, and the support of the 'transferable' rate. A new crop of rumours coming out of the OEEC meeting in July 1955 caused renewed speculation: by then the climax had been reached.

Repeated rounds of rumour were perhaps an inevitable part of the 'collective approach'. The long series of conferences had accomplished little but a general predisposition of governments in favour of convertibility. The advocates of early convertibility necessarily minimized the difficulties in the way; and to them it may have seemed that little more was required to persuade governments to undertake it than the creation of an increasing 'momentum' of opinion in its favour. In this the opinion of those engaged in international finance was part; and their opinion, reflected visibly in the state of 'confidence' in sterling, seemed to this school of thought cogent evidence about the soundness of policies. In particular it was frequently argued that if there was no 'confidence' in sterling, existing policy was wrong; even that it could not long be pursued in face of this lack of confidence. But this kind of argument, if conducted so as to be over-heard, inevitably altered the evidence in its own favour: a general expectation of a 'free floating pound', in the circumstances prevailing, itself immediately reduced the demand for sterling. A renewal of rumour was thus liable to cause a serious loss of reserves; how to amend this trend would in turn be something the central bank would normally discuss with the government. This is a twilight world where facts and motives are hard to disentangle: what could from one point of view be regarded as playing fast and loose with the reserves, as a means of putting pressure on the government, could, from another point of view, be viewed as legitimate technical discussion between one financial expert and another. What is clear is that rumours about policy played a large part in fluctuations of confidence; and it is a feeling difficult to avoid, in rereading the record of these years, that the Bank of England would have been in a better position to deny rumours of impending convertibility if it had not itself, as a strong advocate of this policy, wished them to be true[3].

---

[1] *Economist*, 11 Sept. 1954, p. 791.

[2] *Economist*, 26 Feb. 1955, p. 737.

[3] The importance of rumours was perhaps most evident in 1955. On this episode (discussed further below) Shonfield [1958] remarks that 'the key to the exchange crisis . . . was . . . the authoritative whispers, going the round of the bankers on the continent of Europe, that Britain was about to make the pound convertible . . . There is little doubt where the rumours originated. They came from Basle, where there is a kind of Club of Central Bankers meeting once a month in order to conduct the affairs of the Bank of International Settlements . . . In interpreting British financial policy abroad, no one ever doubted that the Bank of England desperately wanted to make the pound convertible . . . The only question was whether the British Government would give the Bank its head. And the significant fact about the speculative crisis which hit sterling in 1955 was the firm impression abroad that the British Government had. This was the conclusion

The speculation against the pound that broke out in the summer of 1955 drove the Government at last to a firm stand.   The speculation followed the OEEC meeting in July, which was primarily concerned with the annual re-negotiation of the EPU.   The United Kingdom wanted recognition of a right to withdraw in the course of the next twelve months in the event of sterling becoming convertible.   The speculation however appears to have arisen less because of this insistence, than because of the advocacy by some members of the British delegation that the pound should be allowed to float.   Mr Butler, though denying that he had any part in such discussion, refused at first to disown the possibility of floating rates[1].   But in the debate at the end of July, he clearly dissociated himself from this line of policy.   On 25 July he said:

> 'Our foreign exchange position is also being currently affected by many rumours, here and abroad, about our intentions . . . these rumours have reached such unreasonable proportions that I cannot allow them to remain unanswered.   I want, therefore, to make it clear that Her Majesty's Government regard the period in front of us as being one of hard work and

arrived at by the other central bankers, who attended the meetings with their British colleagues in Basle' (pp. 204–6).

Mr Balogh alleges, in his evidence to the Radcliffe Committee that, on the matter of convertibility, the Bank 'succeeded in influencing policy in directions in which hardly any Government would have wanted to go . . . '   He added that, in the absence of any full accounts for recent years 'one can only go by one's impressions' (*Radcliffe, Memoranda,* III. 31 and *Minutes of Evidence* Q 11026–7).

The *Investors' Chronicle*—under the heading of 'convertibility hedge'—remarked on 16 July 1955: 'recent widespread discussion about sterling convertibility has made it plain to the investor that the Government has taken a stand in favour of flexible exchange rates when the time comes'.   On 30 July it commented: 'when [the foreign trader in sterling] is given the bald facts of a UK trade deficit of £456 millions in six months . . . then the movement away from sterling begins to develop in earnest . . .   And when, against this sort of background, the Continent is also bemused by continuing discussions on convertibility, with the stress on "floating rates", then the mood of (quite justifiable) suspicion may grow until it exerts an overwhelming pressure on events and currency policy is determined, not by deliberation and strength, but by events beyond our power to control'.

See below for further references to rumours originating from the OEEC meeting in Paris in July 1955.

[1]See *H.C. Deb.* 19 July 1955, 190–1.   Mr Butler said that 'To do me justice it should be said that I have never departed from the line of the statement which I have given to . . . the House' i.e. that sterling would be made convertible 'when the necessary conditions are satisfied'.   When pressed to say he had no intention of making any changes before the House reassembled in the autumn whereby the £ would be allowed to fluctuate more widely, Mr Butler replied 'it is not reasonable to tie the hands of any Government with regard to the currency of the country'.   *The Economist* commented: 'Mr Butler himself must be believed when he says that no statement on these matters came from him . . . but he cannot, and did not, deny that the British representatives at these talks, and at other recent meetings of bankers and officials in Europe have been among those pleading for greater flexibility of exchange rates' (*Economist*, 30 July 1955, p. 406).

In the debate at the end of July Mr Jenkins also alleged that: 'The Bank of England have been making it clear—not by statements, because that is not the way the Bank operates —that early convertibility is not merely desirable but inevitable because the existing restrictions are impracticable to maintain' (*H.C. Deb.* 26 July 1955, 1041).

consolidation to strengthen the home front before we make any further forward move on the exchange front . . .'[1]

Next day he strengthened this considerably:

'I should like to add that there is no doubt about the policy of the Government in relation to the exchange value of the £ sterling . . . It has been, and will continue to be the maintenance of exchange parity of 2.80 dollars to the £, either in existing circumstances or when sterling is convertible'[2].

Even so, there still appeared room for rumour[3]; and the Chancellor had to restate his pledge even more emphatically in the Fund-Bank meeting at Istanbul in September.

The autumn budget followed the Istanbul denial by a month. Both inevitably had the appearance of a retraction of policy. Mr Macmillan replaced Mr Butler as Chancellor of the Exchequer in January 1956. Convertibility remained a long-term objective, and was in fact to be delayed for three more years; but it was fairly clear from now on—except for a brief spell during the Thorneycroft crisis of 1957—that it was to be convertibility at a fixed rate.

4. TWO YEARS' DISINFLATION, 1956–7

During the next two years, for various reasons, there were two successive Chancellors of the Exchequer. Mr Macmillan succeeded Mr Butler in December 1955, Sir Edward Boyle remaining as Economic Secretary. When Mr Macmillan succeeded Mr Eden as Prime Minister in January 1957, after the Suez affair, Mr Thorneycroft moved from the Board of Trade to become Chancellor, the Financial and Economic Secretaries being Mr Powell and Mr Birch respectively. In January 1958 all three Treasury ministers resigned on a matter of policy. Partly because of the difficulty of making major changes quickly, partly because of the rapidity of these ministerial changes, the broad course of economic policy was less affected than the differing temperaments of successive Chancellors might have been supposed to entail.

The direction of policy had already been turned towards disinflation by Mr Butler before he left the Treasury; and it was pointed more firmly this way by Mr Macmillan as soon as he became Chancellor. How far the subsequent deflationary trend was due to policy, and how far it would have happened anyway, is difficult to determine[4]. However this may be, it is a fact both that, for two or three years, the emphasis of policy continued to be deflationary; and

---

[1] *H.C. Deb.* 25 July 1955, 826.
[2] *H.C. Deb.* 26 July 1955, 1027.
[3] *The Banker* went so far as to say in October:
   'No good was done to sterling by the Chancellor's attempts before the Parliamentary recess to suggest that Britain had not argued in favour of flexibility—because the foreign observers who were to be impressed by this denial had their own sources of inside information' (*The Banker*, October 1955, p. 212).
[4] An answer is attempted at the end of this study: see chapter XV.4.

also that the actual process of disinflation was long drawn out. The pressure of demand fell gradually and the low point was not reached till the middle of 1958. Only then was an expansionary policy resumed. The Anglo-French adventure in Suez at the end of 1956, and the run on the pound at the end of 1957, both caused something like an external crisis. Compared with earlier crises they were, however, curiously unrelated to underlying developments. Each led to some modifications of internal policy: indeed the successive hoistings and lowerings of Bank rate were dictated almost entirely by external considerations. But historical retrospect suggests that the course of the economy was shifted only gradually, and that the 'crisis' measures had less effect than they were credited with at the time.

The course of post-war trade cycles has by no means been exactly coincident in different parts of the world. The British boom of 1955, however, coincided with rapid expansion in most other countries. Europe's expansion accelerated; and the United States of America more than recovered from the recession of the previous year (table 3.2). The consequent increase in our exports was in turn

Table 3.2. *World economic trends, 1952–60*[a]   (*Indices, 1953 = 100*)

	1951	1952	1953	1954	1955	1956	1957	1958	1959	1960
Industrial production[b]										
'World'[c]	91	93	100	101	112	117	121	118	130	139
USA[d]	89	92	100	94	106	109	110	102	116	119
Continental W. Europe[d]	92	95	100	110	122	132	140	144	153	171
UK[d]	98	95	100	108	114	114	116	114	120	129
Primary producers[e]										
Export volume	97	93	100	103	110	117	120	121	131	136
Export prices[f]	118	107	100	102	102	101	101	97	93	94
Overseas sterling area[g]										
Exports	120	103	100	101	111	117	122	113	125	131
Imports	125	117	100	106	121	127	130	133	136	156
United Kingdom[h]										
Export volume	104	98	100	104	112	119	121	116	121	128
Import prices[f]	112	110	100	99	102	104	106	98	97	98

[a]Many series have been subject to frequent revision: for each year latest available estimate is quoted.

[b]Excludes building throughout.

[c]From *UN Statist. Bull.* [Feb. 1961] and [Aug. 1961].

[d]From *OEEC Gen. Statist.* [July 1962].

[e]From *UN Statist. Bull.* [Oct. 1961]: all countries apart from industrial and communist countries: former comprise USA, Canada, OEEC countries and Japan.

[f]Average value index.

[g]From *UN Statist. Bull.*

one cause of expansion here.   During the next three years disinflation caused us to lag behind other European countries, where expansion continued rapidly—as it did in the United States till the further recession of 1958.   Taking the world as a whole, the rapid upsurge in industrial production in 1955 decelerated gradually; was reversed in 1958; and was resumed in 1959.   There were three major consequences for the United Kingdom.   Our exports followed a parallel course—rising till 1958, then dipping, then recovering in 1959: this was one reason, among others discussed below, why the British economy experienced such a slow growth of demand.   Second, the exports of the overseas sterling area followed a broadly similar trend (table 3.2).   Its imports, as usual, expanded more gradually—and, as in other recessions, failed to fall as much as export earnings fell in 1958.   This was one reason (again overlaid by others to be discussed later) for the fluctuations in the reserves.   Thirdly, the recession brought a fall in world commodity prices in 1957-8.   This contributed powerfully to the greater stability which the British price level at length achieved.

When Mr Macmillan took over at the beginning of 1956, though corrective measures seemed necessary, the atmosphere was not one of crisis.   The boom of 1955 had affected almost all kinds of spending (table 3.3): indeed the only item in the national accounts to have shown a fall was defence expenditure, where significant savings had been achieved.   There had been a further large growth in consumption, fed by the April tax concessions; and, despite the reimposition of hire-purchase restrictions in the previous February, this included a very considerable increase in expenditure on durables.   Investment—particularly in industry and commerce—had increased largely, partly as a result of the general expansion, but partly also as a result of the stimulus of the investment allowances granted in 1954.   Monetary restraints notwithstanding, there had also been a very sizeable increase in investment in stocks.   Including the expansion in exports, total final expenditure had increased by about £1,000 million (or five per cent).   Of this well over £400 million had been met from imports, a quite abnormal proportion—a main reason being that the boom required steel and other metals, coal and oil which home production could not supply.   It so happened that the extra imports had had to come from outside the sterling area. Together with a largely accidental decline in invisibles, the balance of payments had declined by £300 million, almost all with the non-sterling area.   This had been the predominant reason for the decline in the reserves in 1955: the worsening in the position of the overseas sterling area, and hostile speculation, had both been minor factors only[1].   On this occasion, home demand had a direct and simple impact on the reserves.

The gold drain had already ceased by the beginning of 1956.   But the level of the reserves seemed uncomfortably low; and the pressure of demand uncomfortably high.   The autumn budget had already raised purchase tax and the

---

[1] *Economic Survey, 1956*, paras. 23 and 52-60.

Table 3.3. *The British economy, 1956–9*

	1955	1956	1957	1958	1959	1960
Changes in final expenditure[a] (£m., 1954 prices[b])						
Consumer durables	100	−125	100	125	200	25
Other consumption	350	250	200	200	350	500
Government expenditure	−75	—	−100	−25	50	75
Fixed investment	125	150	125	—	225	300
of which manufacturing and distribution	150	100	50	—	25	200
Investment in stocks[c]	225	−25	−25	−125	50	375
Exports, goods and services	250	175	75	−100	125	225
TOTAL	975	425	375	75	1,000	1,500
of which imports[d]	450	—	50	25	400	575
Gross domestic product[e] (% change[f])	3·0	2·0	1·5	—	4·0	5·0
Industrial production (% change[f])	5·1	0·5	1·7	−1·1	6·0	—
Labour market						
Percentage unemployment	1·1	1·2	1·4	2·1	2·2	1·6
Index of excess demand[g]	1·5	0·9	—	−1·3	−1·2	−0·2
Prices and wages (% change in year[h])						
Retail prices	6·0	3·3	4·4	1·5	—	—
Wage rates	7·0	7·6	5·7	3·6	1·2	—
Balance of payments[i] (£m.[b])						
Exports	3,075	3,375	3,500	3,400	3,500	3,700
Imports	−3,475	−3,425	−3,575	−3,325	−3,575	−4,075
Invisibles	225	250	275	225	125	25
Current balance	−175	200	200	300	50	−350
Change in reserves (£m.)	−229	42	13	284	−119	177

[a]From *NI & E* [1961] at market prices.
[b]Rounded to nearest £25 m.
[c]Table shows *change* in investment in stocks. Investment in stocks (£m.) was

1955	1956	1957	1958	1959	1960
275	250	225	100	175	550

[d]At factor cost.
[e]Average of changes in production and expenditure series, which often differ appreciably: from *NI & E* [1960].
[f]Change of year's average over previous year.
[g]Roughly twice the difference between % vacancies and % unemployment (see chapter XIII.2 below).
[h]Change during year, measured between successive fourth quarters.
[i]For the sake of continuity, taken from *NI & E* [1961]—not from *BPWP*.
For key to abbreviations see introductory note, p. xiii above.

tax on distributed profits; and various steps had been taken to curtail public investment[1]. Further measures followed in February. Bank rate was raised from $4\frac{1}{2}$ to $5\frac{1}{2}$ per cent; the 'investment allowance' was suspended, 'initial' allowances being restored in their place; public investment programmes were cut; and hire-purchase restrictions were tightened[2]. After this string of measures, those actually made in the April budget were minor, though calculated on balance to be deflationary. The tobacco duty and profits tax were each increased by about £30 million. On the other hand, relief was given on the contribution of the self-employed for their retirement pensions; and various inducements were offered to encourage 'national' savings, of which the most striking—though by no means the most costly to the Exchequer—was the introduction of 'premium bonds'. Both the *Economic Survey* and the budget speech, while calling for a continued restriction of bank lending, included some realistic comment on the difficulty of bringing it about[3]; and the Chancellor probably did not regard action by the banking system as playing a major role in his strategy. Neither *Survey* nor budget speech contained much indication of the developments the Government hoped to bring about: the Government appeared to envisage if not a fall, at least a slower growth in home consumption and investment to permit exports to expand and the pressure of demand to fall— all of which would have entailed, not perhaps a plateau for output, but at least a slower growth[4].

At the end of 1956 came the Suez crisis. Its chief economic result was another run on the reserves: the measures taken to meet this are discussed separately below. Its effects on the home economy were very small. Consumption of petrol and oil had to be restricted first by a higher tax at the beginning of December, and shortly afterwards by temporary rationing. Output however,

---

[1]The investment programmes of the nationalized industries were adjusted; and local authority investment was discouraged by the reduction in the house-building subsidy and by making access to the Public Works Loan Board more difficult and more costly: see *Economic Survey, 1956*, para. 70, and chapter VIII.2 below.

[2]*Ibid.*, para. 82.

[3]See further chapter IX.3.

[4]The way the Chancellor put it was that he was more sure of where he wanted the economy to go than of where it had got to when he spoke in April. 'We cannot' he said 'say with any certainty that we are definitely moving in the direction in which we must go. That is why I have said that any detailed assessment of the course of demand and of production would not help us. For such an assessment would imply a degree of knowledge, which I do not think we possess, as to the exact position at which we stand today (*H.C. Deb.* 17 April 1956, 869–70). He had previously remarked that the statistics came too late to be useful, so that 'we are always, as it were, looking up a train in last year's Bradshaw' (866). Mr Macmillan nevertheless could perfectly well have indicated the changes he wanted by comparison with the previous year, for which he had figures. The *Survey* (para. 85) had in fact indicated that, as compared with 1955, investment even after restraint was likely to show an increase. 'The growth of consumers' demand must' it said 'be checked . . . so that more of our production can be exported, and so that the growth of imports is moderated'.

except in the motor industry, was hardly affected, so that there was minor interruption only of the general policy of disinflation.

Reviewing its effects in 1956, the next *Survey* claimed—with partial, though not quite impartial, justice—that 'on the whole this policy' had been 'successful'[1]. Its impact was very highly selective.   Home demand (table 3.3) grew much more slowly, first, because of the great fall in spending on consumer durables— certainly an induced change; and, second, because the large increase in investment in stocks which had occurred in 1955 was not—it hardly could have been—repeated[2].   The growth of final expenditure was thus only half as large as in 1955; and while there was surprisingly little reduction in demand pressure, the growth of imports at least was very much more moderate.   Since exports continued to expand, the balance of payments swung back into sizeable surplus[3].   The overseas sterling countries somewhat strengthened their position also, and the reserves gained £90 million in the first half year.   The break in confidence over the Suez crisis would however have caused a considerable drop in the reserves in the second half, had steps not been taken to reinforce them[4].

Because of the ministerial changes following the Suez affair, it was Mr Thorneycroft who made the next budget appraisal.   In retrospect of the past year, '1956' he said, 'was a year in which, amid many economic difficulties, we did well'—adding, as he was bound, 'still . . . not . . . well enough'[5]. Nevertheless, in the April of his short term, Mr Thorneycroft viewed the prospects without too much severity.   He stressed the need to rebuild the reserves—both 'for our own security as a trading nation', and 'to honour our commitments as a world banker'.   But 'after making full allowance' for these claims, he could add 'I see some grounds for cheerfulness.   As I see it, the temperature of the economy has been brought down to a more normal level . . . Resources appear to be at least adequate to the demand on them.   It is reasonable to hope for further substantial export gains.   All this seems to be a basis not for standing still, but for going forward.   Expansion must be the theme'— though 'we must do it at a pace and in a manner consistent with our large responsibilities as a trading and a banking nation'[6].

[1]*Economic Survey, 1957*, para. 75.
[2]Investment in stocks was high though not increasing.   The figures on the same basis as in table 3.3 are:

	1954	1955	1956
Investment in stocks	50	275	250
Increase over previous year		*225*	*−25*

A second increase in investment in stocks like that in 1955 was hardly to be expected. The change in 1955 can therefore hardly be attributed at all largely to government influence.

[3]That the improvement was largely with the non-sterling area was due not to a fall in non-sterling imports, but to the continued increase in exports to North America, Western Europe and other non-sterling countries (*Economic Survey, 1957*, paras. 62–8).

[4]See below.
[5]*H.C. Deb.* 9 April 1957, 971.
[6]Same deb. 981–2.

He summed up the existing prospect as 'a fair promise of renewed growth': in addition to higher exports there seemed likely to be 'some increase in consumption and probably a slight increase in fixed investment'[1]. But there still seemed 'some room for manoeuvre', room in fact to 'reduce the burden of taxation by a figure of about £100 million'[2]. The tax remission was spread over income tax, surtax, purchase tax and entertainments tax. Credit restriction, though quite why is not clear, was to be maintained[3].

The crisis of the following August and September thus blew up out of a blue sky. To deal with the previous speculative crisis provoked by the Suez affair, large credits had been obtained: in December the United Kingdom had drawn some £200 million from her quota in the International Monetary Fund; and further credits of about £440 million with the IMF and the United States Export/Import Bank had also been arranged, to be drawn as required. Largely because of such drawing the reserves had risen during the first half of 1957: without such special items they would have been more or less stable[4]. In July there was a small loss: then in August there was a loss of £80 million, and a deficit of nearly £65 million with the European Payments Union. The drain continued in the first part of September. The crisis was important not only in its own right, and because of Mr Thorneycroft's immediate counter-measures in September. It was important also because, by threatening to upset—as had the convertibility issue under Mr Butler—the compromise on which Conservative economic policy had previously rested, it provoked a new crisis in policy itself, and finally Mr Thorneycroft's own resignation in January.

Unlike previous crises, the 1957 crisis was entirely one of confidence. The United Kingdom current account was in comfortable balance; and though

---

[1]*H.C. Deb.* 9 April 1957, 981.

[2]*Ibid.*, 988. The tax changes reduced the yield of taxation in the financial year by about this amount. Those affecting consumers however came to less than this, even in a full year. The income tax/surtax reductions gave in a full year £35 million to surtax payers and £17 million to income tax payers with children over 11. The indirect tax cuts took £24 million off purchase tax on various household goods and £12 million off entertainments. In addition the investment allowance on ships (which had been retained when the general investment allowance was suspended in 1956) was doubled; and tax relief was granted (as recommended by the Royal Commission on the Taxation of Profits and Income which reported in 1955) to a newly-recognized class of 'overseas trade corporation'.

[3]It was not explicit what kind of demand credit restriction was aimed at: but there was an idea that 'long-term investment financed from bank credit' could 'add to the volume of investment without a corresponding increase in real savings' (984–5). Mr Thorneycroft regarded the necessity of restrictions as 'evidence that the monetary machine is working under great difficulties' (985). This was the reason given for the appointment of the Radcliffe Committee, whose appointment was foreshadowed in the budget speech.

[4]The failure of the reserves to rise was largely due to British investors taking advantage of a gap in the exchange control to buy dollar securities. Though Kuwait was in the sterling area it was possible there to buy dollars freely. This export of capital is believed to have cost the reserves about £100 million in the first half of 1957. This was stopped at the beginning of July (*Economist*, 13 July 1957, pp. 141–3). The desire to transfer capital was due to a growing belief among investors that British finances were 'unsound' —a belief discussed further below.

the threat of a new recession in the United States was already giving rise to concern, and though commodity prices were already falling, the overseas sterling area had not yet been seriously affected. Both internal and external factors were widely discussed at the time as causes of the crisis. The policy Mr Thorneycroft adopted to meet it rested on the belief that it was fundamentally due to internal inflation. In retrospect the external factors seem of far greater importance.

In the middle of August the franc was devalued in all but name[1]: this as the next *Survey* said, 'set off an intense wave of currency speculation in Europe'[2]. The persistent chronic surplus in Germany's current account led many, including the British government, to urge an appreciation of the mark. The German government, on the other hand, believed that the mark was not under-valued in terms of the dollar, and that the fault lay with the over-valuation of other European currencies. It therefore urged that the 'collective approach', originally invented by the British, should be implemented; that the European Monetary Agreement, already agreed as successor to EPU when convertibility came, should be put into effect; and that European currencies should be allowed to 'float' within appreciable margins. It was generally expected that in this case the mark would rise and the pound fall. These disputes were widely known[3]; and it was widely expected that an exchange realignment would be announced at the International Monetary Fund gathering in late September.

The prevalence of such expectations might be thought sufficient explanation of the withdrawal of funds from London. But it seems likely that the main reason for the severity of the crisis was that there were in fact some grounds for the rumours. Official Treasury statements continued to emphasize that the existing rate of 2.80 would be maintained. But as the evidence before the Bank Rate Tribunal was later to show in great detail, the imminent likelihood of a new policy was widely believed in the City. There is, indeed, reason to believe that the Government was in fact undecided for a time about allowing the rate to vary—a policy which, it may be presumed the Bank of England must still have favoured[4]. The worst of the crisis seems to have passed as soon as

---

[1]French exports received a 20 per cent subsidy, and French imports other than essential raw materials a 20 per cent tax. The Bank of England treated this as devaluation, by quoting francs at 1,176 as compared with the Paris rate of 980 (*Economist*, 17 Aug. 1957, p. 559).

[2]*Economic Survey, 1958*, para. 70.

[3]There was for instance a heated exchange between the British and German representatives at the June meeting of the Council of OEEC (*The Banker*, September 1957, pp. 564 and 571). The dispute on policy did not prevent the German authorities giving practical assistance in the support of sterling. They agreed to make advance deposits in sterling in London of the £75 million agreed in settlement of Germany's post-war debt to Britain (*Economist*, 17 Aug. 1957, p. 560). They also joined with a British disavowal of any intention to alter exchange rates: these disavowals (19 and 21 August) did in fact abate speculation (*Economist*, 24 Aug. 1957, p. 633).

[4]Among other papers, *The Economist* had discussed the case for a 'widening of the margin within which the sterling exchange rate is allowed to move'. After the measures

H

it was widely believed that freeing the rate was no longer a possibility[1].

Rumours about exchange rates had however fallen on ready ground. For some time financial opinion had been hardening against an economic policy which appeared to tolerate inflation. Concern about the problem was indeed shared by many who did not attribute rising prices entirely to the flabbiness of financial policy. The emergence of the annual wage round as a serious problem

of 19 September, it commented: 'that case has been rejected; the fact that the emergency measures were taken only on Thursday, instead of last month, suggests that there had been a swaying debate within the Treasury and the Bank before rejection, but the die is now clearly meant to be cast' (*Economist*, 21 Sept. 1957, p. 909). It is also known that Mr Gaitskell asked for an assurance from the Chancellor that the Government intended to maintain the parity of sterling; on 13 September Mr Wilson saw the Chancellor and was given this assurance (Mr Thorneycroft's evidence to *Bank Rate Tribunal*, Q 10664–7). This too suggests that government policy had previously been undecided. The Government would hardly have toyed with the idea of a floating rate had the Bank been against it.

[1] The evidence before the Bank Rate Tribunal makes it clear that fear of devaluation (as might be expected if this was in the wind) was far more important, as a cause of selling British bonds, than any anticipation of the change in Bank rate on 19 September whose possible improper disclosure it was the object of the Tribunal to investigate.

The published figures of the changes in the reserves only show that there was a large outflow in August and September, and a large inflow in October. There are however several suggestions in the Tribunal's *Evidence* that the crisis was in fact over several days before the public announcement of policy on 19 September. Deposits at Messrs Lazards, consisting largely of overseas sterling balances, had been heavily affected by the crisis. In the last full week of August these deposits had fallen by £1,600,000; and there had been heavy withdrawals also in the next two weeks (£820,000 and £535,000 respectively). In the week 12–19 September, however, these deposits *rose* by £840,000: almost all, it was agreed, came in before the rise in Bank rate (Attorney-General's opening to the 6th day, and Q 5485 and 5747–8).

Furthermore, as the Tribunal noted in its *Report* (para. 37) there had been a bull market for gilt-edged in the first half of the week before the announcement. After the examination of Mr Alderton of Pearsons on the 6th day, Lord Justice Parker, the chairman of the Tribunal, asked:

'There is only one matter that puzzles me here, and that is why were not more people selling gilt-edged at this time? . . . Just help me as simply as you can. I suppose fifty years ago if there had been pressure on the £, everybody would have said "The Bank of England will raise the Bank rate?" And yet on the 16th, 17th and 18th, on the whole people were not saying that. Is the answer that nobody thought the Government had the courage to do it?'

Mr Alderton replied:

'I would not put it like that. I would say that the real reason was that the Chancellor of the Exchequer had denied that there would be any change in the rate of exchange, and therefore that particular suggestion that there would be a rise in the Bank rate to support such a change no longer existed. I am afraid I have not checked up the actual details of the market at that time, but my recollection is that the market in gilt-edged stocks had been weak during part of those three preceding weeks, but in fact during the week beginning 16th September it had been recovering and was looking much stronger' (Q 4956–9).

The emphatic announcement that the exchange rate would be maintained, and that strong measures would be taken to support it, came only on 19 September. The Tribunal did not pursue the question why before that the market should have acquired new belief in the maintenance of the rate.

dates back at least as far as 1953[1]. In December of that year the government had intervened to avert the threatened railway strike, with the result that the Transport Commission agreed to a larger wage increase than had already been agreed by an independent tribunal. This set the pattern for the wage awards in other industries that followed[2]. In the boom conditions of 1955, wage pressure became even more serious. *The Economist* commented:

> 'In the first six months of this year nearly ten and a half million workers were given wage increases. Already, in mid-August, the majority of those workers have formulated their claims for another rise. This is perhaps the most graphic and disturbing feature of the British economy in 1955. It is now normal for the major unions to demand a new wage increase immediately the old one has been granted. The country has been moving towards this state of perpetual wage inflation for a long time and now it has arrived'[3].

Chancellors recognized that the pace of wage inflation was partly due to the pressure of demand, and attempted to reduce the latter—partly for this reason. But they hardly ever treated wage inflation as a problem that could be met entirely by this means; and never gave up the hope that direct appeals would have some effect[4]. When in July 1957 Mr Thorneycroft set up the Council on Prices, Productivity and Incomes[5], it seemed to be part of this same approach, in which wage pressure was recognized as a phenomenon in its own right, at least partially distinct from the pressure of demand. 'There is clearly no simple act of policy' Mr Thorneycroft said 'which is a remedy for inflation. If there had been, it would have been discovered a very long time ago . . . The Government, the private employers, the trade unions and the nationalized industries all have a part to play'[6].

[1] Though Sir Stafford Cripps had been concerned about wage demands, the pattern was then much less set. Before the 'Korean' price rise in 1951–2 an annual increase in wages was far less general: see chapter XIII.3 below. By 1953 it was clear that wage inflation was to be a continuing problem, not just a problem of the immediate transition from the war.

[2] *Economist*, 19 Dec. 1953, p. 863.

[3] *Economist*, 20 Aug. 1955, p. 595.

[4] In 1956 Mr Macmillan had appealed to industry to maintain a price 'plateau'. Mr Eden also on becoming Prime Minister attempted to utilize his diplomatic experience to secure the unions' agreement to wage restraint—an attempt met, as *The Economist* said, with a 'shattering silence' (19 May 1956, p. 665).

[5] The idea for such a council originated in the proposal made by the Court of Inquiry into the engineering dispute in May 1956 (Cmnd. 159). The position of independent experts on arbitration tribunals had become increasingly invidious; and the Court of Inquiry appealed for some 'authoritative and impartial body' that could give guidance on the general issues that should govern wage settlements. The original idea was for a body including representatives of employers and employees. As finally established, however, the Council consisted only of three 'independent' members (Lord Cohen, Sir Harold Howitt and Sir Dennis Robertson). Its terms of reference were vague: to 'keep under review changes in prices, productivity and the level of incomes . . . and to report thereon from time to time'.

[6] *H.C. Deb.* 25 July 1957, 645.

Ministerial statements about the dangers of inflation, however, necessarily ran some risk of creating alarm about the very dangers they were intended to mitigate. Moreover to those who did not accept the cost-push thesis—and there were many—mere exhortation by the government appeared a blatant abdication from responsibility. The rise in prices had not, in fact, suddenly accelerated. It was the financial world, not the public at large, that was affected by the loss of confidence. The effect therefore was not to turn the creep into a gallop—of this there was probably little real risk—but to make British investors want to get out of sterling. 'The biggest blow to confidence' said Mr Wilson in the debate in July[1] 'has been the frank recognition by the Government of the dangers of the present situation combined with their unwillingness or inability to do anything about it'. It had led, he said 'to an attitude of hopeless resignation about the future of the currency to the point where it becomes not a change of degree but a change of kind, where many people in key positions, from underwriters at Lloyds to those responsible for trust funds, are redisposing their affairs on a scale which reflects their anxiety about the future of the currency'[2].

The alarm was undoubtedly greatest among those who thought the Government most culpable—and the remedy most simple, had the Government but courage to apply it. The Governor of the Bank, though he made the point picturesquely, represented much City opinion, when he put on one side 'learned discussion' of cost and demand inflation by his reference to the 'push-me-pull-you'—'a fascinating creature in one of the nursery books'. 'If we can shoot one end of that animal', he said, 'the other end will not long survive'[3]. Lord Kindersley's informal advice to the Deputy Governor at the beginning of September happens to be on record. 'Bank rate had got to be raised and raised properly' he said 'but it was no good doing it unless the Government were going to make a statement as well'—concerning, in particular, government spending, and wages in the nationalized industries—'so that . . . everybody in this country was going to be made to realize what the situation was and pull their own oar'[4].

There was more than one economist whose views ran at least some way in the same direction. Among those, since Mr Thorneycroft is known to have taken his advice at this juncture[5], those of Professor Robbins may perhaps be quoted. 'All this is very obviously controversial', he wrote later: 'many . . . giving more weight throughout to the push of costs, less to the pull of demand, than I find appropriate. But on one point I hope we should all be agreed; namely,

---

[1]*H.C. Deb.* 25 July 1957, 635–6.
[2]Same deb. 25 July 1957, 624.
[3]Mansion House Speech, reproduced in *Radcliffe, Memoranda*, I, Appendix 1.
[4]*Bank Rate Tribunal, Evidence*, Q 7392 and 7397.
[5]*Ibid.*, Mr Thorneycroft's evidence, Q 10660.

that none of this could happen if there were a sufficiently strong control of the supply of money'[1].

The need for action rose from the external crisis. Mr Thorneycroft's policy at this juncture was remarkable for the whole-hearted way in which he accepted 'rising prices at home' as the cause of the run on the reserves[2]. His response to the situation as he saw it was his 'statement' of 19 September. It had, as Mr Thorneycroft took pains to see it would, a good press. 'The Chancellor sets off for Washington' said *The Economist* 'with every cannon firing in defence of the pound'[3]. Yet it was—and was intended to be—much more an exposition of new doctrine, than an announcement of new measures[4]. 'The Government', it said in paragraph one, 'are determined to maintain the internal and external value of the pound'. 'There can be no remedy for inflation', said paragraph two, 'and the steadily rising prices which go with it which does not include, and indeed is not founded upon, a control of the money supply. So long as it is generally believed that the Government are prepared to see the necessary finance produced to match the upward spiral of costs, inflation will continue and prices will go up'. It went on to declare that the value of various monetary totals—not the same thing as the money supply— must be kept constant: in particular government current expenditure, public investment, and bank advances.

These steps were less drastic than the theory behind them. If, it was argued, the money national income was pegged (as was somehow intended), wages could push up prices only at the expense of employment: the onus of choice was, as it were, to be placed on the unions. To the question whether his measures would lead to unemployment, Mr Thorneycroft said: 'not on our expectations or our intentions, provided moderation is exercised all round'[5].

---

[1] L. Robbins [1958], 'Thoughts on the Crisis', *Lloyds Bank R.*, April 1958, p. 6. Professor Robbins, it should be added, disowned a completely rigid version of the quantity theory. In view of what is said above on the effects of the proposal for a 'floating' exchange rate, Professor Robbins's view on this matter should be quoted also:

'. . . I cannot believe that on this occasion any good purpose could have been served by letting the rate float. The policy of the floating rate is an acutely controversial matter . . . But I think it would be generally agreed that a moment of extreme weakness is not the moment for making such an experiment. The rate would certainly have plunged downward . . . ' (*Ibid.*, p. 10).

[2] Mr Thorneycroft said in his defence of his measures: 'I wish to state at the outset what I believe to be the fundamental truth about [these two problems], and it is that they are the same problem. The value of the £ at home and the value of the £ abroad is, in the last resort, the same thing . . . ' (*H.C. Deb.* 29 Oct. 1957, 46).

[3] *Economist*, 21 Sept. 1957, p. 909.

[4] The full statement was reproduced in the *Bank Rate Tribunal Report* (pp. 9–10). The rise in Bank rate to 7 per cent was referred to in the final paragraph 9—added after the Chancellor's interview with the press on 17 September.

[5] *H.C. Deb.* 29 Oct. 1957, 57–8. Mr Thorneycroft added 'By that I do not mean that we must stick at any cost to an unemployment figure of 1·2 per cent, nor does any thoughtful person of any political persuasion mean it either'. Though the Chancellor no doubt expected that sternness would not have to be pushed far, his policy was intended to be

Mr Thorneycroft was attacked both on the ground that the end of his measures was reactionary; and that, being based on fallacious analysis, the means were ineffective. 'The more I have pondered and considered the words spoken by the Chancellor this afternoon, the more depressed and alarmed I have become. It is very difficult to avoid the conclusion', said Mr Gordon Walker, that one of his main objects 'was really to declare war on the trade unions'[1]. 'The whole trouble' said Mr Wilson 'is that the Chancellor is trying to fight what is a cost-push inflation . . . with the crude techniques which classical theory considers appropriate to a demand inflation . . . merely to freeze the supply of money does not of itself freeze prices'[2].

In January, four months after his crisis measures, the Chancellor resigned, as did his two junior Treasury ministers. The issue on which he resigned was whether government current expenditure should be held absolutely constant, as Mr Thorneycroft was pledged, or should be allowed to rise by £50 million. Though this was made to appear so minor an issue as to leave it mysterious why resignations were necessary, it must be supposed that to him his defeat implied that price stability was not to be the first, chief aim of economic policy[3].

Mr Thorneycroft's September measures have been widely credited with a decisive effect on the course of inflation. This appears exaggerated. That they should be so credited is itself a psychological victory; and even if confined to the financial circles who had previously been most alarmed at inflation, this would itself be important. But their direct impact on the economy cannot in fact have been large. The cuts in investment were marginal and slow-working[4];

stern. It seems fairly clear that the first aim of policy was now intended to be, not full employment, but a 'sound currency'. 'The evolving British view of the subordination of full employment to a sound currency', it was reported, was 'more forcibly expressed in private by the Chancellor's delegation' to the Washington meeting (*Times*, 25 September 1957).

[1] *H.C. Deb.* 29 Oct. 1957, 158.

[2] Same deb. 72.

[3] Mr Shonfield [1958] comments (pp. 248–9):

'The parties to the dispute behaved altogether too well to one another at the time for an outsider to achieve complete clarity on what issues were really involved . . . beyond this argument about the Budget estimates . . . there was a feeling within the Government that Mr Thorneycroft was trying to use . . . the exchange crisis . . . to foist a new internal policy on the Cabinet . . . They were not, and never had been, converted to the idea of holding the supply of money constant as the answer to all our inflationary ills . . . [But] Mr Thorneycroft, and his fellow-ministers in the Treasury, apparently believed that their theory had been accepted as official dogma . . . that there had been a genuine change from earlier Tory policies—of economic expansion, combined with social welfare and increasing scope for private business enterprise—to a party line which put price stability before everything else.'

It may also be relevant that the two senior members of the Government had had first-hand experience of confidence crises: that Mr Butler had got his hand burnt badly with the 'floating-rate' convertibility, and Mr Macmillan had never shown any love for it. It may be wondered whether Mr Thorneycroft's handling of the 1957 crisis commended itself to either.

[4] See chapter VIII.2.

and even the advocates of seven per cent Bank rate did not regard it as in itself crucial[1]. If 1958 turned out to be a year of minor recession, this probably owed more to the continuance, ever since 1955, of a policy of moderate restraint; and to the impact in that year of what had now become a world recessionary trend[2].

5. RE-EXPANSION—AND RENEWED CAUTION, 1958–60

When Mr Thorneycroft resigned in January 1958, Mr Heathcoat Amory moved from the Ministry of Agriculture, and remained Chancellor of the Exchequer till his resignation in July 1960. For a year and a half the post of Economic Secretary was in temporary abeyance, the role being partly filled as one among the other duties of Mr Maudling as Paymaster-General. Mr Barber became Economic Secretary after the general election of October 1959. Under the new Chancellor, through the turn of fortune and his own empirical turn of mind, policy appeared to enter a more auspicious phase. In the course of 1958, the weight of internal policy was gradually shifted towards expansion; and external policy, so long ambiguous, achieved new, perhaps definite, clarification. The publication of the *Radcliffe Report* provoked a more modest, and more rational, assessment of monetary policy. The need, already becoming evident by the end of 1960, to impose new restraints on demand was to provoke even more fundamental heart-searching about the conduct of economic policy.

Mr Amory's first budget made only a cautious move towards expansion. This mood of caution was imposed less by temperament[3] than by what seemed very considerable uncertainties in the spring of 1958. The United States was still in the downward phase of recession: as Mr Amory said[4], 'no one' could 'yet tell' how much further it would go. That both threatened our exports; and, by its effect on the overseas sterling area, promised at least some strain on the reserves[5]—by then recovered from the September crisis. Having regard to all

---

[1]The authorities' justification of Bank rate to the Radcliffe Committee was not that it affected the economy; but that it was 'a symbol of determination to defend the pound', and their 'determination to take unpleasant steps to check inflation' and thus acted directly on foreigners' confidence in sterling. 'It is on this basis that the Bank of England has attached importance to using Bank Rate as only one item in the package deal, in one phase (late 1954) even abstaining from a Bank Rate move because it could not then be part of a package deal' (*Radcliffe Report*, paras. 440–1). Professor Robbins [1958] gave the same defence of the 1957 move: to members of other financial centres, he said, 'the raising of the Bank Rate is a sign that the pound is to be defended'.

[2]See the detailed assessment in chapter XV.4.

[3]'I would like to re-emphasise' said Mr Amory 'that, as a Government, we are convinced that the long-term welfare of this country demands a steady expansion of our national economy. That is the objective of all our policies. We shall not, therefore, keep the brakes on one day longer than we must. We dislike restrictions intensely, and we are eager to resume expansion' (*H.C. Deb.* 15 April 1958, 55).

[4]Same deb. 49.

[5]*Economic Survey, 1958*, paras. 84–5.

these uncertainties the 'budget assessment' was surprisingly explicit. Home demand, said Mr Amory,

> 'should, on the whole, remain firm. But . . . export demand may slacken and this may be reinforced by a fall in business expenditure on stocks . . . industrial production has tended to decline slightly . . . and unemployment has been rising. These trends may well go rather further . . . but I do not believe that a sudden sharp recession in this country . . . is likely'[1].

The Chancellor was in no doubt that the economy was 'capable of meeting a higher level of demand . . . than is likely to be made on it'[2]. But two considerations held him back from resuming 'a policy of general expansion'[2]: First, the danger of provoking wage inflation—where we seemed to 'have only just emerged from a dangerously strained position'[2]. Second, after a series of foreign exchange crises, the Chancellor was naturally 'determined to spare no effort to see that we do not have another'[2]. Like Mr Butler's budget in the similar uncertainties of 1954, it was essentially a 'wait and see' budget. 'Initial' depreciation allowances were increased by a quarter, and a moderate cut was made in purchase tax and entertainments duty.

Looking back a year later, Mr Amory was able to claim, with justice, that his assessment had been broadly correct[3]. Developments during 1958 were to be much coloured by the fall in world commodity prices that had occurred at the end of 1957. It had reduced the incomes of many of our overseas customers; but though exports fell in consequence, it so greatly improved our terms of trade that the 1958 balance of payments surplus was the largest since the war. Perhaps even more important, the overseas sterling area had so increased its long-term non-sterling borrowing that their poor export receipts, contrary to what was feared, imposed no strain on the reserves. Despite the United States recession, the reserves rose by nearly £300 million. Furthermore the fall in import prices produced something much nearer price stability at home[4]. These developments clearly put Mr Amory in a radically stronger position to resume expansion.

At the same time, the need for action to prevent a slide in activity at home had become increasingly clear. By the summer of 1958, industrial production had dipped three points compared with the year before; and the pressure of demand for labour appeared even lower than in the 1952 recession[5]. Industrial

---

[1]*H.C. Deb.* 15 April 1958, 50.

[2]*Ibid.*, 54.

[3]1959 budget speech: *H.C. Deb.* 7 April 1959, 29.

[4]During the calendar year 1958 the index of retail prices rose rather less than 2 per cent. Mr Amory recognized that this could not in any simple sense be claimed as victory for disinflationary policy: 'the most important factor here undoubtedly was the benefit which we had received from lower import prices', but 'the average wage increase, also, was smaller than it has been in recent years' (*ibid.*, 30).

[5]In the third quarter unemployment after seasonal correction was 1·4 per cent. This was not so high as in the middle of 1952, but unfilled vacancies at 1·3 per cent were lower than then.

investment was declining; and with considerable capacity under-employed[1], the decline could easily have become serious.   During the course of 1958 various expansionary steps had indeed already been taken.   The 'ceiling' on bank advances was removed in July; and hire-purchase restrictions were reduced in September, and removed altogether in October.   Mr Thorneycroft's 'ceiling' on public investment was also removed[2].

These measures had produced a rise in demand and output at the end of the year.   At the time of the budget, this trend looked likely to continue.   'But' said Mr Amory:

> 'this rise is not likely to be at all rapid—indeed, if nothing more were done, it might slow down in the second half of the year.'

He concluded:

> 'the prospect for home production as I have set it out does not represent a full enough use of the capital resources which have been created in recent years.   Nor can we be content with the possibility that unemployment might continue at around the present levels . . . [Moreover] we must not forget . . . that we in the United Kingdom have our own contribution to make to the re-expansion of the world economy after the mild recession of last year.   If each nation were to pursue too cautious a policy in regard to its balance of payments, international trade would stagnate.'

On the unsolved problem 'of the interactions of rising money incomes and rising prices', Mr Amory took a middle position:

> 'We must at all costs make it our business not to return to an over-load on the economy, which would make a resumption of inflation inevitable.   At the present time, however, this is clearly not an immediate danger . . . '

Then, having weighed these considerations, Mr Amory concluded:

> 'it would be right for me to seek, through the Budget, to give a further limited but effective impetus to the expansion of our economic activity'[3].

In fact the tax reductions made in the 1959 budget were very considerable indeed.   Purchase tax was reduced by about one sixth, and the duty on beer was also cut: together these incidentally reduced the retail price index by almost a point.   The standard rate of income tax was cut by no less than ninepence; and a start was made on the more rapid repayment of post-war credits—a debt which had been left undischarged for fourteen years.   Furthermore the 1954

---

[1] The National Institute of Economic and Social Research estimated, in the first number of its new *Economic Review* (January 1959), that excess capacity was about 20 per cent in the metal-using industries, and 10–15 per cent in the chemical, paper and steel industries.

[2] Increased investment was permitted for housing, roads and railways (see *Economic Survey, 1959*, para. 2; and chapter VIII.2 below).   Bank rate, also, was reduced from 7 to 6 per cent in March, and by four further stages to 4 per cent in November.

[3] *H.C. Deb.* 7 April 1959, 44–8.

'investment allowance' was reinstated[1].   The tax reductions were calculated to increase consumers' spendable incomes by some £300 million in a full year, on top of which the post-war credit repayments added a once-for-all increase of £70 million.

Together with the likely increase in exports, and some recovery in home investment, the budget concessions looked likely to produce an expansion of industrial production of four or five per cent during 1959[2].   In fact the expansion turned out to be rather more rapid.   Some local bottlenecks developed, notably for steel sheet and for many consumer durables.   But such shortages were exceptional; and the pressure of demand for labour remained remarkably low.   In the light of its full effects, the stimulus provided by the 1959 budget—another pre-election budget—was excessive[3].   But for a while, rapid expansion proved possible without recreating a general excess of demand.

Mr Amory's handling of external economic policy was equally auspicious. His first budget speech contained a notable, though little noticed, defence of the sterling area system—not on the grounds that it contributed to British prestige, but as a serviceable international financial institution.   Sterling, he said,

'finances a large part of the world's trade.   There is no other currency in a position to take its place; nor could one quickly be developed . . . In a world where liquid reserves in other forms are all too scarce, sterling and the sterling area are indispensable to the smooth functioning of a large part of the world's trade . . . Our purpose is that it shall be preserved and developed.'

He added what in the past had been too little recognized, the corollary

'that we must maintain close and continuous consultation with our sterling area partners'.

He added too,

'I believe that the problem of world liquidity . . . is a matter of increasing importance and urgency.   It may well be that a solution can best be found by the steady expansion of institutions such as the International Monetary Fund and the International Bank.   Such a solution would, of course require the active good will and assistance of the chief creditor countries.   It may be that more can be done co-operatively within the Commonwealth . . . I can only say that in this vitally important field of the provision of capital and credit . . . any sound plans . . . will

---

[1]As in 1954, the rates were 20 per cent investment allowance on plant and machinery and 10 per cent on industrial buildings.   But, in addition, there continued to be 'initial' allowances for a further 10 and 5 per cent respectively of such investment expenditure. The total incentive was therefore greater than in 1954.

[2]This was an unofficial contemporary estimate: see *Nat. Inst. econ. R.*, May 1959.   The corresponding increase in total national output between the end of 1958 and the end of 1959 was put at 3 per cent.

[3]See the detailed assessment in chapter XV.4 below.

receive the wholehearted support of Her Majesty's Government'[1].

These questions were discussed at the Commonwealth Economic Conference that met in Montreal in September 1958. At this conference the United Kingdom announced its intention to encourage investment in the Commonwealth. This was important more because it made clear there was to be a conscious policy, than because it promised an early increase in such investment[2]. More important was the general agreement, fully supported by the Commonwealth, at the International Monetary Fund meeting which followed at Delhi, to increase the Fund quotas by 50 per cent. In May 1959 the United Kingdom duly paid £58 million to the Fund as its share, thus increasing our drawing rights by up to five times the amount of the initial gold payment. Other sterling countries made parallel payments.

At the end of December 1958, sterling held by non-residents was made freely convertible into dollars, what had for so long been an object of speculation thus being quietly effected. Mr Amory made it clear that the Government had for some time had this step in mind 'as one to take at a moment convenient for ourselves and our friends in other countries'[3]. The immediate occasion was determined by the decision of the de Gaulle Government, as part of financial reform, to devalue the franc[4]. The move was made in concert with most other European countries; and thus automatically involved the replacement of the European Payments Union by the European Monetary Agreement negotiated in 1955. The move aroused some misgiving, partly on the ground that it ought to have followed, not preceded, the removal of restrictions on dollar imports—a step promised at the Montreal conference in September, but not substantially implemented till the following November. It was certainly a more significant step than the Chancellor made out[5]. But it was still true that

---

[1]*H.C. Deb.* 15 April 1958, 51–3.

[2]The United Kingdom undertook to 'maintain and if possible improve on' the recent average for such investment of £200 million a year. The most important steps were that both independent sterling countries and the colonies were to be given freer access to direct borrowing from the British Government; and that the interest rate was to be ¼ per cent only above the rate the Treasury itself had to pay on long-term borrowing (*Economist*, 27 Sept. 1958, p. 1047).

[3]*H.C. Deb.* 28 January 1959, 1088.

[4]*Economist*, 3 Jan. 1959, p. 11. There was a suggestion that the Bank of England had tried to force the pace. The Chancellor said in the debate that the Government 'had taken no decision on timing' and implied (in Mr Gaitskell's words) that 'the immediate initiative . . . came from the French'. Mr Gaitskell continued: 'inquiries I have made recently in Paris yielded an account of the matter which puts a rather different complexion upon it. I was informed that the Governor of the Bank of England told the Governor of the Bank of France that it was the decision of Her Majesty's Government to introduce convertibility some time between the early weeks of December . . . and the end of January (*H.C. Deb.* 28 January 1959, 1096). If such intervention did occur, it did not necessarily determine the decision, which Mr Amory said (1089) was made by himself with French and German Ministers of Finance at the OEEC meeting in December.

[5]The rate on transferable sterling had been officially supported since 1955. Mr Amory argued

'that the freedom which some have suggested we have to let the transferable rate

since *de facto* convertibility had been maintained for four years, there was good reason to hope *de jure* convertibility would not prove too onerous. Indeed, since so many other currencies now became convertible, the position of sterling was likely to be eased. During the four years from 1958 of *de facto* convertibility in non-convertible Europe, sterling had, perhaps, had the worst of both worlds.

Speculation about the possibility of this step had been so unsettling in the past because it had always gone with an expectation that the exchange rate would be unpegged. The rate now remained at 2.80 dollars to the pound. History may be able to assure us that the institution of convertibility in this way marked the close of an issue which, during the seven years since 1951, had bedevilled British economic policy.

The publication of the *Radcliffe Report*[1], in August 1959, marked, in another sphere, an equally decisive stage. Appointed by Mr Thorneycroft, its conclusions tended to justify not his view of monetary policy, but Mr Heathcoat Amory's much more pragmatic approach. 'The aims of economic policy are various', said the *Report* in its conclusions: 'There is . . . no single objective by which all monetary policy can be conditioned'[2]. 'Monetary measures are . . . part of one general economic policy which includes among its instruments fiscal and monetary measures and direct physical controls'[2]. Therefore, the Committee concluded—while preserving a degree of independence—the role of the Bank of England should be that of 'executant', and its policies 'from first to last in harmony with those avowed and defended by Ministers of the Crown responsible to Parliament'[3].

The Committee, however, marked out no great role for monetary action. Reviewing the experience of the 1950's, it concluded that 'the really quick substantial effects' came from the hire-purchase controls; while a considerable, though rather slower effect probably came in 1956-8 from the 'diffused difficulty of borrowing' resulting from the credit squeeze[4]. On the problem which had immediately provoked its appointment—the difficulty of con-

---

go in times of crisis has been illusory. The move of 29 December will not, in practice, place a greater strain on our reserves nor shall we be under any greater need to keep the economy free of inflation . . . In both these respects the change we have made is not a significant one' (*ibid.*, 1084).
The Opposition were surely right to ask why in this case the step had been delayed for four years (1087); and to point out that support of the transferable rate had originally been defended as a reversible step (1098). The main Opposition misgivings arose out of fear that if ever a new dollar shortage arose, it might in fact be convenient to be able to reverse it.

[1] *Report of the Committee on the Working of the Monetary System*, Cmnd. 827.
[2] Para. 980. A fuller discussion of the conclusions of the *Radcliffe Report* is deferred until chapters IX.8 and XII below.
[3] Paras. 767 and 769.
[4] Para. 472.

trolling bank credit—the Committee had no radical solution to suggest[1]. Thus, 'when all has been said on the possibility of monetary action . . . our conclusion is that monetary measures cannot alone be relied on to keep in fine balance an economy subject to major strains from both without and within. Monetary measures can help, but that is all'[2].

The *Report* had a mixed reception.   Many of its *obiter dicta* were calculated to offend conventional views on the efficacy of monetary measures ; yet it proposed no revolutionary change in existing instructions.   Most economists must have been pleased that it treated monetary policy, not as a magic influence, but as one among other factors capable of affecting the level of demand.   Yet many were puzzled by the *Report*'s emphasis on the 'liquidity' of the economy as a whole, and its suggestion that this could be influenced by 'operations on the structure of interest rates'[3].   The *Report* proposed no cut and dried solutions; and, in the nature of the case, no quick acceptance or rejection by the Government was to be expected[4].   While withholding comment on the more controversial issues—and while feeling that the Committee had 'perhaps underestimated the part that can be played by monetary forces'[5]—the Government generally welcomed the *Report*.

One early result of the *Report* was a subtle, yet important, alteration in the relation of the Bank of England to the Treasury—a matter of small changes, intended, however, to make 'more explicit the understanding that monetary policy must fall within the orbit of general economic policy and that the Government must bear the ultimate responsibility'[6].   The further effects of the

---

[1] 'I remember', said Mr Thorneycroft later, 'telling Lord Radcliffe how the monetary system appeared to us at the Treasury—at least at the Ministerial level.   It appeared like an antiquated pumping machine, creaking and groaning, leaking wildly at all the main valves, but still desperately attempting to keep down the level of water in the mine.   There was, I observed, quite a lot of water in the mine at the time and more was seeping in'. (P. Thorneycroft, 'Policy in Practice', in *Not Unanimous*, edited by A. Seldon [1960].)

The Committee, however, were unable to 'recommend any substantial change in the rules under which the banks operate' (para. 514).   For its views on the 'special deposits' scheme and possible alternatives see further chapter IX.3 below.

[2] Para. 514.

[3] Para. 983.   This aspect of the *Report*, among others, was for instance criticized by Professor Robbins in his maiden speech in the House of Lords as Lord Robbins of Clare Market (*H.L. Deb.* 11 Nov. 1959).   For fuller reference to the discussion, see chapter IX.8 and also chapter XII.

[4] The debate in the Commons followed in November.   The Chancellor was evidently placed in some difficulty in commenting on the more complex matters raised.   'Members may well doubt my personal qualifications for pronouncing on these formidable issues, on which eminent economists hold passionately such divergent views.'   But—he went on—'as has been well said, if only those who were qualified spoke, the world would be filled with a profound silence . . . ' (*H.C. Deb.* 26 Nov. 1959, 576).

[5] Same deb. 575.

[6] Same deb. 578–83.   The Chancellor rejected the Committee's view that the Treasury should issue a formal directive to the Bank when the Bank rate was changed: 'for many years', he said, 'no change in the Bank rate has been made without the approval of the Chancellor'.   But in future a change in Bank rate was to be accompanied by a formal

Report are more difficult to pin down. A major improvement of monetary and financial statistics, early set in train, is likely to appear in time. A renewed emphasis on fiscal policy, and a greater exploration of fiscal flexibility, can also be attributed to its general influence.

Thus by 1960, the course of events had produced a kind of practical settlement, not only of the question of convertibility, but also of the general role of monetary policy. The removal of these contentious side issues was to reveal all the more clearly the central difficulties in the way of managing the economy. 'Our policy in 1959', said Mr Amory in his budget review, 'was to stimulate the revival of business activity, while maintaining price stability, and that policy succeeded'[1]. But in April 1960, the signs of 'incipient overstrain' were, as the Chancellor said, already becoming once more apparent.

In the course of 1959, final expenditure had risen at least six per cent; national output, three or four per cent; industrial production ten per cent[2]. The rise in demand looked like continuing, though more slowly than in 1959[3]. 'On the other hand', said the Chancellor, 'we no longer have the reserves of labour and capacity on which we could count a year ago'. Unemployment (which on a seasonally calculated basis had been 2.3 per cent at the beginning of 1959) had fallen, but was still 1.6 per cent in April. Prices, however, after two years of unexampled stability, looked like rising again. Equally important, the balance of payments surplus had fallen by £200 million between 1958 and 1959—world developments had favoured British exports, but internal expansion had at the same time produced a large rise in imports; and this trend, too, looked

announcement to the press, 'including a statement that the Bank's decisions have met with my approval'.

The Committee had, secondly, proposed a new committee, drawn from the Bank, the Treasury and the Board of Trade, to advise on monetary policy. The Chancellor rejected the proposal, but held that the same aim would be served 'by arranging for the Bank to be permanently represented on the various official committees by which economic policy is already formulated'—with many of which the Bank had indeed already 'been informally associated from time to time in the past'.

In discussing the question of part-time directors of the Bank, the Committee in effect proposed that while they should be consulted about the general direction of policy, they should not be party to decisions about the timing and extent of changes in Bank rate (see particularly para. 785). This view appears to have been accepted. 'In the formation of the Bank's views on monetary policy', the Chancellor said, 'the main responsibility must fall, as it does fall, on the Governors, while the function of the Bank's part-time directors must be mainly advisory . . . At the same time, we attach the greatest importance, as does the Radcliffe Committee, to ensuring that the Bank's position should be maintained as a separate organization with a life of its own, and that its governing body—not only the part-time directors, but all the governing body—should not meet merely as consultants, but should continue to take a corporate responsibility for the formation of the Bank's views'.

[1] *H.C. Deb.* 4 April 1960, 40.
[2] All figures in 'real terms': see *Economic Survey, 1960* (paras. 7–9).
[3] The rate of increase was expected to be less because 'net lending on hire-purchase will probably be lower' and 'investment in stocks is unlikely to exert such an expansionary force as it did in 1959' (same deb. 44).

like continuing. Demand, in short, seemed likely 'at least fully to absorb', and perhaps even to be in 'danger of outrunning', the capacity of the economy[1].

The 1960 budget was therefore a 'no-change' budget as far as consumers were concerned. Taxes were indeed increased by £72 million in a full year, but this was almost entirely accounted for by the increase in profits tax[2]. The main restrictive measures again fell within the field of monetary policy. Bank rate had been raised from four to five per cent in January. At the end of April, hire-purchase restrictions were reimposed; and, for the first time, use was made of the power to call for 'special deposits'[3]. At the end of June, Bank rate was raised to six per cent; and special deposit requirements were further increased.

These measures appear effectively to have checked the rise in consumer debt, and, with it, the rise in consumption. Final expenditure in total continued to grow. But it was met chiefly by imports. The rise in production was therefore, once again, halted for a while. Exports also started to decline, so that, despite the pause in home demand, the balance of payments went once again into deficit. Mr Heathcoat Amory retired in July: his successor as Chancellor of the Exchequer, Mr Selwyn Lloyd, was to find it necessary to restrict demand still further in the middle of 1961.

The history of the previous five years made the need for new restrictions all the more disappointing. The boom of 1955 had been encouraged by policy; policy was reversed very late in the day; and when it was reversed, policy remained restrictive for three years. After this experience, it seemed reasonable to hope that intervention on this scale could in future be avoided; that—while demand would doubtless have to continue to be controlled—small adjustments made in good time would suffice; and that expansion could be allowed to proceed—now rather more, now rather less rapidly—at a fairly steady pace. Yet the expansion induced in 1958 and 1959 had to be severely checked barely fifteen months after it got under way. By 1960, national output was 14 per cent, and output per head $12\frac{1}{2}$ per cent, higher than in 1955. But Britain's neighbours on the continent had been growing at something like twice that rate; and by 1960, this was being made one of the major criticisms of British economic policy.

---

[1] *H.C. Deb.* 4 April 1960, 45.

[2] See chapter VII.3 below. Though the duty on tobacco was increased by £40 million this was almost entirely offset by small income tax reliefs for dependent relatives, widows and widowers, and in connection with national insurance; and by small reductions in the tax on wine and entertainments.

[3] Compulsory deposits by the banks with the Bank of England. Since such deposits are not liquid assets, a call for such deposits reduces the banks' liquidity ratio, and hence their power to lend (see further chapter IX.3 below).

PART II

THE ANALYSIS OF POLICY

CHAPTER IV

INTRODUCTION:

THE BALANCE OF THE ECONOMY, 1945-60

A narration of the events of the last fifteen years, such as given in part I, carries one little further towards distinguishing the effects of policy. Having gone over again these events, one is scarcely in a better position than someone at the time to say what government measures really did. Part II attempts to carry the analysis a stage further. The following chapters aim to single out the main ways in which the government has been able to influence the economy, and to describe policy in terms of these instruments[1]. At the present stage the aim is to describe only the 'first impact' of policy, i.e. upon the level of demand, not its more indirect effects, i.e. upon prices and the balance of payments.

Since the foregoing historical narrative is inevitably diffuse, it may be convenient by way of introduction to summarize the main acts of policy and the main trends in the economy. Table 4.1 is intended to be no more than a one-page summary of the main events of fifteen years. This is bound to be more journalistic than scientific. Most of the crises have been occasioned by sudden large falls in the reserves, and on these occasions it was generally thought necessary to take dramatic action; but many of the acts of policy made during quieter times must have been more important in their impact.

Changes in tax rates are perhaps, as argued later, the most important single measure of policy changes. As the table shows, the most important tax changes were not crisis moves. The three major cuts in rates—Dr Dalton's in 1945-6, Mr Butler's in 1953 and Mr Amory's in 1959—were all undertaken to induce expansion, and were made in years which were not crisis years. The largest single tax increase was that made by Mr Gaitskell in 1951—admittedly a crisis year, but the budget preceded the crisis, and taxes were put up, not because of the crisis, but because of the defence programme[2]. Since 1951 variations in Bank rate have been much more frequent than changes in taxation. When Bank rate was put up, it was always put up as a way of meeting an external crisis. But its increasingly frequent use was accompanied by increasing doubt

---

[1]The aim may be said to be that of singling out the 'instrument variables' which an econometrician would have to take into account when trying to 'explain' trends: see J. Tinbergen [1956], *Economic Policy: Principles and Design*, p. xi.

[2]See further chapter VII.

Table 4.1. *Major acts of policy and the position of the economy, 1946–60*

	Economic situation			Main acts of policy			
	Index of excess demand (%)[a]	Balance of payments (£m.)[bc]	Change in reserves (£m.)[cd]	Budget change in taxes (£m.)[ce]	Change in hire-purchase control	Bank rate (%)	Changes in external policy[f]
1946	2·0	−300	50	−525[e]		2	
1947	2·0	−450	−150	{ 50 / 200[e]		2	CV fiasco
1948	1·4	—	− 50	50		2	
1949	0·8	50	—	−100		2	DV
1950	0·5	325	575	—		2	IC eased
1951	1·4	−400	−350	375		2	
1952	− 0.5	150	−175	− 75	On	2½–4	IC
1953	− 0.1	125	250	−400		4–3½	IC eased
1954	0·6	150	75	—	Off	3½–3	
1955	1·5	−175	−225	{ −150 / 100[e]	On	3–4½	de facto CV
1956	0·9	175	50	—	Tightened[g]	4½–5½	
1957	—	200	25	−125		5½–7	
1958	− 1·3	300	275	−100	Off	7–4	CV
1959	− 1·2	50	−125	−350		4	
1960	− 0·2	−350	175	75	On	4–6	

[a]Roughly twice the difference between per cent vacancies and per cent unemployment: the amplitude of the index is thus twice that originally presented in Dow and Dicks-Mireaux [1958], *Oxford econ. Pap.* (see chapter XIII.2 below).

[b]From *UKBP* [1959] and, for 1950 and later, *NI & E* [1961].

[c]Rounded to nearest £25m.

[d]Excludes in 1949 revaluation of assets on devaluation and includes waiver accounts in 1956 and 1957.

[e]Effect in a 'full year' on revenue of changes in tax rates (see chapter VII, table 7.6). Figures for 1946 include changes announced in October 1945: autumn budgets of 1947 and 1955 shown separately.

[f]CV = convertibility, DV = devaluation, IC = import control.

[g]Restrictions on hire purchase for cars eased later in year.

as to its effectiveness, and, increasingly, by a 'package deal' of other measures about whose effectiveness less doubts were felt.   The tightening of the hire-purchase regulations in 1955 was part of a 'crisis' policy; that in 1952 came rather late in the day for it also to be classed a crisis move; in 1957, this element was not included in the 'package'[1].

The table also shows how loose was the connection between internal conditions and the occurrence of external crises.   Payments deficits often occurred at times of high internal demand, and surpluses when demand was relatively low.   But the correlation, though there, is loose and uncertain.   Thus there were sizeable surpluses in 1950, 1954 and 1956, all years when demand was at least not particularly low[2].   It is equally true that there was a loose connection only between this country's balance of payments and the condition of the reserves. A loss of reserves frequently coincided with an adverse balance of payments for the United Kingdom.   But this was not invariably so: though these were years of surplus, we lost reserves in 1952 and 1959—and also (though this does not appear in the annual figures) during part of 1949 and 1957.

Since the kind of economic policy discussed in this study is intended to obtain its effects via its effect on total demand, the simplest way to chart the course of policy is to look at what happened to the pressure of demand: policy since the war then seems to fall into fairly distinct phases.   The 'pressure of demand' is essentially a relative concept, and implies a comparison between total demand and total available supplies[3].   Throughout the post-war period total available supplies were increasing.   The *pressure* of demand increased only when real demand increased *more rapidly* than potential real supply.   The pressure of demand for labour, as it happens, is easier to measure than that for finished goods and services; but the two are likely to be connected and to vary together. There are various more or less indirect measures of the pressure of demand, which however all tell more or less the same story (figure 4.1).

The statistics of unfilled vacancies provide a direct measure of the unsatisfied demand for labour.   Unemployment statistics also reflect the demand for labour, and tend to confirm the evidence of the statistics of vacancies.   The index of the excess demand for labour shown on figure 4.1 is an attempt to combine the information obtained from both series[4].   When the pressure of demand, so measured, is high, then hours worked tend to be long, and vice versa.   So long as the pressure does not fall, both output and employment tend to rise each year; but when it falls, the rise in output and employment is diminished or even turned into a fall.   This 'fall below trend' in employment

---

[1]See further chapter IX.
[2]See further chapter XV below.
[3]For a fuller discussion see chapter XIII.1.
[4]The index as shown has double the amplitude of the index originally presented in the paper by myself and L. A. Dicks-Mireaux [1958], 'Excess Demand for Labour', *Oxford econ. Pap.*, February 1958.   See chapter XIII.2 below.

Fig. 4.1. Indicators of state of demand

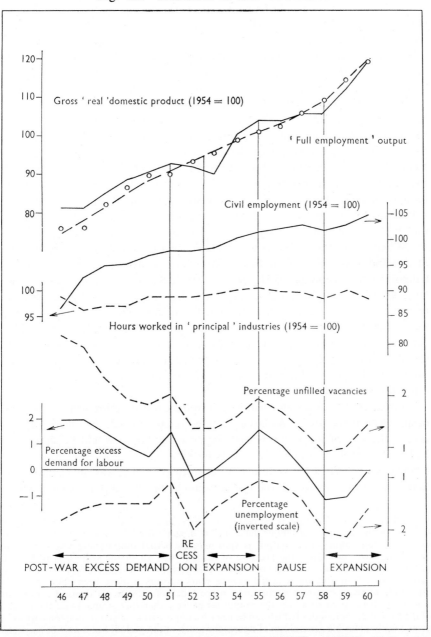

Gross domestic product from output estimates in *NI & E* [1957] and [1960]. '*Full employment*' *output* equals index of output *plus* twice percentage excess demand for labour (as shown below). *Civil employment* is for end-June each year. *Hours worked* is average for April and October each year. *Percentage excess demand for labour* is roughly twice the difference between percentage vacancies and percentage unemployment : the range of amplitude of the index is thus twice that originally presented in Dow and Dicks-Mireaux [1958], *Oxford econ. Pop.* For fuller explanation, see chapter XIII.2.

can be regarded as a sort of concealed unemployment: men and—more particularly—women who would be willing to work, if work were easy to find, do not go to the employment exchanges and consequently are not registered as seeking work.

The 'fall below trend' in output—if it could be measured—would be a measure of unutilized capacity for producing goods and services. The series of dots on the chart about the curve of output represents an attempt to show the growth of full capacity output, i.e. how much would have been produced each year if demand had been neither excessive nor deficient[1]. Accuracy is the last thing that can be claimed for such a constructed statistic; but it may nevertheless indicate in a rough way the development of the productive capacity of the economy. It seems clear that fluctuations about the trend have been pretty wide. Thus both 1951 and 1955 were boom years; while in some intervening and later years, output must have been several per cent below such a maximum.

It seems to emerge from the data that the immediately post-war boom lasted till 1952. The first five or six years therefore constitute one phase, in which the excess demand of the war years was being gradually worked off, and the pressure of demand was gradually falling. This gradual process of disinflation was temporarily interrupted in 1951—partly by the defence programme, which was a large addition superimposed on other existing demands; and partly because fear of war led to a speculative demand for stocks. From this date onward, the economy appears to have oscillated around the 'full employment' point—demand at times growing faster than capacity, and at other times growing less rapidly. These cycles are not necessarily to be thought of as something like the pre-war trade cycle in diminished form; for government policy has now become a much more powerful influence.

To treat 1951-2 as a watershed is to introduce a distinction which was by no means clear at the time. As has already been emphasized, the official expectation at the end of the war was that the post-war boom would be short, as it had been in 1919-20, and would quickly be followed by a post-war slump. This expectation governed Dr Dalton's initial strategy, and it was only during 1947 that it began to be modified: the 1947 autumn budget was a practical recognition

---

[1]'Full employment' output is estimated by adjusting actual output in accord with the fluctuations in the index of labour demand. If demand for labour appears by this index excessive, 'full employment' output is shown *below* actual output; and vice versa. By comparing two years when the pressure of demand was about the same it is possible to gauge the development of 'capacity' during this period. The amplitude of deviation of actual output from this trend in intervening years appears to have been about twice the amplitude of the concurrent fluctuations in the index of pressure of demand for labour. The adjustments used to adjust the output series were therefore simply twice the reading of the labour demand index (which can be negative or positive). Even so simple a correction gives a fairly plausible general run of figures for much of the period; but it may be suspected that it underestimates 'capacity' in the years after 1955.

A very similar construction is given in F. W. Paish [1962], *Studies in an Inflationary Economy*, chapter 17.

that demand could not simply be left to wane of its own accord. The end of inflation and onset of deflation continued to be constantly expected as near and imminent through all Sir Stafford Cripps's budgets.

During the first post-war years, it seemed impossible to form a reliable judgement about the state of demand. Nowadays it seems fairly safe to take the level of unemployment as an index of demand. But to use it in this way, one has to treat quite small changes (changes say of 0·1 points in percentage unemployment) as significant; and at the time it always seemed possible that these might be due to irrelevant factors, such as minor shifts in the pattern of demand or slight inequalities in the seasons. People were, indeed, for lack of better, ready to clutch at straws and shreds of evidence—such as how easy it was to get train seats, or gin from 'under the counter'. There seemed no means of knowing how much excess demand there was, nor how great the danger that policy would overshoot the mark and produce a recession. The 1952 recession now seems a landmark; at the time it was not recognized as occurring till after it had touched bottom, and even in 1953 it seemed a bold statement to say that the post-war boom was over[1].

It is also difficult to judge the extent of a deficiency of demand. It seemed obvious before the war that a shortage of demand would be quickly revealed in a rise in unemployment. But in fact unemployment is not highly responsive, at least to a moderate slackening in demand; for if sales merely stop rising but do not fall, manufacturers are likely to keep workers on their pay-rolls; and the size of the margin of unutilized capacity is then very difficult to judge. Productive capacity may be presumed to have continued to rise; but after some years of slack working, the rate of rise assumed makes a great difference to the estimate of spare capacity; and reliable direct information has been lacking[2]. One lesson which post-war experience seems to have taught is that the division between inflation and deflation is slow and blurred, not precipitous and calamitous. Hesitations in total demand do not rapidly snowball into depressions: small excesses of demand do not have dramatic effects on prices.

Though the various phases of development were not easily distinguished at the time, the development of the situation inevitably coloured the nature of economic policy. In the first post-war years, it was hardly in question, notwithstanding anxieties about a recession in the proximate future, that for the present demand was too high not too low. After the recession of 1952, even though its significance was not immediately fully recognized, this was no longer true. Though conditions changed from year to year, a deficiency of demand was as frequent a possibility as an excess of it. It was a much more real necessity for policy to face both ways and steer a course between; and how high demand was depended much more on what policy was—or, at least, on what

---

[1] See the press comment on the 1953 *Economic Survey*.

[2] There have been unofficial attempts to get direct information: see *Nat. Inst. econ. R.* issues for January (or February) each year.

policy had been followed in recent years[1]. Thus Mr Butler was perhaps the first Chancellor to confront the real task of stabilizing the economy.

The process of disinflation may be dated from Dr Dalton's 1947 autumn budget. It was continued by Sir Stafford Cripps; and proved a slow process. This gave a great continuity to Cripps's budgetary policy: his problem always lay on one side, and his efforts all pointed one way. But in his own mind, Cripps's budgetary policy was probably a subsidiary part only of his general policy. His prime aims tended to be expressed in physical terms: to increase output, invest, and increase exports. The ordinary consumer was therefore to him very much the residuary legatee. Cripps's form of disinflation was biassed disinflation—biassed against the consumer—and thus closely allied with his philosophy of 'austerity'.

The degree of success of his disinflationary policy can indeed almost be measured by seeing how well it succeeded in keeping down the share of national product going to consumers. By 1946 government spending (as compared with the war years) had halved, thus setting free for civilian use some thirty per cent of national output (table 4.2). By 1947 its further fall set free a further eight per cent. By then output was also rising rapidly: between 1947 and 1950 the gross domestic product rose on average by $3\frac{1}{2}$ per cent a year—a higher rate than attained in any subsequent four years. Policy aimed to restrain the growth of consumption relatively to that of national output, so that the growth of resources would in large part be diverted to exports and investment. This was in fact accomplished. Consumption took very much less than its share in the increment of resources; and, as a share of national product, fell four or five percentage points[2]. But despite his reputation for austerity, Sir Stafford Cripps did not raise taxation, but merely kept it high[3].

Thereafter, the share of consumption changed very little. The share of government spending, after being raised by the 'Korean' defence programme, fell back a little; the share of exports fell; and the share of investment rose. What is not consumed has either to be saved by the private sector or taxed away from it by the government. Through most of the post-war years, the proportion of

---

[1]It is sometimes said that the extensive direct controls before 1952 made the economy easier to control, and lessened the risk of unexpected swings in the level of demand and the balance of payments. (See for instance, I. M. D. Little's contribution on 'Fiscal Policy' in *The British Economy in the nineteen-fifties*, edited by Worswick and Ady [1962].) This is questionable. Swings in the balance of payments were considerable; and it is not clear that import controls reduced them—or would, had they been retained, have reduced subsequent ones (see chapter VI.4 below). It is true that, while excess demand lasted, there was relatively little risk of running into a spell of deficient demand; and also true that the persistence of excess demand was connected with the continuance of controls. But it was the excess demand, not the controls, that gave the relative safety—just as a manufacturer's long order book makes it much less likely he will run out of work.

[2]The 1948 Long Term Programme, and the degree of success in achieving its objects, has already been described in chapter II.3 above.

[3]See chapter VII.2.

Table 4.2.   *Disposition of national product, 1938–59 (percentages of GDP*[a]*)*

	1938	Average 1939–44	1946	1947	1952	1955	1959
Consumers' expenditure	77·2	57	69·7	69·2	65·3	65·6	64·1
Public authorities[b]	15·3	55	25·8	17·7	20·3	18·6	18·7
Gross domestic investment[c]	12·9	−3	9·5	14·4	14·7	17·7	17·7
Exports of goods and services	14·2	..	14·1	20·7	25·3	22·9	21·5
Total final expenditure	119·6	..	119·1	122·0	125·6	124·8	122·0
less Imports of goods and services	−19·6	..	−19·1	−22·0	−25·6	−24·8	−22·0
Gross domestic product	100	100	100	100	100	100	100
Index of GDP at constant prices 1946 = 100	*97*[d]	*..*	*100*	*108*	*116*	*130*	*140*

From *NI & E* [1957], [1959] and *NIWP* [1947], [1960].
[a]All items at factor cost.
[b]Current expenditure on goods and services.
[c]Includes value of increase in stocks.
[d]Based on OEEC estimates.   GNP in 1946 was hardly higher than in 1938: though GDP rose, income from abroad fell.

national output that has had to be so saved or so taxed has remained roughly stable at about a third.

There has, however, been a steady and remarkable rise in private saving. Since fiscal policy has been one of the main instruments of stabilization policy, taxation has been adjusted to balance or counteract changes going on elsewhere; and, granted the relative stability of non-consumption expenditures, the main change to which it has had to adapt has been this rise in private saving. Chiefly because of the increase in undistributed profits, private saving rose from $9\frac{1}{2}$ per cent to $12\frac{1}{2}$ per cent of national product between 1946 and 1952.   Between 1952 and 1959—chiefly then because of the increase in personal saving—it rose further to nearly 17 per cent of national product.

Thus, table 4.3 represents an alternative, and more detailed reading, of the trends.   In the first post-war years, private saving was very low; but investment was low also.   Moreover for some years we were disinvesting abroad and living off grants from other countries, which supplemented domestic resources and reduced the need for domestic saving.   During the transition from war to peace it was thus possible to continue for a time deficit government budgets. During the Cripps period, domestic investment recovered, and we also eliminated the foreign deficit.   The government provided most of the extra saving: in 1949, five per cent of the national income was saved through the budget; and to provide

Table 4.3.   *Investment and saving in relation to government expenditure and
taxation, 1938–59 (percentages of GNP)*

	1938	1946	1949	1952	1955	1959
Gross domestic investment[a]	12·7	10·0	14·7	14·4	18·8	19·3
Resources used in foreign investment[b]	−1·4	−5·3	—	1·4	−0·5	0·7
Total saving	11·3	4·7	14·7	15·8	18·3	20·0
of which[c]						
Persons	5·8	4·6	1·7	4·6	5·0	7·0
Corporations	7·1	4·9	7·0	8·0	10·1	9·8
Local authorities	1·4	0·8	0·7	0·6	0·6	0·9
Government[d]	−3·0	−5·6	5·3	2·6	2·6	2·3
Government current expenditure						
Goods and services	8·9	20·8	12·9	15·8	14·0	13·2
Transfers, subsidies and debt interest	12·3	21·1	18·4	16·5	15·5	16·7
Total	21·2	41·9	31·3	32·3	29·5	29·9
Government saving[e]	−3·0	−5·6	5·3	2·6	2·6	2·3
Government revenue[f]	18·2	36·3	36·6	34·9	32·1	32·2
of which 'revenue' taxes[g]	17·4	36·1	35·0	32·5	30·1	29·8

From *NI & E* [1956], [1959] and *NIWP* [1960].

[a]Fixed investment *plus* increase in volume of stocks *less* residual error.

[b]Net investment abroad *less* capital receipts from abroad.

[c]All items *after* provision for stock appreciation, but inclusive of additions to tax (and dividend) reserves.

[d]Revenue surplus *less* capital taxes, *plus* capital transfers.

[e]Excludes capital transfers.

[f]Excludes capital taxes, and after provision for stock appreciation.

[g]As above, but excluding government income from property and grants from overseas governments.

such a surplus, taxes had to be maintained, even though government expenditure by then amounted to ten per cent less of the national income than just after the war.

In the decade of the 'fifties the share of investment continued to grow. It was financed chiefly from personal saving (whose revival has been due in part, but only in part, to lower taxes). Corporate saving, expressed as a share of national income, has not increased since 1956, but has rather tended to fall; nevertheless no less than ten per cent of the national income is still saved as undistributed profits. Government saving has therefore been able to be reduced.

That government taxes are now appreciably smaller in relation to national income than in 1952 is therefore, in some sense, a result of the growth of private saving. But it has to be remembered that the level of taxes was the combined result of many other factors, and dependent also on the restraint of, or failure to restrain, government expenditure; on the expansion of investment, partly government-induced; and on the expansion of, or failure to expand, exports. Taken together these trends during the decade of the 'fifties allowed the burden of taxation to be reduced without upsetting the balance of the economy. Taxes were reduced on average—sometimes more rapidly, sometimes less—by one half of one per cent of the national income (or £100 million) a year. This downward bias greatly eased the political problem of maintaining stability.

CHAPTER V

ECONOMIC FORECASTS AND ECONOMIC POLICY

Policy must rest on some view of the future economic situation; and errors in forecasting are therefore capable of causing serious errors in policy. Before analysing in later chapters the different branches of policy in more detail, it seems useful first to try to assess the accuracy of official economic forecasts since the war[1]. A discussion of economic forecasting inevitably raises many of those questions about the working of the economy, and the effects of policy on it, which it will be the business of later chapters to explore more thoroughly.

The government is bound to take a view about the future, partly because there are delays between action and effect, partly because there are bound to be delays in diagnosing the present situation and taking action. Thus changes of policy require time to put into effect; the reaction of consumers or business men is also likely to be delayed (especially when measures, whether fiscal or monetary, are taken to affect investment demand); and the initial impact of government measures is likely after a time to be joined by further secondary repercussions (e.g. a change of consumption is likely to stimulate or depress investment). Furthermore, government policy cannot be altered every day—partly because the public can only stand a certain amount of change in the conditions within which they have to conduct their affairs; partly because it takes some time for the situation to change so markedly that a revised assessment is possible.

For all these reasons the government must aim to affect the future situation; and, explicitly or implicitly, any kind of macro-economic policy implies a view about the future. In this country policy has rested on explicit predictions; and since the war there have been arrangements for making formal economic forecasts. In the years from 1947 to 1951 forecasts were published in quantitative form. Since then the full quantitative forecasts have not been published; and official pronouncements have usually included only qualitative indications of the view the government took.

The methods used to make forecasts imply a view about how the economy works; and, if for no other reason, it is worth saying something about the methods officially used, in order to illustrate very briefly at this point something of the implicit theory of the behaviour of the economy which has underlain economic policy (§1). It is also necessary to set out the several severe difficulties in the way of comparing forecasts with actual developments (§2). The problem of forecasting was somewhat different before 1952, till when there was continuous excess demand, from what it was afterwards: §3 discusses the forecasts for the years 1947–51, and §4 the forecasts for later years.

[1]An earlier version of this chapter appeared as an article by myself [1962], 'L'expérience britannique en matière de prévisions économiques officielles, 1946–1960', in *B. Banque nat. Belgique*, March 1962. Both text and tables have been substantially revised.

1. METHODS USED IN OFFICIAL FORECASTING

Though there has been no recent account of the methods adopted for making official economic forecasts, some earlier accounts have been published; the official *Economic Surveys* also expose a little of the reasoning underlying the forecasts[1]. General observations on some important aspects are therefore possible. An account covering fifteen years, and based on partial information only, is, however, liable to be unfair to recent practice, which has developed alike with improved statistics and with improved understanding of the working of the economy.

In the conduct of stabilization policy since the war, fiscal policy has played the predominant role. It is chiefly in connection with the budget—in the annual *Economic Survey* and the budget speech—that forecasts, quantitative or qualitative, have been published. Though the government requires to have a continuously revised view of economic prospects, the main purpose of forecasting may still be regarded as assisting the budget decisions.

It is largely for this reason that the official forecasts have been essentially short-term forecasts. Fiscal policy has been decided for one financial year at a time; and the forecasts have referred to a similar period. In the early years, the forecasts referred to the calendar year ahead, and were generally expressed in terms of the average levels of expenditure and output expected to rule during the calendar year. In recent years the development of quarterly national income figures has made it possible to express the forecast in terms of 'terminal rates', so that the forecasts have referred not to developments as compared with the previous twelve months, but to developments expected during the ensuing twelve months. This change would also have made it easy to push the forecast rather further than twelve months ahead. Since the main occasion for the forecasts was the budget in April, the main forecasts have had to be prepared around the turn of the year—say November to February.

The fact that the forecasts have been short-term has meant that for several items of national expenditure there is 'direct' information about probable future trends. This makes it feasible—and, as will be argued more fully later, probably advantageous—not to rely on 'econometric' methods of projection.

---

[1]Early articles by those at one time concerned with official forecasts include R. L. Marris [1954], 'The Position of Economics and Economists in the Government Machine', *Econ. J.*, December 1954—a critical comparison of British methods with the econometric methods used in the Netherlands Central Planning Bureau; and E. F. Jackson [1949], 'The Recent Use of Social Accounting in the United Kingdom', in *Income and Wealth*, Series I, edited by E. Lundberg [1951] for the IARIW. Two more recent articles, which however only touch on the subject, are those by R. C. Tress [1959], 'The Contribution of Economic Theory to Economic Prognostication', *Economica*, August 1959; and Sir Robert Hall [1959], 'Reflections on the Practical Applications of Economics', *Econ. J.*, December 1959. I was concerned with such work in the Treasury till 1954. Mr Neild who was in the Treasury from 1951 to 1956 has described the somewhat similar methods used by the National Institute of Economic and Social Research in an article by himself and E. A. Shirley [1961], 'Economic Review: an Assessment of Forecasts, 1959–1960', *Nat. Inst econ. R.*, May 1961.

By the turn of the year, the level of government expenditure in the year ahead has already been decided, and the estimates are available early in the year[1]. 'Direct' information is also available for the probable course of fixed investment. In the early years fixed investment was partly subject to direct controls and thus was, in theory, within the power of the authorities to determine[2]: the forecasts then were based chiefly on supply probabilities.   In later years, while public investment remains subject to agreement with the government[3], private investment can be estimated from surveys of investment intentions.   Future government expenditure and fixed investment—amounting together to rather over a quarter of total final demand—can thus be treated as 'given' for the purpose of forecasts.

The level of future exports can also be taken as an independent *datum* for the forecasts in that it has to be treated as largely independent of the course of events in the United Kingdom.   The forecast of exports has in fact been based on a mixture of considerations.   As explained more fully below in connection with the balance of payments forecasts, there has been some reliance on an economic assessment of the balance of payments prospects of primary producing countries (which limit what they can *afford* to import) and on the internal prospects of industrial countries (which may determine what they are *likely* to import).   But the government has also various sources of direct information about the prospects for different types of exports in different markets; and no doubt some reliance has continued to be placed on a commonsense appraisal based on such sources.

Forecasts of consumers' expenditure must rest partly on forecasts of consumers' real purchasing power, and partly on forecasts of consumers' saving. Real incomes are largely influenced both by the development of wages and salaries—about which a good deal can be inferred from the current state of wage negotiations; and by the development of prices—which can be forecast in the light of past and probable developments in costs.   Incomes are however also affected by the level of 'non-consumption' expenditure: for, if high, this is likely to raise employment, wage drift and overtime pay.   Such 'cross influences', while not likely to transform the forecast of consumption, may modify it appreciably; and (as explained below) have to be taken account of[4]. The behaviour of saving, having been erratic, has not been easy to forecast. In recent years its fluctuations have been influenced by, and to some extent can

---

[1]Because government expenditure cannot be quickly varied much, the use of fiscal policy for stabilizing the economy has come to depend chiefly on the variation of tax rates, not government expenditure: see chapter VII.1 below.

[2]See chapter VI.3 below.

[3]See further chapter VIII.

[4]This procedure implies a theory about what determines the rate of growth of consumption in a growing economy—an important question which has not been much discussed: see further chapter XV.2 below.

therefore be forecast in terms of, changes in the hire-purchase regulations[1].

Investment in stocks—the fifth major category of demand—has fluctuated largely and erratically; and it seems clear from many remarks in the published documents that the official forecasters have had no great confidence in the forecasts of this component.   In theory it should perhaps be possible to explain fluctuations in stocks in terms of an equilibrium level of stocks, and of departures from the equilibrium position in the past which are likely to give rise to 'corrective' movements in future[2].   There has however been little investigation of how far such an approach is helpful in practice, partly because the statistics have been poor.   It is probably fair to say that official forecasters, by a somewhat intuitive application of such theoretical considerations, have in recent years at least, been able to foresee something of the fluctuations that have occurred.

Since the object of policy has been to keep demand in balance with supply, it is in logic as important to forecast potential supply as to forecast effective demand.   The development of future supply depends on a host of technical factors, about which the government has not proved particularly well-informed. This was especially true in the early years, when output depended almost entirely on supply not demand limitations, and was consistently underestimated.   In later years the problem has been rather different.   If for several years demand has been below the 'full capacity' ceiling, the present level of the ceiling can be estimated only by extrapolation of the vaguely surmised trend from the last year of full capacity working; or by direct enquiries about the under-utilization of capacity—a concept not yet brought fully within the zone of the measurable[3]. It is fair to say that on this matter policy still operates, if not in the dark, at least in the twilight.

Because of the shortage of foreign exchange reserves, as much attention has been devoted to assessing the external as the internal situation.   Since most items in the balance of payments are influenced more by developments in other countries than by developments in the United Kingdom, this has involved a fairly elaborate assessment of trends in the world economy[4].   Basically any such assessment must depend, first, on a forecast of developments in other industrial countries, principally in North America and Western Europe—a forecast which in principle is similar to that undertaken for the United Kingdom itself; and, second, on a forecast of how such developments are likely to impinge on the primary producing countries, principally in the southern hemisphere. Balance of payments forecasts have been made in the light of such assessments. They have, in brief, been a compound of a forecast of exports (as already

---

[1] See chapter XI, §§ 1–3.
[2] See chapter XI.5 below.
[3] See chapter IV above and especially figure 4.1.
[4] In recent *Economic Surveys*, the review of developments in the past year has usually started with a brief survey of world economic developments.

described, depending in part on a view about world trade); a forecast of imports (dependent partly on forecast output at home, partly on a view about stocks of imported materials); a forecast of import prices (also depending on the view about world trade); and a forecast of the invisible items (depending partly on the view of world trade, partly on many items of a governmental nature).

The official forecasters have at times been criticized for not making use of econometric methods; and there are doubtless many who would criticize them on this score[1]. This question cannot be fully discussed here, but it may be useful to indicate some of the main points in the debate. First, it should be emphasized that the replacement of the present informal methods by an econometric forecast would not necessarily change the logical process entirely. Most econometric forecasts treat some items of expenditure (such as government expenditure) as 'autonomous' (and thus to be projected, as now, on the basis of 'direct' information about the government's intentions). It would be possible to replace the present projection of investment, based on 'direct' information about firms' intentions, by an econometric projection involving some knowledge of lagged relationships (e.g. the dependence of investment on, for instance, profits in the previous year). For a forecast extending only a year ahead, this would probably not be an improvement—though, if forecasts extending two years ahead were needed, it might be the only method to use.

Second, the present 'informal' methods already make allowance for what were called above 'cross relationships', e.g. for the influence of high investment or export demand on personal incomes and hence on consumers' demand. In what is essentially an arithmetic method, this involves a process of successive approximation[2]. It is probably correct to argue that this process could be as well done by an econometric model designed on the same scheme of thought. But though the effort to design one might quite possibly improve matters, it would not change the logical process[3].

[1]See Marris [1954], *op. cit.*; and for a general defence of econometric methods, H. Theil [1958], *Economic Forecasts and Policy.* A defence of the alternative—somewhat inadequately described as 'the national income approach' to forecasting—is given by V. L. Bassie [1951], 'Recent Developments in Short-Term Forecasting' in *Short-Term Economic Forecasting* (Studies in Income and Wealth, vol. 17).

[2]Compare Neild and Shirley [1961], *op. cit.*, pp. 14–6: 'Thus the forecast is made by bringing together forecasts of each main item and then juggling them until they fit into a consistent pattern. The main items are estimated independently but allowance is made for the interaction between them. The main interactions are the effect of changes in non-consumption demand on personal incomes and consumption—this emerges in the estimates of employment, hours and incomes—and the effect on private investment of changes in other items of demand. The interactions are, however, generally assumed to be fairly slight in the short period for which forecasts are made'.

[3]In particular, it appears not to be true—as suggested by Marris [1954], p. 771—that the process of successive approximation amounts to begging the main question at the outset. The 'multiplier-accelerator' relations which necessitate the process have to be allowed for. But in an economy operating fairly close to full employment, they modify, rather than transform, the picture.

Third, many of the econometric models so far developed have been unable to produce accurate forecasts.   In their study of the United States, for instance, Messrs Klein and Goldberger congratulate themselves on being able to forecast the national product to within five per cent[1]: but an error of this size would bring down Chancellors, if not governments.   Econometric models have had some success in 'explaining' the pre-war trade cycle in the United States between the wars, for the much wider range of fluctuation in the main economic magnitudes then made it much easier to estimate interrelationships.   But in a managed economy, the range of fluctuation is of an altogether smaller order.   Moreover, policy has to operate within narrow limits.   Deviations of output of plus or minus two per cent matter: yet this is within true statistical error attaching to most econometric forecasts.

However attractive in theory, the practical merits of econometric forecasting are thus not overwhelming.   My own view is that econometric methods have little immediately to offer of practical use; but that, as an investment for the future, it is worth experimenting intensively to see whether better results cannot be obtained.   If, as may well be, forecasts extending two or more years ahead are going to be required in future, econometric forecasting might well have something to contribute.

2. DIFFICULTIES OF ASSESSING FORECASTS

There are many difficulties in making a post mortem on the forecasts.   This makes it possible to make only the broadest sort of assessment.

A first difficulty is that after 1951, quantitative forecasts were not published. Qualitative indications were given in the *Economic Survey* and the budget speech, in most cases designed to give to a careful reader a sufficiently precise indication of what was intended.   But this cryptic method of communication is not always efficient; and even when understood, verbal hints cannot be

---

[1]L. R. Klein and A. S. Goldberger [1955], *An Econometric Model of the United States, 1929–1952*, p. 82.   The authors claim that this model was able to predict the 1954 recession in the United States.   This recession, however, was largely due to a decline in investment in stocks; and while the model contains an equation for fixed investment, it contains none for stock behaviour.   An intuitive guess about stock changes was included: as the authors say (p. 105),

> 'we found it better to correct equations selectively for persistent biases in residuals and independent outside information rather than assume either that all disturbances are zero or equal to the estimated value for the preceding year'.

Success in forecasting the 1954 recession was entirely due to this 'correction' of the investment equation (see pp. 10–3; and—for the basis of the 1954 forecasts—pp. ix and 99).

Klein has also developed a quarterly model for the British economy: see Klein, R. J. Ball, A. Hazlewood and P. Vandome [1961], *An Econometric Model of the United Kingdom*. The forecast of industrial output, the main magnitude forecast, has so far proved to be wildly out: see A. Hazlewood and P. Vandome [1961], 'A Post Mortem on Econometric Forecasts for 1959', *B. Oxford Inst. Statist.*, February 1961; and Neild and Shirley [1961], *op. cit.*

translated back into figures with perfect accuracy   This difficulty is probably a little less serious than it sounds.   Even when forecasts are expressed in figures, they are not intended to be understood as being accurate to the last digit; and quite large revisions are often made within a short space of time.   Even someone working with access to the official figures might therefore not have been able to give a much better picture of what the forecasters intended[1].

The actual course of events, however, also cannot be stated with great accuracy.   The national income estimates have been subject to frequent— almost yearly—revision; and many of the revisions have altered the estimates very considerably.   In many cases, a revision of the estimates for one item, such as consumers' expenditure, will alter the estimates for all years in the same direction, leaving the estimate of the year-to-year changes less affected.   For this reason, in the following comparisons, the absolute figures forecast are not shown, but *forecast changes* are compared with *estimated actual changes*.

Revisions of the estimates of actual changes have however still been considerable.   These have been partly due to additional statistical information, and partly (particularly in the early years) to changes in the definition of different items.   In the following comparisons, adjustments have been made on account of the major definitional changes, so as to put 'forecasts' and 'actuals' on a similar basis; but this is not always possible for minor changes in definition.   For the early years therefore two estimates are shown for the actual changes: first, that made immediately after the event (and likely therefore to be on the same definitional basis); and, second, the latest available estimate (presumably, in other ways, the most accurate).   This gives some idea of the very large range of uncertainty attaching to estimates of the actual out-turn: the *ex post* estimates are, indeed, almost as much likely to be in error, as the forecasts.   For later years, for the sake of simplicity, only one set of 'actuals' is shown; but these, too, are subject to error.

A third difficulty is that the forecasts were made as a guide to policy: and in many cases policy was changed after the forecasts were made in order to correct the situation as originally forecast.   A comparison of events as affected by policy changes with forecasts made before policy was changed would therefore be uninformative.   The only useful procedure seems to be to correct for the effect of policy changes, so as to put both 'forecast' and 'actual' on the same basis.   But (as will be shown at greater length in later chapters) no exact estimate of the effect of policy changes is possible.   Even if one knew how far changes in tax rates had affected consumers' expenditure, it would still be difficult to know how much to allow for secondary effects, for instance, on

---

[1]A contemporary attempt at reconstructing the quantitative forecasts for the years 1953–7 was made by Professor R. C. Tress in the *London Cambridge econ. B.* (issues for June each year).   I have checked my versions against his.   But most of my guesses in table 5.4 could be in error by £50 million either side, and in those cases indicated (by being bracketed) as most dubious, by considerably more.

investment.   In making adjustments for policy changes, only direct effects were allowed for; and no allowance was made for 'multiplier-accelerator' repercussions[1].

Another difficulty is that, as already noted, there has been considerable development in the official forecasts.   Whereas in the earlier years the forecasts in effect tried to predict the change in expenditure and output between one calendar year and another, in recent years they have tried to predict the change which will take place in the course of the ensuing twelve months.   It is possible, with some approximation, to put the later forecasts into the same form as the earlier ones; and for the sake of consistency this has been done.   But the kind of comparison shown is a poor measure of forecasting ability.   An arithmetical example will illustrate this point.   Suppose that actual and forecast developments were as follows:

	Previous year		Current year	
	Average for year	Terminal rate	Average for year	Terminal rate
Actual	100	105	106	107
Forecast	100	105	104	103

Comparison of the yearly averages would suggest that the forecast picked up two thirds of the actual change (a forecast increase of four against an actual increase of six).   Nevertheless, on the example shown, the forecast has misrepresented the direction of change *in the course of the ensuing year*, and misestimated the rate at the end of the year by quite a large amount.   The tables shown therefore need careful interpretation[2].

In assessing the results of official forecasts, it would be wrong to treat them as exercises in unmotivated foresight.   It is for instance tempting, if ten economic magnitudes are forecast, to compare the forecasts with the actual out-turn, award marks for each result and add them up in some kind of total score[3].   This would be misleading, for two reasons.   First, it would involve an element of double counting: for some items forecast are no more than a sum of separate components; and changes in some others may be partly a causal result of changes elsewhere.   Second, the forecasts were prepared as an aid to the formulation of policy; and the only mistakes which matter are mistakes in forecasting magnitudes which it was the main business of policy to control.   For this reason, the following assessment of official forecasting pays most attention to forecasts of total final demand.   In the last analysis, however,

---

[1]Rough estimates of the effect of policy changes will be given in chapter XV.2 below. The adjustment for policy effects in the present chapter is based on these estimates.

[2]As will be clear from the example shown, some of the apparent error in a forecast of changes between annual averages may be due, not to forecasting error, but to later revision of the estimate of the actual change in the latter half of the previous year.

[3]See for example H. Theil [1955], 'Who forecasts best?' *Int. econ. Pap.*, no. 5; and [1958], *Economic Forecasts and Policy*, chapter II.

K

the only proper criterion by which to judge official forecasts is not their technical accuracy, but whether or not they misled policy.

3. THE FORECASTS FOR THE YEARS 1947–51

Economic forecasts were published in each of the *Economic Surveys* for the years 1947–51, which became progressively more quantitative, confident and elaborate. The 1947 *Survey* contained indications so truncated that it is hazardous to guess what changes were in fact expected (table 5.1). Those for 1948–50 all contained forecasts for the *value* of each of at least four main categories of national expenditure, and also for the main categories of national saving (table 5.3). The 1951 *Survey* contained in addition forecasts of 'real' changes in expenditure and output, and hence, by implication, of price changes. As already indicated, up to about 1951 the problems of policy were rather different from what they were thereafter; and since there was general excess demand till about this time, the forecasts were designed to measure the size of the 'inflationary gap'.

There has been considerable theoretical discussion (more especially in Sweden) as to how this should be done, and indeed whether it is logically possible[1]. These theoretical difficulties, which however would seem to have been exaggerated, may be explained as follows. The forecasts were designed to throw light on budgetary policy, whose aim could be taken to be to eliminate excess demand. But excess demand, if unchecked, would tend to diminish itself, i.e. it would cause a rise in incomes which might (through the progressive tax system) disproportionately inflate tax receipts, and (dividends being sticky) disproportionately inflate corporate saving. Forecasts of national income which included a purely realistic forecast of price increases would therefore understate the true budgetary problem. Whether or not there is any sense in forecasting the 'inflationary gap' would thus seem to turn essentially on whether or not prices are in fact 'sticky' in face of excess demand. In the United Kingdom, prices appear sufficiently inflexible for such an estimate to be possible. Nevertheless, they are not completely so; and the theoretical ideal would seem to be to forecast national income at the level of prices which would rule in the absence of excess demand. It was out of deference to such considerations, and as an approximation to this rule, that the 1949 *Economic Survey* showed forecasts at 'end-1948 prices': later *Surveys* were less explicit. But it was in truth a second-order refinement. At no time was any induced price rise likely to go far enough substantially to modify the balance of saving and investment.

For reasons already given, the forecasts are compared in tables 5.1 and 5.3 with two alternative estimates of the changes that actually occurred. These differ so widely as to make only broad conclusions possible. On any reckoning,

---

[1]For a fuller discussion and detailed references see chapter XIII.1 below.

Table 5.1. *Forecasts of changes in expenditure, 1947–51 (£m., year-to-year changes in value[a])*

Change from preceding year to:	1947[d]	1948	1949	1950	1951
Consumers' expenditure					
Forecast	(250)	450[e]	175[f]	275[g]	675[g]
Actual	*600*	*550*	*300*	*475*	*700*
	or 625	*or 600*	*or 350*	*or 500*	*or 725*
Public authorities[b]					
Forecast	(−175)	−100	125	175	475
Actual	*−300*	*−150*	*275*	*−25*	*375*
	or −550	*or 25*	*or 225*	*or 100*	
Gross domestic investment[c]					
Forecast	(425)	−100	−25	—	600
Actual	*725*	*300*	*−125*	*300*	*1,150*
	or 950	*or −50*	*or −75*		*or 1,075*
Net investment abroad					
Forecast	(50)	425	125	125	−325
Actual	*−300*	*500*	*75*	*200*	*−750*
	or −125	*or 450*		*or 250*	*or −700*
***less* Net indirect taxes**					
Forecast	—	−225[e]	—[f]	−75[g]	−75[g]
Actual	—	*−175*	*−25*	*−125*	*−225*
		or −125	*or —*		
Gross national product[c]					
Forecast	(550)	450	400	500	1,350
Actual	*725*	*1,025*	*500*	*875*	*1,250*
	or 900	*or 900*	*or 575*	*or 1,025*	

Forecasts are from *Economic Surveys*, 1947–51. Since in each case consumption was treated as the 'residual' item in the national accounts no adjustment to implied factor cost changes was made on account of budget changes. But to allow for budget changes in indirect taxes or subsidies, adjustments have been made to the forecast changes in consumers' expenditure at market prices and in net indirect taxes (see below).

Actuals are (i) as estimated in *NIWP* immediately after the year forecast and (ii) the most recent available estimates as given in *NI & E* [1957] and [1960].

[a]All figures rounded to £25 million: the forecasts for 1949 were intended to be at prices ruling at the beginning of the year, i.e. presumably below the prices that would have been forecast.

[b]Current expenditure on goods and services.

[c]Includes stock appreciation (not shown separately from investment in the forecasts).

[d]The forecasts shown are a somewhat hazardous deduction from the figures given in the 1947 *Survey*, which gave only a forecast for the value of imports, together with a forecast percentage allocation of national product (including imports) at factor cost.

[e]Adjustment for budget changes, +£75 million.

[f]Adjustment for budget changes, −£25 million.

[g]Adjustment for budget changes, +£50 million.

however, the forecasts for the period 1947–51 were not conspicuously successful. Expenditure by the government was itself badly forecast, the error averaging over £100 million.   The figures for domestic investment here include not only fixed investment (which was partially controlled, though not well forecast), but investment in stocks, and also stock appreciation.   This total was generally underestimated, on average by some £300 million.   The change in the foreign balance was, surprisingly enough, forecast better, the average error being around £150 million (the main failure being in the 1951 forecast).   The increase in consumers' expenditure was also (except in 1951) generally underestimated (which must account for most of the underestimate of the forecast increase in *indirect* taxes).   The increase in the value of total national expenditure and national product was (again, except in 1951) consistently understated—on average by £200–£300 million, or by almost a third of the actual increase.

The major errors, in all cases, probably arose through one major mistake. Throughout the 'inflationary' period, the increase in real output was greatly understated.   It was not till 1951, by which time pockets of excess supply were beginning to appear, that the forecasts caught up with events.   Forecasts were given only for the volume of *industrial* production; but since other parts of national product are less variable, they are a good indication of official expectations.

Table 5.2. *Forecasts of industrial production, 1948–51 (percentage increase over previous year)*

	1948	1949	1950	1951
Forecast	small[a]	about 4	3½	4
Actual	9	6	7½	3

[a]The 1948 *Survey* gave no clear indication.   An attempt to reconstruct in detail the original assumptions suggests that the change assumed may have been negligible.

The general result of increasing output was to permit all types of expenditure to increase.   Resources being partially immobile, different types of output naturally flowed towards different, specific types of final demand.   Unexpected output increases therefore tended to produce unexpected expenditure increases all round.   In particular, the intended proportionate distribution of extra output as between increasing consumption on the one hand, and increasing investment and reducing the foreign deficit on the other, appears not to have been greatly disturbed.   As intended[1], the growth of consumption was kept down, and exports and investment took the greater part of the growth of output. Between the end of 1947 and the end of 1950, tax rates were not much changed; and this diversion of resources away from consumption is roughly what might be expected to follow in the face of expanding output and incomes[2].

[1]See what is said about the 1948 Long Term Programme in chapter II.3 above.   The planned increases *in value* shown in table 5.1 are a poor guide to the intended allocation of the increase in *real* resources.

[2]See chapter VII, §§ 2–3 below.

It is therefore a nice question whether the erroneous forecasts in fact misled policy. Disinflation was more rapid than the government had a right to expect; but at the same time the government probably underestimated the degree of disinflation required. It can be argued that the attempt each year to predict in considerable detail the composition of national expenditure was, as things turned out, largely wasted effort. The chief function of the annual forecasts may in effect have been no more than that of providing arithmetic illustration for an unassailable general argument—that taxes should be kept high to counter inflation.

Table 5.3. *Forecasts of saving and investment, 1948–51 (£m., year-to-year changes in value)*

		1948	1949	1950	1951
Public authorities' saving[a]					
Forecast		425[d]	−75[e]	−125	250[f]
Actual		*775*	*−175*	*200*	*325*
	or	*400*	or *−50*	or *100*	or *300*
Corporate saving					
Forecast		—	25	(100)	100
Actual		*125*	*−50*	*75*	*25*
	or	*150*	or *−125*	or *325*	or *−75*
Depreciation allowances					
Forecast		50	125	25	−125
Actual		*75*	*200*	*100*	*75*
			or *150*		or *50*
Personal saving[b]					
Forecast		−150	25	(100)	25
Actual		*−150*	*−25*	*50*	*−75*
	or	*−200*	or *50*		or *25*
Total investment at home and abroad[c]					
Forecast		325	100	100	250
Actual		*825*	*−50*	*425*	*350*
	or	*425*	or *25*	or *575*	or *300*

Sources as for table 5.1 above. To allow for budget changes subsequent to the forecasts, adjustments have been made for forecast public saving (as noted below); corresponding inverse adjustments have been made to the components of private saving.

[a]Current surplus of public authorities *plus* capital transfers *plus* additions to private tax reserves: no adjustment is made for capital taxes.

[b]For comparability with 1948 *Survey*, includes sums required to meet capital taxes.

[c]Includes stock appreciation.

[d]Adjustment for budget changes, +£25 million.

[e]Adjustment for budget changes, −£75 million.

[f]Adjustment for budget changes, +£325 million.

During these years the budget argument was couched as a deduction from the forecast of the 'combined capital account' (table 5.3). Forecasts were made both of the 'required' national saving—the forecast level of investment at home and abroad—and of the saving likely to be forthcoming either as undistributed profits, or (at current tax rates) in the form of a budget surplus. Unless personal saving made up the difference, taxes (it was argued) would have to be raised. None of the items however was accurately forecast; and the errors could clearly be as great as the tax changes made at any budget[1]. The 'combined capital account' is one way of summarizing the factors about which judgements have unavoidably to be made. But the judgements that can in fact be made are much less precise than the figures suggested. All that can be claimed is that the errors roughly cancelled out in practice. The fact that, till 1951, tax changes were on balance small may be because the forecasts were used only as a rough general guide to policy. As already remarked, the economic arithmetic underlying Sir Stafford Cripps's budgets was never very clearly set out[2]; and this was, perhaps, a practical expression of a justified scepticism.

The forecasts in the 1951 *Economic Survey* were the most ambitious to be published; and the errors thus disclosed have been subject to the most criticism subsequently. It can however be argued that 1951 demonstrates most clearly the usefulness of making explicit forecasts. There were three very large changes, to some extent predictable, which no rational policy could ignore. First, defence expenditure was planned to increase. Second, import prices were expected to rise: this (by raising retail prices more than incomes) was likely to reduce consumers' purchasing power. Third, the defence programme had a highly concentrated impact: cutting consumption therefore would not release the engineering output that the programme required. The conclusion drawn was that though taxes should be raised to reduce consumers' claims on resources, they should be raised by much less than the expected increase in government expenditure. There can be no doubt that the conclusion was correct. Consumption fell a little, as planned (table 5.4); and if there was any mistake, it was that consumption was reduced as much as it was[3]. The policy that brought this about would not have been devised if prospects had not been assessed with some care and detail.

Nevertheless the 1951 forecasts were falsified in several important ways. Both government expenditure, and output, were overestimated—errors which were perhaps partly connected and partly offsetting (table 5.4). More important,

---

[1] The crucial figure is the forecast of personal saving. Errors here are difficult to interpret, for at a time of excess demand personal saving probably depends as much on the availability of supplies as on the propensity to save. Thus the fact that personal saving appears to have been correctly forecast in 1948 does not necessarily mean that persons *wished* to save either as much as they did save or as much as they were predicted to want to save.

[2] See chapter II.3.

[3] This question is considered more fully at a later stage: see chapter XV.5 below.

investment in stocks was enormous, not, as forecast, trivial.   The result was partly to increase the pressure of demand on home resources, and to turn 1951 very pronouncedly into a boom year; and partly, also, to increase imports unexpectedly.   Equally important, income from abroad fell instead of increasing, and the terms of trade worsened more than foreseen (table 5.6)[1].

If it is difficult to judge how far these forecasting errors misled policy, this is chiefly because it is difficult to know what the best policy would have been[2]. If the balance of payments forecast had been correctly foreseen, economic policy would almost certainly have been more cautious.   Nevertheless the balance of payments crisis was not primarily the effect of policy; nor could any change of policy *at the turn of 1950 and 1951* have done much to reduce the severity of the crisis which was to come in the autumn of 1951[2].   Policy may, similarly, be criticized for underrating the dangers of internal inflation: demand certainly carried the economy well beyond the ideal level.   But when would action have had to be taken to deal with this?   Might it not have been *before* 1951?   And may not the steep increase in taxation of consumers in 1951 itself have done something to worsen the stock recession—then quite unforeseen—in 1952?   Such questions suggest that it may have been the theory of fiscal policy, as much as the forecasts themselves, that was at fault.   But it may also be—the forces at work being extremely powerful—that no policy could have availed to stabilize them; and that if policy, though not ideal, was nevertheless fairly sensible, this was largely due to the forecasts, defective though they were.

4.   THE FORECASTS FOR THE YEARS 1951–60

After 1951, the main forecasts were in terms of 'real' expenditure and its conse-quences for output.   This was partly due to development of better estimates of changes in 'real' expenditure in past years.   But in the new situation, with

[1]For various reasons, a fair post mortem on the 1951 balance of payments forecasts is particularly difficult.   The deterioration in invisibles was chiefly due to the Persian seizure of the Abadan oil refinery, which probably reduced invisible income by about £100 million— and which could hardly have been expected to have been allowed for.   Furthermore, because prices changed drastically, the picture is greatly affected by which year one takes as a basis for estimating the changes in the volume of exports and imports and the terms of trade.   The 'actual' changes shown in table 5.4, though adjusted to 1950 prices, are based on subsequent estimates at 1954 prices.   If they had started with estimates at 1950 prices, the change in the volume of imports would have been shown as very much larger; exports instead of falling slightly would have shown a slight increase; and the deterioration in the terms of trade would have been shown as less severe.   But, on any reckoning, the forecasts of each of the items in the balance of payments were over-optimistic; and thus in total largely underestimated the deterioration that took place.   As far as the reserves were concerned, the unforeseen deterioration in the overseas sterling area balance was as important as that in the United Kingdom's balance (see chapter II.4).

[2]This assessment of forecasts and policy in 1951 is one of the passages I have had to rewrite in the light of my own later conclusions in chapter XV.   This illustrates, I think, the difficulty of any simple assessment of the effects of forecasting errors.

Table 5.4. *Forecasts of real expenditure and output, 1951–60 (£m., year-to-year changes at constant factor costs[a])*

| | | | | | | | of which | |
Change from preceding year to	Con- sumers' expen- diture	Public autho- rities[b]	Gross fixed invest- ment	Invest- ment in stocks	Exports, goods and services	Total final expen- diture	Gross domes- tic product	Imports, goods and services
1951								
Forecast	−50[c]	400	(25)	50	100	525	325	200
Actual	*−150*	*175*	*−25*	*675*	*−50*	*625*	*375*	*250*
1952								
Forecast	—[d]	150	(−50)	(−200)	50	−50	250	−300
Actual	*25*	*275*	*—*	*−475*	*−75*	*−250*	*25*	*−275*
1953								
Forecast	(150)[e]	150	150	200	75	(725)[e]	(450)	(275)
Actual	*400*	*100*	*200*	*75*	*75*	*850*	*600*	*250*
1954								
Forecast	(150)	75	(75)	(−100)	(−)	(200)	(200)	(−)
Actual	*450*	*—*	*175*	*−75*	*200*	*750*	*625*	*125*
1955								
Forecast	300[f]	25	150	—	(200)	(675)[f]	(475)	(200)
Actual	*375*	*−75*	*125*	*225*	*250*	*900*	*450*	*450*
1956								
Forecast	(150)	−50	125	(−225)	(250)	(250)	(200)	50
Actual	*150*	*—*	*175*	*−25*	*225*	*525*	*525*	*—*
1957								
Forecast	(250)[g]	−50	100	(−50)	(100)	(350)[g]	(250)	(100)
Actual	*300*	*−100*	*150*	*−50*	*75*	*375*	*225*	*150*
1958								
Forecast	(225)[h]	—	50	(−250)	−100	(−75)[h]	(−75)	—
Actual	*250*	*−25*	*—*	*−150*	*−100*	*−25*	*−75*	*50*
1959								
Forecast	(400)[i]	50	150	(50)	(50)	(700)[i]	(550)	(150)
Actual	*500*	*75*	*200*	*75*	*125*	*975*	*500*	*475*
1960								
Forecast	500[j]	175	350	250	(350)	(1,625)[j]	(1,325)	300
Actual	*450*	*75*	*325*	*425*	*225*	*1,500*	*825*	*675*

Forecasts are based on statements in annual *Economic Surveys* and budget speeches. For years 1953–7, the quantifications given by R. C. Tress in articles in *London Cambridge econ. B.* for June each year have also been consulted; and for 1959–60, the assessment by Neild and Shirley [1961] in *Nat. Inst. econ. R.*, May 1961.   The more hazardous quantifications are shown in brackets.   Forecasts have been adjusted, where appropriate, for effects of subsequent changes in tax rates and credit regulations.   These adjustments are however dubious: the mean of the estimates used in chap. XV.2 below are used, i.e. some delay is assumed before a tax change affects consumption.   No allowance is made for indirect 'multiplier-accelerator' effects.   Estimated *actual* changes are derived from the 1954 market price estimates in *NI &E* [1961], adjusted to price basis of year preceding forecast.

[a]All changes are expressed in prices ruling in year preceding year forecast: all figures rounded to £25 million.
[b]Current expenditure on goods and services.
[c]No adjustment for budget changes, since forecasts assumed subsequent budget.
[d]No adjustment for budget changes, since *Survey* (with forecasts) came after the budget.
[e]Includes £75 million for budget changes.
[f]Includes £50 million for budget changes in April and October.
[g]Includes £25 million for budget changes.
[h]Includes £75 million for budget changes and autumn credit relaxations.
[i]Includes £100 million for budget changes.
[j]Deducts £50 million for April hire-purchase restrictions.

Table 5.5. *Forecasting errors, 1951–60 (£m., constant prices)*

Forecast from preceding year to	Consumers' expenditure	Public authorities	Fixed investment	Investment in stocks	Exports	Total final expenditure	of which	
							GDP	Imports
1951	100	225	(50)	−625	150	−100	−50	−50
1952	−25	−125	(−50)	(275)	125	200	225	−25
1953	(−250)	50	−50	125	—	(−125)	(−150)	25
1954	(−300)	75	(−100)	(−25)	(−200)	(−550)	(−425)	(−125)
1955	−75	100	25	−225	(−50)	(−225)	25	(−250)
1956	(—)	−50	−50	(25)	(25)	(−50)	(−100)	(50)
1957	(−50)	50	−50	(—)	(25)	(−25)	(25)	(−50)
1958	(−25)	25	50	(−100)	—	(−50)	(—)	−50
1959	(−100)	−25	−50	(−25)	(−75)	(−275)	(50)	(−325)
1960	50	100	25	−175	(125)	(125)	(500)	−375
Average error	100	75	50	150	75	175	150	125
Average bias	−50	50	−25	−75	—	−100	—	−100

For sources and notes see table 5.4.

excess demand no longer to be taken for granted, it was a chief object of the forecasts to estimate changes in the degree of under-utilization of capacity; and forecasts in 'real' terms were necessary for this purpose, if they had not been before.

For these years, only a very broad assessment of the forecasts is possible. Table 5.4 is an attempt to 'requantify' the official forecasts, but with the available data this cannot be done with great accuracy. The table shows the forecasts in the form in which in most years they were made, i.e. as forecasts of the change between the average levels expected in the calendar year ahead as compared with the year past. Thus, at the time the forecast was made, something like half the 'forecast' change may (on average) have already occurred; and as already explained, comparison of 'forecasts' and 'actuals' in this form provides an insensitive measure, and appears greatly to exaggerate true forecasting ability.

Figure 5.1 compares the forecast and the actual change each year in total final expenditure; and thus is a convenient summary of the main results. This appears to suggest that in each year the direction of change was correctly foreseen, and that the extent of the change was also fairly well estimated. This however is undoubtedly too favourable an impression. Much of the dip in output 'forecast' for 1952, and again for 1958, must for instance have already occurred by the time the forecasts were made. Similarly the forecasts for 1954 must have greatly underestimated the increase in expenditure that took place after the forecasts were made. The apparent underestimate in 1959 is further considered below.

Fig. 5.1.   Forecasts of final expenditure, 1951–60

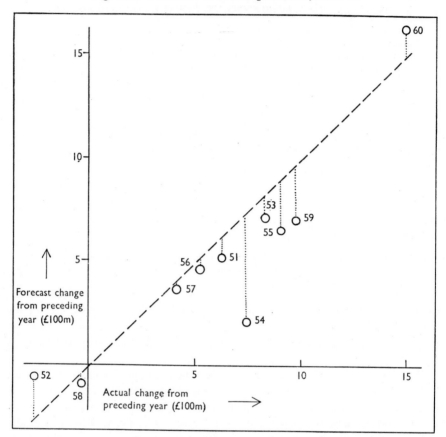

The results are set out in more detail in table 5.4, and the forecasting errors are analysed in table 5.5.   On the 'calendar year' basis shown in the table, most items of expenditure appear to have been forecast to within £100 million: on a 'year ahead' basis the errors must have been larger, and therefore quite appreciable.   The fact that investment in stocks appears to have been rather worse forecast than other items is chiefly due to the big mistake in 1951.   There appears to have been some bias in the forecasts, and a tendency on average to underestimate the increase in expenditure: this appears to account in fact for most of the error in the forecast of total final expenditure.   Similarly the error in forecasting imports was mostly due to a tendency to underestimate the increase that actually occurred.

Official statements about how the balance of payments was expected to develop have been even less precise than those about internal prospects.   Figure

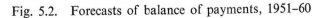

Fig. 5.2.   Forecasts of balance of payments, 1951–60

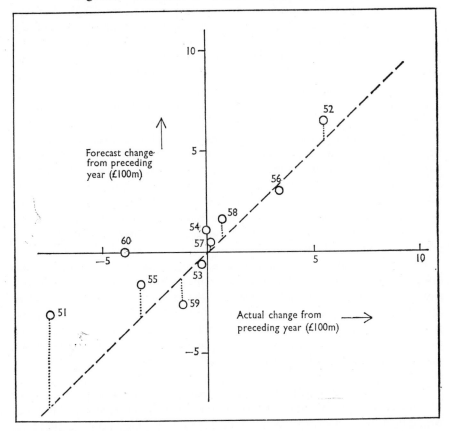

5.2 appears to suggest that the balance of payments forecasts were generally fairly good; and in particular (as with the internal forecasts) that the direction of changes was always correctly foreseen. This again, however, is misleading. It seems clear that *deteriorations* in the balance were usually seriously underestimated. But bearing in mind the form of the forecasts and the date when they were made, it is probably fair to conclude that very little of any further deterioration after the forecasts were made was foreseen. This failure appears to have been chiefly due to the failure to foresee large increases in imports in boom years. The forecasts of *improvements* in the balance appear a bit better: but since there were only two years of marked improvement, there is little to judge by. As might be expected[1], errors in forecasting the terms of trade tended to go with opposite errors in forecasting exports and invisible income.

[1]For analysis of the mechanism of swings in the balance of payments, see chapter XV.5 below.

The general conclusion must therefore be that though they never seem to have told the opposite of the truth, the forecasters, not surprisingly, were not always conspicuously successful. As already argued, a final assessment of how far the imperfections of forecasting mattered must depend on a view of what policy ought to have been; and this cannot be attempted at this stage. Two conclusions of the later analysis may however be anticipated, so as to come to some provisional conclusions on the forecasts.

First, some types of fluctuation are largely self-correcting within a period of two or three years; and also happen to be difficult to control. This is true of stock fluctuations[1]; and also, to a large extent, of short-period fluctuations in the balance of payments. Thus it can be argued that policy measures are bound to be too late to even out the short-term fluctuations in the balance of payments, and can only hope to act on the general trend[2]. While it may be desirable to foresee such fluctuations, it may not be too serious if they are not foreseen. Since policy, in this period, was heavily orientated towards the balance of payments, failure to foresee some of the swings might, paradoxically, even be considered to have had good results.

The decade of the 'fifties, it has already been suggested[3], contained two periods (1952–5 and 1958–60) when demand was expanding more rapidly than productive capacity; and two periods of recession (1952) or pause (1956–7). It will be argued later that these fluctuations can quite largely be attributed to economic policy, which alternated between expansionary and restrictive phases; and that this was one of the main mistakes of policy[4]. The main question, perhaps, may then be whether such mistakes in policy can be attributed to mistaken forecasts.

It is probably fair to say that in the last decade we have learnt more about the way the economy works; and that given the same circumstances again, policy would do better. In particular it would probably be more cautious about the extent to which demand was stimulated at any one time; and by now may have begun to have a longer horizon than the year ahead. But if so, it would be a matter of a more realistic general view of the economy and of the effects of policy, than an improvement in forecasting as such.

On three occasions, however, the mistakes in the forecasts may have contributed to mistakes in policy. Thus—though it is arguable whether the stock recession of 1952 could have been entirely prevented—it was not foreseen, and the 'new monetary policy' of 1952 must, if anything, have made it worse. The second occasion was in 1954, when there was a large surge in demand, which appears hardly to have been foreseen at all. This was the more serious because the boom in demand continued into 1955; and, in the light of hindsight,

---

[1]See chapter XVI.2 below.
[2]See chapter XV.5 below.
[3]Chapter IV, figure 4.1.
[4]See chapter XV.

Table 5.6. *Forecast annual changes in balance of payments, 1951–60 (£m., year-to-year changes)*

	Volume of exports[a]	Volume of imports[ab]	Terms of trade[c]	Net invisibles[d]	Balance of payments
1951					
Forecast	100	200	−250	50	−300
Actual[e]	−50	250	−400	−50	−750
1952					
Forecast	50	−300	150	150	650
Actual	−75	−275	275	75	550
1953					
Forecast	75	275	(200)	(−50)	(−50)
Actual	75	250	225	−75	−25
1954					
Forecast	—	—	(100)	—	(100)
Actual	200	125	−25	−50	—
1955					
Forecast	(200)	(200)	(−150)	—	(−150)
Actual	250	450	25	−125	−300
1956					
Forecast	(250)	50	(—)	100	(300)
Actual	225	—	125	—	350
1957					
Forecast	(100)	(100)	(50)	(—)	(50)
Actual	75	150	75	25	25
1958					
Forecast	−100	(—)	(200)	50	(150)
Actual	−100	50	275	−50	75
1959					
Forecast	(50)	(150)	—	(—)	−100
Actual	125	475	200	−100	−250
1960					
Forecast	(350)	300	−50	(—)	(—)
Actual	225	675	150	−100	−400
Forecasting errors (+ = *overestimate of forecast value*)					
1951	150	−50	150	100	450
1952	125	−25	−125	75	100
1953	—	25	(−25)	(25)	(−25)
1954	(−200)	−125	(125)	50	(100)
1955	(−50)	(−250)	(−175)	125	(150)
1956	(25)	50	(−125)	100	(−50)
1957	(25)	(−50)	(−25)	(−25)	(25)
1958	—	(−50)	(−75)	100	(75)
1959	(−75)	(−325)	−200	(100)	150
1960	(125)	−375	−200	(100)	(400)
Average error	75	125	125	75	150
Average bias	—	−100[b]	−75	75	125

Forecasts from *Economic Surveys* and budget speeches, which generally gave vague indications only, the more dubious guesses being shown in brackets.   Forecasts of volumes are as in table 5.4; this means that imports (and current balances) include small adjustments for budget changes.   *Actuals* are from *NI & E* [1961].

[a]At prices of previous year.

[b]+ indicates increase or overestimate of imports, which however *reduces* total current balance.

[c]Calculated as change in exports less imports at current prices, *minus* change in exports less imports at constant prices.

[d]Includes defence aid.

[e]For the uncertainties surrounding the estimates of the 'actual' changes, see note in accompanying text.

the 1954 budget may seem a good occasion at which to have tried to moderate the pace of expansion before it got out of hand. For any strong restrictive action to have been taken, it would have been necessary for there to have been at the beginning of 1954 forecasts extending not only over 1954 but into 1955 as well. But even a correct forecast for 1954 might possibly have seemed to counsel against the stimulation of investment administered in that year.

The third occasion was 1959. The large expansion in demand in that year was very largely an effect of the sweeping credit relaxations before the budget, and the tax reductions at the budget itself. These were to prove excessive, and restraints on demand had later to be reimposed. Before the forecasts can be compared with the actual course of events, they have to be adjusted to allow for the budget changes; and since these were large, this makes the comparison rather arbitrary[1]. Nevertheless it seems likely that the pace of expansion was under-estimated—possibly because too little allowance was made for the effect of the credit relaxations made some time before—and it is possible that if the full scale of expansion had been foreseen the budget would have been less expansionary.

It has been argued that economic forecasting is likely to be so unreliable that a stabilization policy based on forecasts is unlikely to be successful[2]. It is however difficult to conceive of a practical policy that did not rest on a view of the future[3]. Moreover, however much practical men may distrust forecasting, anyone concerned with practical decisions will in fact be found to have a view; and the result of not making formal forecasts would undoubtedly be that policy would be based on partial views and on exaggerations of the importance of aspects of the future situation.

---

[1]As already noted the adjustments make no allowance for indirect 'multiplier-accelerator' effects; in 1959 such effects must have been appreciable.

[2]Professor Lundberg comes very near to such a position: 'The final conclusion must be one of strong scepticism towards the possibility, through the preparation of a national budget . . . of gaining a clear indication of the line of policy to be pursued in order to achieve equilibrium': E. Lundberg [1953], *Business Cycles and Economic Policy*, [Eng. ed. 1957], p. 201. Professor Phillips, rather than rely on forecasting, advocates stabilization devices based on engineering analogies: 'given the present state of the art of forecasting I believe that better results might be obtained by basing suitable corrective action directly on observations of the economy and its changes rather than on forecasts which are themselves largely derived, perhaps by dubious processes, from those observations': A. W. Phillips [1962], 'Employment, Inflation and Growth', *Economica*, February 1962, p. 7. He advocates in effect something like an 'automatic governor' based not on the rate of the change but on the rate of the acceleration of final demand. But this is essentially a forecasting device, which has not yet been shown to be reliable in economic applications.

[3]It is sometimes argued that fiscal policy is peculiarly dependent on forecasts; but this is perhaps only because it has been used more rationally than monetary policy. Monetary policy has certainly affected the demand for durable goods, and may have affected investment (chapters IX and XI below). In both cases it is desirable to have a view of what is likely to happen in the absence of changes in policy; and in the case of investment, since the effects of policy are slow working, the view should ideally extend one or two years ahead.

The foregoing discussion suggests that some mistakes in policy may have been due at least in part to mistakes in the official forecasts. This by no means implies that policy would have been better if there had been no forecasts of a formal sort. Some mistakes are probably inevitable, and the three chief ones have been indicated. But in most years the forecasts appear to have been good enough to make it seem in retrospect worthwhile for policy to have tried to deal with the situation they indicated.

CHAPTER VI

THE EFFECT OF DIRECT CONTROLS

Controls were retained at the end of the war for one overriding reason—that without controls, it was believed, there would be a repetition of the open inflation that had followed the first world war. This chapter seeks to assess how important direct controls were in the years after 1945 as instruments for controlling total demand. The other purposes served by controls, such as the use of controls as a means of planning the economy, or the effect of food rationing in producing a more equal distribution of food, are not here considered. Consideration of this question involves some consideration of the way the economy responds, when it is not subject to controls, to inflationary conditions.

The system of peacetime direct controls was a continuation of that built up during the war. It is therefore convenient to start with a description of the system of controls as it was when taken over by the Labour Government in 1945 (§ 1). At the end of the war there was general agreement that controls would have to be retained for as long as general shortages persisted[1]. From this presumption, the strategy of decontrol followed naturally ; namely, to retain controls in each case till rising supplies made them unnecessary. In fact, controls were retained for a far longer period than was originally envisaged, and remained of some importance till the early 'fifties.

Considered as instruments for controlling demand the most important types of controls were probably the following: consumer rationing; building licences, together with some other less formal restrictions on investment; import controls; allocation of materials; and price controls. The relative coverage of each of these five types of controls is estimated in §§ 2–6 below, as a first main step towards a judgement of their total effect. Broad conclusions are suggested in §7. Some important types of control—such as those in connection with the utility schemes, or financial controls such as those over capital issues or foreign exchange transactions—are not considered at all, on the grounds that they probably had little impact on total internal demand[2].

1. THE WARTIME SYSTEM OF CONTROLS

The wartime system of controls had been built up piecemeal[3]. Import controls were introduced as it became necessary to economize in imports—at first for currency reasons, later to save shipping space. From this followed allocation

---

[1]See chapter II.1 above.

[2]Capital issues control is considered along with other restrictions on credit in chapter IX. Aspects of foreign exchange policy have already been discussed in chapter III.3.

[3]For a summary of the wartime development see the introductory volume to the Civil Series of War Histories by Hancock and Gowing [1949], *British War Economy*, esp. pp. 319–24, 329–37, 456–63, 494–8 and 502–4.

schemes for most important materials; and also food rationing. As manpower became short, the manpower controls were converted into a system of industrial conscription. In some cases the growth of defence orders was itself enough to limit civilian production. Private motor cars, vacuum cleaners and refrigerators, for instance, disappeared from the home market without formal controls over their purchase—though there were of course controls over the materials that would have been needed for their production. Other civilian supplies were reduced by controls over production, controls over the use of factory space, or—especially in the case of consumer services—by the direction of manpower[1]. Such controls over the means of production were generally adequate without being reinforced by rationing at the final consumption stage. Thus though clothes, furniture and fuel were rationed, most other consumer goods—pots and pans, sports goods, cigarettes and many more—were rationed merely by queues and shortages. Investment demand was fairly comprehensively restricted by the system of building licensing and by machinery licensing.

During the war, controls had a twin purpose. In addition to the negative purpose, which they retained in peace, of reducing civilian demands on the economy, they had also a positive purpose. They served the important purpose of allocating, among competing government uses, whatever could be diverted from civilian needs. It was, indeed, the difficulty of planning the government's own operations, which gave rise to the most serious problems in operating the wartime controls. To ensure that the various controls over war production were mutually consistent, so that what the defence effort needed was efficiently produced, was a matter of continuous difficulty[2].

[1]'For all these reasons, the necessities of supply, the abnormal conditions of risk, the unreliability of market price as an allocation mechanism . . . and the development of severe shortage on the consumption front, it is surely clear that in a major war the fiscal theory of war economy must break down . . . The development of severe shortage takes time; some parts of the economy are more vulnerable than others. But there is a kind of snowball logic about this kind of intervention. You intervene here to fix prices, or to sustain supply, and automatically you are drawn on to prevent developments elsewhere from frustrating your original intentions. Once you are committed anywhere to this kind of policy on a large scale, it is almost inevitable that you will find yourself committed nearly everywhere else.'—Professor (now Lord) Robbins in his 1947 Marshall Lecture, *The Economic Problem in War and Peace*, p. 42.

[2]From one point of view, as Professor Robbins said, there is in war an 'immense simplification' of the planning problem: 'private consumption, which is normally an end in itself, becomes something which is purely instrumental' (Robbins [1947], pp. 46–7). The difficulties of operating wartime controls were the difficulties of very large-scale administration. As Professor Devons says, the government 'was forced, by the difficulties of administration, to delegate decisions to separate, largely self-contained units of administration'. There was therefore a major problem in securing co-ordination. 'This conflict between devolution and centralization appeared at every stage in the administrative hierarchy. At each level the co-ordinators regarded the plans of the individual sectors as futile and wasteful, because they took no account of what was happening elsewhere; and those in charge of individual sectors regarded the plans of the co-ordinators as theoretical, academic, and unrelated to the real facts of the situation' (E. Devons [1950], *Planning in Practice*, pp. 5 and 14).

L

From the point of view of restricting civilian demand, the wartime system of controls was interlocking, self-reinforcing and, in total, almost all-extensive: demand not stopped at one point was stopped at another.   This second negative function was as important as the first.   As has already been shown, wartime fiscal policy, drastic as it was, was by no means drastic enough to eliminate excess demand; and considerable reliance was placed on the 'barrier' of direct controls to prevent demand from having explosive effects on the economy[1]. There can be little doubt that, during the war, the system of direct controls reduced not only the demand for the particular goods affected, but also private demand in total.   Thus private investment was reduced to small if not negligible proportions; and, for years together, consumers were prevented from spending a sizeable portion of their incomes[2].

When the war ended, the system of controls changed its character.   Its positive function—its part in the direction of war production—ceased with the war itself.   Except in one or two cases, controls over production appear to have quickly fallen into disuse.   Though the government continued for some years to go through the motions of 'manpower budgeting'[3], controls over labour rapidly ceased to have operative importance.   With these basic controls removed, the system became far less tightly knit.   The purely negative controls confronting the final consumer remained for some years almost as extensive as in the war;   but they were far less firmly underpinned than before.

2.   CONSUMER RATIONING

Figure 6.1 (and table 6.3, page 173) shows the percentage of consumers' expenditure which was subject to consumer rationing in each of the years 1946–57. Such a statistical summary—and the same applies to the similar summaries given later for other types of control—is a rough indication only of the degree of real control[4].   The existence of a legal control does not necessarily mean that it made much difference: in some cases it made a lot, in others very little. But controls were not generally retained after they had ceased to 'bite'; for it is difficult to persuade controllers to administer, or the public to observe, the form

[1]See the discussion in chapters II.1 and VII.1.

[2]See figure 6.5, below.

[3]A 'manpower budget' continued to be included in the *Economic Survey* until as late as 1950.   As there was little means of ensuring that the targets were reached, the targets were somewhere between a forecast and a qualified hope.

[4]These and following estimates (except those for import controls) are largely the work of Mr D. Friedman.   For the purpose of the estimates, the total percentage of expenditure controlled is *not* current-weighted: this avoids some of the bias towards understatement in a summary measure of this sort.   In table 6.3, consumers' expenditure is divided into ten main categories; for each of which the percentage controlled is calculated.   The total coverage of controls is then calculated as the weighted sum of the separate percentages, using as weights the average value of that type of expenditure over the whole period, 1946–57.

Fig. 6.1.   Extent of consumer rationing, 1946–58

Percentage of consumers' expenditure subject to rationing

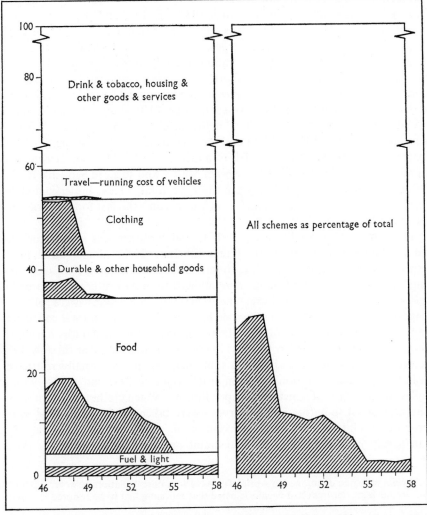

For sources and explanations see notes to table 6.3, p. 173.

of a control which has ceased to have an obvious purpose.   Controls were in general retained until they were 'floated off' on the tide of increasing supplies. In the year or two before the removal of a control, it can be inferred that its effect was becoming marginal.

Consumer rationing was always highly selective and extended only to a few broad categories of goods.   Measured by the amount of expenditure subject to rationing, food rationing was almost as important as all other types of rationing put together.   In the first post-war years food rationing became more extensive, not less: bread, which had not been rationed during the war, was put on ration in July 1946, and potatoes in November 1947.   In 1947 and 1948 about half of consumers' expenditure on food was subject to rationing.   In addition to the staple foods—meat, fats, cheese, eggs, sugar, etc.—a varied assortment of processed or preserved foods was rationed on 'points'.   But fish, fresh fruit and most vegetables, however short, were never rationed.   Nor was the consumer ever prevented from supplementing his rations by taking meals out at restaurants and canteens: there were, till May 1950, limits to what he could spend per meal, but not on how many meals he could have.   With the derationing of bread (July 1948) and jam (December 1948) the share of food expenditure subject to rationing fell to under a third[1].   Milk was decontrolled in May 1950; tea in October 1952; eggs in March, and sugar in September, 1953. By then, rationed food was only a fifth of the total.   Fats, butter and cheese were derationed in May 1954; and meat and bacon—the last foods on ration— two months later in July.

The control of expenditure on clothing and furniture was almost complete during the first three post-war years: till June 1948, almost all domestic expenditure on clothing was subject to rationing; and till March 1949, only those eligible under the docket system[2] were allowed to buy furniture.   Regarded as restraints on total expenditure, the remaining restrictions were of small importance.   Petrol—representing one fifth of one per cent of total consumers' expenditure—was rationed till May 1950, and again for six months during the Suez crisis (December 1956 to May 1957).   Coal was rationed till July 1958. Expenditure abroad (not shown in table 6.3) remained formally restricted[3].

In total, consumer rationing—even at its height, in 1947 and 1948— applied to less than a third of consumers' expenditure[4].   When clothes and furniture— and also bread, potatoes and preserves—were taken off ration in 1948–9, the proportion fell to a mere twelve per cent or so.   Thus even by 1949, rationing can hardly have been much of a restraint on consumption in total.   What

[1]Sweets were first derationed in April 1949—a serious miscalculation, however.   Demand was so much greater than had been calculated that rationing had to be restored in August. Sweets were finally taken off ration in February 1953.

[2]Principally newly-married couples and bombed-out families.

[3]Table 6.3 shows only consumers' expenditure in the United Kingdom.   Hence it omits British consumers' expenditure abroad, which, if not formally rationed, was at times severely restricted.   In the early years the restriction undoubtedly reduced what British holiday-makers spent abroad; but since the end of 1954, the allowance has never been less than £100 a head.   In October 1959 was it raised to £250, being retained then as a restriction not on holiday spending but on capital movements.

[4]See figure 6.1 and table 6.3.   The coverage of consumer rationing when calculated with average 1946–57 weights was 28 per cent in 1946, as against 30 per cent and 31 per cent in 1947 and 1948.   With current weights, the figures would have been 24 per cent in 1946 as against 27 per cent and 28 per cent in 1947 and 1948.

remained of food rationing was dismantled in 1953 and 1954—leaving then, till 1958, little but the rationing of domestic coal.

3. CONTROLS OVER INVESTMENT

During the war, controls over investment had been all but comprehensive. Licences were required not only for all but very small building jobs; they were required too for the acquisition of most types of plant and machinery. At the end of the war, machinery licensing rapidly fell into desuetude[1]. Thus, for six or seven years after the war, the government had four ways of controlling important parts of investment: first, by building licensing; second, as a by-product of steel allocations; third, by inducing the manufacturers to accept export targets for machinery; and fourth, through its influence over public investment.

Until 1955 most building work was subject to control. A licence was required for all private work of 'construction, reconstruction, alteration, decoration, repair, demolition or maintenance' which cost more than the prescribed minimum[2]. Building work by the public corporations, the local authorities and similar bodies, though not requiring a licence, had to be authorized, if above the same limit, by the appropriate government department. Direct work for the government was outside these administrative arrangements. But all work was subject to broad approval by a central official committee in London on which all interested departments were represented. In addition to this central control, the regional offices of the Ministry of Works could specify a starting date when licensing *private* work; and wherever the pressure of demand was highest, this 'starting date' procedure was in fact the operative control. In April 1947, after the weakness of divided control had become very evident, the 'starting date' procedure was extended also to public work.

Most of the building industry consists of very small firms. It is therefore difficult to make estimates either of the amount of building work done, or of the proportion of it subject to control. Moreover a good proportion of building work is done not by the 'building industry' but by building and maintenance workers employed directly by local authorities, public utilities and some private firms. In the early post-war years, something like half the total of building and civil engineering work consisted of repairs and maintenance. The building controls were at first very detailed, so that even minor jobs required licensing or

---

[1]The main statutory regulations were not revoked till 1948, but few licences appear to have been issued after 1946. For wartime licensing of plant and machinery, see the War Histories volume by E. L. Hargreaves and M. M. Gowing [1952], *Civil Industry and Trade*, pp. 540–3.

[2]Defence Regulation 56A. For a fuller description of the machinery of building contro see N. Rosenberg [1960], *Economic Planning in the British Building Industry, 1945–49*.

Table 6.1.   *Building licensing exemption limits* (£ *per year*)

		Industrial and agricultural building	Warehouses, schools and some offices	Other building including housing
1945	August[a]	20	20	20
1948	July			100
	November	1,000	1,000	
1950	February	500	500	
1952	July		200	200
1953	January	2,000	500	500
1954	January	25,000	1,000	1,000
	November	control ends	control ends	control ends

From summaries of *Statutory Rules and Orders* in reports of Ministry of Works.
[a]The limits were fixed for successive six-monthly periods at £10 per period: in addition there was a non-cumulative allowance of £2 per month.

authorization (table 6.1).   The controls must at all times have covered virtually all *new* building work; and, till 1948, by far the greater part of repairs and maintenance work also[1].   The chief effect of the raising of the exemption limits in 1948 must have been to exclude from control the smaller sort of repair jobs—which had never been easy to control.   The limits were substantially raised again in 1953, and again in 1954.   The control was removed entirely in November of that year.

For the first three or four years after the war the building controls were not an effective restraint, simply because they were not rigorously applied.   At least up to 1948, the volume of work licensed or authorized was grossly excessive in relation to the volume of work that got done[2].   For this there were two chief reasons.   First, the system of control was not operated to ration demand, so much as to favour types of investment which the government considered especially urgent, in particular housing.   As the building industry expanded, labour tended in fact to go to repair work, which proved very difficult to control. Mr Bevan, as Minister of Housing, far from being willing to restrict housing to

---

[1]It would seem, from estimates for the years 1946–54 made available by the Ministry of Works, that the value of authorizations and licences amounted in most years to about three quarters of the total value of building and construction work.   In some years when there was overlicensing not all these licences may have been utilized.   The unlicensed sector—at least one quarter—consisted of:

      (a) repair and maintenance work done by local authorities, public utilities and government departments (exempted from the authorization procedure);

      (b) work authorized by local authorities for war damage repairs and conversions and adaptations (figures of authorizations not available); and

      (c) work below licensing limits.

Though work below the licensing limits cannot be estimated directly, it can hardly have been a very large proportion of the total.   From the low level of the exemption limits, it is clear that most new work must have remained subject to control.

[2]This and the next paragraph draw largely on Rosenberg [1960], chapters III–V.

make way for this demand, followed instead the contrary course of freely authorizing the local authorities' housing plans so as to give them every chance to compete for the scarce labour. A second important reason was that the supply of building materials lagged behind the expansion of the building labour force so that the scale of building activity proved much less than expected by the government. This was true not only of steel and timber, which were formally rationed, but even more acutely of other materials which were not rationed, especially bricks. A third contributory factor was that till 1948 there was little co-ordination at the regional level between the various authorities responsible for authorizing building starts.

Up to the middle of 1947 there was an over-issue of licences on an enormous scale. One consequence was that the local authorities started more houses than they had the manpower to complete in a normal time, and the number of houses under construction mounted continually, with little to show in the way of houses completed. This chaotic situation, along with the other disasters of 1947, forced a major reconsideration of policy. The resulting, much more realistic, investment programme[1] was one of the first fruits of Crippsian planning. Its aim was to reduce the load on the building industry: in particular, first, to limit house-building to the number of houses for which timber was likely to be available, and within this total to concentrate not on starting more houses but finishing those already started; and, second, drastically to reduce factory building, chiefly to save steel. Because of the past over-issue of licences, the new restrictions took several months to begin to show; and in the middle of the year the restrictions on house-building were somewhat relaxed. But by the end of the year the restrictions had begun to bite, as was shown by the slight drop in building manpower. Neither the intended cut in investment, nor therefore the intended diversion of resources to exports, took place. Nevertheless, by the end of 1948, building controls had probably begun to limit this part of investment demand.

Investment in plant and machinery and vehicles—roughly one third of total investment in the first post-war decade—was subject to no similar direct control. Nevertheless the government possessed some informal influence: there were various 'arrangements, statutory or voluntary, with the various sections of the engineering industries about the division of the output of plant and machinery between the home and export markets'[2]. In effect the practice of agreeing export targets lasted longer for the engineering industry than in other cases, and only fell into desuetude in the early 'fifties[3]. Partly this may have been because exports of metal goods were so important; partly because many sections of the engineering industry were greatly affected by government defence orders,

[1] *Capital Investment in 1948* (Cmd. 7268).
[2] 'The Long-Term Programme' (in Cmd. 7572), para. 160.
[3] It was only in 1952 that limitations on the number of cars to be sold at home were removed (see *Economic Survey for 1953*, para. 78).

so that the government was forced to consider their effect on exports; and partly, because the existence of steel allocations gave a direct and tangible sanction to compliance with the government's wishes[1]. These restraints were certainly highly effective in the case of cars—where the manufacturers starved the home market for ten years or so in order to export. Considered as a general restraint, not as a planning device, the informal control over investment in plant and machinery may well have been as important as the statutory—but, in practice, highly cumbersome—control of building.

In addition to these general powers of control over investment expenditure, the government had special influence over public investment. It is usual to regard this type of power as something more permanent and inherent than the kinds of control considered in this chapter: it is therefore briefly mentioned here and discussed more fully later[2]. Both for building investment, and for investment in plant, machinery and vehicles, public investment has amounted very roughly to half the total. The kind of control exercised over public investment differs very much according as it is the central government's own expenditure, a mere fifth of the total; or that of the local authorities or the public corporations, which divide the rest. Local authority investment is met for the most part by borrowing, which requires departmental 'loan sanction' (and in some cases approval for separate projects also); and that of the public corporations is subject under the nationalization statutes to ministerial approval. Control over public investment has in fact been exercised at various planning stages, i.e. in the formulation of long-term programmes; in annual examinations of annual programmes; and, at times of crises, at other times too. Until 1948, for reasons already described, public investment was probably not in fact effectively controlled. From 1948 till 1951 the restrictions on public investment must have contributed towards the restraint of inflation. Thereafter, and more especially after 1955, the control of public investment has become a more flexible instrument; and subject not only to downward, but also to upward adjustments.

In the earlier years, the main effects of the controls over investment sprang not from year-to-year changes in the controls, but rather from some long-continued restraints. Thus probably the main effect of the control of *public* investment was to reduce particularly severely some sorts of investment which happened to be easily amenable to control, for instance road building, and railway modernization—an economy which now seems misguided. The building controls, similarly, discriminated heavily against some types of private investment, in particular offices, shops and cinemas. Even though the building control was loose at the edges, it must effectively have reduced the pressure of investment demand, more particularly, perhaps, during the years 1948–51. Even though there was no formal control over investment in plant and

[1]Steel allocations remained extensive till 1953: see §5 below.
[2]See chapter VIII.

machinery, informal rationing by the manufacturers may—during much the same period—have been in total as effective a control.

4. IMPORT CONTROLS

Import controls were first imposed during the war to husband foreign exchange; but it was the shortage of shipping from 1940 on which impelled a drastic control[1]. Since the government had dictatorial power over what was imported, and from where, and what for, it took over much of the business of importing. What was left to private traders was, with few exceptions, subject to licence. Government purchase of imports remained predominant up to the 'fifties. In part this was because, in a world of dollar shortage and trading agreements, the decision to import was not only a commercial but a political decision often involving complex negotiation with foreign governments. The government seemed therefore in a better position than private traders to secure scarce supplies; and by making long-term contracts, seemed also in a position to secure supplies more cheaply. Equally important, the total volume of imports had to be restricted until the early 'fifties because of the shortage of foreign exchange. The degree of restriction, moreover, had frequently to be adjusted to accord with calculations—or miscalculations—of what imports the country could afford. In some cases, government purchase was retained as a convenient form of import restriction. A steadily increasing share of imports was nevertheless handled by private importers, but what they could import remained heavily restricted till 1953—the process of 'liberalization', begun at the end of 1949 being rudely interrupted in 1952 because of the exchange crisis of the previous year.

Figure 6.2 shows the extent of import control in 1946 and subsequent years[2]. In the case of import controls—even more than for the other controls already

---

[1]This section is chiefly based on the various studies of import controls made at the NIESR by Mrs M. F. W. Hemming and her associates: see M. F. W. Hemming, C. M. Miles and G. F. Ray, 'A Statistical Summary of the Extent of Import Control in the United Kingdom since the War', *R. econ. Stud.*, February 1959: W. M. Corden, 'The Control of Imports: A Case Study—The United Kingdom Import Restrictions of 1951–52', *Manchester Sch.*, September 1958; and M. F. W. Hemming and W. M. Corden, 'Import Restriction as an Instrument of Balance-of-Payments Policy', *Econ. J.*, September 1958. An earlier article covering some of the same ground is A. M. Leyshon, 'Import Restrictions in Post-War Britain', *Scott. J. polit. Econ.*, October 1957. For wartime policy see Hancock and Gowing [1949], particularly pp. 113 and 265–7.

[2]These estimates (from Hemming, Miles and Ray [1959]) are more careful than the similar estimates for other controls presented in this chapter. Since import control was strict enough to distort the pattern of imports substantially, some categories being much more restricted than others, an index of its extent using current weights would be particularly misleading. The index shown uses 1955 weights, which, as its authors say, 'underweights the value of items, e.g., dollar consumer goods, which were still controlled— even prohibitively in 1955, and on the other hand overweights certain items, e.g. dollar coal and steel, of which imports were abnormally high in that year' (p. 87).

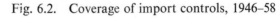

Fig. 6.2. Coverage of import controls, 1946–58

Percentage of imports subject to control

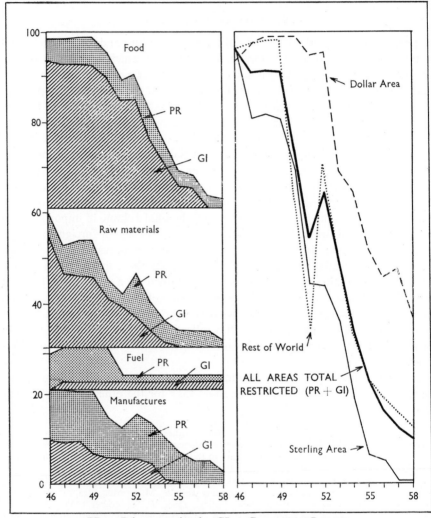

PR = Private restricted. GI = Government Import.

For sources and explanations see notes to table 6.4, p. 174.

described—an index of the *extent* of control is a poor indication of the stringency of its *impact*: right up to the 'fifties import controls were so extensive that the volume of imports could be reduced without extending the list of commodities subject to control.

In 1946 some two-thirds of imports were purchased by the government:

four fifths of imports of food and of raw materials were on government purchase —as were four fifths of imports from the sterling area. Of the third that remained in private hands, nine tenths were subject to restriction. Only a few non-dollar foods and a few other materials from the sterling area were completely free: no manufactures at all were allowed in without licence. The volume of imports was then only about two thirds what it had been in 1938; and there is little doubt that a good part of this contraction was due to control[1]— dollar imports, and manufactures generally, being particularly restricted.

During the first five post-war years, importing reverted gradually to private traders. They were, however, not allowed to import without licence: till 1950 there was little increase in the completely unrestricted field (table 6.4, page 174). The import of raw materials began to revert to private trade fairly soon after the war—wool and iron ore in 1946, rubber in 1947; and, by 1950, flax, hardwood, hides, skins and papermaking materials. Most semi-manufactured industrial materials[2] continued to be bought by the government till after 1950. Government purchase also continued for food imports. All basic (i.e. subsidized or rationed) foods were bought entirely by the government up to 1950, when however the import of cheese, cocoa, tea and various fruits was given back to the trade. By then, government import had been reduced to one half the total.

Restrictions on private trade began to be removed in connection with the OEEC 'liberalization' policy in 1949 and, much more rapidly, with the establishment of the European Payments Union in 1950[3]. The United Kingdom extended this policy also to most other non-dollar countries outside the Soviet bloc. Even before then, imports from the sterling area, though technically controlled, had been admitted relatively freely[4]; and since then, private imports from sterling countries with very minor exceptions have entered free from control. By 1950, restrictions applied to no more than half private imports. Since these in turn now amounted to half total imports, a quarter of the total was now completely free. By 1951, this had been increased to 45 per cent— controls remaining extensive for dollar imports and also (because of government purchase) for food imports.

This steady process of reducing the extent of import control fails to reveal numerous shifts and changes in its effective severity, dictated by changing appraisals, sometimes themselves drastically changed, of the shifting outlook for the balance of payments[5]. For a year or so after the end of the war, the

[1]See further § 7 below.

[2]Classed as manufactures in figure 6.2 and table 6.4.

[3]See chapter III.3 above. Under the liberalization programmes member countries of OEEC undertook to free from quantitative restrictions agreed (and increasing) percentages of their total private imports from each other.

[4]Import control was never applied to sterling imports merely to prevent the accumulation of sterling by sterling countries.

[5]For economic forecasting, see chapter V above. The frequent revisions of import policy were due to changing facts more than to vagaries in the forecasts. If crises had been

American loan having been assured, import policy was relatively lax: in particular, dollar goods were admitted much more freely than they later were.   The
crisis of 1947 compelled a more stringent policy[1].   The main effect of the
import restrictions imposed in the summer and autumn of 1947 was to shift
imports away from dollar sources.   When convertibility of sterling was withdrawn, the principle of non-discrimination (to which we were bound under the
Loan Agreement) was abandoned also.   Between 1947 and 1948, dollar imports
fell in value by almost thirty per cent (in volume, probably more).   Imports
both of machinery and vehicles, and of food and feeding stuffs, were greatly
reduced: some dollar foods—dried eggs, fresh and dried fruit and vegetables,
condensed milk and milk powders—were eliminated almost entirely.   The
volume of imports was not, however, reduced in total, though it rose more
slowly than before[2].

The policy of switching imports from dollar to other sources was an essential
part of the European Recovery Programme adopted by all OEEC countries.
By 1949, the United Kingdom's dollar imports were a third lower in volume,
her non-dollar imports a third higher, than in 1947[3].   This policy was only
possible because, as the years went on, non-dollar supplies gradually became
more plentiful.   But in many cases it meant paying higher prices, and the
process would probably not have been anything like so rapid if there had not
been import controls.   The exchange crisis of 1949, which led to the devaluation
of sterling in September, brought a further twist of the screw.   In July further
cuts in dollar imports were announced, the aim being to restrict them to three
quarters of their 1948 level.   The main items affected were sugar, tobacco,
timber, paper and pulp, non-ferrous metals, steel and machinery[4].   At the
Commonwealth finance ministers' conference in July 1949, the other sterling
countries agreed to make comparable cuts.   Taken together, these cuts
probably played a major part in the improvement of the sterling area's balance[5].

The most spectacular of the post-war import cuts were those implemented by
Mr Butler, occasioned by the payments crisis of 1951.   The crisis was due much
more to the violent rise in the cost of imports than to boom at home; and was,
in any case, as much a sterling area crisis as a United Kingdom one[6].   But to
cut imports was the readiest remedy available.   On this occasion, controls had
to be reimposed on imports which had been freed from control—in earlier

foreseen, changes would have been made more smoothly, but would probably still have
had to be made.
   [1]See chapter II.2 above.
   [2]For volume series and share of dollar imports, see Hemming, Miles and Ray [1959]
charts V and VI.
   [3]*Economic Survey for 1950*, para. 17.
   [4]*H.C. Deb.* 14 July 1949, 690–4, and 26 Oct., 1350–1.   It was at first hoped to implement
the cuts fairly quickly, but in fact it proved possible to bring them into full effect only in
1950.
   [5]See chapter II.3.
   [6]See chapter II.4.

crises the process of decontrol had not gone far enough to make this necessary. The restrictions, moreover, applied not only as before to dollar imports, but to other non-sterling imports. For the first time, too, the restrictions were followed by a fall in the volume of imports—though not all the fall was due to the controls.

Import cuts totalling £600 million were imposed in three bites: in November 1951, in January and in March 1952[1]. Cuts on 'deliberalized' imports (i.e. imports which had been decontrolled and were now recontrolled) were intended to be about a quarter of the total. These probably reduced the import (and consumption) of a wide range of unrationed foods; and also the import (and, in this case, the stocks rather than the use) of timber. Restrictions were also reimposed on paper and papermaking materials and on textiles; but though these imports fell, it is doubtful whether the restrictions 'bit'—demand seems to have fallen even more than the permitted level of imports. The remainder of the cuts were made up—perhaps about equally—of cuts in government imports, and of cuts in imports which were already controlled. The main items affected were non-sterling food; tobacco; and materials for the strategic stockpile.

Total imports in 1952 were some £400 million, or twelve per cent in volume below 1951. Though no refined estimate is possible, it would seem that half of this, or a little more, may have been due to the cuts: the rest would probably have happened in any case[2]. For stocks of imported materials had been built up in 1951[3], and some easing off was anyhow likely for this reason. More important, the recession in demand reduced textiles and furniture output particularly, both heavy import users. Even where they did restrict, the restrictions took time—perhaps six months—to take full effect[4]. This certainly diminished their usefulness as a way of dealing with the payments crisis; and now that the removal of controls is almost complete, there would be even more

[1]The announced cut of £600 million was a cut on a *programme*, not on the actual level of imports in 1951; and included some invisible items: see Corden [1958] on whose study this account is based. The cuts were imposed immediately after the return of the Conservative Government in the election of October 1951, which may explain why the cuts were made in three instalments.

[2]Corden attempted detailed estimates only for 'deliberalized' imports, and concluded that of the fall in value of such imports between 1951 and 1952 of £270 million, between £39 million and £117 million could be ascribed to the restrictions. Little detailed information was released about the other intended cuts. But other food and tobacco imports fell by over £100 million; and a cut in 'strategic' imports was intended, which may have been about £100 million. Corden's 'best guess' is that the cuts reduced imports by about £250 million.

[3]Stocks of those materials for which statistics exist rose by £80 million in 1951—after, however, being run down even more heavily in the previous year: see M. FG. Scott, 'Changes in Stocks of Mainly Imported Goods in the United Kingdom', *B. Oxford Inst. Statist.*, February 1958.

[4]"The evidence suggests that it took some six months before the effects of trade agreement quotas, contracts and hardship allowances and so on had fully worked themselves out, although some effects of the cuts were certainly felt well before six months. The lag would undoubtedly have been greater, however, had the cuts not been reinforced by the effects of the recession in reducing the pressure for concessions': Corden [1958], pp. 23–4.

difficulty in reimposing them in a crisis.   All these limitations, however do not imply that the decision to restrict imports was not justifiable at the time it was taken—if only because the recession in demand in 1952 was not foreseen at that time[1].

By 1953, most of the 'recontrols' of 1951–2 had again been removed, and the process of gradual decontrol was resumed.   Government purchase, though diminished each year, was not to be finally abolished till 1957 (figure 6.2 and table 6.4).   Raw materials had been restored almost completely to private trade by 1954—linseed oil, certain animal fats, and raw cotton in 1952–3; and raw jute and the remaining vegetable and fish oils in the year after.   The impact of semi-manufactured industrial materials (the only manufactures imported by the government) had been virtually restored to private trade by 1954.   Government purchase of food lasted till 1957, and in 1954 it still accounted for a quarter of food imports.

While the share of private trade grew, the extent of restrictions on private imports was reduced, so that a steadily increasing share of imports was freed of all control: by 1953, over half was free; by 1955, over three quarters; and by 1958, nine tenths.   By then, controls were hardly significant except for dollar imports[2].

For the first five post-war years, the control of imports remained almost complete.   During this period, imports were substantially lower in relation to national product than would be expected in view either of pre-war, or of subsequent, experience; and there is little doubt that import controls—together with the other controls that had to accompany them—reduced imports in total[3].   As controls were removed this restrictive effect must have been rapidly weakened.   By 1954 or so, one would guess, they can have had little restrictive effect[4].

5.   ALLOCATION OF MATERIALS

Apart from coal and steel, Britain imports almost all her main industrial materials.   At the end of the war most industrial materials were distributed under allocation schemes.   These, like import controls, were dismantled only gradually, and remained of some importance till 1953 or so.

To get some idea of the quantitative importance of material allocations, an estimate has been made of the value of industrial consumption of the fifteen

[1]See discussion in chapter III.2 above.
[2]Discrimination against dollar imports was substantially ended in 1959: see G. Ray, 'British Imports of Manufactures', *Nat. Inst. econ. R.*, May 1961.
[3]See §7 below.
[4]Restrictions on imports of manufactures were then still fairly extensive.   Imports of manufactures have since risen rapidly, but it is doubtful how far this was due to the removal of controls.   See G. Ray, 'British Imports of Manufactured Goods', *Nat. Inst. econ. R.*, March 1960.

major materials subject to allocation at the end of the war. These materials were: coal, timber and steel; aluminium, copper, tin, lead and zinc; wool, cotton and jute; and rubber, leather, sulphur and sulphuric acid. Estimates were made of the total value of the consumption of these materials in each year, of which that part still subject to allocation could also be calculated[1]. A rough estimate was also made of the total purchases in 1948 of the material-consuming segment of British industry of materials from abroad or from other sectors of the British economy[2]. At this date, the fifteen major materials made up 94 per cent of the value of this total. It seems clear, then, that they include nearly all materials whose value was considerable; and that the total extent of materials allocations can be estimated from the coverage of the controls on these materials.

Coal is consumed by almost all industries; and for many years the value of industry's consumption of coal remained greater than the value of any other single commodity. Coal allocations also lasted longest (till 1958). In the early post-war years, and notably in 1947, the amount of coal allocated to industry was a serious limitation on the level of industrial activity[3]. But after 1952 or so, coal allocations were not very tight, and were probably less restrictive than those of other materials. Other materials are more specific, and allocations impinged particularly on particular industries. Judged by the value of output to which the materials allocated were necessary and whose scale the scale of allocation determined, the two most important of the remaining allocation schemes were those for timber and for steel; allocation of non-ferrous metals, and sulphur and sulphuric acid, had also quite a wide impact.

Material allocations were gradually removed as the balance of payments improved, or as additional supplies became available, this process however being interrupted and reversed during the 'Korean' boom period. Aluminium, wool and rubber were taken off allocation in 1947; tin and cotton—though imports of American cotton continued to be restricted—in 1949. In 1949, too, most sorts of hardwood were taken off allocation, though softwood remained very scarce[4] and had to continue to be allocated up to 1953. In May 1950, steel (except sheet and tinplate) was derestricted, as shortly after was leather.

The Korean war not only raised commodity prices, but made many commodi-

---

[1] For details see table 6.5, p. 175, and notes thereto.

[2] Material-consuming sectors were defined as index of production industries, *excluding* however the following: (i) mining and quarrying (as being a material-*producing* industry); (ii) iron and steel production (also treated as material-producing, since steel was treated as a material to be allocated); and (iii) food, drink and tobacco manufacturing (on the grounds that its purchases from outside the industry are not *industrial* materials).

[3] In 1947 lack of coal was a main reason for the shortage of steel; steel output was no more than in 1946; and there was unutilized capacity for steelmaking (*Economic Survey for 1947*, para. 97).

[4] In 1949 softwood appeared the most persistent shortage: 'Consumption has increased since 1946 less than for any other important raw material, and there is no prospect of improvement in 1949 or indeed in 1950' (*Economic Survey for 1949*, para. 30).

ties scarce[1].   The worst shortage was that of sulphur and sulphuric acid—which threatened wide repercussions on the fertilizer, rayon and many other industries. That of zinc and copper was only less serious; and many other materials became scarce.   Most of the controls which had been removed had to be restored.   Allocations were restored for sulphuric acid (December 1950 to June 1954); steel (February 1952 to May 1953—except for tinplate); various hardwoods (October 1949 to November 1953); and there was a 'voluntary' rationing scheme for aluminium (end of 1950 to July 1953).   This second period of shortage lasted till about 1953.   But by 1954, not only were general steel and sulphur—recently recontrolled—once more free; but so also were softwood and various metals, which had been continuously controlled since the war.   The only important remaining controls were the tinplate control (till December 1956); and the allocations for coal (which lasted till December 1958).

The changing coverage of materials controls may therefore be summarized as follows.   During the war, almost all materials had been allocated[2].   By the beginning of 1951, the coverage had been reduced to well under half (figure 6.3 and table 6.5, page 175).   Reimposition of controls during the 'Korean' period increased their coverage to almost two thirds in 1952.   But by 1954 these and most other controls had been removed: it was only coal allocations which kept the figure as high as a quarter until as late as 1958.   In general, the degree of control over the *allocation* of materials followed very closely the degree of control over *imports* of materials (table 6.4).

Assessment of the effects of material allocations depends partly on an assessment of the organization which administered them.   This organization dated back to the very beginning of the war, and had generally been based, with little change of personnel, on some existing trade association[3].   In many cases, indeed, the control was not even formally administered by the government, but by a trade association or other unofficial body acting as agent for the government[4].   There was in addition an efficient central bureaucracy, whose task it was to impose a degree of co-ordination[5].   But because of the separatist organi-

---

[1]The shortages arose partly because other governments imposed controls over exports to conserve supplies.   The worst case was American limitation of exports of sulphur, the United States producing 95 per cent of the world's natural sulphur.   In addition to the commodities mentioned above, supplies were scarce for cotton, aluminium, nickel, wool and softwood.   This situation led to the establishment of the International Materials Conference, and eventually, to international allocations by that body.   See *Economic Survey for 1951*, paras. 45–56, and chapter II.4 above.

[2]Steel and softwood had been allocated since 1939, most other materials since 1940 or 1941.   See the Civil Series of War Histories volume by J. Hurstfield [1953], *The Control of Raw Materials*.

[3]See Hurstfield [1953], chapter IV.

[4]In some cases, indeed, the trade association acted 'not as the Government's agent, but on its own authority at the Government's request—with no sanction . . . save the threat that if voluntary control failed a compulsory one would take its place': see PEP [1952], *Government and Industry*, p. 71.

[5]For a description of the work of the Materials Committee, see R. S. Edwards and H. Townsend [1958], *Business Enterprise*, pp. 405–8.

Fig. 6.3.   Coverage of material allocations, 1946–58

Percentage subject to rationing of total industrial consumption of materials

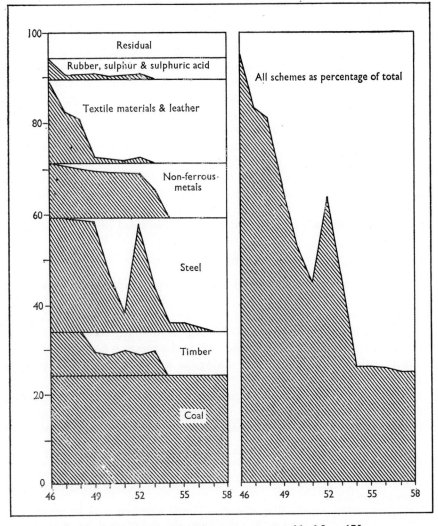

For sources and explanations see notes to table 6.5, p. 175.

zation of different controls, it was co-ordination imposed on otherwise warring tendencies. Ideally, perhaps, the pattern of import and of allocation would have sprung from the pattern of output the government intended. In practice, it was a result of a tussle between different departments and sections of departments. Again, allocations to different firms had necessarily to be made according to some rule of thumb, and were in fact generally based on what

M

different firms had used before the war[1]. This was not necessarily unpopular. After the war black markets were more of a problem than during the war; but they appear to have been marginal[2]. Allocation schemes, if enforced energetically, appear to have been sufficiently enforceable to be fairly effective.

The system had probably two kinds of effect on the macro-economic scale. Along with import controls, which it necessarily accompanied, the allocation of materials probably saved some imports. Nevertheless it was at most times the government's intention to provide all the raw materials which were essential to production, provided supplies were available; and comparison of import ratios before, during and after the period of controls suggests that not many imports were saved through economy with materials[3].

Secondly, materials allocations were plainly a way of organizing for scarcity. Provided the organization continued to be respected, it would make it less likely that businessmen would go out and openly bid for scarce supplies. Allocations schemes must therefore have promoted the acceptance of shortages, and the maintenance of what has been called the 'disequilibrium system'—and thus have reinforced the effects of price control, discussed below.

6. PRICE CONTROLS

At the end of the war, price controls over consumers' expenditure, though not comprehensive, were very extensive. Although, like other controls, gradually diminished, they remained extensive till 1953 or so. But in some fields, control was much tighter than others; and the degree to which control was in fact legally effective is difficult to ascertain. What this meant is best appreciated by considering the difficulties met with during the war in imposing price controls in the first place.

The control of food prices was bound up with rationing and food subsidies, and has to be considered separately. The control of other prices was attempted first under the 1939 Act[4]. Its provisions were, however, for the most part, not

---

[1]Adjustments had been made in various ways to take account of post-war needs (as the PEP [1952] report claims: p. 74). But these were not and could not be complete. Any allocation scheme necessarily inhibits change, competition and new entrants. Since most allocation schemes worked in terms of 3- (or 4-)monthly periods, they also made it difficult for firms to plan ahead.

[2]'Like price control, an allocation scheme . . . must ultimately work by consent . . . In war-time this consent was usually forthcoming. In peace-time it was more difficult to secure. A considerable amount of investigation, checking and tale-telling were needed to make an allocation scheme work tolerably well. A total enforcement would have demanded an expenditure of manpower out of all proportion . . . The existence of a black market was therefore the inevitable accompaniment of allocation.' Edwards and Townsend [1958], p. 408.

[3]See §7 below.

[4]The 1939 Act was the Prices of Goods Act. It was followed by the 1941 Goods and Services (Price Control) Act. The present account is based chiefly on E. L. Hargreaves, 'Price Control of (Non-Food) Consumer Goods', *Oxford econ. Pap.*, November 1947, supplemented by Edwards and Townsend [1958], chapter XV, and other sources noted below.

in fact workable. The Act in its main provisions did no more than specify the principles on which the maximum prices to be permitted should be determined, without however facing the problems of enforcement nor the necessity of prior definition of the goods whose prices were being limited[1]. A subsidiary provision of the Act however also allowed individual 'permitted prices' to be specified; and this permitted a more detailed control to be built up. The Central Price Regulation Committee used this provision to work out a system of permitted prices for various branded goods and later to sanction, often without any formal order, the prices of goods fixed by various trades or trade associations. The 1941 Act gave wider powers to fix maximum prices or margins according to a variety of formulae[2]. Where the Act was more effective than its predecessor, it was chiefly because it was accompanied in some fields by production controls, which limited and defined the quality of the goods being produced. This was chiefly true of clothing and furniture, where 'utility' production was predominant; and for many household goods, where the number of lines available had been limited and standardized. Even so, there were many difficulties in administering the price regulations, and many loopholes in the attempted definition of qualities[3]. Outside this field, price control necessarily remained extremely loose[4].

Price controls extended over the greater part of food expenditure[5]. Most of the major foodstuffs were rationed or subsidized or both; and in either case price control was both necessary and relatively easy. For many other foods, too, the Ministry of Food had control over supplies, and this too made price control feasible. During the war the Ministry's aim was, indeed, to control the price of 'all foodstuffs in common use'[6]. Some of these controls, however—

---

[1] The principle was that the profit earned per article should not be more than what *each firm* had earned on similar goods in August 1939. It would clearly have been difficult in most cases to establish in a court of law what pre-war goods were to be taken as comparable, or what the price or cost or profit then had been. There was moreover no inspectorate, so that action under the Act was initiated only on complaints from the public.

[2] For instance a common arrangement under the Act was 'cost plus' together with an overriding 'maximum price', i.e. either a fixed percentage margin above costs, or the maximum price for the industry, whichever was lower for each producer.

[3] For examples see Hargreaves [1947], pp. 7–10.

[4] Compare Hancock and Gowing [1949] (p. 503): 'Price control under the 1941 legislation was, with all its imperfections, a great improvement on what had gone before. But it must be remembered that it never covered the whole field. Except in a very few industries such as furniture and hosiery it was not considered practicable to achieve anywhere near 100 per cent utility production. Goods outside utility and "near-utility" schemes were covered only by ineffective price controls—the old Prices of Goods Act or later "Standstill" orders.'

[5] Control over food prices was enforced during the war under Defence Regulations under the 1939 [Emergency Powers (Defence) Act] and later by regulations under the 1945 Supplies and Services (Emergency Powers) Act. Wartime arrangements are described in the Civil Series War Histories volume by R. J. Hammond [1951], *Food: The Growth of Policy*, esp. chapter XIV.

[6] Hammond [1951], p. 187.

particularly over fish and home-grown fruit and vegetables—proved, even during the war, almost impossible to operate; and there remained some foodstuffs to which controls did not apply.

The prices of some services were also controlled. Railway fares were already subject to control through the Railway Rates Tribunal; and most 'bus fares, to the supervision of the regional traffic commissioners. Rent control was extended, in 1939, to include ninety per cent of unfurnished accommodation; and during the war, price control was extended to a few other services[1].

At the end of the war price control seems to have covered about one half of total consumers' expenditure (figure 6.4 and table 6.6, page 176). Such a reckoning, however, may perhaps understate the importance of the price controls; for, over much of the uncontrolled field, price control was for one reason or another either inappropriate, or at least less necessary than in the controlled sector. It would have been inappropriate for the central government to peg local authorities' rates; and unnecessary to control gas, electricity and Post Office charges, since these were already subject to government influence or control. Something similar applies to beer and tobacco prices, since half the price of drink, and three quarters or more of that of tobacco, consists of government taxes. Again the imputed annual value of houses occupied by their owners, though it figures in the usual total of consumers' expenditure, is only a notional item, which could not have been controlled. Items of this sort, which for one reason or another should be discounted, amount, it may be suggested, to as much as one fifth of consumers' expenditure (figure 6.4). Price controls therefore covered about sixty per cent of the field which there would have been much sense in controlling.

Some price controls were clearly much more effective than others: in some cases, on the other hand, control was hardly more than nominal. Table 6.6 attempts to classify them into 'tight' and 'loose' controls and to indicate the coverage of each. Such a distinction is admittedly very much a matter of judgement: the main lines of cleavage have already been noted, and further details are given in footnotes to the table.

On the classification adopted, about two thirds of the expenditure subject to price control—i.e. one third of consumers' expenditure in total—was 'tightly' controlled: notably, expenditure on rationed and some other foods, utility clothing and furniture, coal, controlled rents and railway fares. The value of such expenditure was, for the first three post-war years, very much the same as the coverage of rationing schemes—though the boundaries of the two systems of control were not exactly conterminous (table 6.3). Rationing was dismantled more quickly than price control, so that, for the latter part of the period of control, price control was two to three times as extensive in its coverage.

There was no appreciable relaxation[2] of price control till 1949 and 1950 (figure

---

[1]Laundry services, boot and shoe repairing and furniture storage.

[2]At the beginning of 1948 there had indeed been an attempt to tighten up price control,

Fig. 6.4. Extent of consumer price control, 1946–58
Percentage of consumers' expenditure subject to price control

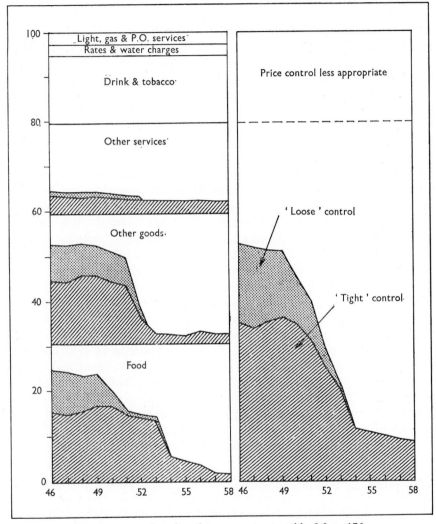

For sources and explanations see notes to table 6.6, p. 176.

as part of Cripps's wage freeze. The Price Control Orders of March imposed a ceiling (the lowest price in the two months ending 31st January) on the price permitted to be charged by any manufacturer, wholesaler or retailer. The government also announced that permitted prices would not automatically be increased to take account of higher costs due to wage awards: see Prime Minister's *Statement on Personal Incomes*, etc. (Cmd. 7321).

6.4).   The relaxations then made abolished some of the least effective parts of price control—fresh fruit and vegetables, fish and poultry; and, in the Board of Trade field, hardware, ironmongery and, with the derationing of clothing, some (non-utility) clothing.

The 'Korean' inflation led to a partial—and rather belated[1]—reintroduction of price controls.   Controls were reimposed on a miscellaneous list of consumer goods—'aluminium hollow-ware, washing machines, carpet sweepers, brooms and brushes, mops, spoons and forks, cutlery, general kitchen utensils, toilet paper, stationery, paper handkerchiefs and so on'[2].   For other controls, the form of control was strengthened[3].   The effect of these measures was probably partly to make controllers try harder to enforce controls; and partly to increase the coverage of the sort of controls it was very difficult to enforce.

The need for control at this juncture was always conceived as a temporary need only.   Nor was the government under any illusions about the difficulties of control in conditions of increasing plenty and variety.   'There are inherent limitations, all the same', said Mr Gaitskell, 'in price control.   It is obviously more effective where the product is more or less standard . . . without standardization and close control of specifications, it is difficult to ensure the maintenance of quality, and a form of price control evasion may develop'.   Again—'Where the costs of different firms diverge there is bound to be a problem of settling what maximum prices are appropriate . . .' If prices were too low, high-cost 'firms may be unable to carry on'; but with higher prices 'the more efficient or maybe more fortunate firms may make substantial profits'[4].

The system of price control was effectively dismantled in 1952 and 1953. With the end of the utility schemes, price controls over furniture and clothing were removed in 1952, along with those over hardware, hollow-ware and many other goods.   The remaining Board of Trade controls expired in 1953 with the repeal of the 1939 and 1941 enabling Acts under which most price controls had been administered.   Most control over food prices ended in 1952 and 1953, as rationing schemes were removed.   Only a few survived the end of food rationing

---

[1]The government knew that prices were bound to rise, as was very clear from the terms of Mr Gaitskell's budget (see chapter II.4).   But the rise in prices, which took some time to become apparent, eventually caused a clamour for government action.   Price controls were not reimposed till July 1951.

[2]The Chancellor's illustrative list: *H.C. Deb.* 26 July 1951, 2341–2.

[3]Mr Gaitskell admitted that there had been 'some impression recently that price control has been less strictly enforced than it was'.   For many goods controlled only by 'maximum cash prices', control by 'cost price' was now to be restored in addition.   Price control over fish and fresh fruit and vegetables was not reimposed (same deb. 2340–2).

[4]Same deb. 2341.   The rapidity of the price rise at this period also greatly increased the difficulties of control.   In some cases the cost-plus controlled price (based on the *historical* cost of materials) came to less than the *current* value of the materials alone— so that if the price had been fixed on the usual principles it would have paid dealers to buy products to treat as scrap for their material content.

in 1954[1]. Coal prices also continued to be controlled, as were rents, 'bus fares and railway fares[2].

Price control thus remained fairly extensive, though in part of the field very loose, for six or seven years after the war. In trying to assess its effects, it should be recognized first of all that, while price control may slow down the rise in prices, it cannot—in an economy subject to internal and external cost pressures—prevent prices rising. The continued administration of price control for something like a decade would have been impossible had not traders, by a process of informal negotiation with government departments, been able to obtain increases in permitted prices when they could show that their costs had risen. Within these limits, price control during and after the second world war seems to have been relatively successful. The trades concerned, however they may have disputed the details of its administration, hardly protested against its principle. Evasion, though not unknown on a minor scale, appears to have been less than scandalous. Prices seem to have risen gradually and in line with costs, and widespread profit inflation does not seem to have been the rule[3].

It has been persuasively argued that, in the United States, the success of price control was due to the fact that most markets are now imperfect, and most prices administered prices[4]. Price control (it is argued) is then perfectly feasible, since its effect 'in markets of this kind is merely to continue accepted rules'. Thus, 'demand in the imperfectly or monopolistically competitive market . . . is subject to an informal control by the seller which is frequently the effective equivalent of rationing'. This is probably true. But it is then necessary to ask whether control added anything to the behaviour that would have been followed anyhow. It is clear that neither in the United Kingdom, nor in the United States, could price regulations be enforced in rigid detail against the opposition of the trade[5]. But if, on the other hand, traders concurred in the purposes of the control, it probably sanctioned and strengthened existing tendencies[6]. As a

---

[1]Price controls over potatoes continued till 1955; over bread, till 1956; and over milk, till 1959.

[2]In table 6.6 and figure 6.4 coal is included in 'other goods'; the services mentioned, under 'other services'.

[3]National income figures do not show any marked shift to profit during the war and post-war boom, as compared with before or after.

[4]J. K. Galbraith [1952], *A Theory of Price Control*, pp. 10–8.

[5]Edwards and Townsend [1958], quote (p. 404) the view of an 'informed' (and presumably official) observer, who remarks that 'where a sufficient number of traders were sufficiently determined to disregard any particular measure, no amount of enforcement was adequate to defeat them'. Katona, in a detailed series of field studies of wartime price control in the United States gives many instances of minor evasion of the regulations (see G. Katona [1945], *Price Control and Business*).

[6]Katona believed (pp. 216–7) that price control could 'play the central role in the fight against inflation, for it can decisively influence the behaviour of businessmen, and consumers'. 'The maintenance of morale' he said, 'depends upon a clear understanding by both businessmen and consumers of the need for and purpose of price control'. Edwards and Townsend's witness concurs (p. 404): 'It is now generally agreed that we succeeded here in the administration of price control not only to a much higher degree than did the

legally enforceable code price control may have appeared a frail instrument, but there can be little doubt that at least in the early post-war years it provided a strong moral reinforcement of customary pricing procedures.

7. THE GENERAL EFFECTS OF DIRECT CONTROLS

There are various points of view from which the effectiveness of direct controls might be assessed. The Labour Party, coming into office at a time when an extensive system of controls was in existence, tended to view them as heaven-sent instruments for economic planning[1]. But with the waning of war expenditure, controls tended increasingly to be negative, prohibitory devices. The government had only a few, very general, ideas about the strategy of the transition period and the priorities of national expenditure. An attempt was made to use controls to restrict some types of expenditure—chiefly consumers' expenditure—specially severely so as to show others—especially exports—relative favour. This however was no more than restricting home demand with a certain bias against consumer demand in particular. Any control scheme has to go into great detail, and constantly calls for the exercise of detailed decisions. These made a great call on the energies of ministers and officials. But though all these decisions were sometimes represented as part of a national economic strategy, they were for the most part merely decisions called for by the existence of a complex system of controls.

Particularly strenuous attempts were made to use controls as instruments of economic planning during several of the early post-war economic crises. Instances, already referred to, were: the attempts to cut investment in 1947-8, and again in 1949-50; the cuts on imports, particularly dollar imports, in 1947, and the more general and extensive cuts in 1951-2; and the renewed reliance on price control in 1948 and again in 1951. The memory of these attempts is accompanied by a certain air of failure. In announcing their measures on each occasion ministers certainly spoke as if the situation was going to be more completely under control than events bore out, so that the apparatus of control came to appear a cumbersome and vexatious way of not doing precisely what was intended. In fact on such occasions controls often did something of what they were meant to do; but—like other methods used later—they were not highly efficient as a means of making short-term adjustments.

The continuous operation of the widespread system of controls had also, however, a more general and continuous effect on the pressure and pattern of demand; and this may be judged their most important effect. Figure 6.5 illustrates two crucial trends in expenditure. During the war, not only did

Americans, but also more than did the Germans. If this is so, it is largely due to the measure of general consent accorded to the theory of price control . . . Price control seems to me to be more than any other form of legislation one which demands the consent of the governed'.

[1]See chapter II.1; and, for Sir Stafford Cripps's attitude, II.3.

Fig. 6.5. Saving and investment in the period of controls

Percentages of GNP

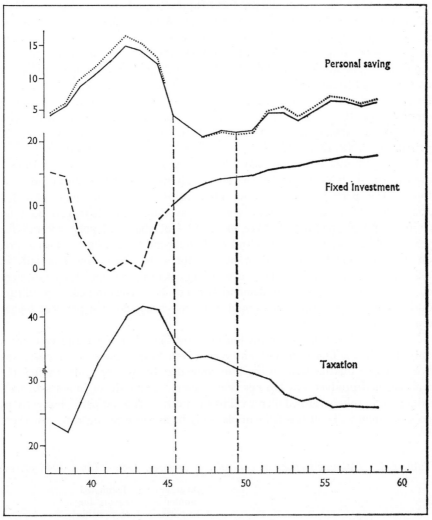

1938–45 from *Statistical Digest of the War;* 1946–8 from *NI & E* [1956]. Wartime figures of personal saving are adjusted to be (as later years) gross of capital taxes. The dotted line shows saving as a percentage of personal income (not GNP). Wartime figures for fixed investment are residual estimates of *total* domestic investment. Taxation figures include central government taxes only.

consumers have an unusually large part of their income taxed away from them, but they spent an unusually low proportion of what was left. Personal saving as a proportion of disposable personal income rose from around five to over fifteen per cent (as a proportion of national product it was hardly less). Equally important, investment was drastically curtailed. Gross fixed investment fell from fifteen per cent of national product to approximately zero during the middle of the war. Both these trends were the result of a combination of controls and shortages, allied perhaps with a certain patriotic acquiescence—in proportions to be considered in a minute. Between them they may be considered to have reduced the pressure of demand by as much as 25 per cent (for personal saving can be judged to have been 10 per cent *more*, and investment some 15 per cent *less*, of gross national product than would then have been normal). Controls and shortages thus seem to have been as important a way of preventing demand as the steep wartime increase in taxes (an increase corresponding to some 20 per cent of GNP: figure 6.5).

In the post-war transition—say, the four years between 1945 and 1949—these restraints, it is clear, rapidly became less powerful. But they still had some force. The personal saving ratio, after being abnormally high, now fell abnormally low. But, if goods had been available and there had been no controls, people might well have *dis*-saved—for they had gone without for years, and had the money saved and ready to spend. Investment expenditure, on the other hand, continued to be low for some years—low especially in relation to what must have been a very high pent-up demand for investment deferred during the war. If demand had not been constrained, expenditure during the first post-war years could well have been, say, ten per cent higher than it was.

A second effect, equally conspicuous, was the diversion of demand away from imports. In the first four post-war years (1946-9) the volume of imports was lower by one quarter than in the four immediately pre-war years, though the real national product was ten per cent higher. The ratio of imports to final sales had, in other words, fallen by thirty per cent. A good part—but perhaps no more than half—of this fall can plausibly be ascribed to controls. A recent

Table 6.2. *Estimated effect of controls on imports, 1946–9 (£m., 1948 prices)*

	Average annual imports	Estimated saving due to controls
Food	890	over 200
Drink and tobacco	70	—
Materials	580	40
Fuels	140	some
Manufactures	250	70
	1,940	over 310

From M. FG. Scott [1963], *A Study of United Kingdom Imports*, pp. 17 and 71-2.

and careful estimate, taking account of this and other identifiable influences, suggests that controls reduced imports by something like one seventh below the level that would otherwise have ruled (table 6.2). The greater part of the saving was in food imports. Restrictions on manufactures also appear to have been relatively important. Control of raw materials, on the other hand appears to have saved little—as might be expected, since policy aimed to import materials adequate to support full-employment production.

That import controls could have so large an effect is not surprising, given the extensiveness of the controls. During the first four years after the war (as already seen) import control was all but complete. Practically the only relaxations made in this period were in respect of raw materials from the sterling area: other categories of imports remained 95–100 per cent subject to control. But saving of imports on a really substantial scale required, in addition to the control of imports, food rationing, material allocations, and also some fairly severe production controls[1]. In the early 'fifties, the coverage of controls was sensibly diminished; and, by 1954 or so, their effect on the total, as distinct from the composition, of imports must have become much less.

To assess the effects of controls on internal demand raises more complex issues. Demand (it has been suggested) was appreciably constrained. But controls were far from comprehensive. This being so, the question is: how were they capable of acting as a dam to hold back demand? For a dam has to be complete, or very nearly so, to be effective. Rationing, it will be recalled, never covered more than a third of consumers' expenditure, and already in 1949 had been greatly reduced. Investment controls were hardly more comprehensive. Though building controls covered most new building, they were not till 1948 applied in such a way as to restrict demand; nor, after that, can they have done very much to limit it. There were agreements about the allocation of engineering output as between exports and home demand; but this was generally a case of the government relying on private manufacturers to do its rationing for it.

The remaining types of controls hardly gave a more direct handle over demand. Admittedly, in 1949, raw material allocation was two thirds complete, and till 1948 had been eighty per cent complete. But this control applied only to the early stages of production. Output may have been limited by the materials producers were allocated, but this did not restrict the prices which traders could charge for this limited output. Price control, in turn, was both incomplete, and incompletely effective. It covered one half of consumers' expenditure—itself only half of final demand; and much price control was very loose.

The conclusion therefore seems inescapable that if—as seems certain for the

---

[1]Till 1952 the amount of timber allowed for each house was limited to 1·6 standards— four fifths of the pre-war average. Till December 1956 newspapers and other papers were severely limited as to the number of pages they were allowed to include.

war years, and very probable for the transition—demand was constrained, it was constrained in very large part by private traders operating what amounts to their own schemes for rationing their sales, and their own constraints over prices. That such private 'controls' existed in many lines is indeed a matter of common knowledge: commodities ranging from cars to cigarettes and drink were either queued for, or kept 'under the counter' and handed out to old customers, usually at standard prices.   Unless this had been the case, official controls would not have had much effect, for they were too partial in their coverage to be, on their own, an effective barrier to total demand.   Moreover, very similar reactions to high demand have continued to be observable after controls were dismantled.   In recent booms, the economy has continued to react not by open price inflation, but with queues and shortages and all the symptoms of repressed inflation[1].

It may be the case, as Galbraith argues[2], that it was only possible to impose and operate public controls, because of the existing habit of operating what amounted to private 'controls'.   But it must equally be true that statutory regulations strengthened private habits, which might otherwise have disintegrated.   Price inflexibility—the habit of not charging what the market will bear—is likely to break down once a minority starts cashing in on scarcity; and traders are only likely to go on 'following the rules' if they feel others are going to be made to do so also.

The overriding reason why controls were retained at the end of the war was, as already noted, to prevent an outbreak of open inflation, such as had followed the first world war.   The conclusion of this chapter must be that they were effective in this respect.   Their effect nevertheless was as much moral as legal.   They strengthened tendencies that would have existed without them: without both a pre-existent tendency towards 'controlled' behaviour, and also a general concurrence with the aims of control, statutory controls would hardly have been effective. All types of control had it in common that they imposed an orderly procedure in place of what might have been an inflationary scramble; and in this, they must therefore have tended to reinforce each other, success in one sector facilitating success elsewhere.   Not only price control, but the system of controls as a whole, tended to underpin the inflexibility of prices, which is the economy's natural resistance to inflation.

It is however probably possible to consider the use of controls as an anti-inflationary device only in conditions of very considerable excess demand. Direct controls are necessarily detailed and specific and refer to particular kinds of goods and services.   They can only be imposed or retained while these particular goods and services are scarce.   Direct controls cannot be extensive enough to be a serious barrier to total demand unless shortages are widespread.   The war and post-war record suggests that this is unlikely to happen unless there is a very severe degree of excess demand.

[1]See further chapter XIII.1 below.
[2]See quotation in §6.

Table 6.3. *Extent of consumer rationing, 1946–57 (£m.: expenditure on controlled items in italics)*

Year[a]	1946	1947	1948	1949	1950	1951	1952	1953	1954	1955	1956	1957
Food	1,816	2,104	2,245	2,448	2,699	2,949	3,246	3,502	3,782	4,116	4,365	4,533
	746	*1,031*	*1,098*	*757*	*790*	*834*	*951*	*726*	*586*			
Drink and tobacco	1,328	1,439	1,590	1,526	1,527	1,598	1,623	1,654	1,673	1,746	1,839	1,924
Housing	656	718	745	756	793	845	904	982	1,053	1,065	1,123	1,211
Fuel and light	278	298	324	332	353	388	421	447	486	522	590	610
	119[f]	*126*	*140*	*140*	*151*	*165*	*178*	*189*	*208*	*220*	*246*	*249*
Clothing	638	736	902	1,013	1,063	1,116	1,097	1,115	1,205	1,297	1,377	1,439
	611	*712*	*879*									
Durables *plus* other household goods	442	557	615	706	800	892	920	1,060	1,226	1,354	1,318	1,455
	167	*215*	*263*	*49*	*57*							
Travel (including running cost of vehicles)	397	435	419	452	479	527	582	618	642	714	772	817
	18[g]	*20*	*12*	*22*								
Other goods[b]	407	455	502	518	525	574	590	612	640	700	753	792
Other services[c]	963	992	1,068	1,023	1,044	1,098	1,153	1,190	1,234	1,295	1,379	1,424
Total[d]	6,925	7,734	8,410	8,774	9,283	9,987	10,536	11,180	11,941	12,809	13,516	14,205
Percentage controlled[e]	*28*	*30*	*31*	*12*	*11*	*10*	*10*	*8*	*6*	*2*	*2*	*2*

Information on rationing from Statutory Orders: expenditure data from *NI & E* [1960], except that years 1946–7 are from *NI & E* [1957] and 1948 from *NI & E* [1959] adjusted as noted below, and supplementary sources.

[a] Items italicized when controlled on 30 June (which is normally an indication they were controlled for the greater part of the year).
[b] Books, newspapers and magazines, chemists' goods, recreational and other goods.
[c] Communication services, entertainments, insurance, domestic and other services.
[d] Total expenditure (by British consumers and foreign tourists) in UK omitting income in kind: British tourists' expenditure abroad is thus omitted.
[e] Not current weighted: weighted average of percentage of each main group shown in table that was rationed each year, weights being average expenditure on each group during period 1946–57.
[f] Coal rationing: not abolished till July 1958.
[g] Petrol rationing: reimposition in 1956–7 lasted 6 months only.

Table 6.4. Extent of import control, 1945–58 (percentage of imports purchased by government or subject to government restrictions[a])

Year[b]	1946	1947	1948	1949	1950	1951	1952	1953	1954	1955	1956	1957	1958
Total imports													
Government import[c]	64	58	57	54	46	38	37	24	13	6	6	2	—
Restricted private import[d]	32	33	34	37	27	16	28	24	21	16	10	7	10
Total controlled imports	96	91	91	91	73	54	65	48	34	22	16	9	10
Controlled imports[e] by commodity class[f]													
Food	97	98	97	97	88	72	78	55	37	20	17	6	6
Raw materials	96	73	75	74	48	36	53	32	19	12	8	8	6
Fuels	82	100	100	100	100	32	31	32	32	32	32	32	32
Manufactures	100	100	99	99	68	61	73	65	48	34	24	24	13
Controlled imports[e] by currency area													
Dollar area[g]	94	98	98	98	98	95	95	68	64	52	46	47	37
Non-dollar non-sterling	96	98	98	98	63	44	70	51	33	23	18	15	12
Sterling area[h]	97	81	81	81	69	44	43	36	18	7	5	—	—

From Hemming, Miles and Ray, 'A Statistical Summary of the Extent of Import Control', *R. econ. Stud.*, 1959: estimates based on licensing regulations and *Annual Statement of Trade*. . . .

[a] Not current weighted: each category of imports weighted by value of imports in 1955.
[b] Items are shown as controlled in any year if controlled on 30 June (which generally indicates controlled for more than half the year).
[c] Commodities bought exclusively by government departments or by agents acting on their behalf: thus imports by National Coal Board and by Raw Cotton Commission are included, while imports by British Iron and Steel Corporation (a private body) are not.
[d] Private imports not on 'Open General' or 'Open Individual' licence.
[e] Government purchased *plus* private restricted imports.
[f] Classification accords with United Nations *Standard International Trade Classification* throughout.
[g] US and dependencies, Canada, Liberia, the Philippines, Colombia, Costa Rica, Cuba, Dominican Republic, Ecuador, Guatemala, Haiti, Honduras, Mexico, Nicaragua, Panama, El Salvador and Venezuela; and from 1948 on Bolivia, and in 1948 only Chile and Peru.
[h] Australia, New Zealand, India, Pakistan, Ceylon, South Africa, Ireland, Iraq and Burma; UK colonial dependencies: excludes Anglo-Egyptian Sudan and Palestine from 1948, Faroë Islands from 1949, and Jordan in 1948–9, but includes Libya from 1952.

Table 6.5. *Estimated consumption and allocation of materials, 1946–54 (estimated industrial consumption in £m.)*

Italics indicate that commodity was more than half freed from control[a]

Year[a]	1946	1947	1948	1949	1950	1951	1952	1953	1954[b]
Coal	246	290	363	380	381	428	486	514	*534*[b]
Timber	88	*153*	*132*	*140*	*128*	261	206	197	*205*
Steel	222	259	296	339	341	406	520	536	540
Aluminium	12	17	*18*	*21*	*26*	33	44	*36*	*42*
Copper	38	71	*72*	*67*	*94*	121	148	*115*	*144*
Tin	8	11	*14*	*13*	*17*	26	22	*14*	*16*
Lead	15	27	*32*	*34*	*35*	55	39	*28*	*32*
Zinc	12	22	*25*	*25*	*39*	49	38	*18*	*25*
Wool	48	75	123	137	272	220	147	224	194
Cotton	44	56	106	121	*161*	259	128	107	*126*
Jute	3	5	9	10	13	17	14	12	*13*
Rubber	43	29	33	22	60	161	103	57	51
Leather	27	54	38	49	54	69	33	47	50
Sulphur and sulphuric acid	7	8	10	10	12	14	15	18	21
Total of above	813	1,077	1,271	1,368	1,633	2,119	1,943	1,923	1,993
Estimated 'industrial input' of materials[c]	(865)	(1,146)	(1,352)	(1,455)	(1,734)	(2,254)	(2,067)	(2,046)	(2,120)
Total allocated[d]	813	954	1,092	943	811	905	1,315	968	561
Allocated as % of 'industrial input'	*94*	*83*	*81*	*65*	*47*	*41*	*64*	*47*	*26*

Rough estimates of home consumption based on (i) estimates of the quantities imported into or produced in the UK less (where important) exports or sales to consumers; and (ii) estimates of the average price paid by industrial consumers. Information on controls from Statutory Orders.

[a] A commodity (or grade of commodity) is counted as allocated in any year if allocated on 30 June (which in general indicates it was allocated for more than half the year).

[b] Coal rationing continued till 1958; apart from this, allocation schemes were not important from 1954 on.

[c] 'Industry' is here defined as industries included in index of production excluding mining and quarrying, iron and steel production, and food, drink and tobacco manufacturing. The total input of materials to these industries is taken as input of 'non-competitive' imports *plus* purchases of the output of agriculture, mining and quarrying, and iron and steel production. The value of this total in 1948 is taken from the Cambridge 50-industry input-output table (*London Cambridge econ. B.*, Dec. 1958), in which year it was estimated to exceed the consumption of the 15 major materials by 6 per cent: the ratio was assumed to be the same in other years also.

[d] The figures include not only statutory allocation schemes, but also 'voluntary' schemes run by the trades concerned at the government's request: as explained in the text, the difference was one of degree only. The total allocated is the sum of the *separate grades* of each commodity (not shown in table but shown in fig. 6.3) to be allocated each year.

Table 6.6. *Extent of consumer price control, 1946–58, selected years (consumers' expenditure in £m.)*

Year[a]	1946	1949	1950	1951	1952	1953	1954	1958
Food								
Tightly controlled[b]	934	1,336	1,430	1,395	1,493	1,540	642	338
Loosely controlled[c]	537	545	303	130	143	125	—	—
Not controlled[d]	345	567	966	1,424	1,610	1,837	3,140	4,334
Total	1,816	2,448	2,699	2,949	3,246	3,502	3,782	4,672
Other goods[e]								
Tightly controlled[f]	864	1,307	1,294	1,334	604	210	233	306
Loosely controlled[g]	491	632	600	599	220	—	—	—
Not controlled[h]	369	557	795	990	2,161	2,988	3,292	4,281
Total	1,724	2,496	2,689	2,923	2,985	3,198	3,525	4,587
Other services[i]								
Tightly controlled[j]	381	408	409	424	442	471	476	554
Loosely controlled[k]	75	85	85	90	86	—	—	—
Not controlled[l]	1,255	1,394	1,436	1,523	1,637	1,790	1,886	2,295
Total	1,711	1,887	1,930	2,037	2,165	2,261	2,362	2,849
Sector where controls not appropriate[m]								
Drink and tobacco	1,328	1,526	1,527	1,598	1,623	1,654	1,673	1,984
Rates and water charges	159	197	207	226	243	272	288	406
Gas, light and Post Office services	187	220	231	254	274	293	311	461
Total	1,674	1,943	1,965	2,078	2,140	2,219	2,272	2,851
Total consumers' expenditure[n]	6,925	8,774	9,283	9,987	10,536	11,180	11,941	14,959
Tightly controlled	2,179	3,051	3,133	3,153	2,539	2,221	1,351	1,198
Loosely controlled	1,103	1,262	988	819	449	125	—	—
As percentages								
Tightly controlled	*32*	*35*	*34*	*32*	*24*	*20*	*11*	*8*
Loosely controlled	*16*	*14*	*11*	*8*	*4*	*1*	—	—

Information about prevalence of controls from Statutory Orders. The estimates of expenditure, in some cases fairly rough, are based on *Annual Reports* of National Food Survey Committee; and for non-food items on estimates in *NI & E*, supplemented by information relating to taxes and other sources.

aItems shown controlled if controlled on 30 June (which in general indicates they were controlled for more than half the year).

bStaple foods, i.e. bread, potatoes, meat, fats, sugar, tea, milk, etc.

cMainly fish, fresh fruit and vegetables.

dAt first, mainly (food component of) meals in canteens and restaurants, some fruits, some confectionery, etc.

eGoods other than food, drink, tobacco and gas and electricity.

fUtility furniture and clothing and also coal and petrol.

gMainly non-utility clothing, hardware, radio and electrical goods and some chemists' goods.

hAt first, mainly motor cars, books and most stationery, recreational and chemists' goods.

iServices other than Post Office services and rates and water charges: includes owner-occupiers' imputed rent.

jRailway and some other fares and most unfurnished rents.

kLaundry services, boot and shoe repairing, furniture storage and funeral charges.

lEntertainments and betting, hotel and restaurant services; insurance, health and educational fees; domestic servants, etc.

mA miscellaneous grouping: for justification, see text.

nTotal expenditure in the UK on consumer goods and services, i.e. as official estimates except that British consumers' expenditure abroad is not included, foreigners' expenditure in UK is not deducted, and income in kind is excluded.

N

CHAPTER VII

FISCAL POLICY AS AN INSTRUMENT OF STABILIZATION POLICY[1]

There is probably no country in the world that has made a fuller use than the United Kingdom of budgetary policy as a means of stabilizing the economy. Since 1941, almost all adjustments to the total level of taxation have been made with the object of reducing an excess in total demand or of repairing a deficiency. This chapter analyses the 'first impact' upon the economy of such tax adjustments. It is concerned only with tax adjustments as an instrument of stabilization policy; and analyses both the properties of the tax system as an 'automatic' stabilizer, and changes in tax rates made since the war. Questions concerning the social incidence of taxation are ignored completely. It need hardly be said that in practice the social impact is equally important; nor that in practice Chancellors of the Exchequer have, so far as possible, to devise their budgets, not only to stabilize the economy, but also to get by the political pressures which beset them.

1. THE IDEAS UNDERLYING POST-WAR FISCAL POLICY

British budgetary policy since the war has been based, to an extent unusual in matters of economic policy, on relatively clear and articulate principles. The new responsibilities of government for maintaining full employment and for controlling the course of the economy were carried into effect chiefly by means of budgetary policy; and it was this branch of policy therefore which bore most clearly the impress of Keynesian ideas. For various reasons, explained below, adjustments of the impact of public finance came to be much more a matter of adjusting the level of taxation than of the level of expenditure; and since adjustments were made within a framework of annual budgets, stabilization policy has had a short-term character. When embodied in practice, general ideas are inevitably applied in particular directions. Policy is never determined only by theoretical ideas. It is inevitable that administrative convenience, civil service traditions, political pressures of all sorts—indeed, what the people want—should be important also. Thus, what has now become the current British tradition may be seen as one limited application of the general ideas which it has absorbed in the last twenty years and which have forced it into a

---

[1]This chapter was submitted to the 1961 Warsaw Congress of the Institut International des Finances Publiques and is being reprinted in an IIFP Conference volume entitled *Les Prévisions budgétaires dans le Cadre des Prévisions économiques et leurs Adaptations.*

new mould. This process was gradual and only half-conscious, and is worth recapitulation.

The evolution of modern budgetary policy owes much to the group of economists working inside the government; this may indeed be considered one of their major contributions. The part played by Keynes in the formulation of wartime budgetary policy, and, in particular, of the crucial 'stabilization budget' of 1941, has already been described by Professor Sayers[1]. The ideas underlying it had already been set out by Keynes himself in the small book on *How to Pay for the War*, published immediately before he went back into the Treasury[2]. These in turn were one application of the general ideas set out in his *General Theory*, published four years before[3]. Almost continuously since that date[4], economists inside the government have been in a position to consolidate and refine the application of this body of ideas—ideas of which Keynes was if not himself always the father, at least one of the grandfathers. British budgetary policy is therefore unusually interesting, not only as an example of the impact of ideas upon practice, but as a case where new ideas were translated in practice remarkably quickly[5].

It may nowadays be forgotten that the use of budgetary policy had practically no place among the proposals for action suggested in the *General Theory*. Keynes had there argued for 'a large extension of the traditional function of government', in that the government should make itself responsible for 'adjusting to one another the propensity to consume and the inducement to invest'[6]. But there are many possible ways by which this may be done; and in fact both Keynes and similar-minded economists at the time proposed other avenues of intervention. They emphasized in particular—to remedy the current state of under-employment—low interest rates, public works, and, perhaps, direct

---

[1]R. S. Sayers [1956], *Financial Policy, 1939–45*, especially chapter III.

[2]J. M. Keynes [1940], *How to Pay for the War*.

[3]J. M. Keynes [1936], *The General Theory of Employment, Interest and Money*.

[4]For a year or so in 1946–7 there were no economists in close touch with Treasury matters. Keynes had died and the other economists who had been in the Treasury during the war had left. The Economic Section was in the Cabinet Office; and until the Central Economic Planning Staff was taken into the Treasury at the end of 1947, the economists there tended to be more concerned with 'physical' planning than financial questions.

[5]Keynes was in fact able to eliminate, as far as his own ideas were concerned, the 'cultural lag' which usually intervenes before new ideas are accepted, and to which he had alluded in the confident conclusion to the *General Theory*: 'Practical men, who believe themselves to be quite exempt from any intellectual influences, are usually the slaves of some defunct economist . . . I am sure that the power of vested interest is vastly exaggerated compared with the gradual encroachment of ideas. Not, indeed immediately, but after a certain interval; for in the field of economic and political philosophy there are not many who are influenced by new theories after they are twenty-five or thirty years of age, so that the ideas which Civil Servants and politicians and even agitators apply to current events are not likely to be the newest. But, soon or late, it is ideas, not vested interest which are dangerous for good or evil'.

[6]Keynes [1936], pp. 379–80.

credits to consumers[1]. Tax cuts would have been equally to the point, but they were in fact hardly mentioned[2]. The idea that the level of taxation should be adjusted to bring total demand into balance with total supply, was, however, applied very boldly and simply to the problem of *How to Pay for the War*. There, as it happens, the emphasis has remained.

Changes in tax rates have been made chiefly with the object of changing consumers' expenditure. It would be equally rational to try, as a remedy for deflation, to increase (or as a remedy for inflation, to reduce) other branches of national expenditure; and it may be asked how it came about that the aim of policy was to throw the bulk of adjustment on private consumption. The answer lies partly in the procedure of budget-making, partly in more fundamental reasons.

Budgets have always been decided annually. This means that, even if preliminary consideration is given to them somewhat earlier, decisions about the level of taxation in the financial year commencing in April have to be taken during the first three months of each year. At this date, the level of most items of government expenditure has very largely been already determined[3]. The only items of expenditure which it will then be easy to alter greatly are subsidies; transfer payments—particularly if an increase is being considered but is not yet committed; and services, such as the Health Service, for which a direct charge is, or could be, made. In terms of economic analysis, subsidies are

---

[1]The latter was suggested by J. E. Meade [1936], *Economic Analysis and Policy*.

[2]The sole reference in the *General Theory* appears to be a remark, almost in parenthesis, to the effect that 'the aggregate propensity to consume' is also affected by 'Government sinking funds for the discharge of debt paid out of ordinary taxation. For these represent a species of corporate saving . . . . It is for this reason that a change-over from a policy of Government borrowing to the opposite policy of providing sinking funds (or vice versa) is capable of causing a severe contraction (or marked expansion) of effective demand'. (Keynes [1936], p. 95.)

[3]As Sir Herbert Brittain has explained, government expenditure is planned well in advance. 'Two years before' $(X - 2)$ any given year (X), 'the departments provide the Treasury with forecasts' of the Civil Estimates. 'The forecasts made at the beginning of year $X - 2$ are revised at six-monthly intervals. Very soon after Budget day for year $X - 1$ is over, the revised forecasts for the year X must be examined more closely; and . . . the Chancellor must begin to consider whether he must take any special steps ahead of the formal Estimates procedure to keep the total within reasonable bounds . . . such a proceeding involves many inter-ministerial battles and most probably references to the Cabinet . . . These battles . . . overlap the first formal stages in the preparation of the actual Estimates to be presented to Parliament. These begin on or about October 1st each year, when the Treasury sends out an official invitation to departments to submit formal Estimates by December 1st . . .'

The defence estimates are handled separately but in a broadly similar manner: ' . . . the Chancellor and the Minister of Defence in the first place will normally consider many months before the beginning of each financial year what the overall expenditure should be in that year . . . High policy may be involved and the questions at issue may often have to be put to the Cabinet or to its Defence Committee. But sooner or later agreement is reached on the total and the agreed figure is then divided' between the various defence services. (H. Brittain [1959], *The British Budgetary System*, pp. 216–20.)

indirect taxes in reverse; transfer payments, the reverse of direct taxation. That these items are flexible is then only an apparent contradiction to the rule that at the time budgets are decided, it is on the revenue not the expenditure side that large adjustments are possible.

Keynesian principles of budgeting require that government revenue should be determined not merely in the light of the government's own expenditure, but so as to keep the economy as a whole in balance. The aim may be defined as reducing private expenditure (by raising taxes) when total prospective demand looks like exceeding the capacity of the economy to produce; or stimulating it (by reducing taxes) when it looks like being deficient. Alternatively—since excess demand implies that prospective investment demand exceeds prospective saving—it may be defined as increasing government saving through the budget surplus (by raising taxes) when private saving looks like being deficient; or reducing the budget surplus (by reducing taxes) when private saving looks like being excessive. In order to carry out such a policy it is necessary to have estimates of future private income, private saving and private demand, and of potential capacity. The system of forecasting which has been developed to meet this need has therefore to provide forecasts of all the main items in the national accounts. As already explained[1] the procedure of official forecasting is designed to fit in with the procedure of budget-making. The forecasts are prepared around the turn of the year for the ensuing year. For the reasons and with the qualifications given below, investment expenditure, like government expenditure, is treated in the forecasts as being already determined. Consumption is thus the main variable element; taxation the main instrument by which it may be varied.

This procedure is not simply a matter of historical accident. The procedure itself arises from more fundamental characteristics of the problem of exercising foresight and control over the economy. Forecasting is imperfect: errors are bound to arise even in forecasting one year ahead; and—rightly or wrongly—forecasting two years ahead has seemed too hazardous to be worth attempting. By the time the situation is appraised and action decided, some elements of total demand are therefore already determined. That decisions about government expenditure are long-term decisions has already been argued. Not only is a considerable organization required to carry them out, but also the government only spends money for reasons which seem good, and these do not vary greatly year by year. Investment goods being complicated, investment requires advance preparation and takes time to carry out. Though decisions can and are adjusted in the light of current circumstance[2], adjustment in midstream usually

---

[1]Chapter V.1 above.
[2]The extent to which public investment can be varied to suit the needs of trade is discussed in chapter VIII below.

involves loss.   Decisions to invest in stocks are not long-term decisions: but on the other hand an effective way of controlling investment in stocks has not yet been devised.   Any one country, also, has little influence on overseas demand for its exports.

Consumers' expenditure, however, can be influenced; and it can be influenced with little notice, because consumers do not have to plan their expenditure in its entirety according to long-range plans.   Consumer demand, moreover, is a large part of the whole—two thirds of the national product, or one half of final demand—so that it would be difficult to make any large adjustment of the total without affecting consumption.   That fiscal policy has aimed to affect consumption is the main part of the truth.   What attempts there have been to affect other types of national expenditure—government expenditure, or fixed investment both public and private—have generally been crisis measures, have generally been less well considered, and have generally been less successful.

Calculations of the 'inflationary' or 'deflationary gap'—would have been impossible without a great development in the statistical sources of information about the economy.   This need was obvious from the beginning.   Keynes's *How to Pay for the War* contained estimates of the current national income as a basis for the estimates of the wartime inflationary gap.   It was the poverty of these estimates that led directly to the official work on national income estimation[1].   The subsequent progressive elaboration of the national income and other statistics consitute nothing less than a revolution.   Strangely enough, however, this revolution has not been carried through completely in the organization of the government's own accounts.   For use in a system of national accounts or of national income forecasting, the definitions adopted for the accounts of the government sector need to be consistent with those used in the estimates for the private sector.   In the traditional Exchequer accounts, as summarized for instance in the *Financial Statement* published each year at the time of the budget, this is not the case.   These refer only to the transactions of the Exchequer, which is not the same as the whole government sector but only its inner sanctum.   Government purchases of goods and services are not always distinguished from loans, nor sales of financial assets from tax and other receipts; current outlays are not always distinguished from capital expenditures; and expenditure is classified primarily according to administrative divisions, rather than so as to show its economic impact.   Numerous adjustments have therefore to be made by the Central Statistical Office to the traditional

---

[1]The first National Income White Paper was published in 1941 under the title *An Analysis of the Sources of War Finance and an Estimate of the National Income and Expenditure in 1938 and 1940.*   It was prepared by J. E. Meade and J. R. N. Stone: see Stone [1951], 'The Use and Development of National Income and Expenditure Estimates' in *Lessons of the British War Economy*, ed. D. N. Chester [1951].

accounts in order to obtain the 'national income' version of the public accounts[1].

The running of a dual system of accounts suffices for the internal work of budget-making, but complicates the public discussion of a matter already complicated enough. The traditional Exchequer accounts have constantly to be explained away as misleading; and indeed at times appear to have misled the Chancellor of the Exchequer himself. Thus Sir Stafford Cripps included his 'Special Contribution' above the line and defended it as an anti-inflationary measure, though it probably had relatively little impact on spending[2]. The most blatant case of mispresentation was when Dr Dalton in 1947 took credit for 'clawing back' into the Exchequer sums previously issued to departments but not spent[3]—transparently an unreal item of revenue. Resulting criticism of the public accounts was the reason for Sir Stafford Cripps's introducing into the *Financial Statement* an 'alternative classification' of the government accounts[4].

At Sir Stafford Cripps's request, too, Professor Hicks undertook a study of the accounting problem: this substantially endorsed the statisticians' rather than than the accountants' solution to the problem[5]. The accountants' procedure is designed primarily to facilitate 'accountability' for money spent; the statisticians' to give a brief 'operating account', not necessarily perfectly accurate to the last penny, for the guidance of government policy. The two purposes are not necessarily incompatible. A radical solution would involve some reform of the government accounting system: a compromise solution would involve merely the addition of an 'economic classification' to the present *Financial Statement*. Neither has yet been adopted[6].

A system of accounts, like words, classifies events; and, like language, implies a theory about the world it is used to describe. National income accounting has in large part been evolved to meet the needs of budgetary policy; and its system of classifications implies a theory of budgetary policy. The national accounts treat income tax and surtax as a deduction paid out of income and as a reduction of 'disposable income'. Death duties on the other hand are treated as being paid out of capital not income, i.e. as not reducing 'disposable income',

[1]See Central Statistical Office [1956], *National Income Statistics: Sources and Methods*, chapter VIII.

[2]Chapter II.3.

[3]Chapter II.2.

[4]The alternative classification was in fact an unsatisfactory compromise which made no major changes, but rearranged some items in the traditional accounts. It was included in the *Financia Statements* for the years 1948/49 to 1954/55, and then dropped.

[5]J. R. Hicks [1948], *The Problem of Budgetary Reform*.

[6]The compromise solution was essentially that recommended in the *Report* [1950] of the Crick Committee on the Form of the Government Accounts (Cmd. 7969). An economic classification of government expenditure was included in the *Estimates* for 1962/63 (see *Estimates, 1962–63, Memorandum by the Financial Secretary to the Treasury*, table XIV).

but involving a unilateral transfer of property. Again, government borrowing from the private sector is treated as a financial transaction, i.e. the exchange of one asset (money) for another (bonds).

The justification for these distinctions rests on the view that the transactions distinguished have different effects. Budgetary policy has been chiefly concerned with influencing personal consumption and the distinctions rest chiefly on a theory of consumer behaviour. 'The fundamental psychological law', Keynes said, 'upon which we are entitled to rely with great confidence both *a priori* from our knowledge of human nature and from the detailed facts of experience, is that men are disposed as a rule and on the average, to increase their consumption as their income increases, but not by as much as the increase in their income'[1]. Expenditure then can be affected by altering 'income'. The question is, what is 'income'? The national income accounts in effect define disposable income—i.e. the income which affects expenditure—as income after deduction of taxes on income, but without deduction of taxes on capital; and, of course, without deduction of purchases of government debt.

If the budget surplus or deficit is likewise defined to exclude these capital items, this is probably as near as one can get by accountancy to measure the overall economic impact of the budget[2]. But accounting conventions have to make black and white distinctions, though reality itself is different shades of grey. The 'national income' definition of the budget surplus can be defended only as being as little misleading as possible. It may be taken to imply that an increase in income tax or in indirect taxation produces an *equivalent* reduction in personal spending. In fact the effect is probably *less* than the rise in tax; so that the convention tells only the better part of the truth. Again it implies that an increase in death duties has *no* effect on spending. In fact it probably has some; but it is probably much less than the increase in tax. The exclusion from current revenue of receipts from loans is rather more clearly justified. How much a person saves or spends is not likely to be influenced by how much he lends to the government; if anything, the connection is in the reverse direction[3]. The 'national income' definition of the budget surplus or deficit is then a moderately good measuring rod of the impact of budget policy. For purposes

---

[1]Keynes [1936], p. 36. For subsequent, more sophisticated theories of the consumption function, see chapter XI.1 below.

[2]In the official British national income estimates, taxes on capital are included among government current receipts, but deducted in the estimate of the government's contribution to the finance of investment: see CSO [1956], *National Income Statistics: Sources and Methods*, p. 193, and tables 35 and 47 of *NI & E* [1960].

[3]Even in some post-Keynesian writing it is argued that the receipts of long-term government loans should be included in government revenue. See for instance F. Neumark [1959], 'Fiscal Policy as a Weapon to Control Inflation' in *Inflation*, edited by D. Hague [1962] for the International Economic Association. The argument may perhaps stem from the still-prevalent belief that some sources of government finance are 'inflationary'; others, like long-term borrowing, not—for a refutation of which see chapter XII below.

of public presentation, it is necessary to have one measure, not many, and discussion in these terms can give a roughly accurate impression.

But in the formulation of policy, or in its detailed and expert assessment, discussion in such simple terms is not adequate. In fact tax changes are likely to have, not an equivalent effect on consumption, but less, and in some cases much less. It has already been argued that the impact of death duties on consumption expenditure is small. But there are other taxes, normally classified as taxes on income, where the impact is hardly greater. An increase in the tax paid by companies is likely, in the short run at least, to reduce corporate saving more than it reduces dividends and thus personal spending. At the other extreme are taxes, direct or indirect, paid by the poorer sections of the community, which are likely to have the largest impact on spending. To calculate the impact of a budget in terms of the effect of tax changes on the total revenue or the total surplus or deficit is therefore bound to be partially misleading. In fact all taxes are likely to fall partly on saving, partly on consumption: they differ only in degree. The only satisfactory procedure is to differentiate, and to weight changes in each class of tax by the marginal propensity to consume of the population affected by that class of tax: such an estimate is attempted in tables 7.5 and 7.6 below. The fact that official estimates on these lines are not published does not necessarily mean that such considerations are ignored. In the early wartime days, it seems clear, no great refinement was attempted; but the basis for performing the budget arithmetic, in the absence of good national income estimates, and amid the unknowns of war, was crude in the extreme[1]. It is probably true that nowadays, wherever it is important, more sophistication is applied; but the imperfections of forecasting make any vast sophistication out of place. If it is not clear to within £50 million by how much private expenditure ought to be changed, the effects of tax changes do not need to be gauged with much greater accuracy.

A more serious defect of post-war budgetary policy has been its unresolved attitude towards the possibility of influencing investment expenditure by tax changes. As already made clear, the working theory of budgetary policy has given emphasis to the effect on consumption. At the same time practical necessities have forced Chancellors of the Exchequer from time to time to attempt to influence investment. But how much could be expected, and how quickly, has not been clearly defined.

---

[1]It seems clear from the argument in *How to Pay for the War*, and from the account given by Professor Sayers, that the 'budget gap' to be closed by higher taxation was simply equated to the amount that private consumption had to be curtailed (see Keynes [1940], p. 28 and Sayers [1956], pp. 67–74). In fact a much larger sum would surely have been needed. But one has the impression that at that date the figures served more as arithmetical examples of a line of argument, than as exact estimates. To some extent this remains the case today.

The basic reason for this obscurity is that the theory of what determines investment expenditure has been in a far less satisfactory state than the theory of consumer demand.   Theoretical discussion in this country had left us with an almost exclusively 'marginalist' theory of investment demand.   Keynes's summary runs: 'There will be an inducement to push the rate of new investment to a point which forces the supply-price of each type of capital asset to a figure which, taken in conjunction with the prospective yield, brings the marginal efficiency of capital in general to approximate equality with the rate of interest'[1]. On such a theory the impact of taxation (by affecting the *net* return on capital) could be no more important than the rate of interest; and by 1945 opinion had come to think, probably with justification, that the rate of interest had relatively little impact on risk investment.   This line of argument also implies that entrepreneurs are indifferent as to the source of funds; i.e. that investment will be pushed to the same 'margin' whether it is financed out of retained profits or from new issues on the market.   Other writers had stressed the importance of the 'availability of funds', and argued that how far an entrepreneur pushed his investment plans was likely to depend very greatly on how much of it he was able to finance from sources internal to the firm[2].   This, however, was not sufficiently an orthodoxy for it to displace marginalism from its central position in the theory of investment; nor for its implications to be carried through into the theory of budgetary policy, still less, for it to be applied in practice.   Post-war policy has, as a result, been exposed to all the *ad hoc* inconsistencies of common sense[3].

Post-war emphasis on fiscal policy as the means of controlling the economy was not foreshadowed (as already noted) in the pre-war theoretical literature. Nor, more surprisingly, was it foreseen in the wartime White Paper on *Employment Policy*.   This is partly because the problem of control has turned out to be very different from what was expected.   The White Paper was haunted by the fear of the recurrence of the pre-war trade cycle; and for this reason, the main danger seemed to be 'the inherent instability of capital expenditure'.   It proposed two lines of attack.   The first was to counter this instability directly, not by monetary policy[4], but by the contra-cyclical variation of public investment.

The second line of defence was to try to stop a recession so initiated from spreading, should such direct action not immediately be sufficient—to stop the 'multiplier' working should there be anything to 'multiply'.   For this purpose it proposed that, not tax rates, but national insurance contributions should be

[1]Keynes [1936], p. 248.
[2]For instance, M. Kalecki [1937], 'The Principle of Increasing Risk', *Economica*, November 1937, and B. Tew [1952], 'The Finance of Investment', *Oxford econ. Pap.*, July 1952: see further chapter XI.4.
[3]See further §4 below.
[4]'Monetary policy alone, however, will not be sufficient to defeat the inherent instability of capital expenditure' (Cmd. 6527, para. 60).

varied; and that they should be varied, not in a 'discretionary', but in a 'quasi-automatic' manner[1]. In fact the problem has not been that of dealing with an occasional trade cycle superimposed on a state of affairs otherwise satisfactory, and capable of being handled by 'normal' measures. The fluctuations requiring correction have been much less catastrophic than this, but much more continuous; and the problem of dealing with them has required to be integrated continuously with the continuously changing objects of government spending and of social policy.

Another reason why fiscal policy did not figure more largely in earlier discussion was the distrust aroused in orthodox financial breasts by the idea of unbalancing the budget[2]. On the plane of ideas this fear is absurd. But on the plane of practical wisdom, it is still not clear whether the economist who mocks the fear is not being too clever by half. The fear rests on the belief, not altogether unfounded, that governments are weak and shortsighted and not always able to resist the even more shortsighted pressure of their supporters. Taxation is never popular. Once taxes are reduced—say for the perfectly respectable object of unbalancing the budget in a deflation year—is it altogether certain that the government will ever manage to get them back again?

A British Chancellor of the Exchequer is in a position of unique strength among the finance ministers of the world. Though backed up by Cabinet solidarity he has barely to consult his colleagues, except the Prime Minister himself, about his budget. The cohesion of parties is such that what the government proposes is rarely denied: tax changes take effect immediately, are debated later, and rarely reversed. It is probably also true that there is a higher standard of honesty in the declaration of income and the payment of taxes in this country than in most others; without this, too, the modern use of fiscal policy would have been impossible.

These conditions explain why fiscal policy has been given a more central role in this country than in any other—except perhaps the other protestant democracies bordering the North Sea. Nevertheless there have been definite

---

[1]The Appendix to the White Paper proposed that variations should be geared, on a scheme agreed in advance, to changes in percentage unemployment. Power to introduce such a scheme was taken in the 1946 National Insurance Act, but was never used.

[2]An instance is provided by the White Paper itself. Its references to fiscal policy are highly confused, no doubt precisely because there was here a major conflict between the economists and the guardians of the older Treasury tradition. Thus at one point the White Paper cautiously admitted the possible desirability of varying tax rates:
'If experience should show that variation of social insurance contributions was of value in keeping employment steady . . . it might well become a matter for consideration whether in prosperous times rather more taxation should be raised than was necessary for the Budget requirements of the year and that excess treated as a credit repayable to the taxpayers in bad times' (para. 72).
But the section on 'Central Finance' started out with the words:
'None of the main proposals contained in this Paper involves deliberate planning for a deficit in the National Budget in years of sub-normal trade activity' (para. 74).

limits beyond which Chancellors of the Exchequer would prefer not to have to push fiscal policy.   The experience of the last fifteen years tells something of where the political limits to fiscal policy lie.

2. THE POST-WAR TAX STRUCTURE

Table 7.1 shows the composition of taxation in selected post-war years as compared with before the war.   As an instrument for controlling the economy, local taxation may be ignored: it is decided by a multitude of authorities, and cannot readily be varied in accord with the changing needs of the situation. National insurance contributions, on the other hand, though constitutionally outside the budget, are controlled by the central government.   They could be used as a means to stabilize the economy, though they have not been.

Table 7.1.   *The structure of taxation, 1938–59 (percentages of GNP)*

	1938	1946	1951	1959
Taxes on personal income				
On incomes from employment[a]	1·1	5·6	4·8	ɔ·1
On dividends, interest, rent and trading incomes	4·6	6·5	4·4	3·5
Taxes on corporate incomes	1·8	7·4	5·8	4·6
Taxes on capital	1·5	1·6	1·5	1·0
Taxes on expenditure	8·0	14·6	14·8	11·9
Total	16·9	35·8	31·4	26·1
National insurance contributions	2·1	1·9	3·5	4·3
Total including N.I. contributions	19·0	37·7	34·9	30·4
of which affecting consumers' expenditure:				
Insured persons' N.I. contributions[b]	1·1	0·9	1·9	2·3
Other taxes on personal income	5·6	12·0	9·1	8·6
Taxes on personal expenditure[c]	8·6	14·4	14·0	11·4
Total	15·3	27·3	25·0	22·3
Local authority rates	4·1	3·1	2·8	3·4
Central government subsidies	0·6	4·3	3·5	1·7

From *NI & E* [1956] and [1960].

[a]Includes taxes on transfer incomes.

[b]Contrary to the standard treatment, employers' insurance contributions are here treated as an indirect tax, since only employees' contributions directly affect take-home pay.

[c]Official estimate of total indirect taxes on consumption (adjusted to exclude local authority rates) *plus* one half of employers' national insurance contributions, presumed to fall as an indirect tax on consumption.

In 1946 central government taxes, including national insurance contributions, were nearly 38 per cent of gross national product, as compared with almost exactly half this proportion in 1938.   Since then the proportion has fallen gradually—by about half a percentage point a year, or 5 percentage points a decade. Government expenditure as a share of national product has fallen. But, as already explained[1], this is not the main reason for the fall in taxes. Taxation has been used as the main balancing item in the national accounts. It has therefore been used to offset the net effect of a multitude of other influences. In fact the main influences which it was necessary to compensate, if demand were to be kept in balance, were, first the growth in the share of gross national product going to investment; and second—working the other way, and even more important—the growth in private saving. Because private saving has grown, the need for public saving—i.e. a budget surplus, has been reduced.

The greater part of taxation is borne by consumers. It can indeed be argued that in the last resort all taxation falls on consumers; and, for instance, that an increase in the taxation of profits will lead entrepreneurs to put up prices. But this effect, if it occurs, is a long-run effect[2]. The first impact of a rise in profits tax must be to reduce company saving or company investment, rather than to increase gross profit margins. For short-term stabilization policy, it is useful to know which are the taxes which impinge fairly directly on consumers, and in particular which are the taxes where a change in tax rates will have immediate impact on consumer purchasing power. In recent years these may be reckoned to come to about three quarters of the whole (in 1959, 22 per cent of national product). Of this, half is indirect taxation (11 per cent of gross national product); half direct—mostly income tax and surtax, but partly insurance contributions[3].

It is this part of taxation which it is sensible to vary, if the object is to affect consumer demand. The remainder consists, first, of taxes on corporate income; second, of taxes on capital (i.e. death duties); and third, that part of indirect taxation which may be reckoned to fall not on consumption, but on investment goods, exports, or goods bought by the government. Changes in some of these taxes may affect investment demand on the part of business. In the same way, changes in taxes on consumers, in addition to affecting consumers' expenditure, may also affect investment demand (for some of those called 'persons' in the national income accounts are owners of unincorporated businesses).

The incidence of taxes on consumers' expenditure is highly uneven (table 7.2).

---

[1]Chapter IV.

[2]For instance N. Kaldor [1955], *An Expenditure Tax*, p. 169:
> 'Our conclusion therefore is that provided sufficiently long periods are taken into account, the taxation of business profits *does* tend to get "passed on" in the form of higher profit margins, and thus its true incidence is shifted from the shareholders to the general consumer.'

[3]Tabe 7.1 departs from the standard conventions regarding the classification of taxes. In the national income accounts, employers' national insurance contributions are treated as a supplement to personal income, and their payment to the state is classed as a tax on income. From the present point of view it seems better to treat employers' contributions as an indirect tax entering (like, e.g. local rates) into the cost of production.

Table 7.2. *Incidence of taxes on consumers' expenditure in 1959 (£m.)*

	Taxes[a] on expenditure	Expenditure net of taxes	Taxes as % of 'pre-tax value'
Tobacco	769	292	264
Alcoholic drink	368	571	64
Running cost of vehicles	116	273	42
Durable goods	235	1,066	22
Chemists' goods	43	189	23
Recreational goods	24	141	17
Total of above highly taxed items	1,555	2,532	61
Food	55	4,743	1
Other goods and services	622	6,208	10
Total consumers' expenditure	2,232	13,483	16

From *NI & E* [1960].

[a]Excludes taxes not allocated in *NI & E* by expenditure heading; and also subsidies.

Expenditure on food accounts for over a third of consumers' expenditure 'before tax', and is barely taxed (it bears indeed a negative tax in the shape of subsidies not shown in the table). Then there is a large block of expenditure, amounting to almost half the total, which is taxed on average at about ten per cent. Finally there are a few highly taxed items where the taxation increases the price by sixty per cent on average. Though they amount to under a fifth of the 'pre-tax value' of consumers' expenditure, they account for two thirds of the tax revenue. Tobacco alone, which is a mere two per cent of the 'before tax' value of consumers' expenditure, accounts for one third of the taxes on consumers' expenditure.

The uneven incidence of taxes on consumers' expenditure somewhat diminishes its use as an instrument of stabilization policy. For it is difficult to make any considerable change in the aggregate of taxation without altering tax rates on the narrow range of heavily taxed goods. This would have a heavy, disporportionate effect on the demand for these particular goods—not the general effect on demand which is usually desired. The variation of income tax has a more widely-spread effect. Nevertheless little of the revenue is raised from the half of the population earning less than £500 a year, so that only half the population is much affected by income tax changes.

Fiscal policy is not entirely a matter of altering tax rates. The tax structure will only by accident be 'neutral' in the face of rising incomes and rising consumption; and the maintenance of constant tax rates may, if continued, itself have an appreciable effect on the pressure of demand. Suppose for instance that the 'marginal' rate of tax greatly exceeds the 'average', so that as incomes rise, taxes take an increasing share: then if incomes grow and tax rates are unchanged, the pressure of demand will *ceteris paribus* be reduced. It is therefore worth examining what the 'marginal' rates are. Such an examination shows that, notwithstanding the progressiveness of income tax, the post-war British tax system has not been important as a 'built-in' agent of disinflation; and that other parts of the economic system are more important in this regard[1].

Table 7.3 presents an estimate of the marginal rates of tax affecting persons. The method of estimation used is to correct each year's tax yield for changes in tax rates, in order to estimate the change in yield that would have occurred in the absence of changes in tax rates. Expressed as a ratio of the change in the tax base—i.e. personal incomes, or alternatively consumers' expenditure—this gives an estimate of the marginal rate of tax between each pair of years. The corrections made to allow for tax changes are estimated from the forecasts, published each year in the *Financial Statement*, of the effect of proposed tax changes. These are certainly not perfectly accurate; but any alternative method of estimation is probably even more misleading[2].

---

[1]The concept of a 'built-in disinflator', used in the present analysis, is an application of the concept of a 'built-in stabilizer'. The latter concept is variously defined in the literature. When incomes rise, tax yields rise; and, in the case of a progressive income tax, they rise in *greater proportion* than the rise in income. If the rise of incomes were supposed to leave the money value of national expenditure unchanged apart from the effect of rising tax yields, then any increase in tax yields could be considered to reduce the pressure of demand; and thus, in a situation of excess demand, to be stabilizing. Some writers therefore define the stabilizing properties of the tax system in terms of the proportion of an increase in incomes that is 'withdrawn' as taxation: for instance P. H. Pearse [1962], 'Automatic Stabilization and the British Taxes on Income', *R. econ. Stud.*, February 1962.

But it seems more nearly realistic to assume that when incomes rise, all branches of national expenditure will tend (apart from the tax effect) to rise in proportion. This is certainly the more realistic assumption when it is a case of pure price inflation and even when the rise in incomes is due to a real increase in national output, there will certainly be some tendency for expenditures to rise *pari passu*. But if expenditures rise in proportion to income, and tax yields merely do likewise, there will be no change in the balance of demand and supply. It therefore seems better to define the 'built-in' disinflationary properties of the tax system in terms of the degree to which tax yields rise more than in proportion to the rise in income (as by R. A. Musgrave and M. H. Miller [1948], 'Built-in Flexibility', *Amer. econ. R.*, March 1948); or alternatively in terms of the degree to which the marginal rate of tax exceeds the average rate of tax (as here and as by various other authors).

This 'automatic' effect of the tax system is certainly *stabilizing* when there is a condition of excess demand, for the effect is to reduce the pressure of demand. But in the reverse situation the effect is not necessarily, or even probably, stabilizing. In the United Kingdom, money incomes have continued to rise even through periods of deficient demand; and, in such a situation, the tax effect will be to reduce the pressure of demand still further, and thus be destabilizing. The term 'built-in stabilizer' is therefore avoided here in favour of 'built-in disinflator'.

For full references to the literature see R. A. Musgrave [1959], *The Theory of Public Finance*, p. 506; and P. H. Pearse [1962], *op. cit.*

[2]Since these estimates were made, two other estimates of the marginal rate of British taxes on income have been published. That by A. R. Prest [1962], 'The Sensitivity of the Yield of Personal Income Tax in the United Kingdom', *Econ. J.*, September 1962, uses a method very similar to that here used. The estimates for separate years are however not shown, and indeed Prest appears to distrust the divergencies shown. The article by Pearse [1962], *loc. cit.*, is estimated from a cross-section tabulation of aggregate tax paid and income earned by different income brackets in 1959. Both estimates agree fairly well with the present estimates: both only apply to taxes on income.

Table 7.3.   *Average and marginal tax rates, 1947–59 (taxes as percentages of income or expenditure)*

	Taxes on personal income[a]	Taxes on personal expenditure[b]
1947–53		
Marginal rates		
1947–8	22·1	−0·7
1948–9	7·7	−9·0
1949–50	16·8	7·3
1950–1	12·5	6·0
1951–2	21·9	−13·0
1952–3	18·4	7·1
Average marginal rate	16·5	0·7
Average average rate[c]	13·0	17·0
Ratio of marginal to average rate	*1·3*	—
1953–9		
Marginal rates		
1953–4	19·3	11·0
1954–5	17·4	13·2
1955–6	16·7	3·0
1956–7	24·8	9·7
1957–8	17·4	11·9
1958–9	29·3	26·7
Average marginal rate	20·2	12·9
Average average rate[c]	12·5	14·4
Ratio of marginal to average rate	*1·6*	*0·9*

The estimates start from calendar year figures of tax accruals on incomes, and payments of taxes on consumption, from *NI & E* [1960]. An estimate is then made of what each figure would have been if (a) tax rates ruling up to April, and (b) those ruling after April, had ruled throughout each year. This makes it possible to calculate what the change in taxes between each pair of years would have been if tax rates had remained unchanged. The marginal rates shown above are the adjusted change in tax yield divided respectively by the change in income and change in expenditure between each pair of years.

The estimates of the effect of tax changes are derived from the figures given in the *Financial Statements* each year of the effect of prospective changes in tax rates—figures which are not necessarily precisely accurate. Two further steps were required. First, an estimate had to be made (as for table 7.5 below) of the effect on persons as distinct from companies; and of the effect on consumers' expenditure as distinct from investment and other types of expenditure. Second, the financial year figures had to be adjusted to a calendar year basis. The following proportions of what the *Financial Statement* calls the 'effect in a full year' were taken as adjustments to put each calendar year's tax yield on to an 'old rate' or 'new rate' basis respectively: for taxes on income under Schedule E and surtax, *plus* three quarters, or *minus* one quarter respectively of a tax increase at an April budget (except for purchase tax where, because of the lag in collection, the division was half and half); and for an autumn budget, a division depending on how far through the year the budget came.

[a]*Taxes* equal payments plus additional 'current liabilities' for tax, the latter being *part* of the figure shown in the official estimates for personal 'additions to tax reserves' each year. National insurance contributions are not included. *Personal income* is as usually defined *less* employers' insurance contributions and *less* government transfers to persons (which have varied considerably and on which little tax is charged).

[b]Central government taxes only, thus excluding (as in table 7.1) the share of local rates estimated to fall on consumers' expenditure.

[c]Includes employees' national insurance contributions as well as income tax and surtax. (Being a poll tax, the *marginal* rate is zero.)

The table shows, as might be expected, that the marginal rate of tax on personal income is usually, though to a varying degree, well above the average rate. But for indirect taxes, the opposite is true. The reason is that the most important indirect taxes are 'specific' taxes: the taxes on tobacco, drink and petrol—three great revenue raisers—and some import duties, are specified as so much per pound or per gallon. The '*ad valorem*' taxes—principally purchase tax and most import duties—are less important. (Although expenditure on drink and tobacco has a relatively low income elasticity, petrol and goods subject to purchase tax have a high income elasticity. Income effects therefore do not help to explain why the marginal rate of indirect taxes as a whole is lower than the average rate.)

The table suggests, further, that the marginal rate of tax is subject to great fluctuations from year to year. Especially is this the case for indirect taxation, where the marginal yield is subject to a host of special influences. The large negative rate in 1948/49 was associated with a fall in the consumption of tobacco and drink[1]; and that in 1951/52 was associated with a fall in the consumption both of drink and of durable goods. Similarly, the drop in the marginal rate in 1955/56 was associated with a drop in spending on durables in 1956[2].

Looking at the broad trend, the marginal rate of indirect taxes was negligible until 1953 or so, but has since risen to something like the average rate. The explanation is probably twofold. During the war years, because other things were scarce, consumers spent more on drink and tobacco than they otherwise would have done. As shortages eased during the early post-war years, this process was reversed: consumption both of drink and tobacco was less in 1953 than it was in 1946[3]. Second, supplies of durables did not expand much till 1952. It was only after then that the boom in durables got under way, to the great benefit of the yield of purchase tax.

With direct taxation, also, there has been a less marked but still perceptible rise over the period in the marginal rate[4]. The main reason is that in the early years—till 1951 or so—both dividends and profits received by persons grew much less rapidly than wages and salaries. Since the typical recipient of dividends or profits is richer than average and is thus taxed at a higher rate, this tended to depress the yield of income tax and surtax. Since 1951 the profits of

---

[1]Both had, however, fallen also between 1947 and 1948. The duties on both beer and tobacco were raised in 1948, and the former reduced again in 1949.

[2]Purchase tax was raised substantially in the autumn budget of 1955, but hire-purchase controls, changed several times during 1955 and 1956 (chapter IX.5), were less stringent during 1956 than 1955.

[3]This cannot have been due to a shift in relative prices. Retail tobacco prices rose more than the average, but not much; and the relative price of drink fell.

[4]The year to year variations in the marginal rate of direct taxes are hardly worth trying to account for. The tax 'due' on profits in one year is assessed on the basis of the *previous* year's profits, and in the calculation of the table, no attempt was made to 're-date' such tax accruals and relate them to the year in which the profits were actually earned.

O

personal businesses have still tended to grow less than other classes of income, but dividends have kept pace; so that the marginal direct tax rate has been higher.

During the early years, the combined marginal impact of taxation bearing on consumers, direct and indirect, was very low indeed. The total marginal rate was well below the total average rate of tax; so that the tax system, far from acting as a 'built-in disinflator', had the reverse effect. As a result of the various trends discussed above, this is no longer the case: the total marginal rate is now above the total average rate of tax. But the 'built-in disinflationary impact' is still relatively small. It will be seen that the effect of indirect taxation is now practically neutral, whereas the marginal rate of direct tax is nearly twice the average. But direct taxes amount to under ten per cent of income. In recent years, incomes have risen by, say, six to eight per cent a year. The effect of the tax system is thus to siphon off about one half of one per cent of consumer purchasing power each year for which tax rates are kept unchanged[1]. Since consumer demand is only half of total final demand, this is not a large effect: the tax changes made at many budgets have had a much larger impact (see §3 below).

The working of the tax system is, however, only one part of the process by which spending power is diverted away from consumption goods. Part of the national income never reaches consumers, chiefly because companies do not distribute part of their profits[2]. Of the part which does reach consumers, the state deducts part as taxes on income. Consumers save part of this; and the state taxes part of what is spent. Table 7.4 is an attempt to show how all these processes have worked out. All 'diversions' of purchasing power are for comparability expressed as shares of national product. In interpreting the table it should be noted that it embodies a certain amount of reconstruction of history. It shows what would have happened if tax rates had not changed; and also, if the share of state benefits and grants had remained constant. In the hope of improving the regularities to be observed, the usual definition of national product has also been modified[3].

The object of the table is to show how it is that, as national income increases, some of the increase is diverted from consumption. In the six-year period 1947-53, some 45 per cent of the increase of national income was diverted away from consumption by the four 'diversionary' factors included in the table, i.e. abstracting from the effect of changes in tax rates or state benefits and grants[4].

[1]For reasons already given, this estimate of the 'built-in' disinflationary effect takes credit only for the excess of the marginal over average rates of tax.

[2]Personal income equals gross national product *less* that part accruing to the state or retained by companies *plus* national debt interest paid to persons and benefits and grants from the state.

[3]See notes to table 7.4.

[4]The table also ignores the effects of changes in relative prices. Changes in the price of food and other imports have sometimes made a considerable difference to consumers' real purchasing power, notably in 1951-2.

Table 7.4. *Diversion of national income from consumption, 1947–59 (percentage shares of gross national product[a])*

	Share not reaching consumers[b]	of which through corporate saving[c]	Share of taxes on personal income[d]	Share of taxes on personal spending[d]	Share of personal saving	Total diversion from consumption
1947–53						
Marginal rates						
1947–8	47	35	12	—	−15	43
1948–9	7	2	7	−6	23	30
1949–50	55	52	7	4	−1	66
1950–1	22	24	10	4	3	38
1951–2	−244	−200	75	−29	186	−12
1952–3	31	28	13	5	8	57
Average marginal rate	20	19	13	—	11	45
Average average rate	15	17	11[e]	13	3	42
Marginal *less* average rate	6	2	2	−13	8	3
1953–9						
Marginal rates						
1953–4	38	31	12	8	−15	43
1954–5	6	8	16	9	23	54
1955–6	11	9	15	1	28	56
1956–7	17	12	21	7	4	49
1957–8	−14	−15	20	18	−17	7
1958–9	32	27	20	21	17	90
Average marginal rate	17	14	17	10	10	53
Average average rate	15	16	11[e]	11	6	42
Marginal *less* average rate	2	−2	6	−1	4	11

From *NI & E* [1956], [1959] and [1960] except that changes in tax yields are corrected to eliminate effects of changes in tax rates as for table 7.3.

[a]GNP here includes stock appreciation, since corporate and personal saving are gross of this item and tax is levied on income gross of stock appreciation. Furthermore the residual error is not deducted, as in the official estimates; and employers' insurance contributions are excluded.

[b]Excludes employers' insurance contributions and government benefits and grants.

[c]The surplus of companies and public corporations gross of tax and of stock appreciation.

[d]Marginal shares are corrected for tax changes as in table 7.3.

[e]Employees' national insurance contributions are included only in 'average rates of taxes', since the yield does not change automatically with income.

Since the marginal rate exceeds the average, it can be concluded that the 'diversions' between them tended to reduce the share of consumption. For each ten per cent rise in national product, the share of consumption would tend to be reduced by three percentage points.

Other factors were more important than the tax system in producing this effect. In the first period (1947 to 1953) the tax system itself worked strongly in the other direction; but this was more than offset by the rise of corporate and personal saving. In the second six years, there was (as already explained) a marked rise in the marginal rate of tax, so that the tax system became a 'built-in disinflator'. The continued rise in personal saving was equally important. Assessment of these effects is deferred till §5.

3. CHANGES IN TAX RATES, 1945–60

This section presents an analysis of changes in tax rates made since the war. In the period from the end of the war to 1960 there were fifteen normal budgets and three autumn budgets. A main object of the present analysis is to estimate the effect of tax changes on consumer demand.

The accompanying tables are based on the estimates given in the *Financial Statement* issued at each budget of the expected effect on the revenue of proposed tax changes. These estimates cannot be perfectly accurate. On the other hand, it is unlikely that anyone else could make better estimates than the Inland Revenue and Customs and Excise departments made at the time, and the error is likely to be small[1].

There were two further stages of estimation. The first was to allocate the effect of tax changes according to the category of income or expenditure affected. Changes were classified according as they affected (a) employment and transfer incomes, or dividends, interest and trading incomes; (b) the income of companies; or (c) not income, but capital; or, alternatively, affected (d) taxes on expenditure, and within that, consumers' expenditure. The *Financial Statement* estimates analyse tax changes only according to the type of tax. Changes in the standard rate of income tax or in depreciation allowances under income tax, however, affect both personal incomes and companies; and such changes had to be roughly allocated to these two classes of income. Some indirect taxes, too, do not fall or do not entirely fall on consumers' expenditure; and in such cases also a rough allocation had to be made. The results of this analysis are set out

---

[1] In making estimates of future tax revenue, the tax departments have often underestimated the growth of revenue, presumably because they have underestimated the growth in national income and expenditure. For this reason they probably underestimated the effect of *changes* in tax rates. But the likely error is small.

The effect of tax changes on the revenue may also have been mis-estimated for another reason, which is, however, irrelevant to the present purpose. This is that the estimates of the Inland Revenue and of the Customs and Excise departments are prepared separately. Hence the former do not attempt, when estimating the yield of taxes on income, to allow for the growth in incomes caused by any cut in indirect taxes; nor do the latter attempt, when estimating the yield of taxes on expenditure, to allow for the growth in incomes caused by any cut in direct taxes. The error caused by this omission could be considerable, i.e. 10–20 per cent. But, from the present point of view, such induced changes are 'secondary' effects and should be disregarded anyhow. The estimates as given probably give quite a good measure of the first impact of tax changes.

The *Financial Statement* gives both the expected effect on the revenue in the current financial year, and the effect in a 'full year'. The former is less than the latter because some tax changes may not take immediate effect and because the revenue is collected in arrear. For present purposes, estimates of the effect in a 'full year' have been used.

in detail in table 7.5, the notes to which explain more fully the processes of estimation indicated above.

The foregoing analysis permits an estimate of the impact of tax changes, both direct and indirect, upon personal purchasing power (see bottom of table 7.5). The impact upon consumers' expenditure can be assumed to be less than this; but it can only be estimated roughly. The marginal propensity to consume almost certainly varies widely according to the type and size of income. But there is practically no statistical information on the matter. It is indeed quite possible that the values do not remain unchanged, but vary according to other circumstances[1]. It was nevertheless felt to be worthwhile to make an estimate of the impact on spending, using what are no more than guesses about the marginal propensities to consume. These guesses were as follows:

Type of income affected	Proportion of change of income spent
Income from employment	
Lower ranges	1·0
Upper ranges	0·67
Dividends, interest and	
trading incomes	0·5

The weighted average of these propensities comes to 0·8. This therefore was taken to be the effect on consumption of a change in real purchasing power brought about by changes in indirect taxation. The effect on spending of a change in the taxation of capital was assumed to be 0·1 of the change in such taxation.

The average budget changed taxes by £150 million—up or down. The average impact on consumers' purchasing power (neglecting sign) was £100 million, or two thirds of the total tax change. But this proportion varied considerably. In one year it was only one third of the total tax change; in other years the impact on consumers exceeded the total tax change. The average impact on consumer spending—roughly estimated by the method described above—was £80 million. This was eighty per cent of the impact on consumer purchasing power (or some fifty per cent of the total tax change). There was, however, little variation in the relations between the 'impact on purchasing power' and the 'impact on spending'. This suggests that to estimate the impact on consumption it is essential to make an analysis of the social impact of tax changes (first stage of estimation); but that it is not worth making elaborate allowance for the propensity to consume (second stage of estimation).

---

[1] In particular, changes in income probably affect consumers' spending only with some delay: see chapter XI.1 below.

Table 7.5.   *Analysis of budget tax changes, 1945–60:*

	1945 Oct.g	1946	1947	1947 Nov.	1948
Taxes on personal incomes					
Incomes from employment[a]					
By income tax allowances, and changes in reduced rates	−157	− 70	−70		− 80
Changes in standard rate or in surtax	− 54[h]				
Dividends, interest and trading incomes					
Income tax rates and allowances and surtax	− 77	− 7	−17		− 24
Profits taxation[b] and depreciation allowances	− 4	− 5			
Total	−292	− 82	−87		−104
Taxes on company income[a]					
Income tax rate	− 27				
Profits taxation[b]	− 56	− 70	20	47	
Depreciation allowances					
Total	− 83	− 70	20	47	
Taxes on capital[c]		22	9		105[k]
Taxes on expenditure					
Drink				56	45
Tobacco			77		20
Petrol and oil			− 4		
Entertainment and betting		− 1		15	7
Purchase tax	− 10	− 15	16	79	− 24
Stamp duties			25		
Other			− 2		
Total	− 10	− 16	112	150	48
of which on personal expenditure[d]	− 10	− 16	89	150	48
Total change in taxation	−385	−146	54	197	49
Impact on personal purchasing power[e]	+302	+ 98	− 2	−150	+ 56
Estimated impact on consumption[f]	+242	+ 87	8	−120	+ 42

Forecast change in revenue in a 'full' year, from annual *Financial Statements*.

[a] The allocation of the tax effects as between incomes from employment, personal trading incomes, and company income is based on estimates of tax under the various heads as given in *NI & E* and in the annual reports of the Inland Revenue.   The allocation, between income from employment and other personal income is necessarily somewhat arbitrary, since where taxpayers pay under more than one head, the tax reliefs are only arbitrarily divisible.   The allocation shown is based on the number of incomes assessed to tax, and the total tax paid, under the various income tax schedules.   It attributes to incomes from employment: 80 per cent of effects of changes in personal allowances; 70 per cent of 'reduced rate' reliefs; and 60 per cent of changes in standard rate.

[b] 'Profits taxation' comprises profits tax, excess profits tax and excess profits levy; and *includes* any consequent changes in yield of income tax.

[c] 'Taxes on capital' comprise death duties and the 'Special Contribution' of 1948.

[d] The portion of indirect taxes treated as falling on personal expenditure excludes stamp duties and also one half of the duties on petrol and oil and the share of purchase tax estimated to fall on business purchases.

[e] Item 5 *plus* item 19 (positive tax change gives negative impact and *vice versa*).

[f] The estimated impact of tax changes on consumers' expenditure is intended to allow for the fact that the impact of tax increases is in part on saving, not spending, the degree depending on the class of income affected.   The various tax change effects are therefore multiplied by factors

effects in a 'full' year on the revenue yield (£m.)

1949	1950	1951	1952	1953	1954	1955	1955 Oct.	1956	1957	1958	1959	1960
9	− 57	13	−174	− 53		− 57		−11	− 39	− 5	− 75	−20
		15[h]		− 13[h]		− 20[h]					− 31[h]	
1	− 25	20	− 56	− 32		− 33		−42[i]	− 17	1	− 54	
−14		31[j]		− 16[j]						− 4[j]		
− 4	−82	79	−230	−114		−110		− 53	− 56	− 8	−160	−20
		32		− 44		− 42			− 28		− 69	
		62	100	−126			38	30	− 7	− 16	− 3	64
−62		139		− 68	− 4				− 12	− 19		
−62		233	100	−238	− 4	− 42	38	30	− 47	− 35	− 72	64
20					− 2					− 1		− 2
−32	− 3									− 3	− 33	− 4
								28				40
	73	36	66						− 12	− 14		− 7
6	10				− 4				− 24	− 41	− 82	
	11	29		− 60		− 3	75					
− 2			− 3					− 7		− 6	− 3	
−18									8		− 9	
−46	81	75	63	− 60	− 4	− 3	75	21	− 28	− 64	−127	29
−44	40	50	33	− 52	− 4	− 3	74	28	− 28	− 58	−114	29
−92	− 1	387	− 67	−412	−10	−155	113	− 2	−131	−108	−359	71
+50	+42	−131	+197	+166	+ 4	+113	−74	+25	+ 84	+ 66	+274	− 9
+38	+37	− 84	+176	+128	+ 3	+ 90	−59	+10	70	+ 52	+215	− 4

ranging from unity to one tenth:

Incidence of tax changes	Share assumed spent
On income from employment	
By allowances or reduced rates	1·0
By standard rate or surtax	0·67
On dividends interest and trading incomes	0·5
Taxes on capital	0·1
Taxes on personal expenditure	0·8

The first three factors imply a weighted average propensity to spend out of marginal income of 0·8; this therefore is the weight given to indirect taxes on personal expenditure.

gExcept for purchase tax the changes took effect only in April 1946.

hStandard rate of income tax was changed as follows: 1945 (Oct.), 10/- to 9/-; 1951, to 9/6; 1953, to 9/-; 1955, to 8/6; 1959, to 7/9.

iOf which relief on premiums for retirement pensions some £40 m. of which £10 m. attributed to incomes from employment and £30 m. to trading incomes.

jOf which change in initial allowances: 1949, −£14 m.; 1951, £31 m.; 1953, −£16 m.; 1958, −£4 m.

kThe Special Contribution, being a once-for-all levy, had no permanent effect on the revenue. Since the 'full year' effect cannot be shown, the total yield (expected to accrue over several years) is included in the year of the levy.

Table 7.6.   *Budget changes: summary, 1945–60*

	Taxes on personal income	Taxes on company profits	Taxes on capital	Taxes on expenditure	Total tax changes	Total tax change	Impact on consumers' purchasing power[a]	Estimated impact on consumption[b]
			(£ m.)				(As % of GNP)	
Dalton								
1945, Oct.[c]	−292	−83		−10	−385	−4·4	+3·4	+2·8
1946	−82	−70	22	−16	−146	−1·6	+1·1	+1·0
1947	−87	20	9	112	54	0·5		+0·1
1947, Nov.		47		150	197	2·0	−1·5	−1·2
Cripps								
1948	−104		105[d]	48	49	0·5	+0·5	+0·4
1949	−4	−62	20	−46	−92	−0·8	+0·4	+0·3
1950	−82			81	−1		+0·3	+0·3
Gaitskell								
1951	79	233		75	387	2·9	−1·0	−0·6
Butler								
1952	−230	100		63	−67	−0·5	+1·4	+1·2
1953	−114	−238		−60	−412	−2·7	+1·1	+0·8
1954		−4	−2	−4	−10	−0·1		
1955	−110	−42		−3	−155	−0·9	+0·6	+0·5
1955, Oct.		38		75	113	0·6	−0·4	−0·3
Macmillan (1956), *Thorneycroft* *(1957) and Amory* *(1958–60)*								
1956	−53	30		21	−2		+0·1	+0·1
1957	−56	−47		−28	−131	−0·7	+0·4	+0·3
1958	−8	−35	−1	−64	−108	−0·5	+0·3	+0·3
1959	−160	−72		−127	−359	−1·7	+1·3	+1·0
1960	−20	65	−2	29	72	0·3		
Summary (Tax changes as % of GNP)								
Dalton	−5·1	−1·0	0·3	2·4		−3·4	+3·0	+2·6
Cripps	−1·7	−0·5	0·2[d]	0·7		−0·4[d]	+1·3	+1·1[d]
Gaitskell	0·6	1·7		0·6		2·9	−1·0	−0·6
Butler	−3·0	−0·9		0·4		−3·4	−2·7	+2·3
Macmillan, Thorneycroft and Amory	−1·4	−0·3		−0·8		−2·5	+2·1	+1·7
Total, 1945–60	−10·4	−1·0	0·5[d]	3·3		−6·8[d]	+8·1	+7·1[d]

Forecast change in revenue in a 'full' year from annual *Financial Statements*.

[a]Change in taxes on personal income *plus* change in taxes on personal expenditure (for which see table 7.5).

[b]Estimated effect on spending of impact on personal purchasing power *plus* small allowance for effect of changes in taxes on capital: see notes to table 7.5.

[c]The changes apart from purchase tax took effect only in April 1946.

[d]The Special Contribution, here attributed entirely to 1948, was a once-for-all levy and is therefore excluded from totals for the period.

The story told by table 7.5 is summarized in table 7.6. This shows clearly how considerable was the impact of budget changes. The tax cuts by Dr Dalton immediately after the end of the war increased consumer purchasing power by an amount corresponding to 6 per cent of national product—which probably increased consumer demand by an amount corresponding to 4 per cent of national product. His 1947 autumn budget though in effect it reversed only one third of these previous tax cuts, nevertheless stands out as one of the major tax increases since the war, and the one with the largest impact on consumption.

Sir Stafford Cripps in his three budgets left total taxation little changed. The Special Contribution in 1948, though spectacular, was a once-for-all levy without permanent effect, and probably had little of the disinflationary effect which was claimed for it as its justification. Sir Stafford Cripps, despite his name for austerity, and despite the tenacity with which he strove to disinflate by fiscal means, in fact reduced taxes affecting consumption at each of his three budgets; and in three years, more or less undid Dr Dalton's last act of disinflation.

Mr Gaitskell as sponsor of rearmament faced the Mr Gaitskell who was Chancellor of the Exchequer with a problem quite as difficult as his predecessors', and he was even more ready than Sir Stafford Cripps to follow the logic of economic argument. His 'defence' budget resulted in the largest increase in taxes since the war. Less than half fell on consumers. Company income was heavily affected because profits tax and income tax were raised at the same time as the 'initial' depreciation allowances were abolished. The last step was specifically intended as a measure to reduce investment expenditure—and thus to direct engineering output to the defence programme[1].

Mr Butler, in his four normal budgets and the autumn budget of 1955, went through successive phases of caution and expansiveness. 1952, a year of internal recession, followed a year of external crisis: tax changes therefore were on balance inflationary, but relatively small. In 1953 the situation seemed secure enough to reduce taxes quite largely: among other changes, the 'initial' depreciation allowances were restored. In 1954 it was feared—as it turned out, needlessly—that recession in the United States would bring both internal recession, and balance of payments difficulties. To prevent the first would have meant tax cuts; to mitigate the second, tax increases. Caught between opposing fears, the 1954 budget was as near as might be a 'no-change' budget—except that the 'investment' allowances were substituted (with no effect on the tax revenue) for the 'initial' allowances. In 1955, relying unduly on monetary policy to restrain the developing boom, Mr Butler reduced taxes in April. By October he felt forced to put taxes up again. Analysis of the effects of Mr Butler's budgets shows that they stimulated consumer demand quite largely in 1952 and 1953; thereafter, with the no doubt important exception of the six months between April and October 1955, they were almost neutral.

[1] See §4 below.

Table 7.7.   *Changes in national insurance contributions and food subsidies as compared with changes in taxes on personal income and expenditure*

	Taxes on personal income[a]	National insurance contributions[b]	Taxes on consumers' expenditure[a]	Less change in food subsidies[c]	Taxes affecting persons	National insurance contributions	Food subsidies[c]
			(£ m.)			(As % of GNP)	
Dalton							
1945, Oct.[d]	−292		−10		−3·4		−0·2
1946	−82	74	−16	−17	−1·1	0·8	
1947	−87		89	−16			−0·2
1947, Nov.			150		1·5		
Cripps							
1948	−104	118	48	−88	−0·5	1·1	−0·8
1949	−4		−44	63	−0·4		0·6
1950	−82		40	88	−0·3		0·7
Gaitskell							
1951	79	9	50	47	1·0	0·1	0·4
Butler							
1952	−230	23	33	103	−1·4	0·2	0·7
1953	−114		−52	94	−1·1		0·6
1954			−4	−5			
1955	−110	54	−3	129	−0·6	0·3	0·7
1955, Oct.			74		0·4		
Macmillan (1956), Thorneycroft (1957), and Amory (1958–60)							
1956	−53		28	28	−0·1		0·2
1957	−56	40	−28	−19	−0·4	0·2	−0·1
1958	−8	120	−58	44	−0·3	0·6	0·2
1959	−160		−114	36	−1·3		0·2
1960	−20		29				
Summary (As % of GNP)							
Dalton	−5·1	(see	2·1	(see	−3·0	0·8	−0·2
Cripps	−1·7	right	0·4	right	−1·3	1·1	0·5
Gaitskell	0·6	of	0·4	of	1·0	0·1	0·4
Butler	−3·0	table)	0·3	table)	−2·7	0·5	2·0
Macmillan, Thorneycroft and Amory	−1·4		−0·7		−2·1	0·8	0·5
Total, 1945–60	−10·6		2·5		−8·1	3·3	3·2

For notes to table see foot of next page.

For the next three years the bias of policy was towards caution.   The budgets of 1956, 1957 and 1958—for which Mr Macmillan, Mr Thorneycroft and Mr Heathcoat Amory were successively responsible—made only moderate reductions in taxation.   After this pause, Mr Amory's tax reductions in 1959 made a considerable political impact, though their economic impact was not larger than those made by Mr Butler in each of his first two years as Chancellor. 1960 was, again, a year of pause.

Over the whole period, in fits and starts, tax rates came down.   Between 1946 and 1959 central government taxes fell from nearly 36 to just over 26 per cent of gross national product (table 7.1), or by nearly $9\frac{1}{2}$ percentage points. Most of this was due to the reduction in *rates* of tax, which (as table 7.6 shows) amounted to about 8 percentage points over the period.   The rest was due to the tendency of taxation at unchanged tax rates to grow more slowly than national income (a trend which, as the discussion in §2 above has already shown, was marked only in the first part of the period).   Except for Mr Gaitskell each successive Chancellor lowered tax rates during his period of office.

There was also an apparent shift from direct to indirect taxation.   *Rates* of tax on personal income were heavily reduced, while *rates* of tax on personal expenditure were slightly raised.   Most of this shift took place under Dr Dalton right at the beginning of the period, though Conservative Chancellors too have tended to reduce income tax in preference to indirect taxation.   It must be remembered, however, that the burden of indirect taxation tends automatically to be reduced as national product grows (§2 above).   The budget bias towards reducing the burden of direct taxes was accompanied by an 'automatic' bias which reduced the burden of indirect taxes.   As a share of national product, both taxes on personal income, and taxes on consumers' expenditure, fell between 1946 and 1959, and by about the same amount (table 7.1).

National insurance contributions have been changed almost as frequently as

Notes to table 7.7

[a]As in table 7.5.

[b]Changes in insurance contributions were made in January and September 1946; and, after the inception (July 1948) of the National Insurance scheme, in October 1951, October 1952, June 1955, September 1957, and in February and July 1958.   The estimates are shown for the 'full year effect', as it might have been estimated at these dates.   They were obtained from weighted averages of the changes in individual contributions, and by interpolation from the calendar year estimates given in the national income accounts; and are probably accurate only to £5 m.

[c]The estimates measure changes in 'rate' of subsidy per volume unit of food consumption, and discount changes in the subsidy bill attributable to changes in the value of food consumed.   They are based on year-to-year changes in the calendar year figures in *NI & E* [1955] and [1959] and (for 1945–6) in *NIWP* [1948].   Changes in subsidies were not in fact made at specific points of time between which there was no change.   But in the table a difference between the averages for two calendar years is entered as occurring in the second year.   Since a reduction in subsidies increases net indirect taxation, it is shown with a *positive* sign; and vice versa for subsidy increases.

[d]Except for purchase tax changes took effect only in April 1946.

tax rates.   They have always been increased; so that this has in effect offset some of the reductions in direct tax rates (table 7.7).   National insurance deductions are now twice as important, expressed as a share of national product, as in 1946 (table 7.1).   But contributions have not been varied as part of stabilization policy.   Each increase in the contributions has been made to pay for an increase in benefits; since persons pay only part of the former, the net effect, at least at first, was to increase the pressure of demand.

The changes in food subsidies have been more nearly an integral part of budgetary policy[1].   There was a steady rise in the subsidies in the first post-war years till Sir Stafford Cripps called a halt to this process in 1949[2].   Thereafter the subsidies were fairly steadily reduced; and they are now considerably smaller in relation to national product than they were in 1946.   Subsidies have not been treated as on a par with indirect taxes, to be varied like them according to the dictates of stabilization policy.   Rather there has been a fairly consistent effort gradually to reduce them as an undesirable branch of government expenditure, whose reduction would make possible a reduction in taxation.

Cuts in subsidies have been less obvious than increases in tax rates.   Thus the rate of subsidy ruling at any time is not publicly specified as are tax rates; and reductions in subsidies could be made any time, and be timed to be as inconspicuous as possible.   It is, however, somewhat misleading to look at tax changes without considering subsidy changes at the same time.   In many years changes in subsidies have been more important than changes in taxes.   The increase in subsidies in Sir Stafford Cripps's first year as Chancellor, was bigger than the yield of his Special Contribution; and the reductions brought about in the next two years just about offset the reductions in tax rates.   The main reduction in subsidies came during Mr Butler's term of office.   In an economic sense, this undid nearly half the effect of his tax reductions.   Changes in taxes net of subsidies have been smaller than changes in taxes alone.

4.   THE IMPACT OF TAX CHANGES ON INVESTMENT DEMAND

In the previous section tax changes have been considered primarily for their impact on consumers' purchasing power and consumers' expenditure.   Tax

---

[1]The only substantial central government subsidies are those on food and on housing. The size of the latter depends on considerations quite different from stabilization policy; and has increased slowly as the number of houses eligible for them has increased.

[2]In table 7.7, a rise in subsidies is shown as negative, since, as an indirect tax in reverse, it reduces the net rate of indirect taxation.   The table treats a change in subsidies as consisting of two elements (a) that increase which would have occurred with an increase in the value of food consumed, if the rate of subsidy per £ of food consumed had remained constant (b) the difference between this and the total change in the cost of subsidy, here considered as a change in the 'rate of subsidy'.   The table shows only the latter element, i.e. changes in the 'rate of subsidy' in this sense.

changes have probably also had a less heralded impact on investment demand. To some extent this has been consciously exploited, in particular by the variation of the depreciation allowances under the tax laws.

The scheme of 'initial' allowances was introduced in 1945 as a way of increasing the finance available for post-war reconstruction[1]; and as some sort of recognition of the fact that the current aggregate of depreciation allowances, assessed on the original cost of the capital in use, was insufficient for its replacement at post-war prices. It was a scheme of accelerated depreciation. In addition to the proportion (depending on the assumed life of the asset) normally allowable in the first year, a further proportion of the cost of an asset was allowed free of tax in the year of purchase. The additional allowance was twenty per cent for plant and machinery and ten per cent for building works. Correspondingly less was allowed in the later years of the asset's life, so that over the whole agreed life of the plant, the same aggregate was granted in depreciation. The effect could be considered to be that of an interest-free loan from the government—the amount of the loan being something like half the allowance (since the rate of tax was fifty per cent). Considered in this light, the additional inducement to invest was small—say, something like a reduction in the rate of interest by $\frac{1}{2}$ per cent. But unlike most loans, the amount made available in effect constituted an addition to the finance available to a firm from internal sources.

In 1949 Sir Stafford Cripps doubled the initial allowances, still on the general grounds that investment ought to be encouraged; and that, with 'the further rise in prices . . . current depreciation allowances on machinery'—even with the twenty per cent initial allowance—'are not sufficient to allow replacement'[2]. In 1951 Mr Gaitskell announced the suspension of these arrangements with effect from April 1952. He recognized that since 'the planning and execution of most investment takes a considerable time, the scope for restriction this year, 1951, is obviously limited' and he expected the effect to be seen, not only in 1951, but in 'later years'[3]. In 1953, Mr Butler felt able to restore the initial allowances but only at the original rate of twenty per cent (with immediate effect), to help meet the 'urgent' need for 'more investment in productive industry and agriculture'; and he expected (at least some) 'increased demand for investment this year'[4].

In 1954, Mr Butler made the allowances even more clearly into an instrument for influencing investment by substituting for the initial allowances a new allowance called the 'investment allowance'. This was not accelerated depreciation, but a permanent exemption from taxation. Thus, while the

---

[1]Partial refunds of wartime payments of excess profits tax, and war damage payments, were also thought of as a financial facilitation of reconstruction.
[2]*H.C. Deb.* 6 April 1949, 2105.
[3]*H.C. Deb.* 10 April 1951, 842.
[4]*H.C. Deb.* 14 April 1953, 49–50.

Table 7.8.   *Value of 'initial' and 'investment' allowances, 1946–59 (£m.)*

	Companies	Persons	Total	Changes
1946	97	17	114	
1947	85	17	102	− 12
1948	95	20	115	+ 13
1949	185	36	221	+106
1950	227	42	269	+ 48
1951	238	43	281	+ 12
1952	111	41	152	−129
1953	104	46	150	− 2
1954	157	56	213	+ 63
1955	205	62	267	+ 54
1956	227	74	301	+ 34
1957	267	73	340	+ 39
1958	334	79	413	+ 73
1959	352	91	443	+ 30

From *NI & E* [1957] and [1960].

Table 7.9.   *Rates of 'initial' and 'investment' allowances, 1945–59 (percentages of investment expenditure allowed under (A) 'initial' or (B) 'investment' allowances)*

Announcement	Effective date	Plant and machinery[a]		Indus-trial building		Agri-cultural works and buildings		Mining works		Con-struction of ships	
		A	B	A	B	A	B	A	B	A	B
1945	April 1944	20	..	10	..	0	..	10	..	20	..
1949, April	Immediate	40	..	10	..	0	..	10	..	40	..
1951, April	April 1952	0	..	0	..	0	..	0	..	0	..
1953, April	Immediate	20	..	10	..	0	..	40	..	20	..
1954, April	Immediate	..	20[b]	..	10	..	10	40	or 20[c]	..	20
1956, February	Immediate	20	..	10	..	0	..	40	..	..	20[d]
1957, April	Immediate	20	..	10	..	0	..	40	..	..	40
1958, July[e]	April 1958	30	..	15	..	0	..	40	..	..	40
1959, April	Immediate	10	20	5	10	..	10	20	20	..	40

[a]Capital expenditure for scientific research was also eligible for initial and investment allowances but at times treated differently from expenditure on plant and machinery.

[b]Did not apply to cars for business use which continued to be eligible for initial allowances.

[c]For mining works *either* an initial allowance of 40 per cent *or* an investment allowance of 20 per cent could be claimed.

[d]The investment allowance remained in force only for ships (and here were indeed soon doubled).

[e]An increase of allowances to 25 and 12½ per cent was announced in the April 1958 budget: in July these were further increased to 30 and 15 per cent.

initial allowances gave 'extra help in the year in which investment was under-taken . . . at a cost of smaller allowances for that investment in later years', the new allowance gave similar help in the first year, but with no reduction in subsequent years[1]. The rates of allowance were twenty per cent of expenditure on plant and machinery and ten per cent on new industrial and agricultural buildings. Thus, it gave the same help to firms' liquidity as the previous initial allowances. But, by excusing tax[2] on the amount of the allowance, it gave a subsidy of about ten and five per cent respectively on plant and buildings.

The boom and accompanying balance of payments crisis of 1955 led to the investment allowances being withdrawn early in 1956, the old initial allowances being restored in their place. When two years later policy began to become re-expansionary again, one of Mr Amory's first steps was to increase these moderately. In his 1958 budget he proposed an increase of the allowances by a quarter, which was later (in July) changed to an increase of one half. In his 1959 budget, the investment allowance was again reinstated—at the same rates as in 1954 but this time with an initial allowance, half as large, in addition. These successive changes are tabulated for convenience in table 7.9.

The ten years since 1949 thus saw the emergence of a new fiscal instrument, at first intended as a general encouragement for investment, and later becoming an adjustable means of influencing investment as the situation required. It has already been pointed out that policy was hampered by the lack of an accepted theory of the factors determining investment expenditure. Perhaps for this reason, it has never been quite clear how much effect the authorities expected to have. Though there has been some tendency to belittle the initial allowances as no more than an interest-free loan, this has not prevented their use as an instrument of policy. But when the government has wished to make a pro-nounced impact on investment, it has resorted to the investment allowances.

Much investment expenditure appears notably insensitive to the rate of interest; and would be expected therefore to be insensitive also to small induce-ments by way of subsidy. The subsidy element in the investment allowances may, however, have been large enough to be effective. Both types of allowance —initial and investment allowance alike—have also a 'liquidity effect'. They have considerably increased the amount of investment which firms could undertake without resorting to outside finance. This too could be expected to be a stimulant to investment; and reasons are given at a later stage of this study for thinking that the effect of this additional finance may have been appreciable[3]. The extent of extra finance has been considerable. The value of the initial allowances plus the investment allowances has increased in ten

---

[1] *H.C. Deb.* 6 April 1954, 225. Mr Butler remarked that the effect of the initial allowances was 'limited', 'since its effect is essentially that of an interest-free loan. As the cash resources of companies increase, this incentive becomes of less importance' (same deb. 224).

[2] The rate of income tax plus profits tax on undistributed profits was then 47½ per cent.

[3] Chapter XI.4 below.

Table 7.10.   *Effects of tax changes on business finance (£m.)*

	Companies	Small traders and partners[a]	Total	of which Initial or investment allowances	Total as % of GNP
1945–6[b]	−153	−30	−183		−2·0
1947[c]	67	− 4	63		0·6
1948		− 6	− 6		−0·1
1949	− 62	−14	− 76	−76	−0·7
1950		− 6	− 6		
1951	233	36	269	264	2·0
1952	100	−14	86		0·6
1953	−238	−24	−262	−84	−1·7
1954	− 4		− 4	− 4	
1955[c]	− 4	− 8	− 12		−0·1
1956	30	−10	20		0·1
1957	− 47	− 4	−51	−12	−0·3
1958	− 35	− 4	− 39	−23	−0·2
1959	− 72	−13	− 85		−0·4
1960	65		65		0·3

Estimates of 'full' year effects on revenue from table 7.5.
[a]Effect of changes in profits tax and in initial or investment allowances *plus* one quarter of effect of other tax changes on personal incomes from dividends, interest and trading.
[b]Includes effects of autumn budget of 1945.
[c]Includes effect of autumn budget.

years from £100 million or so to well over £400 million (table 7.8).   The additional finance provided was some 40–50 per cent of these amounts (this being the rate of tax on corporate profits[1]).

Changes in income tax and in profits tax have also made a substantial difference to the finance available to firms.   The possible effects on investment expenditure have, however, been little remarked on.   The greater part of the effect of tax changes on business falls on companies (table 7.10).   The effect on unincorporated businesses is more difficult to estimate, since their finances are part and parcel of the personal finances of their owners.   But it seems reasonable to assume that a good part of the impact of a change in tax falls not on their spending as consumers, but on their means to finance the investment in their businesses[2].   Table 7.10 shows that changes in the rates of income tax and profits

[1]The allowances apply also to non-corporate enterprise, the rate of tax probably being somewhat higher than the standard rate of income tax (as above) because many owners of unincorporated businesses pay surtax.
[2]The figures in table 7.10 are guesses based on the estimates in table 7.5.   They assume (1) that the whole effect on small businesses of changes in profits tax and the depreciation allowance falls on saving not personal consumption, (2) that one quarter of the effect of other tax changes on personal incomes from dividends, interest and trading falls on small business saving on the grounds (a) that trading incomes are half the total of this group of incomes (b) that the propensity to save is high and perhaps 0.5.

tax have been far more frequent, and their financial effect often a lot larger, than changes in the rate of initial investment allowances.

This line of reasoning suggests that changes in income tax and profits tax may therefore have had as much effect on investment as the changes in either the initial or the investment allowances.   Such effects were not intended.   On the theoretical plane therefore, fiscal policy may well have been inconsistent and incomplete[1].   It should be added that what in practice was done was perhaps very much what would have been done if the possible effects on investment had been taken into account.   For, as it happened, other changes in taxation always worked in the same direction as the changes in the initial and investment allowances (table 7.10) and in general supported the current emphasis of policy towards investment.

The total impact on investment demand must therefore have been considerable.   The main doubt must indeed be whether in the formulation of policy the full effects were allowed for.   The main impact of fiscal—or any other—measures to affect investment probably occur later rather than sooner, and take perhaps two years rather than one to appear.   Policy, however, has been shaped by current pressures, not remote contingencies.   The wisdom of the timing of policy is discussed further in the next section.

5.   THE EFFECTIVENESS OF FISCAL POLICY AS AN INSTRUMENT OF STABILIZATION

This analysis in general supports the view that fiscal policy has been a powerful instrument for keeping demand in balance with supply; but it also suggests that it has had, and probably must always have, some limitations.

The best measure of the impact of fiscal policy is the extent of tax variations. If fiscal policy is to compensate for fluctuations elsewhere in the economy, it has to compensate not only for variations in government expenditure, but also for variations in investment and in the net foreign balance and possibly also in investment.   Fluctuations in government expenditure have as a rule—though with the important exception of defence expenditure in 1950–1—been relatively unimportant.   Nor, as already argued, can government expenditure be varied quickly from its planned level.   Short-period adjustments have therefore to be made chiefly via the adjustment of tax rates.

The previous analysis suggests that tax changes are likely to have large effects.   Fiscal policy has traditionally been chiefly conceived as a way of influencing consumers' expenditure.   Any change brought about in consumers'

[1]The taxation of profits necessarily raises major questions of equity.   That changes in the taxation of profits were usually made on social or political grounds is therefore not necessarily a criticism of policy.   But changes in the allowances were treated as a technical matter outside the realms of equity.   In fact changes in the allowances and other changes in the taxation of profits raise similar issues both of social justice and of economic effect.

P

purchasing power is likely to be reflected in changes of consumer demand some-what smaller but of the same order.   Tax changes which do not affect consumers' purchasing power seem likely to have some appreciable effect on investment demand.   But the problem of utilizing these two effects is quite different, because the investment effects are likely to be delayed.   Consumer tax changes are bound to be the more important as a means of stabilizing the economy in the short run.   The effects of tax changes on consumer purchasing power in the last fifteen years have at times been appreciable.   But this in itself does not show that no mistakes were made, nor that fiscal policy was the one all-powerful factor at work in determining the level of demand.   The long-run trends—chiefly, the growth in private saving—have been such as to make possible a gradual reduction of the burden of taxation over the period as a whole[1].   To a large extent the impact of fiscal policy came from going 'slower than trend' at some times (e.g. 1948–50, or 1955–8); and more rapidly at others (1953, or 1958).   On three occasions, taxes were actually raised.   But on two of these (autumn 1947 and autumn 1955) policy was correcting what by then was clear had been a previous mistake (i.e. the tax cuts of 1945–6 and April 1955); and in the other case (1951), the circumstances (the defence programme) were, luckily, exceptional.

During the first part of the period, up to 1951, policy was trying to right a long-standing and persistent state of excess demand, rather than to deal with short-period fluctuations.   At the time it was thought both that demand might ebb rapidly, and that policy was contributing actively to its decline.   In retrospect it seems clear that the implicit strategy of policy was long-drawn and slow-working.   Taking the period from 1945–51 as a whole, taxes were not raised, but merely kept high.   The economy did eventually disinflate itself.   This was not due to any properties of the tax system which caused it to act as a 'built-in disinflator': indeed the reverse was true.   It was due fundamentally to the fact that private saving increased, and increased more than the increase in investment and the improvement in the foreign balance[2].   Given time, as produc-tion rose, wartime shortages both of consumer and of investment goods were bound to ease.   It is greatly to the credit of Dr Dalton and Sir Stafford Cripps that they did not follow a less austere fiscal policy, which would have been positively inflationary.   Nevertheless it seems clear in retrospect that the role of fiscal policy was then passive, rather than actively disinflationary.

Since 1951, the role of fiscal policy has been to act as a stabilizing instrument in a fuller sense.   The three-year pause in tax reductions in 1956–8 (see table 7.6) certainly played its part in disinflating the economy, as had the earlier phase of passive fiscal policy under Sir Stafford Cripps.   This was flanked by two periods when fiscal policy was expansionary: Mr Butler gave a large stimulus, first to consumption in 1952 and 1953, and then to investment in 1953 and 1954; and

[1]See chapter IV, especially table 4.3.
[2]See table 7.4 above.

Mr Amory in 1959 gave a large stimulus both to consumption and to investment (tables 7.6 and 7.9). These injections of purchasing power were relatively considerable. The average increase in national product over the later decade has been 2 or $2\frac{1}{2}$ per cent a year. The impact of tax cuts on consumer demand in 1952 and 1953, and again in 1958, were of the order of one per cent of the national product. They must therefore have caused a relatively large addition to the rate of growth in these years.

Whether the variations of fiscal policy were well-judged from the point of view of stabilizing the economy is a different question, and one where it is always easier to be wise in the light of hindsight than it is at the time. There now seems little doubt that policy was at times too much influenced by the superficial current appearance of events, and in particular by the state of the reserves; and that likewise the ability of policy to work a quick correction was over-estimated. The continued apparent success of policy in Mr Butler's first three years undoubtedly gave an illusion of security; and the very considerable stimulants supplied by policy in this period, reinforced as late as the April budget in that year, must have contributed largely to the boom and crisis of 1955. The tax increases in the autumn of 1955 came far too late to undo what had been done over the last three and a half years.

There are signs that some of the lessons of these mistakes have since been learned. A full appreciation of the logic of the situation might indeed require forecasting the trend of events over two or three years, and taking account of the repercussions of present action over a period as long as this. But short of this, it is a good deal if policy moves cautiously step by step, waiting for more remote repercussions to emerge before intervening further. If such a policy had been followed throughout the last ten years, policy interventions would almost certainly have been smaller, more gradual, more even and less dramatic. If *small* tax cuts had been made in 1952–4, it might not have been necessary to go slow with tax cuts during the 'cautious' phase 1956–8.

If this is true, it is a serious criticism of policy. It suggests that the major variations of fiscal policy were in fact not stabilizing, but rather themselves one of the main causes of instability; and that demand would have remained much more nearly in balance with supply if fiscal policy had, throughout the whole period, been less actively interventionist. It is indeed a question whether we have not been too clever by half; whether the economy cannot get on quite well without a hand on the steering wheel; whether even a good driver is an improvement on no driver at all. These are fundamental questions, which will have to be discussed further at a later stage[1].

Similar doubts apply to the wisdom of fiscal policy towards investment demand. Since the effects on investment demand take longer to work through there is even greater danger of measures being inappropriate by the time the effects appear. There are indeed at least two major instances where, in the

[1] See chapter XV below.

light of hindsight, policy was probably working in precisely the opposite direction to what would have been desirable. The first was in 1951–2: notice was given in April 1951 that the initial allowances would cease a year later; but by then demand was falling, and investment might more appropriately have been stimulated than discouraged. The second was in 1954–5: the investment allowances of 1954 must have contributed to the unwanted and unforeseen investment boom of 1955.

It is possible that such mistakes would have been avoided if more care had been taken to allow for the long-run effects of the measures themselves, and this alone would probably have helped. But a rational policy of active intervention would also need some view of the other factors influencing the state of the economy two or three years ahead. It is, however, doubtful whether it will ever be possible to make reliable forecasts so far ahead. It is therefore a serious question whether policy towards investment should not be confined to the passive role of not creating large fluctuations, rather than the active role of offsetting fluctuations arising for other reasons.

The experience of the last fifteen years also illustrates the political limitations to the use of fiscal policy. These apply chiefly to the use of fiscal policy to control consumption expenditure. To be effective, tax changes must affect most consumers, which is most of the electorate; no one likes taxes; and a tax change which to an economist is a mere fraction of a per cent of the national income, may well to a Chancellor of the Exchequer seem to spell life or death to his political future.

It is probably true to say that the most blatant weakness to be feared has not arisen: Chancellors of the Exchequer have not simply ignored such considerations as the likelihood of inflation, and lowered taxes merely to gain popularity[1]. The case has indeed at times been almost the contrary: Chancellors have at times been reluctant to lower taxes till the need was more than clear lest, if they were mistaken, they had later to put them up again. The trends have fortunately been such as to call, in most years and over the whole period, for taxes to be lowered not raised. This has eased the conduct of fiscal policy very greatly indeed. It is no doubt very largely coincidence, but it is also a fact that, of the three Chancellors who raised taxes substantially, all had ceased to be Chancellors within six months[2].

---

[1] The possible exceptions are April 1955 and April 1959, on both of which occasions taxes were lowered before a general election. The danger of inflation could be claimed to have then been clear; but the facts permitted misinterpretation at the time: see for 1955, chapter III.2; and for 1959, chapter III.5.

[2] Dr Dalton had to retire immediately after his autumn budget in 1947 through his slip in being too confidential with the press before the budget speech. Mr Gaitskell raised taxes in April 1951, and his party was defeated at the election in October. Mr Butler raised taxes in October 1955, and became Home Secretary next January. Both the autumn budgets of 1947 and 1955 appeared as something like admissions of the failure of past

Since 1951 Chancellors of the Exchequer have for such reasons sought, to varying degrees, to use monetary policy or other extra-budgetary measures as at least a partial alternative to fiscal policy. 'Classical' monetary policy has the advantages of affecting businesses, not consumers—a far smaller part of the electorate—and to be capable of appearing to being worked by a hidden hand not the government's. Credit restraints and hire-purchase controls—more obvious and, as this study argues, more effective instruments than monetary policy of the older type—have appeared as acceptable alternatives to fiscal policy: for in contrast to taxation, they curtail only the right to spend beyond one's income. Increased attempts have also been made to vary public investment contra-cyclically. Later chapters describing these measures conclude that they have been found either not particularly effective, or to have disadvantages of their own. But the political strains of operating fiscal policy will probably continue to make it desirable, where possible, not to rely on fiscal policy alone.

policy. The Labour Party would probably have lost the 1951 election in any case; but the tax increases cannot have helped. (This review goes up to 1960: subsequently Mr Selwyn Lloyd raised taxes in July 1961—and remained Chancellor for a year.)

CHAPTER VIII

VARIATIONS IN PUBLIC INVESTMENT AS AN INSTRUMENT OF STABILIZATION POLICY

The level of investment by the central government, the local authorities and the public corporations is all, in various ways, under the government's control. But since investment has to be planned a long time in advance, it has not been easy to alter its level quickly; and it has not proved possible to use variations in public investment—as economists at one time hoped it would be—as a major instrument of stabilization policy. This chapter is therefore short, and hardly more than an appendix to the previous chapter on fiscal policy. It describes the various powers of control over public investment (§1); and the various post-war attempts to cut public investment, from which has gradually evolved a flexible method of long-term control (§2).

1. GOVERNMENT POWERS OF CONTROL

Wartime thinking on employment policy treated the control of public investment as one of the most important of the means the government could use to influence demand. In the 1944 White Paper as much emphasis was given to this as was given to another device then in favour, the variation of national insurance contributions. The government announced that it would aim at least to prevent public investment falling in a slump, and if possible would go some way towards *contra-cyclical* variation[1]. In order to carry out this policy, the local authorities—and, said the White Paper, probably also, public utilities—'will be required to submit each year a programme of capital expenditure for five years ahead'—the latter part of which would be 'tentative and provisional'. The programmes 'will then be assembled by an appropriate co-ordinating body under Ministers and will be adjusted, upward or downward, in the light of the latest information on the prospective employment situation'. These ideas stemmed from the debate, going back perhaps to before the first war[2], which ranged widely in the inter-war years—from Keynes's scornful advocacy of pyramid building, or burying bank notes in old bottles so that private enterprise

---

[1]Cmd. 6527, *Employment Policy*, para. 62. The White Paper noted the 'practical limits': 'a large part of the capital expenditure of public authorities—for example on housing, schools and hospitals—is dictated by urgent public needs, the satisfaction of which cannot readily be postponed to serve the purposes of employment policy'.

[2]Henderson suggests that the idea of using public works 'goes back to the days of the pre-war Poor Law Commission, and was first, I think, put forward by Professor Bowley': H. D. Henderson [1935], 'Do We Want Public Works?' reprinted in the posthumous selection of his writings *The Inter-War Years* [1955], p. 155.

could dig them up again, to Henderson's carefully classified degrees of caution[1]. The ideas in the White Paper were indeed particularly close to those Meade had espoused[2].

Orientated entirely at this time against the danger of depression, it took many years to adjust these ideas to the actual post-war situation. Until 1947 or 1948, as already noted[3], though the situation was highly inflationary little real attempt was made to control public investment. Controls were rather used as a means of favouring some types of public investment, in particular housing, than as one of the means to restrict investment in total. Attempts were made to accumulate a reserve of works for use in a slump. But it proved impossible to persuade local authorities or public corporations, on whom detailed planning depended, and who were already doing all the investment which they were able or the government permitted them to do, to take this seriously. Control was at this time very much a short-term control. It was not perhaps till the later 'fifties that longer-term, and presumably more effective, means of control were developed.

The practice of making annual 'investment programmes' dates from 1948. These referred at first to all investment, both public and private. But when building controls were abolished in 1954, it was no longer possible to treat private investment as subject to control; it could be forecast, but no more. The annual programming procedure continued to apply to public investment. and since 1960 there has been a yearly White Paper describing the programmes[4]. Though programmes are compiled not only for the year immediately ahead but for the two succeeding years also, only those for the year ahead have been published.

The bodies responsible for public investment are very various, and the form and degree of control by the central government accordingly varies[5]. The central government's own investment (i.e. direct expenditure by government departments and other expenditure financed from votes) amounts to about one fifth of total public investment. Until the 1961 Post Office Act this was all subject to direct ministerial control through the appropriate spending depart-

---

[1]Keynes [1936], *General Theory of Employment, Interest and Money*, p. 129: Henderson, *op. cit.* A more practical study was that by R. F. Bretherton, F. A. Burchardt and R. S. G. Rutherford [1941], *Public Investment and the Trade Cycle in Great Britain*, one of whose main conclusions was the inadvisability of public works of a 'relief' character.

[2]See J. E. Meade [1936], *Economic Analysis and Policy*, chapter V. In 1944 Professor Meade was deputy director of the Economic Section, then in the Cabinet Office.

[3]See chapter VI.3: and the work there quoted: N. Rosenberg [1960], *Economic Planning in the British Building Industry, 1945–49.*

[4]*Public Investment in Great Britain* [1960], [1961] and [1962], Cmnd. 1203, 1522 and 1849.

[5]As the 1960 White Paper (para. 12) says, 'there are 27 gas and electricity boards, some 180 local education authorities, over 950 local government water undertakings, over 1,600 sewerage authorities and about 1,700 local housing authorities'. On the government's powers of influence see the 1960 White Paper and also the local authority associations' and the public corporations' evidence to the Radcliffe Committee (*Radcliffe, Memoranda*, IX and X).

ments; and to direct parliamentary control, since the expenditure is from votes. The bulk of the money goes on Post Office investment—since 1961 treated in the same way as investment by other nationalized industries[1]—the main roads, atomic energy development, the universities and hospitals.

Investment by the public corporations accounts for about two fifths of total public investment. Of this, nearly a half is due to the various electricity authorities, about a quarter to the Transport Commission, the rest being divided between the coal boards, the gas boards and the air corporations. The public corporations' investment is subject, under the nationalization statutes, to the approval of Ministers. Each authority operates on a long-term investment programme extending over five or ten years; and programmes have to obtain the general approval of the appropriate Minister (i.e. of Power or Transport). In addition, there is a detailed Treasury control on a year-to-year basis under the investment programmes procedure. The Boards' borrowing is also subject to limits approved from time to time by Parliament.

The remaining two fifths of public investment is the capital expenditure of the local authorities. This is financed as to ninety per cent by borrowing: investment then requires a 'loan sanction' from the appropriate Minister—a highly effective control[2]—as well as Treasury approval under the Control of Borrowing Order, 1958. Housing and education, comprising some two thirds of the local authorities' investment, are subject also to more detailed control: the acceptance of housing tenders has to be approved by the Ministers for housing; educational projects, by the Ministers for education.

2. THE CONTROL OF PUBLIC INVESTMENT, 1945-60

The long-term effects of government control over public investment have to be distinguished from the effects of efforts made at various times to make speedy adjustments in the level of public investment. For the first years after the war, as already noted[3], though investment was subject to widespread controls, the controls were hardly operated to have much restrictive effect—chiefly because Mr Bevan, as Minister of Housing, was chiefly anxious to get houses built. During the middle part of the period—say from 1948 till 1958—the general effect was to restrict public investment. In more recent years the general effect has been much less restrictive.

Restraint pressed much more hardly on some types of investment than others:

---

[1]Under the 1961 Post Office Act which gave much greater freedom of commercial operation, the Post Office is no longer required, as hitherto, to get specific parliamentary sanction and Treasury approval for all expenditures.

[2]'Through the granting or withholding of Ministry loan sanction, the Government has always had a very effective control over the greater part of the county council capital expenditure and borrowing, and capital projects are generally not brought forward where there is no likelihood of obtaining loan sanction' (*Radcliffe, Memoranda*, IX.2, para. 65).

[3]See chapter VI.3

Table 8.1. *Contra-cyclical public investment policy*

Action taken	Result seen	Action	Out-turn
1947		Cuts primarily on private investment	Little effect
1949	1950	Reduction in public programme	Some effect
	1951	*1951 boom not foreseen: restriction of private investment only for defence programme*	*Local authority house-building (though not public investment in total) fell because of bad weather*
	1955	*No action—1955 boom not foreseen*	*Local authority house-building reduced for non-economic reasons*
1955–6	1956	Public programmes reduced over £50 m.	Effect questionable
1957 end	1958	Ceiling on public investment (in 'money terms')	Ceiling effective: volume of public investment reduced
1958	1959	Public investment increased	Large increase resulted
1960	1961	Restraint of public investment	Effective

Episodes italicized were occasions when public investment fell for reasons unconnected with stabilization policy.

hardly, for instance, on roads, schools and hospitals, and also on railway modernization; less hardly on electricity expansion or coalmining re-equipment. During the last five years or so, some of these priorities have been reversed: thus local authority house-building has been restricted, while investment in roads and railways has increased.   Taking the post-war period as a whole, public investment has grown, but (unlike private investment) no more rapidly than total national product[1].

Superimposed on the more or less routine 'programming' of public investment, there have been five or six occasions when the government has sought to bring about rather a rapid change in the level of public investment.   In most cases this took the form of an attempted cut, as an emergency operation taken outside the normal proecedure of annual reviews.   Table 8.1 lists the chief episodes (more fully described below).   It also notes two occasions when public investment fell—1951 and 1955—for accidental reasons or for reasons

---

[1]Public investment as a proportion of the GNP rose from about 6 per cent in 1948 to nearly 9 per cent in 1953, and has since declined to about $7\frac{1}{2}$ per cent in 1960.   Private investment during the same period has risen from $7\frac{1}{2}$ per cent to 10 per cent of gross national product.

unconnected with stabilization policy[1]. By an ironic chance, these were both boom years—in which a reduction of public investment happened therefore to be particularly timely. The actual course of public investment is summarized in table 8.2.

The decision to cut investment in 1947–8 was one of a series of measures that followed the fuel crisis of February and the convertibility crisis in August[2]. The new programme was intended to produce a cut in total investment of about £130 million between 1947 and 1948[3]. Most of the cut was clearly intended to fall on private investment, but some sorts of public investment were also to be restricted[4]. In fact, total investment rose between 1947 and 1948—by just about as much as it had been supposed to fall. Public investment certainly shared in this increase: one reason why it did not fall is that the original policy was in part not enforced or was later reversed[5].

After the devaluation of 1949, there was a similar, though less ambitious, attempt to restrict investment in order to provide space for greater exports. Before the cuts it seems to have been intended that investment should rise by about £140 million between 1949 and 1950; and the new restrictions appear to have been intended to prevent this increase[6]. On the side of public investment, the restrictions involved a large cut in two expanding sectors, investment in fuel and power and in education. But in total, public investment was apparently intended to rise a bit. It is difficult to judge what effect the measures had. Investment in total increased by £80 million or so instead of remaining constant; and within this total, public investment also appears to have risen more than intended. Nevertheless, the 'cuts' probably prevented it rising as much as

---

[1]See further below.   Mr S. Please [1959] has tried to assess the counter-cyclical behaviour of public investment in an article on that subject in *Pub. Finance*, vol. XIV, no. 3–4 [1959]. His analysis is however based on statistics of what happened; and this is not a reliable index, for changes in public investment were by no means decided entirely for stabilization reasons.   He contends that in both the boom years 1951 and 1955, public investment was reduced; and, primarily on this evidence, concludes that public investment was consciously used as a stabilizing factor.   But (see chapter V above) neither boom was foreseen. It seems better to start with the intentions of policy.   Mr Please's figures also seem more favourable to his case than are the latest official estimates.

[2]See chapter II.2.

[3]Total gross fixed investment was expected to fall from a roughly estimated 'mid-1947 rate' of £1,550 million to an average 1948 rate of £1,420 million. (*Capital Investment in 1948*, Cmd. 7268, paras. 5 and 9).

[4]The main object of the new building programme was to finish houses already started: this meant getting more labour on to local authority house-building, and restricting other demands for building.   Much of the cut in 'plant and machinery' was in fact a cut in road vehicles for the home market—mostly classified as private investment.   But various public investment projects were postponed, e.g. telephone extensions, the Severn Bridge, the Great West Road/Cromwell Road extension, the Notting Hill Gate reconstruction, the rebuilding of Euston Station, and the deferment of replacement of railway coaches and permanent way. (Cmd. 7268, paras. 11 and 17 and appendices A and B.)

[5]See *Economic Survey for 1949*, and chapter VI.3 above.

[6]*Economic Survey for 1950*, para. 117.

Table 8.2. *Public investment, 1948–60 (£m. 1954 prices)*

	Central govern-ment	Public corpor-ations[a]	Local authorities House-building	Other in-vestment	Total public in-vestment[a]	*Total annual change*[a]	*of which house-building*
1948	142	233	324	145	844		
1949	143	334	321	151	949	*105*	*−3*
1950	155	350	315	185	1,005	*56*	*−6*
1951	190	351	296	199	1,036	*31*	*−19*
1952	217	364	330	199	1,110	*74*	*34*
1953	217	429	385	216	1,247	*137*	*55*
1954	184	494	355	220	1,253	*6*	*−30*
1955	181	514	284	222	1,201	*−52*	*−71*
1956	203	500	257	247	1,207	*6*	*−27*
1957	212	549	243	257	1,261	*54*	*−14*
1958	206	566	205	255	1,232	*−29*	*−38*
1959	214	617	207	283	1,321	*89*	*2*
1960	209	605	210	313	1,337	*16*	*3*

Estimated from *NI & E* [1959] and [1961].

[a] The steel industry was nationalized with effect from 1951; and denationalized gradually from 1953. To preserve comparability, investment in steel has been excluded throughout. For similar reasons the investment of British Road Services has also been excluded.

it would otherwise have done[1].

There were no 'investment cuts' in 1951 or 1952, though a general attempt was made to restrict *total* investment in order to favour exports and, in 1951, also to make way for the defence programme. But action was confined to financial discentives, in particular withdrawal of the initial allowances; or to agreeing with the producers to export more cars or capital goods. Such action was calculated to affect private investment. There appears to have been no parallel attempt to slow down public investment. Total investment in fact rose little between 1950 and 1952; and public investment continued to rise moderately rapidly[2].

The fall in public investment in 1955 (table 8.2), though it might appear so, was not a successful attempt to counter the 1955 boom—which was not foreseen at the time action would have had to be taken. It was due to a fall in local authority house-building, a decline which had started two years before, and which was part of a policy pursued by the Conservative government not as part of stabilization policy, but out of dislike of local government house-building.

[1] The programme given in *Economic Survey for 1950* shows public corporations' investment about stable, and local authorities' investment rather higher than in 1949. The public corporations in fact spent about the same in the two years (table 8.2), but local authorities spent quite a lot more. The effect of the 'cuts' on public investment may nevertheless have been £10–20 million.

[2] House-building fell off in 1951 (table 8.2); but this appears to have been due to bad weather (see *Economic Survey for 1952*, para. 81), and the government appears to have had no intention of cutting the housing programme (*Economic Survey for 1951*, para. 76).

The next attempt to restrain public investment was at the end of 1955 and in the early months of 1956. At the time of the autumn budget, local authorities were asked to keep investment other than housing in the next financial year down to the level ruling in the previous year 1954/55[1]. Though steps were also taken to restrict the investment of the nationalized industries and of the central government, the intention may have been to reduce future expansion rather than to produce a positive cut[2]. In February these restraints were greatly strengthened. The nationalized industries agreed to reduce their expenditure in 1956 by £50 million below the level to which it had already been restricted, and the 'same principles' were applied to the local authorities[3]. The practical effect of these measures was more or less to stabilize public investment: far from falling between 1955 and 1956, it rose slightly.

The next measures against public investment came, only eighteen months later, as part of Mr Thorneycroft's crisis measures. The 'ceiling' then imposed on public investment was intended to secure that public investment during the next two years was held constant, in money terms, at the level of 1957/58[4]. This involved a ten per cent cut on 'what at one time was forecast or planned' for the fuel and power industries; a cut in the Transport Commission's plans; and, more gradually, a twenty per cent reduction over the next two years in local authority housing[5]. Developments in 1958 followed this intended course remarkably closely. Public investment cost exactly what it had in the previous year. In terms of volume, it fell three per cent—chiefly, it would seem, because local authority housing fell more than intended. Had it not been for the cuts, public investment in 1958 might well have been £50 million higher.

This policy was, however, fairly rapidly modified. It was probably being less stringently applied by April 1958—when initial allowances were raised. By August, the public authorities concerned had been asked to expand their investment again, especially in housing, roads and railways[6]. Between 1958 and 1959 the volume of public investment rose seven per cent. Finally, in the middle of 1960, steps were taken to 'stabilize' public investment. The 'approved

---

[1]*H.C. Deb.* 26 Oct. 1955, 213: local authority house-building was not expected to increase.

[2]None of the cuts mentioned were for more than a few £ million. They included deferment of work on government offices on the Westminster Hospital and Horseferry Road sites—sites still unused eight years later.

[3]*H.C. Deb.* 17 Feb. 1956, 2678–9.

[4]' . . . these limits are expressed in money terms. If costs rise, the amount of work will have to be reduced so that expenditure limits will not be exceeded. We do not intend to finance the inflation . . . ' (*H.C. Deb.* 29 Oct. 1957, 55).

[5]Same deb. 53.

[6]*Economic Survey, 1959*, para. 2. Local authority housing was expected to increase by 2 per cent (*ibid.*, App. B, para. 26). The Electricity Council was also asked to expand investment, 'although to a relatively modest degree' (*Radcliffe, Memoranda*, X, para. 15, note).

total' of public investment in 1961/62 was to be the same as in the previous financial year[1]. The measures seem to have been effective[2].

The decade and a half since the war have thus seen the gradual evolution of a flexible procedure for the long-term control of public investment. In the late 'forties the control of public investment was part of a general effort, year in, year out, to contain inflation; or, in an emergency, to cut demand in a crisis. During the first four years of Conservative rule, it seemed possible to believe there was going to be less need for such action. But then came a series of new investment cuts; and these caused much the same complaints of disruptive government action by those on whom they were imposed, as did, in a different sphere, the frequent variations of purchase tax and of hire-purchase controls. The present procedure is therefore designed to give those who have to carry out public investment sufficient assurance for long-term planning, while preserving some degree of flexibility. But this has meant giving up the hope of being able to bring about rapid major changes in public investment as a way of controlling the economy[3].

This conclusion of policy appears entirely realistic. The government no longer hopes to alter public investment by more than £50 million in the course of a year or so: but no post-war attempt to cut it has probably succeeded in affecting public investment more severely. There are indeed three good and fundamental reasons for not trying to elevate the control of public investment to being a major instrument of stabilization policy. First, public investment accounts for well under ten per cent of total final demand: fluctuations would therefore have to be enormous to compensate for major fluctuations elsewhere. Second, as already argued in connection with fiscal policy, consumers' expenditure (which can be affected by fiscal policy) is much more readily changed at short notice than is fixed investment. Third, reliable forecasts of the situation two or three years ahead will probably never be possible. Given two or three years' notice, large changes can be made in public investment—and indeed have to be made now in the light of the situation thought likely. But if events do not go according to plan, and quick adjustments are needed, fiscal policy and monetary policy are bound to be more important instruments of control.

---

[1] *H.C. Deb.* 23 June 1960, 651; and Cmnd. 1203.

[2] Public investment in 1961/62 was over £50 million larger in volume than in the previous year (1954 prices). But this was because investment in 1960/61 had fallen below 'approvals' —largely it seems due to errors in programming and to pressure on the building industry (Cmd. 1522, para. 13).

[3] 'We doubt,' said Mr Amory, 'whether action of this kind could alter the aggregate of public sector investment within a period of 12 to 18 months by more than 2 or 3 per cent without causing harmful dislocation or defeating its own object by reason of the delays inevitable in carrying the action through.' (Speech to Association of Municipal Treasurers reported in *Economist*, 25 June 1960, p. 1357). Mr Selwyn Lloyd later stated the same doctrine in other words in putting the possible variation up or down as '£30 million to £50 million' (*H.C. Deb.* 9 Nov. 1960, 1057).

CHAPTER IX

MONETARY POLICY, 1945–60

In contrast to budgetary policy, there has been no generally accepted theory of how monetary policy operates. The ideas of the authorities have changed; policies pushed far in one direction have later come to be thought mistaken; and aspects of policies neglected at some times have later been given greater emphasis. The range of outside opinion has been even wider; what by some are regarded as mere aspects are by others elevated to prime objects of policy. The *Radcliffe Report*[1] has had the effect of putting much of the controversy into proportion; but some of its conclusions are, as yet, controversial.

The present account is intended to be, as far as possible, a 'neutral' account of post-war monetary policy that does not prejudge the controversial issues; but leaves them to be discussed separately at a later stage[2]. It aims to give, first, a historical narrative of monetary measures, so as to describe the changing attitudes of the authorities. Secondly, it aims to describe the main monetary trends which are frequently singled out as having an important effect on the economy; and which could have been influenced by the authorities, whether or not the authorities chose to exert this influence. The behaviour of the banks may at times influence the 'real' economy; but the way the authorities influence the behaviour of the banks is from the present point of view of subordinate interest, and is therefore given only a secondary place in the following discussion. The emphasis throughout is on the *internal* effects of monetary trends and policy: repercussions on capital movements from or to other countries are briefly considered only at the end.

The arrangement of the chapter is as follows. §1 deals with the cheap money policy of 1945–7; §2 with subsequent trends in long-term interest rates, debt management, and the volume of money. §3 deals with restrictions on bank advances; and §4 deals with trends in capital issues and the capital issues control. §5 discusses the control of hire purchase; and §6 the effect of monetary policy on building society lending. To pull these various strands together, and to give some idea of what the authorities expected of more active monetary intervention, §7 gives a résumé of monetary policy since 1951.

Some conclusions about monetary policy are relatively easy to draw: thus the authorities' ideas about what monetary policy could do were at times plainly exaggerated. But there remain many issues which are far from simple. The

[1] The *Report* of the Committee on the Working of the Monetary System (Cmnd. 827, August 1959) is here referred to as the *Radcliffe Report;* the Committee's Minutes of Evidence as *Radcliffe, Minutes;* and the Memoranda of Evidence as *Radcliffe, Memoranda.*

[2] The present account incorporates material, often in much revised form, from the paper submitted by myself to the Radcliffe Committee (see 'The Economic Effect of Monetary Policy, 1945–57', *Radcliffe, Memoranda,* XIII. 9, pp. 76–105).

final §8 is therefore intended only to get the more obvious points out of the way, and to list the issues which will have to be discussed more fully at a later stage (chapter XII).

1. CHEAP MONEY, 1945-7

During the first two years of peace, the rate of interest on bonds was brought down, as a matter of policy, from 3 to 2½ per cent. Thereafter it rose fairly steadily, though with some setbacks, to a level by 1960 around 6 per cent (fig. 9.1). But this was not deliberate policy: after 1947—and until perhaps 1958— the authorities ceased to have a conscious policy toward the long-term rate. The rise in the rate was, however, assisted by a policy of funding the national debt pursued for other, more limited, reasons.

Because the cheap money policy of the first two post-war years has come to be associated with Dr Dalton, it may now be forgotten that a policy of at least moderately cheap money was then in favour with almost all strands of opinion. The cheap money view rested on a combination of considerations. It had been possible to finance the war on the basis of three per cent for long-term government borrowing, and to keep short rates down to one per cent[1]; and there seemed advantage in maintaining this—at least for the post-war transition. From the narrowly budgetary point of view, the argument for reducing the service of the national debt remained almost as pressing as during the war. At the same time, there was general scepticism about the effects of interest rates upon investment, and thus upon the economy at large[2]. There was general agreement that during the transition period, controls would have to remain in force, including controls on investment[3]: this seemed to make high interest rates even if otherwise desirable, unnecessary. The transition period was, moreover, expected to be short; and beyond it, the danger foreseen was not inflation but deflation[4]. So far as interest rates could help at all, it would, after this phase, be low interest rates that were going to be needed.

The cheap money policy pursued from the middle of 1945 to the middle of 1947 was, however, given a strong personal flavour by the active interest of the Chancellor of the Exchequer, Dr Dalton. It may be said that, both as regards

---

[1] For wartime policy, see R. S. Sayers [1956], *Financial Policy, 1939-45*, chapter V.
[2] Thus the 1944 White Paper on *Employment Policy*, published by the Coalition Government, was tepid in advocating the interest rate as an instrument of stabilization policy:—
    ' . . . the possibility of influencing capital expenditure by the variation of interest rates will be kept in view . . .
    'Monetary policy alone, however, will not be sufficient to defeat the inherent instability of capital expenditure. High interest rates are more effective in preventing excessive investment in periods of prosperity than are low interest rates in encouraging investment in periods of depression'. (Cmd. 6527, paras. 59–60.)
[3] See, for instance, the White Paper on *Employment Policy*, para. 16.
[4] The White Paper is its own evidence for the seriousness with which this prospect was taken: see also chapter II.2 above.

its end and as regards its methods, he converted a cheap money policy into a cheap money campaign. In his thinking, the redistributional effects of cheap money were paramount: the interest of the nation, no less than that of the government, stood opposed to that of the lenders of money. 'So long as the National Debt endures', he said, '—and that may be for a long time yet—the Chancellor of the Exchequer must be on the side of the borrowers of money as against the money lenders, on the side of the active producer as against the passive *rentier*'[1]. Though the Opposition did not endorse these reasons for the pursuit of cheap money, it was at first in full sympathy with the policy itself. Even in April 1947, its complaint was only that the Chancellor was 'in too great a hurry' to get down to 2½ per cent; even as late as November, Opposition spokesmen could declare they had never opposed cheap money as such[2].

---

[1]Dr Dalton's defence of his policy, made in the course of his budget speech in April 1947 when cheap money was already under some attack, is worth quoting at greater length:

'I have heard some criticism from time to time of my cheap money policy, in defence of which therefore, I now ask leave to say a few words. The steady and progressive reduction in the rates of Government borrowing over the last 18 months has brought great and solid benefit, not to one section only, but to the nation as a whole. . . First and foremost comes the relief to the taxpayer, on whom falls the burden of servicing the National Debt, now grown to gigantic proportions as a consequence of two great wars . . .'

'But cheap money benefits not only the central Government. It benefits the local authorities; it benefits the great public boards; it benefits private industry at large; and indeed it benefits other members of the British Commonwealth of Nations'.

' . . . Finally, I repeat these are gains which benefit the whole community, section by section, right throughout the national life. But I would add that these are only a beginning. The volume of borrowing which has taken place so far, during the period of the cheap money drive, is small compared with that which we have in prospect during the next few years . . . So long as the National Debt endures— and that may be for a long time yet—the Chancellor of the Exchequer must be on the side of the borrowers of money as against the money lenders, on the side of the active producer as against the passive *rentier*.

'There has been a long Debate about cheap money. The late Lord Keynes . . . was very definitely in favour of cheap money . . . Lord Keynes wrote a famous Tract on Monetary Reform, in which he said :—

"The active and working elements in no community, ancient or modern, will consent to hand over to the *rentier* or bond holding class more than a certain proportion of the fruits of their work. When the piled up debt demands more than a tolerable proportion, relief has usually been sought" either in straight-out Repudiation of the Debt or in devaluation of the Currency . . . But there is another way of partial relief from these tremendous debt burdens, and that is by the pursuit of cheap money and low interest rates. If rates of interest now were what they were at the end of the first World War, where should we be? What would be the annual cost of the National Debt? What would the Income Tax be? What would the other taxes be?'

H.C. Deb. 15 April 1947, 61–4: Dr Dalton's quotation was from Keynes [1923], *A Tract on Monetary Reform*, p. 64. Dr Dalton later was somewhat ashamed of his defence of cheap money on this occasion, describing it as 'rhetorical and even a bit shrill' (Dalton [1962], *High Tide and After*, p. 230).

[2]Sir John Anderson as he then was, as ex-Chancellor and chief Opposition speaker in the budget debate of October 1945, was in complete agreement:

'As the Chancellor knows, studies on this whole question of interest rates had been in progress within the Treasury for some time before he assumed his present

It can be argued that Dr Dalton, in order to produce the fall in interest rates he wanted, ought to have been ready to countenance a substantial increase in the money supply. The argument rests on the belief that the amount of money people wish to hold depends on how much they sacrifice by holding money rather than bonds, i.e. that the rate of interest on bonds and the quantity of money are interrelated[1]. On this argument, then, open market purchases of bonds, designed to raise their price, financed by expansion of short-term debt and involving an increase in bank deposits, ought to have been accepted as a corollary of a cheap money policy.

Dr Dalton's view was different. Keynes had remarked that the rate of interest was a conventional or psychological phenomenon, its present value being 'largely governed by the prevailing view as to what its value is expected to be'[2]. If this were the whole truth, then nothing more was required than to work on market expectations: any obstacles, being psychological, could be overcome by a species of psychological warfare. As Dr Dalton said in March 1947, 'we have been gradually conditioning the capital market to a long-term rate of $2\frac{1}{2}$ per cent for gilt-edged. We have met some psychological resistance, but I am convinced that it is in the national interest that this should be overcome'[3].

The process culminated with the issue of the famous 'Daltons' in October

office. I do not hesitate to say that if I had been in his position I should have done exactly what he has done' (i.e. reduced short-term rates).

'The whole problem of interest rates is rather fascinating. Interest rates, as far as I understand the position, do not respond fully to the ordinary economic laws of supply and demand. There is what may be called a psychological factor to be taken into account. . . . Not only are the Government in a position to exercise a greater control than was previously possible over short-term rates, but the question which, in my view, is the important question in connection with interest rates, the question of the proper relation between longer term and short-term rates, can now be tackled. I was glad to hear that the Chancellor is going into that matter. He has very competent advisers in the Treasury who, I am sure, will serve him well' (*H.C. Deb.* 24 October 1945, 2019–20).

A year and a half later in the April budget debate of 1947, Sir John Anderson spoke again, and less enthusiastically; but his opposition to cheap money was not outright: 'I have always said . . . there was a danger of carrying that policy forward too quickly and too far, and I think the Chancellor has fallen into that danger. I think he was in too great a hurry to get down to the $2\frac{1}{2}$ per cent basis' (*H.C. Deb.* 16 April 1947, 203). Again as late as November 1947 Mr Oliver Stanley could declare: 'We have never complained of cheap money as an objective; what we have complained of are the methods he has adopted in order to reach it'. He went on to complain (illogically enough) of capital gains (*H.C. Deb.* 13 November 1947, 563).

[1] Full consideration of this matter must be deferred until chapter XII.

[2] J. M. Keynes [1936], *General Theory of Employment, Interest and Money*, p. 203. Dr Dalton later claimed that, 'contrary to what some have alleged', Keynes 'was not weakening at all, at the end of his life, in support of cheap money, or of the immediate steps required to cheapen it further' (Dalton [1962], p. 161). At the time of Keynes's death in April 1946, Dr Dalton's attack on the long rate had not been pushed very far.

[3] *H.C. Deb.* 10 March 1947, 1076.

Q

1946—2½ per cent undated Treasury stock redeemable in 1975 or after. In total £482 million of 'Daltons' were issued[1]. But it was believed at the time that much of it was in fact taken up not by the public but by the departments; and that the failure to persuade the public to buy bonds necessitated heavy borrowing from the banks, of which the rapid rise in bank deposits during much of 1946 was the reflection[2]. Such complaints were angrily received by Dr Dalton as seeming to cast doubts on the success of his policy; and were met, not by a defence that the rise in bank deposits was justifiable, but by denial that deposits were still rising or would do so in future[3].

By then bank deposits had in fact ceased to rise so rapidly. The reason for the earlier rise, and subsequent deceleration sprang, however, less from debt policy, than from the scale of Exchequer borrowing. During the first year or two of peace, the Exchequer deficit was only less large than during the war itself. But by the end of 1946, the Exchequer was no longer borrowing on a large scale (table 9.1)[4]. Equally important, the proceeds of the American loan were by then available. Instead, therefore, of large-scale borrowing from the public, the Exchequer started to repay internal loans on a considerable scale. The authorities could, of course, had they so wished, have continued to borrow heavily from the banks, and repaid even more long-term debt that they in fact did. But, as already noted, this was never intended to be part of Dr Dalton's strategy of cheap money.

The fact that bank credit ceased to rise rapidly, may nevertheless be one important reason for the failure of the policy. Equally important was the mounting tide of criticism[5], and the effect on the market of the convertibility crisis of August 1947. This led to a collapse of gilt-edged prices which pushed the yield on irredeemables to over three per cent. Financial commentators noted not only that the government broker was inactive, but that the Chancellor omitted to reaffirm his faith in low rates[6]. When Sir Stafford Cripps succeeded

[1]Of this, £305 million was in exchange for Local Loans Stock called in, and £177 million was for cash.

[2]See, for instance, W. T. C. King, 'Gilt-edged and the Volume of Money', *Banker*, October 1946.

[3]*H.C. Deb.* 10 March 1947, 1069–70.

[4]Table 9.1 summarizes the quarterly statistics of Exchequer borrowing which have subsequently been published (*Econ. Trends*, December 1961). The quarterly figures show that in the second half of 1946, long-term debt with the public was reduced at the same time as short-term debt was increased—most of the latter increase coming from the banks. But this was on a relatively small scale and only lasted a short while, and was probably intended to be a merely temporary phase. In the earlier period—from the end of the war to the middle of 1946—precisely the reverse was true: long-term borrowing was sufficient to permit a reduction of the short-term debt.

[5]Criticism began to be vocal from about the time when 'Daltons' were issued in October 1946: see for instance the article by W. T. C. King [1946], already cited, in the *Banker*, October 1946; and Dr Dalton's reply in his Mansion House speech in October (quoted in Dalton [1962], pp. 164–5). The annual 'statements' by the chairmen of the joint-stock banks at the beginning of 1947 were almost unanimously critical of the cheap money policy.

[6]See *Banker*, September 1947.

to the Exchequer in November, he formally reaffirmed the cheap money policy. But two months later he in effect wrote its epilogue by issuing Transport Stock at three per cent, and fixing the same rate for long loans from the Public Works Loan Board.

It remains, however, an open question whether the cheap money policy could not have succeeded in getting the long-term rate down to $2\frac{1}{2}$ per cent and keeping it there. The fact that it failed gives an air of inevitability to the failure; but it constitutes no proof[1]. Still less does it show that the rate of interest depends on 'market forces' and is in principle beyond the reach of the authorities to control—though their later attitude suggests that they draw something like this conclusion.

2. DEBT MANAGEMENT AND THE LONG-TERM RATE OF INTEREST, 1948–60

After the collapse of the cheap money policy, the authorities ceased to have any very active policy of monetary intervention. Sir Stafford Cripps was Chancellor of the Exchequer for three years from November 1947 to October 1950. This period might be described as the St Lucy's day[2] of monetary policy: for a year or two in the middle of the period there is scarcely a sentence in any official statement which mentions credit or interest rates[3]. It is probably correct

---

[1]Compare Joan Robinson: 'All goes smoothly so long as the authorities are working with the grain of market opinion. But if they . . . begin to buy bonds at a time when the long rate is generally expected to rise, they come sharply into conflict with market opinion . . . If they persist resolutely, a moment will come when the bears are convinced that the new low rate has come to stay . . .

'But if the authorities' nerves are shaken by the ferocious growls with which the bears have been deafening them all this time, and once allow bond prices to relapse, the growling of the bears turns to joyous yelps of "I told you so" and the expected future bond rate is so much the higher for ever after'. J. Robinson [1951], 'The Rate of Interest' reprinted in *The Rate of Interest* [1952], p. 30. (But see further chapter XII.3 below.)

[2]St. Lucy's day is the 22nd December: compare John Donne:
'Tis the yeares midnight, and it is the dayes,
Lucies, who scarce seaven houres herself unmaskes'.

[3]Within a few days of his accession to the Exchequer, Sir Stafford Cripps was found defending cheap money. His defence recognized the criticism made of cheap money that it encouraged capital expenditure. To this his reply was that if interest rates were to be an effective brake they would have to be very high; that the effect of this would be 'wholly unselective'; and that the government therefore preferred to use physical controls. (*H.C. Deb.* 17 November 1947, 939–43.)

References to monetary policy were thereafter very sparse indeed. In the budget speeches of 1948, 1949 and 1950 there is no mention of monetary policy; unless a very oblique one can be seen in 1950 in the statistical recitation of changes in the volume of the National Debt and note circulation, or in the phrase that the fiscal policy of the government is 'the most important single instrument' for maintaining a balance between inflation and deflation (*H.C. Deb.* 18 April 1950, 62). The *Economic Survey for 1949* contained the sentence: 'continued restraint in the provision of credit is desirable if investment is not to be excessive' (Cmd. 7647, para. 112). The fullest explanation of policy was Sir Stafford Cripps's statement in the 'devaluation' debate in October 1949: this was concerned chiefly with the question of bank advances: see §3 below.

Table 9.1.   *Exchequer financing, 1945/46 to 1960/61 (£m.)*

Financial years, April to March

	Exchequer borrowing			External finan-cing[b]	Total internal borrow-ing	of which		
	For above-the-line deficit	Other require-ments[a]	Total			Treasury bills and TDR's	Net sales of bonds[c]	Other borrow-ing[d]
1945/46	2,207	−78	2,129	64	2,065	320	992	753
1946/47	586	261	847	277	570	320	−38	288
1947/48	−636	840	204	902	−698	−50	−463	−185
1948/49	−831	479	−352	428	−780	−769	67	−78
1949/50	−549	325	−224	91	−315	56	−323	−48
1950/51	−720	407	−313	−661	348	182	81	85
1951/52	−380	633	253	1,063	−810	−1,608	834[e]	−36
1952/53	−88	691	603	−127	730	306	433	−9
1953/54	−94	555	461	−341	802	284	459	59
1954/55	−433	502	69	−175	244	48	18	178
1955/56	−397	756	359	120	239	38	232	−31
1956/57	−290	484	194	201	−7	−364	180	177
1957/58	−423	528	105	−139	244	235	−110	119
1958/59	−377	349	−28	−250	222	−111	−64	397
1959/60	−386	674	288	−81	369	462	−519	426
1960/61	−147	418	271	−289	560	−288	292	556

From *Econ. Trends*, October 1959 and December 1961 and *MDS*.

[a]Below-the-line deficit *plus* borrowing for capital requirements of nationalized industries and Post Office *less* receipts from extra-budgetary funds.

[b]Sterling receipts of Exchange Equalization Account *plus* American Aid *plus* net external loans to UK government.

[c]Issues *less* redemptions of government and guaranteed stocks.

[d]Increase in fiduciary note issue *plus* small savings, tax reserve certificates and other non-marketable issues.

[e]Includes issue of £1,000 million of 1¾ per cent Serial Funding Stock in exchange for Treasury bills (see text).

to say that the aim was a 'neutral' money policy, which would not work against the general aim of disinflation—as Dr Dalton's policy was, by then, generally thought to have done[1].

[1]The *Banker* commented in February 1951:
'   . . . the authorities have never given any sign of intent to use control over the volume of money as a positive instrument of economic discipline; all the evidence confirms that the principles evolved in the post-Dalton phase were designed to ensure a *neutral* policy, in which the monetary trends would conform to the pattern set by Budgetary policy and by the other instruments (such as control of investment and of imports) of economic policy in its wider sense.   The objective in short, was chiefly to avoid the errors of the Dalton phase, in which monetary policy was working in a direction precisely opposite to that of economic policy as a whole.'

Table 9.2. *Bank deposits and bank lending, 1945/46 to 1960/61*
(changes during financial year[a], £m.)

London clearing banks only

	Deposits	Liquidity ratio, end of period[c]	Liquid assets[b]	Treasury deposit receipts	Invest-ments	Advances
1945/46	290	24	332	−238	93	82
1946/47	807	30	535	−126	209	169
1947/48	238	30	83	−164	31	277
1948/49	21	31	83	−197	10	121
1949/50	−32	37	299	−512	7	174
1950/51	254	39	214	−210	49	160
1951/52	−150	32	−701	—	383	192
1952/53	166	33	121	—	187	−148
1953/54	190	33	65	—	147	−38
1954/55	159	30	−141	—	12	264
1955/56	−316	33	95	—	−288	−119
1956/57	75	33	−5	—	—	71
1957/58	204	34	153	—	101	−59
1958/59	266	31	−107		−166	529[d]
1959/60	416	32	164	Special deposits	−427	642
1960/61	142	30	−30	143	−314	348[e]

[a]Change from mid-March to mid-March, corresponding roughly to fiscal years (for comparison with table 9.1).

[b]Cash and balances with Bank of England (excluding special deposits), money at call and short notice, and bills discounted.

[c]Liquid assets as percentage of total deposits.

[d]Old series March-October, new series October-March.

[e]For 1960/61 *Bills* include and *Advances* exclude re-financeable export credits up to 18 months.

During this period, the Exchequer was in a relatively easy position. Due partly to receipts of Marshall Aid, and partly to the big surplus on the National Insurance Fund, it was able to repay internal debt on a considerable scale. Contrary to what might have been expected in view of later developments, this was not accompanied by any pronounced emphasis on funding the debt. In fact almost as much long-term as short-term debt was paid off in the four years 1947/48—1950/51 (see table 9.1). The banks' holdings of short-term assets were reduced each year[1]. But this still left the banks with very large holdings of liquid assets (table 9.2)—and still therefore left the volume of bank deposits beyond the reach of formal control.

[1]As will be noted, changes in the London clearing banks' holdings of liquid assets (table 9.2) do not correspond at all closely, during these years, with the Exchequer figures of total changes in bills and TDR's (table 9.1).

In fact, however, bank deposits rose only moderately—by about four per cent in the financial year 1947/48, hardly at all in the next two years, and by another four per cent in 1950/51 (table 9.2). The reasons probably were that bank advances—the assets the banks were most anxious to expand—were subject to an informal policy of restraint (see §3 below); that the banks at this date were not anxious to increase their holdings of bonds; and possibly, also, that the policy of restraint applied in a still less formal manner to the rate of growth of deposits[1].

One important aspect of the 'new' monetary policy of 1951 was the attempt to restore the authorities' control over the volume of money. The fact that the floating debt was bound to continue to be large, and that much of it was bound to be held by the banks, implied that the banks were immune from the classical method of control via their 'cash' ratio: the banks could readily replenish their cash holdings, if these were reduced by the authorities, merely by failing to maintain their holdings of bills. A new method of control had therefore to be devised. This consisted first in the formalization of a rule which had previously been at best an informal working convention—namely, that the banks should not reduce their 'liquid' assets below thirty per cent of their deposits[2]. Second was the 'forced funding' of £1,000 million of Treasury bills in exchange for a new short-dated serial funding stock bearing interest at $1\frac{3}{4}$ per cent—an operation which incidentally involved the demise of the old Treasury Deposit Receipt. The point of this manoeuvre was that the new stock was to count not as 'liquid assets', but as 'investments'. As the *Radcliffe Report* comments, 'The banks were in effect instructed to take about £500 million out of the total: by this stroke £500 million was switched in the banks' balance sheets from "liquid assets" to "investments", the liquid assets ratio thereby being reduced from 39 to 32 per cent'[3].

Since 1952, the Exchequer has been almost continuously a net borrower on a large scale. Considerable budget surpluses have been insufficient to finance the investment of the nationalized industries—and until 1956, when the Exchequer ceased to be their main channel of finance—of the local authorities (table 9.1). The aim of debt policy in this period was to meet the resulting Exchequer

[1] Requests by the government for 'restraint' on the part of the banks were always couched in terms of advances. Nevertheless, too rapid a rise in bank deposits did occasion outside criticism; see, for instance, the article 'Return to Monetary Policy?', *Banker*, January 1949.

[2] Little was heard of this rule until it began to be referred to in official statements about the end of 1951. It may be surmised that its formalization at this date was due to the initiative of the authorities, who, since then, have certainly regarded it as a rule that the banks were bound to obey (see *Radcliffe Report*, para. 352).

[3] *Radcliffe Report*, para. 406. Of the £1,000 million issue of serial funding stock issued in November 1951, £450 million was to mature in November 1952, £200 million in November 1953, and £350 million in November 1954. Apart from nomenclature, the 'forced funding' amounted in effect to little more than a rise in the rate of interest paid to the banks for holding floating debt—something which the banks appear to have argued for unsuccessfully under Mr Gaitskell's Chancellorship. See *H.C. Deb.* 26 July 1951, 2342-5, and the article, 'The Eclipse of Hugh Gaitskell', *Banker*, September 1951; and §3 below.

deficit by borrowing long, not short—so as to be able to keep bank liquidity within reach of thirty per cent, and thus maintain a handle over bank lending[1].

In fact, since 1952 the greater part of Exchequer borrowing has been long-term, and there has indeed in some years been a notable contraction of unfunded debt (table 9.1). Between March 1952 and March 1960, the liquid assets of the clearing banks rose less than twenty per cent, so permitting an increase in their deposits of little more than two per cent a year (table 9.2).

Since the collapse of the cheap money policy in 1947, and up to at least 1957, the authorities appear to have had no conscious policy towards the long-term rate of interest[2]. The long-term rate, nevertheless, crept fairly steadily upwards —the yield on consols, for instance, rising from three per cent at the end of 1947 to about five per cent in 1957, and to nearer six per cent in 1960 (figure 9.1).

Theoretical considerations—of the sort already touched on in discussion of the earlier cheap money policy—suggest an explanation on the following lines. One would expect the rate of interest to rise, if the volume of money were reduced. Taking the period as a whole, there has been no absolute reduction in the quantity of money: it has risen, not fallen. But because of the restraint imposed on the growth of bank deposits, the volume of money has grown less rapidly than the value of the national product (which has grown on average by seven per cent or so a year). This relative restriction, in an economy where both real output and the price level is rising, might be expected to have similar effects to an absolute contraction of the money supply in a static economy. There is in fact a fairly clear inverse relation between the long-term rate of interest and the ratio of money supply to the national product[3]. An explanation in these terms clearly does not explain all the observed movements in interest rates. Nevertheless it would seem reasonable to explain the general upward drift in long-term rates as a result of the *relative* restraint imposed on the money supply[4].

If this is true, the rise in interest rates was a result of monetary policy. But it was an unintended result, and one somewhat contrary to what the authorities themselves believed to be possible. In evidence to the Radcliffe Committee,

[1]See *Radcliffe, Memoranda*, I. 4 and II. 10. Equally important in the eyes of the Bank was the desire to increase the maturity of the funded debt, on the view that the total of short-dated bonds was excessive, and that longer bonds would be more 'firmly held': see *Radcliffe Report*, para. 549.

[2]Speaking of the later part of this period, the *Radcliffe Report* remarks that the authorities were 'entirely passive, indeed fatalistic, in their attitude to the movement of long-term interest rates' (para. 552).

[3]See figure 12.1 (chapter XII below) which follows the similar diagram given in F. W. Paish [1959], 'Gilt-edged and the Money Supply', *Banker*, January 1959. A curve through the points on the diagram may be interpreted as representing a liquidity preference schedule. But while the points for years 1921–33 and 1947–60 seem to lie roughly on one curve, those for 1934–46 appear to lie on a lower one.

[4]It can be argued that the causal sequence was the reverse of that stated here: that the use of Bank rate raised bond rates, and that this permitted a relative restriction of the money supply. This question is discussed more fully in chapter XII below.

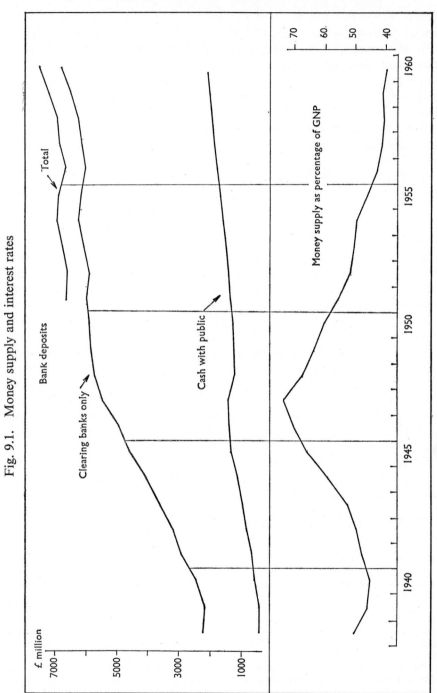

Fig. 9.1. Money supply and interest rates

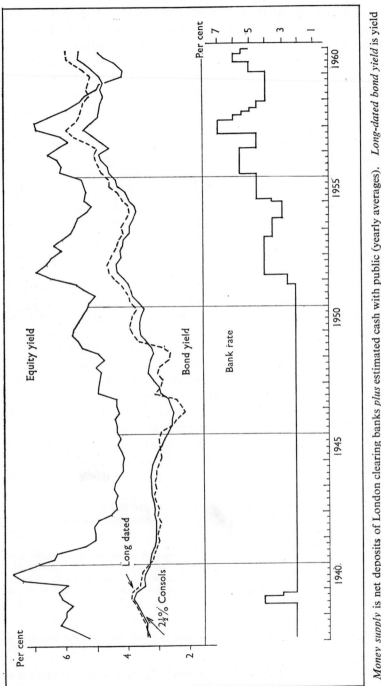

Money supply is net deposits of London clearing banks *plus* estimated cash with public (yearly averages). *Long-dated bond yield* is yield of 3½ per cent War Loan for years up to 1956 and for years thereafter yield on selected long-dated stocks (as in *MDS*).

the Bank of England argued strongly that bonds could only be sold in any quantity on a rising market, and that the demand for them could not be stimulated by dropping prices i.e. raising interest rates[1]. In asserting this, the Bank was no doubt thinking chiefly of the short-term problem of managing the market for a particular new issue. Nevertheless, even a gradual rise of interest rates and infliction of capital losses of the sort that did in fact occur in the years after 1947, if pursued as a conscious policy, ought still to have been regarded by the Bank as unwarrantable 'juggling' with the market[2].

By 1958 there had been some change in the attitude of the authorities, who by then began to be willing to exercise a degree of conscious influence over yields and security prices[3]. 'When general circumstances made for a broad swing downwards in interest rates . . .', noted the Radcliffe Committee, 'the authorities, by their instructions to the Government broker, have given the market a positive lead, resisting the tendency of gilt-edged prices to rise sharply. They had been able to make their view prevail . . . because they had been prepared—indeed have been delighted— to sell as much of the long bonds as the market would absorb'[4]. But, though largely motivated by considerations of funding policy, it was also influenced by a general view that in the current economic situation, 'a pronounced reduction in the cost of long-term capital' would have been inappropriate[5]. 'Never before, in peacetime', said the Committee, 'has the level of prices in the gilt-edged market come so near to being decided by official action'[6]. This restricted degree of intervention has continued to be in evidence. Thus in 1960, long-term interest rates tended to rise— partly at least as an indirect result of the imposition of 'special deposit' requirements, which led the banks, not to restrict their advances, but to reduce their holdings of bonds (which must have reduced bond prices and raised interest rates). While it is clear that this was not the intended result of curbing the banks[7], the rise in rates appears to have been not unwelcome to the authorities[8].

In historical perspective, this is a major evolution of policy. For a decade, debt policy had been dominated by the objective of funding, as a means to

---

[1]The *Radcliffe Report* remarks that this 'view is not easy to accept', and notes that in the first half of 1955, the authorities 'did succeed in unloading large amounts despite the downward drag in markets' (para. 551).

[2]See *Radcliffe Report*, para. 551.

[3]Attention was drawn by the Bank to this shift in policy when the question of debt policy was re-examined by the Radcliffe Committee in November 1958. The Bank's main evidence on this question had been given in October 1957 (see *Radcliffe, Minutes*, Q 11919). The shift in policy was presumably due to earlier discussion with the Bank and the Treasury before the Committee.

[4]*Radcliffe Report*, para. 553.

[5]*Radcliffe, Minutes*, Q 11919.

[6]*Radcliffe Report*, para. 553: this is perhaps to underrate the importance of the Dalton experiment.

[7]See §3 below.

[8]*Economic Survey, 1961*: 'The authorities did not resist some upward movement of medium and long-term gilt-edged rates' (para. 82).

avoid reliance on bank credit for the government's financial requirements. Though there was an idea that reliance on bank credit was in some sense inflationary, it is fair to say that the policy of funding was pursued without clear conception of its impact on the economy—and thus as though it were itself an independent object of policy. The emphasis has, however, now begun to shift from funding as an independent objective, to funding as a means of affecting long-term interest rates. In the thirteen years since policy deliberately aimed at low rates of interest, the authorities moved a long way towards the conscious adoption of the opposite policy of dear money. Gilt-edged rates have risen from three to over six per cent; and by the end of the period the authorities were ready to moderate falls and encourage rises in the long-term rate of interest. Behind this lay the idea that in the likely future situation of full employment and brisk demand for investment, high long-term rates are appropriate.

The advantage of high interest rates is disputable—and will be disputed at a later stage of this study[1]. This aside, it should be emphasized that the new official concern with the long-term rate has certainly not gone along with a belief on the part of the authorities that long-term rates have a quick and marked economic impact, or that changes in such rates can be used to keep the economy in short-term balance. When it comes to seeking quick effects on spending, the authorities in practice continued to rely much more on restricting various sorts of borrowing. The methods were various; were evolved piecemeal; and were of very varying degrees of effectiveness—and are described in the following four sections.

3. THE RESTRICTION OF BANK ADVANCES

Ever since the war years, the level of bank advances has been something to which the authorities attached importance. But at no time have they been subject to formal control: the authorities have chosen to work, and in effect still do, by means of informal pressure. During the war, there had been a loose control of bank advances as auxiliary to the standing control of new issues[2]. The banks were then expected to avoid any expansion of credit which would 'contribute to any general rise in prices or cause a diversion of resources towards non-essential needs'; and, in particular, to restrict advances except those needed directly for defence production, the export trade, coalmining and agriculture[3]. In fact, in wartime conditions of direct control, this financial

---

[1]See further chapter XII.5 below. By 1962 the authorities appear to have come round to the view that they should work to reduce interest rates rather than raise them.

[2]R. S. Sayers [1956], *Financial Policy, 1939–45*, chapter IV: 'The banks themselves were quick to complain that they were being left without advice about the policy of the authorities, and this complaint led to acceptance, by both sides, of the Governor of the Bank of England as the natural channel of contact' (p. 184).

[3]Letter from the Chancellor of the Exchequer to the Governor of the Bank of England, 26 September 1939, quoted by Sayers [1956], p. 185.

control hardly mattered; but the banks became accustomed to operating, on very loose instructions, a 'voluntary' type of control.

The Bank of England Act of 1946 gave the Treasury power to direct the Bank of England; and the Bank power, with Treasury consent, to give such directions to bankers as were deemed necessary in the public interest. Though this power could have been used to issue directions about bank advances[1], it has never been formally used. New instructions were given to the Capital Issues Committee at the end of the war, and partially revised at the end of 1947 and on later occasions, listing the purposes for which permission for new issues would normally be granted[2]. The banks were expected to 'observe the intentions' of these instructions and to continue 'restricting credit facilities to conform with the general policy of the Government'[3].

Under Sir Stafford Cripps, the control of bank advances thus became part— though a minor part—of his general policy of 'democratic' planning by 'voluntary' restrictions. Almost the only, and certainly the fullest, explanation of policy was contained in his statement during the devaluation debate of October 1949[4]. 'Many people', said the Chancellor, 'are concerned on the question of the credit policy that is now being followed and the possibility that the whole of our policies of disinflation may be frustrated by inflationary credit. I have carefully considered both the question of short-term money rates and the policy of advances by the clearing banks. I have reached the conclusion that . . . there is no advantage to be gained by raising the short-term money rates.'

'With the rise in costs, the increase in production, and the increased export drive by many smaller firms, it is natural that there should be a rise in advances made by the banks to their clients compared to the period before the war. More money is needed to keep the wheels of industry and trade moving. But inflationary pressure can set up a chain-reaction. In a seller's market anything which leads to higher prices can be passed on, all down the line, and there is always the danger that advances, justifiable though they may be on the credit-worthiness of the client, may create the conditions which themselves sustain a general upward pressure.

'The banks, whose co-operation I have had throughout, are fully aware of this danger. But in order to make sure that everything is done to avoid inflationary credit, I have discussed the matter with the Governor of the Bank of England, the Chairman and Deputy Chairman of the Clearing Banks Committee. As a result, I have written to the Governor asking

---

[1] For the fears aroused during the passage of the bill, see *The Economist*, 16 Feb. 1946, pp. 259–60.

[2] See §4 below. The permitted purposes were inevitably defined in very broad terms. The prohibition (except in special cases) of some categories, such as finance for the distributive trades and hire purchase, was probably more important than the listing of 'approved' classes.

[3] *H.C. Deb.* 2 December 1947, 199.

[4] *H.C. Deb.* 26 October 1949, 1352–3.

Fig. 9.2. Bank advances, 1946–60 (£ million)

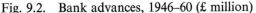

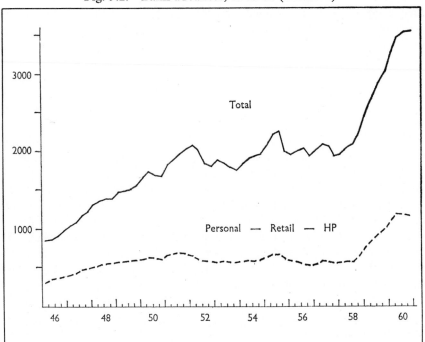

Quarterly figures from British Bankers' Association: dotted curve shows advances classified as to retail trade, personal and professional, and (from 1955) to hire-purchase finance companies (which before 1955 were very small).

him to inform the banks and accepting houses of the importance of their co-operation and requesting them, in their credit policy, to use every endeavour to ensure that inflationary pressures are held in check'.

Though in form like many other similar 'requests' to be made in the next decade, in tone it was much gentler. Under the Labour Government, bank advances in fact increased relatively rapidly. In the first six post-war years, they increased fairly steadily by about fifteen per cent, or nearly £200 million, a year; and in mid-1951 were two and a half times what they had been at the end of the war[1]. How serious this was is another question. They started from a very low level; and in relation either to national income, or to bank *deposits*, they were, even in 1951, far below what they had been before the war.

By 1951, the trend was beginning to be powerfully affected by the 'Korean' inflation. This led both to an enormous inflation of commodity prices, and to an abnormal build-up of physical stocks: in 1951, expenditure on stocks was thus three or four times as high as normal[2]. Though bank credit is by no means

[1]See figure 9.2. The dip in the curve in the second half of 1950 was chiefly due to the repayment of advances by the Central Electricity Board from the proceeds of new loans.
[2]See chapter II.4 above.

the typical way of financing stocks, there is little doubt that the need for marginal finance created a strong demand for bank advances; and that this explains the surge in their trend[1]. For this very reason, however, the government was especially concerned to limit the rise in bank credit. Mr Gaitskell, then Chancellor, emphasized the 'renewed importance' of credit restraint in April[2]; and felt called upon to repeat his request 'with emphasis' in July[3]. In view of the great pressure which must have existed for bank credit, the further rise in bank advances seems relatively moderate; and thus was, perhaps, a triumph for 'restraint'.

From the spring of 1952, bank advances began to fall; and (with an interruption in the trend in the spring of 1953) went on falling until the autumn of 1954. This phase coincides with the active phase of the 'new' monetary policy[4]. As Mr Butler was to say, monetary policy was 'working . . . with the tide of economic forces'[5]: by then the stock cycle had gone into reverse, and this must have greatly reduced the demand for bank credit. Nevertheless, the efforts of the banks to restrict their advances probably also had some effect. The November measures had given the authorities greater control over the banks; they probably used this power to press the banks to reduce advances; in particular, bank managers appear to have been noticeably more stringent; and the

---

[1]See A. Luboff [1956], 'Some Aspects of Post-War Company Finance', *Account. Res.*, April 1956, particularly §6.

[2]The October statement was:
    ' . . . Advances in the past year have increased. This is inevitable, particularly in view of the rise in the cost of raw materials and imports. . . I am certain that the banks fully appreciate the renewed importance . . . of the Government's disinflationary policy, and I am confident that I can continue to rely on them to maintain a restraint in their credit policy, and in particular to ensure that advances are not made for any speculative purposes or for capital expenditure or investment which would conflict with the intentions of the revised principles of guidance, which I propose to issue in the next day or two to the Capital Issues Committee' (*H.C. Deb.* 10 April 1951, 841–2).

[3]The need for repeating the request seems to have arisen through a dispute with the banks. 'It has been suggested sometimes', said Mr Gaitskell, 'that every tightening of credit control requires an increase in the short-term rates of interest which the Government pay to the banking system. . . I do not agree with this'.
    'I have explained my views on this matter to the Governor of the Bank of England and asked him to repeat with emphasis the request which my predecessors and I have addressed to the banks on credit restriction. . . The Governor has since informed me that the banks will endeavour to do their utmost to carry out the policy I have indicated to restrict any extension of bank credit for any but essential purposes.'
    'I value this renewed assurance of co-operation by the banking system. . . It is they who, without derogating in any way from their accepted standards, will have to exercise from day to day the selection and discrimination which our present circumstances clearly demand. Should they need further guidance from the Government, which must be of a fairly general kind, I shall, of course, be willing to provide it' (*H.C. Deb.* 26 July 1951, 2343–5).

[4]Bank rate was raised to 4 per cent in March 1952, and kept there until September 1953 (see §7 below).

[5]*H.C. Deb.* 14 April 1953, 36.

rates charged on advances also increased noticeably[1]. By the autumn of 1953, advances were scarcely higher than they had been three years previous (figure 9.2): without a deliberate squeeze, they would, one might guess, have been at least a third as high again. Though the effect on advances may thus have been quite large, its impact on the economy is much more difficult to gauge. One major result of the squeeze of bank credit was merely to force industry to raise new issues and 'fund' outstanding bank advances: this was true of the Central Electricity Authority and other nationalized boards—and must also have been true of private industry.

With the expansionary bias of policy in 1953, 'the degree of pressure on the monetary system' (in the words of the Treasury later), 'was somewhat eased'[2]. For eighteen months or so, until the middle of 1955, bank advances rose rapidly. There then followed three years in which, in various ways, repeated efforts were made to curtail bank advances. Mr Butler's handling of the 1955 boom has already been described elsewhere[3]. His reliance on monetary measures, as a counterpoise to an inflationary budget, appears to have led to a considerable friction with the banks. Evidently to the Treasury's surprise, the monetary measures taken in February did not check the rapid rise in bank advances[4]. In July, the government called for a 'positive and significant reduction' in bank advances. This appears to have been interpreted by the banks as calling for a reduction of at least ten per cent—so that, as the *Radcliffe Report* says, 'what had hitherto been merely a qualitative control thus became also quantitative'[5].

There followed Mr Butler's disinflationary budget of October 1955; and, under Mr Macmillan, further restrictive measures in February 1956. These included a request to the banks 'to continue their efforts to reduce the total of their advances'[6]. In his budget speech, Mr Macmillan alluded to the 'many problems' in implementing monetary policy, 'especially as between the Exchequer and the monetary system'[7]. As he said, 'carrying out a disinflationary policy is

[1]For the November measures, see §2. Though less emphasis was given to direct controls over credit, these continued: new instructions were given to the Capital Issues Committee and the banks were requested to follow similar criteria. In June there was a specific request to the banks to reduce credit for hire purchase by 10 per cent (*Economist*, 22 March 1952, p. 703). By then the rates on advances were between 4 and 5 per cent, or more—a considerable increase on the rates ruling twelve months previous.

[2]*Radcliffe, Memoranda*, II.6, para. 62. The Bank of England appears to have regarded the aims of the monetary policy at this stage as being more restrictive than the Treasury thought they were: see *Radcliffe Report*, para. 410.

[3]Chapter III.2.

[4]It is not clear from any of the documents whether the banks in February had been specifically requested to restrain advances. If they were, this was not mentioned in Mr Butler's statement: see *H.C. Deb.* 24 February 1955, 1457–8.

[5]See *Radcliffe Report*, para. 417, and *The Economist*, 6 Aug. 1955, p. 490. The Banks themselves appear to have asked for a directive from the government: see *Radcliffe, Memoranda*, II. 6, para. 68.

[6]*H.C. Deb.* 17 February 1956, 2677.

[7]*H.C. Deb.* 17 April 1956, 855–6.

not pleasant. . . for the banks and for their managers and staffs throughout the country'[1]. In July, the Chancellor took the unprecedented step, instead of dealing with the banks through the Bank of England, of himself summoning their representatives to a meeting—to obtain their assurance that credit contraction would be 'resolutely pursued'.

Bank advances then fell[2]. But three months later, they started to rise again. When Bank rate was reduced in February, both the Chancellor and the Governor stated that this was not intended as a sign that 'monetary discipline' should be relaxed; and the Chancellor again summoned the representatives of the banks to obtain their assurance that they would continue to be restrictive[3]. 'But', as Mr Thorneycroft said in his budget speech, 'the very fact that these arrangements have to be made is evidence that the monetary machine is working under great difficulties'[4]. Bank advances, in fact, continued to rise throughout the first half of 1956—and there was some impression that the banks were, in fact, being less stringent in vetting advances[5].

Finally, Mr Thorneycroft's 'crisis measures' of September 1957 included a request that 'the average level of bank advances during the next twelve months should be held at the average level for the last twelve months[6]. Since they had been rising, this involved an equally steep absolute fall. Advances did in fact fall[7].

In July 1958, along with other easements, pressure for restraint in making advances was withdrawn entirely. At the same time, a new method, already

---

[1]*H.C. Deb.* 17 April 1956, 871. The 1956 *Economic Survey* commented similarly on the difficulty of procuring a contraction of bank advances in the previous year: 'the course of bank advances', it said, 'illustrates the resistance which the economy offers to a restrictive credit policy at a time of great prosperity, when business expectations are optimistic and many expansion plans are in the course of execution, but when no abnormal speculative activity is taking place. Several months elapsed between the first action by the banks to limit borrowing and the beginning of a decline in the total of advances outstanding' (para. 71). The increase in advances in the first half of 1955 was in fact the largest six-monthly increase that had up to then occurred.

[2]The authorities at this period failed to fund as much debt as they wanted, and the liquidity ratio of the banks was well above 30 per cent. The *Radcliffe Report* (para. 422) remarks that 'the banks' holdings of maturing debt enabled them to escape pressure on their advances'. This was presumably a reason for the failure of funding policy.

[3]*H.C. Deb.* 9 April 1947, 983–4.

[4]Same deb. 985: he went on to announce the appointment of a committee (the Radcliffe Committee) 'to inquire into the working of the monetary and credit system'.

[5]*Economist*, 6 April 1957, p. 66.

[6]*Bank Rate Tribunal Report* (Cmnd. 350), p. 9.

[7]The Radcliffe Committee reported that 'the branch bank managers who gave evidence to us were disposed to attribute [the reduction in advances in the last quarter of 1957] not so much to the raising of interest rates or to any positive action by the banks to restrict advances after September 1957 as to the cumulative effect of a long period of credit restriction and customers' expectations of a decline in the level of activity' (para. 425). Investment in stocks and stock appreciation appear to have been low at this juncture, which might account for a fall in the demand for credit. But in view of what happened in previous and later years, it would be surprising if credit rationing had not also been a main influence.

'negotiated' with the banks, was introduced for use as required in future. Under this scheme, the Bank of England could call for 'special deposits' from the banks. The important point was that such deposits, as explicitly agreed, 'would not qualify for inclusion in the banks' liquid assets'; and that 'the banks would continue to maintain their usual minimum ratios between liquid assets and total deposits'[1]. The 'usual ratio' was understood to be thirty per cent in the case of the London clearing banks[2]; but the same convention had never been held to apply to the Scottish banks, and the scheme provided for them to be called on for deposits in different ratio from those called for from the London clearing banks[3].

Both the Bank and the banks had 'repeatedly impressed' on the government that the method of 'official requests', if used too long or too often, hampered ordinary banking; and the 'special deposits' scheme was designed as an alternative way for the authorities 'to restrain an increase of total bank advances'[4]. But in fact all it gave was power to control deposits. As such, it was no doubt a way of putting pressure on the banks, which might presumably be used to persuade them to fall in with the authorities' wishes about advances. To eyes outside the city, this might well seem no more than an old-style 'request' dressed up in pseudo-financial arithmetic; and though the Chancellor hoped to dispense with 'requests' in future[5], time was to reveal this basic weakness of the scheme.

Meanwhile, however, with their new-found freedom, the banks increased advances very rapidly indeed. Between the autumn of 1958 and the middle of 1960, total advances rose by nearly £1,500 million, or by some seventy per cent (figure 9.2). This is some indication of the severity of the previous repeated doses of 'restraint', which had kept advances on an undulating plateau for the previous seven years. There was a notable development of 'personal loan' facilities—in effect, a rival to hire-purchase finance; and most of the banks also acquired interests in hire-purchase finance companies.

By the spring of 1960, the time seemed to have come to impose a brake. The first call for special deposits was made at the end of April, to take effect on 15

---

[1]See the exchange of letters between the Chancellor and the Governor reprinted in *H.C. Deb.* 3 July 1958, 1604–5.

[2]*Radcliffe Report*, para. 352.

[3]The scheme was introduced in the first place as 'a temporary arrangement pending the recommendations of the Radcliffe Committee'. The Committee found 'little to choose' between this and other methods. It inclined 'towards a straight-forward power to raise the 30 per cent liquidity requirement to some higher percentage' (para. 508). Alternatively, if stronger measures were needed, it suggested that restrictions should be imposed on the ratio of advances to deposits (para. 527). The 'special deposits' scheme appears not to have rested on statutory authority, but to have been 'negotiated' by the Governor of the Bank with the banks (para. 353).

[4]Chancellor's letter, already referred to.

[5]Same deb. 1599.

R

June[1].   The banks responded by selling investments; and advances in the second quarter rose as before[2].   At the end of June, further special deposits were called for[3].   The rise in bank advances then slowed down, but did not stop—the banks again selling investments, though at a slower rate.   Three categories of advances most closely associated with consumer spending—those to personal and professional borrowers, hire-purchase finance companies and retail trade—showed, however, a marked fall.   Since the *Economic Survey* singled this fact out for mention[4], it may be presumed that the effect was intended.   It is not quite the behaviour that might have been expected of the banks in the absence of official hints.   In July 1961 (to look for a moment beyond the end of the period covered by this survey) when special deposits were next called for, the Governor gave public intimation that the impact 'should fall on advances'[5].

It is therefore debateable how far the special deposits scheme has helped to control advances.   Nevertheless, by one means or another, the authorities have been and still are able to exert marked influence over the level of advances. It seems likely that the credit squeezes so induced had, at times, and in the short term at least, some significant influence on demand—even though, in the slightly longer term, its chief effect was to drive borrowers to alternative sources of finance[6].

4. CAPITAL ISSUES AND CAPITAL ISSUES CONTROL

Capital issues control dates back to the beginning of the war, when the 'public offer of securities for sale' had been prohibited except with Treasury consent, and the Capital Issues Committee had been appointed to advise the Treasury on the exercise of this power.   The memorandum of guidance with which it was provided indicated that new issues would be approved only for purposes directly connected with defence, essential supplies and services, or exports.   The new-issue control had originally been intended as a control over investment expenditure.   But the development of physical control quickly made financial control unnecessary for this purpose; and it appears in fact soon to have become primarily a way of 'grooming the market in favour of the War Loan issues'[7].

[1]The London clearing banks were called on to deposit 1 per cent of deposits; Scottish banks, ½ per cent.

[2]The comment in the next *Economic Survey* suggests that the disposal of bonds by the banks was not welcomed by the authorities.   But this must have contributed to the rise in long-term interest rates; it should be added that in itself this rise was not unwelcome to them: see *Economic Survey, 1961*, paras. 76 and 82 (ii).

[3]The clearing banks were called on for 1 per cent of deposits in two equal instalments on 21 July and 17 August: the Scottish banks, for half these percentages.

[4]Para. 78.

[5]*Economist*, 29 July 1961, p. 468.   In the year up to July, total advances had risen by over £300 million or around 10 per cent.   The London banks were called on for a 1 per cent deposit in two instalments, to take effect in August and September: the Scottish banks again for half these percentages.

[6]For the theory of a credit squeeze see chapter XII.4 below.

[7]Sayers [1956], chapter VI.

Despite doubts about its usefulness[1], the control was not discontinued at the end of the war. Under the Labour Government's Borrowing (Control and Guarantees) Act, 1946, the Treasury was given permanent power to control borrowing and the raising of capital by issue of shares; and the Capital Issues Committee remained in being, still in a non-statutory and advisory capacity. In preparation for the end of hostilities, new terms of guidance had been promulgated by the Treasury in 1945. The approved purposes included exports, public utilities, transport, housing, and the production of capital goods and of 'essential' consumer goods[2].

In intention, at least, the control was much tightened at the end of 1947—when Sir Stafford Cripps, newly become Chancellor, was endeavouring to cut investment. In effect the Committee was enjoined to refuse permission for capital outlays unless for the 'basic' industries, or unless the expenditure promised a considerable increase in exports or saving of imports. Equally important, the Committee were required to get the 'definite assurance' of departments that proposed issues were in 'full accord' with the government's investment programme[3]. During the next ten years, the 'approved purposes' were to be amended many times—notably in April 1951, to take account of the new defence programme; in December 1951, at the beginning of the new monetary policy; in February and July 1953; and February 1955[4]. The categories, however, remained throughout of a very broad and general character. As the Treasury said in summarizing the 'guidance' under which the Committee was operating in 1957, the Committee was asked to recommend in favour of investment 'judged by them to be urgent and for essential purposes, with particular regard to the production of exports, the saving of imports or the earning of foreign exchange'[5]. Only at one juncture, at the turn of 1955–6, was the Committee asked, not merely to discriminate between new issues, but to go some way towards restricting their total[6].

[1] In 1945 Keynes in particular had been strongly opposed to its continuance: see Sayers [1956], pp. 181–2.

[2] White Paper on *Capital Issues Control* (Cmd. 6645), May 1945. Consent was required for all issues above £50,000 a year. For issues above £100,000, Bank of England consent as to the timing of issues was also required. New issues were not normally to be allowed for purposes of retail trade and distribution or hire purchase; nor for bonus issues or the acquisition of existing firms.

[3] *H.C. Deb.* 17 Nov. 1947, 939–40. It is difficult to believe that the control was anything like as fierce as intended. It may be that the building controls were in fact the operative control; and building consent having been obtained, financial approval followed easily. Taken as a whole, the apparatus of investment control was, in any case, not particularly effective—see chapters II.3 and VI.3 above.

[4] For details of changes since 1951, see *Radcliffe, Memoranda*, II. 8. In March 1956 the exemption limit was reduced from £50,000 to £10,000 a year.

[5] Same memorandum, para. 19.

[6] In October 1955 the Committee was asked 'not to relax their critical attitude'; and in February 1956, to recommend consent only when 'an application had definite urgency, (same memorandum, paras. 16–7).

The control probably had little impact on investment demand. Because the categories were so vaguely defined, it appears to have been easy to frame most applications in a way to bring them within the range of 'approved purposes'[1]. The Capital Issues Committee—as it was quick to insist—was, indeed, instructed to concern itself, not with the amount, but only with the 'purpose', of applications[2]. Nor, had this been intended, was the machinery adequate for anything approaching a quantitative control[3]. It was these reasons which led the Radcliffe Committee to conclude, in one of its more stinging phrases, that capital issues control had been 'negligible, to the point of irrelevance'[4]; and to recommend that it should not be retained, at least in normal times[5]. The control was in fact suspended, except for overseas issues, in February 1959, shortly before the Radcliffe Committee reported.

This, however, does not imply that the new issue market was unimportant as a channel of finance. During the years 1949 to 1953, nearly one quoted company in three had resort to a market issue, and the total sum raised amounted to nearly thirty per cent of their net investment[6]. It has been suggested that, quite apart from the effects of control, monetary policy may affect the ease of floating new issues; and in particular that a rise in interest rates may cause a temporary freezing up of the new issues market. The course of new issues is shown in figure 9.3. The chart shows extremely wide swings from quarter to quarter, which appear random and accidental; and the general course of new issues is probably best judged by something like the moving average shown on the chart. The curve mounts fairly steadily to the boom of 1955; then drops for three years; and after the economic revival of 1958, again climbs. It seems clear that the flow of new issues depended chiefly on the scale of investment[7].

There were, however, occasions when, for a short while, the market appears to have become 'congested', and the flow of new issues was temporarily slowed down. The first occasion was immediately after the inception of the 'new'

---

[1] *Radcliffe Report*, para. 970.

[2] *Radcliffe, Memoranda*, II. 8, para. 4.

[3] Applications were dealt with rapidly, without time for detailed discussion; and the Committee's recommendations were almost always accepted automatically by the Treasury. As the Radcliffe Committee remarked, it would not have been possible to make decisions in this way on the advice of an unofficial committee, had they been executive decisions of real moment. (*Report*, paras. 967–8 and 975.)

[4] *Report*, para. 471. Earlier the *Report* suggests that the control 'probably contributed somewhat to the "diffused difficulty of borrowing" ' (para. 463).

[5] Para. 977. The Committee suggested, however, that a stronger, quantitative, control of capital issues might be useful in 'emergency' conditions (para. 526).

[6] *Studies in Company Finance*, edited by B. Tew and R. F. Henderson [1959], pp. 65–6. 'Non-quoted' companies had much less resort to new issues.

[7] Applications to the Capital Issues Committee for permission to make new issues also varied widely from year to year; though the series does not match closely with the actual new issues, the humps occur (as might be expected) somewhat earlier. The volume of non-government issues do not appear to be related in any way, either negatively or positively, with the volume of government bond issues; nor with the level, or change, of long-term interest rates.

Fig. 9.3.   New issues, 1950–60 (£ million)

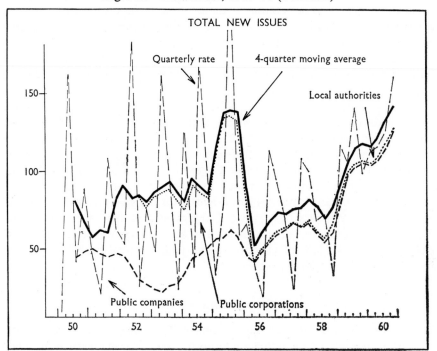

Bank of England quarterly estimates for United Kingdom borrowers only.

monetary policy in November 1951.   Security prices then fell; but the flow of
new issues appears to have been resumed when prices became stabilized again[1].
A similar, and equally temporary, 'congestion' appears to have followed the
increases in Bank rate in January and February 1955, apparently because the
insurance companies withdrew from the new issue market[2].   But by the late
spring the market recovered and in the third quarter new issues reached a post-
war peak (figure 9.3).   The Radcliffe Committee concluded that though a rise
in interest rates may put 'difficulties in the way of borrowers because the change
causes a freezing-up of the new issue market . . . any such interruption of
market activity is very short-lived'[3].   The identifiable occasions of market

[1]Kenen notes that in November nearly all of an Imperial Chemical Industries debenture
passed into the hands of the underwriters, and comments that (through official intervention)
'gilt-edged prices were quickly stabilized, bringing forth new capital issues that had been
postponed because securities prices were falling'.   (P. B. Kenen [1960], *British Monetary
Policy and the Balance of Payments, 1951–1957*, p. 82.)
[2]Kenen notes 'some new issues were left with the underwriters; some that had been
announced were postponed; and the local authorities withdrew entirely from the market'
(Kenen [1960], p. 171: see also p. 181).
[3]In the opinion of the new issues market, perhaps only 'for a week or two' (*Radcliffe
Report*, para. 454).

congestion certainly fail to show up in the quarterly figures of new issues, which are anyhow highly erratic.   Since the timing of new issues is not closely related to actual investment, it is to be doubted whether temporary periods of 'congestion' have much effect on expenditure.

There is, indeed, another consideration which tends to reduce the significance, on their own, of the figures of new issues.   As already noted (in §3 above), one result of the successive 'squeezes' on bank advances was to force industry to raise new issues and 'fund' its bank advances.   This was especially true for the nationalized industries[1], and probably applies to private industry to some extent.   The credit 'squeezes' of 1952, 1955 and 1957 probably each contributed to the rise in new issues that occurred at these periods (figure 9.3)—an effect fully in line with the Radcliffe Committee's conclusion that their main effect 'was to drive frustrated borrowers to other sources of credit'[2].

The control of bank advances was originally instituted as an ancillary to the control of capital issues (§3).   In fact things worked the other way round: the control of advances, though intended to be ancillary, was in fact the more effective; while the lack of effective capital issues control probably made its impact less than it might have been.

5.   HIRE-PURCHASE CONTROL

Hire-purchase credit has been chiefly regulated, not directly, but by statutory regulations prescribing the minimum terms on which hire-purchase deals might be undertaken[3].   Restrictions specifying the minimum 'down-payment' and maximum period of repayment were imposed for the first time in February 1952[4].   The 1952 regulations were retained practically unchanged for two and a half years.   They were removed entirely in July 1954.   Controls were reimposed as part of the pre-budget restrictions of February 1955, strengthened in July and again in February 1956.   The terms for car purchase were greatly eased in December, but strengthened again in May 1957.   For other goods, they

[1]Notably in 1952–3, and in the second half of 1955.

[2]*Radcliffe Report*, para. 460.

[3]In addition, hire-purchase finance companies were subjected to financial restraints. From 1945 and till February 1959, except for the six months from August 1954 to February 1955, they were debarred from making capital issues—of a size that required Capital Issues Committee assent—or from obtaining finance from the banks.   The companies were, however, able to obtain finance in the form of direct deposits by the public and other ways.   The restrictions may have retarded the spread of hire purchase, by making it more expensive.   They did not amount to a control over hire purchase.   (See *Radcliffe Report*, particularly paras. 464–5).

[4]There had previously been restrictions under the price control regulations of the finance charge permitted on goods sold under hire-purchase agreements.   (See F. R. Oliver [1961], *The Control of Hire-Purchase*, chapter XIII).

For details of the 1952 and later restrictions on terms, see *Radcliffe, Memoranda*, IV. 10; and also R. Harris, M. Naylor and A. Seldon [1961], *Hire Purchase in a Free Society*, Appendix A: 'The Law on Instalment Credit'.

ran on practically unchanged till September 1958, when the terms for electrical goods were eased. In October 1958, all controls were again removed. In April 1960, relatively mild restrictions were reimposed. Changes in the statutory terms for the main categories of consumer durables are summarized in table 9.3.

Table 9.3. *Minimum hire-purchase terms*

		Minimum deposit (percentage)			Repayment period (months)		
		Cars	Radio and electrical goods	Furniture and floor coverings	Cars	Radio and electrical goods	Furniture and floor coverings
1952	Feb.	33⅓	33⅓	12½	18	18	18
1954	July	Controls off			Controls off		
1955	Feb.	15	15	15	24	24	24
	July	33⅓	33⅓				
1956	Feb.	50	50	20			
	Dec.	20					
1957	May	33⅓					
1958	Sept.		33⅓				
	Oct.	Controls off			Controls off		
1960	April	20	20	20	24	24	24

Hire purchase is only a minor form of business finance, and appears chiefly to be used by small firms[1]. In spite of the stiff rates charged, it has been rapidly growing, no doubt because it is a way for a firm to expand without weakening financial control. The control of the terms of hire purchase was extended to cover its business use in February 1956. This had the effect of reducing business hire-purchase debt from £70 million to £50 million during the year[2].

The effect of hire-purchase restrictions has however fallen chiefly on the demand for consumer durables, since it is these goods for which hire purchase is chiefly used. Almost half the consumer durables bought are bought on hire purchase. Expenditure on these goods has been increasing rapidly and now accounts for some ten per cent of total consumer expenditure. Even so, however, it is only four per cent of total final demand. Since the easing of restrictions on bank advances in 1958 (§3 above) bank credit has probably become in recent years an important source of consumer credit. Restrictions on bank credit have, however, generally accompanied restrictions on hire purchase.

[1] See J. A. Bates [1957], 'Hire Purchase in Small Manufacturing Business', *Bankers' Mag.*, Sept. and Oct. 1957.
[2] *Radcliffe Report*, para. 467.

Since alternative means of borrowing are not available to most consumers, restrictions on their access to bank credit or hire-purchase finance are bound to affect their demand.   The precise effect of such restrictions is however difficult to estimate.   This is partly because the demand for durables has been subject to many other influences—in particular, by the shift in the pattern of consumer demand towards durables as incomes rise; and also by the changes in purchase tax.   This question will be more fully considered in chapter XI, where it is concluded that the effect on consumer demand is approximately to be measured by the amount of new (bank and hire-purchase) credit extended.   The most striking effects occurred in late 1958, when restrictions were removed; and in late 1960, when restrictions were reimposed.   It would appear that easier credit may well add £100-£200 million to the level of demand; and when first imposed, it would appear that restrictions may well reduce demand by a like amount[1].

An effect of this size amounts to 0·5 per cent of total final demand.   Most, though perhaps not all, of the effect, however, probably falls on the demand for durables—which thus stand to be trimmed or swollen by something of the order of ten per cent.   The operation of the controls, as used in the past, is therefore disrupting for the trades concerned—a consideration which, as the Radcliffe Committee was at pains to emphasize, should weigh heavily against the type of control operated in the 1950's[2].

6.   RESTRICTION OF BUILDING SOCIETY FINANCE

Though there has been no formal control of advances by the building societies, monetary policy has in fact exerted an influence over their lending; and though this has not been a conscious aim of policy, the influence has been in some ways similar to a direct control, or rationing, of their lending.   The societies assist in the finance of about two thirds of private house-building.   Their operations have been an important influence over investment in housing only since 1953 or 1954, before which private house-building was effectively limited by direct controls[3].

The societies are reluctant to adjust their lending and borrowing rates; and though their rates do move in response to movements elsewhere in interest rates, they do so with some delay.   Their finance is obtained by what are in effect deposits by the public, liable to withdrawal at short notice.   Such deposits are therefore competitive not only with bonds, but also with bank deposits,

---

[1]See chapter XI.2 below and especially figure 11.2.   This conclusion accords with the order of magnitude suggested by the *Radcliffe Report* (paras. 471–2).

[2]*Radcliffe Report*, paras. 468–9.   As the *Report* said (para. 472) the effect 'is far removed from the smooth and widespread adjustment sometimes claimed as the virtue of monetary action'.

[3]See chapter VI.3 above.

local authority mortgages and national savings. When the yield on such assets rises, building society rates tend to lag behind, and the flow of new deposits to the societies tends to fall. In such a case the societies are compelled to ration their advances to customers[1].

This process was well in evidence in the period 1955–7. Other interest rates were rising fairly steadily from the beginning of 1955 to the end of 1957; throughout this period, building society rates were rising also, but always, as it were, one step behind (figure 9.4). New borrowing by the societies fell off from £180 million a year in 1954 to £90 million in 1956; and though it then began to recover, it did not regain the 1954 level till 1959. Then, with tighter monetary policy, outside rates again began to rise; and the flow was again reduced.

The finance available for new advances by the building societies depends also on the flow of repayments of old advances—which (since the societies have been expanding) have, in recent years mounted fairly steadily (figure 9.4). New advances therefore fell off only in 1956 (from £395 million in 1955 to £335 million); recovered a bit in 1957 and 1958 (£375 million in both years); and rose markedly in 1959 and 1960 (£510 and £560 million respectively). From the middle of 1959, the finances of the building societies were supplemented by loans from the government under the House Purchase and Housing Act of May 1959. This was introduced to increase the finance available for the purchase of old houses—hitherto heavily discriminated against by the building societies. In 1960, £40 million was provided through this scheme. Though not originally intended as a stabilization device, the scheme was to be suspended in the 'little budget' of July 1961[2].

The interest rate on mortgages has risen from four per cent in 1950 to over six per cent in 1960. A rise in rates of this order might be expected to have a considerable effect in depressing the demand for new houses. But it has been working against the trend—in particular, the influence of rising incomes; and the demand for new private houses has nevertheless risen very rapidly (figure 9.4). All that can be said is that the demand might have been even larger than it has been without the rise in interest rates[3]. Because of the way the building societies operate, the rise in mortgage rates over the last ten years has been

---

[1] See *Radcliffe Report*, paras. 285–96. Deposits with the societies are called either 'deposits' or 'shares'—the latter being, however, only a slightly less liquid form of deposit.

[2] The suspension of the scheme must indirectly have reduced the demand for new houses. But if the government wanted this effect, it would have been better to have sought it directly, rather than suspend a scheme whose general effects were entirely beneficial.

The 1959 Act provided for Exchequer advances to approved building societies in respect of loans to pre-1919 houses valued at £2,500 or less (in London, £3,000 or less). Societies entering the scheme undertake to make loans on not less favourable terms than on houses of a similar value built between 1919 and 1940. See *House Purchase—Proposed Government Scheme* (Cmnd. 571, November 1958) and *Report of the Ministry of Housing and Local Government*, 1959, pp. 53–4).

[3] For evidence of the interest rate effect on the demand for housing, see part 3 (chapter XI.4) below.

Fig. 9.4.   Building society lending and private house-building, 1950–60

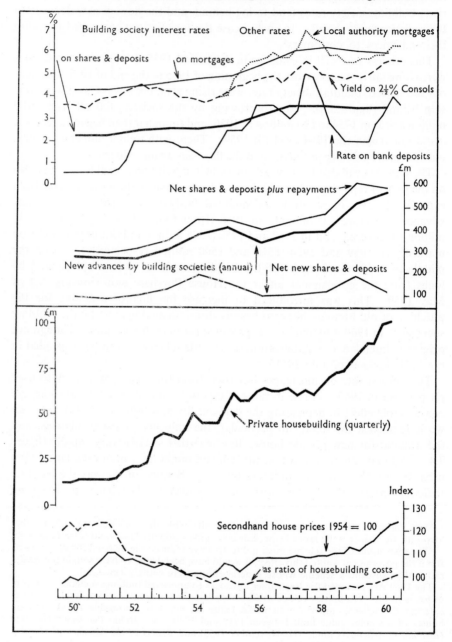

For notes to figure see foot of next page.

gradual. It does not therefore account for short-run fluctuations in the demand for new houses; nor, on the present system, could adjustments of mortgage rates easily be used by the authorities for this purpose.

Some of the short-run fluctuations can, however, probably be accounted for in terms of the availability of building society finance. Private expenditure on new houses rose particularly fast in two periods: 1951 to 1953 and 1958 to 1960. The first was associated with the easing of direct controls over private house-building[1]. The second coincides with the rapid spurt in building society advances (already noted) in 1958. Fluctuations in the availability of building society finance were to some extent offset by loans by the insurance companies against mortgages on house property; but this was a relatively small factor[2]. During this period, private house-building increased by well over £100 million a year—as did building society advances (figure 9.4). The evidence does not permit any good estimate of the impact of monetary policy on house-building; but it could possibly have been of this order.

One may conclude that because of the stickiness of building society rates, the general rise in interest rates in the years 1955–7 had an appreciable effect in limiting the availability of building society finance; and that this in turn probably appreciably reduced private demand for new houses. These effects were probably reversed in the years 1958–9, when interest rates were stable or falling. The impact of these changes in building society finance, though probably less than the impact of hire-purchase restrictions, may well have been appreciable. In the past such effects have not been brought about as part of conscious policy. Whether they are to be utilized in future or not, it is desirable that the authorities should take conscious account of such possible side effects of their actions.

[1] See chapter VI.3.
[2] In 1957 loans by the insurance companies on private houses were about a fifth as large as those by the building societies. (*Radcliffe Report*, paras. 248 and 289). Their grants had been stimulated by the non-availability of building society finance; and the insurance companies expected them to stop increasing when such finance became more readily available (*Radcliffe, Minutes* Q 7118–7125).

Notes to fig. 9.4

Rates of interest: building societies' rates on mortgages, and shares and deposits (annual figures for all societies) from Registry of Friendly Societies; local authority mortgage rates (from 1955 only: quarterly) from *Fin. Statist.*; bank deposit rates (quarterly) from *Bank England quart. B.*

Building societies' advances, repayments, and net shares and deposits (annual figures from all societies) from Registry of Friendly Societies.

Private house-building (seasonally corrected quarterly figures) from *MDS*: and for years before 1955, based on yearly or half-yearly figures from Ministry of Works. *Second-hand house prices* (quarterly figures for all houses) and *house-building costs* from Co-operative Building Society: the latter index is based on material costs and wage rates without allowance for improvements in productivity in the building industry, on the grounds that these have affected large building projects not house-building.

7. RÉSUMÉ—THE INTENTIONS OF MONETARY POLICY

Previous sections have described separately the main elements of monetary policy. By way of synthesis, it is convenient now to relate the measures taken to the intentions of the authorities as revealed in official statements at the time. Since 1951, monetary policy has been used, not smoothly, but to have a kind of shock effect. The typical cycle has been for a collection of measures, intended to have a deflationary impact, to be imposed amid some publicity, all together at one date; and then to be followed by piecemeal, gradual and unpublicized relaxation. The authorities have retained enough faith in Bank rate always to include changes in the rate among such measures, though not enough to use it alone. Bank rate is therefore a convenient index of policy. The nine years since the end of 1951 may conveniently be divided into four cycles of alternate stringency, and—greater or less—relaxation (table 9.4).

The 'new' monetary policy, 1952–4

Mr Butler became Chancellor of the Exchequer at the height of the payments crisis of 1951. Internal demand had been high in 1951; but by the beginning of 1952 it was already clear that consumer industries were going to be in difficulties. Despite the payments crisis, therefore, the 1952 budget was not deflationary, but rather the reverse.

Bank rate, after being raised from 2 to $2\frac{1}{2}$ per cent in November 1951, was raised to 4 per cent at the time of the budget in March. The first rise was officially justified, not as a means of influencing the economy directly, but as one of 'a number of closely inter-related steps . . . taken to make it possible to control credit as rigidly as might be required'[1]. It can hardly have done more than impress the banks that a new era had begun: it had been at two per cent since 1939. But the 'forced funding' operations, and consequent reduction of bank 'liquidity' must have been more important (§2 above).

The second rise in Bank rate in March was described as 'an essential part of the effort to fortify the currency and improve the balance of payments, and also to provide a further reminder of the need for caution and economy in our present circumstances'[2]. In more rational terms, it could plainly only be justified not as a measure of general deflation, but as a step to curtail investment —and Mr Butler made considerable claims for it in this respect. 'The use of the Bank Rate . . .', he said, 'can make an important contribution towards the right economic climate, particularly towards the diversion of resources from investment, above all, to export . . . The Bank Rate will reinforce the other factors already operating to restrict investment at home'[3].

---

[1] *Economic Survey for 1952*, para. 108.
[2] *Economic Survey for 1952*, para. 112.
[3] *H.C. Deb.* 11 March 1952, 1284–5.

Table 9.4. *Monetary measures, 1952–60*

		Bank rate (per cent)	Other monetary measures	Other measures announced with monetary measures[a]
1951	Nov.	$2\frac{1}{2}$[b]	'Forced funding' operation	
	Feb.		HP restrictions	
1952	March	4	Restraint of bank advances	Initial allowances withdrawn (restored in April 1953)
1953	Sept.	$3\frac{1}{2}$		
1954	May	3		
	July		(HP restrictions removed)	
1955	Jan.	$3\frac{1}{2}$		
	Feb.	$4\frac{1}{2}$	HP restrictions	(Support of rate for transferable sterling)
	July		HP restrictions tightened 'Quantitative' control of bank advances	
1956	Feb.	$5\frac{1}{2}$	HP restrictions tightened	Investment allowances withdrawn: public investment cut
	July		Chancellor meets bankers about bank advances	
1957	Sept.	7	'Quantitative' control of bank advances	Stabilization of public investment[c].
1958	March	6		
	May	$5\frac{1}{2}$		
	June	5		
	July		Control of bank advances removed	
	Aug.	$4\frac{1}{2}$		
	Sept.		HP restrictions relaxed	
	Oct.		HP restrictions removed	
	Nov.	4		
1960	Jan.	5		
	April		HP restrictions. First call for special deposits	
	June	6	Second call for special deposits	
	Oct.	$5\frac{1}{2}$		
	Dec.	5		

[a]Includes only those other measures announced as part of a 'package' including monetary measures: for other measures taken at budget and other times, see text.
[b]Previously 2 per cent since 1939.
[c]Stabilization of government current expenditure rejected by Cabinet.

The other 'factors' were probably far more effective—the initial allowances were suspended; and 'voluntary arrangements' made with the manufacturers about the share of engineering goods to be exported. (Hire-purchase restrictions had been, for the first time, imposed in February: §5 above).

These measures were expected 'to lead to a marked reduction in civil investment, particularly in plant and machinery, and in stocks'—possibly partly offset by an increase in investment for defence and in building[1]. Despite the passing reference to stocks, the authorities, accustomed as they were to continuous excess demand, were unprepared for the stock recession of 1952, which was to cause something like a ten per cent decline in output in the first half of the year (chapter III.2.). Investment by the industries affected also fell off. At the same time, the balance of payments righted itself—chiefly for reasons unconnected with policy. Bank advances fell, largely as a result of a stock recession that would have occurred in any case. The policy of restricting bank advances must have exaggerated the depth of the recession: this was not intended, nor, probably, would restriction have been pursued if the effect had been realized in time[2].

For the next two years, budgetary policy leant steadily towards reflation; monetary policy was almost forgotten. Bank rate was reduced, though only by $\frac{1}{2}$ per cent, in September 1953; and not till May 1954 was it reduced a further $\frac{1}{2}$ per cent to 3 per cent. The hire-purchase controls remained in force till July 1954 (§5). Official references to monetary policy were non-committal and brief. In the 1953 budget speech, for example, Mr Butler promised to continue to use 'the monetary weapon' to keep investment in stocks 'within reasonable bounds'[3]—but it is difficult to feel that this was a very firm intention[4]. *The Economic Survey, 1954* reviewed the past year without making reference to monetary policy[5], and equally ignored it in discussing the year ahead[6]. The budget speech had one, delphic allusion to monetary policy[7].

---

[1]*H.C. Deb.* 11 March 1952, 1284–5.

[2]In the middle of the year the government tried to mitigate the effects of the recession in textiles by giving special defence orders (chapter III.2).

[3]*H.C. Deb.* 14 April 1953, 47.

[4]Stocks in total stopped rising in 1952—but did not fall—while stocks in the textile and some other consumer industries fell heavily. The *Economic Survey for 1953* concluded that it was 'impossible to say' whether this was 'a once-for-all adjustment to new economic and monetary conditions, or a temporary reaction that will later be reversed' (para. 130). It discussed the prospects for fixed investment without reference to monetary policy (paras. 126–8).

[5]See particularly the 'general assessment' at paras. 66–78; there was a purely factual description of interest rates and certain financial flows at paras. 63–5.

[6]Paras. 95–101 and 108–9.

[7]'Interest rates generally fell during the year. But few have made the mistake of interpreting those movements as a change of direction in monetary policy'; and 'I will not offer any predictions on the role that monetary measures are likely to play in the coming year. Bank rate and the rates that depend on it will be kept flexible and free for use in either direction as circumstances may require' (*H.C. Deb.* 6 April 1954, 217).

The 1955 crisis

Renewed signs of crisis in 1955 led to a new resort to monetary measures. Bank rate was raised to 3½ per cent in January 1955, and to 4½ per cent in February—the second increase being accompanied by reimposition of the hire-purchase controls—and also by the announcement that in future the authorities would support the rate for transferable sterling. The reserves recovered; and this appears to have been taken as indicating that the problem was solved, and that the way was open for the expansionary budget of April 1955. But the boom continued to grow.

The summer of 1955 saw further attempts to tighten monetary policy. In face of the continued rise in bank advances, something approaching a quantitative control was imposed in July (§3 above). At the same time, hire-purchase restrictions were tightened, and measures were taken to slow down public investment. But the main step was the autumn budget, which in broad effect, though not in detail, reversed much of the April tax cut.

Further measures to check the boom were taken in February by Mr Macmillan (who became Chancellor of the Exchequer at the end of 1955). Bank rate was raised from 4½ per cent to 5½ per cent; hire-purchase restrictions were tightened further; and the request to the banks to control advances was reaffirmed. (At the same time, the investment allowances were withdrawn, and further steps were taken to control public investment: the budget in April made relatively minor changes.)

As Mr Macmillan said, the government, in its 'efforts to check inflation . . . relied very largely on monetary policy'; he went on to allude to 'problems, especially as between the Exchequer and the monetary system'[1]. There had been considerable friction with the banks, which culminated in the Chancellor breaking with tradition and himself summoning a meeting of the bankers' representatives (§3 above). Only then did advances fall. In view of these same difficulties, Mr Thorneycroft felt it necessary to summon a similar meeting in February 1956 (§3).

The 1957 crisis

The exchange crisis of the summer and autumn of 1957 came at a time when the British balance of payments was in surplus. It was due primarily to what the *Economic Survey* called 'an intense wave of currency speculation'[2]—speculation, however, probably much intensified by rumours about British exchange policy (chapter III.4). Mr Thorneycroft treated it as primarily due to inflation at home.

His counter-measures were, at least in the manner of their announcement, the most spectacular of the post-war resorts to monetary policy. In September,

[1]*H.C. Deb.* 17 April 1956, 855–6.
[2]*Economic Survey, 1958*, para. 70.

Bank rate was raised to seven per cent, its highest level since 1921.   Once again, a rise in Bank rate was accompanied by a list of other measures intended to be equally impressive.   The banks were 'required'—not 'requested'—to hold the level of advances to the average of the preceding twelve months; and restrictions on lending abroad were tightened. (Public investment was to be stabilized at its present level; and, as would seem from the issue on which he resigned, Mr Thorneycroft's plan included also a stabilization of government current expenditure.)

The intention behind the deeds was more drastic than the deeds themselves. 'So long as it is generally believed', ran the Chancellor's crisis statement, 'that the Government are prepared to see the necessary finance produced to match the upward spiral of costs, inflation will continue and prices will go up'[1].   If then (his argument ran) the supply of money—and various other 'monetary' totals not strictly to be equated with the supply of money—were limited, inflation would run up against an immovable obstacle.   Rising prices would be prevented—if necessary, at the cost of falling activity and falling employment[2].

There are good reasons for thinking that these measures could never have had these effects—though they may have had some effect on the holding of stocks[3]. Though the Cabinet refused to endorse the restriction on government spending, the other measures continued in force after Mr Thorneycroft's resignation. The trend of demand continued downward; and if the rise in prices was slower, this was very largely due to the world-wide fall in commodity prices (chapter III.4).

When Mr Thorneycroft resigned, the extreme emphasis on monetary measures ceased.   The 1958 *Economic Survey* made little of monetary policy[4]; and the new Chancellor, Mr Heathcoat Amory, referred only briefly to it in his budget speech[5].   In the course of 1958, there was a gradual shift in the emphasis of policy, and a series of measures were taken with the conscious intention of

---

[1] The Chancellor's statement is quoted in the *Bank Rate Tribunal Report*, para. 2.

[2] See *Radcliffe Report*, para. 424.   The same impression of a new leaf being turned was given by the Governor of the Bank, when he referred to the 'decisive effects' which can sometimes be looked for from a sharp increase in interest rates, and underlined the Chancellor's emphasis on 'the fundamental importance of the supply of money' (Mansion House Speech, 8th October 1957: see *Radcliffe, Memoranda*, I, Appendix I).

[3] See chapter XV.2 below.

[4] "By mid-March 1958, the exceptionally high level of short-term interest rates was no longer justified in order to support the international position of sterling, which had greatly improved, while at home inflationary pressures were moderating.   Bank Rate was reduced from 7 per cent to 6 per cent on 20th March 1958' (*Economic Survey, 1958*, para. 36). The epilogue (paras. 77–86) discussed prospects without mentioning monetary policy.

[5] "The September measures succeeded in restoring confidence in the £, and I was able, last month, to approve a reduction in the Bank Rate from the exceptionally high level of 7 per cent . . .   It is still necessary for the banks to hold down the level of advances and for hire purchase restrictions to be kept on.   The Capital Issues Committee will continue for the present to maintain its critical scrutiny' (*H.C. Deb.* 15 April 1958, 55).

raising home demand and producing a 'resumption of economic growth'[1].

Bank rate was reduced from seven to six per cent in March and by four further stages to four per cent in November. Hire-purchase restrictions were relaxed in September and removed entirely in October (§5). In July, bank advances were freed entirely from restriction—for the first time since the war; and the banks used their freedom to expand advances rapidly (§3). At the same time that bank advances were freed, the Chancellor also announced the 'special deposits' scheme—intended as a measure, for use as required, for influencing bank advances in future (§3). These monetary measures were followed by the even more expansionary budget of 1959—which, with them, produced a rapid rise in expenditure and output in the course of 1959.

Restraint in 1960

By early 1960, the authorities felt it desirable to moderate the course of expansion. The 1960 budget made practically no difference to consumers' purchasing power; and the first series of measures were all of a monetary nature. At the end of April, relatively mild hire-purchase restrictions were reimposed (§5 above); and the first call was made on the banks for special deposits (to take effect at the end of June— §3). Bank rate, which had been raised from four to five per cent in January, was raised to six per cent in June; and a further call was made for special deposits. After some delay, this resulted in a slower growth in advances, and—presumably with hints from the authorities—a fall in those types of lending most closely connected with consumers' expenditure (§3). The authorities also went a long way towards encouraging a rise in long-term interest rates (§2). Later, in the middle of 1961, these monetary measures were to be reinforced by fiscal action.

8. CONCLUSIONS: THE ECONOMIC IMPACT OF MONETARY POLICY

The previous section has attempted to describe the intentions of the authorities since the inception of an active monetary policy at the end of 1951. Such an account cannot be entirely fair. Policy had many aspects, not necessarily well integrated; the views of the Bank of England may not have coincided—indeed sometimes clearly did not coincide—with those of the Treasury; and, policy not being much explained in public, such comments as were made, chiefly by the Chancellor of the Exchequer, may have been a partial account only of what was intended by those who had a say in policy.

Nevertheless it is clear that for much of the time, while the aims of monetary policy were exceedingly ambitious, the conception of its method of working was left extremely vague: monetary policy was indeed invested with many of the

---

[1]*Economic Survey, 1959,* para. 1.

S

properties of magic[1].   It was often employed as if it, and it alone, would cure inflation, or, alternatively, right the balance of payments; and as if it would do so without impinging openly or painfully on any specific class of demand.   It is scarcely surprising that Chancellors of the Exchequer grasped at monetary policy as a heaven-sent alternative to budgetary policy.   Even when specific effects were attributed to monetary policy—as when it was stated to be intended to curtail fixed investment or investment in stocks—such claims were not based on much reasoning or evidence; and may, one feels, have come near to being rationalizations of what had been decided anyhow.

Resort to monetary policy was generally prompted by the balance of payments situation.   But the vagueness concerning the route by which monetary policy was expected to take effect was especially great when it came to the use of monetary policy to right the external balance.   Since advocacy of monetary measures was often allied with a tendency to judge the balance of payments by the movement of the reserves, there was a constant danger of being satisfied with favourable capital movements without considering that the effect on the underlying trading position might be far from comparable.   This weakness in the formation of policy is typified by the continued emphasis on Bank rate: it was never clear whether a rise in the rate was intended to attract external capital—either by providing an interest incentive, or as a symbol of intentions; or whether it was expected to have effects of a more fundamental nature via effects on internal demand.

During the last few years, however, there has been a change: the aims of monetary policy have become less grandiose; and the measures taken, more closely adapted to the achievement of precise aims.   Of this change, the *Radcliffe Report*, and the discussions that accompanied and followed it, is both a sign and a cause.   Some of the conclusions of the *Report* have been disputed, and will no doubt for long go on being discussed.   But the *Report* as a whole is more important than the detailed conclusions scattered throughout—and sometimes difficult to unearth from—its lengthy discussions of the facts.   If the Committee failed to say the last word on some matters, this would not be surprising.   But to have discussed monetary policy fully and carefully, and in an empirical commonsense tone, is itself an achievement which becomes more impressive the more it is studied; and which has already had, and is bound to continue to have, a powerful influence on the spirit of policy.

Any subsequent discussion of the impact of monetary policy during these years has to start from the conclusions proposed by the Radcliffe Committee which, however, having been much discussed, need only be briefly restated here. One of the most important negative conclusions of the Committee was its

---

[1]'Indeed, there is still a tendency to speak in magical rather than scientific terms of the use of interest rates and of monetary controls generally.   The economy is to be given a potion or dose, and wonderful results will follow.'   (Sir Robert Hall [1959], 'Reflections on the Practical Application of Economics', *Econ. J.*, December 1959, p. 648.)

scepticism about the short-run impact of changes in interest rates, and of changes in Bank rate in particular.   Thus, said the *Report*, 'changes in rates of interest only very exceptionally have direct effects on the level of demand'[1]. If they did have some effect, they, like other internal effects, would in turn affect the balance of payments—but not with 'any rapid impact'[2].   Nor did the Committee believe that changes in short-term rates have much effect on movements of short-term international capital—'a jump in short-term rates seems . . . to have lost much of its power to effect any real immediate improvement in Britain's international balance sheet'[3].   But Bank rate still had effects on 'the foreigner's confidence in sterling'.   'The rise in Bank Rate is symbolical': however foolishly, it was still taken as 'evidence that the United Kingdom authorities have the determination to take unpleasant steps to check inflation'[4].

The *Report*'s more positive conclusions upon the internal impact of monetary measures are worth quoting at length[5]:

'In investigating the effects of these various measures we have had in mind that a marginal adjustment in the pressure of demand may be all that is required . . . we should look upon a minimum effect of the order of £100 million over a year as an adjustment worth seeking.   We have tried to decide whether any of the measures which we have been reviewing has had effect of this order. . .   While we have no statistics firm enough to warrant any assurance, we find it difficult . . . to believe that any of the changes in interest rates have by themselves had an impact of this order of magnitude.   The squeeze on bank advances in 1955–56 perhaps would, if the impact could be measured, qualify by this criterion.   Almost certainly the changes in hire purchase control, when at all substantial, did have effects of this order.   The capital issues control was negligible, to the point of irrelevance . . .'

'If we look at the actual experience of the 1950s—as far as the evidence has allowed us to trace it—we come to the conclusion that the really quick substantial effects were secured by the hire purchase controls, just those which have the most concentrated directional effects.   A considerable, though rather slower, effect probably came in 1956–58 from the "diffused difficulty of borrowing" which resulted from the tighter and dearer money —particularly the squeeze of bank credit—of 1955–56. . .   The monetary instruments employed left untouched the large industrial corporations that

---

[1] *Radcliffe Report*, para. 487.   It is difficult to give a fair summary of the *Report* by brief quotations, since most statements are qualified by other passages.   For the theory that interest rates affect 'the state of liquidity', see further below.

[2] Para. 437.

[3] Para. 439—but this 'power might revive as exchange markets take on a more settled appearance'.

[4] Para. 441; but 'we find it difficult to believe that such veneration for Bank Rate can persist if there develops a general scepticism of the power of interest rates over the internal economic situation'.

[5] Paras. 471–2.

control more than half the investment in manufacturing industry; and neither their planning nor that of the public corporations appears to have responded seriously to changes in interest rates. In the more fractionally organised parts of the private sector there has been pressure here and pressure there, though nothing of great moment. . . We are driven to the conclusion that the more conventional instruments have failed to keep the system in smooth balance, but that every now and again the mounting pressure of demand has in one way or another (generally via the exchange situation) driven the Government to take action, and that the quick results then required have been mainly concentrated on the hire purchase front and on investment in the public sector which could be cut by administrative decision. The light engineering industries have been frustrated in their planning, and the public corporations have had almost equally disheartening experience. That these two should be the "residuary legatees" for real resources when sharp adjustments were called for is not a comforting thought. It is far removed from the smooth and widespread adjustment sometimes claimed as the virtue of monetary action; this is no gentle hand on the steering wheel that keeps a well-driven car in its right place on the road.'

The review of monetary measures since 1951 in preceding sections of this chapter suggest some amendment, but no radical revision, of these conclusions. The most important conclusion—to be more fully justified in chapter XI.2— is that the main impact was obtained by hire-purchase regulation: the impact could well have been even larger than the £100 million suggested by the Radcliffe Committee. The present assessment suggests that variations in building society lending (brought about indirectly by monetary measures) may also have had some appreciable impact—an effect hardly mentioned by the Committee. As against this, it is difficult to believe that the squeeze of bank advances, even in 1955–6, had effects as large as the Radcliffe Committee's quantum of £100 million a year. This is not to deny that it had some impact— including perhaps some impact on stocks[1].

These appear to be the main conclusions of practical importance. It would seem, then, that the effect of monetary measures on internal demand was considerably more restricted than the effect of budgetary policy (as discussed in chapter VII above). The effect of hire-purchase controls on consumers' expenditure was at times appreciable, but the impact was concentrated on a narrow range of expenditure. The effect of variations in building society lending was probably less than that of changes in the initial or investment allowances—or of changes in local authority house-building.

---

[1]The Committee suggested (para. 460) that the impact was on fixed investment ('capital projects in their earliest planning stages'), not on 'holding of stocks of commodities'. The present assessment suggests that credit restrictions may have affected the level of stocks, particularly in 1957–8: see chapter XV.2 below.

In addition to these practical conclusions, there are two issues of some theoretical complexity, which should be noted at this point since they have some practical relevance, though their full discussion must be deferred (till chapter XII).

The Radcliffe Committee suggested that changes in interest rates, quite apart from any direct effect they may have on the demand for investment goods, altered the liquidity position of financial institutions; and this affected the availability of funds to borrowers through particular channels[1]. For this reason, said the Committee, monetary policy should seek to influence 'the state of liquidity of the whole economy'[2]. This idea, which has offended economists by its vagueness, will be further discussed in chapter XII below. It is there conceded that monetary policy may be able to interrupt the flows of short-term finance; and that, the capital market being imperfect, this may cause sufficient short-term embarrassment temporarily to curtail business expenditure on stocks or investment. But it is also argued that this effect is most likely to be provoked, not by interest-rate changes as the Radcliffe Committee suggested; but by direct restriction of bank advances, for which the Committee left little place[3]. If this view is correct, there is a case for finding better means to control bank advances than the 'special deposit' provisions—whose inadequacy in this regard has already become evident (§3 above).

Very little has been said in this chapter about the volume of money. That a fixed quantity of money is no barrier to price inflation or to excess demand is perhaps sufficiently evident from inspection of the facts[4]. The role of money will be further discussed later; and it will be argued that by controlling the volume of money, the authorities can control interest rates—an argument in some ways similar to the Radcliffe Committee's emphasis on National Debt policy[5].

The Committee also thought that the level of interest rates had some direct effects, at least in the long run, on investment; and ought in consequence to be the subject of conscious policy[6]. In recent years, and largely as a result of the Radcliffe discussions, the authorities have been making increasingly deliberate use of their ability to control interest rates, and by 1960 had come near to a positive policy of 'dear money' (§2 above). The argument as to the advantage of such a policy is highly complex (chapter XII.3). But high interest rates worsen both the budget and the balance of payments; and it seems time to reconsider again the case for 'cheap money', which since Dr Dalton has been forgotten[7].

[1]Paras. 387–97.
[2]Para. 981.
[3]The Committee emphasized that banks were 'key lenders' in the system (para. 395). But, compared with its emphasis on interest-rate manipulations, it gave little emphasis to the need to control bank advances (see, for instance, para. 397 (i)).
[4]The volume of money, as usually defined, was, for instance, falling between 1954 and 1956, i.e. during the 1955 boom: see figure 9.1 above.
[5]See further chapter XII.1 below.
[6]*Report*, paras. 495–8.
[7]See chapter XII.5 below. Since 1960, as already noted, the policy has changed, and the authorities now appear to favour a reduction of the long-term rate of interest.

THE GENERAL BEHAVIOUR OF THE ECONOMY

CHAPTER X

INTRODUCTION: QUESTIONS TO BE CONSIDERED

The aim of the present part III of this study is to give a rough picture of the main relationships determining the behaviour of the economy. Since the war (it is roughly true to say) the government has tried to control the economy by operating on the level of demand. Only, then, if one knows how policy affects demand, and how demand in turn affects output and investment, imports, exports, and the price level, can one say what policy did, and how useful it was.

To answer these questions it is necessary at this point to turn from the straightforward analysis of previous chapters, and consider more general or theoretical questions. This may appear a digression, though one hardly to be avoided, in what is essentially an empirical study of a particular phase of history. The following discussion will go no further into things than is necessary to establish the elements needed to arrive at broad conclusions on the important questions about economic policy. It seems useful first to set out the general conclusions which seem to emerge from this study so far, and then to try to list the main questions as yet unanswered to which an answer must now be sought (§1). Second, since much of the argument is interconnected, it may help to give a brief preview (§2) of the line of argument to be followed in part III of this study together with an indication of questions left over for part IV.

1. FIRST CONCLUSIONS AND QUESTIONS RAISED

This study so far has aimed to carry the analysis only up to a certain point: it has been content to analyse acts of policy without going into very detailed discussion of how the economy responds to them. Some conclusions emerge even at this stage of the analysis; and the following paragraphs summarize what seems to emerge from the account given in part II of the effects of direct controls, public investment policy, and budgetary and monetary policy, and, finally, of official forecasting.

Experience with direct controls tells something of the normal working of the economy and the general problem of controlling it, and is thus of more than historic interest. The Labour Government in 1945 took over an economy subject to full wartime controls; and tended to regard them as instruments, available by this lucky chance, for economic planning. The administration of this complex network required frequent detailed specific decisions both of officials and of ministers. Such decisions were necessary merely to keep the system operating, whether or not it had strategic impact; and the constant drain on the energies of policy-makers probably hampered economic planning. The first post-war years were beset with frequent 'crises'. The government tried to use controls to force rapid adjustments on the economy (e.g. cuts in imports or investment) as a way of meeting the crises. These attempts were only partially successful—much as were later attempts, by means other than direct controls, to bring about quick adjustments. But such short-term effects were not the main result of controls, nor reason enough alone to keep the system in being.

The main reason for retaining controls at the end of the war was as a means to prevent a post-war burst of open inflation. The general conclusion of chapter VI was that extensive controls were justified by their general effect in containing the pressure of demand, and in keeping down the volume of imports. It was suggested earlier that during the war the apparatus of direct controls played as large a part in reducing civilian demand as did steep wartime taxation. After the war their effect must have been only less important. For instance, during the four years 1946–9, controls may have reduced the pressure of demand by ten per cent or so, and have saved fifteen per cent or so of imports. But experience of operating direct controls in peacetime suggests that they are conceivable as an anti-inflationary device only in conditions of grave and widespread shortage. General concurrence with the purposes of control is unlikely except in national emergency. Furthermore, controls are always specific: a system of controls widespread enough to affect total demand is therefore only possible when shortages are serious and numerous.

Controls may nevertheless not have altered business behaviour greatly. Firms left to themselves tend to 'ration' customers when demand is high; and the economy, faced with high demand, does not react with violent price inflation (see further chapter XIII). The stickiness of prices may thus provide in normal times much the same protection against inflation as controls did during the war and for some years after.

British stabilization policy, to a degree probably not surpassed elsewhere, has relied predominantly on fiscal measures. In the early years, when the demand behind the 'barrier' of controls was seriously excessive, the aim was to deflate demand by fiscal means. Only after this first heavy excess of demand was removed—only after, say, 1951 or 1952—was the economy, as it were, free to fluctuate. Till then the effects of fiscal policy were, like the inflationary pressure it sought to remove, concealed from view. Taking the post-war period as a whole, various features in economic development—in particular the growth of private savings—have made it possible gradually to reduce taxes (chapter IV). Most of the impact of fiscal policy has come by going 'slower than trend' at some times (e.g. 1948–50 under Sir Stafford Cripps and 1955–8 under Mr Butler's successors as Chancellor); and 'more rapidly than trend' at other times (e.g. 1953–4 and 1958).   Taxes were actually raised only on three occasions —in the autumns of 1947 and 1955 (in correction of what was by then clear was a previous mistake) and in 1951 (on account of the defence programme).

It is clear even on a superficial view that the big changes in tax rates must have affected demand considerably.   The average growth of output over the last decade has been $2\frac{1}{2}$ per cent or rather under.   On several occasions tax changes, both up and down, have been of this same order, i.e. 2–3 per cent of national product.   Even though their effect on spending will have been somewhat less than this, they must at such times have caused a large reduction, or addition, to the rate of growth of real demand.   One major question is whether these changes contributed towards 'stability', or whether the effect was not rather the reverse. The growth of output has gone in steps, periods of rapid growth alternating with periods of little or none.   These steps coincide with the alternating phases of fiscal policy just described—which may therefore have been the cause of the other.   (This question will be further discussed in chapter XV.)

It is clear that the major impact of tax changes was on consumer demand not investment demand.   This was the effect intended, and the taxes whose rates were changed were selected to have this effect.   But there is room for argument as to the scale and timing of the effect.   (The argument in chapter XII.1 suggests that the effect on consumer spending is by no means instantaneous, and that the full effect may take longer to work itself through than has usually been allowed.)   In so far as tax changes do not affect consumption they affect saving—partly personal saving, and more important, the retained profits of companies.   There have been important changes in the taxation of profits; and successive introductions and suspensions first of the 'initial' and then of the 'investment' allowances.   Though they do not affect consumers' expenditure much, such tax changes may still affect investment; but there is little agreement how much they do.   (This question is discussed in chapter XI.4 as part of the general question of what determines investment.)

The use of fiscal policy to stabilize the economy undoubtedly makes great calls on the firmness and courage of those in charge of the fiscal machine, in particular of the Chancellor of the Exchequer.   One conclusion might be that it is unwise to rely on fiscal policy alone.   But other policy instruments have lesser effects, and also different effects, on the economy—which limits the choice (chapter XVI.2.)   So far, fiscal policy has not been put to too much strain, for the trends have been such as to make it possible gradually to reduce taxes.   Another possible conclusion is that ways must be found to let this continue—which would have implications for the growth of government expenditure and of investment.

One alternative to fiscal policy is the control of public investment. Pre-war discussion emphasized the 'contra-cyclical' variation of public investment as a means of stabilizing the economy; but experience since (chapter VIII) seems to show that it cannot be an instrument for taking *rapid*, major action.

For it is difficult to vary investment (whether public or private) at short notice; and public investment is anyhow a small part only of total demand. Experience suggests that public investment can only be varied by £30–£50 million within a period of twelve to eighteen months.

In the first years after its revival, great hopes were rested on monetary policy as a means of controlling the economy. But much of the talk was insubstantial, since it left it vague precisely how monetary policy was expected to impinge on the economy. Chapter IX proposed two chief types of monetary influence: first, the hire-purchase controls; and, second, the effect on housebuilding of the rationing of mortgage credit by the building societies; it allowed some effect also to the restraint of bank credit. It remains to consider more closely the size of their impact. Hire-purchase changes probably affect not only the demand for durables, but that for other goods and services also; and their impact has to be assessed along with the other things that affect consumers' expenditure (chapter XI.2). The effect of the restriction of building society credit is probably smaller (chapter XI.4). There also remains to consider (chapter XII) a tangled skein of questions concerning monetary policy, which have hitherto been deferred, and which amount to this: whether monetary policy does not have other effects (through interest rates, or 'liquidity') more pervasive than those (like the two rationing effects listed above) which can be easily pinpointed.

Granted that the effects of policy measures can be roughly quantified, there emerge several questions as to the laws of response of the economy to them. Foremost among these is the debated question of rising prices. Are rising prices entirely due to high demand, and hence to be prevented by a reduction in the pressure of demand? If so, policy is to blame. Or can prices also be forced up by cost pressures—a process more difficult to stop? Chapter XIII summarizes recent research on this question.

There remain more general questions as to whether the 'strategy' of government intervention was well devised. It has already been suggested that the 'stops and starts' in economic growth may have been due to the 'stops and starts' of economic policy. The direction of policy has necessarily depended on forecasts of the situation to be dealt with; and one prior question is how far mistakes in policy can be attributed to failures in the official forecasts. Till recent years the forecasts (as noted in chapter V) were not in a form best suited to guide policy; and by comparing the level of expenditure expected to rule *on average* in the year ahead with the *average* level in the year elapsed, they obscured the view taken of prospective developments over the next twelve months.

In most years, nevertheless, they appear not to have been seriously misleading; but there were occasions when the forecasts, if not positively misleading, appear to have been seriously inadequate. The three main occasions of this sort were the failure to foresee the check to output in the 1952 recession; the failure to foresee the pre-boom build-up in 1954; and the failure to foresee in full the pace

of expansion in 1959.   In each case the policy pursued on the basis of the forecasts may be judged, in the light of hindsight, to have taken the economy further
from the ideal level.   This does not mean that the attempt to forecast was a
waste of effort.   The risk of error is inevitable, and may be reduced in time; but
there is little question that systematic forecasting, however imperfect, resulted
in a radically better picture of future developments than would have been
possible without forecasting procedures.

It is, too, a question how far any mistakes in policy on these three occasions
should be ascribed to the erroneous forecasts, and whether they should not
rather be ascribed to an inadequate picture of the working of the economy and
an inadequate analysis of the problems with which policy was faced.   It is
possible to suspect that policy made insufficient allowance for the *delayed*
effects of policy, and for indirect repercussions springing from the dynamic interactions of different sectors of the economy—repercussions which may only
become important over periods of more than a year.   The practice of dividing
time into yearly periods, both for the formulation of policy at successive budgets
and for the forecasts that accompanied them, may have tended to obscure such
effects.   In a sense, therefore, the main weakness of the forecasts may have been
that they were too short-term.   An attempt to forecast over a longer term, even
though not reliable as a forecast, might direct attention to influences and interactions that at present can be ignored.   The benefit of systematic diagnosis is
not to be measured solely by the accuracy of the forecasts; an equally important
result of a careful analysis is that it may sort out which of the trends in view are
relevant for the direction of policy.

The criterion according to which policy should properly be directed will be
reconsidered in the final part IV of this study.   Most acts of intervention were
prompted by short-run swings in the balance of payments.   One set of subsidiary questions therefore is: what caused these swings?   How far were they due
to the state of home demand?   And how quickly could induced changes in home
demand be expected to affect the balance of payments?   All these questions
affect the proper direction of policy: it can well be argued that internal policy
cannot prevent swings in the balance of payments.   Then there is the question
of why the economy has grown, in comparison with some other countries,
relatively slowly.   If slow growth has been partly due to a failure of policy, it is
worth considering how far this in turn has made more difficult the achievement
of other objectives: in particular, price stability, and a satisfactory balance of
payments.   The strategy of policy may need to be rethought (chapter XVI).

2.   NATURE OF THE ARGUMENT TO FOLLOW

The following chapters attempt to summarize the evidence relevant to such
questions.   They do not aim to present new empirical results, but attempt rather

a progress report on research and a provisional synthesis of results. Since different aspects of the economy are interrelated, the argument of the following chapters is necessarily interlocking: wherever one broke into the circle, answers would have to be begged on some questions only to be discussed later.

It seems simplest, first, to start straightforwardly with a discussion of the determinants of consumers' expenditure, fixed investment and investment in stocks; and to summarize the evidence about the size of the various influences affecting each class of expenditure (chapter XI). This permits some sort of conclusion about the most obvious ways in which policy may affect demand.

The relative insensitivity of most investment to interest rates argues that the capital market is imperfect, so that there is, as it were, a gulf fixed between 'real' and 'monetary' assets. This provides a basis for a new attack (chapter XII) on the old tangle of questions concerning monetary policy—whether the quantity of money, interest rates and the state of 'liquidity' affect real spending.

The discussion so far concerns the effect of policy on demand. The third question discussed is the impact of changes in demand on the price level. This question has to be discussed (chapter XIII) along with other factors affecting prices: in particular, account has to be taken of the way in which changes in wages, changes in prices and changes in productivity are interrelated.

Finally (in part IV) it is necessary to put the pieces together into a rough 'model' of the economy. From this, conclusions follow about the influence of past policy on the fluctuations in demand to which the economy has been subject since the war; and about its influence on the balance of payments and on the rate of economic growth.

The above order of argument has been chosen because it suits the line of argument, which means that it may not suit those who disbelieve the argument. There is no way round this kind of difficulty. It is impossible to approach reality without a theory in one's mind about what kind of events are inter-related and roughly how. In interpreting economic developments, one has to start with the relationships that one thinks are relatively sure; fit other events on to this initial 'core', so as to enlarge the area which one thinks one under-stands; and use this, in turn, as a base on which to try to fit yet further aspects intelligibly into the picture.

If, for instance, one regards it as certain that prices rise only when there is an excess of demand, then a rise in prices can be taken as a reliable and sufficient index of excess demand. Other possible indices would have to be interpreted in this light; and some theory would be needed to 'explain away' their evidence, when contradictory. Yet other symptoms would also be interpreted in this light, as evidence of how the economy reacts to excess demand. If however it is believed—as will be argued here—that prices may rise for other reasons also, then a rise in prices cannot be taken as a reliable index of excess demand; and some other index has to be sought, such as for instance the level of unemploy-ment. Far from starting with price trends, one has, on the contrary, to treat them as one of the phenomena to be 'explained', i.e. related to something else.

Much the same applies to the role allotted to the volume of money. If one regards an increase in the volume of money as an invariable cause or necessary accompaniment to an excessive level of demand, one would have to make this the starting point of one's interpretation of events; and other developments, such as the balance of payments or the state of employment would have, if possible, to be made sense of in this light. If however one regards the volume of money as a secondary and relatively unimportant factor—as will be argued in this study—it will be one of the last things to be fitted into the picture.

The price level, and the role of money, happen to be foci of dispute in economists' rival pictures of the world. Each is here given a chapter to itself. Argument between those who set out from different starting points is however always difficult. What one would ideally like from one's opponent would be suspension of his disbelief in one's own argument, so that he could view the flux of events in terms of one's own categories, and see how well the facts then fit. It is asking a lot to expect one's opponent to see the world, even experimentally, through one's own eyes. But, in complicated disputes, it is not detailed theories but rival attitudes to the world that are in collision.

In principle, many of the matters to be discussed in the following chapters could be dealt with as deductions from a mathematical 'model' describing the workings of the economy. But deductions are only simple if one's basic knowledge is detailed and sure. As has already been made plain, this is not the case in this field at this moment. One has therefore to base conclusions not on tight logical deduction from known premises, but rather on a sceptical and reasoned review of scanty basic evidence.

A mathematical model of the economy must rest on the statistical measurement of numerous relationships. But just as one cannot approach reality without a theory, so it is also true that the selection of relations to measure is as important as their measurement. The choice of hypotheses to test ought to depend on careful theoretical reasoning from existing knowledge. In some cases, where questions are the subject of lively theoretical dispute, it would be premature to try to settle the issue by econometrics. If reason has anything to contribute, it is better to spend time worrying about the prior questions of theory. Questions, for instance, concerning the role of money are complicated questions, on which it is easy to make muddles, which careful thinking might avoid; and where an immediate uncritical recourse to econometrics could certainly not settle the points under dispute[1].

[1]My object here is to defend myself for not having chosen to follow the method adopted by Professor Tinbergen [1956], in *Economic Policy: Principles and Design*. He there deduces many propositions about economic policy from a series of models describing different aspects of the economy. Logically the procedure may be impeccable: propositions about policy should depend on the nature of the economy. At the same time, if the premises are doubtful, this can easily be obscured in such a treatment. For instance, Professor Tinbergen (*op. cit.*, p. 73) is able to assume away a whole world of doubt and difficulty

Since the questions at issue affect fundamentally one's general picture of how the economy works, it seems impossible to get straight down to the task of specifying a model of the sort econometricians need.   To by-pass difficulties in order to state conclusions more quickly and to refrain from setting out the arguments which might convince those who take a contrary view, would hardly advance the cause of economic science.   'If we are to make any progress at all, we must', Lord Robbins has said, 'go on seeking to set forth the ultimate reasons for our own attitudes'[1].

by one equation describing the role of money.   Professor Tinbergen's equation, it so happens, seems to me to imply a wrong theory: to justify this view of mine requires some pages of argument, not the line or two of text which Professor Tinbergen devotes to the equation.

[1]Lionel Robbins [1958], 'Thoughts on the Crisis', *Lloyds Bank R.*, April 1958, p. 2: ' . . . if we are to make any progress at all we must go on exchanging opinions and seeking to set forth, with mutual respect and toleration of other points of view . . . the ultimate reasons for our own attitudes'.   Lord Robbins, as it happens, has taken a rather different view from that taken here on both of the two crucial questions of prices and the role of money: see this same article, p. 6.

CHAPTER XI

THE DETERMINANTS OF DEMAND:

A SUMMARY OF THE EVIDENCE*

It would scarcely be possible to determine the influence of economic policy on the British economy merely from direct inspection of the post-war record. Changes in policy have been accompanied by other powerful influences operating at the same time, so that the effects of policy are obscured. Moreover some of the shifts in policy, particularly long-term interest policy, have been slow and within a limited compass. A broader and more analytical approach is inevitable: it seems possible to indicate the scale of policy influences only by calling in aid inference from general theoretical presumptions, and by consulting empirical evidence drawn from other periods and other countries.

This chapter therefore discusses what it is that determines the level of each of the three broad classes of private demand: consumers' expenditure (§§ 1–3); fixed investment (§4); and investment in stocks (§5). In each case, policy measures are one type of influence among others; and in each case the aim is to give some quantitative indication of the magnitude of the influence[1]. A summary of conclusions is appended in the final section (§6). At a later stage (chapter XV) it is intended to 'apply' these conclusions to post-war trends, and use them as one ingredient in their interpretation.

Essentially, the present chapter seeks to identify the main routes along which policy influences can be expected on general grounds to impinge on the economy; and to summarize the evidence of such empirical studies as have been made, here or abroad, as to the scale of influence. The implications for monetary policy are discussed in chapter XII along with some general issues concerning monetary policy not easily dealt with at this stage.

1. THE DETERMINANTS OF CONSUMPTION: THE EFFECT OF
CHANGES OF INCOME AND OF CHANGES IN TAXES

Pre-war discussion of economic policy assumed that consumers' expenditure was dependable and stable, and related in a simple way to their disposable

---

*The discussion in this chapter is more technical than in most others. The argument is outlined in the introductory paragraphs and conclusions are stated in §6.

[1]Some of the ground covered in this chapter was covered in a memorandum submitted to the Radcliffe Committee, part 2 of which was entitled 'The Scale of Monetary Influences: A Summary of the Evidence' (see Dow [1958], 'The Economic Effect of Monetary Policy, 1945–57' in *Radcliffe, Memoranda*, XIII.9). I am now less sure than I was about some matters, in particular the effect of hire-purchase controls (§2 below) and the dependence of investment on finance (§4).

income. In the fifteen years since the war, however, personal savings have varied greatly from year to year; and, while changes in consumption have clearly been affected by changes in income, it is clear that any relation between them is complex, and that other factors have also been important. This section summarizes the present evidence about the effect of income—a question closely connected with the effect of *taxes* on income. (§§ 2 and 3 deal more specifically with the effect of changes in hire-purchase controls, which have also been an important influence; and with the effect of changes in interest rates, which— whether direct, or via capital gains and losses—probably have not.)

Keynes asserted it as a 'fundamental psychological rule of any modern community that, when its real income is increased, it will not increase its consumption by an equal *absolute* amount', and that 'as a rule . . . a greater *proportion* of income' will be saved as real income increases[1]. While much of the evidence which has become available since then seemed to confirm Keynes's hypothesis, study of national income data for the United States suggested the need for some modification. Thus Kuznets's estimates seemed to show that despite a substantial rise in income during the last half century, savings had not increased their share in national income[2]. Partly in order to reconcile this seemingly well attested—though still rather isolated—finding about the long-term, with the apparent short-term behaviour of savings, various writers have suggested more sophisticated versions of the consumption function[3]. These have two features in common: first, they assume that not only current but past levels of income affect consumers' expenditure[4]; and second, they assume that the long-run propensity is for a constant proportion of income to be spent. Thus, a rise in income (it is supposed) takes time to have full effect, so that at first less than the normal proportion will be spent; but in the end only the same fraction of income will be spent as before.

There has been less work with the British data, largely because estimates do not extend far back. Though there are estimates of consumers' expenditure before the war, those for consumers' income cover only the post-war years: the main series, expressed throughout at 1954 prices, are summarized on figure 11.1. In the fourteen-year period 1946–60, consumers' real disposable incomes rose about fifty per cent. The tax figures only permit this to be divided into three broad components: wages, salaries and other incomes from employment; national insurance benefits and government grants and other transfer incomes;

[1]J. M. Keynes [1936], *The General Theory of Employment, Interest and Money*, pp. 96–7.
[2]For instance S. Kuznets [1952], 'Proportion of Capital Formation to National Product', *Amer. econ. R.*, May 1952.
[3]Notably Duesenberry, Milton Friedman and Modigliani and Brumberg; see J. S. Duesenberry [1949], *Income, Saving and the Theory of Consumer Behavior*; M. Friedman [1957], *A Theory of the Consumption Function*; F. Modigliani and R. Brumberg [1954], 'Utility Analysis and the Consumption Function: An Interpretation of Cross-section Data'; and also M. J. Farrell [1959], 'The New Theories of the Consumption Function', *Econ.. J.*, December 1959.
[4]This is an over-simple description of Friedman's 'permanent income' hypothesis,

and all other incomes—rent, interest, dividends and incomes from self-employment. Of these three components, the increase in wages and salaries accounts, according to the official estimates, for most of the increase in real incomes since the war.

The increase in real personal income has not been quite continuous. Total real disposable income fell two per cent in 1948 (because of Dr Dalton's autumn budget, and also, perhaps, Sir Stafford Cripps's wage freeze). It was 'profit' incomes which were then most affected. Again in 1951, disposable income fell one per cent (partly because of Mr Gaitskell's budget, but chiefly because of the rise in commodity prices produced by the Korean war). Again 'profit' incomes were most affected. Thereafter real incomes have risen continuously: especially rapidly during the 1955 boom; and less rapidly after, especially in 1958 (when aggregate wages and salaries fell in real terms).

Consumers' expenditure has clearly reflected the development of real incomes to some degree. The rise in total real consumers' expenditure was checked in 1948 (when real income fell) and in 1951 and 1952 (real income fell in 1951); and was also affected by the 1955 boom and the subsequent reaction. Spending on durables has been affected by hire-purchase controls and by tax changes. This matters here since spending on durables is in some ways an alternative to saving, so that one might expect the total of saving and spending on durables to be more stable than either separately. This does indeed appear to be the case in the period after 1952—the period when the use of hire purchase was expanding, and changes in the regulations were important. Since then, spending on non-durables has grown distinctly less rapidly (25 per cent or so) than the growth of real incomes (35 per cent) and the total of savings *plus* durables distinctly more rapidly (it has in fact grown two-and-a-half-fold).

This trend to greater personal saving—as noted in the discussion at an earlier stage[1]—has been of great importance for policy; but it runs somewhat counter to the theoretical expectation suggested by the recent theorizing. The data available for the United Kingdom are insufficient to enable final conclusions to be drawn about consumers' behaviour; nor have they yet been the subject of any full study[2]. While it is difficult to believe the trend to greater saving will

[1] Chapter IV.
[2] The general study of the British economy by Professor Klein and his associates contains various consumption equations estimated from 'time series': see L. R. Klein, R. J. Ball, A. Hazlewood and P. Vandome [1961], *An Econometric Model of the United Kingdom*. Previously Klein was associated with the savings surveys made by the Oxford University Institute of Statistics. Some main results are conveniently summarized in L. R. Klein [1955], 'Patterns of Saving—The Surveys of 1953 and 1954', B. *Oxford Inst. Statist.*, May 1955. Estimates of different income groups' marginal propensity to save based on this 'cross-section' data are in L. R. Klein [1958], 'The British Propensity to Save', *J. roy. statist. Soc.*, A, 1958, part 1.

An earlier study of time series was by J. R. N. Stone and D. A. Rowe [1956], 'Aggregate Consumption and Investment Functions for the Household Sector considered in the Light of British Experience', *Nat.-økon. Tss.*, vol. 94, parts 1–2, 1956. This study was based on pre-war data and post-war data for the period up to 1954.

Fig. 11.1. Consumers' incomes, expenditure and saving, 1946–60
£000m. at 1954 prices

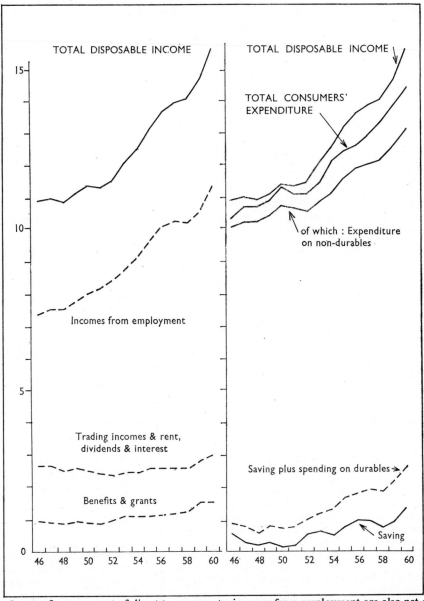

Income figures are net of direct tax payments; incomes from employment are also net of (employers' and employees') national insurance contributions and employers' other insurance contributions. Incomes and savings are deflated by average value index for total consumers' expenditure (1954 = 100). Expenditure in total and on durables and non-durables are official estimates revalued at 1954 prices, except that those for years 1946–7 are obtained by linking official constant value series at 1948 prices.

T

continue indefinitely, it is difficult also to point to the special factors which have brought it into being in recent years. This makes any explanation of recent experience somewhat provisional and unsatisfactory[1]. But whatever doubts remain, it is clear that changes in incomes are of fundamental importance in explaining changes in spending, and that most of the variation in the latter is to be explained in these terms. It remains somewhat uncertain how rapid the effect is. A change in income might after two years cause a rise in spending almost as large; but the effect on spending within the same year might still be fairly low, i.e. in the first year spending might only increase by, say, one half the increase in personal income net of tax[2].

It is clear that some classes of the population do most of the saving, and that these classes save a fair proportion of *increases* in their income. In the early 'fifties, the largest savers were the self-employed (table 11.1), much of whose saving must go direct into their own businesses[3]. They were followed by the 'managerial and technical' group and by the skilled manual workers. Clerical and sales staff, and unskilled manual workers, appeared to save—or dis-save— little. The fifth of the adult population which is retired or unoccupied, on the other hand, were considerable dis-savers. Estimates of the marginal propensity to save of different classes suggest that the *marginal* propensity of the self-employed is much higher than the average and that they may save as much as a third or a half of any increase in their income. For the upper ranks of employees

---

[1] If an equation fitted to recent data explaining saving in terms of income etc. includes a time trend, the numerical values would inevitably be such that if projected for a decade or so, they would indicate a huge proportion of income saved: see for instance the equations in Klein and associates [1961], pp. 30 and 96.

The statistics of personal income, and hence of personal saving, include employers' contributions to private pension schemes, which have been growing rapidly. These are a rather special form of income or saving, since the individual consumer does not see them as income nor decide to save them. This may be one reason for the trend towards greater saving; but it does not by any means explain the whole of the trend.

[2] The equations in Klein and associates [1961] were fitted to data for 1948–56 and give some idea of what the data imply. The aim was to explain separately the changes in the four main divisions of consumers' expenditure, namely food, durables, other goods and services. Quarterly data were used. In each case most of the variation could be explained in terms of the current quarter's income and a term representing a weighted average of past income experience. Generally speaking a change in income would seem to have a considerable effect on spending even within the current quarter, and the values obtained for the other term suggest that a good part of the effect would be exhausted within four quarters. But there is room for alternative formulations giving rather different results. (Compare p. 96 with pp. 30 and 103.)

This kind of result is comparable with experimental calculations made at the National Institute of Economic and Social Research. The earlier study by Stone and Rowe [1956] concluded that the short-period (i.e. current year) propensity to consume was of the order of one half.

[3] The fact that it is impossible to reconcile the figures in table 11.1 with the national income aggregates suggests that the saving of the self-employed may have been understated. The trend of incomes since then has however favoured other income groups, and may have increased their share of saving, even though the self-employed save a high proportion of increases in their incomes.

Table 11.1. *The distribution of personal saving (£m.)*

	% of population	1951–3	1953–5
Self-employed	6	170	115
Managers and technical staff	8	25	100
Clerical and sales staff	12	−15	5
Skilled manual workers	37	10	90
Unskilled manual workers	15	—	10
Retired and unoccupied	22	−95	−80
Total	100	95	240

Based on surveys made by the Oxford University Institute of Statistics: see Klein [1955], *op. cit.* Each column shown is an average of estimates for two years. The figures are adjusted to a 'national income' basis, but the total is much smaller than that shown in the national income estimates. The saving of the self-employed may be much understated.

(i.e. managerial and technical groups) the marginal share of saving, though appreciable, is much less. For the retired and unoccupied there appears to be no relation: the rate to which they live on past saving appears unrelated to their current income[1].

These conclusions mean that fiscal policy is as important as has always been thought. But the effects on consumption may take longer to come through than has usually been allowed. They also justify the usual belief that if a tax cut is made which affects the mass of the population, most of it will be spent; while if it affects the wealthier classes, an appreciable part will be saved. But they suggest too that this saving will be concentrated in the hands of the self-employed, whose saving is often the counterpart to investment in their own business. Even in this case the effect of a tax change on total spending (i.e. consumption plus investment) may therefore be rather high[2].

2. THE EFFECT OF CONSUMER-CREDIT REGULATION

There is little doubt that changes in the availability of consumer credit have had a large effect on the demand for consumer durables: but the effect on total consumer spending is harder to establish. For most consumers, hire purchase

[1]See Klein [1958] who also cites comparable findings for the United States. These estimates, being based on cross-section data, have to be interpreted cautiously, for instance the propensities should probably be regarded as *long-period* propensities. There are however probably corresponding differences in the short-period saving or spending propensities.

As already noted, the development of wages and salaries and of other incomes has been far from parallel. An explanation of consumers' expenditure in terms of changes in different classes of income ought to be an improvement over an explanation in terms of changes in total income. The consumption equations in Klein etc. [1961] suggest that this is sometimes helpful; but experimental calculations at the National Institute show that the gain is far less clear-cut than might be expected.

[2]See §4 below for effect of taxes on investment.

remains the only readily available source of consumer credit; and the matter can best be discussed in terms of hire purchase in the first instance[1]. Since 1959 personal bank loans have however become important (see figure 11.2).

Almost half all sales of consumer durables are bought on hire purchase[2]. This is however still a small part of total demand: consumer durables now account for about 8 per cent of total consumers' expenditure, or $4\frac{1}{2}$ per cent of total final sales. About one household in four seems to make use of hire purchase: chiefly people with enough income (say £500–£1,000 a year) to meet the instalment payments, but with few liquid assets (£100 or less)[3]. Restriction of access to hire-purchase credit is thus likely to restrict expenditure on durables.

The nature of the effect is more difficult to determine: in particular whether credit restrictions have a permanent effect (so that demand for durables is lower for as long as the restrictions remain in force) or a temporary effect (so that the restrictions reduce the demand for a time only, after which the effect wears off).

Deductive reasoning from the nature of hire-purchase transactions might seem to point to a merely impact effect. If a durable good is purchased outright, the whole cost has to be saved in advance. If, on the other hand, it is possible to hire the piece of equipment in return for an annual rent, payments are spread over its whole life, and nothing has to be saved in advance of enjoying the benefit of owning the equipment. A hire-purchase arrangement is half way between, thus being aptly named. One might therefore expect that a restriction of hire-purchase facilities would simply postpone the demand of those dependent on hire purchase. Thus if hire-purchase facilities were completely abolished, and if the hire-purchase element in the purchase of a durable good (i.e. value less initial payment) represented two years' savings, one might expect purchase to be postponed for two years; and thereafter, demand to recover to its old level. This is an extreme case. Moreover, as already noted, only about half durables purchases are hire-purchase transactions; and some of those who use hire purchase might still be able to purchase without it. But the proportion of demand that might be expected on this simple model to be postponed for a while would still be very sizeable—e.g. perhaps a quarter of the total.

[1]The following general sources have been used: A. Kisselgoff [1952], *Factors Affecting the Demand for Consumer Instalment Sales Credit*; K. H. Straw [1956], 'Consumers' Net Worth: the 1953 Savings Survey', *B. Oxford Inst. Statist.*, Feb. 1956; J. A. Bates, 'Hire Purchase in Small Manufacturing Business', *Bankers' Mag.*, Sept. and Oct. 1957; J. R. Cuthbertson [1961], 'Hire Purchase Controls and Fluctuations in the Car Market', *Economica*, May 1961. The following were also consulted: F. R. Oliver [1961], *The Control of Hire-Purchase*; R. Harris, M. Naylor and A. Seldon [3rd ed. 1961], *Hire Purchase in a Free Society*; and the U.S. Report [1957] on *Consumer Instalment Credit* to the Board of Governors of the Federal Reserve System.

[2]*Nat. Inst. econ. R.*, Sept. 1960, table 4; and *Radcliffe, Memoranda*, XIII. 10, p. 238. Consumer durables comprise motor vehicles, furniture and floor coverings, radio and electrical goods and household appliances.

[3]Straw [1956], *op. cit.*

It is a corollary of this view that consumers' demand *in total* would be reduced by the same amount as the reduction in durables demand. The demand for other goods would be unaffected. The sums which previously had gone to hire-purchase down-payments and instalments would now be set aside as liquid balances till the end of the waiting period. Saving on the usual definition would therefore be increased (for the acquisition of durables would be reduced, and that of other goods would remain unchanged). One may think of saving as made up of two parts: first, changes in consumer debt; and, second, the remainder. This second part, defined as disposable income *plus* the increase in consumer debt *less* consumers' expenditure, may be called 'cash saving' equal to income *less* cash outlay. In this example, 'cash saving' would also be increased, though less than total saving (for total saving rises by the amount of the fall in durables, while consumer debt declines, but by less than the reduction in purchases).

This example implies that consumers are as ready to sacrifice other pleasures for the sake of durable goods tomorrow as they are for the sake of durable goods today—which is unrealistic. Not all those who would have bought durables on hire purchase will, when denied it, staunchly save for a later purchase the money they would have laid out on hire purchase; they will divert their demand to other goods. If all consumers diverted their demand in this way, the reaction to a tightening of credit terms would be the same as to an increase in the price of durable goods: on this second line of reasoning, one would expect the effect of stiffer credit terms to be *permanent*, i.e. to persist as long as terms remained as tight.

If, as supposed in this second model, the whole effect were one of diverting demand from durables to other goods, the effect on total consumer demand would be *less* than the effect on the demand for durables alone. Suppose that one third of the value of the durables that would have been bought on hire purchase would have been paid for in cash in the current year. This one third would (on this model) be diverted to other things. The reduction in total demand would thus be two thirds the effect on durables alone. Total savings would therefore still rise, but they would rise less than in the first model: 'cash savings', however, instead of rising, as in the previous case, would now be expected to remain unchanged.

A third possibility is that easy access to hire-purchase credit might cause people who would have bought durable goods anyhow to buy them on hire purchase instead of buying them outright, so setting free more of their income to buy non-durable goods. In this case—as opposed to the second case—restrictions on hire purchase would have a *greater* effect on total consumer demand than on the demand for durables alone; and total savings, when restrictions were imposed, would therefore rise even *more* than in the first model: 'cash saving' would therefore also rise.

In practice, all three of these possibilities are likely to occur in combination.

Hire-purchase restrictions are likely to cause some people to postpone demand for durables, some to divert their demand to other goods, and some (who had in effect borrowed to buy non-durables) to contract their demand for other goods. The effect on total saving and on 'cash saving', could this be observed, might help to identify the dominant reaction.

Consumer credit has been controlled chiefly by changing the statutory minimum terms for hire-purchase credit.   But this control was initiated only in 1952, and its active use as a means of regulating the economy dates only from 1954. In recent years personal bank loans have become increasingly important: personal loans have gone up and down in much the same way as hire-purchase debt, and such changes have been almost as large as those in hire-purchase debt (figure 11.3).   But this has been the case only since 1957.   The evidence therefore can hardly provide more than impressionistic and provisional conclusions[1].

Figure 11.2 shows quarterly figures for consumers' expenditure on durables for the period 1954–61, together with indices of prescribed hire-purchase terms[2] and of relative prices (influenced at times by tax changes).   Changes in prescribed terms have been very frequent.   Consequently there is little evidence as to whether changes in hire-purchase regulations have a 'permanent' or a 'temporary' effect on demand (in the sense discussed above).   On various occasions, too, changes in hire-purchase regulations have occurred at about the same time as tax changes working in the same direction, which must therefore be held to account for some of the fluctuations in expenditure.

Expenditure on motor vehicles has fluctuated much more than other types of durable expenditure: expenditure on radio and electrical goods has fluctuated less, and expenditure on furniture and furnishings very little.   Much of the fluctuation in expenditure on vehicles can probably be accounted for in terms of changes in the hire-purchase regulations.   Such expenditure fell at the end of

---

[1]Some United States evidence supports the view that people react to an increase in the size of permitted instalments in the same way as to price changes (as in example II above). Thus Kisselgoff's [1952] study suggests that a 10 per cent increase in the size of the instalment might reduce hire-purchase sales by 10–30 per cent.   Consumers in this study were found to be insensitive to the size of the hire-purchase charge.

There have been various studies of the demand for durables in the United Kingdom, which however have not introduced hire-purchase terms as an explanatory variable: see especially J. R. N. Stone and D. A. Rowe [1958], 'Dynamic Demand Functions: Some Econometric Results', *Econ. J.*, June 1958; and also Klein, Ball, Hazlewood and Vandome [1961], *op cit.*   In the course of the latter study (p. 59), an attempt was made to determine the effect of hire-purchase restrictions but without success.   A study, however, by L. Needleman [1960], 'The Demand for Domestic Appliances', *Nat. Inst. econ. R.*, Nov. 1960, found significant short-term 'credit' effects on the demand for selected durables in the United Kingdom.

[2]The index of hire-purchase terms represents a combination of the minimum deposit required and the maximum repayment period allowed.   In constructing such an index, it is difficult to know to which factor most weight should be given.   The index shown is based on the percentage of the total cost paid in the first year and thus gives fair weight to both factors.

1956, and recovered in 1957. The fall in 1956 followed the stiffening of credit terms in February 1956—and also the stiff increase in purchase tax in the preceding October, and the reintroduction of petrol rationing during the Suez crisis. The rise in demand in 1957 was probably due both to easier credit, and to the ending of petrol rationing. The next major change in trend was in 1959, when demand for cars rose steeply throughout the year. Both the decontrol of hire purchase in the preceding October, and the tax cut in April, must have been important influences. The reimposition of hire-purchase controls in April 1960 was followed by a very large fall in car sales. But the effect was delayed because it took some time to work off a backlog of orders built up in the previous boom, and much of the fall in sales was due to these arrears having been worked off. Hardly any of the major swings in the demand for cars can therefore be accounted for entirely in terms of changes in the hire-purchase controls. The same probably applies to the rather less evident swings in demand for radio and electrical goods[1].

The best way of gauging the effects of consumer credit is, perhaps, to compare the changes in consumers' debt with their expenditure on durables (figure 11.3). The most spectacular changes in debt were the surge in new extensions—both of hire purchase and of bank credit—in the last quarter of 1958; this was followed by fifteen to eighteen months when credit continued, with some interruptions, to be expanded, but at a much less spectacular pace; and eventually by a contraction of credit in the second half of 1960. In a rough sort of way, these movements seem to have been reflected in durables spending. In the eighteen-month period comprising 1959 and the first half of 1960, total spending on durables was distinctly higher than before or after (figure 11.3): in this period it seems, as it were, to have fluctuated around a faster rate of growth.

In the last quarter of 1958 extensions of hire purchase rose over £50 million; if extensions of bank credit are included also, the rise was over £100 million. In the second half of 1960, both fell almost as much. The impact on the quarterly rate of spending on durables appears to have been on a rather smaller scale. The rise in spending in late 1958 might be put at *less* than £100 million (at quarterly rates), as might the fall in late 1960. This suggests that a part of the impact of credit changes may fall on *non-durables* demand.

It is difficult to put an exact figure to the size of such a credit effect. Very high rates of expansion—or of contraction—of new credit could not be continued indefinitely. A very rapid expansion of credit may, on the present evidence, add something of the order of £100 million or more to consumer demand in a period of three to six months. But if concentrated in a few months, it is unlikely to be long continued. The effect on consumer demand *in the space of a year* of a transition from tight to very easy credit might perhaps be at most to add £200 million to demand.

[1]The study by Needleman [1960] found significant 'hire-purchase effects' on the demand for washing machines and vacuum cleaners, but not for television sets nor for refrigerators,

Fig. 11.2.   Hire-purchase terms and sales of durables (£ (1954) million and indices)

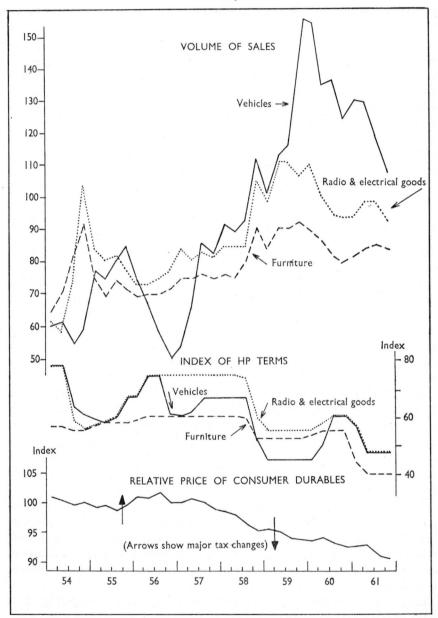

Expenditure on durables is seasonally corrected and from *Econ. Trends*, Oct. 1962 (adjusted from 1958 to 1954 prices).   Index of *hire-purchase terms* is statutory minimum down-payment *plus* first year's minimum instalment as percentage of purchase price. From July 1954 to Feb. 1955 and from Sept./Oct. 1958 to April 1960 controls were removed entirely: chart shows estimate of average actual terms.   *Relative price* of durables is average value of durables divided by average value of all consumer goods and services.

Fig. 11.3.   Consumer credit and sales of durables

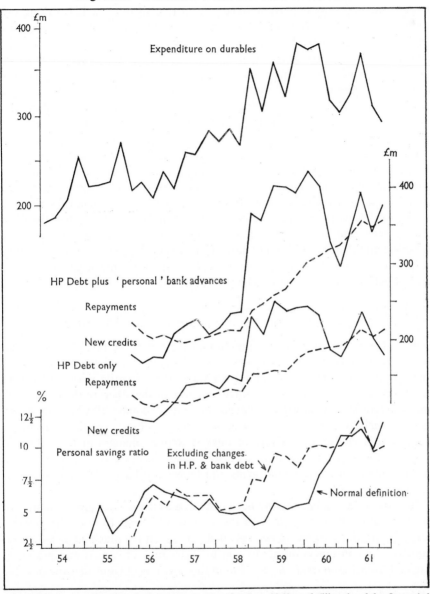

Expenditure on durables is from *Econ. Trends*, Oct. 1962 and (like the debt figures) is not seasonally corrected. Repayments of *hire-purchase debt* are estimated from official figures of debt outstanding and of new extensions, except for 1956–7 which are NIESR estimates. New extensions and repayments of *bank credit* refer to advances by London clearing banks for retail trade, personal and professional and hire-purchase finance companies; and are rough NIESR estimates based on the assumption that total debt being stable in 1957 and part of 1958, repayments approximately equalled advances, and that the average loan was for 2 years. *Personal savings* are shown, seasonally corrected, as a percentage of personal disposable income; the adjusted series is personal savings (as in official estimates) *plus* increases in hire-purchase and bank debt (as above).

The trend of savings may give some support to this conclusion.   The trend of 'cash savings' only departs markedly from that of total savings during the credit upsurge of 1958–60 (figure 11.3) and, as might be expected on the previous reasoning, it is somewhat the smoother of the two series.   There is little obvious tendency for 'cash savings' to be deflected, one way or the other, at times of rapid credit expansion.   This might indicate that the total effect on demand was of the same order as the total expansion of credit.   But the course of savings is clearly affected by several other factors also; and, without a good explanation of savings behaviour as a whole, it is difficult to judge the effect of any one factor singly.

These conclusions, tentative as they are, confirm the view that the regulation of hire purchase, though more limited in impact than fiscal policy, deserves to rank as an important instrument of economic control.   They also suggest that the effect of such regulation may not be confined to the demand for durable goods, so that its impact may be somewhat less narrow and selective than has usually been supposed.   But it remains true that most of the effect falls on durables; and that, as used in the past, the control has produced severe fluctuations in demand in this narrow sector.   The scope for a much gentler type of control will be considered later (chapter XVI.4 below).

3. INTEREST-RATE EFFECTS ON CONSUMPTION

Nineteenth-century economists believed that the higher the rate of interest, the higher would saving be and the lower consumption: the modern view is that since general considerations point both ways, there is little reason to expect saving and consumption to be sensitive, one way or the other, to the level of the rate of interest[1].   What direct evidence there is to support this belief is by no means conclusive; but there seems little chance of ever getting conclusive evidence.   A *change* in the rate of interest implies changes in the values of stocks and shares.   There are also reasons, again inconclusive, to believe that, in this country at least, capital gains and losses also have little effect on consumption.

The rate of saving has usually been discussed as if it were simply a matter of the disposal of the current flow of income—which seems to limit the possible range of variation that has to be explained.   In fact it is a much larger question: namely, why consumers decide to add to their stock of capital and gradually extend it, *rather than run it down*.   Put in this way it is obvious that the possible

[1]Marshall, for instance, concluded that 'a strong balance of evidence seems to rest with the opinion that a rise in the rate of interest . . . tends to increase the volume of saving'. But he did not believe it would be much affected; and he recognised that those 'who have determined to secure an income of a certain fixed amount for themselves or their family will save less with a high rate than with a low rate of interest'. (A. Marshall, *Principles of Economics* [8th ed. 1920], pp. 533–4.)   Later writers in effect give more emphasis to this latter consideration.

range of behaviour is very wide: people could dis-save on an enormous scale. But the evidence seems to suggest that over recent centuries consumers in advanced countries have wished, year in, year out, to add gradually to their capital stock.   This makes it seem likely that the desire to maintain and increase wealth has little to do with variations in the rate of interest, at least within the range met with in advanced countries; and that it has much more to do with 'real' factors—in particular, the desire to be secure, to provide for old age, to improve property and to develop small businesses[1].

If the rate of interest were very high (say twenty or thirty per cent) there seems admittedly little doubt that people would find it worth doing without many things this year for the sake of having more of the same things in a later year. This would cause a shift in the life cycle of saving and consumption, which would for a while increase saving: people would save more in early life and dis-save more in later years.   While the adjustment to this new cycle was taking place, there would be a (long-drawn-out, though temporary) increase in saving: for saving would increase now but dis-saving only later.   In so far as people saved more to leave more to their heirs, there would be an increase in saving even in the long term.   But it is only if interest rates change a great deal that such effects seem likely.

The fact that the capital market is imperfect means that different classes of savers are partially isolated from each other and from 'market forces'.   Most consumers have poor credit standing; and many would be glad not to save but to borrow and dis-save more than they do.   Their borrowing is limited not by interest rates but by what people will lend them; and they are willing e.g. to pay high rates on hire-purchase loans.   Most consumers too have no ready access to the capital market, so that small savers have not been deterred from investing in National Savings, even though the rate of interest has often been little if anything above the rate of increase of prices.   The saving of the self-employed— as already seen, a large element in positive saving—is likely to be influenced not by what they can earn by lending it to others, but by the profits to be earned by investing it in their own business: these are typically much higher than, and little affected by, the market rate of interest.   So-called 'contractual' saving also seems unlikely to respond to higher interest rates.   Mortgage repayments stand to be increased (though building societies tend to lengthen the repayment period rather than the annual amount).   But saving for old age, in so far as it is saving for a fixed sum or fixed income, might even be reduced by higher rates. The dis-saving of the retired who live on their past savings also seems unlikely to be affected.

Whatever the effect of low or high interest rates, the *transition* from low to high rates involves capital losses, and the transition from high to low involves capital gains, to those who own stocks and shares.   Many believe that such

---

[1]See further discussion in chapter XII.1 below.

losses or gains have an independent effect in temporarily reducing or increasing consumption. This cannot be a general effect. It is not for example an instance of what happens when people get wealthier; for, historically, increased wealth has not stopped people saving: if it had, they would not have accumulated wealth. Similarly, if *everyone* tried to realize capital gains, this would so reduce stock prices that the gains would not occur. Nevertheless it seems likely that some of the gains will accrue to people who have rather limited ambitions to hold wealth; and there is certainly evidence that some forms of windfall gains, such as football-pool prize money, lead to greater spending[1].

Capital gains and losses have been very considerable (table 11.2): even if only a small fraction of gains had been spent, this would have had a big effect on spending. Moreover, ownership of stocks and shares is fairly restricted, and individual holdings large[2], which means that capital gains would generally be worth realizing in relation to the trouble and cost of doing so. Nevertheless there are reasons for doubting whether capital gains and losses do affect spending much. To judge from a single survey of the savings of the rich (i.e. those with incomes of over £2,000 a year—who probably own the larger part of personal holdings of stocks and shares), even among the rich relatively little account seems to be taken of capital gains, and the tendency to spend them seems even smaller[3].

It may therefore be that, in this country at least, capital gains and losses have little effect on spending. No recent attempts to explain saving and consumption

---

[1]Klein's [1958] study of the British propensity to save seemed to show that some sorts of people (the retired, but not the self-employed) spent a fraction of any windfall gains (*op. cit.*, pp. 75 and 83).

Some other cross-section studies have seemed to show an inverse relation between saving and liquid-asset holdings. This could indicate a similar inverse relation between saving and total assets. But the apparent correlation might reflect the fact that the ownership of assets enables people to be *erratic* about saving, not that it reduces their desire to save on an average of years.

[2]There is some conflict of evidence. One direct survey of asset holding suggests that three quarters of personal holdings of stocks and shares are owned by persons who own £2,000 or less (H. F. Lydall [1955], *British Incomes and Savings*, table 46). But this is difficult to believe and is impossible to reconcile with the estate duty figures (see 104th Inland Revenue *Report*, Cmnd. 1598, pp. 128 *et seq.*).

[3]See L. R. Klein, K. H. Straw and P. Vandome [1956], 'Savings and Finances of the Upper Income Classes', *B. Oxford Inst. Statist.*, November 1956, pp. 310–1:

'Although we have a sample concentrated in the upper end of the income distribution and providing a fair representation of surtax payers we do not find much response to questions about capital gains or capital realization. Many respondents did not see the point of, or even understand the meaning of [such questions] . . . Somewhat under one-half the units expressed a preference for capital gains as opposed to . . . income from investments . . .

As far as capital realization is concerned, three-quarters of the sample had no such transactions. Very few of those who had realized capital did so for ordinary living expenses' i.e. many reinvested or repaid debt.

These findings may in part be due to the fact that the period in question (mid-1955 to mid-1956) was not a period when stock prices were rising much.

Table 11.2. *Capital gains or losses on personal holdings of securities, 1946–60*
(*£ million*[a])

	Due to changes in:		
	Interest rates[b]	Profits, actual and expected[c]	Total
1946	500	750	1,250
1947	−750	—	−750
1948	—	−250	−250
1949	−1,000	−250	−1,250
1950	—	250	500
1951	−1,500	1,000	−500
1952	−250	−250	−500
1953	750	500	1,250
1954	500	2,000	2,250
1955	−1,250	750	−500
1956	−750	−250	−1,250
1957	−750	—	−500
1958	500	2,250	2,750
1959	1,250	3,750	4,750
1960	−750	−250	−1,000

Based on estimated values of personal holdings of British government bonds and debentures of non-financial companies, and of ordinary and preference shares of non-financial companies in 1953 (from E. V. Morgan [1960], *The Structure of Property Ownership in Great Britain*, table 62) projected backwards and forwards by means of index of bond prices (weighted average of indices for consols and 3½ per cent War Loan) and Actuaries' Investment index of equity prices. The estimates are necessarily very rough because of errors in the 1953 estimates, and because the indices used are imperfectly representative; changes in the *volume* of stocks and shares held by persons are also ignored. (Earlier, and rather different, estimates were given in Dow [1958], *Radcliffe, Memoranda*, XIII.9, p. 93).

[a]All figures are rounded to £250 m., hence components may not sum to total.

[b]Shows what would have happened if the price of personal holdings of stocks *and shares* had moved in line with index of bond prices.

[c]Shows the effect on the value of holdings of equities of the *differential* change in equity prices over and above the change in bond prices.

have found it useful to include capital gains and losses among the explanatory factors[1]. But none of this evidence is conclusive, nor, in particular, sufficient to rule out the possibility that a minor part of capital gains are spent. Even if the proportion spent were no more than one or two per cent, this could still cause fluctuations in consumer demand of £50–£100 million from year to year.

[1]Tinbergen in an early study of the United States suggests that one quarter of capital gains are spent: see J. Tinbergen [1939], *Statistical Testing of Business Cycle Theories*, Vol. II, *Business Cycles in the United States of America, 1919–1932*. The effect as estimated seems very high, and was indicated by Tinbergen as uncertain. Later work has not confirmed it.

4. THE DETERMINANTS OF FIXED INVESTMENT

In spite of much discussion among economists, there remains at best a rather general degree of agreement as to the determinants of investment, which leaves room for doubt as to precisely how important various possible influences in fact are[1]. The results of empirical studies so far have not eradicated these uncertainties. It is argued below that government policy affected investment chiefly via changes in the depreciation allowances granted under the tax laws, and that other methods of influence—in particular interest changes and other effects of general credit policy—were barely significant. But while this can be strongly argued it can hardly be conclusively demonstrated.

The following rough picture would probably be fairly generally accepted as a starting point. First, the incentive to invest must depend primarily on the prospective evolution of final demand, and the degree to which productive capacity is at any time under- or over-employed in meeting demand. Second, the anticipated profitability of investment may, in some cases at least, be modified by the cost of borrowing (i.e. the rate of interest). Third, the pace at which firms exploit investment opportunities may be limited by their unwillingness or inability to rely beyond a point on external finance. Since direct empirical evidence is still scanty and inconclusive, some general theoretical considerations are worth summarizing briefly.

Economists in the past have given great emphasis to 'marginalist' considerations; and most of what needs to be said can be said by way of qualification of this emphasis. 'If there is an increased investment in any given type of capital . . . the marginal efficiency of that type of capital will diminish . . .' said Keynes[2]; and went on: 'now it is obvious that the actual rate of current investment will be pushed to the point where there is no longer any class of capital-asset of which the marginal efficiency exceeds the current rate of interest.' Such emphasis demands at least to be heavily qualified[3].

The prospective return on investment is inevitably uncertain. Firms therefore usually require a high prospective return on new investment projects, so that it may 'pay off' within a few years; and the implicit allowance for uncer-

---

[1]J. R. Meyer and E. Kuh [1957], *The Investment Decision*, give in chapter II of their book a convenient summary of current theories of investment. See also L. R. Klein [1947], *The Keynesian Revolution*, pp. 61–9.

[2]J. M. Keynes [1936], p. 136. Note that in this passage there seems some confusion between *capital* and *investment*, i.e. *additions to capital*. Thus, it may be that there are decreasing returns to capital as the stock of capital is increased. But investment in any year is very small in relation to the existing stock. It is therefore barely plausible that (within any practical range) the return to *capital* should be high or low as *investment* is small or large.

This point is important for the theory of monetary policy: see chapter XII.3 below.

[3]The interest sensitivity of investment was central to the *General Theory*. But it is fair to add that Keynes himself stated most of the necessary qualifications. 'If we speak frankly, we have to admit that our basis of knowledge for estimating the yield ten years hence of a railway, a copper mine, a textile factory, the goodwill of a patent medicine,

tainty and obsolescence much exceeds the rate of interest[1]. In these circum-stances, as Hubert Henderson said, 'it is hard to suppose that a difference in interest rates, which could only represent a small item in the calculation, could play a material part in the decision reached'[2]. As Professor Shackle has shown more formally, the length of life assumed for new equipment is likely to be the crucial factor in governing the sensitivity of investment to changes in interest rates[3]. Thus, if businessmen require their investment to 'pay off' in three years one might expect investment to increase by less than, say, two per cent in response to a 'unit' fall in interest rate (i.e. a fall in the percentage rate of interest from say five to four). Even with a required pay-off period of seven years, the effect on investment is still likely to be only a few per cent. Only with an effective horizon of forty years would the effect of a unit interest-rate change rise to, say, ten per cent.

For these reasons it is not at all surprising that businessmen, when questioned, have usually pleaded more or less complete immunity from the effects of changes in the rate of interest. Since the first, now famous, enquiry by the Oxford Economists' Research Group in 1938–9, there have been various direct enquiries into investment motivation, chiefly in America, of which the enquiries made by the Radcliffe Committee deserve to be included as the latest[4]; and on the face of it, at least, this evidence is by now impressive. But one should be sceptical of

an Atlantic liner, a building in the City of London amounts to little and sometimes to nothing . . .' (pp. 149–50). 'Most probably of our decisions to do something positive, the full consequences of which will be drawn out over many days to come, can only be taken as a result of animal spirits . . .' (p. 161). For such reasons Keynes (at one point) declared himself as 'somewhat sceptical of the success of a merely monetary policy directed towards influencing the rate of interest' (p. 164).

[1]Though there is no systematic evidence about the target rate of return expected by British industry from new investment, a rate of 15–30 per cent would seem a common requirement: see the evidence cited in my memorandum to the Radcliffe Committee (*Radcliffe, Memoranda*, XIII. 9, para. 88) and also the oral evidence to the Committee of some of the directors of large industrial companies (particularly QQ 10760, 11352, 11476 and 11622).

[2]H. D. Henderson [1938], 'The Significance of the Rate of Interest', reprinted in *Oxford Studies in the Price Mechanism*, edited by T. Wilson and P. W. S. Andrews [1951].

[3]G. L. S. Shackle [1946], 'Interest Rates and the Pace of Investment', *Econ. J.*, March 1946. The quantitative statements that follow in the text above are not quite of the same form as Shackle's conclusion, and follow from it only on certain assumptions not made by him, which are however fairly plausible.

[4]For the Oxford enquiries see J. E. Meade and P. W. S. Andrews [1938], 'Summary of Replies to Questions on Effects of Interest Rates'; P. W. S. Andrews [1940], 'A Further Inquiry into the Effects of Rates of Interest'; and R. S. Sayers [1940], 'Business Men and the Terms of Borrowing'; all reprinted in *Oxford Studies in the Price Mechanism*.

For convenient reviews of subsequent enquiries, see W. H. White [1956] in 'Interest Inelasticity of Investment Demand—The Case from Business Attitude Surveys Re-examined', *Amer. econ. R.*, Sept. 1956; and R. Eisner [1957], 'Interview and Other Survey Techniques and the Study of Investment' in *Problems of Capital Formation*. Of the indivi-dual investigations discussed, the two chief are by J. F. Ebersole, using the case studies of the Harvard Graduate School of Business Administration (see 'The Influence of Interest Rates upon Entrepreneurial Decision in Business—A Case Study', *Harvard Bus. R.*, Autumn 1938); and the Minnesota Business School Survey (see W. W. Heller, 'The Anatomy

this kind of evidence.   Of the complex considerations underlying investment decisions, businessmen are likely to cite only those which are in the forefront of their minds.   Interest-rate changes have, moreover, historically been small: and most investment projects undertaken could in any case be expected to remain profitable, and most projects rejected to remain unprofitable, at slightly different rates of interest[1].   The most such evidence can be taken to show is, perhaps, that risky investment is not vastly sensitive to interest rates.

The riskiness of investment has further consequences.   In particular, it means that the capital market is highly imperfect, so that funds do not flow smoothly and without impediment to the most profitable investment opportunities.   One would therefore expect a certain sort of 'financial' consideration to be important. Established firms are in a much more favourable position to exploit investment opportunities in their own field of business than are outsiders to this field. But most firms are unwilling to rely without limit on external finance[2] in order to exploit such opportunities—possibly because in many cases, as Professor Tew has persuasively argued, controlling groups are unwilling to weaken their hold over the control of firms' policy[3].   The chief internal sources of finance are retained profits and depreciation allowances.   One might therefore expect the flow of profits to set a limit to the pace of investment; and one might also expect changes in the statutory depreciation allowances to be an important influence.

A firm's assessment of risk is subjective, in the sense that it will be more unwilling to undertake further risky projects if its marginal financial resources have already been committed[4].   This is one reason for expecting firms to expand only gradually: there have been many examples in post-war years of excess demand resulting only in a slow, delayed expansion of capacity[5].   But how risky

of Investment Decisions', *Harvard Bus. R.*, March 1951).
For the Radcliffe Committee's summary of the evidence presented to it, see *Radcliffe Report*, paras. 451–2.
[1]For a fuller critique of such evidence see White [1956] and R. Eisner [1957], *op. cit.*
[2]Companies in aggregate appear to have financed the whole of their investment at home out of retained profits in most post-war years (*NI & E* [1960], table 28).   But there are many differences between companies.   Large, i.e. 'public quoted', companies in aggregate financed about seven eighths of their investment out of profits in the years 1949–53 (see the volume edited by B. Tew and R. F. Henderson [1959], *Studies in Company Finance*, table 3.1); but they differed widely (table 1.20).   Similarly several very large companies whose directors were interviewed by the Radcliffe Committee relied much more extensively on external finance (see particularly *Radcliffe, Minutes*, Q 10763 and 11643)
[3]B. Tew [1952], 'The Finance of Investment', *Oxford econ. Pap.*, July 1952, p. 113: '*Most* enterprises *are* severely limited in the amount of new equity they can issue without weakening the existing controlling interest, and most controlling groups are more or less reluctant to weaken their position . . . [Moreover] only a limited amount of fixed-interest finance can be accepted without causing a more highly geared capital structure.'
[4]As was argued by M. Kalecki [1937], 'The Principle of Increasing Risk', *Economica*, Nov. 1937.
[5]The speed of adjustment is likely to depend on how oligopolistic the industry is.   As Meyer and Kuh [1957] (*op. cit.*, p. 203) observe: 'In a less competitive atmosphere, firms can wait a longer period of time before expanding and permit the expansion to take place out of internal funds as these become available'.

expansion seems will clearly depend also on the kind of expectations firms have about the future; and the risks will seem less if they expect a rapid general expansion of the economy. Expectations of expansion, in short, are likely to help to bring expansion about[1].

The results of most of the now fairly considerable number of econometric studies of investment behaviour appear to bear out these presumptions. Most of the studies[2] appear to show that variations in investment can be explained in part by the variations in profits in a previous period. This holds both for studies of aggregate investment over time, and for comparisons—perhaps less convincing—of different firms' investment at the same time[3]. The model of the British economy constructed by Professor Klein and his associates[4]—a 'time series' study—attributes considerable importance to the previous year's profits as a determinant of investment in plant and equipment in the current year: in the equation, profits are shown net of tax, so that equal importance is implicitly attached to changes in the depreciation allowances. The role of profits in such an explanation remains however somewhat ambiguous. It could be a measure of the ease of financing investment (on the lines argued above); alternatively, it could be a measure of the expected profitability of investment. In the American 'cross-section' study by Meyer and Kuh, for instance, it was found that changes in investment could be explained almost equally well by changes in sales as by changes in profits, since the two varied together. But the fact that variations in depreciation allowances—not an indication of expected profitability—helped to explain investment suggested that the flow of finance was both important in this case and, by analogy, suggested that the role of profits was financial.

[1] The implications for government policies to encourage growth are considered further in chapter XVI below.

[2] A useful summary of the literature is given by J. R. Meyer and E. Kuh [1957], *The Investment Decision*. Perhaps the chief of these studies have been: J. Tinbergen [1939], *Statistical Testing of Business Cycle Theories*, Vol. I, *A Method and its Application to Investment Activity*; J. Tinbergen [1951], *Business Cycles in the United Kingdom, 1871–1914*; L. R. Klein [1950], *Economic Fluctuations in the United States, 1921–41*; and L. R. Klein and A. S. Goldberger [1955], *An Econometric Model of the United States, 1929–1952*. Three more recent studies (by Klein etc., Eisner and Grunfeld respectively) will be noted separately.

[3] There is reason to be sceptical of 'cross-section' studies in this field. The size of the firm inevitably affects both the size of the variable to be explained (investment) and many of the variables invoked as explanations (e.g. profits or sales). In an attempt to eliminate this it is usual to divide all variables by some index of the size of the firm (e.g. gross assets of the firm). But there inevitably remains some doubt whether what is being compared is not then simply the difference between 'good' and 'bad' firms. Thus 'good' firms might well both enjoy a high ratio of profits to capital, and also be expanding rapidly, e.g. have a high ratio of investment to capital. In this case, the correlations would reflect differences in the characteristics of different firms, not differences in external circumstance to which they were responding. The relation between profits and investment would not, then, indicate what would happen to investment if profits rose—which is the sort of question such enquiries set out to answer.

[4] Klein, Ball, Hazlewood and Vandome [1961], *op. cit.*, pp. 55, 95 and 226.

U

Hardly any study has been able to show that the rate of interest has caused investment in aggregate to be different from what would be expected as a result of the other forces at work.   Interest rates however appear to influence private house-building and investment in public utilities: and various studies suggest how much.   To judge from pre-war experience in various countries, a unit change in the rate of interest (e.g. from four to five per cent) seems likely to reduce private house-building by something between ten and fifty per cent[1]. A study of investment in electrical utilities in the United States of America (1919–41) suggests that the interest effect here might be as large as the higher of these two figures[2].   The same study suggests that the effect on railway investment (USA, 1919–41) was smaller (15–20 per cent change in investment from a unit change in the rate of interest).   Such estimates should probably not be taken too literally, but they seem to show that interest rates affect some sorts of investment considerably; they also suggest that the effect is not instantaneous, but takes at least a year.   The fact that public utilities are now almost entirely nationalized has probably greatly diminished the influence of interest rates[3].   In post-war years house-building must have been affected less by interest rates than by credit rationing by the building societies[4].

The reasoning and the evidence reviewed so far have all pointed in one direction: that liquidity flows are an important influence on investment, but that, in the general case, interest rates are not.   But in econometric studies of this sort, there are often several explanations that appear to explain the data; and which appears to explain them best often depends very much on the precise formulation of the hypotheses being tested.   It is therefore disturbing that two recent studies appear to cast doubt on these conclusions.   The first—by Eisner[5] —suggests that investment can best be explained not by past profits, but by the past change in sales.   Though profits, taken separately, appear to be related to investment, this may be appearance only; for in a multiple correlation of investment against both profits and change in sales, the relation between profits and investment disappears.   An explanation in terms of changes in sales is on the face of it plausible.   The study suggests that investment is affected by the changes in sales over the previous four years—which would help to explain the observed gradual adjustment of capacity to demand.

---

[1] J. Tinbergen [1939], *op. cit.*

[2] L. R. Klein [1951], 'Studies in Investment Behavior' in *Conference on Business Cycles.*

[3] 'Representatives of the nationalized industries showed much the same independence of interest rate changes: although they have to take interest changes into account, the pace of their capital developments seems to have been decided by availability of materials or labour or by administrative decision—by anything but the rate of interest.' (*Radcliffe Report*, para. 451.)

[4] See chapter IX.6.

[5] R. Eisner [1960], 'A Distributed Lag Investment Function', *Econometrica*, Jan. 1960. This is another 'cross-section' study—to which however some of the cautions suggested earlier do not apply.

A similar but different sort of reinterpretation is proposed in a second study— by Grunfeld[1]. He too observes that profits appear to explain investment. But he finds it can be even better explained by the valuation of the firm implied by stock market prices—which, quite plausibly, he interprets as an indication of what the market thinks a firm's profits are going to be. Again, when a multiple explanation of investment is attempted, the apparent influence of profits seems to disappear. The 'market valuation' of a firm moreover, depends partly on the rate of interest. It is an even more disturbing result of this study to suggest that the rate of interest (if treated as one among the other specified influences) was related to the investment of these eight firms[2].

The conclusions of all these studies should be treated with some reserve; for none of them give anything like a complete explanation of investment behaviour and, in a more complete explanation, things might look very different. Econometric studies of this type are probably the only way in which quantitative answers can be arrived at on this sort of question. But it is only in the last decade or so that such studies have become at all numerous; and it is still too soon to say what conclusions can, and what conclusions cannot, be established. The foregoing studies have seemed worth summarizing separately, so as to show the dangers of jumping to hasty conclusions on the basis of one study alone.

The two most important questions from the present point of view, are whether interest-rate changes are important; and whether changes in the depreciation allowances or other changes in taxes have mattered. The present argument has chiefly been concerned with the short-term impact of interest-rate changes; and the balance of argument and evidence seems to me still against the view that changes in interest rates have been an important cause of short-term changes in investment. It follows that interest-rate policy is probably not useful for dealing with the situation in the short-term. The government nevertheless probably still needs to have an interest-rate policy, since interest rates are probably still capable of having some impact in the longer run—a question considered at greater length in chapter XII.

Changes in the depreciation allowances and other changes in taxation have made a considerable difference to the financial position of firms[3]. The question of whether they have affected investment is part of the more general question of whether profits affect investment because profits are a source of finance. On

---

[1] Y. Grunfeld [1960], 'The Determinants of Corporate Investment' in *The Demand for Durable Goods*, edited by A. C. Harberger [1960]. This is a 'time series' study of eight large American companies for the period 1935–54.

[2] Grunfeld's own interpretation of this result is perhaps not the end of the matter. For (as he points out) he does not explain what determines 'market valuations'; and until he has done that he has not done a great deal. One would suppose that stock market prices were affected among other things by past profits, and Grunfeld's own results indeed imply that they are correlated. In taking his analysis one stage further Grunfeld might well have had to bring profits back in by the back door.

[3] See chapter VII.4 above.

this matter the evidence seems inconclusive. Thus *a priori* reasoning would lead one to expect that 'financial' limitations were important. The econometric evidence is consistent with this view, but is inconclusive. Such more direct evidence as there is also seems somewhat contradictory. Thus, in evidence to the Radcliffe Committee large companies claimed to be completely unmoved by the large changes in depreciation allowances in recent years[1]. As against this, a recent study—by Mackintosh[2]—of the finance of smaller firms in this country suggests that the investment of such firms was affected by tax changes. But it also suggests that tax changes had an effect on investment much less than one to one. This perhaps is the best provisional conclusion to hold to.

5. THE DETERMINANTS OF INVESTMENT IN STOCKS

Economists have generally tended to dismiss the possibility that changes in taxes, interest rates or credit terms could directly affect the volume of stocks held[3]. It is argued here that this general view nevertheless needs to be reconsidered; and that the volume of stocks being very large, even a very 'weak' effect would in practice be important.

The reasons for desiring to hold stocks of a certain size are rooted in the technical conditions of production, and are thus 'powerful' reasons. Among the reasons for holding stocks[4] are: (i) the necessity for storing crops through the season; (ii) the economy for each enterprise of procuring in bulk rather than in small quantities; (iii) the economy of a stable level of production in face of a fluctuating or erratic flow of demand; (iv) uncertainty about the future demand for goods (where as usual they are not produced to order) and the commercial disadvantage of being unable to supply on demand. The expectation of price

---

[1]The Committee devoted considerable time to questioning the directors of large industrial companies about this matter. They replied, with impressive unanimity, that their investment had to be planned for years ahead, and that they had therefore to treat changes in the allowances as a temporary upset which should be ignored. (See *Radcliffe, Minutes,* Q 10773–6, 11404, 11426, 11466, 11491–2 and 11693.)

[2]See A. S. Mackintosh [1963], *The Development of Firms*—which reports an empirical study of the behaviour of a group of 36 firms over a period of 7 to 10 years and extending up to 1955–6. Only in about half the firms did financial constraints seem operative. Mackintosh suggests that for each £100 by which taxes were reduced, investment (in fixed assets and stocks) would increase by about £20 (see p. 126).

Carter and Williams [1957], *Industry and Technical Progress*, on the evidence of a rather wider enquiry, emphasize (p. 150) the psychological effect of the investment allowance as 'evidence of official approval for investment'.

[3]Of the many economists who have discussed the effect of the rate of interest on stockholding, Hawtrey seems to be alone in believing it important: see for instance R. G. Hawtrey [1932], *The Art of Central Banking*, pp. 363–71, as against J. M. Keynes [1930], *A Treatise on Money*, Vol. II, pp. 130–47; H. D. Henderson [1938], *op. cit.*; F. A. Lutz [1945], 'The Interest Rate and Investment in a Dynamic Economy', *Amer. econ. R.*, December 1945; and R. F. Harrod [1936], *The Trade Cycle*, p. 122.

[4]Compare F. Modigliani [1957], 'Business Reasons for Holding Inventories and their Macro-Economic Implications', in the NBER [1957] volume, *Problems of Capital Formation*.

changes might provide a further reason for holding more (or less) stocks; this also is a 'powerful' reason.

In most of the above cases, the advantages of holding more stocks do not suddenly disappear when stocks have reached a certain size, but rather taper off. Yet the advantage of holding further stocks seems likely to decline rather steeply. For instance given the inevitable uncertainties, the advantage of carrying part of an annual crop into a second year will be much less than carrying it through a single season. Or again, the increase in stocks required to reduce by a given amount the risk of being caught without stock is beyond a point very large[1]. Furthermore, the cost of holding more stocks probably increases rather steeply. This is not simply because new storage facilities would have to be built, which would be expensive; or that stocks would deteriorate, which must also be important. The main factor must be that such stocks would be held for sale in a remote future; and the universal reaction to a highly uncertain world is to take decisions only when decisions have to be taken, and to preserve an uncommitted position towards the more distant future.

The reasons noted above for holding business stocks ought to tend to produce a constant relation between the *desired* level of stocks and the level of sales. In fact both the actual level of stocks, and the stock-sales ratio, vary a lot. Most actual stock changes are not planned, but are the unintended result of unforeseen changes. It takes time to adapt production to changes in demand; and since a falling off in demand can rarely be fully foreseen, it is likely to cause a depletion of stocks[2]. Such a depleted state moreover may well take a long time to

---

[1]See T. M. Whitin [1952] ('Inventory Control in Theory and Practice', *Quart. J. Econ.*, Nov. 1952, p. 502) who quotes the following figures for the Bell Telephone Company:

Risk of items going out of stock once in year	Required inventory
1·0	76
0·5	100
0·2	134
0·1	167
'nil'	276

[2]Theoretical models embodying a lagged response of output to changes in sales, and hence involving the distinction between *actual* and *desired* stocks, have engaged the attention of many economists. See in particular E. Lundberg [1937], *Studies in the Theory of Economic Expansion*; L. A. Metzler [1941], 'The Nature and Stability of Inventory Cycles', *R. Econ. Statist.*, Aug. 1941 and [1947], 'Factors Governing the Length of Inventory Cycles', *R. Econ. Statist.*, Feb. 1947; R. Nurske [1952], 'The Cyclical Pattern of Inventory Investment', *Quart. J. Econ.*, Aug. 1952 and J. R. Hicks [1950], *The Trade Cycle.*

The empirical study by M. Abramovitz [1950], *Inventories and Business Cycles, with special reference to Manufacturers' Inventories*, showed fairly conclusively that the simplest hypothesis, that stock-sales ratios are constant, was untrue. There have so far been few empirical attempts to explain the behaviour of stocks in terms of lagged responses. A major exception is the recent study by M. Lovell [1961], 'Manufacturers' Inventories, Sales Expectations, and the Acceleration Principle', *Econometrica*, July 1961, who gets impressively good explanations of quarterly movements of manufacturers' stocks in the United States in the period 1948–55. Lovell's calculations suggest that the gap between actual and desired stocks can be substantial (e.g. at times, one quarter of actual stocks) and that discrepancies between them may take as much as two years to correct.

correct; for an attempt to do so may be defeated by a further unforeseen increase in demand, so that production merely keeps pace with but does not overtake the expansion of sales.   Hence if sales are increasing unusually fast, stocks are likely to be below 'normal', and vice versa when sales are lagging.

Thus even 'powerful' reasons for holding stocks are in the short run ineffective in determining the actual level of stocks.   Any influence that interest rates may have on the volume of stockholding is therefore likely to be swamped by very large unintended changes arising from the lagged response of output to sales. But this does not necessarily mean that the influence is negligible.   No statistical correlation has been found between investment in stocks and the level of interest rates[1]; but in the circumstances this can hardly be regarded as relevant.   The evidence presented to the Radcliffe Committee was taken by the Committee itself to indicate that the holding of stocks was insensitive to the rate of interest[2]. This interpretation has been challenged; but it is probably true that any direct evidence that stockholding is interest-sensitive is very dubious[3].   But it should be said here again that doubts about the value of direct questionnaires apply with redoubled force to questionnaires on this topic.

It may therefore be worth falling back on more general considerations.   There are three pointers, which, taken together, suggest that the size of any possible interest-rate effect would anyhow be small: (i) as argued above, the benefits of stockholding probably decline steeply; (ii) the costs of stockholding (including 'subjective' costs) probably rise steeply; (iii) the interest charge is only a portion of the total carrying charge[4].   It seems clear therefore that the interest elasticity of stockholding must be at best small—so that if, for example, interest rates

---

[1]J. Tinbergen and J. J. Polak [1950], *The Dynamics of Business Cycles*, state that 'it has never been possible to obtain any statistical verification' of the effect on investment in stocks of changes in the short-term rate of interest (p. 182).

[2]'But we have found that stocks of commodities are extremely insensitive to interest rates [i.e. short-term rates], and in any case they are often financed with long-term capital . . .' (*Radcliffe Report*, para. 489).

[3]R. G. Hawtrey [1960], 'Stocks of Commodities, Fixed Capital and the Interest Rate', *Bankers' Mag.*, May 1960.   Hawtrey challenges the Committee's conclusion in the light of the detailed evidence submitted to it and printed in the *Minutes* and *Memoranda of Evidence*.   But the Committee had the opportunity of cross-questioning witnesses; and its summary of the evidence doubtless reflects not only what was said but the quality of the evidence.

[4]In the lengthy debate between Keynes and Hawtrey before the war, it seemed to be agreed between them that, for staple raw materials, interest charges constituted about half the total carrying cost.   'For some goods, such as non-ferrous metals, which occupy little space in proportion to value, the cost in addition to interest is almost negligible.   For very bulky goods the cost may considerably exceed interest.   This particularly applies to cereals . . .   As a rule fairly compact manufactured goods would be cheap to store' (Hawtrey [1932], p. 368).   This is consistent with Keynes's statement that for primary commodities, deterioration, warehouse and insurance charges and interest 'seldom cost altogether less than 6 per cent per annum, and 10 per cent per annum may be regarded as a normal figure' (Keynes [1930], Vol. II, p. 136).

changed from five to six per cent (i.e. by twenty per cent) business would desire to reduce stocks by only a small fraction of twenty per cent[1].

But it has always to be remembered that the total value of stocks is large. In 1961 it was of the order of £10,000 million, or almost half the value of a gross national product of £24,000 million. A change in stocks of even one per cent (£100 million) would therefore be sizeable in relation to the balance of the economy. It would be, say, one third the annual change in national expenditure (say £300 million) or one half the average annual change in stocks (about £200 million). General considerations suggest that interest-rate changes might well have effects of this order. The present negative evidence is certainly too crude to justify the contrary conclusion. It may be possible to devise ways of obtaining more refined evidence; but meanwhile it would seem best to assume that stocks can be affected to some degree by interest rates.

Similar considerations apply to the possibility that investment in stocks is affected by restrictions on bank credit—as has been frequently suggested in the political discussion of the last decade[2]. Bank advances are by no means the predominant source of finance for stocks. For large companies the value of stocks amounts to ten times their bank advances[3]; and about half make no use of bank overdrafts[4]. It is hardly surprising that in most years there appears little correlation between changes in stocks and changes in bank advances. The one exception appears to be that during the Korean boom when the increase in the value of stocks was enormous, all industries increased their bank advances; and reduced them when stocks subsequently fell[5]. But it may

---

[1]Two further considerations tell in the same direction. Most stocks are not held by merchants—who make their living purely by holding stocks, and who are thus forced to pay close attention to margins between costs and returns; but by those engaged in production or distribution—for whom stockholding is an entirely subsidiary function, and for whom small changes in interest charges may well be not worth taking account of. Secondly, only a small part of stocks are financed on short-term loans; and if no decision to borrow is required, the cost of finance may pass unnoticed, provided short-term interest rates do not vary outside the usual range.

[2]See for instance Mr Butler's 1952 and 1953 budget speeches (*H.C. Deb.* 11 March 1952, 1285 and 14 April 1953, 47).

[3]NIESR [1956], *Company Income and Finance, 1949–53,* tables 4 and 5; and (for later figures) *Econ. Trends,* November 1961.

[4]B. Tew and R. F. Henderson [ed. 1959], *Studies in Company Finance,* chapter 6. See also Carter and Williams [1957], *Industry and Technical Progress,* p. 143: ' . . . despite the supposed limitation of bank lending to short-term finance, we have found it to be extremely important in supporting the long-term capital investment programmes of firms. The connection is usually nominally indirect, the bank taking over the finance of stock and work in progress, and thus releasing resources which the firm uses to buy capital equipment. Nevertheless to a number of firms we have visited the condition of their adoption of a new method has been an ability to raise a bank loan.'

[5]See A. Luboff [1956], 'Some Aspects of Post-War Company Finance', *Account. Res.,* April 1956. There appeared a correlation between stocks and advances in only two of the seventeen industries examined. But in 1951–2 all industries increased both the value of stocks and (by a quarter or a third as much) bank advances; and subsequently all industries reduced both.

well have been that 'real' not 'monetary' forces were then the operative ones, i.e. that bank advances were adjusted (as bankers often say they are) to the 'needs of trade'. The evidence to the Radcliffe Committee suggested that the 1957 credit restrictions had little direct effect on the holding of stocks[1]—perhaps because the banks tried to the best of their ability not to embarrass their customers[2]. But the evidence is not conclusive[3].

Nevertheless despite all the doubts, it seems reasonable to conclude that credit restrictions if vigorously pushed may have some effect on stockholding. Though nominally temporary, bank credits can normally be expected to be renewed; and the withdrawal of a facility that has come to be relied on can hardly fail to be upsetting, particularly if it comes at a time of falling profits or general uncertainty and financial stringency[4]. And as already argued, even a 'weak' effect might be important in the aggregate.

6. SUMMARY OF CONCLUSIONS: THE SCALE OF POLICY INFLUENCES

The conclusions of this chapter are probably not novel, but in most respects seem to confirm the prevailing opinion about the efficacy of the various instruments of economic policy.

The analysis confirms fiscal policy in its primary role, both as a means to influence consumption, and (though with more reservations) as an influence on investment demand. It confirms the importance—and the limitations—of the regulation of hire-purchase terms; it also points to the control of personal bank advances as an increasingly important part of the same operation. Together with the restriction by the building societies of their lending (whose effect on house-building was discussed in chapter IX.6) these have probably been the main points at which policy has impinged on the economy. It was argued earlier (chapter IX.4) that the control of borrowing, in particular the control of new issues, could have had a major effect on business investment, but in fact it probably had little.

The conclusions may be summarized in more detail as follows :

(1) Consumers' expenditure is heavily influenced by changes in taxes; so that, since large tax changes have been made, fiscal policy through its impact

[1]'We have not been able to find that the squeeze had any marked effect on holdings of stocks of commodities.' (*Radcliffe Report*, para. 460.) See also H. F. Lydall [1957], 'The Impact of the Credit Squeeze on Small and Medium-Sized Manufacturing Firms', *Econ. J.*, Sept. 1957.

[2]'On the industrial side, the banks on the whole managed to avoid positive reductions of existing advances, though they had to be discouraging to applications for new advances' (*Radcliffe Report*, para. 460).

[3]See the discussion of trends in investment in stocks in chapter XV.3 below.

[4]Nurkse, in his review article on Abramovitz [1950], *Inventories and Business Cycles*, suggests this as part of the explanation for the fact that in the United States periods of supernormal stocks (when trade declines) are typically shorter than periods of subnormal stocks (when sales increase): see R. Nurkse [1952], *op. cit.*

on consumers' expenditure has been the most important single means of controlling demand. The impact of tax changes probably takes longer to be felt than has usually been allowed: the full impact may (according to differing estimates) be delayed till six to eighteen months after the tax change.

(2) Consumers' expenditure has also been greatly influenced, more particularly since 1954, by the hire-purchase regulations. Since 1958 changes in restrictions on personal bank loans have also been important, though probably less so. Though much of the impact falls on durable goods, part may also fall on other types of consumer demand. Thus the impact of credit controls is probably rather less narrow than usually assumed. The total impact on spending seems of the same order as (though probably less than) the change in consumer indebtedness. It has probably therefore, at times, been of the order of £100 million in a year.

(3) Consumers' saving and spending are probably not affected by the level of interest rates. The transition from high to low interest rates implies capital gains; and the reverse transition, capital losses. Such gains and losses have been large. It is unlikely that any large part of capital gains are spent. But, though there is no direct evidence, a small proportion may be. Even if only a small minority spent their gains, it could add £50 million to spending in some years.

(4) Recent research into investment behaviour (chiefly in the United States of America not in this country) has been considerable. Nevertheless it remains uncertain whether any of the conventional policy influences on investment have much effect on investment demand. Many studies suggest that the internal sources of finance available to firms are a major influence on their investment. Changes in the taxation of profits, and in particular changes in the 'initial' and 'investment' allowances affect firms' financial position more directly than anything else the government can do. If investment is susceptible to policy influences at all, one would therefore expect it to be affected by such tax changes. Inconclusive evidence suggests that if they do affect investment, the induced change in investment may be much smaller than the change in tax-free profits.

(5) The bulk of the evidence—again, however, not quite conclusive—suggests that most investment is not sensitive to changes in the rate of interest. Various institutional developments, moreover, now mask the effect on those types of investment which potentially are sensitive to interest rates. Thus most 'utility' investment is now done by public corporations. Private house-building has been affected less by changes in mortgage rates (which have been relatively stable) than by the informal rationing of advances by the building societies. (The discussion in chapter IX.6 suggested that the latter had significantly influenced the rate of house-building.)

(6) The present argument disputes the usual view that policy has little direct impact on the holding of stocks. This is a matter on which it is extremely hard to get evidence one way or another. For fluctuations in stocks are largely

caused by delays in adjusting output to changes in sales, so that any changes in conditions take a long time to work themselves out. A change in interest rates, or in bank lending, is likely to make at best only a minor change in the desire to hold stocks. But even a one per cent change would alter the level of demand by £100 million.

It will be clear that present knowledge permits only broad and tentative conclusions, and even so leaves gaps in which it is possible only to guess or suspend judgement. There is need for a great deal more research in this field.

CHAPTER XII

MONEY, INTEREST RATES AND 'LIQUIDITY'*

It is now necessary to deal with a group of questions so far only touched on—questions concerning the role of money in the economic system; how this is related to interest rates, and how interest rates, in turn, affect the demand for real assets; and what the *Radcliffe Report* called the 'liquidity' of the economic system. These questions have so far been left on one side because argument about them has to be on a higher plane of abstraction and generality than in other parts of this study. If the chapter appears long, it can only be pleaded that the questions are difficult, and that an attempt to take a balanced view of the main issues can hardly be done more shortly. The conclusion will be that for purposes of practical policy, the issues are of secondary importance only: nevertheless they are of some importance, and how they are important needs to be defined.

It is the more difficult—and the more rash—to take a view on this group of questions, in that they have been of major concern to economists for at least sixty years, and have been debated with particular intensity for the last thirty. The earlier discussion may be considered to spring from Wicksell's theory of the 'money' rate and the 'natural' rate of interest[1] and in this country to include pre-eminently Keynes's three main works[2]. It was motivated by a strong policy interest: economists' main object was to find how to deal with the trade cycle. By the 1930's, the rate of interest had been elevated, at least in the English discussion and largely under Keynes's influence, to be the main instrument for controlling the economy[3].

---

*The discussion in this chapter is more technical than in most others. The argument is outlined in the introductory paragraphs and conclusions are stated in §5.

[1] Knut Wicksell [1898], *Interest and Prices*, English ed. by R. F. Kahn [1936]. Wicksell himself explicitly built on the English controversies of the 1830's and 1840's between the 'Currency School', who (to put it shortly) wished to regulate the volume of money; and the 'Banking School' who (to quote Wicksell's summary, p. 82) 'maintained that on the assumption that the banks issue notes *purely by way of lending* on adequate security—and not through advancing large sums to the government and the like—the banks are entirely dependent on the requirements of the business world for means of payment and have no means of affecting these requirements or of influencing prices'.

[2] J. M. Keynes [1923], *A Tract on Monetary Reform*; [1930], *A Treatise on Money*; and 1936], *The General Theory of Employment, Interest and Money*.

[3] Professor Sayers in his review of opinion regarding the rate of interest remarks that the 'belief that changes in the rate of interest powerfully influence economic activity reached its high-water mark in Keynes's *Treatise* . . . Looking back now, I am astonished at the confidence and simplicity of Keynes's argument . . . ' (R. S. Sayers [1951], 'The Rate of Interest as a Weapon of Economic Policy) in *Oxford Studies in the Price Mechanism*, edited by Wilson and Andrews [1951], pp. 1–2). See also the discussion on the functions of Bank rate—'a most delicate and beautiful instrument'—in the Macmillan Report [1931], Cmd. 3897, paras. 214–21.

Though the interest sensitivity of investment remained central to the *General Theory*,

The main line of discussion since then has centred on questions of high theory. Keynes's theoretical treatment of these questions was one-sided and misleading: discussion since has been concerned to formulate a more satisfactory general statement of the role of money in the equilibrium of the system[1]. This is inevitably difficult: the more peculiar monetary phenomena, themselves sufficiently complex, have to be related to an abridged but adequate model of the economic system as a whole. The discussion is voluminous, and being highly abstract, policy considerations have fallen from view. We have now almost reached the stage where those who know the argument do not care about policy, while those who care do not know[2].

It seems necessary to start (§1) with fundamentals and describe, in terms of the post-Keynesian discussion, what it is that the authorities do when they alter the volume of money and alter interest rates. Second, it is necessary (§2) to consider further the question of how far the community's need for money is elastic—an important question in its own right, which also throws light on the nature of 'liquidity', to be considered later.

The discussion so far is meant to lead up to a reconsideration of a question already discussed (in chapter IX.4)—the impact of interest rates on investment. It is argued (§3) that if bonds and real assets are substitutes, then not only does the rate of interest affect investment, but the return on real capital helps to determine the rate of interest on paper assets. If they were close substitutes, it would be hard for the authorities to alter the rate of interest, but even small changes would produce big adjustments to the stock of capital. In fact this does not occur: the imperfections of the market impose many brakes on the attainment of the theoretical 'equilibrium'. Since in the short run at least, paper and real assets are poor substitutes, it is easy, but of little use, for the authorities to alter interest rates.

The last stage of the argument (§4) is to suggest that monetary policy has

Keynes there also heavily qualified his belief in its importance (see quotations noted in chapter IX.4, p. 286 n., above).

[1]Professor Harry Johnson, for instance, notes: 'the fundamental contention of Keynesian monetary theory is that a monetary economy is essentially different from a barter economy . . . To examine the validity of this contention it is necessary to investigate the role of money in an economy with wage and price flexibility, allowing for the wealth effect of price-level changes. Such investigation is the object of the two major works in monetary theory published since the *General Theory*—Patinkin's *Money, Interest and Prices* and Gurley and Shaw's *Money in a Theory of Finance*' (H. G. Johnson [1961], 'The *General Theory* after Twenty-five Years', *Amer. econ. R.*, May 1961).

[2]In his review of the discussion since 1945 of the rate of interest, Professor Shackle refers to 50 books and articles; and in a similar but wider review (published as this book was nearly finished), Professor Johnson refers to 129. Neither is an exhaustive list. (See G. L. S. Shackle [1961], 'Recent Theories concerning the Nature and Role of Interest', *Econ. J.*, June 1961; and H. G. Johnson [1962], 'Monetary Theory and Policy', *Amer. econ. R.*, June 1962.) Shackle concludes: 'It seems likely that the interest rate . . . will continue to receive . . . the homage due to a ceremonial monarch, without in fact counting for more than such a monarch in the real affairs of western nations.'

effects arising out of the imperfections of the capital market: these, though important in practice, an 'equilibrium' method of argument is bound to neglect. Bankers, following a different approach from economists, often emphasize the importance of 'confidence', as the *Radcliffe Report* has emphasized that of 'liquidity'; and these ideas can be given a clearer meaning in the light of the previous discussion of the 'need' for money. A credit 'squeeze' can be shown to be capable of important effects: whether they are useful is another matter. The general conclusions for policy are summarized in §5.

Various elements of the present argument have been set out by previous writers. A series of articles have sought to broaden the Keynesian theory of 'liquidity preference' into a general theory of asset holding; see in particular those by Mrs Robinson and Messrs Kragh, Day and Turvey[1]. The question of whether transactions balances are sensitive to interest rates has been treated by Professors Tobin and Baumol and by Mr Turvey[2]: §2 goes, I believe, a bit beyond their arguments. The essential points in §3 about the relation between the demand for real and paper assets are, I believe, to be found, albeit briefly, in articles by Professors Musgrave and Tobin, and in Professor Milton Friedman's 'restatement'[3]. What is said in §4 about 'availability effects', though provoked by the *Radcliffe Report*, follows exactly neither the *Report* itself nor the various comments on it that have since appeared[4].

1. CHANGES IN THE VOLUME OF MONEY

The belief that an increase in the quantity of money causes an increase in prices has a great hold over the popular mind, and dies uncommonly hard even among economists. It seems as well to start by setting out again why this idea will not do. For to do so, it is necessary to make clear how the monetary authorities

[1]Joan Robinson [1951], 'The Rate of Interest', reprinted in her book [1952], *The Rate of Interest*; B. Kragh [1955], 'The Meaning and Use of Liquidity Curves in Keynesian Interest Theory', *Internat. econ. Pap.*, No. 5; A. C. L. Day [1957], *Outline of Monetary Economics*, especially chapter 17, 'A Conspectus of Interest-Rate Theory'; and R. Turvey [1960], *Interest Rates and Asset Prices*.

[2]W. J. Baumol [1952], 'The Transactions Demand for Cash', *Quart. J. Econ.*, Nov. 1952; J. Tobin [1956], 'The Interest-Elasticity of Transactions Demand for Cash', *R. Econ. Statist.*, Aug. 1956; and R. Turvey [1960], *op. cit.*, chapter III.

[3]R. A. Musgrave [1951], 'Money, Liquidity and the Valuation of Assets' in *Money, Trade, and Economic Growth* (essays in honour of John Henry Williams); and J. Tobin [1961], 'Money, Capital, and Other Stores of Value', *Amer. econ. R.*, May 1961; and M. Friedman [1956], 'The Quantity Theory of Money—A Restatement', in *Studies in the Quantity Theory of Money*, edited by M. Friedman [1956]. (For Friedman's position see further §1 below.)

The argument in §3 is, I think, in line with what Professor Johnson calls the 'new approach' that 'has been emerging . . . as an outgrowth of the formulation of monetary theory as part of a general theory of asset holding' (see Johnson [1962], §14 C). But §3 attempts also to show the limits to the practical usefulness of this line of argument.

[4]*Report* of the Committee on the Working of the Monetary System [Cmnd. 827: 1959]. For references to the discussion on the *Report* see §4.

can change the volume of money, and what they have to do to induce the public to hold more or be content to hold less.   The following paragraphs attempt this essentially expository task as a preliminary for the argument to follow in later sections.

The reason why people have been disposed to give such emphasis to the volume of money may be that, throughout history, governments in financial difficulties have resorted to the creation of money to cover a budget deficit.   No one should deny that this may add powerfully to the pressure of demand.   But such action compounds two effects, which must be distinguished.   First, there is the effect of the government spending in excess of its current receipts—an effect usually considered under the heading of fiscal policy[1].   Such deficit spending adds to effective demand irrespective of whether the deficit is *financed by the creation of money or by loans.*

To analyse the second, 'monetary' effect[2], it is necessary to isolate it from the effect of deficit spending.   Let us then ignore the effects of the deficit as such, and consider only what difference it makes to finance it alternatively by borrowing, or by creating money.   This is the same as supposing the deficit to be zero, and considering the effect of the government switching its debt between money and bonds, e.g. considering the effect of an increase in the stock of money, and an equivalent reduction in the stock of government debt held by the public.   To understand this, one needs an idea of what determines the public's demand for different types of assets.

Assets are of various sorts: money, bills, bonds, equities, and real assets of miscellaneous variety, and may be arranged in a 'spectrum' according to their liquidity[3].   Roughly speaking, assets with the greatest liquidity earn the smallest interest, and vice versa, the return on the most liquid asset, money, being frequently zero.   In this sense, the rate of interest may be considered to be— as Keynes said it was—'the reward for parting with liquidity'[4].

People do not want unlimited liquidity.   The more they have, the less they want more; and beyond a point, they would rather hold wealth in a form that yields a monetary return.   Hence, the higher are rates of interest, the smaller the proportion of their wealth that people are prepared to hold as money; or—to put the same thing the other way round—to be willing to hold a small amount as money, people require a high return on other ways of holding wealth.   The converse holds for assets other than money: the higher the return to be earned on any assets (or the lower the price of fixed-interest assets) the larger the proportion of their wealth will people be prepared to hold in this form.

It follows that at any time, stocks of existing assets being what they are,

---

[1]See chapter VII above.

[2]Or in Musgrave's terminology, the 'asset' effect, as distinct from the 'income' effect.

[3]The quality of liquidity includes saleability (i.e. the ability to sell it quickly without loss) and also certainty as to its capital value: see J. Robinson [1952], p. 6.

[4]Keynes [1936], p. 167.   The desire for liquidity will be considered further in §2.

there is an equilibrium set of prices and yields, at which people would be prepared to hold the existing stocks of assets, and wish neither for more nor less of any asset.   Since prices in financial markets are flexible, equilibrium here is likely to be reached quickly and to obtain continuously.   If people have more than they want (at existing prices) of any financial asset, their efforts to sell will bring prices down to the point where the supply is willingly held.

From this, in turn, it follows that the monetary authorities can only induce the public to hold more or less money by altering the terms on which they offer substitutes for money.   At these new terms, the public will be *willing* to hold a different quantity of money: there is no question of the public being forced to hold 'excess' liquid assets against their will, nor of their being starved of them.   The higher the public's holding of money, the lower must interest rates be, and vice versa.   Thus, the authorities can determine the volume of money, or the level of interest rates; but not both[1].

'Open market' operations in bonds are an example of such action by the authorities.   The public holds some money and some government bonds.   If, then, the authorities wish to increase the volume of money held by the public, they must induce it to exchange some bonds for money.   Action by the authorities will itself affect expectations and hence the preferences of the public for money as against bonds.   But this complication can be left on one side for a moment, on the grounds (argued more fully below) that changes in expectations cause only short-term deviations from what the public's underlying preferences dictate.   If this is so, it follows that the only way in which the authorities can in the end get the public to exchange bonds for money is by buying bonds from it at a little above the initial price.   Conversely to get the public to exchange some of its money for bonds, so reducing the volume of money, bonds must be sold to it at a little below the initial price[2].

Money nowadays consists less of notes and coin than of bank deposits; and the authorities, to affect the public's holding of money, have to operate on

---

[1]Compare the *Radcliffe Report*, paras. 373 and 375:
   ' . . . National Debt is spread over four significant classes: cash . . . ; Treasury Bills . . . ; short bonds . . . ; and long bonds . . . ;' ' . . . in redistributing the National Debt between the four maturity classes . . . the Bank is not a dictator but a market operator.   All the non-cash classes of debt carry interest, and it is by offering interest at varying rates (or frequently by dealing at varying prices for fixed interest securities) that the Bank induces holders to shift from one maturity to another . . . except so far as its views influence market expectations (an important exception), it cannot choose both a rate of interest and the quantity of debt to be held at that rate.'
[2]The argument abstracts from the practical question of how the market should be handled. It can be argued that if the authorities lower their selling price, they will create an expectation of a further fall in bond prices, in anticipation of which the public will hold off the market. In evidence to the Radcliffe Committee the Bank of England made much of the alleged impossibility of selling bonds on a falling market (see *Radcliffe Report*, paras. 551–3). But the reaction of the market would seem to turn on how the market is handled.   It is clearly not impossible to sell bonds when the market believes the price *has already fallen* as far as it is likely to go.

bank deposits.   A reduction in the volume of money may be brought about by a 'funding' operation in which the government sells bonds (as before), and uses the proceeds to reduce short-term debt predominantly held by the banking system.   The public's deposits with the banks will fall by the same amount, for they have given the government money for its bonds.

The process may also have further stages.   The fall in liquid assets may reduce the banks' liquid-asset ratio below the conventional thirty per cent minimum[1], so forcing the banks to reduce non-liquid assets (including, quite possibly, their holding of government bonds) thus further reducing deposits.   Alternatively the government may call for special deposits[1], resort to moral pressure, or instruct the banks to reduce deposits.   The manner of operating is, from the present point of view, of secondary importance: what matters is the effect on the holdings of the non-bank public of notes and coin and bank deposits on the one hand, and on the other hand their holding of government debt.

For purposes of analysing the authorities' actions designed to affect the volume of money and the level of interest rates, it is thus simpler to regard the banks as, by one means or other, controllable, and within the financial sector of the public authorities.   The banks have a dual role in the financial system.   On the one hand they are money-creating agents: from this point of view it is their total deposits that matter.   On the other hand they are a form of financial intermediary constantly lending, getting repaid, and relending short-term finance: it is from this point of view that their advances matter[2].

The long-term rate of interest is also influenced by expectations as to its future value: indeed, if expectations were clear and uniform, it could be said that the long-term rate of interest *would be what it was expected to be.*   Thus a change in the rate implies a change in the market valuation of existing securities: if the rate on a gilt-edged security rises from 3 to 4 per cent, its price falls 25 per cent. If anyone expects interest rates to fall, he expects to make a capital gain by buying now and selling later: and were this general, the rush to buy would force up the price immediately.   From this it would seem that any attempt to alter the rate of interest (i.e. by varying the volume of money) would have small effect unless market expectations were changed at the same time[3].   At first

[1]See chapter IX.3 above.

[2]This duality of function was noted by Lavington, who remarks: 'all the complex and highly specialized processes which form the organization of the market are tributary to two functions . . . the first is that of supplying a stock of money; the second is that of facilitating the transport of capital' (Lavington [1921], *The English Capital Market*, pp. 6–7).

The *Radcliffe Report* appears in places to lay little emphasis on control of the volume of money.   For instance, after saying that the authorities have to have 'a special care' for the effect of their actions on the banks, the *Report* added that measures should be 'aimed at the banks as key lenders in the system, and not at the banks as "creators of money" ', and that it is 'the level of bank advances rather than the level of bank deposits that is the object of this special interest' (para. 395).   There are however passages in the *Report* which treat 'control of the money supply' as 'an important facet of debt management' (para. 514).   See also paras. 373 and 375 (already quoted, p. 303 n.).

[3]It would have *some* effect, since expectations are not likely to be uniform.

sight this seems to reduce the rate of interest, as Keynes said, not only to a 'highly psychological', but to a 'highly conventional', phenomenon[1]. If the rate of interest has to be what it is expected to be, it might (one would think) be anything.

But this is not the whole story. The market is not ruled entirely by arbitrary expectations; the preference of investors for different types of assets still counts and the price of any particular class of asset seems, in fact, to be affected by the volume of them on the market. The market cannot properly be compared to a blind sage who holds to his own view regardless; and if the government sold bonds, operators would not necessarily buy in equal quantity and hold them indefinitely on some view of their 'proper' price. The price would probably fall, implying that expectations were in some sense changed. The demand for money seems to be governed fundamentally by liquidity preference considerations, though, in the very short run, the vagaries of expectations certainly cause temporary fluctuations away from what such considerations would dictate.

Empirical evidence shows that most of the year-to-year variation in long-term interest rates can be explained in these terms. Liquidity preference theory suggests—to put it rather shortly—that the rate of interest (measuring, on this argument, the marginal convenience) should vary in inverse relation to the volume of money. But one would also expect that the demand for money balances would depend on the volume of transactions to be effected; so that, if the national product rose and the volume of money were not increased, one would expect interest rates to rise. As a first approximation, one might expect the rate of interest to vary in inverse relation to the volume of money expressed as a percentage of the value of national product.

Figure 12.1 is a first look at the data for the United Kingdom for the years 1921–60[2], and, in a very rough way, bears out this expectation. It suggests that the demand for money varies according to the rate of return that is sacrificed by holding wealth in the form of money. But the elasticity is not extreme: the figures suggest that the volume of money has to be varied a good deal to alter interest rates by, say, one percentage point[3]. But the points do not lie neatly

---

[1]Keynes [1936], p. 203.

[2]The statistical series used are necessarily rather crude. The rate of interest is represented only by the yield on 2½ per cent consols. The volume of money is represented by cash and notes with the public *plus* the net deposits of the London clearing banks, figures for other bank deposits not being obtainable: it could be argued that holdings of other liquid assets ought also to be taken account of. To explain rates of interest in terms of the *ratio* of 'money' to the value of national product may also be crude: changes in the volume and the price of output might, for instance, affect the demand for money differently.

[3]For what they are worth, the figures suggest that the elasticity of the demand for money with respect to interest rates is about unity. Thus an increase in the volume of money, at present values, of £1,000–2,000 million (or 15–30 per cent) seems to be associated with a reduction in bond yields of one percentage point (or about 20 per cent).

V

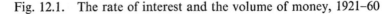

Fig. 12.1.   The rate of interest and the volume of money, 1921–60

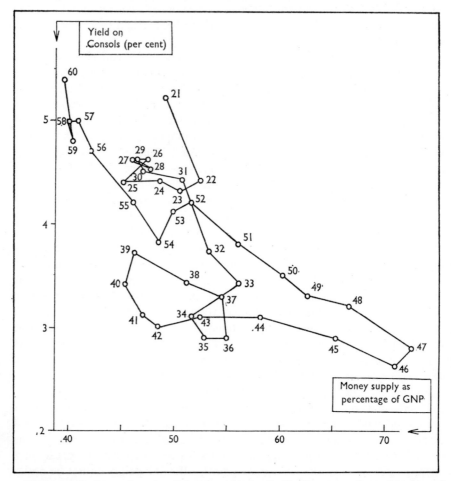

Money supply is net deposits of London clearing banks (averages of monthly figures) *plus* estimated notes and coin with public.   Inter-war estimates of GNP are from *London Cambridge econ. B.*

on one line, which suggests that there are other influences not taken into account which also affect the demand for money[1].

More systematic attempts at explanation date back to Professor Brown's [1939] correlation study, which attempted an explanation of bond yields

---

[1]Some types of liquid asset (including deposit accounts, which are here classified as 'money') yield interest.   Liquidity preference theory, strictly speaking, explains not the long-term rate of interest, but its excess over the rate on highly liquid assets.   The level of Bank rate may therefore explain some of the 'divergencies' on figure 12.1.

primarily in terms of the money supply or the volume of 'idle balances'[1]. An approach in many ways similar was followed in Dr Khusro's post-war study of British data[2], and in Mr Turvey's recent study of American bond yields[3]. Both take account not only of changes in the quantity of money but also of changes in the quantity of bonds—or, in Turvey's case, National Debt; the former is notable too for investigating the influence on bond yields of changes in the dividends earned on equities. Both appear to 'explain' changes in interest rates very successfully in these terms[4], and thus appear to confirm that the rate of interest is closely dependent on the volume of money. They also seem to confirm that the volume of money has to be changed a good deal—perhaps by something like ten per cent—to alter the bond yield by one percentage point[5]. This kind of relationship appears moreover to hold over a wide range of experience. During extreme inflations, the cost of holding money is represented not so much by the money rate of interest as by the rise of prices which constantly diminishes the value of money. This naturally makes people hold smaller money balances. It seems a fairly typical rule that the cost has to double to make people halve the size of their money balances[6].

---

[1]A. J. Brown [1939], 'Interest, Prices, and the Demand Schedule for Idle Money' reprinted in *Oxford Studies in the Price Mechanism*, edited by T. Wilson and P. W. S. Andrews [1951]. This study was based on data for the United Kingdom for the period 1921–36. The procedure of estimating 'idle money' could be criticized as an arbitrary and unnecessary step in the analysis, but probably did not affect the general nature of the results. The other main explanatory variables considered were past changes in interest rates and recent changes in wholesale prices, neither of which however appeared to be important.

[2]A. M. Khusro [1952], 'An Investigation of Liquidity Preference', *Yorkshire B.*, Jan. 1952. The study was based on data for the United Kingdom for the period 1919–48. It shows also that the increase in marginal tax rates, which since 1919 has almost halved the *net* return on bonds, is another important influence.

[3]R. Turvey [1960], chapter VI. Other studies include J. Tobin [1947], 'Liquidity Preference and Monetary Policy', *R. Econ. Statist.*, May 1947; and M. Kalecki [1943], *Studies in Economic Dynamics*, chapter 2.

[4]Khrusro 'explained' some 95 per cent and Turvey some 90 per cent of the variation of the interest-rate changes they were examining.

[5]Brown's estimates suggest (*Oxford Studies*, p. 39) that, to vary the bond yield by one percentage point, the volume of money would have to be varied by about 20 per cent. Khusro tries various formulations which, though he does not discuss this, appear to give rather different results. His first two equations (pp. 3 and 6) suggest that the volume of money might have to be varied by 30 per cent or so to alter *net* bond yield by 1 percentage point; or (at present rates of tax) by perhaps 10 per cent to have a similar effect on the gross bond yield. His later formulations in terms of the idle money/liquid assets ratio seem to imply that the required change in the volume of money is less than half as great. Turvey's results for the United States suggest (p. 76) something like a 10 per cent change in money to alter the (gross) bond yield by 1 percentage point—or rather less if one assumes (as one should) that through open market operations the stock of bonds varies inversely with the volume of money. However inexact, these estimates probably suffice to establish the main point of the present argument.

[6]See the excellent study by P. Cagan [1956], 'The Monetary Dynamics of Hyperinflation', in *Studies in the Quantity Theory of Money*, edited by M. Friedman [1956]. The statement in the text is a very rough summary of Cagan's results; the elasticity of demand for money appeared to rise as the expected price rise increased.

Khusro's study also seems to show that interest rates are affected by changes in industrial profits. As he says, a 'rise in the profits of enterprise, or the expectations of such a rise, other things remaining unchanged, will lead the investors to seek to switch their assets from bonds and idle balances to equities'. But bonds are closer to equities than money; and his study appears to confirm that the level of dividends has a significant effect on the bond yield, and that changes in dividends help to explain some changes in the bond rate that could not otherwise be explained. This result is important. But it raises intricate questions (whose further consideration will however be deferred till §3 below) as to how far interest rates affect the demand for real assets; and as to how far, *per contra*, the return on real assets governs the rate of interest on financial assets.

The discussion so far has attempted a straightforward account of how the monetary authorities operate in financial markets to affect interest rates and the volume of money held by the public. Most common confusions as to how monetary policy works spring from one form or another of the 'quantity theory' of money—which seems, like a cat with nine times ninety lives, however many times discredited never to die. Three confusions are worth singling out. First, monetary policy is often discussed as though the volume of money were something which the authorities could directly determine—rather like the level of water in a mine—without the public being in any way involved in deciding the size of their money balances[1]. Second, the velocity of circulation is often supposed to be fixed, or at least inelastic, so that an increase in the quantity of money, thus brought about, somehow becomes a force pressing more or less directly on the price level. Alternatively, and somewhat more sophisticatedly, the increase brought about in the quantity of money is considered to result in 'excess liquidity', surplus to what the public wants to hold, which, in turn, leads the public to spend more than before and thus force up prices[2].

---

[1] '. . . the monetary system . . . an antiquated pumping machine . . . desperately attempting to keep down the level of the water in the mine' (Peter Thorneycroft [1960], 'Policy in Practice' in *Not Unanimous*, edited by A. Seldon [1960]).

[2] Passages in the *Radcliffe Report* seem to speak in these terms: see paras. 45, 401, 404 and 478. It is probably true that the public's holdings of liquid assets were abnormally high during the war; but this was a consequence of rationing and price control.

Modern attempts to rehabilitate the 'quantity theory' do not avoid this manner of reasoning. Milton Friedman, for instance, attempts to distinguish 'between the determinants of the nominal stock of money, on the one hand, and the real stock of money, on the other . . .' He supposes a 'society in which money consists exclusively of a purely fiduciary currency *issued by a single money-creating authority at its discretion*. The nominal number of units of money is then whatever amount this authority creates. *Holders of money cannot alter this amount directly*. But they can make the real amount of money anything that in the aggregate they want to. *If they want to hold a relatively small real quantity of money, they will individually seek to reduce their nominal cash balances by increasing expenditures*. This will not alter the nominal stock of money to be held—if some individuals succeed in reducing their nominal cash balances, it will only be by transferring them to others. But it will raise the flow of expenditures and hence money income and prices and

None of these ideas bears examination. In determining the volume of money, the monetary authority is, as the *Radcliffe Report* said, 'not a dictator but a market operator'[1]. The only permanent way to get people to hold more money is by altering the terms on which they hold it, i.e. by making it worth their while to hold more money. At these new terms, there is no question of their holding more than they want, nor of their being in some way displaced from an equilibrium position to which they seek to return by spending more. This implies that the relation between the volume of money and the value of transactions—in other words, the velocity of circulation—may vary. So much is indeed an observed fact[2]. Nor, were the velocity of circulation immutable, would it be possible for the authorities to vary the public's holdings of money.

The Radcliffe Committee denied that there was any obvious limit to the velocity of circulation[3]—a conclusion which is surely right (see further §2 below). This does not imply that the velocity can change *without affecting the rest of the system*: a rise in velocity raises interest rates—which has some effect, however small, on investment (§3 below); and sudden action of this sort might have disruptive effects on the flow of funds (§4 below), and hence also on the course of investment.

2. REASONS FOR HOLDING MONEY

In §1 it was assumed without close argument that the demand for money is sensitive to the rate of interest. But quite how it is sensitive has been the subject of argument. A convenient starting point is Keynes's division of the reasons for holding money into three: the 'transactions motive', the 'precautionary motive' and the 'speculative motive'.

The need for money depends among other things on the value of transactions to be effected. As Keynes put it: 'One reason for holding cash is to bridge the interval between the receipt of income and its disbursement. The strength of this motive in inducing a decision to hold a given aggregate of cash will chiefly depend on the amount of income and the normal length of the interval between its receipt and disbursement . . . Similarly, cash is held to bridge the interval between the time of incurring business costs and that of the receipt of the sale

thereby reduce the real quantity of money to the desired level . . .' (M. Friedman [1959], 'The Demand for Money: Some Theoretical and Empirical Results', *J. polit. Econ.*, August 1959: *my italics*).

[1]Para. 375.

[2]See for instance figure 12.1; and also A. J. Brown [1955], *The Great Inflation, 1939–1951*, chapter 8, and P. Cagan [1956], *op. cit.* As already noted, Cagan found that the elasticity of demand for money increased as the expected price rise increased—which, as he says (p. 88) 'contradicts the often stated view that the degree to which individuals can reduce their holdings of a depreciating currency has a limit'. Coming from the Chicago stable, this is an important admission.

[3]' . . . we cannot find any reason for supposing, or any experience in monetary history indicating, that there is any limit to the velocity of circulation' (*Report*, para. 391).

proceeds . . . The strength of this demand will chiefly depend on the value of current output . . . and on the number of hands through which income passes'[1].

The timing of payments and expenditures cannot be exactly foreseen. There is therefore a strong reason for people holding more money than on an average run of probabilities they are likely to need. One can say (as Keynes did) that there is need to provide 'for contingencies requiring sudden expenditure and for unforeseen opportunities of advantageous purchases'[2]. But it is better to recognize that almost all transactions have this character to some degree. Life is inherently uncertain, and it is at least an embarrassment, and possibly a source of disproportionate hardship, not to be able to meet payments when expected of one. Thus though this motive for holding money could—perhaps following Keynes[3]—be called the 'precautionary motive', it might equally well be regarded as a part and parcel of the 'transactions motive', since the timing of transactions is inevitably uncertain.

Keynes laid chief stress on his third category, the 'speculative motive' for holding money. Long-term interest rates, and the prices of securities—as already argued—must in some sense be what 'the market' expects them to be. The market, however, will not always be of one mind; and Keynes supposed it was often divided—in the terminology of the *Treatise*[4]—into 'bulls' and 'bears'. *Some* of the public may sometimes think that the price of non-monetary assets is going to fall (since they are a minority, their opinion does not itself force the price down); and anyone who thus 'differs from the predominant opinion as expressed in market quotations may have a good reason for keeping liquid resources in order to profit, if he is right', from the fall in prices he expects[5]. Keynes regarded the 'transactions demand' for money as inelastic, and supposed that it was 'speculative' balances that accounted for the sensitivity of money balances to interest rates[6]. Both sides to this proposition seem to me untrue.

For, first, speculation of the type involved in the 'speculative' motive seems of too *recherché* a nature to be typical. Most people who hold money do not

---

[1]Keynes [1936], pp. 195–6.

[2]*Ibid.*, p. 196.

[3]As Professor Johnson notes, Keynes gave different meanings to the term in the two chapters in the *General Theory* which discuss these matters: 'the precautionary motive starts as the senior partner, entrusted with the important business of avoiding uncertainty about future rates of interest, while the speculative motive is the junior partner who looks after the possibility of profiting from a fall in security prices . . . But when next we meet them, the speculative motive has taken over the whole business of asset management, and the precautionary motive has been reduced to a poor relation eking out his existence in the household of transactions demand' (H. Johnson [1961], p. 8).

The question of how far balances can be held in forms *other* than money is further discussed below: this creates uncertainties of a different sort, which also provide a motive for holding money balances as a precaution.

[4]Keynes [1930], Vol. I, pp. 251–2.

[5]Keynes [1936], p. 169.

[6]Keynes [1936], pp. 171–2.

actively speculate on future movements of the rate of interest, because their total assets are too small to make active trading on the stock exchange worthwhile[1]. The number of those who feel sure enough of themselves to take up a position opposed to the prevailing market opinion must be smaller still. Even if some do back their own view against the prevailing view, it appears like taking up a risky and exposed position which operators are unlikely to maintain for long. Financial institutions are better placed than most to take such a view and to act on it; but their working rule appears, for quite intelligible reasons, to keep themselves fully 'loaned up'[2]. These considerations suggest that the speculative motive is important, if at all, only as a short-term influence. Were this not the case, it would not be possible—as in fact appears possible[3]—to explain changes in interest rates in terms of objective factors[4].

If so, transactions balances (defined, as above, to include balances held against uncertainties) are left as the major element; and there are two sorts of reason for supposing them—contrary to Keynes's supposition—to be sensitive to interest rates. The argument so far has assumed that the timing of payments and receipts, however uncertain, is given and unchangeable. But this is not in fact the case. They can be retimed in such a way as to reduce the need for money balances. Perfect timing could indeed reduce the need for money to vanishing point. For the flow of money, as the older writers used to say, is circular; or, as national income statisticians constantly remind us, national income, expenditure and output are identically equal. If all payments to factors of production for work done, and by them for products bought, and between productive units for intermediate output, were *continuous*; or if they were made discretely, but in all cases were *synchronous* at the same moment (say at the end of the month); then the need for money for effecting transactions could in principle be reduced to zero, i.e. the velocity of circulation could become infinite. It seems likely that every rise in the rate of interest will induce some retiming of payments of a kind which results in a greater degree of synchronization; and will thus go some way towards eliminating the need for money.

There is an alternative way of putting the same argument, which may conveniently be spelt out in terms of considerations advanced by Professor Tobin

---

[1]As already pointed out, few people own stocks and shares on a substantial scale; and even among those who do, little account seems to be taken of capital gains and losses (see references in chapter XI.3 above).

[2]See the *Radcliffe Report* on the behaviour of insurance companies (para. 245) and investment trusts (para. 271).

[3]See figure 12.1 and further below.

[4]Tobin has suggested (as an alternative to the Keynesian theory of 'speculative' balances) that people hold 'investment' balances of money because they are averse to the capital risks of holding bonds (J. Tobin [1958], 'Liquidity Preference as Behavior towards Risk', *R. econ. Stud.*, February 1958). Such a reformulation escapes many of the above objections. But it still seems to me doubtful whether it is such balances, rather than transactions balances, that can account for the interest elasticity of the demand for money.

and Professor Baumol on the one hand, and Mr Turvey on the other[1].   Tobin has argued as follows: 'the failure of receipts and expenditure to be perfectly synchronized certainly creates the need for transactions balances.   But it is not obvious that these balances must be cash . . .   Why not hold transactions balances in assets with higher yields than cash, shifting into cash only at the time an outlay must be made? . . .   The advantage of this procedure is of course the yield.   The disadvantage is the cost, pecuniary and non-pecuniary, of such frequent and small transactions between cash and other assets . . .' Thus, 'when the yield disadvantage of cash is slight, the costs of frequent trans- actions will deter the holding of other assets, and average cash holdings will be large.   However, when the yield disadvantage of cash is great, it is worth while to incur large transactions costs and keep average cash holdings low'. Professor Tobin concludes it is thus plausible 'that the share of cash in trans- actions balances will be related inversely to the interest rate on other assets . . .'

Turvey has argued that the matter is less simple.   There are two ways of economizing in transactions balances: (1) by lending an unused cash balance (as in Tobin's argument) till the cash is needed to effect payments; and (2) by borrowing someone else's cash balance till receipts come in.   A high rate of interest should encourage the first, but discourage the second.   Turvey there- fore draws the conclusion, which he himself finds paradoxical, that the 'net effect of a general change in interest rates may therefore be in either direction' (i.e. it may either raise or lower average cash balances).

This apparent paradox arises from considering individuals as if they were separate.   In fact different people have unused cash balances *at different times*, as follows necessarily from the causes that create the need to hold transactions balances.   Being paid monthly, my balance is highest at the end of the month, and falls continuously through the month: my employer's cash balance, on the other hand, is likely to follow exactly the inverse pattern.   The same timing of payments that makes my cash balance low is bound to mean that someone else has a large balance temporarily unused.   Thus if we were all perfectly skilled in borrowing each other's unused cash balances, we could in theory reduce them to nothing at all.

One factor determining the need for transactions balances is the fact that employees are paid in arrear weekly or monthly or sometimes at longer intervals. They thus have to hold balances averaging (unless they are clever with the time they pay their bills) at least half a week's wages or half a month's salary—as does the business sector as a whole which employs them.   The simplest way to eliminate this need for holding balances would be for the 'business sector' to allow 'persons' to settle their bills at the time that persons themselves were paid. The effect of extension of credit in this manner is however precisely that of

---

[1]See the articles already cited by Baumol [1952] in *Quart. J. Econ.* and by Tobin [1956] in *R. Econ. Statist.* and chapter III of Turvey's [1960] *Interest Rates and Asset Prices.*

securing a greater synchronization of payments and receipts throughout the system. In this example, employees, by being paid in arrear, give implicit credit to their employers; and it is generally true that *if each unit received at each point of time as much credit, explicit or implicit, as it gave itself, all could get by without transactions balances.*

The market for short-term credit of this sort is very imperfect. The terms for trade credit appear to be conventional and insensitive to market forces. The same applies even more strongly to the implicit credit extended by employees to their employers: they do not get more for doing this when market rates of interest rise. The response to changes in interest rates must therefore be highly imperfect. Nevertheless there are many ways open to the community to economize in transactions balances; and a sufficient rise in interest rates must make people wish to do so. It seems plausible to conclude that a rise in interest rates leads people to find ways of economizing in their money balances.

The imperfection of the market has, however, other important consequences. It means that people are unable to rely on being able to effect money-economizing transactions at will: they are unable to rely with any certainty on being able to obtain short-term credit at anything like 'market' rates of interest. Most people therefore like to hold a precautionary balance over and above what is normally likely to be needed for transactions purposes; and the fact that the demand for money is as large as it is can be explained only in these terms[1].

Balances held for this kind of precautionary motive must also be presumed to be sensitive to the level of interest rates. The benefits from holding them as cash, rather than as interest-bearing assets, consists in the real or imagined risk of loss or difficulty in converting such assets into cash if a sudden need arose—or, equally, the cost or difficulties of getting a short-term loan to permit a more leisurely disposal of them. The marginal advantage of holding a money balance for this reason may be presumed to decline the larger the balance is; for the larger it is the less likely it is that it will in total actually be called on; and this declining advantage has to be balanced against the rate of interest[2].

The imperfection of the market, and the inflexibility of interest rates, has one further consequence. This is that the supply of short-term credit is governed

---

[1] The stock of money (as usually defined) has in this country since the war varied between 70 and 40 per cent of the annual national income (see figure 12.1 above). This seems far larger than can be accounted for as being required to meet the main classes of periodic payments that one can think of (such as wages, salaries, tax payments, etc.). It may be surmised that most people's cash balance always stands above zero; and that their minimum cash balance (in, say, a year) is substantial in relation to their average daily cash balance.

[2] Compare what is said in chapter XI.5 on the advantages of holding stocks of goods, and the example there quoted from Whitin [1952]. It has however to be admitted that the advantage of precautionary balances is greatest to those whose credit-standing is least. These must chiefly be people without ready access to the capital market, who are thus likely to be least sensitive to what is happening to the rate of interest. Simply because they enjoy better credit facilities, the 'precautionary' component in firms' money balances may be quite small.

much more by informal rationing than by the price mechanism: credit either is, or is not, available—irrespective of the rate of interest offered—from a particular source at a particular time. This greatly increases the uncertainties (and indeed, in a sense, accounts for the 'precautionary' demand for money balances). Credit restrictions seem thus capable of having general effect: one man refused credit is in turn unable to oblige his customers as freely as usual, who in their turn are forced to behave restrictively. One would therefore expect the demand for transactions balances to fluctuate considerably according to the state of financial confidence (see further in §4 below).

3. INTEREST RATES AND THE DEMAND FOR REAL ASSETS

The argument so far has sought to show how the monetary authorities can affect the price of financial securities and hence the rate of interest on them. It is now necessary to show how the demand for real and financial assets are inter-related. Keynes's 'liquidity preference' theory—the contention that the rate of interest represents 'the reward for parting with liquidity'—was developed in conscious opposition to the 'classical' doctrine that the rate of interest is 'the factor which brings the demand for investment and the willingness to save into equilibrium with one another'[1]. But he also believed that the 'rate of current investment will be pushed to the point where there is no longer any class of capital-asset of which the marginal efficiency exceeds the current rate of interest'[2]. These two articles of belief—as stated—are inconsistent. For the latter contention is equivalent to saying that bonds and real assets are substitutes for each other as far as the investor is concerned; and from this it follows that not only does the price of bonds affect the demand for real assets, but also that all the factors affecting the demand for real assets affect the price of bonds. Since Keynes wrote it has been one of the vexed questions of economics whether the rate of interest is a monetary phenomenon, or alternatively, is a creation of the real forces of 'productivity and thrift': in fact it must surely be both.

The best way of describing the effect of changes in interest rates on the demand for real assets is in terms of changes in the price of assets; for, in the market for assets, it is the *price* of assets that is determined. The price of *new* capital assets, being dependent on current costs of production, may be taken as given from the present point of view. The price of *existing* real assets, on the other hand—in so far as there is a market price for second-hand houses, shops, offices, factories, machinery and vehicles—is not unrelated to the price of financial securities, and the two must to some extent vary in sympathy. A rise in bond prices therefore raises the price of old real assets relatively to their replacement cost; and thus makes it more desirable to maintain or add to the existing stock, i.e. it increases investment demand to some degree.

[1]Keynes [1936], pp. 167 and 175.
[2]*Ibid.*, p. 136.

In operating on the composition of the National Debt as between money and bonds, the authorities are thus in effect, though at several removes, operating on a vast market—on nothing less than the demand to hold the stock of national wealth. The different categories of assets range in a sort of spectrum from money and bills, through bonds and equities, to real assets. At first sight it may seem difficult to believe that manipulations at the 'monetary' end of the spectrum have large effects on the market for real assets. In order to illustrate the orders of magnitude, it is convenient first to give a highly simplified picture, in which the differences between different capital goods are ignored, so that it is possible to speak of 'the stock' of real capital. To show the effect of monetary action, it is also necessary to have an idea of the other forces affecting the demand for real assets.

Interest-rate effects, though usually discussed in terms of savings and investment should properly be framed in terms of the stock of capital. Thus there may be reasons to think that if the stock of capital were greatly increased (the state of 'technique' being assumed as given), the 'rate of return' would fall: but there is no reason to think it would fall off quickly. Since the annual rate of investment is small in relation to the stock, there is therefore no reason to think that the rate of *investment* affects the yield materially[1]. The yield on capital expressed as a ratio of the replacement cost of capital assets can therefore at any one time be taken as given for all practical purposes.

The argument about saving (as already noted[2]) also needs to be formulated in terms of the desire to hold assets. People start by owning assets, and the alternatives open to them include not merely the possibility of adding to their assets, but of living off their capital: thus to speak only of decisions to save obscures the range of choice to be explained. That savings should be positive, and that communities should add fairly steadily to their economic wealth, seems an almost invariable concomitant of economic progress. It is difficult to believe that the precise level of interest rates has much affected the process of accumulation, which has surely to be explained rather in terms of the advantages of being wealthy. Moreover even if it were true that a higher interest rate, for instance, increased saving (as Marshall believed), it would still be true (as Marshall added) 'that the annual investment of wealth is a small part of the already existing stock, and that therefore the stock would not be increased perceptibly in any one year by even a considerable increase in the annual rate of

---

[1]The illegitimate transition in Keynes's argument in *The General Theory* from 'stocks' to 'flows' has already been pointed out (chapter XI.4, p. 286 n.). Thus Keynes concluded on this point that 'for each type of capital we can build up a schedule, showing by how much investment in it will have to increase within the period, in order that its marginal efficiency should fall to any given figure' (Keynes [1936], p. 136). His argument admittedly depended partly on the consideration that pressure on production facilities would raise the supply price of capital goods—a short-term 'disequilibrium' consideration best ignored on the present plane of argument.

[2]See chapter XI.3 above.

Fig. 12.2.   Productivity of capital (CC) and desire to hold real assets (MM)

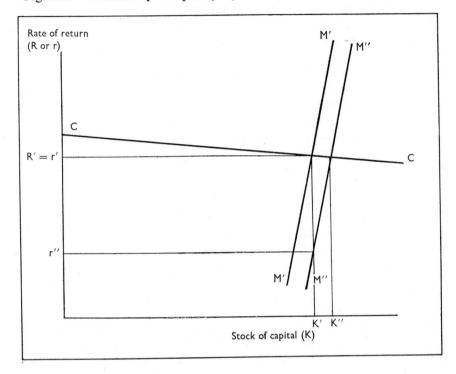

saving'[1]. The desire to hold wealth, rather than to dissipate it in dis-saving, cannot then depend critically on the rate of interest.

It may be concluded that, at any moment of time, the rate of return on new additions to the stock of capital is what it is; and that the stock which people desire to maintain is what it is more or less irrespective of the rate of return. Their desired stock may however change for other reasons: with the passage of time, it normally grows, and it is affected by the actions of the monetary authorities.   The present plane of argument leaves out many qualifications but contains the essentials needed to show the effect of monetary intervention.

Fig. 12.2 shows the equilibrium position at a point in time[2]. The 'productivity of capital' curve (CC) can be expressed directly in 'real' terms: the curve shows the return (R) on capital (K) expressed as a ratio of the *replacement* cost.

[1]A. Marshall [1920], *Principles of Economics*, [1938 ed.], p. 236.
[2]Compare the discussion in J. R. Hicks [1960], 'Thoughts on the Theory of Capital—The Corfu Conference', *Oxford econ. Pap.*, June 1960, pp. 125–6.   Fig. 12.2 follows Hicks's notation.

MONEY, INTEREST RATES AND LIQUIDITY   317

This falls only slowly as the stock is increased. The demand to hold assets is insensitive with respect to the rate of return so defined (and so would in these terms be represented by a vertical line). The 'demand for assets' curve (*MM*) on the diagram relates the *volume* of assets desired to be held to the rate of return (*r*) expressed as a ratio of the *market value* of existing assets (which may be above or below the replacement cost). This curve, while nearly vertical, probably falls to the left[1].

In stationary equilibrium, people would desire to maintain the capital stock at its present size: the market price would equal the replacement cost ($r' = R'$), so that it paid neither to add to the capital stock (K') nor to run it down. Now suppose that people want to increase their stock of assets (i.e. to save) and this is not immediately matched by an increase in the stock of assets (i.e. by investment). This is represented on the diagram by the shift from $M'M'$ to $M''M''$. One adjustment to close this disequilibrium would be for asset prices to be bid up, so providing an incentive to investment. The fall in the 'money' rate of interest to r'' implies a rise in asset prices, which causes an expansion of the capital stock from K' to K'', which in turn brings an eventual return to a position where $r = R$ at a point very little below R'. If the economy is working below full employment, the disequilibrium between *ex ante* saving and investment may also be closed by the familiar multiplier mechanism, i.e. by induced changes in income; and for reasons to be stated in a moment, this second type of adjustment is much more rapid, and thus more important. If the economy is at full employment, this type of adjustment is not available. Apart from deliberate budgetary action, saving and investment are brought into equilibrium—if at all—only by price movements, i.e. by the adjustment mechanism portrayed in the diagram.

Now one way by which a shift in the asset demand curve may come about is by open market operations on the part of the monetary authorities. To reduce the rate of interest the authorities must buy bonds from the public for money, so bidding up the price of bonds and lowering their yield. This must induce a diminishing trail of price adjustments along the 'spectrum' of assets: a smaller rise in the price of equities, and a still smaller rise in the price of real assets. Only in so far as the desirability of holding real assets is affected do interest-rate changes have a real impact.

The scale of the impact depends on the degree to which paper securities and real assets are substitutes. In practice, the degree of substitution is small;

---

[1]Hicks argues that 'in the classical conception' we should think of *MM* as a *horizontal* line, but he later gives reasons for supposing that it should be drawn sloping downwards very sharply.

One reason for believing that the curve is not absolutely vertical is that the demand to hold assets is probably to some extent a demand for a certain *value* of assets. The quantity of assets demanded should therefore vary inversely with the price of assets; or directly with *r*, the return expressed as a ratio of the price.

but it cannot be entirely negligible. If substitutability were perfect, the intervention of the authorities would have the same effect as if the authorities were buying not bonds but real assets. It is for instance conceivable that the banks should increase the public's holding of money by making loans against the security of real property, i.e. by monetizing part not of the National Debt but of the national wealth, or in effect by making 'open market purchases' of real property. There would then be an additional demand for real property coming from the banks in addition to the previously existing demand to hold real assets on the part of the public—which would analytically amount to a shift in the *MM* curve.

It may be helpful at this point to give some idea of the possible scale of action by the monetary authorities. In a country like the United Kingdom with a large National Debt, the possible range of action is large. All the following figures refer to the years 1953–5[1]. For these years the volume of money held by the public has been estimated at £9 billion; and the value of floating debt and British government bonds (not held by the banks or by the government itself) has been estimated at about £9 billion also. This compares with about £14 billion for the value of the liabilities of public and private non-financial companies[2]; and about £22 billion for the value of real assets other than those owned by the government[3]. The total net assets held by the private sector, excluding its holding of money, but including its holding of National Debt, were therefore of the order of £31 billion.

Figure 12.1 showed that the ratio of the money supply to the national product fell (as there defined) from 0·7 in 1947 to a little under 0·5 in 1953–5 (and fell more by 1960). Suppose that this had not happened, but that the government had issued more money as national income rose and reduced its debt in inverse correspondence. The public's holding of money in 1953–5 would then have been almost half as large again, or £4 billion larger; and the value of National Debt £4 billion smaller. This is appreciable in relation to the public's total holding of financial *plus* real assets of £31 billion: had the money-income ratio been kept constant, this total would have been smaller by fifteen per cent. The price it was willing to pay for assets—chiefly financial assets, but also to some extent real assets—might therefore be expected to have been appreciably higher.

This gives some idea of the authorities' possible range of action: in principle, this could be much wider than the actual change over these seven years. The conclusion must be that operations of the open market type can be more than minor manipulations of the monetary end of the 'spectrum' of assets, and can

[1]See E. V. Morgan [1960], *The Structure of Property Ownership in Great Britain*, especially table 65.

[2]This excludes the liabilities of foreign companies and British companies operating abroad.

[3]The real assets of the central government, the local authorities and the public corporations were put at another £8 billion.

represent sizeable additions to or subtractions from the demand for non-monetary assets.   But though in the short run the authorities may effectively manipulate the level of yields and asset prices, in the long run one would expect this to set up forces which restored rates or yields to something like their original level—a level determined by the real productivity of capital.

This account of the mechanism of adjustment, based on the distinction between the market price of real assets and their replacement value, is however a vast simplification of reality.   The market for financial securities and for real assets is far from being one market.   The financial capital market is often said to be imperfect: the property market is at least equally so, and that for most other sorts of real assets is so imperfect that one can hardly speak of there being a market at all.

If the market were as perfect as implied hitherto, small changes in asset prices (induced let us say by the actions of the monetary authorities) would induce sizeable adjustments to the stock of capital.   Again, if the market were perfect, the adjustments would be rapid, so that one would see extreme variations in the rate of investment.   Indeed, if the market were perfect, no discrepancy between *ex ante* saving and investment could arise.   In practice, the market does not operate in this way; investment is by no means so sensitive.   The notion that *ex ante* saving and investment may differ, so that excess demand may emerge, is a keystone of modern macro-economic theory: it is clear that the pricing system is *not* perfect enough to eradicate such divergencies, and that the idea of excess demand is based on a valid intuition.

The reason for the imperfection of the market for real assets is that their productiveness, and hence their value, depends very much on who it is that is putting them to use.   Most capital goods are therefore, in this sense, highly specific: they have a higher value in their present use than elsewhere.   They may have some value if sold separately; but if their 'second-hand' price falls, it does not necessarily reflect a low value in use, nor necessarily imply that it is less economic for their present owners to replace them when worn out.

The converse also holds.   Real assets tend to be managed by those who think they can make best use of them; but there are so many uncertainties that their productivity is very difficult even for those managing them to judge.   Consequently, probably profitable lines of investment are not exploited to the full immediately.   The *management* of property is part and parcel of getting a profit; and, being a demanding task, entrepreneurs extend their commitments only gradually, making a second investment only when a first has proved successful[1].   A rise in second-hand asset prices, therefore, does not necessarily imply that entrepreneurs find it worthwhile to extend their investment.

The market price of real assets, in short, is a poor reflection of their value in use.   The fact that real assets are not interchangeable among themselves means

[1]See the discussion of the 'principle of increasing risk' in chapter XI.4 above.

also that as a class they are not good substitutes for paper assets. It follows that the authorities are able within wide limits to vary the rate of return on interest-bearing paper assets (by themselves buying and holding more or less) without greatly affecting the demand for real assets. There is little immediate tendency to bring the market rate into equilibrium with the return on real assets. Indeed, when the riskiness of capital is allowed for, the 'return' on real assets becomes a misty and subjective entity.

The theoretical conclusion is then this: in the short-term, the rate of interest is primarily a 'monetary' phenomenon determined by the forces of liquidity preference as described by Keynes. Since paper securities and real assets are poor substitutes, there is no rigid link between the returns on each. Precisely because of this, it is relatively easy—and also relatively useless—for the authorities to vary the rate of interest. Nevertheless, the division between paper and real assets is not absolute. Hence the fact that real assets yield a return may still be regarded as the reason for there being a positive rate of interest at all: it is for this reason that the government cannot borrow free, but has to pay interest on its debt. Even in the short term, this link with real forces will cast its shadow before it, by providing some vague norm for the expectation of the market, so preventing security prices departing too far from what the market expects real forces will eventually dictate they should be[1].

Equities also provide a bridge between the two markets. Since equities are 'standardized' real assets, they are fairly close substitutes for bonds; so that, in the absence of dividend changes, equity prices and bond prices move closely parallel[2]. But dividends—or expected dividends—bear some relation to firms' profits. Hence changes in profits affect the rate of interest on paper assets[3].

There being a significant connection between the two markets, it follows that at least in the long term it matters what the authorities do to interest rates. If it is true that, in the long term, 'real' forces tend to predominate in fixing the level of interest rates, this is so only because in the long term the effects on the stock of capital can be expected to be appreciable. The effectiveness of monetary intervention is to be measured not by how greatly interest rates can be changed, but by how far even small effects on interest rates affect the volume of

---

[1] See discussion in §1 above. The market opposition to cheap money in 1947 probably sprang in part from the feeling that interest rates were lower than could be maintained.

[2] See for instance I. M. Sahni [1951], 'A Study of Share Prices, 1918–1947', *Yorkshire B.*, February 1951.

[3] Empirical confirmation of this conclusion is provided by Khusro's [1952] study already quoted (in §1 above). It is however disputed. Mr Kennedy, for instance, attempting to reinstate a purely Keynesian view, has recently argued that, while expected dividend increases (arising from the expectation of continued inflation) 'must lead to an alteration in the relative yields of bonds and equities, there is no reason why equilibrium should not be restored by a rise in equity prices rather than by a fall in bond prices' (C. Kennedy [1960], 'Inflation and the Bond Rate', *Oxford econ. Pap.*, October 1960, p. 272). Khusro's results suggest, on the contrary, that in such a case bond yields in fact rise and bond prices fall.

capital which the community wishes to maintain.   But what precisely interest-rate policy should be is still a complicated question, whose consideration will be deferred to §5.

4.   THE CAPITAL MARKET AND 'AVAILABILITY' EFFECTS

Previous sections have sought to show how a theory of monetary policy may be derived as a corollary of the general theory of asset holding.   This approach, by and large and with varying degrees of thoroughness, has been the one usually favoured by economists.   This 'equilibrium' approach to monetary policy differs markedly from that of bankers and practical men, who tend to regard its influence as depending on business attitudes, which are capable of being changed by the actions of the banks.   This second approach appears to have something in common with the general philosophy of the *Radcliffe Report*, which has recently emphasized the importance of 'liquidity' effects[1], without however making it entirely clear in what they consist, and how they may be induced.   Some of the steps in the preceding argument seem to provide a basis for a more exact analysis of such matters, which seems to show that they are much more important than economists have often allowed.

It is clear that liquidity preference depends on attitudes which may change; and also that the capital market, far from being perfect, as supposed by static equilibrium analysis, is 'divided into an infinite number of pockets between which money does not readily "spill over" in either direction as soon as an established price differential is disturbed'[2].   It will be argued that this means that the flow of funds is liable to be interrupted, and that it is possible to say something fairly precise both as to how policy may cause such disruption and as to its effects.   Such an analysis also makes it possible to describe in their proper context direct controls over certain flows of funds.

As a first step it is convenient to divide the flows of funds into two distinct types—a distinction whose sharpness will later have to be modified.   First are *money-economizing transactions*.   As already noted, the holding of paper assets is to some degree an alternative to holding money.   Balances so held will occasionally be spent.   A continual flux is therefore to be expected in the ownership of (primarily short-term) non-monetary assets held for this purpose as some people encash them to meet current payments, while others buy them with cash temporarily redundant.   This class of transaction should be understood to include the constant ebb and flow of trade credit, on the grounds that though the rise and fall of trade credits may appear to by-pass the capital market, it is an alternative to transactions routed through it.

Second are *transactions connected with the transport of loanable funds*.   Some economic units save more than they themselves invest, and thus acquire financial

[1]For references see further below.
[2]Sayers [1951], p. 11.

assets; while others invest more than they save, and to cover the difference have to sell financial assets. The transfer may either be direct through the sale and purchase of what may be called 'primary paper', or indirect through financial intermediaries, in which case it may involve the issue of 'secondary paper'[1]. Such transactions may for the greater part be conceived of as being long-term (i.e. not quickly reversed). Most acts of saving are fairly permanent (i.e. the savings are not quickly spent). Some categories of economic units are fairly consistently year in, year out, 'surplus units'; and others equally consistently 'deficit units'[2]. In recent years, the central government has been consistently a 'surplus' sector, as has, in aggregate, the personal sector; whereas the public corporations and the local authorities have been consistently 'deficit' sectors[3]. The company sector may in aggregate have been a 'surplus' sector, but many individual companies have been consistent borrowers[4].

It is possible to conceive of these two sorts of flows proceeding without relation one with another, most long-term investment being matched by long-term finance, and most money-economizing transactions being in short-term securities. But the division is clearly not absolute. Firms may expect to be able to rely on short-term credit either from the banks or from other traders for part of their finance: if this is not occasional but normal practice, it reduces their need for long-term finance. Long-term financial arrangements, also, may not synchronize with long-term investment expenditure, so that firms may need temporary short-term 'bridging' finance, or have abnormal amounts of finance temporarily available for short-term lending.

In addition to trading in 'new' long-term securities there is continuous trading in 'old' securities. It is this which creates a ready market in long-term paper, and which gives long-term paper a degree of liquidity. Similarly it is only the confidence that short-term finance can be obtained as needed that makes it possible for people to consider money-economizing transactions. The more perfect the market, the more completely can money be dispensed with.

The extension of trade credit as needed is, in principle, the simplest form of money-economizing transaction to consider: for it amounts to a retiming of payments, and the object of retiming payments is to make payments and receipts synchronize more closely[5]. But such transactions can equally easily be conceived as taking place through the banks. Thus it comes to the same thing whether firm A lends to firm B directly (i.e. runs down its deposit), so making it unnecessary for firm B to ask for a bank loan; or, alternatively, repays an advance from its bank who then relends to firm B. In practice, the intermediary action of banks must often be important, because the circle of any firm's

---

[1]To adopt a convenient recent terminology: see J. G. Gurley and E. S. Shaw [1960], *Money in a Theory of Finance*, p. 93.

[2]*Ibid.*, p. 21.

[3]*National Income and Expenditure* [1961], table 48.

[4]See chapter XI.4.

[5]See §2 above

immediate customers and suppliers is limited. The intermediary action of the banks can therefore greatly extend the possibilities, and the banks are uniquely placed to play such a role.

If the banks restrict credit, the effect can be widespread. For if a bank restricts credit to firm A, firm A is likely to be more restrictive towards other firms, and they in turn towards firms dependent on them. The effect of such a credit restriction springs from the fact that the market is imperfect, i.e. credit refused by banks or trade connections cannot easily be replaced. Since the market is imperfect, the effect is likely to be not a moderate rise in interest rates (which would not be so bad); but rather a blocking up of many usual channels, combined in some cases with the payment of very high short-term rates necessary to obtain funds from unconventional sources.

Furthermore, restrictions, like a servo-mechanism, tend to reinforce each other. An initial restriction reduces the perfection of the market. It thus makes each firm more anxious to maintain its own liquidity, and, with any given degree of liquidity, more reluctant to lend to others. This further spreads the restrictiveness. Various forms of short-term asset become less like money than they were before; so that the demand for money balances is increased.

If money were the only form of liquid asset, and people suddenly wanted more of it, the only way people could get more money would be to reduce expenditure. A credit squeeze produces a pale imitation of this situation. If everyone is trying to take cash balances off each other, they cannot all succeed in doing so: but it is the *desire* to do so that is relevant. The stock of money is a large fraction of the national income[1]. If people aimed to increase their own cash balance by only a small proportion, the cut in expenditure could therefore be appreciable in relation to total demand. Thus it seems possible to account in rational terms for the pervasive effects which bankers attribute to a credit squeeze.

This view of money and credit seems to have much in common with that of the *Radcliffe Report*[2]—which, it has been said, 'regards the monetary system primarily as a complex of institutions and markets supporting numerous flows

---

[1]Of the order of half the national income: see figure 12.1.

[2]It has seemed best not to attempt at this point to summarize the doctrine of the *Radcliffe Report*. Other people have written articles discussing the theory underlying the *Report*, and what must have been meant by terms such as the 'state of liquidity' of the economy. The fact that interpretation has been thought necessary—and that interpretations differ—makes the *Report* a difficult starting point for a discussion. It has therefore seemed best to deal piecemeal with points of similarity and difference between the view put forward here and that of the *Report*.

For other comment on the *Report* see for instance R. F. G. Alford and H. B. Rose [1959], 'The Radcliffe Report and Domestic Monetary Policy', *London Cambridge econ. B.*, December 1959; A. E. Jasay [1960], 'The Working of the Radcliffe Monetary System', *Ox. econ. Pap.*, June 1960; M. Gaskin [1960], 'Liquidity and the Monetary Mechanism', *Ox. econ. Pap.*, October 1960; D. C. Rowan [1961], 'Radcliffe Monetary Theory', *Econ. Record*, December 1961; and Lord Robbins [1960], 'Monetary Theory and the *Radcliffe Report*', reprinted [1963] in his collection of essays *Politics and Economics*.

of funds, rather than as a group of institutions providing a stock of means of payment'[1]. Thus the *Report* placed great emphasis not merely on holdings of liquid assets, but also on the ease of borrowing[2]. But on one important matter, namely the question of trade credit, it differs from the foregoing analysis.

The *Report* rightly emphasized the importance, and complementarity of bank credit and trade credit; but, so it seems to me, stated only half the truth. Thus it emphasized the key position of banks[3]. It also rightly criticized the usual view that trade credit is merely passing on to others credit obtained elsewhere, and pointed out that the effect on 'net takers' and on 'net givers' of credit may not be opposite and equal[4]. This point should however be put more strongly. The effects are most unlikely to be equal: the 'net giver' has cash to spare, and the 'net taker' has not; and (as already argued) the total effect is to economize in cash, and to make it unnecessary to cut spending in order to get it. Furthermore, the *Report* treats changes in trade credit and bank credit *as likely to be unconnected*; so that it is possible for it to argue that a 'small lengthening of trade credit' might 'offset quite a large proportionate reduction in bank credit'[5]. But, as already argued, it seems more likely that a reduction in bank credit will *provoke* a contraction of trade credit.

What the *Report* had to say on how a credit squeeze might be set in motion is one of its most disputed parts. The Radcliffe doctrine was that 'movements in interest rates have significant effects on the liquidity structure' so that the 'authorities thus have to regard the structure of interest rates . . . as the centrepiece of the monetary mechanism'[6]. 'A rise in rates makes some less willing to lend because capital values have fallen, and others because their own interest rate structure is sticky. A fall in rates on the other hand, strengthens balance

---

[1]Gaskin [1960], *op. cit.*, p. 274.

[2]For instance:

'The spending is not limited by the amount of money in existence; but it is related to the amount of money people think they can get hold of, whether by receipts of income . . . by disposal of capital assets or by borrowing' (para. 390).

' . . . the monetary authorities may bring to bear another influence which can be altogether more peremptory. This is the availability of funds to borrowers through particular channels . . . if the money for financing the project cannot be got on any tolerable terms at all, that is the end of the matter.' (para. 387.)

[3]'In the liquidity structure as we have described it, the banks hold a special position, in that they are, for most borrowers and for most short-term purposes, much the most convenient source of funds and often the only source. The authorities therefore need to have a special care, in framing a particular course of action, for its effects on the banks . . . We emphasise that . . . [it] is the level of bank advances rather than the level of bank deposits that is the object of this special interest; the behaviour of bank deposits is of interest only because it has some bearing, along with other influences, on the behaviour of other lenders' (para. 395).

[4]Para. 299.

[5]Para. 300.

[6]Para. 397. It has to be remembered that the *Radcliffe Report* discussed liquidity effects as one way in which monetary policy might have *quick effects* on the economy, and that it had dismissed various other possible methods of achieving quick effects as not likely to be effective.

sheets and encourages lenders to seek new business'[1].

This has not generally been found acceptable as an account of the impact of interest-rate changes on financial institutions. The one clear example of the 'sticky-rate' effect is the building societies; who borrow short, but try to keep lending rates and hence borrowing rates steady: when other short rates rise, they have therefore to ration credit[2]. But this is an exceptional case. What the *Report* said on 'capital loss' effects is also unconvincing. As the *Report* elsewhere admits[3], the banks, precisely in order to avoid the risk of capital losses, hold a substantial cushion of short-term bonds; and some of the evidence to the Committee makes it clear that not only the banks, but insurance companies and other institutions are in fact prepared to sell securities at a loss[4].

The foregoing analysis suggested that restrictions on bank lending may induce further restrictions on the giving of private credit; and that the banks are in a unique position to start this cycle off. It would seem that this jamming of the flow of short-term finance is much more likely to be induced by quantitative restriction of bank advances, than by a rise in the rates charged for them; for doubt as to whether bank credit can be obtained at all seems likely to be much more potent than fear that it will cost more. In this process, the 'stickiness' of rates matters only in as much as it is part and parcel of the business of rationing credit. Nevertheless it could be that if the banks raised the price of credit, traders themselves might react by quantitative restriction of credit to customers or suppliers. Moreover, when banks raise rates, they usually ration as well. A rise in rates might, too, be taken as a signal that credit was going to get tighter, so inducing caution among lenders[5]. It is more doubtful whether the flow of long-term finance is liable to comparable interruption[6].

The present argument therefore suggests that changes in the availability of credit—as distinct from the effects of changes in interest rates discussed in §§ 1–3 above—can have an appreciable impact. It also suggests that they are better induced by credit restrictions than by changes in interest rates. It is chiefly the flow of short-term credit that is likely to be affected. The impact seems likely to fall on business expenditure (on fixed investment or investment in stocks), since businesses make more use of short-term credit than persons[7].

[1]Para. 393.
[2]See chapter IX.6 above.
[3]Para. 144.
[4]See H. B. Rose [1960], 'Financial Institutions and Monetary Policy', *Bankers' Mag.*, July 1960.
[5]This seems to be a main point in the article by Rosa which started the recent discussion of the effects of interest rates *on lenders*: see R. V. Rosa [1951], 'Interest Rates and the Central Bank' in *Money, Trade and Economic Growth*; p. 286.
[6]See chapter IX.4 above.
[7]In reviewing the effects of the 1957 credit squeeze, the Radcliffe Committee reported it was unable 'to find that the squeeze had any marked effect on holdings of stocks of commodities'. The Committee therefore believed that the blow fell on fixed investment—'not on projects already in train but on capital projects in their earliest planning stages' (para. 460). This question is further considered in chapter XV.2 below.

The argument also suggests that the jamming up of credit flows is essentially a temporary phenomenon. It must, for instance, be highly disconcerting to a trader who has come to rely on bank credit to finance his stocks to be refused it. But if the stringency continued long, he could increase his long-term finance, and in future be immune to such disruption. For the same reason the impact must be largely one way: the effect of an easing of credit is probably much less than the effect of a restriction. Whether such effects are useful will be considered in §5.

It remains to reconsider one provisional conclusion reached earlier: namely that there is no sense in the idea of 'excess liquidity', nor, therefore, harm in high holdings of liquid assets[1]. It might be argued that too high a stock of liquid assets renders the economy relatively immune from the short-term restrictions of credit of the sort discussed in this section. It has already been argued[2] that existing money holdings are larger than strictly required for transactions purposes, and that much therefore is, in some rather vague sense, 'idle money'. If there is much 'idle money', it seems likely that the interruption of money-economizing financial flows will cause less disruption than if there is little 'idle money'. Precautionary balances are held precisely because money may be much more liquid than other assets in an emergency: if people can be lulled into not taking precautions against it, they should be more vulnerable to a credit squeeze when it comes. But a credit squeeze can never catch everyone; and even with high liquidity in general, some people will be in a vulnerable position. It is always possible moreover to operate severer restrictions. A community which has come to rely on bank advances is always likely to be embarrassed if they are restricted. The final answer therefore seems much as before: it is no use trying to control a 'flow' (like the expenditure of the public) by operating on a 'stock' (like its holding of money, or liquid assets).

5.   CONCLUSIONS REGARDING MONETARY POLICY

The first parts of this chapter were concerned to define the place of the rate of interest in the scheme of things. Changes in the rate of interest, it was concluded, had little effect in the short run; but if pushed vigorously enough in either direction, interest-rate policy could in the long run stimulate or retard investment significantly. The authorities therefore must have a policy regarding the rate of interest. What should the policy be? Should interest rates be high or low?

This conclusion is very much that of the *Radcliffe Report*. The rate of interest, said the *Report*, while not much use as a 'major short-term stabilizer of demand', has effects in the longer term. The *Report* concluded that the authorities 'should take a view as to what the long-term economic situation

[1]Conclusion to §1 above.
[2]See §2.

demands'—without however specifying whether it was high or low rates that were likely to be required[1]. During the last decade there has been a movement of opinion in favour of high rates of interest; and in interpreting the Radcliffe recommendations, the authorities appear at first to have tried to keep rates relatively high[2]. But this conclusion can be criticized. For the economic argument provides very imprecise guidance. It seems therefore legitimate to take other considerations also into account, in particular, the budgetary burden of high interest rates. In short, the case for cheap money needs to be reconsidered[3].

The level of interest rates which 'the long-term economic situation demands' is, in fact, exceedingly difficult to judge. There is a sizeable range of rates any point within which could well be defended—partly because, within a range, the level probably makes no crucial difference; partly because it is difficult to predict what level of investment any given rate will produce; and partly because it is difficult to judge whether that level, if predictable, would be desirable or not. Moreover there probably are more potent, and quicker, ways of affecting investment, for instance by variation of the depreciation allowances.

The level of rates affects the composition of investment. Thus low rates encourage longer-lasting investment, such as power stations and houses. It could therefore be argued that 'unduly' high or 'unduly' low rates 'distort' the structure of investment by 'unduly' encouraging or 'unduly' discouraging investment in the more durable type of asset. In principle everyone would admit this; but in application one cannot specify 'distortion' because it is impossible to say precisely what rates are 'unduly' high or low. The only practical solution seems to be for the government to take a view both on the desirable total of investment, and on any features of its composition that seem particularly desirable. Here again, there are more direct ways than interest-rate changes to affect the composition—though for private house-building the rate of interest is important.

As against this, the government has always a valid, though not overriding, interest in securing low rates in order to reduce the cost of the National Debt. Since 1946, short-term rates have risen from $\frac{1}{2}$ per cent to nearly five per cent, and the rate on government bonds from under three to over six per cent. This has probably added £300–400 million to the cost of National-Debt interest[4]; and has probably also increased interest payments abroad by £50–100 million[5].

[1] *Radcliffe Report*, paras. 492–9. This doctine has attracted less attention than the Committee's denial of quick interest-rate effects, or their emphasis on the alleged effects of interest-rate changes on 'the structure of liquidity' (paras. 384–94: see §4 above).

[2] See chapter IX.2 above.

[3] This represents a revision of my view of four years ago (which now seems to me unsatisfactory): see my memorandum to the Committee, *Radcliffe, Memoranda*, XIII.9, paras. 153–4.

[4] Debt interest has risen from £480 million in 1946 to £870 million in 1960. But this is partly because the size of the gross debt is larger; and something approaching a fifth of the gross debt now corresponds to relending to local authorities and the public corporations.

[5] It has been estimated that a rise in short-term rates of 1 per cent costs about £15 million a year to the balance of payments (*Radcliffe Report*, para. 438).

The effect of the level of interest rates on the economy has certainly to be taken into account.   But if, as argued, there is in practice a 'range of indifference' the bias should surely be towards keeping interest rates down to the bottom end of the range.

Recent practice is certainly anomalous.   The authorities think interest rates ought to stay fairly high, presumably because investment demand is high.   But at the same time they subsidize investment through the investment allowances; and the budget *suffers on both counts*.   One might not wish to reduce interest rates to what they were in Dr Dalton's day.   But his instinct that the rate of interest should be as low as possible may well have been right.   Lower interest rates imply (on the argument of §1) higher money holdings by the public: it has already been argued (conclusions to §§ 1 and 3) that fears of consequent excess liquidity are mistaken.

Two qualifications should however be made.   The 'range of indifference' for the bond rate might for example be put at 3–8 per cent *during times when prices were expected to be stable*.   But by now the market makes some allowance for a continuation of rising prices.   If 4 per cent were now to be classed as a low rate, bond yields of $6\frac{1}{2}$ per cent (as in 1962) should perhaps still be rated as moderately high.

Secondly, the market for financial securities is becoming much more international.   It would therefore be difficult for one country on its own to maintain very low rates of interest.   But this only means that the argument has to be conducted on an international plane.   There has been a movement of opinion in all countries since 1950 in favour of high interest rates.   But the present arguments apply not only to this country but to others.   The world-wide movement of opinion may have gone too far.

The argument of this chapter seems to run inescapably to the conclusion that the rate of interest is of little use as a means of controlling the economy.   Can more be hoped from credit restrictions? It was argued in §4 that there is a constant ebb and flow of short-term credit between different units of the economic system, to some of which the banks are intermediary.   A restriction of credit by the banks will have two effects.   First, since the market is imperfect, restriction by the banks will lead those directly affected to impose quantitative restrictions on their short-term lending to others.   Second, it will reduce the certainty of being able to obtain financial accommodation when needed, which also will make non-bank lenders less willing to lend, and thus reinforce the first effect.

The effect of a credit squeeze can be compared, graphically if perhaps too picturesquely, to the effect of dropping bombs on a city's traffic system. A few bombs may for a time close some traffic routes, but there are ways round.   Most of the traffic gets through, many people are inconvenienced, some may be deterred from travelling—and quite who is affected is random and arbitrary. Firms seriously affected by a credit squeeze will be those who by accident are in a vulnerable position at the time of the squeeze; many will be made more anxious, and most will be made more careful.

In previous decades, credit restrictions may have had further, even more serious, effects. For, first, economic fluctuations were not controlled; an initial fall in sales could therefore induce traders to contract their purchases out of fear of worse to come, thereby themselves contributing to a cumulative downswing in activity. Second, prices appear to have been more flexible—a fall in activity could therefore cause production to become not merely less profitable, but a cause of actual loss. Both these effects must in turn have greatly reinforced firms' financial restrictiveness. The importance traditionally ascribed to monetary policy can probably be explained historically in these terms.

Now that confidence in full employment is well engrained, and now that, partly as a consequence, prices are much less flexible, serious cumulative disruption of this sort is perhaps not to be feared. But it is still questionable how far a credit squeeze can usefully be pushed. A credit squeeze it would appear, is effective in so far as it worsens the perfection of the capital market. Its effects are essentially random: the firms hit are not necessarily either the least economic, or those engaged in lines of activity which it is desirable for some reason to contract. Moreover, it is only to a limited extent that the banks are willing to act as agents in this process; understandably, they have little enthusiasm for deliberately embarrassing their customers.

It seems, then, that a restriction of credit is far from being a beautiful and delicate market mechanism. In a mild form, credit restrictions may still be useful as a preliminary to the government taking more purposive and long-term action to restrain demand. If more permanent financial restrictions are needed, however, they will have to be of another form. Rather than seeking to utilize the arbitrary effects of market confidence, they must be more in the nature of direct controls in the financial sphere. To be effective, such controls must straddle a flow of funds which is difficult to replace. Hire-purchase controls work because most consumers have few financial assets, and are in a poor position to borrow in other ways. Similarly a quantitative control of capital issues—as opposed to the loose and ineffective control operated till 1959— could, as the Radcliffe Committee implied[1], effectively restrict firms' access to long finance. The occasions when it might be desirable to resort to such measures will be considered later (chapter XVI below).

[1] The *Radcliffe Report* (para. 526) proposed such a capital-issues control only as an emergency measure.

CHAPTER XIII

DEMAND INFLATION AND PRICE INFLATION*

The object of the present chapter is to consider the evidence about the forces that have caused prices to rise since the war, and to come to a view about how far a different policy with regard to the pressure of demand would have slowed down the rise in prices.

It seems necessary first (§1) to review very briefly some of the theoretical discussion of inflation.   It is sometimes argued on general or theoretical grounds that cost pressures cannot operate without excess demand, and cannot accordingly be regarded as an independent force.   It is argued here that in a modern industrialized economy prices are to some degree 'inflexible', and that under such conditions prices can be affected by cost pressures.   The relative influence of cost and demand pressures is then a question of fact which can only be settled by empirical investigation.   It is argued too that under such conditions excess demand may be persistent and is capable of at least rough measurement.   The statistics of unemployment and unfilled vacancies appear in fact to provide a good index of the pressure of demand for labour, and to tell a credible story of post-war fluctuations in the pressure of demand (§2).   The course of prices and costs since the war is summarized in §3.

Previous chapters have shown how policy affected the pressure of demand. To say how this, in turn, affected prices, one has to have a general explanation of price changes, in which demand is treated as one among other causal influences.   During the last decade, there has been a respectable amount of research, more especially in this country, into various aspects of this question: this is summarized in §4.   The proper interpretation of the results is not however entirely straightforward.   Wages seem likely to rise less rapidly with a lower pressure of demand: but the main doubt is whether the latter is likely to slow down the rise in output per head—in which case the effect on the rise in *prices* might be negligible or even perverse.   It is argued here (§5) that the chief effect on output per head is a transitional effect, associated with a transition from a high to a low (or a low to a high) pressure of demand, i.e. that a steady but lower pressure of demand in the post-war years would have slowed down the rise in prices.   How far it is desirable to try to stop prices rising by this means is a different question, reserved for later discussion[1].

---

*The discussion in this chapter is more technical than in most others.   The argument is outlined in the introductory paragraphs and conclusions are stated in §5.
[1]See chapter XVI.2 below.

1. SOME THEORETICAL PRELIMINARIES[1]

There has been much argument as to whether the post-war rise in prices is to be explained as a result of high demand, or alternatively is a result of cost inflation. The view proposed here is an intermediate one. There seems much evidence that the price structure of an advanced industrial country is fairly inflexible, so that prices remain only moderately sensitive to demand influences[2]. It will be argued that prices have been affected also by cost pressures. Cost pressures are of various sorts, some tending to continue a price rise started by other forces, while others (such as pressure by trade unions) are capable of initiating a price rise. Both, it will be argued, have been important.

Later an attempt will be made to estimate the relative importance of these various factors. But some theoretical points have to be discussed first. Some writers argue, on the basis of attempted deductions from the general body of accepted economic theory, that cost pressures cannot be regarded as an independent cause of rising prices. It is therefore necessary to say why such arguments seem mistaken; and to define some of the ideas underlying the present approach.

If prices were highly flexible, this alone would mean that in the short run they were not determined by costs. In analysing the behaviour of the prices of individual goods, economists are accustomed to regarding prices as dependent in the short run on demand, and profits as a residual between costs incurred and prices so determined; and for analysing the nature of economic 'equilibrium' this may be a useful approach. Much thinking about the general problem of inflation regards prices and profits in the same way. Thus Keynes's *Treatise*[3] gave emphasis to profit inflation as the first response of the economy to high demand. Much the same idea is repeated in Keynes's pamphlet on *How to Pay for the War*[4]—which though a small book has since had both practical and theoretical influence. If prices were demand-determined and always such as to clear supplies in particular markets, they could not at the same time be 'fixed', and determined in some relation to costs.

This however is no objection to the theory of cost inflation. The assumption of perfect price flexibility is merely unrealistic[5]. Profits are not in fact highly

---

[1]A fuller discussion of some parts of the present argument was given to an International Economic Association conference on inflation in the summer of 1959: see my [1959] paper, 'Internal Factors Causing and Propagating Inflation' in the IEA conference volume *Inflation* edited by D. Hague [1962].

[2]See for instance the comments in chapter VI on the working of price controls. The rigidity of the price of manufactures is especially striking in comparison with the volatility of commodity prices; and the swings in the terms of trade of countries like the United Kingdom, which sell the one and buy the other, is itself evidence of the relative rigidity of their price structure.

[3]J. M. Keynes [1930], *A Treatise on Money*, especially chapter 10.

[4]J. M. Keynes [1940], *How to Pay for the War*.

[5]The idea of profit inflation implies that while final prices are highly sensitive to demand, wages (the price of labour) are not. Keynes assumed (Keynes [1940], pp. 62–6) that there was a delay in the distribution of profit incomes, and that it was only after some time that wages increased—so that inflation proceeded by stages. If there were not these delays,

variable[1]; and if prices are sensitive to the pressure of demand, this appears to be chiefly because wage costs are sensitive, and because prices are related to costs. One important sort of cost increase has been a rise in the price of imported materials. From the point of view of the world as a whole, such a rise is due to a rise in demand. But it may not coincide with high demand for these materials in each individual country; and despite a lack of demand, it may still result in an increase in prices[2]. If it is possible for a cost increase originating from outside the economy to push up prices, there is no logical reason why an increase in costs due to pressure by trade unions for higher wages should not do so likewise.

Another objection often argued against the theory of cost inflation is that if trade unions raised wages and producers accordingly raised prices in this way, there would be insufficient demand to take up the goods. But what from one aspect are costs are, from another, incomes; so that if costs rise, so will incomes and hence demand. In an open economy part of costs are imports, while exports constitute part of demand; and these will not rise *pari passu*. But home costs and internal demand are much the greater part of the whole. Similarly, it is sometimes argued that such inflation could not continue unless the money supply were 'elastic'[3]. But prices, in fact, can and do rise when the money supply is constant. This will admittedly raise interest rates and thus reduce investment demand a little; but even a doubling of the price level would produce by this route only a small reduction in the pressure of demand[4].

The inflexibility of prices typical of an advanced economy probably stems from the oligopolistic conditions found in many manufacturing industries. In an industry dominated by a few firms, open price competition is unlikely; and prices are likely to be inflexible[5]. Each firm will have a market position consisting of its reputation and relations over the years with its customers. This it will be unwilling to risk by putting up prices when its rivals do not; and since all firms will feel the same way, prices are unlikely to be increased except for reasons which affect all firms and to which all can be counted on to respond. Firms will likewise be reluctant to put down prices without some 'reason'. For this would be liable to force their rivals to follow suit, from which the first

there would be no limit to the pace of inflation. Any realistic theory of demand inflation has therefore to assume considerable delays in response.

[1] See §3 below.

[2] A striking instance is the behaviour of textile prices in 1951–2. The price of wool and cotton rose steeply in 1950–1; the increase in costs was passed on only with some delays, so that retail prices continued to rise despite the onset of the textile recession in 1952.

[3] The argument for instance in W. A. Morton's [1950] paper on 'Trade Unionism, Full Employment and Inflation' (*Amer. econ. R.*, March 1950) rests entirely on the contention that if the money supply is limited, wage increases cannot be passed on to the consumer but must come out of the employers' profits.

[4] See chapter XII.3 above.

[5] For a fuller statement of this line of thought, see J. S. Duesenberry [1958], *Business Cycles and Economic Growth*, chapter 6.

firm like the rest would lose.   A rise in costs which affects all firms will however not only make each firm wish to put up prices, but will make each think others will do likewise, and so remove the inhibition against unilateral price increases. In oligopolistic conditions firms have to have a price 'policy'; and in practice this has to be based on some simple rule of thumb, such as 'full-cost' pricing (i.e. prices sufficient to cover average variable costs plus a margin for over-heads).   This does not mean that costs are the only thing that affects prices; but such a procedure provides a link between costs and prices so that an appreciable general rise in costs is likely to cause prices to rise too[1].

Prices are nonetheless likely to be affected by the pressure of demand.   But it is difficult to say much in general about the extent of the influence.   To take the simplest case first, an entrepreneur seems less likely to resist cost increases if he is aware that, at present prices, he could sell more than his present output, i.e. if he is faced with excess demand.   By definition, he has some distaste for adjusting his prices; so that even in such conditions, he is likely to retain some resistance to cost pressures.   But little can be said about the likely strength of his resistance, nor consequently about the relation between the extent of excess demand and the pace of price inflation.   Much is likely to depend on how accustomed entrepreneurs are to meeting cost pressures and yielding to them.

How much difference does it make if the entrepreneur is not faced with excess demand?   An increase in costs and prices will in this case lead to lower sales, unless it is accompanied by parallel increases in the costs and prices of other firms.   Such developments are not within the control of any particular entre-preneur.   It can be argued that it will seem uncertain to him whether they will happen; and that this uncertainty will deter him from increasing his prices and from accepting any cost increases he can avoid.

Nevertheless this deterrent must be greatly reduced by three circumstances. First, an entrepreneur's calculations are chiefly concerned with his position *vis-à-vis* his competitors in the same industry.   His resistance to a cost increase which affects all firms in an industry may thus be very small.   Second, many cost increases will seem outside his control altogether; he has no choice but to

---

[1]This does not imply support for the 'full-cost' or 'normal-cost' theories of pricing in the sense in which they are usually discussed.   In the hands of Miss Brunner, the normal cost theory becomes no more than the contention (i) that prices are 'administered'; (ii) that prices are fixed after taking *some account* of costs; but (iii) that the margin above costs is variable.   Thus to say that a businessman 'uses his own costs as a guide in determining prices . . . is not to say that he will not revise this downwards immediately if he discovers that other firms are quoting below it' (Elizabeth Brunner [1952], 'Competition and the Theory of the Firm', *Econ. int.*, August and November 1952).

This is probably valid as a description of procedure.   It is probably also legitimate to deduce from it something about firms' reactions to general, external changes in costs. But it is probably not legitimate to deduce from it anything about inter-firm competition or profit maximization.   The main importance of the 'full-cost' theory may thus be in its macro-economic, not its micro-economic application.   Evidence of the prevalence of full-cost pricing obtained through direct inquiry may chiefly reflect not the way firms compete but the broader question of their reaction to general changes in costs.

'accept' increases in the cost of imports, or of other purchased input. Third, experience of a period of rising prices, and of being able to 'pass on' cost increases, will make the latter too normal to require deliberation. In this country entrepreneurs have had thirty years' experience of passing on cost increases.

All that one can say in general is perhaps, then, that whatever the pace of inflation before, *excess* demand is likely to accelerate it. The reason why one cannot say more than this is that the pace of inflation depends essentially on attitudes and habits, which differ from country to country, and may well change over time. In some countries the convention against taking abnormal profits when demand is high is stronger than in others. The pace of a wage-price spiral depends on the frequency of wage adjustments, and on the delays between changes in prices and wages on the one hand, and changes in costs and prices on the other hand. All these may change—and are likely to be changed by the process of inflation. Experience of being able to 'pass on' cost increases reduces the resistance to cost pressures; and reduces the lag between cost and price increases, and between price and cost increases[1]. Similarly, 'cost plus' pricing is a convention, which may break down when prices rise rapidly[2], and leaves prices more sensitive to demand than before.

It is again often argued that there is some 'equilibrium' level of demand above which prices will rise, and below which prices will fall[3]. But it seems that theoretical reasoning is able to produce little in the way of positive conclusions about inflation: in particular, there is nothing in economic theory which tells us how quickly prices are likely to rise in response to a given degree of demand pressure. Consequently it is impossible to say how far the absence of pressure from the side of demand will offset pressures coming from the side of costs—or even whether, if demand were reduced low enough, there is some point at which a price rise would be halted. It may be that in extreme depression, the rigidity of prices would break down, and entrepreneurs would be ready to countenance price cuts. But it seems equally likely that the inflexibility of prices would hold, and that the system would remain open to cost pressures[4]. Prices and

---

[1]It is reported that in Sweden the trade unions now take account of the price increases their own wage claims are likely to provoke.

[2]During the 'Korean' inflation, prices rose so rapidly that it was difficult to apply 'cost plus' principles in operating price controls: see chapter VI.6 above (p. 166n).

[3]Keynes argued that as soon as full employment is reached, prices will rise; but he did not argue that below that point they would fall (Keynes [1936], p. 295). Many later writers have sought to qualify Keynes's conclusions by making this assumption. It was the basis for Pigou's [1945] *Lapses from Full Employment*, and an essential element in later discussion in what Patinkin called the 'Pigou' (or, later, the 'real balance') effect (see D. Patinkin [1948], 'Price Flexibility and Full Employment', *Amer. econ. R.*, Sept. 1948 and [1956] *Money. Interest and Prices*, p. 21).

[4]Compare A. J. Brown [1955], *The Great Inflation, 1939–1951*, p. 89: 'there is, however, no obvious reason why the spiral should not work in a situation in which real output is expansible in response to increments in spending power; the existence of full employment is not an essential condition of the spiral's operation'.

wages in the United Kingdom were rising in the late 'thirties, even though there was then ten to fifteen per cent unemployment. Beyond a point, a reduction in the pressure of demand is probably therefore ineffective as a way to stop prices rising.

In the present discussion much use is made of the concept of 'excess demand', which must now be considered more carefully. There has been dispute as to whether the degree of excess demand can be considered a precise magnitude[1]. The doubt is best explained by taking an extreme case. As prices and money incomes rise, taxes and saving are likely to increase disproportionately, so reducing the pressure of demand. If prices were completely flexible, the rise in prices would proceed very rapidly to the point where excess demand was eliminated, so that it would be difficult to get a true measure of the motive force which was propelling prices upward. But—as already argued, and as will be further evidenced in later sections—prices are not flexible to this degree; and excess demand in fact seems capable of being a persistent condition, often lasting years. It seems possible, then, to treat it as a magnitude capable of at least rough measurement.

This being granted, it is still necessary to consider how the concept may be applied in an economy where the price level is being driven up by cost pressures, and where home supplies may be supplemented by imports. The idea of 'excess demand' involves a comparison: the value of the goods and services which people would buy if they were available is to be compared with the goods and services which are available[2]. But even in a closed economy, the concept of 'available supplies' is not clear-cut; for even at very high levels of demand, output may always be capable of being increased if demand were higher still. But beyond a point output will begin to rise more slowly in response to an increase in demand (figure 13.1, curve OO). This point must be reached where excess demands start to build up appreciably in some lines and exceed 'excess supplies' in other lines, i.e. where there is *net* excess demand.

Beyond this point it is also likely that imports will rise more rapidly (curve II) so that the import content of final sales increases. But there are impediments to importing, so that beyond a point the sum of output and imports (the expenditure curve EE) will start to diverge appreciably from the demand curve (DD): if this were not so it would be impossible to have excess demand in one country

---

[1]See R. Turvey [1949], 'A Further Note on the Inflationary Gap', *Ekon. Ts.*, June 1949; B. Hansen [1951], pp. 78–82; and E. Lundberg [1953], *Business Cycles and Economic Policy*, pp. 202–9.

[2]A definition of excess demand in terms of available supplies is called by Bent Hansen the 'inflationary gap' formulation—which he traces to Keynes's *How to Pay for the War*. He contrasts this with a definition in terms of the inconsistency between the *expectations* of buyers and the *plans* of sellers, which is in the tradition of Swedish '*ex ante*' theory. The latter appears to me far less useful for analysing conditions of fairly continuous excess demand; for both sides may come to know what is in fact likely to be available, and buyers not to *expect* to get more even though they would like it. See Bent Hansen [1951], *A Study in the Theory of Inflation*, chapter III.

Fig. 13.1.   Available supplies and excess demand

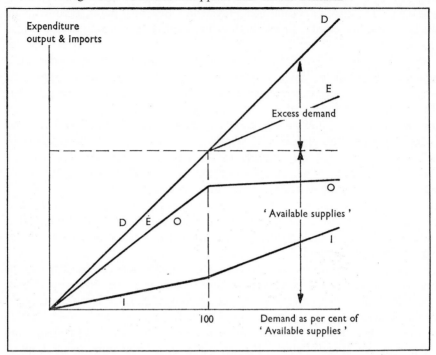

so long as supplies were available anywhere in the world. 'Available supplies' may then be defined as the supplies available at the point of zero net excess demand.

Excess demand may perhaps most conveniently be defined as the excess of demand over 'available supplies' so defined: for this is the amount by which demand would have to be reduced in order to eliminate excess demand[1]. The extent of excess demand is best measured in proportionate or percentage terms, e.g. as a percentage of available supplies. Since a comparison with two aggregates is involved, this measure of excess demand will not be greatly affected by a moderate rise in prices. Thus a price rise of ten per cent would raise the money value of total available supplies by this amount, and the money value of total demand by almost as much[2], so that the relation between them will be little affected. It is convenient to use as synonyms for 'excess demand' phrases such as 'a high pressure of demand' or, less precisely, 'high demand'.

---

[1] This will generally exceed the amount of demand left unsatisfied (i.e. the gap between the DD and EE curves). For above the zero point, supplies are being swollen by output and imports only available when demand is excessive: see figure 13.1.

As already conceded, the inflation may slightly increase the share of taxes and saving; but for a small rise in prices, this is a second order point.

On these definitions, a constant 'pressure of demand' is consistent with a rising trend in the value of national output and expenditure.   This will be the case if the price level is being forced up by cost pressures.   Equally important, when the volume of available supplies is being expanded by rising productivity, demand will have to rise too if the relation between them (i.e. the pressure of demand) is to remain unchanged.

When the government acts to affect the level of demand, it is convenient to define its actions in terms of their effect on the pressure of demand.   A policy which makes no change in the pressure of demand may be regarded as a neutral policy.   Such a policy is consistent with allowing a steady increase in the value of national income in the face of cost pressures—and indeed requires that this should take place.   Those who believe that demand is the sole source of inflation can argue that to allow such an increase is itself inflationary: for they dispute the thesis that cost pressures are enough to force up prices.   But if cost pressures are powerful, an attempt to prevent national expenditure increasing would result, not in stable prices, but in a falling volume of output.   In practice this could only be done, if at all, by restrictive measures of extreme severity— measures which, since they would reduce the pressure of demand, seem best described as deflationary.

2. THE PRESSURE OF DEMAND, 1946–60[1]

The argument of §1 has sought to show that the measurement of excess demand is theoretically valid.   In practice, such indications as we have of the pressure of demand for final products are imprecise and impressionistic.   But there happen to be two statistical series—the statistics of unemployment and of unfilled vacancies—which seem to provide a fair measure of the pressure of demand for labour.   Excess demand for labour may be defined as the amount of labour employers would hire *less* the amount willing to be hired if employment were available.   Since the demand for labour is a derived demand, this may reflect, to some extent, the pressure of final demand.

Neither statistic is a perfect index of labour demand.   The statistics of unfilled vacancies record the number of vacancies reported to the employment exchanges which remain unfilled at the end of each month: it purports therefore to be a direct measure of unsatisfied demand.   There are however prima facie reasons for distrusting statistics of this sort.   For they neither record actual transactions, nor register decisions, but rather represent a queue.   The size of the queue may be either more or less than the real unsatisfied demand: people may either duplicate orders, i.e. join several queues; or they may give up trying

---

[1]This section is a summary of material first given in a paper by myself and Mr Dicks-Mireaux [1958], 'The Excess Demand for Labour', *Oxford econ. Pap.*, February 1958.   In one important respect, the presentation has been revised.

Y

and not join a queue at all. Thus the vacancy statistics might 'overstate' or 'understate' the true position.

The unemployment figures, by contrast, are 'hard' statistics: a person can register only once as unemployed, and he has financial reason for doing so. Unemployment fluctuates inversely with the pressure of demand, so that the unemployment series provide an indirect indication of the pressure. However, it would appear that when demand is low, many people (in particular, many women) do not register as unemployed, so that statistics based on registrations (as the British figures are) understate the position that would be revealed by house-to-house surveys (as are the figures in the United States of America)[1]. An indication of the extent of this understatement is provided by the figures of 'participation rates' (figure 13.2.) The number of men and women of working age who are in employment or are registered as seeking work has tended to increase in recent years. But if this trend is allowed for, it will be seen that the proportion fell when demand was low and unemployment high, and rose when demand was high. This movement out of the statistical labour force when demand is low may be regarded as a form of 'concealed unemployment'; and the figures suggest that the growth of such concealed unemployment at such times is of roughly equal magnitude to the growth of registered unemployment. This relationship is probably not constant but may well vary with the extent and phase of economic fluctuations; but the recent figures suggest that the unemployment statistics may have understated *fluctuations* in 'true' unemployment by a factor of about two[2].

The vacancy figures bear a fairly systematic relation to the unemployment figures; and the more closely their behaviour is examined, the clearer it seems that up to a point, taken together, they provide a rather reliable indication of the pressure of demand for labour. There is a striking inverse parallelism between the seasonal swings of the two series (figure 13.3, part A). It is equally striking that when seasonal movements are removed, changes in demand still appear to be equally reflected in both series. In part B of figure 13.3 unemployment has been inverted, so that a rise in demand is associated with a rise in both series as charted: though there has been a slow divergence between them, a striking parallelism remains. These observations give one a certain confidence in the vacancy statistics, which more detailed analysis in general confirms[3].

---

[1]See H. A. Turner [1959], 'Employment Fluctuations, Labour Supply and Bargaining Power', *Manchester Sch.*, May 1959; and E. Kalachek and R. Westebbe [1961], 'Rates of Unemployment in Great Britain and the United States, 1950–1960', *R. Econ. Statist.*, November 1961.

[2]The conclusion is intentionally phrased in terms of *changes* in unemployment, and says nothing about the relation between the level of 'true' unemployment and the level of registered unemployment. This latter relation must clearly vary.

[3]See Dow and Dicks-Mireaux [1958], appendix (3), which analyses the figures for separate industry groups, and also the seasonalities of the two sets of statistics.

Controls over engagement were in force (see figure 13.3B) for much of the period. With

Fig. 13.2.   Unemployment and concealed unemployment

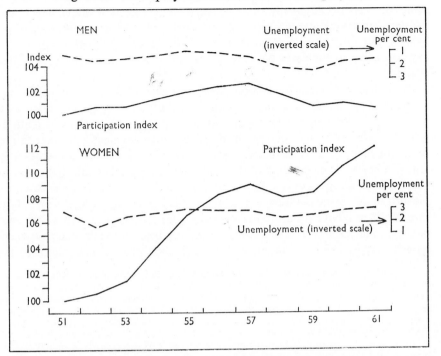

The participation index measures the proportion of the population of working age who are in work or registered as unemployed.   In order to eliminate the effect of changes in the age composition of the population, participation rates were calculated for separate age groups and applied to the 1951 age structure.   The index shows the percentage effect on the working population of changes in participation rates: changes in unemployment are shown on a comparable scale.   The participation index is based on figures for the working population for May each year.   Unemployment figures are annual averages.

Taken together the statistics of unemployment and of unfilled vacancies seem then to provide a good indicator of changes in the excess demand for labour, though not a direct measure of its magnitude.   The long-period 'divergence' between the two series may be taken as showing that one or other or each was being affected not only by the demand for labour but for something else as well.   The most probable reason is that, over the post-war period, the pattern of labour supply has become better adapted to the pattern of demand. The fact that unfilled vacancies for some sorts of labour coexist with the unemployment of other sorts implies that there is some 'maladjustment', i.e.

some exceptions, employment had then to be obtained through the employment exchanges, But this does not appear to have affected the number of unfilled vacancies which got reported to the exchanges.

that the kinds of labour demanded differ from those on offer[1].   If 'maladjustment' of this sort gradually diminished, *both* registered unemployment and registered unfilled vacancies will have been reduced (v lowered and u raised on figure 13.3B, where unemployment is inverted).   Most of this shift appears to have occurred in the early post-war years and is not much in evidence after 1949[2].

The index of demand for labour shown in figure 13.3C is derived from the statistics of unemployment and of vacancies, both series being expressed as a percentage of the labour force; and is an attempt to combine the best features of each.   However high the level of demand, unemployment will never fall to zero.   Beyond a point, therefore, unemployment must become a decreasingly sensitive index of the pressure of demand; and beyond this point it is better to rely on the evidence provided by the vacancy statistics.   The *index* is based on the idea that at some point net excess demand is zero, i.e. the excess demand for some types of labour equals the excess supply for other types.   Above the zero point, the index is based on the vacancy statistics; below it, on the unemployment series[3].   Apart from the question of scale (to be discussed in a moment) the

[1]The causes are very various.   Most of the unemployed have been unskilled, while most of the vacancies have been for skilled workers; and vacancies for young people have been many times the number of young people unemployed.   Other causes (perhaps partially overlapping those above) are geographical maldistribution; seasonal variation in demand; and the effect of turnover of labour between firms (in manufacturing, 30–40 per cent a year).

[2]Another explanation of the long-term 'divergence' between the two series would be that as time went on employers increasingly understated (or decreasingly overstated) their true demand for labour.   Reasons for rejecting this hypothesis are given in appendix (3) of the 1958 study.

[3]The derivation of the index may be explained more fully as follows, all magnitudes being expressed as percentages of the labour force.

Let v = recorded unfilled vacancies
          s = the proportion of true vacancies that is recorded
hence v/s = true vacancies
          u = recorded unemployment
          t = the proportion of true unemployment that is recorded
hence u/t = true unemployment
          m = maladjustment, which may be defined as the amount of unemployment (u/t) at that pressure of demand where $u/t = v/s$
          d = net excess demand for labour, being positive for excess and negative for deficient demand.

Assuming that m, s and t are constant, u will decrease and v increase as the pressure of demand increases.   Because u is a decreasingly sensitive index of demand, a plot of u and v will lie on a curve convex to the origin.   Assuming further that this curve can be approximated by a rectangular hyperbola, $\sqrt{uv/ts}$ will be a constant, and may be taken to measure m.

The index measures excess demand (d) as true vacancies *less* maladjustment ($v/s - m = v/s - \sqrt{uv/ts}$) when excess demand is positive ($u/t < v/s$); and as maladjustment *less* true unemployment ($\sqrt{uv/ts} - u/t$) when excess demand is negative ($u/t > v/s$).   For reasons briefly indicated in the text it is further assumed that $s = 0\cdot5$; and that at or below the point of zero excess demand, $t = 0\cdot5$ also.

The principles of construction were more fully set out in Dow and Dicks-Mireaux [1958], appendix (1)—where, however, no account was taken of the possibility that recorded unemployment might understate the position.

index is little different from what would be obtained by subtracting percentage unemployment from percentage vacancies, but it gives a more responsive index with a wider amplitude of variation than would be got from this simpler procedure.

The index is shown on the diagram along with the unemployment and vacancy statistics from which it is derived. In constructing the index, it seemed best to assume (for reasons already stated) that the unemployment statistics showed only half the changes in 'true' unemployment and that, since the inverse fluctuations in registered unemployment and unfilled vacancies in response to changes in demand were generally of similar size, the vacancy statistics also understated 'true' vacancies by a factor of two. For these reasons the index of excess demand is given an amplitude of variation twice that of its component series. (Compare the scales on parts B and C of figure 13.3)[1]. The scale of the index—which for many purposes is not of first importance—is probably the least accurate thing about it.

A certain interest attaches nevertheless to the quantitative extent of excess demand. The index (which is on a quarterly basis) suggests that excess demand for labour was never more than 3 per cent; and that when there was a deficient demand for labour, the deficiency was never as much as two per cent. The question thus arises whether this somewhat narrow range can be regarded as plausible. General impressions might lead one to suppose that the pressure of demand had varied much more than this. But such impressions are based chiefly on what one knows about the demand for final products; and there are reasons to think that this has fluctuated more widely than the demand for labour[2]. There are various factors that might produce this result. In the early years, direct controls were extensive, and these probably reduced the effective pressure of demand; and in later years, when controls had been removed, the sluggishness of response to excess demand may almost as effectively have inhibited the transmission of demand down to the labour market[3]. In many cases labour may not have been the shortest factor: the bottleneck has often been plant capacity; or in earlier years, materials; or skilled labour so that for other kinds of labour (relative wages being fairly rigid) there may have been no great pressure. There has, too, been 'collusion' between firms to avoid 'spoiling' the labour market by bidding up wages or by 'poaching' labour.

Thus it seems likely that in an economy whose price structure does not 'explode' when confronted with excess demand, the fluctuations in demand will not be fully transmitted to the labour market. It was suggested earlier[4] that

[1]This interpretation differs from that of the original 1958 study, where the possibility of 'understatement' by the unemployment statistics was not allowed for. Thus the index as originally presented (and as continued in the statistical series in the *Nat. Inst. econ. R.*) had half the above range of variation.

[2]See figure 4.1, chapter IV above.

[3]Compare the argument in chapter VI.6.

[4]Chapter VI.7.

Fig. 13.3.   Indices of pressure of demand for labour
Percentage of total employees

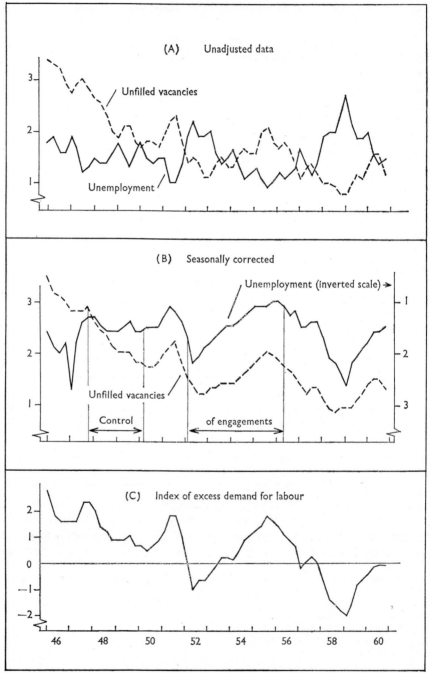

For notes to figure see foot of next page.

direct controls were mutually reinforcing as barriers to demand, each set of restrictions supporting and being supported by those elsewhere. The same is probably true of market inflexibilities: the partial insulation of the labour market must have reinforced the inflexibility of the price structure, and makes more intelligible the latter's partial insensitivity to demand influences.

This insulation and this insensitivity were not however complete. The demand for labour, though for the most part a derived demand, must vary with the demand for final products; and the index of labour demand accords with common impression about the successive phases through which the economy has passed since the war. In particular it shows the high demand of the immediate post-war years, gradually ebbing; the new peak caused by defence spending and the 'Korean' boom in 1951; the 1952 recession in textiles and other consumer industries; the build-up to the 1955 boom; the gradual ebbing of demand—perhaps in response to government contractionary policies—in the years 1955–7; and a moderate increase in the pressure of demand in 1960, which was to continue into 1961.

3. PRICE AND COST CHANGES, 1946–60

Before trying to explain why prices rose, it is best to outline the main trends. Though the pace of price inflation has varied considerably, prices and wages have risen in each of the 25 years since 1935[1]. The course of prices and costs since 1946 is shown in figure 13.4. The most general measure of the price level is an index of the price of all goods and services entering into final expenditure[2]. Over the fourteen years 1946–60 final prices rose 77 per cent, or $4\frac{1}{2}$ per cent (compound) a year. Most of the rise occurred in three short bursts: first, in 1946–8; an even larger burst in 1950–2; and a smaller burst in 1954–7. In one or more years in each of these periods the pressure of demand was parti-

---

[1] *London Cambridge econ. B.*, statistical appendix.

[2] The index used is an 'average value' series obtained by dividing the value of final expenditure at current prices by its estimated value at 1954 prices (see notes to table 13.1). Final expenditure consists as to half of goods and services bought by consumers; and for the rest, of public authorities' expenditure, gross fixed investment and investment in stocks, and exports. Since estimates of gross domestic product at constant prices obtained by revaluing national expenditure differ somewhat from measures of the volume of output, somewhat different price estimates would be obtained by using the latter. But over a period of years the difference is slight. Analysis of price changes on these lines was set out in the article by myself [1956], 'Analysis of the Generation of Price Inflation', *Oxford econ. Pap.*, October 1956.

Notes to fig. 13.3

The method of calculation of the *index of excess demand for labour* is as explained in the text. The index is as given in Dow and Dicks-Mireaux [1958], *Oxford econ. Pap.* and for later years in *Nat. Inst. econ. R.*, statistical appendix, except that (for reasons given in the text) the scale of the index has been doubled. Thus what was previously shown as an excess demand of 1 per cent would now be shown as 2 per cent. The unemployment figures for 1947 have been roughly adjusted to eliminate the effect of the fuel crisis in the first quarter.

Fig. 13.4.   Changes in costs and prices, 1946–60
1954 final prices = 100

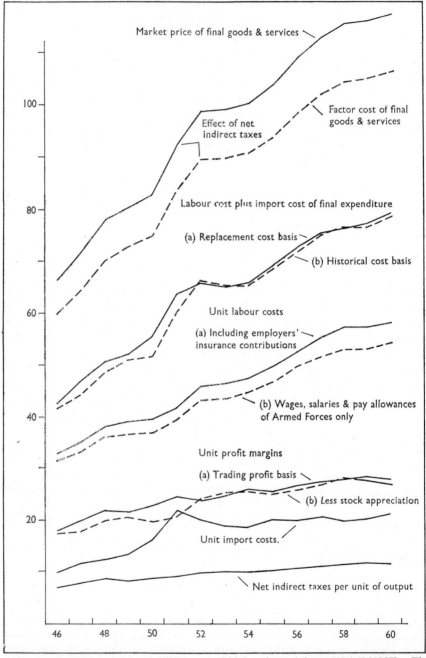

Years 1950–60 from *NI & E* [1961]: years 1946–9 estimated from *NI & E* [1957].   The general method of calculation is explained in table 13.1.   In each case the appropriate current value series is divided by the value at 1954 prices of total final expenditure so giving price and 'unit cost' estimates.   Labour costs *plus* import costs *less* stock appreciation gives 'historical' unit costs.

cularly high (figure 13.3). Price inflation has been slower in the second part of the period: in the six years 1946–52 prices rose on average $6\frac{3}{4}$ per cent (compound) a year: in the eight years 1952–60, by only $3\frac{1}{4}$ per cent a year.

Labour costs constitute almost half, and profits and other home factor costs constitute another quarter, of the value of final expenditure (table 13.1). The remainder is accounted for by the cost of imports and by net indirect taxation. A simple arithmetical calculation shows the contribution of these elements to the change in prices. Division of the total by the *volume* of final expenditure gives the index of final prices; and division of each of the components by the same volume total gives (table 13.1, bottom half) the contribution of each type of cost to the price index. The results are shown graphically on figure 13.4.

During the early years, the rise in import costs contributed appreciably to the rise in prices. In the period 1946–52, import costs account directly for 10 of the 32 percentage points rise in the price index (table 13.1). There were probably also indirect effects (see further §4 below); for the rapid rise in import costs, particularly in 1950–1, caused a steep rise in retail prices, and this probably accounts in part for the large wage increases; and in a sense (given constant profit margins) for some also of the rise in the value of profits. The rise in import prices is not *enough* to explain the rise in prices up to 1952, but it could explain why prices rose more rapidly in these years than later. In the years since 1952 import costs have changed much less, and in 1960 were little higher than in 1952. Thus the price rise since 1952 has by and large to be ascribed to purely internal factors.

Table 13.2 shows changes in money wages and salaries and output per man, and thus of changes in 'labour costs per unit of output'. During the fourteen years 1946–60, the average wage/salary rose 138 per cent or nearly $6\frac{1}{2}$ per cent a year (compound), thus exceeding the rise in prices by some $2\frac{1}{4}$ per cent a year. This increase in real wages and salaries is thus roughly in line with the average increase in output per head of about $2\frac{1}{4}$ per cent a year—which can hardly be entirely accidental (see further §4). The rise in wages and salaries went in bursts, the most rapid bursts occurring—much as with prices—in 1946–8, 1950–2 and 1954–6. The central year in each case was a year when the pressure of demand was at a peak.

Wage earnings increased rather more rapidly than nationally agreed wage rates. Thus between 1948 and 1959 (figure 13.5) wage earnings increased $6\frac{1}{4}$ per cent (compound) a year, and wage rates $5\frac{1}{4}$ per cent. The divergence is even more striking in absolute terms. Thus average weekly earnings in manufacturing rose by 109 shillings between these dates: of this the rise in wage rates accounted for 67 shillings; overtime for 10 or 11 shillings; and 'supplementary payments' for 32 shillings. These 'supplementary payments', which were apparently negligible before the war, now account for no less than a quarter of standard weekly

Table 13.1.   *The cost components of final prices, summary for 1946–60*

	1946	1952	1954	1960	*1946–52*	*1952–60*
Current value series (£ m.)						
Imports of goods and services	1,668	3,960	3,967	5,540		
Labour incomes[a]	5,732	9,097	10,253	15,111		
Trading profits and other incomes[b]	3,137	4,598	5,497	7,153		
less stock appreciation	−125	50	−75	−127		
Net indirect taxes[c]	1,164	1,871	2,059	2,916		
Total final expenditure	11,576	19,576	21,701	30,593		
Volume series (£m. 1954 prices)						
Total final expenditure	17,427	19,891	21,701	26,097		
Average value series (1954 = 100)					Points	change
Contribution of						
Imports	9·6	19·9	18·3	21·2	*+10·3*	*+1·3*
Labour incomes[a]	32·9	45·7	47·3	57·9	*+12·8*	*+12·2*
Trading profits, etc.[b]	18·0	23·1	25·3	27·4	*+5·1*	*+4·3*
less stock appreciation	−0·7	0·3	−0·4	−0·5	*+1·0*	*−0·8*
Net indirect taxes[c]	6·6	9·4	9·5	11·2	*+2·8*	*+1·8*
Price of final expenditure	66·4	98·4	100·0	117·2	*+32·0*	*+18·8*

From *NI & E* [1957] and [1961].   For explanations of method see text and Dow [1956], *Oxford econ. Pap.*

[a]Income from employment, i.e. wages, salaries, pay of Armed Forces and employers' insurance contributions.

[b]Gross trading profits of companies, public corporations and other public enterprises; incomes from self-employment; and rent.

[c]Indirect taxes *less* subsidies.

earnings[1].   There was no year in which this wage-drift component of earnings in manufacturing showed an absolute fall.   This suggests that 'supplementary payments', once granted, are not easily compressible, i.e. that increases in nationally agreed rates will lead to increases in actual earnings.   This is an important question, open to dispute (see further §4 below), which greatly affects one's view of the trade unions' role in the inflationary process, and of the way wages react to price changes.

The rise in labour costs has been partially offset by the rise in output per head since the war.   But the increase in output per head has been erratic.   Most large

[1]These estimates are from a paper by L. A. Dicks-Mireaux and P. G. Elkan, 'The Extent of Supplementary Payments', included in L. A. Dicks-Mireaux [to be published], *Studies in Cost and Price Behaviour.*   Outside manufacturing, 'supplementary payments' are less important, so that for all industries they accounted for a fifth of standard weekly earnings in 1959.

Table 13.2. *Changes in labour costs*

Annual percentage changes

	Average wages and salaries per employee	Output (GDP) per man	Labour cost per unit of output	Percentage excess demand for labour[a]
1946/7	8·9	2·3	6·4	1·8
1947/8	9·4	5·6	3·6	1·7
1948/9	6·1	4·3	1·7	0·9
1949/50	3·9	3·0	0·9	0·6
1950/1	9·7	0·8	8·8	1·3
1951/2	7·9	−0·8	8·8	−0·2
1952/3	4·4	3·1	1·3	−0·2
1953/4	4·9	2·6	2·2	0·4
1954/5	8·0	2·8	5·1	1·3
1955/6	8·3	0·0	8·3	1·2
1956/7	5·6	1·7	3·8	0·1
1957/8	3·9	1·2	2·7	−0·9
1958/9	2·9	3·6	−0·7	−1·6
1959/60	6·0	3·4	2·5	−0·3
Average for period	6·4	2·3	4·0	0·4

From Dicks-Mireaux [1961], *Oxford econ. Pap.*, and Dow and Dicks-Mireaux [1958], *Oxford econ. Pap.*; and for later years *Nat. Inst. econ. R.*

[a]Excess demand is taken as twice the value originally estimated in Dow and Dicks-Mireaux [1958], 'Excess Demand for Labour' for reasons set out in text (§2).   The average shown is that presumed to have affected the wage/salary change: for 1946/7 it is the average of 1946 fourth quarter and 1947 first three quarters; and so on for other years.

increases came when the pressure of demand rose *after a period of low demand* (1952–5, and to a less marked extent, 1959–60); for output then increased rapidly, and productivity generally varies with output. (Some spurts, e.g. in 1947–9, probably originated on the supply side.) Similarly years of low productivity increase were years when the pressure of demand fell after a period of high demand (1951–2 and, to a less marked degree, 1957–8).

Since the average wage/salary rose by almost $6\frac{1}{2}$ per cent a year, and output per man increased on average by about $2\frac{1}{4}$ per cent a year, 'labour cost per unit of output' rose four per cent a year on average. Since both components were erratic, the movement of unit labour costs was even more so: in some years they rose nine per cent or so, in one year they fell. But years when money wages and salaries rose most rapidly were generally years when unit labour costs (as here calculated) also rose more than average. (As will be argued more fully later, there is some reason to believe that entrepreneurs discount some of the temporary fluctuations in productivity in determining prices, so that a moving average of unit labour costs may provide a better indication of the pressure of labour costs on prices: see further §4).

Table 13.3.   *Aggregate profit margins (percentages of value of final output)*

	Corporate profits[a]		Non-corporate profits[b]		Total profits	
	Trading profits basis	*Profits less stock appreciation*	Trading profits basis	*Profits less stock appreciation*	Trading profits basis	*Profits less stock appreciation*
1946	12·8	*12·3*	9·8	*9·7*	22·6	*22·0*
1947	13·2	*11·2*	9·6	*9·4*	22·8	*20·6*
1948	13·5	*12·4*	9·3	*9·1*	22·8	*21·5*
1949	13·3	*12·4*	9·2	*9·1*	22·5	*21·5*
1950	13·9	*11·6*	8·4	*8·4*	22·3	*20·0*
1951	14·1	*11·2*	7·5	*7·2*	21·6	*18·4*
1952	12·6	*12·7*	7·7	*7·7*	20·3	*20·4*
1953	12·8	*13·0*	7·6	*7·5*	20·4	*20·5*
1954	13·5	*13·2*	7·3	*7·3*	20·8	*20·5*
1955	13·6	*13·1*	7·1	*7·0*	20·7	*20·1*
1956	13·0	*12·6*	6·8	*6·7*	19·8	*19·3*
1957	12·9	*12·6*	6·7	*6·6*	19·6	*19·2*
1958	12·8	*12·5*	6·6	*6·5*	19·4	*19·0*
1959	13·1	*12·9*	6·6	*6·7*	19·7	*19·6*
1960	13·4	*13·2*	6·5	*6·5*	19·9	*19·7*

From *NI & E* [1957] and [1961].

[a]Gross trading profits of companies *plus* gross trading surpluses of public corporations as a percentage of the value of final output.

[b]Income gross of depreciation of professional persons, farmers and other sole traders and partnerships as a percentage of the value of final output.

It also appears to be the case that cost increases are passed on in prices after some delay. Thus when costs are rising, the cost of materials embodied in goods currently being sold (the 'historical' cost) is less than the current cost (or 'replacement' cost) of materials. Figure 13.4 shows the total of import *plus* labour costs on both a historical and replacement cost basis[1]: the diagram suggests that prices follow the former rather more closely than the latter. This implies that profits tend to be stable, and to show rather more stability if measured as a margin above historical costs than as a margin above replacement costs. The first is roughly measured by the accountants' concept of 'trading profits': the latter by the national-income statistician's concept of profits adjusted for stock appreciation[2]. Table 13.3 shows that the share of the value of output taken by profits has been fairly stable, but has declined slightly since 1946. Profits have often been a little higher in years of high demand:

[1]Current costs *less* stock appreciation provides a fair measure of 'historical' costs: see Dow [1956], pp. 261–3.

[2]See Dow [1956], pp. 261–3.

Fig. 13.5.   Wage rates, wage earnings and wage drift in manufacturing industry, 1938, 1948–59

Shillings

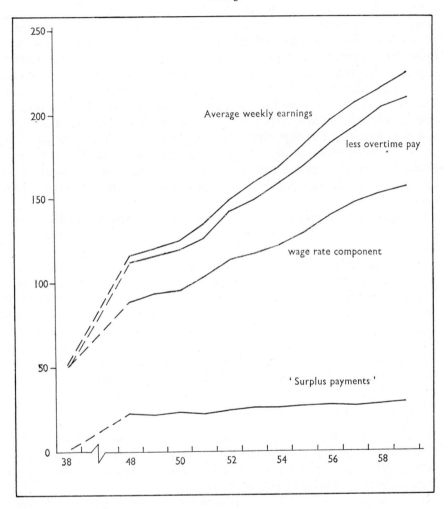

From Dicks-Mireaux and Elkan, *op. cit.*   The contribution of wage rates to average weekly wage earnings in manufacturing is estimated by comparing Ministry of Labour estimates of the effect of changes in wage rates on the wage bill with changes in the wage-rate index.   Subtraction from average weekly earnings, adjusted for overtime, gives a rough estimate of 'surplus payments'.   The idea of estimating the importance of wage drift in this way was first suggested by Sir Donald MacDougall.

but some of the fluctuation in profits can be regarded as due to the tendency (noted above) not fully to adjust prices to short-term fluctuations in output per head.

From this inspection of price developments since the war, there emerges a general picture of the main inflationary mechanisms at work. First, since profits (apart from transitional fluctuations) appear fairly stable, prices appear to be linked, probably with a lag, to costs. Costs principally comprise import costs, which at times have risen steeply; and labour costs. Second, wages (and probably salaries also) appear to be linked, probably again with a lag, to prices. These two relations between them mean that if there is a rise in prices for any cause, it will be followed by a (possibly rapidly diminishing) series of further price and wage increases: one important initiating cause (at least in the first post-war years) was rising import prices. Third, wages appear to be sensitive to demand pressures. Since prices are linked to costs, and wage costs are sensitive to demand, the whole wage-price complex appears to be open to influences from the side of demand.

To suggest that inflationary developments are to be explained in these terms is not novel: a similar picture was proposed by Professor Brown in 1955[1]. But this is still too imprecise. Even if the general picture of the system is right, its behaviour depends crucially on the 'magnitude' of the various responses, e.g. *how much* wages respond to price changes or to the pressure of demand. It is only in recent years that research has sought to provide quantitative answers of this sort. But detailed statistical work must start with a hypothesis about which events are causes and which effects. The general picture that has emerged so far, however plausible, is no more than a hypothesis in this sense. It remains to be seen just how far the facts can be explained in these terms, and, in so doing, to indicate the size of the response of prices to various influences.

4. ESTIMATES OF THE DETERMINANTS OF PRICE CHANGES

The survey in §3 suggested various hypotheses to account for post-war price developments, and in particular that prices were partly determined by costs, and costs partly determined by prices, and both also influenced by other factors. Thus it seems reasonable to suppose that:

(a) changes in wages and salaries are determined partly by previous price changes, partly by changes in output per man, and partly by the pressure of demand for labour; and that

(b) changes in prices are determined partly by past changes in wages and salaries, partly by changes in import costs, and partly by changes in output per man.

---

[1]A. J. Brown [1955], *The Great Inflation, 1939–1951*, especially p. 289.

At first sight it might seem an impossible task to unravel these interconnections; but in fact, with care, it seems possible to make estimates of the strength of the various separate causal links. This is partly because the various reactions do not occur simultaneously, but with some delay, e.g. the reaction of both wages to price changes and prices to wage changes is delayed, so that the 'feedback' on wages of a wage change is not instantaneous. As it happens, too, changes in the pressure of demand, import costs and output per man, have tended not to occur at the same time; and this absence of correlation between the 'explanatory' factors also helps estimation of their separate effects[1].

In the past decade there have been a number of statistical studies which have attempted to unravel these interrelationships by means of correlation analysis. Most work has been done on the determinants of wage increases, but some studies have attempted to explain both wage and price changes as part of one interconnected causal system. In all cases the method is essentially the same: if for instance it is wage changes that are being analysed, the analysis tests how far wage changes larger or smaller *than average* are associated with previous price changes larger or smaller *than average*, or with a demand for labour higher or lower *than average*.

The results of these studies are certainly illuminating; but they may tell only half the story. In the first place, analysis on these lines cannot explain why wages should rise at the average rate in the absence of disturbing factors: in each case there is a 'constant' term in the equations as fitted, which merely states without explaining that (other things being 'neutral') there is a constant tendency for wages to rise. Secondly, analysis of this sort can test only fairly quick reactions. Thus it is possible to test the reaction of wages in one year to price changes in, say, the current and the previous years; but with the rather small number of years available for analysis, it is hardly possible to test whether some of the wage change is a reaction to price changes in years before that. It is therefore possible that the 'constant' term in the equations should really be regarded as an omnibus item which sums up various long-delayed reactions which have not been separately unravelled. The results have to be interpreted with this limitation in mind.

These problems have been chiefly studied at the London School of Economics (by Professors Phillips and Lipsey and Professor Phelps Brown); at the Oxford University Institute of Statistics (by Professor Klein and his colleagues as part of their work on a statistical model of the United Kingdom); and at the National Institute of Economic and Social Research. The following account is for the most part a progress report on work done at the National Institute, other studies

---

[1]For a fuller discussion of the technical problems of estimation see for instance L. A. Dicks-Mireaux and J. C. R. Dow [1959], 'The Determinants of Wage Inflation: United Kingdom, 1946–56', *J. roy. statist. Soc.*, *A*, 1959, part 2; and L. A. Dicks-Mireaux [1961], 'The Interrelationship between Cost and Price Changes, 1946–1959', *Oxford econ. Pap.*, October 1961.

being referred to more briefly[1].   It is convenient to summarize the results in an order rather different from that in which they happen to have been published; and to deal first with *wage drift*, secondly with the behaviour of *wage rates*, and thirdly with wages and other costs as determinants of *prices*.   Finally it is necessary to consider the way demand affects the growth in output per head, and how the latter affects prices.

Wage drift

Five or ten years ago, the difference of view between those who believed that prices rose because of demand, and those who believed they rose because of cost pressures focused on the interpretation of what has come to be called 'wage drift'.   Common observation suggested that trade unions were able to force up wage rates.   It seemed reasonable to believe 'that full compensation for price increases is something which trade unions aim at and which both sides to wage negotiations accept as a standard of reference'[2].   'Cost-inflationists' could afford to admit that, though this was the 'norm', wage rates would increase rather more than normal when demand was high, and less when it was low.   But such variations seemed a minor matter[3].   As far as wage rates were concerned, both sides seemed ready to accept this as a fair description. If this were all, there would have been little point in trying to stop prices rising by lowering demand.

The 'demand-inflationists', however, could still argue that actual earnings depended, not on national agreements, but on hundreds of local bargains at the 'work place'—and that these were sensitive to demand.   Consequently, if demand were high, earnings would drift upward even if agreed rates did not. One of the first empirical studies was a study by Professor Hansen and Dr Rehn of wage drift (in Sweden) couched in these terms[4].   This seemed to show that the rate of wage drift did in fact depend on the pressure of demand.

---

[1]Studies at the National Institute include four papers already referred to: Dow [1956], 'Analysis of the Generation of Price Inflation'; Dicks-Mireaux and Dow [1959], 'The Determinants of Wage Inflation: United Kingdom, 1946–56'; Dicks-Mireaux [1961], 'The Interrelationship between Cost and Price Changes, 1946–1959'; and Dicks-Mireaux and P. G. Elkan, 'The Extent of Supplementary Payments'.   One further study is a paper by L. A. Dicks-Mireaux and J. R. Shepherd, 'The Dynamics of Wage Drift'.   The latter two papers will appear in a volume by L. A. Dicks-Mireaux [to be published], *Studies in Cost and Price Behaviour*, which will also include in revised form the previous studies listed; a first summary of results was given in L. A. Dicks-Mireaux and J. R. Shepherd [1962], 'The Wages Structure and some Implications for Incomes Policy', *Nat. Inst. econ. R.*, November 1962.
    References to studies made elsewhere are given below as relevant.
[2]Dow [1956], para. 38.
[3]*Ibid.*, para. 99.
[4]B. Hansen and G. Rehn [1956], 'On Wage Drift' in *25 Economic Essays in Honour of Eric Lindahl*.

Fig. 13.6.   The relation between changes in wage rates and changes
in wage earnings

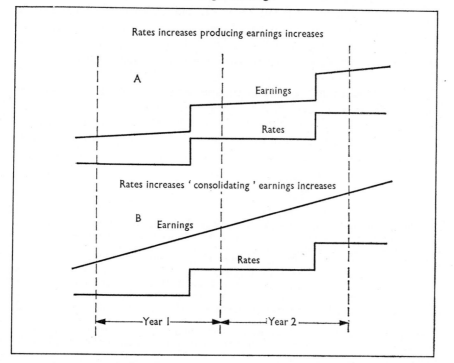

Belief in the primacy of 'work-place' bargaining can be held in even stronger form.   It can be argued that nationally agreed wage rates are causally irrelevant; that earnings are determined by market forces at local negotiations; and that increases in rates negotiated at the national level represent only a 'catching up on what has happened in the market since the completion of the previous negotiations'[1].   On this view, nationally agreed wage rates would be a mere epiphenomenon, reflecting events but not influencing them.   Increases in rates would merely 'consolidate' increases in earnings that had already taken place.

Wage awards occur discontinuously at something like annual intervals.   On the 'consolidation' hypothesis one would expect that a wage award would not itself raise earnings, so that 'drift' would fall.   On the contrary hypothesis, one would expect earnings to increase and drift not to fall (figure 13.6).   Or reality might be half-way between these two extremes: drift might fall, but not by as much as rates rose.   The relation between rates and earnings was examined

[1]The quotation is from the OEEC report, *The Problem of Rising Prices*, produced by a committee consisting of Mr Milton Gilbert and Professors W. Fellner, B. Hansen, R. Kahn, F. Lutz and P. de Wolff [1961]—who however mention (p. 68) this view as one they are 'absolutely clear' is wrong.

Z

by Mr S. Marris in the course of an OEEC study; and more exhaustively in studies by Professor Phelps Brown and Mr Browne, and by Messrs Dicks-Mireaux and Shepherd. The latter seems to show fairly convincingly that the preponderant relation is for changes in wage rates to cause changes in wage earnings—not the reverse, as implied by the 'consolidation' hypothesis. It shows too (as did an earlier study by Mrs Marquand) that wage drift is affected—though only to a limited extent—by the pressure of demand[1].

These findings justify the (entirely commonsense) view that national negotiations between trade unions and employers' associations are not irrelevant, but affect the level of earnings. Since it must chiefly be through national negotiations that price changes affect wages, this is an important link in the 'cost-inflation' argument. But this does not dispose of the 'demand-inflation' case.

---

[1]See J. Marquand [1960], 'Earnings-drift in the United Kingdom, 1948–57', *Oxford econ. Pap.*, February 1960; S. Marris [1961], 'Wage Determination in Selected Countries', being appendix 4 to the OEEC [1961] report already quoted; L. A. Dicks-Mireaux and J. R. Shepherd, *op. cit.*; and E. H. Phelps Brown and M. H. Browne [1962], 'Earnings in Industries of the United Kingdom, 1948–59', *Econ. J.*, September 1962.

In practice the relation of rates and earnings cannot be inferred from direct inspection, as suggested by figure 13.6; for (i) different groups of workers get wage awards at different dates, so that in most cases an index of wage rates for all workers in any industry rises fairly continuously; and (ii) the level of wage earnings is known only at six-monthly intervals, so that when steep rises in rates occur one cannot see precisely how earnings have been affected. The study by Dicks-Mireaux and Shepherd attempted to deal with this difficulty by explicitly allowing for the possibility of a dual causal relationship, the hypotheses being:

$$E = a + bR + cH \qquad (1)$$
$$R = w + xP + yD + zE \qquad (2)$$

where E = (six-monthly) change in wage earnings
R = „ „ wage rates
H = „ „ hours worked
P = „ „ retail prices
D = index of pressure of demand

It was known from other work that most of the variation in wage rates could be explained in terms of price change and demand pressure (see later text). Equation (2) therefore contains these two factors, with earnings change as an additional variable. The results however showed that the coefficient b was much larger than z, i.e. that the predominant relation was for changes in wage rates to cause changes in earnings, not vice versa.

Marris's study appeared to show that wage drift increased most rapidly when there was a lull in wage awards: this could be interpreted (though Marris did not do so) as evidence for the 'consolidation' hypothesis. Dicks-Mireaux and Shepherd estimated the coefficient b to be of the order 0·6 or 0·7. This means that when wage rates increase, earnings increase *less than proportionately*. But this is what would happen if the 'supplementary payments' component of earnings (about 0.3 of total earnings: see Dicks-Mireaux and Elkan [to be published], *op. cit.*) remained constant in absolute terms. The apparent relative sluggishness of earnings is therefore not proof of 'consolidation'.

Demand appeared to have a moderate effect on drift: a rise in the pressure of demand enough to reduce unemployment 1 percentage point was associated with an increase in drift of 1 per cent a year. The excess demand of the post-war years could therefore explain the gradual increase in the 'wage drift component' of earnings (§3 above). This study (unlike Mrs Marquand's) found no relation between earnings and changes in productivity.

Wage rates

There have been several studies of the behaviour of wage rates of which that by Mr Dicks-Mireaux and myself is perhaps the most detailed for the post-war period[1]. These seem to show, first, that (contrary to what might be supposed) wage rates are much more sensitive than wage drift to the influence of demand, i.e. that it is mainly at the national level, not at the level of local negotiations, that the influence of demand appears to make itself felt. Second, the results also seem to show—though the interpretation to be put on this conclusion is open to question—that the effect of price changes on wages is, in the short term at least, much less than one to one. Third, there is an unexplained 'constant' tendency for wage rates to rise—which might be due at least in part to trade union pressure[2].

---

[1] L. A. Dicks-Mireaux and J. C. R. Dow [1959], 'The Determinants of Wage Inflation' (already referred to); A. W. Phillips [1958], 'The Relation between Unemployment and the Rate of Change of Money Wage Rates in the United Kingdom, 1861–1957', *Economica*, November 1958; R. G. Lipsey [1960], 'The Relation between Unemployment and the Rate of Change of Money Wage Rates in the United Kingdom, 1862–1957: A Further Analysis', *Economica*, February 1960; R. G. Lipsey and M. D. Steuer [1961], 'The Relation between Profits and Wage Rates', *Economica*, May 1961; L. R. Klein and R. J. Ball [1959], 'Some Econometrics of the Determination of Absolute Prices and Wages', *Econ. J.*, September 1959; L. R. Klein, R. J. Ball, A. Hazlewood and P. Vandome [1961], *An Econometric Model of the United Kingdom*, pp. 114–26 and appendix III; and (for the United States) O. Eckstein and T. A. Wilson [1962], 'The Determination of Money Wages in American Industry', *Quart. J. Econ.*, August 1962.

[2] The study by Dicks-Mireaux and Dow [1959] showed that an increase in the pressure of demand sufficient to reduce unemployment 1 per cent was associated with an increase in wage rates of about 3 per cent; and that an increase in prices of 1 per cent was associated with an increase in wage rates of about ½ per cent.

The study related to the period 1946–56. But the earlier years were difficult to deal with, partly because wage rates in 1948–50 appeared to be affected by the government's policy of 'wage restraint'. For the years 1950–6 the following equation was obtained:

$$R = 2.6 + 0.52P + 3.64D \qquad (1)$$

(this being an approximate transcription of an equation originally estimated in logarithmic form) where:

R = change (over a year) in wage rates
P = „ „ „ „ „ retail prices
D = index of pressure of demand (as originally defined in Dow and Dicks-Mireaux [1958]: see §2 above)

For the years 1946–56 the equation was also fitted with an additional explanatory variable (F) purporting to measure trade union 'pushfulness'—which thus takes account of the effect of 'wage restraint'. The results were:

$$R = 2.6 + 0.60P + 2.63D + 0.03F \qquad (2)$$

This seems to show that the effects of demand and price changes on wage rates is not entirely mechanical, but depends also on trade-union attitudes. The study by Klein and his colleagues [1961] made a similar attempt to allow for the effect of a 'political factor'.

It could be argued that the apparent response of wage rates to high demand is in reality a response to high profits. But profit margins have not varied greatly; and what variation there has been has been correlated with the pressure of demand. There is therefore little to be gained by this reading of the results: see Lipsey and Steuer [1961]. Eckstein and Wilson [1962] claim that, in the United States, profits (as well as unemployment) have affected wage rates; but their results also show that the course of wage rates can be as well explained in terms of unemployment and *price changes*.

The results have other general implications. Analysis of wage movements in separate industries seemed to show that wage negotiations are affected by demand conditions *in the economy as a whole*—not the 'local' demand conditions obtaining in each industry[1]. The same appears to be true of the United States[2]. This suggests that the effect of demand is to affect the climate of negotiations in a semi-political manner, and is not a purely economic response in the strict sense. Furthermore, there is no reason to think that correlations based on a short period of history reflect unchanging fundamental laws: the sensitivity of wages to demand may well vary[3].

There is one other question of some importance. It is possible that a rise in wages is discouraged not only by *low* demand, but also by a *fall* in the level of demand. If this were the case, a policy of deflation would have some impact effect (while demand was falling) which would later cease (since no government would reduce demand indefinitely)—so that, as time went on, its first success in stopping wage increases would be reduced. Some of the results appear to confirm the existence of this impact effect; but the question is still obscure[4].

The fact that wage rates appear highly sensitive to demand might seem to suggest that wages could be prevented from rising at all if demand were sufficiently reduced. This deduction is however highly questionable. When demand is high—as in the post-war period—variations in the pressure of demand appear to make a big difference. But when demand is low, the sensitivity of wages to the pressure of demand is almost certainly much less[5]. This line of reasoning acquires its plausibility from the idea that there is some 'equilibrium' point of demand, at which prices or wages would stop rising. But as already argued (§1 above), there seems no reason to believe that there is such a point.

Costs and prices

Thus far it has been shown that wage rates are affected by demand and by price changes, and that wage drift is also affected to a less extent by demand. These two factors must then account for changes in wage earnings. They probably

---

[1]Dicks-Mireaux and Dow [1959], §4.

[2]See Eckstein and Wilson [1962].

[3]Some evidence of changes in the sensitivity of wages to demand—and to price changes— is provided by Lipsey's [1960] study.

[4]Lipsey's [1960] analysis suggests that there was such an effect in the period 1948–57, and also in 1923–9—but not in the 'thirties or before 1914. He suggests (p. 27) that the results are better explained as due to the fact that when unemployment has increased in recent years, it has affected some industries or areas much more than others.

[5]See Phillips [1958] and Lipsey [1960] each of whose studies referred to the last century, during most of which demand was much lower (unemployment much higher) than since the war.

A reworking of the post-war data, however, in which the parameter measuring the effect of demand was estimated separately for periods of 'excess' and 'deficient' demand, failed to reveal a conclusive difference. (See Dicks-Mireaux [to be published].)

also account for changes in salaries—since salaries have on the whole risen as fast as wages.   Mr Dicks-Mireaux's study of the interrelationship between costs and prices[1] shows that changes in the labour bill as a whole can be explained in these terms.   It shows also that price changes, in turn, can be explained in terms of changes in the labour bill, of import prices and of output per head.

His results can best be explained by setting out the two equations obtained. The first 'explains' changes in wages and salaries; the second, changes in prices; and each equation includes the other factor as part of the explanation.   The equations were:

$$L_{(t)} = 3.90 + 0.30P_{(t)} + 0.16P_{(t-1)} + 2.78D_{(t-\frac{1}{2})} \cdot \cdots \cdots \cdots \quad (1)$$
$$P_{(t)} = 2.47 + 0.27L_{(t)} + 0.21I_{(t-\frac{1}{2})} - 0.54X_{(t)} \cdot \cdots \cdots \cdots \quad (2)$$

where all variables except D measure percentage changes between the annual averages of one year and the next, and where:

L = change in labour bill per person employed (average wage/salary)
P = change in final prices
I = change in import prices
X = change in output per head
D = index of demand for labour (as originally defined in Dow and Dicks-Mireaux [1958]: see §2 above)
t = time subscript measured at yearly intervals

Figure 13.7 illustrates the results, and shows that a great part of the variation of costs and prices can be explained in these terms.   But, for reasons already noted, the results have to be interpreted with care: for neither equation deals with responses delayed more than a year, and each contains a large constant term.

Several features of the results, as they emerge from the calculations, call for remark.   First, the effect of the two main 'exogenous' factors comes out much as one would expect.   The estimate of the 'demand' coefficient implies that a rise in demand sufficient to cause a fall of unemployment of one per cent is associated with a rise in wages and salaries of about $2\frac{3}{4}$ per cent: this squares with previous estimates.   The estimate of the 'import cost' coefficient implies that prices rise by one fifth of any rise in import prices: this too is roughly what one would expect in view of the average 'import content' of final output.

Second, the estimates of the effects of the two 'endogenous' factors are each relatively low.   The estimates of the price coefficients in the first equation, taken at face value, imply that wages and salaries rise by only about half any rise in prices.   The estimated wage/salary coefficient in the second equation implies that prices rise by only one quarter of any rise in wages and salaries—though wages and salaries account for three quarters of the cost of final output[2]. On the face of it, this means that the internal links in the system are 'weak'. If this were all there was to it, the wage-price spiral would be quickly damped,

[1]Dicks-Mireaux [1961], *op. cit.*
[2]Defining 'cost' as the cost of imports *plus* the cost of labour.

Fig. 13.7.   Explanation (A) of changes in wages and salaries and (B) of changes
in final prices

Annual percentage changes

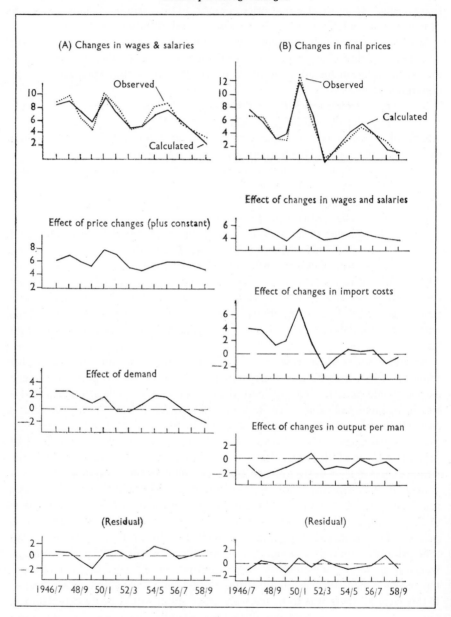

From L. A. Dicks-Mireaux [1961], 'The Interrelationship between Cost and Price
Changes, 1946–1959'.   For equations fitted see text, p. 357 above.

the element of feedback being reduced to one eighth of any initial disturbance after only one round.

But, as already argued, this may not be the full story: there may well be other, delayed, responses, neglected by the analysis, which greatly alter the picture. Historically, wages have tended to rise *more* than prices, not less; and wages and salaries have tended to keep their share in national output, and thus their share in costs. The equations do not deny this: though the degree of 'cost compensation' in the price equation is much below unity, the incompleteness of cost compensation has, as it were, been made good by the effect of the constant term. But this makes full compensation appear a historical accident. In fact the tendency of prices in the long run to keep pace with costs is probably as well established a law as any other; and it would be more satisfactory to have a form of explanatory equation which formally provided for this. In the study referred to, experiments were made with a 'long-run' equation which incorporated delayed responses[1]. If these are allowed for, it is clear that the internal links in the system—i.e. between prices and costs, and costs and prices—are much strengthened. The wage-price spiral may then, after all, be quite strong and perseverant[2].

Third, an increase in productivity can be regarded as a cost-reducing factor, tending to offset increases in money wages. Mr Dicks-Mireaux's results seem to show not only that prices are affected by changes in output per head, but are more quickly affected by such changes than by changes in wages and salaries. Thus, if both wages and salaries and output per head rose four per cent a year more quickly than average, the equations suggest that the effect of the first would be to increase the rate of price rise by about one per cent a year, and the effect of the second would be to reduce the rate of price increase by about two per cent (see equation (2) above). These results have to be interpreted with the same qualifications that apply to the other results of this type of analysis: namely, that they reflect only the short-term response. In the long term, the response to changes in output per head (like that to changes in wages and salaries) must be supposed to be larger; and it seems reasonable to suppose

---

[1]Dicks-Mireaux [1961], §5. Constant factor shares can be accounted for *either* by full cost compensation in the price equation; *or* by full price compensation in the wage/salary equation (plus a factor to allow real wages to keep pace with productivity); or by both. The study showed that the first, but not the second, hypothesis was plausible. Thus the following equation (without a constant term) explained the data as well as the original equation containing the constant:

$$
\begin{aligned}
P_{(t)} = \quad & 0{\cdot}27\,L_{(t)} & + \;\; 0{\cdot}21\,I_{(t-\frac{1}{4})} & \;\; - \;\; 0{\cdot}54\,X_{(t)} \\
+ \;\; & 0{\cdot}20\,L_{(t-1)} & + \;\; 0{\cdot}02\,I_{(t-1\frac{1}{4})} & \;\; - \;\; 0{\cdot}08\,X_{(t-1)} \\
+ \;\; & 0{\cdot}14\,L_{(t-2)} & + \;\; 0{\cdot}015\,I_{(t-2\frac{1}{4})} & \;\; - \;\; 0{\cdot}06\,X_{(t-2)} \\
+ \;\; & 0{\cdot}09\,L_{(t-3)} & + \;\; 0{\cdot}010\,I_{(t-3\frac{1}{4})} & \;\; - \;\; 0{\cdot}04\,X_{(t-3)} \\
+ \;\; & 0{\cdot}04\,L_{(t-4)} & + \;\; 0{\cdot}005\,I_{(t-4\frac{1}{4})} & \;\; - \;\; 0{\cdot}02\,X_{(t-4)} \quad .. \quad (3)
\end{aligned}
$$

[2]For a general analysis of wage-price spirals in a system with 'strong' internal links, see Dow [1956].

that an increase in output per head would fully compensate for an equal rise in wages and salaries[1].

These results are consistent with the belief that the rise in prices has been partly due to pressure by trade unions for higher wages—which there are general reasons to believe was important. They are themselves not however very strong evidence for the existence of such a pressure. The presence of a constant term in the equations is not necessarily an indication that it has been a force, for there are other possible reasons why wages might rise at what is here defined as 'zero' excess demand[2].

5. INTERPRETATION OF THE RESULTS

The empirical results previously summarized seem to show that the pressure of demand for labour has a marked effect on the rate of increase in money wages and salaries. From this it does not necessarily follow that the pressure of demand has a similar effect on the rate of increase in prices. For the results show that the rate of increase of output per head also affects prices, and it remains to consider how the latter is affected by the pressure of demand. It is for instance frequently argued that a reduction in the pressure of demand, aiming to reduce the rise in wages, will also reduce the rise in output per head, and the net effects on prices will be negligible or even perverse. Here again short-term and long-term effects need to be distinguished.

A *reduction* in the pressure of demand means that output grows less rapidly than productive capacity—which in the post-war period seems to have expanded fairly steadily (figure 4.1 in chapter IV). When output grows less rapidly than usual, this is likely for a time at least to have little effect on employment so that output per head rises less rapidly than usual; and when output falls, the effect on employment is likely to be less than proportionate, so that the immediate effect is likely to be to reduce output per head. Thus output per head fell after the 1951 boom and failed to rise in the year after the 1955 boom (table 13.2). Conversely when the pressure of demand is increased after a period of some slack, output per head is likely to increase unusually fast (as e.g. in 1952–5 and 1958–60)—though if the pressure of demand is further increased when there is already little slack (as perhaps in 1950–1) this will not happen.

---

[1] See the 'long-term' equation (3) already quoted, p. 359n.

[2] Even if there is no *net* excess demand, there may be excess demand in some sectors and deficient demand in others; and the former may have more effect in raising wages than the latter has in slowing their rise. Furthermore, too much should not be built on the precise way excess demand has been measured; and this affects the value of the constant term. If a lower pressure of demand had been called zero, the constant term could have been eliminated. This type of analysis can only be expected to tell something about factors which varied over the period, not about those which were fairly constant. Pressure for higher wages may have varied a bit, as the Dicks-Mireaux/Dow study surmised; but it is difficult to measure and was probably always a factor.

The transition from a low to a high, or a high to a low pressure of demand is thus likely to have a marked effect on the rise of output per head at least in the short run. This could mean that a policy of deflation will not have a *quick* effect in slowing down the rise in prices: for though the lower pressure of demand may slow the rise in wages, the transition to it will reduce the rise in output per head.

The effect on output per head of the *level* of demand (i.e. apart from the transitional effects just discussed of a move from a higher to a lower pressure of demand) is even less clear. Some argue that it is the government's policy of restraining demand that accounts for the slow growth of productive capacity in the decade of the fifties. My view, more fully argued later[1], is that the causes are more deep-seated. Government policies of restraint were intermittent; and it seems fairly clear for instance that when demand was allowed to expand rapidly (as in 1952–5) there was not an equally rapid expansion of productive capacity. The statistical evidence of other periods and other countries shows many cases of economies expanding relatively rapidly despite a low pressure of demand[2]. My own belief is that if the pressure of demand had been somewhat lower, and the margin of unused capacity somewhat larger, than in most of the post-war years, there could have been steady expansion of expenditure, output and output per head as rapid as that which in fact occurred. Since the *alterations* of policy were probably to some extent disrupting, the preservation of a steady but lower pressure of demand might even have resulted in faster growth[3].

If this is so, and if it is accepted that the pressure of demand may affect the rise of wages, it follows that a different long-term policy towards the pressure of demand could have had a marked effect on the rise of prices. How large the effect would have been is no doubt beyond precise calculation. It may nevertheless be worth showing what Mr Dicks-Mireaux's equations—on my interpretation of the effects on output per head—imply. Figure 13.8 is intended to illustrate the effect of a lower, stable level of demand as compared with the fluctuations that actually obtained. Unemployment actually averaged $1\frac{1}{2}$ per cent. Curve A shows the hypothetical effect of zero excess demand (as

---

[1]See chapter XVI.1.

[2]The statistics suggest that productivity increases as rapidly at a stable low level of demand (e.g. the inter-war years as a whole in the United Kingdom) as at a stable high level (e.g. the post-war period as a whole): see the figures for this and other countries in A. Maddison [1959], 'Economic Growth in Western Europe, 1870–1957', *Banca naz. Lav. R.*, March 1959; and D. Paige [1961], 'Economic Growth: the Last Hundred Years', *Nat. Inst. econ. R.*, July 1961.

It has also been argued that if deflation did stop prices rising, this itself would slow down economic expansion, chiefly (it is argued) because investment would be less attractive (see for instance N. Kaldor [1958], 'Monetary Policy, Economic Stability and Growth': *Radcliffe, Memoranda*, XIII.20). The statistics of growth seem to provide little evidence for this idea either.

[3]See further chapter XVI.1.

Fig. 13.8. Reconstruction of price trends to show effect of lower pressure of demand

Index of factor cost of final expenditure 1947 = 100

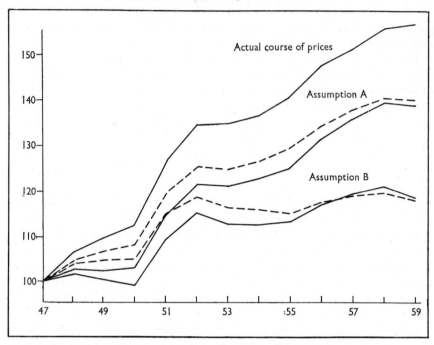

A   assumes zero net excess demand (unemployment of $1\frac{3}{4}\%$).
B   assumes deficient demand corresponding to unemployment of $2\frac{1}{4}\%$.
Dotted lines assume steady in place of fluctuating growth in output per head.

The calculations assume that a lower pressure of demand would in each year have caused wages and salaries to rise less rapidly than in fact they did; and that this would have produced a smaller rise in prices. They also assume that wages would have risen less because prices had risen less in the immediately previous period. The calculation in effect amounts to the generation of artificial history, assuming some factors unchanged (import price changes) and others different (the pressure of demand). It further assumes (except for the dotted curves) that with a steady pressure of demand, output per head would have increased steadily but *on average* at the same rate as before. The calculation is based on the 'wage' and 'price' equations estimated in Dicks-Mireaux [1961], *Oxford econ. Pap.*: see equation (1) set out on p. 357 above and equation (3), p. 359n. The latter equation assumes that a cost change will *in time* generate an equiproportionate price change.

measured by the index discussed in §2) which corresponds roughly to unemployment of $1\frac{3}{4}$ per cent. Curve B shows the effect of a level of demand somewhat lower again, corresponding roughly to unemployment of $2\frac{1}{4}$ per cent. In each case it is assumed (on the argument already outlined) that if the pressure of demand had been lower but steady, output per head would have risen steadily and at its average actual rate[1]. (To give some idea of the effect of this latter assumption, the dotted curves are calculated from actual changes in output per head.)

If price increases had been much smaller, as these results suggest, this would have changed the character of wage negotiations, and one can hardly believe that the outcome could be predicted by any mechanical formula[2]. But whatever qualifications are made, the results appear to me to justify the belief that with a lower pressure of demand, the rise of prices would have been considerably less. How far policy in future should go in trying to slow down prices by this means is quite a separate question which will be considered later.

For reasons already indicated (§1 above) the results do not appear to me to show that manipulation of the level of demand would alone have been enough to stop prices rising. Nor can they show that this is the only way to slow down the rise in prices. As already argued (§1), the pace of inflation depends on customs and institutions, which a wages policy might well modify; the possibility of dealing with inflation partly by this means is further discussed later[3].

[1]The calculations are based on Mr Dicks-Mireaux's modified equation which assumes that, in the long term, cost changes produce equiproportionate changes in prices (see notes to figure 13.8).

[2]The calculations are probably also unrealistic in suggesting that there would have been absolute falls in prices in some years: assumption B produces falls in 4 of the last 7 years shown. But even if these are discounted there would still have been only a very moderate rise in the period after 1951.

[3]See chapter XVI.2.

PART IV

CONCLUSIONS

CHAPTER XIV

INTRODUCTION: THE BROAD ISSUES

The success or failure of policy needs to be seen from various points of view. Economic policy affects the well-being of the people, and its success or failure in meeting social objectives is, in the last analysis, the only thing that matters. Many criticisms of post-war policy raise more restricted, and more difficult, economic issues. Before going on (in the next two chapters) to discuss these, it is as well to try to see post-war policy first in broad perspective.

This study has traced the conduct of policy since the early days after the war when the government had newly accepted the maintenance of full employment as one of its primary responsibilities. In assessing the success of this experiment it is well to remember how new it is in the eyes of history, and how theoretical and untested the whole conception initially seemed. 'Not long ago,' said the 1944 official statement 'the ideas embodied in the present proposals were unfamiliar to the general public and the subject of controversy among economists. Today, the conception of an expansionist economy and the broad principles governing its growth are widely accepted . . . But the whole of the measures here proposed have never yet been systematically applied as part of the official economic policy of any Government . . .'[1]

In terms of its fundamental aim—the desire so to manage the economy as to prevent the heavy unemployment that accompanied the pre-war trade cycle— modern economic policy has clearly been a success. For some years after the war, high employment required no specific intervention: wartime arrears of demand were more than enough to ensure full employment. In the decade of the 'fifties, however, there probably would have been more unemployment if the government had not intervened to increase demand when unemployment showed signs of increasing: and, perhaps equally important, if the world of business had not acquired some confidence that governments could and would so intervene when necessary.

There was some tendency, in the wartime formulation of employment policy

---

[1] The White Paper continued, somewhat grandiloquently: 'in these matters we shall be pioneers. We must determine, therefore, to learn from experience; to invent and improve the instruments of our new policy as we move forward to its goal . . . ' (*Employment Policy*, Cmd. 6527 [1944], para. 80).

to consider it as a separate and, as it were occasional, aspect of policy[1]. The case has in fact been far otherwise. By taking on responsibility for full employment, the government took on responsibility for much more; and it is on failure, or partial failure, in these related matters, that criticism fastens: we now expect much more of economic policy than the mere avoidance of mass unemployment. The criticisms of policy to be considered are chiefly these five:

(1) First, something like the old trade cycle remains, in much attenuated form. There have been oscillations in the pressure of demand; and though output and employment have hardly ever registered a decline, yet there has been a sort of cycle in the rate of growth of output.

(2) Second, there have been frequent adjustments of policy which have led both the trades chiefly affected, and the public at large, to feel— justly or unjustly—that they were being subjected to unnecessarily frequent reversals of policy.

(3) Third, in spite of the measures taken by the government, prices have risen continuously.

(4) Fourth, there has been frequent trouble with the balance of payments. It has tended to be weak: the current surplus has often been less than our long-term lending. It has also fluctuated; and there have been even larger and more erratic fluctuations in the reserves.

(5) Fifth, though output has grown almost continuously, it has not during the last decade, grown as rapidly as some other countries—chiefly France, Germany, Italy, Russia and Japan.

Failure in these respects has been relative failure only. By pre-war standards, economic fluctuations have been very minor: what recessions there have been have been few, and either very minor, or very brief. Though growth has not been as rapid as the recent record of a handful of some other major countries, it has been as rapid as this country or most other countries have achieved over the last century[2]. The increase in production has been enough to make people far better off than before the war. Most industries have been able to count on every year being a record year for sales. For industries specially hit by temporary government restrictions, there have been interruptions. But on the whole it is in these industries that the *trend* of production has shown the most rapid

---

[1]The 1944 White Paper for instance placed much emphasis on the accumulation of a 'shelf' of public investment projects—which could be taken 'off the shelf' and put into effect if a slump threatened. It also attached great importance to a scheme for varying national insurance contributions in inverse relation to percentage unemployment; and this scheme was to be 'automatic', not 'discretionary', to operate alongside the budget. Little emphasis was placed on budgetary policy—indeed the White Paper (para. 74) specially disowned the idea of deficit budgeting in a recession. In fact it was chiefly through its integration with budgetary policy that employment policy has become incorporated as one essential aspect of economic policy.

[2]The best measure is the rate of growth of output per head. For a review of rates of growth during the last century, see D. C. Paige [1961], 'Economic Growth: The Last Hundred Years', *Nat. Inst. econ. R.*, July 1961.

rise: even though every year was not a record year, every second or third beat previous records by a wide margin. Prices have gone up steadily. But the same is true of every country in the world; and the rise, if faster than in other countries, has been only marginally so[1]. It is only to a minority that this seems a serious disadvantage. The constant rise in prices is a nuisance, and may in the end be dangerous. But if their incomes rise too, most people hardly complain. The balance of payments has been a constant anxiety *to the authorities*. But it has not been so unfavourable as to force the government to relinquish high employment, nor to do more than at times slow down the rate of growth. These points are too obvious to require argument: but they are also too important not to be said.

It is nevertheless clear that there is room for improvement in the management of the economy. One of the main questions is how far policy was responsible for the fluctuations in internal demand, and in the balance of payments. An important issue underlying this question is how much can be expected of economic policy, and how quickly the economy can be expected to respond to treatment. It is suggested in chapter XV that policy has, in effect, expected too quick a response; that long views have to be taken; and that the failure to take them has resulted in unnecessary fluctuations. It is also argued that fiscal and monetary policy, however well devised, are not by themselves able to ensure rapid economic growth, nor, probably, reasonable price stability; and that these objects need to be sought directly by greater government initiative in economic planning and in wages policy. These questions are discussed in chapter XVI, which considers a general strategy for future policy.

---

[1]See for instance the OEEC Report by Fellner, Gilbert, Hansen, Kahn, Lutz and de Wolff [1961], *The Problem of Rising Prices*, especially tables 1 and 2. Between 1953 and 1960 most countries of Western Europe and North America experienced a rise of prices of between 10 and 35 per cent. The rise of prices in the United Kingdom was 21 per cent.

CHAPTER XV

POST-WAR FLUCTUATIONS AND THE IMPACT

OF POLICY

It is tempting to regard post-war fluctuations in demand as a pale remnant of the pre-war trade cycle. But post-war fluctuations have not been uncontrolled; and it is a major question whether there has been anything like an autonomous cycle at work. This chapter discusses why demand fluctuated as it did, and what part policy played.

Fluctuations in demand are reflected in the trend of output (figure 15.1). During the post-war period, output has grown fairly continuously. The annual figures of national output in total show only one year in which output failed to rise: in all other years, it rose, at varying rates[1]. In place of fluctuations of the pre-war type, when all the main indicators went up or down together, there have merely been fluctuations in the rate of growth. Output tended to grow in steps, years of fairly rapid growth being interspersed with years when output grew little. Not output, but the rate of growth of output, shows therefore a wave-like movement (the *arrows* in figure 15.1 indicate years when output grew more, or less, than average). The range of fluctuation has been fairly narrow. Thus the average growth in real final expenditure and output has been a little over $2\frac{1}{2}$ per cent a year; and the fluctuations in the rate of growth have been within the range of *plus* or *minus* $2\frac{1}{2}$ per cent from this mean.

The period 1948–60 may be divided into five phases: three years when output continued to grow fairly rapidly, as it had since the war (the *pressure* of demand was high, rising to a peak in 1951); one year (1952) when output hardly changed (and the pressure of demand fell); four more years when output grew fairly rapidly (the pressure of demand again gradually mounting to a new peak in 1955); two years when output grew little (and the pressure of demand fell); and finally two more years of fairly rapid growth (the pressure of demand again beginning to mount). These phases are, by and large, also reflected in the movement of employment and hours worked (shown together on the chart as the change in man-hours worked); and were also reflected, though more erratically, in the behaviour of imports[2].

---

[1]The use of annual data reduces the width of some fluctuations (for example, output fell sharply *in the middle* of 1952).

[2]The series for man-hours has fluctuated less erratically than the separate series for employment and average hours worked. The figure shown for 'man-hours' is admittedly a hybrid statistic; for employment refers to the whole employed population (excluding only the self-employed), whereas the figures of hours worked refer only to the 'principal industries' (about half the working population). But since overtime is paid above standard rates, percentage changes in 'man-hours' roughly measure the proportionate effect on wage and salary incomes. Changes in imports (shown as a percentage of *gross domestic product*) also reflect changes in stocks of imported commodities, which were erratic.

Fig. 15.1.   Fluctuations in the British economy, 1948–60

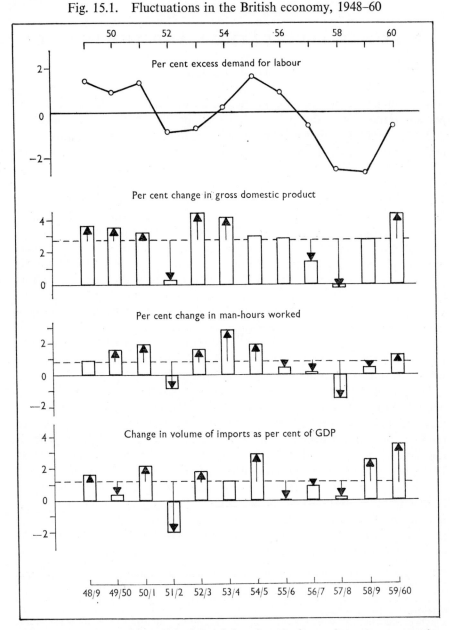

The measure of *excess demand for labour* is based on the figure of percentage unemployment and percentage unfilled vacancies: see chap. XIII.2 above.   Changes in *gross domestic product* and *imports* of goods and services are at 1954 prices from *NI & E* [1959] and [1961]. Change in *man-hours worked* is the percentage change in employment *plus* the percentage change in hours worked in the Ministry of Labour's 'principal' industries.

The first step in explaining these fluctuations is to estimate the effect of changes in policy. §1 brings together the estimates made in previous chapters of the 'initial impact' of changes in policy (e.g. the effect of changes in taxes affecting consumers' expenditure). There are likely also to be secondary repercussions: if consumption is stimulated, this is likely to affect fixed investment and investment in stocks, and if investment is stimulated, this is likely to affect consumption. 'Multiplier' and other mechanisms of this sort are discussed in §2. An interpretation of post-war trends in demand, incorporating these elements of the argument, is given in §3. Fluctuations in the balance of payments and their relation to internal demand are discussed in §4. Conclusions are summarized in §5.

1. THE IMPACT OF POLICY CHANGES

It is possible to make only rough estimates of how policy changes affected consumers' expenditure. One of the main difficulties is that it remains uncertain how quickly consumers react to changes in their disposable income[1]. It is therefore uncertain whether the main impact of a tax change made in April is to increase consumption in that year (as compared with the year previous) or whether the main increase comes only in the following year[2]. The estimates of the impact of tax changes shown in figure 15.2 are therefore based on alternative assumptions: first, that spending responds without delay to a change in income, and hence to a change in tax rates; and, second, that the effect on spending is gradual and takes two years to appear in full. These are probably extreme assumptions[3].

Apart from changes in taxes, there have also been major changes in national insurance contributions (which are very similar to taxes); in subsidies (which are indirect taxes in reverse); and in national insurance benefits and other grants to persons (akin to direct taxes in reverse). There is here a further difficulty: there are figures of subsidies for each calendar year, but no information as to precisely when within the year the rate of subsidy was changed. A rather

---

[1] See discussion in chapter XI.1 above.

[2] The present analysis is in terms of changes in expenditure between successive *calendar* years.

[3] The first assumption means that if a tax change occurs in April of year B (i.e. one quarter of the way through the year) spending in year B (as compared with the previous year) is increased by three quarters of the full-year effect. Spending in year C as compared with year B is therefore increased by a further quarter of the full effect. The second assumption of 'distributed lags' implies that, say, a quarter of the full effect impinges on year B, a further half on year C, and the remaining quarter on year D.

In all cases the 'full-year' effects are as estimated in chapter VII, table 7.5, and thus make allowance for the propensity to spend being less than unity, i.e. for the effect on spending being less than the effect on government revenue.

AA

Fig. 15.2.   Estimates of initial impact of government measures
£ *(1954) million*

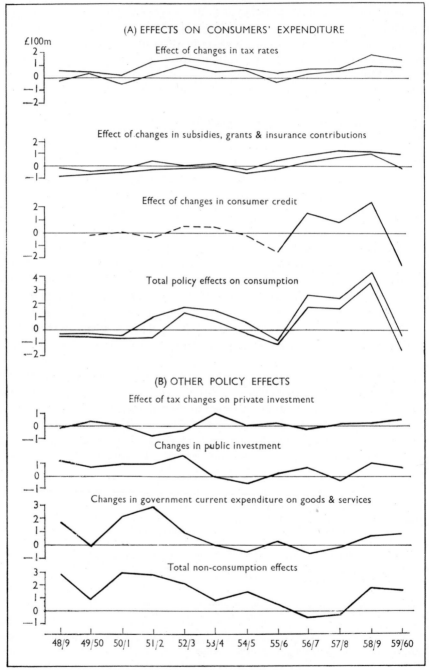

For notes to figure see foot of next page.

rough treatment had therefore to be adopted[1]. The estimates are again shown on alternative assumptions about the speed of response.

The uncertainty as to timing is not so serious when estimating the effect of changes in consumer credit. Consumers may take time to react to changes in *credit terms*. But it seems reasonable to assume that they do not borrow money much in advance of the time they want to spend it. The timing of the effect should therefore be indicated by the changes in consumer debt. The difficulty here is that of knowing the scale of the effect[2].

Since the effects can be estimated only roughly they are only worth showing

---

[1] The change of subsidy was estimated as the change between one calendar year and the next, and it was assumed that the change *took effect at the turn of the year*. The date when changes in national insurance contributions and benefits took effect is known; but it seemed better to treat changes in subsidies, grants and contributions as a group, and to adopt the same treatment for all. Changes in 'rates' of subsidy were as estimated in chapter VII, table 7.7. It was assumed that the marginal propensities to consume appropriate to changes in subsidies, insurance contributions and grants were respectively 0·8, 0·8 and 1·0 (compare table 7.5).

[2] It is assumed that the increase in spending induced by a change in consumer debt is the change in hire-purchase debt, plus half the change in the 'personal and professional' advances recorded by the British Bankers' Association (see chapter XI.2).

There are no good estimates of changes in hire-purchase debt for years before 1955.

Notes to fig. 15.2

All the above estimates are intended to indicate the effect of changes in policy in contributing to *year-to-year changes in final expenditure*.

The estimated *effects of changes in tax rates* are taken from table 7.5 and thus allow for the effect on consumers' expenditure being less than the effect on government revenue. All estimates are adjusted to 1954 prices. Because of the uncertainty regarding the speed with which expenditure is likely to be affected, two alternative assumptions are made (*a*) that the effect is instantaneous (*b*) that the effect gradually increases, the full effect being reached in two years. The area between the two lines of the diagram indicates the general range of possibilities on these alternative assumptions: the exact consequences of assumption (*a*) or assumption (*b*) *are not* shown separately. *Subsidies, grants and insurance contributions* are central government subsidies on consumers' expenditure; national insurance and other central government grants to persons; and the national insurance contributions of insured persons and half of those of employers (half being the portion of the latter assumed to enter the cost of consumers' expenditure). Changes are year-to-year changes in total payments as given in *NI & E* [1959] and [1961]: subsidies are adjusted for changes in the volume of consumption, as in table 7.7. It is assumed that grants are spent in full, and that the effect on spending of a change in subsidies or insurance contributions is 0.8 of the change in total subsidies or contributions (compare table 7.5). Alternative assumptions are made as to timing, as for tax changes. *Consumer credit* effects are taken to be the change in hire-purchase debt (figures available only for 1955 and later years) and half of the change in 'personal and professional' loans recorded by the British Bankers' Association (dotted line for years before 1956): the changes are adjusted to 1954 prices.

Taxes affecting private investment are taken to be profits tax, depreciation allowances and the portion of income tax paid by companies (as estimated in table 7.5). The effect on investment is taken to be one third of the change in government revenue, adjusted to 1954 prices; and is assumed to operate with a lag of about a year. Changes in *public authorities' current expenditure on goods and services* and in *public investment*, both at 1954 prices, are from *NI & E* [1959] and [1961].

graphically, and only large changes are worth taking notice of[1]. Tax rates were on balance reduced, the expansionary effects on consumption being especially marked in the period 1953–5, and again in 1959–60: there were probably small contractionary effects only in 1951 and possibly 1956. The 'other fiscal' effects (shown together on figure 15.2) reflect various changes. Subsidies were reduced fairly steadily in the period 1949–53. National insurance benefits were increased on many occasions (most notably in October 1952 and again in February 1958). Contributions were then increased also; but the increase in contributions from insured persons was generally much less than the increase in benefits to them, and especially in 1957–9 the net expansionary effect was considerable. In recent years, the effects of changes in consumer credit were probably even larger than that of tax changes.

In total, there were two chief phases when policy was markedly stimulating consumption. First, there were three years in 1952–4 of moderate continued expansionary impact—chiefly due to the tax cuts of these years. Then there were three further years of expansionary impact in 1957–9—in this case largely due to the growth of consumer credit, to which were added large tax cuts in 1959. As will be shown later, an appreciable part of the expansion of consumption during these periods must have been due directly to these stimuli.

The picture looks rather different when the effects of policy on other branches of national expenditure are also taken into account (part B of figure 15.2). Changes in taxes may be assumed to have some effect not only on personal consumption, but also on private investment; but it is questionable whether this has been very considerable[2]. It may have been sizeable only in 1952—following the suspension of the 'initial' depreciation allowances in the previous year; and in 1954—following their restoration in 1953[3].

The level of public investment and of government current expenditure was chiefly determined by reasons other than stabilization policy[4]. Nevertheless some of the changes were important and have to be taken account of to get a complete picture. For a variety of reasons, both were increasing steadily throughout the first five years shown on the diagram; and these increases far outweighed any contractionary effects that policy had on consumers' expenditure. For the next five years both tended on the whole to fall—to some extent for extraneous reasons, but to some extent also as part of the general policy of

---

[1]The estimates of 'policy' effects are all corrected for price changes, and thus show how far 'policy' changes contributed to year-to-year changes in real consumer spending, i.e. expenditure at 1954 prices.

[2]See discussion in chapter XI.4 above.

[3]The estimates shown in figure 15.2 take account only of changes in profits tax, in depreciation allowances and in the income tax paid by companies (from chapter VII, table 7.5). It is assumed that the induced increase in private investment is *one third* of the tax change (after deflation to 1954 prices) in the *previous* year. It is probable that monetary policy reduced private house-building particularly in 1957 (chapter IX.6): had this effect been included, it would have altered the look of the curve a bit.

[4]See chapter VII.1 and VIII.2 above.

restraining demand. In 1959 and 1960 both as it happened increased, thus adding appreciably to the build-up of demand.

The total impact of all these 'policy' effects is summarized on figure 15.5 (see bottom of chart). It will be seen that at times 'policy' effects must have contributed substantially to the growth in demand; and this appears to be especially true of the early stages of the two successive bursts of expansion to which, after 1952, the economy was subject. But these effects do not by any means explain the whole of the fluctuation experienced. The 'dips' in the rate of growth in 1952 and again in 1957–8 appear—at any rate at first sight—to have owed little to government action. Before drawing final conclusions, it is necessary to take account of the secondary repercussions of policy changes.

2. 'MULTIPLIER' EFFECTS AND OTHER REPERCUSSIONS

It is now necessary to consider how consumers' expenditure, private investment and investment in stocks respond to changes in other parts of the economy. What we are here interested in is how far a larger-than-average growth in expenditures other than consumption itself, causes a larger-than-average growth in consumption; and similarly for investment. 'Multiplier' and 'accelerator' effects are well known to economic theorists; but how far comparable mechanisms determine the short-term behaviour of an expanding economy has not been much studied.

Figure 15.3 shows (part A) the change in consumers' expenditure, and the change in the rest of final expenditure, each year. The 'ringed' points show *actual* changes in consumption: the points connected by the line indicate that part of the change in consumers' expenditure which cannot be explained as an effect of policy changes (as estimated in §2 above). The change in final expenditure—and hence 'non-consumption' as shown on the chart—has been roughly adjusted to eliminate changes in stocks of imported commodities: for such stock changes do not generate incomes in this country, and so could not be expected to cause consumption to increase[1]. The 'ringed' points again show the actual change in 'non-consumption' (estimated as above); and the points joined by the line show the latter *plus the estimated policy effects on consumption*. For a policy-induced change in consumption should cause a further increase in consumption, in the same way as does a change in 'non-consumption'.

There are several reasons why one might expect sizeable 'multiplier' effects. First, when output rose fast, employment and hours worked also increased unusually fast (figure 15.1). Such fluctuations, at their largest, may well have

---

[1]The same is true of the import constituent of other types of national expenditure. But, apart from fluctuations in stocks of imported commodities, this is probably a fairly constant proportion of national expenditure. An abnormally small or large increase in imports in relation to the change in GNP was treated as a change in stocks of imported commodities (see figure 15.4 and notes to it).

Fig. 15.3. 'Multiplier' and other effects

£ (1954) million, year-to-year changes

£*100 m.*

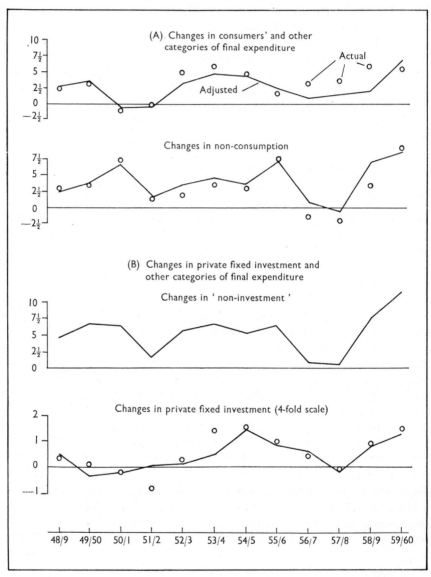

For notes to figure see foot of next page.

added something approaching one per cent to the 'normal' growth in personal incomes, or subtracted as much from it. Second, unusually rapid increases in output go with unusually rapid increases in output per head; and these seem to affect prices.[1] Thus when output rises unusually fast, prices tend to rise more slowly *relative to wages*, so that wage-earners' real purchasing power is increased. This effect too, at its largest, might well add (or subtract) one per cent to (or from) the 'normal' growth of real personal income[2]. Third, a high pressure of demand produces an unusually rapid rise in wages; and this increase in wages is unlikely to produce immediate, fully proportionate, price increases[3]. Again, then, there will for a time be a rise in wage-earners' real purchasing power, which, again, might be appreciable[4].

It would seem that the fluctuations in consumption can be partly explained in these terms. Figure 15.3 perhaps suggests that that part of the increase in consumers' expenditure which cannot be explained as a direct effect of policy changes tends to be large when the increase in other types of expenditure was large. Admittedly there were two years—1951 and 1956—when a large increase in 'non-consumption' did not produce a large increase in consumption; but these exceptions can perhaps be explained away. Consumption was depressed in 1951 by the steep rise in import prices, which reduced consumer purchasing power; and

[1]See chapter XIII.4.

[2]This stimulus may occur only if output *in consumer goods industries* is affected, e.g. by a spurt in exports of consumer goods. An increase in the home or export demand for investment goods might affect output (and hence prices) in investment industries, but leave consumer prices unaffected.

It would occur also only when there was 'slack' in consumer goods industries, and when an increase in demand might thus lead to a rapid increase in output and output per head. At the peak of a boom this kind of multiplier would cease to operate.

[3]Again see chapter XIII.4.

[4]Strictly speaking, this effect is to be expected only when demand is increasing more rapidly than productive capacity (so that the pressure of demand rises). In practice, this is much the same as a larger-than-average increase in demand.

Notes to fig. 15.3

Estimates of annual changes in final expenditure from *NI & E* [1959] and [1961]. Changes in 'non-consumption' and 'non-investment' are the changes in total final expenditure *less* the change in consumption, or in private fixed investment, respectively. The figures of total final expenditure changes here used are however roughly adjusted to eliminate changes in stocks of imported commodities (as explained in the notes to fig. 15.4).

Actual changes in consumers' expenditure are shown by the 'ringed' points. Points connected by the line are after adjustment for the estimated policy effects shown on fig. 15.2 (mean of alternative estimates), and thus purport to show how consumption would have changed in the absence of policy changes. The actual change in 'non-consumption' is similarly shown by the 'ringed' points. The points connected by the line are the actual change in 'non-consumption' *plus* the estimated policy effect in each case—since the latter, like the former, might be expected to have secondary effects on consumption.

The figures used for private fixed investment exclude investment in the steel industry (since for some years it was in the public sector) and also private house-building. Actual changes in private fixed investment are shown by the 'ringed' points: points connected by the line are after adjustment for policy effects on private investment (as estimated for fig. 15.2).

in 1956 there was a sudden large increase in personal saving (as there had also been in 1952).   (Both in 1951 and 1956 the large rise in 'non-consumption' reflected a massive and probably involuntary investment in stocks—figure 15.5— which might perhaps have less 'multiplier' effect than other types of spending.)

If 1951 and 1956 are accepted as explicable exceptions, it seems fair to say that a rise in 'non-consumption' larger or smaller than average will tend to make the rise in consumption to be larger or smaller than average.   Figure 15.3 suggests that the induced change in consumption is likely to be rather less than the change in 'non-consumption' which induced it, but is likely to vary a good deal[1].   One would not anyhow expect the kind of 'multiplier' relation here being discussed to be perfectly regular.   Consumption might well take time to respond.   Then again, the marginal incidence of taxation in an expanding economy is erratic, since it depends very much on what kinds of goods consumers spend their extra money on[2].   Consumption may, too, have been affected not only by income effects but also by capital losses or gains[3].

The next thing to consider is how far private investment is liable to be affected by changes in consumption and other types of expenditure.   Since private house-building is determined by different sorts of considerations, figure 15.3 shows (part B) the growth each year of private investment other than in houses[4]. As already indicated, little of the fluctuation seems to have been due to direct policy influences: on the diagram, actual changes (as in part A) are shown by 'ringed' points, and the points on the line show the change in investment after adjustment for the effect of tax changes (as estimated in §1).   The change in final expenditure other than private investment is also shown—on a scale, however, one quarter that used to show changes in private investment.   Here again, any correlation is pretty rough.   But there seems some tendency for fluctuations in the rate of growth of private investment to go with fluctuations in the growth of other types of expenditure.   There seem some grounds for thinking that fluctuations in 'non-investment' induce—and induce fairly rapidly—fluctuations in private investment perhaps one quarter as large[5].

---

[1]The size of this relationship, here approximately indicated, has little to do with the size of the multiplier usually discussed.   As reflection will show, none of the three 'multiplier' mechanisms discussed above can be more than a short-term mechanism.   In the long term, *and assuming full employment*, the relation between the increase in (say) investment and the increase in consumption is either entirely arbitrary, or depends on the marginal propensity to save.   Resources can be moved to investment, but only at the expense of consumption.   Investment in excess of voluntary saving will generate an excess demand for consumer goods.   This could be removed by higher taxes, or might merely be tolerated; in either case investment could then be what the authorities chose.

[2]See chapter VII.2, especially table 7.3.

[3]See chapter XI.3.

[4]This omission in fact makes little difference to the shape of the curve.

[5]This is not an 'accelerator' relation in the strict sense.   Changes in sales are here related to changes in investment, not to changes in the capital stock.   It is an open question whether the suggested effect on investment is a direct effect of the change in sales, or an effect of induced changes in profits: see discussion in chapter XI.4.

Next to be considered is the way investment in stocks has been affected by changes elsewhere in the economy. Figure 15.4 shows only changes in 'domestic' stocks, i.e. excluding changes in stocks of imported commodities (roughly estimated by methods already indicated). These are shown along with changes in total final expenditure excluding investment in stocks: this total will be referred to as final 'sales'.

In the years up to 1956, *investment in* stocks shows a striking inverse correlation with the change in other sorts of final expenditure. This suggests that in these years most of the short-term change in 'domestic' stocks was 'involuntary'—a conclusion entirely in line with theoretical expectations[1]. Since 1956 this mechanism seems less clearly to have been in operation. In 1957 and 1958, if the figures are to be believed, there was a fall in stocks. This could hardly have been involuntary (for demand was not then buoyant): but it could possibly have been a once-for-all effect of the tight money policy[2]. The fall in stocks in 1959 is explicable in terms of the rapid rise in 'sales' in that year; but their rise in 1960 is not so easily explained[3].

For most of the period it seems clear that the first result of a rapid rise in 'sales' was not a rise in output, but a fall in stocks. But stocks cannot be depleted (or accumulated) indefinitely: the effect on output is only delayed. A curve of the *change in investment in stocks* therefore follows a highly erratic course (figure 15.4). The rate of change of output is given by the rate of change of final expenditure including the change in investment in stocks (bottom of diagram). This typically shows dips and peaks occurring some time after the dips and peaks in the curve of final 'sales' (top of diagram).

An increase in sales is likely to lead not merely, first to a depletion, then to a restoration, of stocks, but to a net increase. Over the whole period stocks have grown. The average increase in stocks has amounted to about a third of the increase in other types of expenditure. This means that when 'involuntary' stock fluctuations have had time to right themselves, the rise in output will be rather greater than the increase in sales.

There remains one other type of effect to be considered. Part of any increase in expenditure is met not by home output but by imports. Expenditure on imports generates income abroad, and thus—to some rather limited degree— increases the demand for British exports. In the case of a fairly close trading

---

[1]See chapter XI.5.

[2]It may have been due to the higher interest rates and to the credit squeezes that followed the 1955 crisis (see chapter IX.3). The Radcliffe Committee found no evidence that stocks had been affected. But firm evidence on such matters is hard to come by; for it is only a 1 or 2 per cent reduction in the volume of stocks that is involved (see discussion at chapter XI.4). If monetary policy can be supposed to have caused a *small* reduction of this sort in 1957 and again in 1958, the puzzle is solved.

[3]The official estimates of stock changes are not highly reliable; and the fact that the 'residual' in the national income estimates has fluctuated a lot casts special doubt on the stock figures in recent years. The adjustment used here to exclude 'imported' stocks is also very rough, and is probably especially unsatisfactory for recent years.

Fig. 15.4.   Changes in stocks

£ (1954) million, year-to-year changes

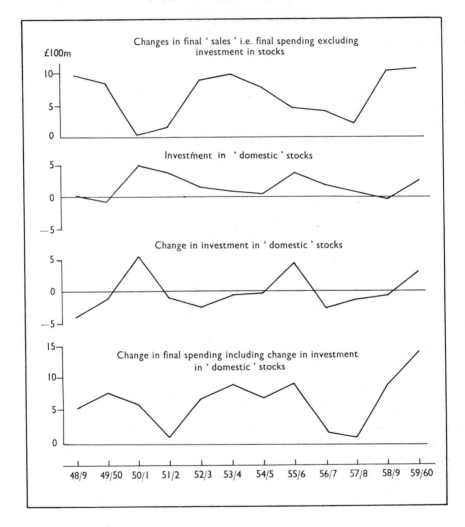

Annual changes from *NI & E* [1959] and [1961].   Change in 'domestic' stocks is the total change in stocks roughly adjusted to eliminate changes in imported stocks.   The change in the 'consumption' of imports is taken as 40 per cent of the change in GDP; and the change in imported stocks is taken as the actual change in the volume of imports (of goods and services) less 'consumption' of imports so estimated.   The change in 'domestic' stocks is thus the official estimate of the total stock change *less* the change in imported stocks so estimated.

network, like the sterling area, the 'feedback' is significant. Though these proportions are now decreasing, for most of the post-war period half our imports came from countries of the sterling area; and half their imports came from the United Kingdom. If their foreign earnings increase, they tend to spend it on more imports.

One result of a faster expansion of demand in the United Kingdom is thus, later on, to produce a ripple in the demand for British exports. An extra £100 million expenditure in this country might raise the volume of total imports by £20 or £25 million, and would also tend to raise their price. This, in a year or two, might increase British exports to the sterling area by £5 million or so— i.e. by perhaps a twentieth of the original increase in demand. In trade with other areas the 'feedback' must be even smaller. The subsequent effect on total demand in this country is therefore fairly unimportant; and most of the fluctuations in world demand for British exports have certainly not arisen as a result of fluctuations in demand in this country.

The present discussion is too brief to give more than a rough idea of the quantitative importance of the various mechanisms discussed. But the evidence, fragmentary as it is, suggests that taken together they are fairly important. The immediate effect of a tax cut in increasing consumers' expenditure seems likely to lead to a large secondary effect on consumption, perhaps half as large as the initial effect or perhaps more. Taken together these might induce increases in fixed investment, and later in investment in stocks—and also to some extent in exports—which together might again be perhaps almost half as large as the initial effect. Many of these 'magnifying' mechanisms seem to work fairly quickly. But 'involuntary' stock depletions in the early stages of a boom must tend to mask their effects; and seem capable of delaying their effect on output for several years. This has probably led the government on occasions to underestimate the amount of stimulus that had already been given to the economy. One conclusion is that the effect of policy measures is better judged by watching the trend of total final 'sales' (i.e. excluding investment in stocks) than by the more conventional total of final expenditure (in which investment in stocks is included).

3. AN INTERPRETATION OF POST-WAR FLUCTUATIONS IN DEMAND

Changes in the main constituents of final expenditure are shown on figure 15.5. The arrows indicate the estimated effect of policy changes[1]. Developments in the years 1950–2 were dominated by the repercussions of the Korean war;

[1]The position from which the arrows start shows the change in expenditure that might have occurred if there had been no change in policy. The estimates of policy effects on consumers' expenditure and on private investment are as given in §1 (the *average* of the alternative estimates of fiscal changes being shown). Changes in public authorities' current expenditure on goods and services and in public investment are included (at the bottom of the diagram) in the total effect of policy changes on total final expenditure.

and the questions are thus different from those raised by later phases, when policy effects were more predominant.

The outbreak of the Korean war in mid-1950 caused a huge rise in commodity prices, which was a main cause of the 1951 British payments crisis, and produced a steep rise in internal prices; and it led also to a steep increase in government spending on defence.   In the United Kingdom, demand was already fairly expansionary in 1949.   In 1950 the boom in world demand caused a further surge in exports; and there was also a large rise in consumers' expenditure, partly in anticipation of shortages and dearer prices.   In the next year, despite the rise in defence expenditure, the rise in final 'sales' was brought to a halt. For commodity prices, after the enormous rise of the previous year, fell; and thus reduced world demand and brought a fall in United Kingdom exports. Consumers' expenditure also fell—partly because taxes were raised, partly perhaps in reaction to the previous 'forestalling'; and partly because the previous rise in import prices had by now worked through to prices in the shops, so that consumers' purchasing power was reduced.   In 1952 final sales again failed to rise much: for though defence spending again rose, consumption and exports again both showed a further fall.

The impact on output of these large swings in demand was cushioned by the behaviour of stocks.   Even in 1949, it may be supposed, sales rose fast enough to prevent accumulation of stocks; and the further rise in 1950 appears to have caused some depletion (figure 15.4).   When sales ceased to rise in 1951, stocks seem to have been rebuilt on a striking scale, and continued to increase in 1952. The change-over from stock depletion to stock accumulation kept output rising in 1951 despite the stagnancy of final sales.   But, in the nature of the case, this could not be repeated in 1952[1].   Hence, a year after the check to sales, the rise in output was brought to a halt.

Action to produce steady growth despite these swings in demand would require to have been both massive and farsighted.   It would perhaps have been an ideal policy to have restrained consumption in 1950 so as to allow stocks to rise: the restocking boom of 1951 might then have been mitigated.   But this might have needed a tougher budget not only in 1950 but also in 1949.   It would have been better if consumption had not fallen in 1951 and again in 1952: the steep dip in final 'sales' would then at least have been mitigated.   For this, Mr Gaitskell's 'defence' budget of 1951, and that of 1950, would have had to have been laxer.   Had all this happened, both the boom of 1951 and the recession of 1952 would have been lessened.   But it would have required an unattainable degree of foresight.   In fact it took six months after the outbreak of the Korean war for a fair view of its immediate consequences to be taken—in time for the 1951 budget.   The conclusion must be that world developments on

[1]For *investment* in stocks to have shown as large an increase in 1952 as it had in 1951, stock accumulation might have had to be twice the already large accumulation that took place in 1951: see figure 15.4.

this scale can hardly be completely countered.

The events of 1950–2 are perhaps a special case, now only of historical interest. The cycle of events leading up to the boom of 1955, and reaction from it, are, on the other hand, of central interest for post-war history. It again seems best to concentrate attention on the development not of final expenditure but of final 'sales'; and this somewhat alters the usual picture of these years. Final 'sales' rose very rapidly in 1953 and again in 1954 (figure 15.5). By 1955, surprisingly enough, their growth had already moderated: in 1956 it again moderated, and continued to sag till 1958. Growth in the first three years rested very largely on the rapid rise in consumer spending, but was increasingly supported also by the revival both of exports and of private investment. The check in 1955 was due to a fall in public spending and a check to consumption; in 1956, to a further check to consumption; and in 1957–8, to the slower growth of exports and private investment.

If one looks for the initiating causes of the renewed expansion of demand in 1953, one cause is clearly the expansionary budget: others are probably the revival of exports, and of private investment after the recession. All these must have had secondary repercussions on consumption; and one might guess that the budget accounted, directly and indirectly, for a good half of the expansion of demand in that year. The 1954 budget provided no further stimulus to consumption, but some of the effects of the 1953 tax cuts were probably still operative. Private investment was probably likewise stimulated by the 1953 restoration of the 'initial' allowances. Thus, though some of the expansion in 1954 was due to the further expansion of exports, policy influences must again have been considerable.

By 1955 the effects of policy—contrary perhaps to the common impression —were not so clear-cut. The April budget gave some further stimulus to consumption, and there may also have been some effect from the 1954 investment allowances. But against this, hire purchase was restricted (the effect of which is not shown on figures 15.3 and 15.5, for lack of earlier figures); and, as it happened, government real current spending and public investment both fell. By 1955 final 'sales' (as already noted) had ceased to rise so rapidly. The boom and crisis of 1955 are often blamed on Mr Butler's 'pre-election' budget of April 1955. The present analysis suggests that the seeds were sown much earlier; and that to have avoided the excess of the peak, the whole pace of expansion would have needed to be more moderate. But 'involuntary' stock changes in 1953 and 1954 served to conceal the full inflationary impact of the stimuli given to the economy in these years. From 1953, sales were probably growing faster than productive capacity, and appear to have been met in part by some depletion of stocks. For from 1953 to 1955, investment in stocks looks abnormally low (figure 15.4). Only in 1956—after the rise in final sales fell off—did investment in stocks recover.

It is difficult to disentangle how far policy contributed to the subsequent phase

Fig. 15.5.   Changes in final expenditure

Percentages of total final expenditure

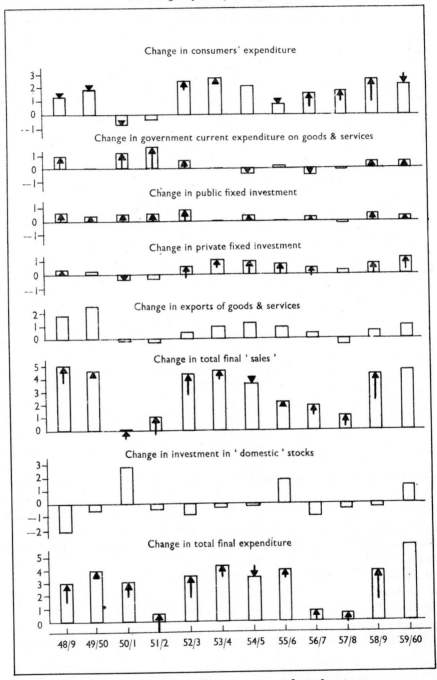

Arrows indicate policy effects: see notes at foot of next page.

of stagnation. After the large replenishment of stocks in 1956, stockbuilding was bound to fall off. But the fact that it became negative, so that stocks actually declined in 1957 and 1958 may, as already suggested, have been due to the credit squeeze (§2 and figure 15.4). This in turn would help to account for the slower growth of consumption—as does the slow growth of exports in 1957 and the decline in exports in 1958. The slow growth of private investment also helps to explain the slow growth of consumption—but it has itself to be explained[1].

Government current expenditure on goods and services, and public investment, both declined in 1955 (the latter was due to Conservative policy in discouraging local authority house-building)[2]. This helps to explain the dip in the growth of final 'sales' in that year. Thereafter the effect of direct public spending was more or less neutral. Both government real spending and public investment remained almost unchanged in 1956: in 1957, defence spending fell again, but public investment rose: in 1958, as a result of Mr Thorneycroft's 1957 crisis measures, there was a small fall in public investment. One would expect government spending and public investment to grow as national income grew. The fact that for three years they showed little change can itself be regarded as a restrictive influence.

In 1955 credit policy and budgetary policy had a restraining influence on consumers' expenditure (figure 15.2); but in 1956 and 1957 their influence was as clearly expansionary. The *basic* restrictive factors operating in these years must then have been these three: the falling trend in exports; the lack of growth in public spending; and, possibly, the effect of the credit squeeze on stockholding. Whether one believes that policy was responsible for the standstill in output in these years thus turns very largely on whether one believes that the credit squeeze affected stocks: the evidence is, and will probably remain, quite insufficient for a firm view.

The evidence is far clearer for the two years of rapid growth that followed 1958. To a minor extent this was due to the renewed expansion of exports (figure 15.5). For the rest it was, in the first phase, due almost entirely to government policy. Under the influence of tax cuts and, equally important, credit relaxations (figure 15.2), there was a surge in consumer spending in 1959.

[1]'Initial' allowances replaced 'investment' allowances at the beginning of 1956: figure 15.2 assumes that this had little effect on investment.
[2]See chapter VIII.2.

Notes to fig. 15.5

Annual changes from *NI & E* [1959] and [1961]. The change in investment in stocks, and in total final expenditure is after rough adjustment to eliminate changes in stocks of imported commodities: see notes to fig. 15.4. Policy effects (shown by the *arrows*) are as estimated on fig. 15.2: the start of the arrow purports to show how each category of expenditure would have changed in the absence of changes in policy (including changes in the real expenditure of the public authorities and in public investment). Only the initial impact, not the secondary repercussions, of policy changes is shown (see discussion in text)

Government real expenditure and public investment also rose. Stocks in this first phase appear to have fallen, so again masking some of the expansionary impetus.

The further rise in final 'sales' in 1960 was less clearly a result of government policy. Consumption demand again rose quite steeply—despite credit restrictions, and presumably as a result of the surge in other branches of demand. For this surge, policy was partly responsible. It was responsible, not for the rise in exports, but for the rise in government spending and public investment; the considerable rise in private investment probably owed something to the boom in demand in 1959 and thus, indirectly, to government policy. There seems little doubt then that the pace of expansion of demand in 1958–60 would have been much more moderate but for the encouragement of policy. Subsequently the government felt obliged in 1961 again to restrain the growth of demand.

The conclusion then is that the rapid expansion of demand and output in the years 1952–5, and that in 1958–60, were both due, directly and indirectly, to the influence of policy. Though this is less certain the same may be true of the slow expansion of demand and output in the years 1955–8: even if due to causes other than policy, policy was certainly not directed to counteract them. The major fluctuations in the rate of growth of demand in the years after 1952 were thus chiefly due to government policy. This was not the intended effect; in each phase, it must be supposed, policy went further than intended, as in turn did the correction of these effects.

As far as internal conditions are concerned then, budgetary and monetary policy failed to be stabilizing, and must on the contrary be regarded as having been positively destabilizing. Tax reductions were made in two or three steep steps, and changes in the regulation of credit were extremely severe. Had tax changes been more gradual, and credit regulations less variable, demand and output would probably have grown much more steadily. (As will be argued more fully in chapter XVI, there would still have been some fluctuations in the growth of demand—if only because export demand would still have fluctuated.)

Many adjustments of policy were occasioned by the balance of payments. It remains to consider how the balance of payments would have fared if internal growth had been steady.

4.   AN INTERPRETATION OF BALANCE OF PAYMENTS FLUCTUATIONS

The balance of payments over the period 1948–60 was on average in surplus by something over £100 million a year[1]. It fluctuated from year to year—the average swing, up or down, being £250 million. There are two chief questions. First, what was the cause of *year-to-year fluctuations* in the balance of payments,

[1] The official balance of payments estimates have been subject to frequent revision. The following analysis is based on the estimates contained in the 1961 edition of *National*

and, in particular, could crises have been avoided by a different internal policy? And second, could the *whole level* of the balance of payments have been bettered?

When internal expansion was rapid, imports also tended to grow rapidly (figure 15.1 above). This has been the chief short-term effect of internal policy on the balance of payments. Rapid expansion may also at times have hampered exports; but most of the short-term fluctuations in exports have clearly not been due to internal trends but to fluctuations in world demand[1]. The balance of payments has also been largely affected by swings in the terms of trade—chiefly due to changes in the world price of the commodities we import. It has been affected too, to a less degree, by changes in net property income from abroad (changes chiefly due to changes in the profits on British-owned investments abroad); and by changes in net grants and transfers (chiefly reflecting the changing size of grants made by foreign governments to this country).

The four latter factors all reflect conditions overseas rather than conditions in the United Kingdom. As will be seen from table 15.1, most of the year-to-year fluctuation in the balance of payments has been due to changes in these. The volume of imports has been on a rising trend—in line with the general expansion of activity. After allowing for this trend, the average swing in the volume of imports has been of the order of £150 million up or down on the previous year; and of this, most has probably been due to swings in stocks of imported commodities—a random factor, perhaps not dependent entirely on the rate of expansion of internal demand. On an average for the period, therefore, probably no more than one quarter or one fifth of the total year-to-year fluctuation in the balance of payments can be ascribed to fluctuations in internal demand[2].

Income and Expenditure (August 1961)—or, for the first two years covered, on the 1959 edition. Substantial revisions were made in particular in the March 1962 *Balance of Payments* White Paper (Cmnd. 1671). These raised the estimate of the current balance in 1959 and 1960 by about £60 million as compared with the 1961 estimates. Since the working for this section was completed, revised estimates for earlier years have also been published (in *NI & E* [1962]); but these revisions do not greatly affect the estimated *year-to year* changes on which the following analysis is chiefly based.

[1] As far as I know, no study has succeeded in demonstrating any close inverse connection between the level of exports and the level of home demand. This is because home demand has tended to be high at the same time as demand in overseas markets, so that exports have tended to rise fastest at times when internal demand was also increasing most rapidly (see figure 15.5). It is thus very difficult to sort out the effect of home demand on exports. It seems probable that there is such an effect, but it seems likely to be much less important than the effect of home demand on imports.

[2] See bottom line of table 15.1: 'swing corrected for trend'. Because fluctuations were partially offsetting the sum of the average swing for separate items is more than the average swing for the total current balance.

Most of the 'price effects' shown reflect changes in the terms of trade. But since imports usually exceeded exports, a *general* rise in prices worsens the balance, and such effects are also included among 'price effects'.

A good deal of the fluctuation to which the balance of payments is subject is of a random nature; and, to this extent, favourable or unfavourable movements are unlikely to go far, or for long, without being halted or reversed. As already argued, many of the factors depend on the trend in world trade: but there are limits to the swings in world trade. Our terms of trade are chiefly determined by world commodity prices, which in the short term are very variable; but any

Table 15.1. *Analysis of year-to-year changes in balance of payments, 1948–60 (£m., year-to-year changes[a])*

	Volume of exports[b]	less volume of imports[bc]		Effect of price changes[d]	Net property income from abroad	Net grants, transfers, etc.	Current balance of payments
		'stock changes'[e]	'consumption of imports[e]				
1948–9	250	−25	−150	25	−25	−50	25
1949–50	325	+100	−150	−225	175	25	250
1950–1	−25	−100	−150	−400	−50	—	−750
1951–2	−75	+350	—	275	−100	100	550
1952–3	75	—	−275	200	−25	—	−25
1953–4	200	+125	−250	−25	25	−75	—
1954–5	250	−275	−175	−25	−75	−25	−300
1955–6	175	+175	−175	150	50	−25	350
1956–7	75	−50	−100	75	25	−25	25
1957–8	−100	−50	+ 25	225	—	—	100
1958–9	150	−225	−175	75	−50	—	−250
1959–60	250	−300	−275	—	−50	—	−400
Average swing[f]	150	150	150	150	50	25	250
Trend[g]	125	−25	−150	25	—	—	−25
Swing corrected for trend[h]	75	150	50	125	50	25	225

From *NI & E* [1959] and [1961], tables 7 and 13.

[a]All figures rounded to nearest £25 million.

[b]Changes in the volume of exports and imports are valued at prices ruling in the first of each pair of years.

[c]The signs of all items show the effect on the balance of payments: hence an *increase* in imports is shown as *negative*.

[d]The effect of price changes is estimated as the change in the value of exports of goods and services *less* the change in volume of exports (as above) *less* the change in the value of imports of goods and services *plus* the change in the volume of imports (as above).

[e]As for fig. 15.4, 'consumption' of imports is taken as 40 per cent of change in GNP at constant prices; the remainder of the change in imports is attributed to a change in stocks of imported commodities.

[f]Average change neglecting sign.

[g]Average change taking account of sign.

[h]Average of (average change *less* trend).

large movement in prices tends after a time to effect an adjustment of supplies calculated at least partially to restore the position. Moreover, the immediate effect on our import prices is likely to be accompanied after a year or so by compensating changes in other items of the external account: booming world trade may cause us to pay more for imports, but we can then also sell more exports, and profits on overseas investments are high. Finally (as noted) a good deal of the fluctuation has been caused by erratic swings in stocks of imported commodities; but stocks are not run up or down indefinitely, and any large movement is likely sooner to or later to produce a reaction.

The speed with which these compensating factors work themselves out varies from item to item; and it is this which is the fundamental cause of short-period fluctuations in the balance of payments. A year is too short a period in which to expect all factors to balance out smoothly. But taking a two- or three-year view, there seem only two factors affecting our balance of payments, both under our own control. The first is our competitive position, which—it will be argued later—is primarily determined by the level of prices in this country compared with those of our competitors. The second is the rate of expansion of demand in this country (which—price levels being given—determines the rate of growth of imports) as compared with the rate of expansion in other countries (which—price levels again being given—determines the rate of growth of exports)[1].

In order to analyse more easily the course of the balance of payments since 1948, the analysis of table 15.1 is repeated in graphical form in figure 15.6. In interpreting the diagram, it has to be remembered that in an expanding economy in an expanding world, the volume of both exports and imports should be expected to grow; it is only changes larger, or smaller, than average that call for comment. Changes in the volume of imports are shown, as it were, upside down—since an increase in the volume of imports helps to worsen the balance. The *arrows* indicate that part of the change in imports which was due to changes in stocks of imported commodities[2].

The diagram also shows (top part) not only changes in the balance of payments but the size of the surplus or deficit each year; and with it, the change in the foreign exchange reserves. In some years the actual change in the reserves means little. In the early years, for instance, the loss of reserves would have been far greater but for Marshall Aid. In 1956 the reserves were bolstered by drawings from the IMF and in 1958 by the loan from the Export-Import Bank: and in 1959 and 1960 these loans were repaid. The dotted line in the diagram shows how the reserves would have changed apart from these transactions—which may all be considered more or less of the nature of compensatory finance[3].

[1] For simplicity, the argument ignores such factors as military expenditure overseas. For, whatever its level, there are (on the present argument) ways of adapting to it. The same is true, e.g. of loss of protection previously enjoyed in sterling markets.

[2] As roughly estimated: see notes to table 15.1.

[3] What items to allow for is a matter of judgement: for details see notes to figure 15.6.

Fig. 15.6.   Balance of payments fluctuations
£100 million

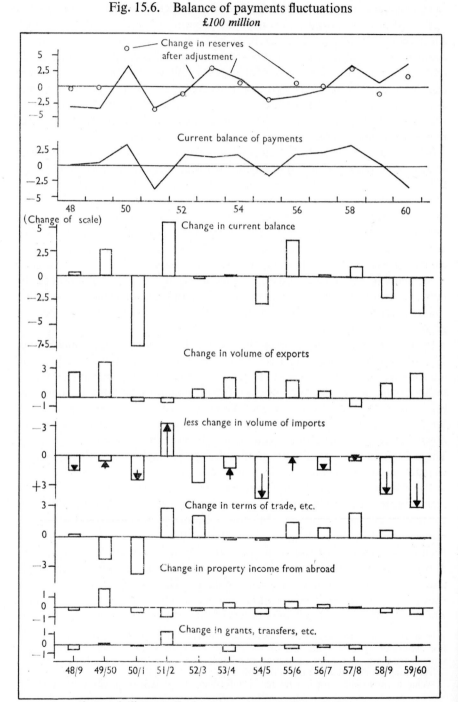

Arrows indicate stock changes: see notes at foot of next page.

The reserves have been influenced not only by the United Kingdom's balance of payments, but also by that of the rest of the sterling area, and by swings in confidence. Thus the large gain in reserves in 1950, and the subsequent loss in 1951, were due as to about one half to the successive surge, first, in the exports, then in the imports, of the outer sterling area[1]. The loss in 1952 was made worse by a movement out of sterling associated with doubts about British exchange policy[2]. Some confidence crises were short-lived and do not show up in the annual figures: this is true of the devaluation crisis of 1949[3], and the crisis in the summer of 1957[4]. The 1955 crisis was again made the more severe by lack of confidence in sterling associated with renewed rumours about exchange policy[2]; while in 1960 the reserves were bolstered by a movement in favour of sterling.

The reserves were plainly affected also by the current balance of payments. Such an effect is clear in 1950–1, in 1955, and in 1959—though not in 1960. In the longer run, the reserves must depend primarily on the current balance; and in analysing the effects of internal and budgetary policy on the external situation, it is more profitable to look to this than to changes in the reserves.

Each of the three occasions when the balance of payments fell into deficit (1951, 1955 and 1960) came after a period of rapid growth in internal demand; and each was accompanied, and quite largely caused, by an abnormal growth in imports[5]. This does not mean that the deficits should be attributed solely to

[1]See chapter II.4.
[2]See chapter III.3.
[3]See chapter II.4.
[4]See chapter III.4.
[5]Some of the increase in imports in 1959 and 1960 was a 'trend increase', which would probably have occurred whatever the trend in home demand (see G. F. Ray [1960], 'British Imports of Manufactured Goods', and the same author [1961], 'British Imports of Manufactures', *Nat. Inst. econ. R.*, March 1960 and May 1961). One reason for this trend was the reduction of import restrictions. Another probably was the unfavourable trend in prices in the United Kingdom compared with that elsewhere—an important consideration further discussed later.

Notes to fig. 15.6

From *NI & E* [1959] and [1961] except for changes in reserves which are from *UKBP* [1959] and subsequent *Balance of Payments* White Papers. Actual changes in reserves are shown by the 'ringed' points. Points connected by the line show changes in reserves after adjustment for certain transactions of the nature of 'compensatory finance'. They show changes in official reserves *plus* drawings on (or *less* repayments to) the IMF, *plus* drawings on (or *less* repayments of) the US and Canadian lines of credit, ERP loans and grants, and Export-Import Bank credits. Adjustment is not made for changes in the UK balance in the EPU nor for subscriptions to the IMF.

Balance of payments items are as estimated in *NI & E* [1961] and for years prior to 1950 in *NI & E* [1959]. The change in the volume of exports and imports (of goods and services) and the effect of changes in the terms of trade and other price effects are estimated as described in the notes to table 15.1. Changes in imports are shown 'upside down' in order to show their effect on the balance of payments. The effect of changes in stocks of imported commodities (roughly estimated as explained in the notes to fig. 15.4) is shown by the *arrows*: the start of the arrow purports to show how imports would have changed in the absence of such stock changes.

the level of home demand *in the crisis year itself.* A period of unusually rapid growth in home demand necessitates a more rapid growth of imports and this worsens the trend in the balance of payments and makes it more likely to be thrown into deficit. Each of the three payments deficits came after a period of rapid growth of internal demand. Similarly, the stagnation of internal demand in 1952[1], and again in 1957–8, favoured the balance of payments. If throughout the period, the internal demand had grown at a steady rate instead of fluctuating, the balance of payments would also have fluctuated rather less; and, in particular, such deficits as occurred would have been, at least, much reduced.

In each of the three deficit years, however, the rise in imports was partly due to stockbuilding (see *arrows* on figure 15.6)[2]. It is difficult to say how far this stockbuilding of imported commodities was a result of high demand at home, and would have been reduced if home demand had fluctuated less. If as is possible the level of such stocks is only loosely connected with internal conditions there would still have been considerable fluctuations in the balance of payments for this reason among others.

The argument so far has been that the balance of payments might have been made more stable. But this by itself would have done nothing to make it on average more favourable—and thus done nothing to remedy one of the most persistent of post-war problems. It can however be argued that if the economy had been run not only at a more stable, but at a lower average pressure of demand, this would have reduced the rise of prices; and that this in turn would have produced a greater expansion of exports. These two contentions have figured in most of the political discussion of economic policy; but many economists have come to doubt one or other or both.

I myself believe both contentions to be true. The reasons, such as they are, for believing that prices are sensitive to the pressure of demand have already been set out in chapter XIII. There have been many academic studies of the sensitivity of exports and imports to relative prices. But in my view, relevant evidence is hard to come by, and conclusions have to be based chiefly on study of the effects of major devaluations and tariff changes. Their evidence seems to suggest that international trade is greatly affected by prices. Thus a recent study of British imports suggests, for instance, that a one per cent fall in the price of British substitutes for manufactures we at present import might in

---

[1]For the relative importance of import restrictions and internal deflation as factors causing the fall of imports in 1952, see chapter III.2 above, and the article by W. M. Corden [1958], there quoted.

[2]The method used here to estimate changes in stocks of imported commodities is not accurate. At times of boom the marginal propensity to import is probably particularly high: this is ignored by the method adopted (see M. FG. Scott [1963], *A Study of United Kingdom Imports*, pp. 53–8).

time reduce the volume of such imports by as much as, say, ten per cent[1]. What is true of other countries' exports in our markets must also be true of our exports in theirs.

Control of internal price developments is not the only way in which export prices could have been made more competitive—the exchange rate could have been altered. Nor is a different policy with respect to demand the only way by which the rise in prices might have been mitigated. The problem of prices and the balance of payments is likely to continue to be of importance in future, as more emphasis is placed on a rapid rate of economic growth; and is more fully discussed in the next chapter.

5. CONCLUSIONS: THE MANAGEMENT OF DEMAND

The problem of managing the level of demand only emerged after the excess demand built up during the war had been worked off. But for the Korean war, general excess demand might have been eliminated in 1950 or so. The repercussions of the Korean war caused very great fluctuations in demand. To have appreciably mitigated the boom of 1951 and subsequent recession of 1952, would have required massive counter-measures taken well in advance. The analysis in §3 suggests that internal policy could hardly have been expected completely to counter the effects of world developments on this scale.

The analysis also suggests that the fluctuations in the growth of demand in the years 1952–60 were due in large part to fluctuations in policy. The trend over the whole period was for tax rates to be reduced; but they were reduced not gradually but in two or three steep steps. Had tax reductions instead been gradual, and had alternate restrictions and relaxations of credit been avoided, the growth of demand would probably have been much smoother. Some important causes of fluctuations would still however have remained. Some of the fluctuation in the growth of demand arose from three- or four-year cycles in the growth of overseas demand for British exports. However well demand had been managed, it would, too, have been difficult to eliminate fluctuations in investment in stocks. But so far from countering such basic causes of instability,

[1] M. FG. Scott [1963], *A Study of United Kingdom Imports*, esp. pp. 43–4 and chapter VIII. Scott estimated the price elasticity of demand for imports of manufactures into the United Kingdom as between -5 and -15. He also discusses the general problem of estimating such elasticities. He argues that since the demand for different manufactures is price-elastic, observed divergencies between the prices of competing imports and home products do not emerge in normal times; and that the usual econometric demand study is therefore fruitless. Scott's own conclusions rest chiefly on an analysis of the effect on imports of the imposition of tariffs and devaluation of the pound in 1931–2. A study of recent changes in tariffs in Germany, and their effect on imports suggests similar conclusions: J. Wemelsfelder [1960], 'The Short-term Effect of the Lowering of Import Duties in Germany', *Econ. J.*, March 1960. Sir Donald MacDougall has previously estimated that the price elasticity of substitution as between British and American products in world markets was in the long run of the order -5 (G. D. A. MacDougall [1951], 'British and American Exports', part 1, *Econ. J.*, December 1951).

the influence of policy seems rather to have exaggerated their effects.

One reason for this partial failure of policy was probably that it was difficult to form a reliable view as to the rate of growth of demand which the economy was capable of meeting.   The difficulty was perhaps especially great in the early 'fifties, before much experience had been gained; but since the 'potential' rate of growth may well change, it is likely to remain a problem.   Another reason probably was that there was a tendency to take too simple a view of the economy, and to regard it as quickly responsive to treatment.   The discussion in §2 suggested that policy measures designed to stimulate demand had, in addition to their initial impact, secondary effects which in total were liable to be as important.   It also suggested that, largely because of the behaviour of stocks, the full impact on output was likely to be delayed, sometimes for several years. It is difficult not to feel that too little weight was given to such secondary and delayed effects of policy changes; and that the long train of repercussions out of which, over years, a boom builds up, was not reckoned with.   For this neglect, it has already been suggested, the practice of making annual forecasts of developments to be expected in the year ahead was partly responsible[1].   For short-run forecasting may often be best done by what amounts to short cuts— which fail to focus attention on basic causal sequences.   This weakness can only be overcome if a conscious effort is made to do so by interpreting the forecasts in the perspective of developments over several past years.

Periods of rapid expansion of demand led to a rapid growth of imports and thus to balance of payments deficits; and this was a main motive for the switch to a restrictive policy in 1955-6 and later in 1961.   Had policy been more effectively directed to securing a steady growth of demand, and had rapid expansions of demand, later to prove excessive, been avoided, one important reason for balance of payments fluctuations would have been removed. But this, again, would not have removed all causes of fluctuation.   However well internal demand is managed, short-period fluctuations in the balance of payments, of a more or less random nature, are to be expected.   Furthermore, if internal demand grew steadily, while cycles in export demand continued, this would bring longer-period fluctuations in the balance of payments of a new sort[2].

Though a steadier growth of internal demand would probably have reduced fluctuations in the balance of payments, it would probably have done little to make the balance of payments on average more favourable.   But the pressure of demand not only fluctuated, but was also on average relatively high.   The general high pressure of demand (it has been argued earlier) accelerated the rise in prices; and this in turn (it was argued in §4) tended to reduce the rise in exports and also to increase imports of manufactures.   Precisely how high a pressure of demand the economy should be run at depends on a complex of considerations more fully argued in chapter XVI.

[1]See chapter V.4.
[2]See chapter XVI.2.

ECONOMIC GROWTH AND ECONOMIC STABILITY

The analysis of past experience in chapter XV suggested that a different management of fiscal and monetary policy might have avoided much of the fluctuation in the rate of growth of internal demand, and some of the fluctuations in the balance of payments.   But it did not suggest that this alone would have been enough greatly to accelerate the average rate of growth, or greatly to improve the balance of payments on average.   The conclusions so far are thus somewhat negative.

This concluding chapter steps beyond the analysis of past trends to suggest how the performance of the economy might be more radically improved.   On matters where views differ so widely, it seems possible only to set out the main considerations, and to state a personal view.   During the 'fifties the government sought to manage the economy chiefly by controlling the level of demand by means of budgetary and monetary policy.   More recently the government set up arrangements for some degree of central organization of economic planning, and has begun to develop a wages policy.   These methods used along with budgetary and monetary policy, it is argued, might help to achieve faster economic growth with a reasonable degree of price stability.

This chapter first discusses briefly the problem of securing faster growth (§1) and then considers the management of prices and the balance of payments in relation to economic growth (§2).   A possible general strategy of policy is then outlined (§3).   The last part considers in more detail the possible respective roles of fiscal and credit policy in a strategy aiming more explicitly than in the past at faster growth (§4).

1. THE RATE OF ECONOMIC GROWTH

During the years 1948–60 national output grew on average by $2\frac{3}{4}$ per cent, and output per head by two per cent, a year.   The discussion in chapter XV was confined to trying to explain fluctuations about this average rate of growth. But what determines the average rate of growth itself?   It would hardly be useful to try to answer this question by detailed analysis of post-war experience, such as was found useful in dealing with the essentially short-term questions discussed in chapter XV.   In the nature of the case there can be little firm evidence, and any answer must be in the nature of supposition.   But reflection on the short-term mechanisms previously discussed suggests some implications for the longer-term process of economic growth[1].

---

[1]A full-scale study of economic growth and of the longer-term prospects for the British economy is being undertaken at the National Institute of Economic and Social Research under the direction of Mr W. Beckerman.   I can hardly hope to anticipate his conclusions, but have some hope that the present tentative views will not be too far out of line with his.

The pace of the growth of output from year to year has been due to changes in demand. This has caused capacity to be more fully employed in some years, and less so in others. But the economy's capacity to produce has fairly certainly grown much more steadily[1]. Over the period 1948–60, it must have grown at much the same rate as the actual increase in output over this period[2]: by and large—and with all the fluctuations already noted—the government has had to keep the growth of real demand within the limits set by the growth of the economy's capacity. The question here is to explain, not these fluctuations in the degree of utilization, but why the economy's capacity to produce grew at the rate it did, and in particular not more rapidly.

It seems clear in the first place that the growth of productive capacity cannot be explained simply as a result of the growth of capital, i.e. of investment. There have been a series of statistical studies which have examined the relation over the last century or so between, on the one hand, the growth of output and, on the other, the changes in working population and in the stock of capital[3]. These studies suggest that only the lesser part of the growth of output can be explained in terms of greater input of the factors of production: most leave an unexplained residual, amounting to half or more of the growth of output. This, it has to be surmised, is due to the adoption of better techniques and the gradual, piecemeal refinement of ways of work. Though better methods frequently require better equipment, the resulting investment seems best regarded as a necessary accompaniment rather than a full explanation of the increase in output.

It seems reasonable to argue that the pace at which new methods are adopted is not rigidly determined by technical factors, but depends on human habits and attitudes; and also that habits and attitudes can be changed. The possibilities of amendment are perhaps not always obvious at the time. For there would seem to be various processes which tend to make what firms do appear the only thing they could have done, or could do in future—though they would equally well tend to underpin a faster rate of growth, could this be once achieved.

Economic expansion normally requires that 'business' sells to 'consumers' an

---

[1]Compare E. F. Denison [1962], *The Sources of Economic Growth in the United States*, pp. 3–4: 'it is absolutely essential to distinguish between (1) the growth of the nation's "potential" production, its *ability* or *capacity* to produce marketable goods and services, and (2) changes in the ratio of actual production to "potential" production. The former depends on changes in the quantity and quality of available labor and capital, the advance of knowledge, and similar factors, while the latter is governed mainly by the relationship between aggregate demand and potential production.'

[2]Even if capacity was less fully employed in 1960 than in 1948—and no accurate measure exists—the scale of 'under-employment' would hardly be large enough greatly to affect a twelve-year average.

[3]See for instance R. Solow [1957], 'Technical Change and the Aggregate Production Function', *R. Econ. Statist.*, August 1957; O. Aukrust [1959], 'Investment and Economic Growth', *Productivity Meas. R.*, February 1959; W. B. Reddaway and A. D. Smith [1960], 'Progress in British Manufacturing Industries', *Econ. J.*, March 1960; E. D. Domar [1961], 'On the Measurement of Technological Change', *Econ. J.*, December 1961; and the general discussion in the article by E. Lundberg [1959], 'The Profitability of Investment', *Econ. J.*, December 1959.

ever-increasing volume of goods and services.   The argument developed below is that, not only (as already shown) does the rate of increase in productivity affect prices[1]; but, also, that what may be called the aggregate pricing policy of 'business' towards 'consumers' affects real purchasing power, and hence in turn the rate of growth of production and productivity.   This interdependence, or circularity in the logic of the process, means that production and pricing developments have to keep in step.   It may therefore be that 'conservative' pricing policy imposes a brake on the whole process, and results in a 'conservative' rate of growth.

The argument can best be developed by considering first an economy where output consists entirely of consumer goods and services, which are consumed entirely by the members of that economy, and paid for out of the income earned in producing these goods and services.   In such an economy consumption, and hence output, could only grow if consumers' real purchasing power increased; and for this to happen, product prices would have to fall *relative to wages and other incomes*.   The case is not essentially different if, as in any real case, there are other types of expenditure than consumption[2].

Over the last decade and a half real wages have about kept pace with the growth of productivity.   The benefits of rising productivity have been passed on through product prices advancing less rapidly than wages and other factor costs[3]; and most of the steady increase in purchasing power has come about in this way.   In this field, Say's law holds: increases in supply create their own demand.   Purchasing power has also been increased by the reduction of taxes over the period; but this accounts for the lesser part of the increase.   It is thus a normal part of the process of growth that consumption should grow fairly steadily[4].

[1] See chapter XIII.4.

[2] A continuous growth of consumption still appears a basic requirement for continued growth.   For, first, consumption is itself a large part of demand: even in an open economy like the United Kingdom, consumption is one half of final demand.   The growth of exports has admittedly contributed to the growth of demand, but this only shifts the problem of explanation: what is foreign demand for one country is home demand for another.   Investment demand, again, is essentially a 'derived' demand, and depends on a parallel growth in the demand for the things capital equipment produces.

[3] Economic growth requires other relative price adjustments also.   Because of different rates of increase in productivity in different industries the price of services has tended to rise more, and that of durables less, than the average of consumer prices in most countries. (See the OEEC report by Fellner, Gilbert, Hansen, Kahn, Lutz and de Wolff [1961], *The Problem of Rising Prices*, esp. table 3.)

[4] This has implications for forecasting and econometric models of the economy.   The process has not usually been made explicit either in the latter, or in growth models of the theoretical sort.   Sir Roy Harrod, for instance, concentrates most of his attention on the growth of capital (see R. F. Harrod [1948], *Towards a Dynamic Economics*).   His formulae imply that investment causes consumption to grow; for s (the fraction of income saved) is (if not absolutely yet for practical purposes as good as) constant (pp. 78–9).   This assumption rests on an analysis (Lecture II) of the likely rate of saving out of growing personal real incomes.   But he does not examine the question here under scrutiny—how it is that personal real incomes come to grow.

The reason for emphasizing this aspect here is to suggest that the speed with which the process operates is a main determinant of the rate of growth. What may happen is that the 'productivity benefit passed on' is less than the increase in productivity which could be obtained if maximum advantage were taken of opportunities to expand output; what is 'passed on' may be much less, determined perhaps by the rate of productivity increase achieved in the recent past.

A distinction has already been drawn between, on the one hand, short-run changes in output per head, associated with the transition from a lower to a higher, or a higher to a lower, degree of utilization of capacity—which have been marked, and which have been obviously affected by government policy; and, on the other hand, the underlying growth in capacity to produce—which has probably gone on fairly steadily.

Now the system is not, as it were, 'self-righting' with regard to capacity working. If the economy is working below capacity, output could, by definition, be increased. If all entrepreuneurs lowered prices (relative to factor costs) they would increase purchasing power and stimulate spending—and thus induce the increase in output and output per head that would 'justify' their (relative) price reductions[1]. In fact this does not happen, or not quickly.

Much the same may apply to the speed with which productive capacity is increased. The long-run growth of productivity depends to some extent on the speed with which known better methods are introduced. One may say, if one likes, that the limit is set by the scarcity of 'entrepreneurship'. But this is to admit that it depends on the quality of management, and the choices that management makes[2].

If the pace of advance is unnecessarily slow, are there any forces that will right this state of affairs? Will not the outcome, on the contrary, appear to justify itself? For if the pace is slow, the reduction in prices (relative to factor costs) will be slow also. Consumers' purchasing power will grow at a moderate pace only, and entrepreneurs will feel justified in having planned for only a moderate increase in productive capacity.

Failure fully to exploit productive opportunities clearly implies a certain muting of the forces of competition. Under perfectly competitive conditions it should pay firms to expand faster, cut their costs more, and get their prices lower than their rivals. But under oligopolistic conditions firms are restrained from aggressive competition by fear of retaliation; and tend to fall back on the more limited goal of preserving their share of their markets. This being so,

---

[1]What is implied is a reduction in prices relative to total labour costs; not (as it turns out) a reduction relative to unit labour costs. Thus it does not imply profit-cutting. The aggregate *value* of sales might remain as it would have been, with lower prices and a larger volume being sold. Profits might take the same share of sales revenue; and in real terms be worth more.

[2]For a study of different firms' policies for growth, and of the importance of the quality of management, see the study by T. Barna [1962], *Investment and Growth Policies in British Industrial Firms.*

their plans to expand must be greatly coloured by whether they expect their environment to be a rapidly, or a slowly expanding economy[1]. In practice such expectations must be based very largely on what they have come to know from experience; thus a slow—or a fast—rate of growth seems likely to perpetuate itself.

It is often argued that if the government permitted demand to expand quickly, this alone would be enough to cause an equally rapid expansion of productive capacity. The foregoing analysis suggests that if this treatment could be continued for long enough at a time, it might work. Repeated experience of being able to sell more than they were able to produce might well lead manufacturers to quicken the pace with which they expanded capacity; and once the faster growth of productivity got reflected in their pricing policies, the process would be self-sustaining and would cease to be dependent on continued fiscal stimulation of purchasing power. But a high level of demand does not appear to lead quickly to a faster growth in productive capacity: the typical reaction of the British economy to excess demand seems, rather, not to react to it very much[2]. There have been times when government measures have produced a rapid expansion in demand. Thus during the four years 1952–6 the volume of final expenditure grew at well above its average rate[3]. This may have accelerated the growth of capacity to some degree; but clearly not to the degree needed to prevent demand outrunning capacity. The consequent emergence of excess demand prevented the policy being continued for longer.

It is often argued also that the 'stops and starts' of official policy have constantly interrupted business plans, and made firms less willing to plan for expansion. This is probably true to some extent. Yet it may be doubted whether a relatively passive policy of keeping the pressure of demand as steady as possible would alone be enough to make a radical difference to the rate of economic growth. To achieve this a different approach seems to be required, aiming to influence the rate of growth of supply directly, not via the manipulation of demand.

[1]Compare W. J. Baumol [1959], *Business Behavior, Value and Growth*. Writing of American conditions, he says (p. 99) 'past experience has prejudiced firms to look with favor on expansion programs. When they expanded in the past they have often found demand waiting for them just because so many other firms were increasing their production at the same time. If every executive is convinced that the growth of his enterprise will be lucrative, the general expansion which results may turn out to have justified this belief'. He adds, 'it is essentially a matter of faith'.

Barna [1962], *op. cit.*, also emphasizes (p. 51) the importance of long-run expectations: ' . . . the growing belief in the stability of the economy kept fluctuations in confidence within bounds. There has been a widespread belief that demand could not fall much without the government taking counter measures and this belief has prevented any substantial fall in investment expenditure'. As Barna describes them for the United Kingdom, expectations have been an anti-contractionary influence, rather than a positively expansionary one.

[2]Compare the argument of chapter XIII.1.

[3]See figure 15.5, chapter XV.

The reasons for the slow growth of the British economy seem then deep-seated, and not due chiefly to government policy.   They are probably not unconnected with the reasons which underlay the sluggishness of its response to inflation. The pace of inflation is dependent (it was suggested) on customs and habitual expectations; and the prevailing rate of growth seems to depend on them too. How quickly firms expand depends on how quickly they expect sales to expand; how quickly sales can expand depends on how quickly real incomes grow: and how quickly real incomes grow depends on how fast firms introduce improved methods.   To some extent therefore the rate of growth is the collective result of numerous decisions which have hitherto been taken—and which hitherto could only be taken—individually.   There has been no mechanism by which any conscious collective decision could be made.

There seems then a logical case for the organized, mutual discussion by private firms and public corporations of their plans for expansion.   The result could be to persuade the main body of firms that faster growth was possible; and to enable some sort of collective decision to be taken as to the rate of growth.   If each firm knew that other firms were planning for a faster rate of growth than in the past, it would have good reason to believe that faster growth was not only possible, but likely; and good reason therefore for expanding more rapidly itself.   Such an exercise, it may be said, would be no more than a psychological conjuring trick.   But the foregoing analysis of the relation between pricing policies and the expansion of real output suggests that it matters what kind of faith business works on, and that left to itself nature does not necessarily produce the best answers.

The resurrection of the idea of economic planning after a decade of eclipse, has been the result of a disillusion with past policies, in which there were perhaps three main currents.   First was the feeling in government circles that effective control of public investment and government current expenditure required a long-term programme, and that this in turn required to be seen against the prospects for the economy as a whole[1].   Second was a feeling in industry that economic policy had been too much governed by short-run considerations, and gave too little emphasis to economic growth[2].   Third was the dawning realization that other European economies had succeeded in growing much

---

[1]The idea of the National Economic Development Council was first bruited in Mr Selwyn Lloyd's statement on economic policy in July 1961.   'The controversial matter of planning at once arises', he said; 'I am not frightened of the word'.   He went on: 'one of the first things I did when appointed Chancellor was to ask for a plan of the programme for development and expenditure in the public sector for five years ahead . . .   In addition . . . developments in the economy as a whole are studied by a number of bodies.' Instancing the Economic Planning Board and various other advisory bodies, he said that it was time for 'better co-ordination of these various activities' (*H.C. Deb.* 25 July 1961, 220).

[2]This feeling emerged strongly at the conference organized by the Federation of British Industries in Brighton in November 1960.

more rapidly than the British; in the case of France it was possible to associate this with French procedures for economic planning[1].

The constitution of the National Economic Development Council, with a secretariat of its own, and in an independent position half-way between the government and business, may enable it to play a positive role in the co-ordination of plans[2]. How effective this will prove, and how much scope for faster growth there will prove to be, remains to be seen. The belief that economic growth in this country could be faster rests almost entirely on the fact that during the last decade it has been about twice as fast in the other main European countries: and in five years' time the facts may look very different. My own belief is that faster growth will prove possible and that the institution of planning procedures will have made an important difference.

2. GROWTH, THE BALANCE OF PAYMENTS AND PRICE STABILITY

It is now necessary to discuss how the balance of payments would fare if the rate of internal growth were both more steady and more rapid than in the past. The effect of steady growth is different from that of more rapid growth, and may be discussed separately. The latter question, it will be argued, is closely connected with the question of price stability.

Analysis of past balance of payments fluctuations suggests that if internal growth had been steady, part of the fluctuations in the balance of payments would have been avoided[3]. Nevertheless, some fluctuations would remain. To a large extent these are likely to be self-correcting. They are likely also to be difficult to foresee, and hence difficult to correct by adjustments of the level of internal demand. Furthermore, adjustments to the level of demand designed to offset other factors affecting the balance of payments would have to be large. They would therefore be incompatible with a policy designed to produce steady internal expansion.

The conclusion is that if policy is to aim at producing steady growth, it must, as it were, drive straight through fluctuations in the balance of payments. Whatever the average balance of payments is to be, the authorities ought to view with equanimity a surplus in some years less than this, and in other years

[1]A conference on French planning organized by the National Institute of Economic and Social Research in April 1961 aroused much interest. The conference was addressed by M. Massé and others associated with the Commissariat Général du Plan. A record of the conference, which I edited, was published in August for the NIESR by PEP, *Economic Planning in France*.

[2]The NEDC, at its second meeting in May 1962, instructed its secretariat to investigate the possibilities of a 4 per cent annual rate of growth and to discuss its implications with a cross-section of major industries. Such a rate would be half as fast again as the rate of growth in the 'fifties. The terms of reference of the Council are 'to study centrally the plans and prospects of our main industries, to correlate them with each other and with the public sector, and to see how in aggregate they contribute to and fit in with the prospects of the economy as a whole'.

[3]See chapter XV.5 above.

more.   (It may be assumed that the authorities will continue to aim at a balance of payments on average in surplus, in order for instance to finance grants and loans to underdeveloped countries.)

Some causes of balance of payments fluctuation (such as swings in stocks of imported commodities) are likely to be fairly short-lived.   Others are likely to last much longer.   Thus world trade has in the past grown in bursts, two or three years of rapid growth alternating with two or three years of slow growth or actual decline; and this has caused a parallel uneven growth in British exports[1]. But a steady growth of internal demand is likely to cause a steady growth in the volume of imports.   If world trade continues to grow unsteadily while growth in this country is steady, this would tend to make the balance of payments worse than average for several years together in a slack time for world trade, and better than average for several years together in a boom.   The extent of the swing in the balance of payments to be expected is probably to be put at at least £200 million either side of its average value.

This consequence of the pursuit of steady growth has probably not yet been accepted by financial opinion either at home or abroad.   It may be that the present level of reserves would be adequate to finance such swings in the balance of payments provided that they did not provoke parallel swings in confidence. But past fluctuations in the reserves have been due less to fluctuations in the trade balance than to swings in confidence in sterling.   The remedy for the present instability in the mechanism of international payments will surely be found to be, as the *Radcliffe Report* urged, in getting away from the present reliance on one or two national currencies as the media for international reserves, and in 'increasing the resources and through them the facilities of international organisations for the provision of credit'[2].   But meanwhile the world is some way off from a major development in this direction; and the lack of it may well prove to be a constraint on policies designed to promote steady growth.   The world being what it is, there remains therefore a case for building up reserves by running a larger balance of payments surplus than would other-wise be required—provided that this itself does not inhibit the internal growth it should be intended to facilitate.

So far we have discussed only the consequences of *steady* growth.   A rate of growth which was also more rapid than in the past would have two further consequences for the balance of payments.   First, it would tend to produce a more rapid growth of imports; and hence, to be sustainable, it would require a more rapid growth of exports.   Second (as will be argued here) it would tend to promote greater price stability; and this (as will also be argued) would tend to promote the expansion of exports required.   But the two effects would not necessarily match each other automatically; and further action, either by exchange-rate adjustments, or by greater control of internal inflation, might well

[1]See figure 15.6, chapter XV.
[2]*Radcliffe Report*, para. 985: see also chapter VIII of the *Report*.

be required. The various considerations involved need to be set out at greater length.

On the question of whether exports are sensitive to prices there has been a good deal of disagreement. Governments and monetary authorities have continued to believe that they are, and to emphasize the importance for this reason of controlling price developments. Many economists have been sceptical. My own view, for reasons set out[1], is that the less sophisticated opinion is correct; and that the volume of exports, and also the volume of imports of manufactured goods, is markedly affected by the level of prices in one country as compared with those of its competitors. If this is the case, it is possible to prevent the balance of payments—or more simply, inability to pay for the volume of imports required—from acting as a constraint on the sustainable rate of internal growth. But this still leaves a choice of methods. Competitive export prices can be assured either by control of the internal price level, or by devaluation of the external value of the currency[2].

The method of devaluation cannot be dismissed out of hand. A degree of orderliness in the conditions of world trade is certainly advantageous; and this justifies international rules limiting a country's freedom to devalue. But internal price developments are not perfectly within the control of governments. It is therefore hardly conceivable that the world can get by, decade after decade, without adjustment of the rates of exchange between major currencies. This being so, there is much to be said for permitting countries to make *strictly limited* adjustments in rates, whenever they like, rather than forcing them to wait till a major disruption of the system of rates is inevitable. If countries were allowed to adjust their exchange rates by no more than two or three per cent a year, and if such adjustment were permitted to be cumulative, many of the upsets hitherto associated with devaluation might be avoided[3].

In the present state of opinion, however, a system of limited exchange-rate flexibility will undoubtedly be difficult to introduce with general agreement, and without provoking an immediate effect on confidence and hence on international liquidity even more disadvantageous than the ultimate advantages to be

---

[1]See chapter XV.4 above.

[2]Import controls, it could be argued, are another alternative. If extensive enough they could reduce imports appreciably (see chapter VI.4). But even if they were maintained indefinitely, the benefit would be once-for-all; and thus would hardly solve the balance of payments problem of an expanding economy. But the main reason against the permanent use of import controls by a country like the United Kingdom is that it would lead other countries to retaliate. It would also compel extensive material allocations and other controls over business.

Other possible alternatives are export subsidies and import taxes. These are cumbersome and inferior substitutes for a devaluation.

[3]The present IMF rules require countries to declare an exchange-rate 'parity' and enjoin on them that their rate should be kept within 1 per cent of this. It might well be enough if they were permitted to make *cumulative* adjustments of two or three times this amount. For a fuller account of the argument, see M. FG. Scott [1959], 'What should be done about the Sterling Area?', *B. Oxford Inst. Statist.*, November 1959, pp. 244–51

obtained.   If such a system is not at present practical politics, the only way to get rapid growth without running into balance of payments difficulties would seem to be by better control of internal price inflation.   Moreover, even in a different world, the amount of exchange-rate flexibility which could be easily tolerated would still be strictly limited.

There seems good hope of preventing the rise of prices being anything like as rapid as in the past.   First, the previous analysis of inflation[1] suggested that the rise in prices had been due in part to cost pressures, of which the pressure by trade unions for higher wages was an important part; and that the pace of inflation depended on customs and attitudes—which presumably can be changed.   There have been attempts by various Chancellors to influence the course of wages, of which the attempt by Mr Selwyn Lloyd was perhaps the most persistent, and—by being linked with a parallel attempt to increase the rate of economic growth—perhaps also the most imaginative.   It is too soon to pass judgement on the success of this new emphasis in policy[2].   But governments have more power of influence than they have yet chosen to exert, and the possibilities of governmental wages policy have not yet been fully explored.

Second, if it were possible to speed up the rate of growth, along the lines suggested in §1, this would make it much easier to keep prices stable.   Annual increases in wages have become increasingly prevalent, and the custom would now be difficult to change[3].   The size of wage awards which can be granted without increasing prices depends on how fast productivity increases.   If productivity in future were to increase not by an average of two per cent a year as in the past, but by say twice as much, there would be better hope of keeping wage awards to the same order.

Third, the rate of increase in wages seems to have been much higher during periods when the pressure of demand was high.   It can be argued that to run the economy at a lower pressure of demand would prevent output per head from

---

[1]Chapter XIII above.

[2]The new developments in wages policy under Mr Selwyn Lloyd date from his statement of economic policy in July 1961 when, at the same time as proposing new arrangements for economic planning, he announced the 'pay pause' (*H.C. Deb.* 25 July 1961, 223).   The 'pause' was officially ended in March 1962, and was replaced by a policy—soon called the 'guiding light'—of trying to limit increases in agreed wage rates to $2\frac{1}{2}$ per cent.   This line of policy was carried a stage further in July 1962 by the announcement of a new National Incomes Commission, to provide 'an impartial and authoritative view on the more important or difficult pay questions' (*H.C. Deb.* 26 July 1962, 1759).   Though neither the 'pause' nor the 'guiding light' was fully observed, policy nevertheless probably slowed down the rise in wages to some extent.

The case for a wages policy was impressively set out in the report prepared for OEEC by Mr Milton Gilbert and Professors Fellner, Hansen, Kahn, Lutz and de Wolff [1961], *The Problem of Rising Prices.*   This report must have had some influence on the evolution of British policy.

[3]The number of wage-earners is now 13–$13\frac{1}{2}$ million.   The annual number getting an award averaged 6–7 million in the five-year period 1946–50; 11·0 million in the period 1951–5 and 10·4 million in 1956–60 (*M. of L. Gaz.*, January 1959, p. 3 and *Statist. Incomes and Prices*, April 1962, table B5).

rising fast, and would therefore be of little avail as a means of slowing down the rise of prices. My own view (already stated in chapter XIII) is that there would be a transitional effect of this sort if it were necessary to start by *reducing* the pressure of demand; but that if the pressure of demand were kept steady at a somewhat lower level, the rate of growth should be as rapid. On this view, such a policy ought to have a considerable effect in reducing the rise of prices[1].

The effect of demand on prices is one thing: how far it should be utilized is a different question. If demand has an effect on prices, then lower unemployment means a faster rise in prices, and vice versa. Most people would agree that price stability has some importance as an aim of policy: its absence results in some injustice and some inconvenience. The previous argument also suggests that, granted the practical difficulty of exchange-rate adjustments, greater price stability may be required if the balance of payments is not to be a constraint on the rate of economic growth.

Views differ about the force of these arguments for moderating the rise of prices, and also as to the means to do this. My own view is that though wages policy may prove effective, it may not, at least for some years, prove enough alone; and that it should be accompanied by a policy of running the economy at a lower pressure of demand than in most post-war years. If unemployment were kept at 2 to $2\frac{1}{2}$ per cent, instead of the post-war average of $1\frac{1}{2}$ per cent, this would probably make a major difference to the rate of rise in prices. This is of course not the only consideration: we have a case here where the various objectives of policy cannot all be achieved in full. Greater unemployment has to be weighed against the advantages of greater price stability—and in particular for the effects of this on the expansion of exports and the means of paying for the imports required for faster growth.

3. A POSSIBLE STRATEGY FOR POLICY

The general conclusion of the present argument is that the strategy of economic policy needs to be broadened, and more emphasis placed on the longer-term objectives of price stability and economic growth. In such a strategy, economic planning and wages policy would have an important role: fiscal policy and monetary policy, though still important, would cease to be the sole instruments for managing the economy.

The argument, to recapitulate, is *first*, that the pursuit of faster growth requires action aimed directly at accelerating the growth of capacity. A faster expansion of demand without such action seems likely to lead to an insupportable degree

---

[1]Though opinion on this question is divided, most economists would probably not disown this line of thought completely. Thus it would be possible to run the economy at a much higher pressure of demand than in the post-war years—as it was run during the war, when unemployment was much lower than since; the reason why few advocate this is presumably because of the effect it would have on prices.

of excess demand, i.e. any induced acceleration of the growth of capacity seems unlikely to be sufficiently rapid.

Second, fiscal and monetary policy should:—

(i) aim to produce a steady growth of demand in line with the growth of capacity: this seems desirable partly because 'stop/go' policies probably upset the process of growth; partly because such policies would produce periods of excess demand, which would speed up the rise in prices.

(ii) aim to keep demand at a point which left a rather greater margin of spare capacity than on average in the past. This seems desirable because a wages policy on its own seems unlikely to be sufficiently effective, at least at first; and greater price stability seems desirable, partly for its own sake, but largely as a means of getting the growth of exports to pay for the imports needed for faster growth[1].

These objectives would probably require less active intervention through fiscal and monetary policy than in the past. It has already been argued that the growth of real purchasing power has in the past arisen not chiefly through tax cuts or other acts of policy, but as a natural result of the process of growth. If the rate of growth of capacity were accelerated, so that entrepreneurs could count on a faster increase in productivity, they could afford to absorb larger wage increases before putting up their prices. This itself would therefore produce most of the increase in real purchasing power required to take up the more rapidly growing stream of goods they were able to produce.

Some of the increase in purchasing power in the past has however come by a reduction in rates of taxation. Over the decade and a half since the war, tax rates have, now more quickly, now more slowly, been reduced. There are two main reasons why there has been scope for tax cuts. First, chiefly because of the progressiveness of direct taxation, a growth of incomes tends to produce a disproportionate growth of government revenue if tax rates are left unchanged[2]. Second—to summarize various trends very briefly—private saving has increased more rapidly than investment. This has made it possible to reduce not only statutory tax rates, but the share of national income taken in taxation[3]. It is difficult to foresee what scope there will be for tax cuts in future, but it seems quite likely that the same factors will be at work as in the past. On a broad perspective, then, the main business of fiscal policy may be to compensate for this shifting balance between saving and investment, which might otherwise

---

[1] This view of the strategy of policy is in some respects similar to that of Professor Paish: see for instance F. W. Paish [1962], *Studies in an Inflationary Economy*, especially chapter 17. It is similar in its emphasis on the importance of price stability, and on running the economy with a margin of spare capacity as a means to this end. It differs, I think, in its emphasis on the prior importance of rapid economic growth and in placing less reliance on the power of 'market mechanisms' alone to bring about either price stability or rapid growth.

[2] See chapter VII, especially table 7.3.

[3] See chapter IV, especially table 4.3.

create a growing deficiency of demand; and this balance is likely to shift only slowly.

Though a less active fiscal and monetary policy seems to be required than in the past, this does not mean that it would be simple to carry out. What ideally is required is that the authorities should take a view of the prospective balance of demand over a longer period than in the past, and keep the trend as steady as possible. But since foresight is limited, it may also be useful to have some rule of thumb to work to. During the period 1950–60, the net reduction in tax rates affecting consumers averaged 0.4 of the national product—or, at present prices, £90 million each year[1]. If growth were more rapid than in the past, taxes might be able to be reduced more rapidly. Thus it might be a good rule to make reductions in taxation of £75–150 million a year, unless unwanted fluctuations in demand could be foreseen, requiring modification of the general rule[2].

It has been argued that the economy should be run with a small extra margin of spare capacity. But this depends partly on the success of policy in other directions: if growth were faster, and wages policy proved successful, little extra margin might be needed. Assuming that an acceptable solution is possible on these lines, the practical decision as to how much slack is needed should probably depend on whether the balance of payments is proving, or is likely to prove, a brake on expansionist policy. For though, as argued above, short-term swings in the balance of payments should not be made the touchstone of policy, a trend towards an uncovered deficit in the balance of payments cannot be allowed to continue indefinitely. If internal expansion is not to be slowed down, and if the last-resort cure of devaluation is to be avoided, this requires an adequate control of price inflation. But the effective action would have to be taken long in advance—and, therefore, before the trends become obvious. This would seem to necessitate a highly sophisticated scrutiny of balance of payments trends. It is not the current year's balance of payments that matters, for this may be affected by temporary factors; but rather the underlying trend. Since this is likely to be difficult to identify, analysis of the balance of payments itself may be less useful than analysis of such indicators of the underlying trend as the share of British exports in world trade, and of price movements here as compared with elsewhere.

[1]See table 7.7.

[2]This proposed rule of thumb has some similarity with the principle which we are told is followed in Japan: see *Economist*, 1 Sept. 1962, p. 799. 'For every 0·1 per cent of the agreed target rate of growth in national income the Japanese reckon that they can expect a stated amount of extra tax revenue on the basis of existing tax rates.' This 'is then assumed to be available for deliberate increases in government expenditure or for new tax reliefs'.

If taken as a fixed rule this however seems too rigid a procedure, since unwanted fluctuations in demand may well still occur: see §4 below.

4. THE ROLE OF FISCAL AND MONETARY POLICY

There has been a wide debate on the relative merits of fiscal and monetary policy. It is however misleading to consider them as simple alternatives, for they have different effects. The previous discussion suggests that the main role of fiscal and monetary policy should be, while maintaining an appropriate margin of spare capacity, to even out fluctuations in the growth of demand. One way of defining the respective roles of fiscal and monetary policy is to consider the kind of fluctuations that are likely to arise, and the most effective means of control in each case[1].

The scale of past fluctuations in demand is not a good guide to what may be expected in future. Some of the large swings in the growth of consumers' expenditure have been due to over-large adjustments of policy which have subsequently had to be corrected. If policy had been less variable, and the growth of consumption accordingly more steady, some of the fluctuation in fixed investment and investment in stocks would probably also have been avoided. But demand would not have grown perfectly steadily; and left to itself cannot be expected to do so in future. There will therefore remain a problem of trying to compensate for these residual fluctuations as far as possible.

It is a major question how far the economy can be protected from fluctuations in sympathy with fluctuations in the world economy. Exports are likely to continue to grow more rapidly when world trade is expanding rapidly than during pauses in the expansion of world trade. From some points of view (as already argued) it would be desirable for the growth of internal demand not to follow these fluctuations, as it has tended to in the past, but to be *contracyclical* to them. There are two difficulties: first, the possible inadequacy of foreign exchange reserves (§2 above); and second, the difficulty of matching a fall in exports by an increase in home demand for similar goods.

The extent to which fixed investment and investment in stocks can be directly affected by policy measures seems rather limited; but they are affected by the course of sales, and are likely to be steadier the steadier is the growth of other sorts of demand. Ideally it might be desirable that consumption should grow more rapidly when exports grow less rapidly. A more practical aim might be to stabilize as far as possible the growth of consumers' expenditure, not only because it amounts to one half of total final demand, but also for the indirect effects on investment.

It has already been suggested that to stabilize the growth of *consumers' expenditure* may require a gradual reduction of tax rates year by year. Even so, there may be some fluctuations; for even in the absence of policy changes, there would undoubtedly have been some fluctuations in the growth of con-

[1]These issues were considered in a series of three articles by myself [1960] on 'Fiscal Policy and Monetary Policy as Instruments of Economic Control' in the *Westminster Bank R.*, May, August and November 1960. I have had second thoughts on several points of the argument.

sumption in the past[1]. In some cases it may be possible to foresee them long enough in advance to correct for them[2]. Consumers' expenditure may for these reasons need to be stimulated, or restrained, by up to, perhaps, £200 million a year.

Consumers' demand has in the past been influenced by changes in tax rates, and by changes in hire-purchase regulations. The disadvantage of the latter is that practically the whole effect is concentrated on expenditure on durables. Since no type of monetary measure has anything like a general impact on consumption[3], it seems clear that the role of controlling consumers' expenditure —perhaps the most important aspect of stabilization policy—must lie with fiscal, not monetary, policy.

In the last 20 years tax policy has become a major instrument for controlling the economy. But despite adaptations the system of taxation is still largely an inheritance from an earlier age, effective in a rough and ready way, but not perfectly fitted to its present use. Some of its limitations have recently been mitigated by the powers taken by Mr Selwyn Lloyd in 1961 to vary taxes between budgets[4].

The first disadvantage has been that it was difficult to vary taxes between April budgets. Special budgets have always been possible, and once decided are quickly dispatched; but they have been treated as crisis measures, carrying a distinct implication that 'normal' policy had failed. Mr Lloyd's innovation of the 'economic regulators' in 1961 may therefore prove an important change. The fact that there is advance agreement that the 'regulators' may properly be used may have broken the old barrier to flexibility in the timing of fiscal policy.

[1]See chapter XV, especially figure 15.3.

[2]As an example, a large change in import prices can have a significant effect on real purchasing power: since it takes time to affect prices in the shops, its effect can be foreseen some time in advance.

[3]Monetary measures, besides affecting durables expenditure may also bear on some special types of consumers, e.g. those with bank overdrafts or possibly those who own stocks and shares.

[4]In his 1961 budget, Mr Selwyn Lloyd introduced two 'economic regulators'—'means of stimulating or restricting the economy', as Mr Lloyd said (*H.C. Deb.* 17 April 1961, 805) 'by measures which can be brought into operation quickly at any time of the year, and the effect of which will be reasonably rapid and widespread'.

First, he took power to apply a special surcharge, or special rebate, of up to 10 per cent 'to all the main Customs and Excise revenue duties and to purchase tax'. The possible addition to or subtraction from consumers' purchasing power resulting from the exercise of this power was estimated at about £200 million a year. This power was first used in July 1961, when a surcharge of the full 10 per cent was imposed. In the 1962 budget this surcharge was consolidated with the pre-existing tax rates; and powers were taken to impose a similar surcharge or rebate on these new rates.

Second, Mr Lloyd took power in his 1961 budget to impose 'a special surcharge on employers, analogous to a pay-roll tax', of up to four shillings per employee per week. At this maximum the surcharge was calculated to withdraw £200 million a year of purchasing power—though only about half would be likely to have affected consumers as such. This proposal attracted much criticism; was never used; and was dropped in the 1962 budget.

The second disadvantage is that none of the present taxes is very broad-based, nor therefore appropriate for influencing mass consumption. Income tax is the most general tax we have, but little is paid by the half of the tax population with incomes below £500 a year. Indirect taxation also is unevenly spread, so that even if all the main taxes are varied—as they are by Mr Lloyd's indirect-tax surcharge or rebate—the impact is still very concentrated[1].

Chiefly because it has been difficult to affect consumption as a whole, policy measures in the past have fallen with disporportionate emphasis on *consumers' expenditure on durables*. It has already been argued that to influence such a narrow sector is not a useful way of trying to control the economy; and for the trades concerned, it has caused recurrent dislocations and loss. For the purpose of producing steady growth it would seem better not to make major changes in purchase tax or in the hire-purchase regulations.

Had these been avoided in the past, there is no doubt that demand for consumer durables would have grown more steadily. Most of the fluctuations in expenditure on durables seem to have been caused by changes in policy[2]; and demand would undoubtedly grow more steadily if in future large changes in purchase tax or in the hire-purchase regulations are avoided. But even so some fluctuations may still occur[3]; and it might be desirable—could these be foreseen—to compensate for them. There may therefore be need for the government to have means of influencing the demand for durables in addition to any influence it exerts over total consumer demand—not, as unintentionally heretofore, to create fluctuations in this class of demand, but to smooth out any marked swings that remain. What this would amount to, and how difficult it would be, can hardly be foretold in advance; but it may be supposed that the need for intervention would be rather infrequent.

Though hire-purchase control as operated in the past has had a very jerky effect on the demand for durables, such a control could probably be operated with smoother effect. It would probably be an improvement from this point of view if changes in the regulations affected not the minimum down payment, but the size of the subsequent monthly instalments[4]. It would also be possible

---

[1]Drink, tobacco, petrol and oil, and goods subject to purchase tax represent (at factor cost) one seventh of consumption; but they bear three quarters of all taxes on expenditure.

The second 'regulator', the pay-roll tax, in so far as it bore on consumption, would have much the same incidence as a poll tax—which is something like what is required if it is to have a wide impact. An alternative would be to institute a 'value added' tax in substitution for some existing indirect taxes; and then to impose surcharges or rebates on this new base. (See the second of the articles referred to: Dow [1960], 'The Possibilities of Fiscal Policy', *Westminster Bank R.*, August 1960.)

[2]See chapter XI.2, especially figure 11.2.

[3]One reason for which fluctuations in expenditure on consumer durables may arise is that, despite the best efforts of policy, consumers' real incomes are unlikely to grow perfectly steadily—and the demand for durables happens to be particularly sensitive to changes in income (see chapter XI.2). If fluctuations have occurred in the past, this is likely also to give rise to cycles in replacement demand.

[4]See chapter XI.2 above.

to operate by changes, more finely graded than hitherto, in the rates of purchase tax[1].

The government may wish to influence *private fixed investment* for two sorts of reasons. It may wish to increase the general level of investment in relation to the national product; and may also wish to even out cycles in investment demand. For both purposes it may well be that the kind of development planning likely to be carried out under the National Economic Development Council may prove more effective than any financial device; and it seems an open question whether other means of influence are going to be required.

It also seems doubtful whether financial stimulants or restraints are effective. It has already been argued that the best way to prevent fluctuations in investment demand is to prevent fluctuations in the demand for the goods that investment is required to produce. It may well be that faced with a fall-off in sales, entrepreneurs will be reluctant to invest, whatever inducements they are offered. In the reverse situation, however, restraints on investment may be more effective.

The analysis of previous chapters suggests that 'fiscal' means to influence investment demand are more effective than 'monetary' means proper. The most serviceable instrument appears to be variation of the depreciation allowances. For changes in the 'initial', or in the 'investment', allowances (which directly affect the amount of finance available from within the firm) have a much more powerful effect on firms' liquidity than credit restraints (which can at best only affect the difficulty of getting finance from outside). At a rough guess, and merely to indicate possible orders of magnitude, the withdrawal from (or granting to) firms of £100 million a year might affect private investment by one third as much after a delay of perhaps a year[2]. Changes in interest rates are probably not very effective[3]. But it could be argued that in an incipient investment boom, before it was clear that the situation called for a change in depreciation allowances, it might be useful to raise interest rates as an interim measure. This would serve to keep business in touch with the authorities' intentions, and perhaps have a 'psychological' influence.

There is however likely to be one serious difficulty in controlling investment by any sort of financial means. They all take time to take effect, and it may

---

[1]Under the 'economic regulator' procedure, purchase tax may be increased, or reduced, by up to 10 per cent of its existing level. For gas and electric fires, refrigerators and washing machines this was (in 1962) 25 per cent; for cars, radios and television sets, 45 per cent. The 10 per cent variation therefore probably causes a change in the retail price of these two groups of durables of about $1\frac{1}{2}$ per cent and $2\frac{1}{2}$ per cent respectively.

This may not appear a large change; but it probably is enough to have a marked effect on sales. As already argued, it is a weakness of the 'economic regulator' procedure that its impact is concentrated on a fairly narrow range of goods (of which durables are an important part). It may also be undesirable to have to vary the demand for durables at the same time as consumer demand in total requires stimulation or restraint.

[2]See chapter XI.4.

[3]See chapter XII.

well be difficult to foresee the need for stimulation or restraint sufficiently far in advance. It is therefore conceivable that in the event of serious miscalculation, other measures might be needed as a 'long stop'. If this situation did arise, the imposition of a quantitative form of capital issues control would probably be effective. Thus a ceiling might be imposed on the new issues permitted in each period, applications being dealt with as a queue, so knocking the head off an investment boom. If severe restraints are needed, this appears preferable to, because less erratic in its incidence than, a severe restraint on bank advances; and as a temporary measure, it might be both more tolerable, and more feasible to administer, than for instance the reimposition of building controls[1]. But the need for such measures of last resort appears exceptional and hardly worth legislating for.

In one respect the government has intervened fairly continuously with the composition of investment, by affecting the level of house-building. It has largely determined public authority housing; and monetary policy has probably had some indirect effect on private house-building by affecting building society lending. This latter effect has occurred largely by accident; and it seems desirable that it should be more explicitly taken account of in future. The problem is however likely to look rather different. The long-term investment plan to be formulated by the NEDC is probably bound to make provision for the growing need to redevelop towns and cities; and if there is a long-term plan, there may be less need for short-term measures.

Fluctuations in *investment in stocks* are likely to remain both the main cause of fluctuations in final expenditure, and the most difficult type of fluctuation to control. Most fluctuations in stocks are probably due to output being adjusted late to changes in the trend of sales, so that large adjustments in output are subsequently required. They have probably had little to do with monetary policy, and may well prove too powerful to be much influenced. Stocks cannot pile up or be run down indefinitely and any large movement is likely to be reversed within two or three years. It is therefore not disastrous for policy if it proves impossible to stabilize their fluctuations. Nevertheless, as already argued, it would be desirable to do so if possible.

There seem two chief possibilities. First, there seems some ground to hope that the level of stocks held by business could be *slightly* affected either by restrictions on bank credit or changes in the interest charged on it. Since stocks are large in relation to national product, a slight effect would be enough[2].

---

[1] The strictures of the Radcliffe Committee against the capital-issues control applied to the loose and ineffective control that was operated up to 1959 (see chapter IX.4 above). A control over access to credit is likely to be more palatable than a direct control over expenditure, since people are more prepared to have to justify what they want to do when borrowing money, than when it is a case of disposing of their own. The effect of credit restrictions is highly arbitrary: but for a strictly temporary measure this might be acceptable.

[2] See chapter XI.5 and (for the possible effect of the 1957–8 credit restrictions) chapter XV.2.

An active use of credit policy for this purpose might well entail some changes in the behaviour of the banks. Credit rationing would probably be more effective as an influence on stockholding if in its detailed application it were consciously and purposively aimed at affecting the stocks held by the banks' customers. Alternatively, there might be greater influence on stockholding if, when credit was restricted, the rates charged on bank advances were raised more steeply than hitherto[1].

To operate a policy designed to stabilize stockholding, much more would have to be known about what stocks were held and how and why they were changing: otherwise policy might easily make things worse. But the question then arises whether, if full information were available, business would not make the necessary adjustments more effectively than the government could. Wide swings in stocks are a defect in the working of the economy, due primarily to inadequate knowledge. They are contrary to the interest of business itself: in any trade subject to serious stock cycles, the vagaries of retailers' stocks causes much cost and dislocation to producers and distributors lower down the line. The cost and dislocation could be reduced if such firms knew what was happening to final sales. There is therefore hope that the provision of full information would itself mitigate stock cycles. An effective policy would certainly require fuller information; it is in the interest of all that there should be better information, and that stock cycles should be prevented[2].

This review suggests that, within a policy for promoting steady growth, fiscal policy will, if anything, have a more important role relative to monetary policy than in the past. There seems little question that fiscal policy will continue to be the chief means of exerting a stabilizing influence on consumers' expenditure. If there proves to be a need to stabilize investment, tax incentives seem the best method to use here also. Monetary policy appears likely to be useful only for subsidiary purposes—before other measures are taken to affect investment; to help to mitigate cycles in the demand for durables; or, possibly, to influence the level of stocks.

One of the major conclusions of this study is that the attempt to manage the economy by means of fiscal and credit policy alone has shown them to be not enough. They need to subserve a policy for directly promoting economic growth, and to be flanked by a wages policy. The institution of the National Economic Development Council is likely to affect the conduct of fiscal and monetary policy in future. The plan for investment which emerges from it will

[1] It is the rate on advances to business that here matters, not that on Treasury bills, nor Bank rate: there is no necessary merit in making government borrowing more expensive because the government is trying to restrict business borrowing. But it remains true that only a small proportion of stocks are held on bank finance, partly because only a small proportion of firms borrow from the banks (see chapter XI.5).

[2] Since stock changes reflect an excess or deficiency of sales over output, the basic information required includes much fuller information about final sales. Some firms, and some market research organizations, have already found that it pays them themselves to bear the cost of collecting the current facts about the final sales of their goods.

have to extend over a term of years; and this will inevitably have implications not only for business, but also for government policy. It would be neither possible nor necessary for the Chancellor to give pledges about future rates of taxation. But it would seem necessary for the government to give a general idea of the rates of expansion in both consumer and investment demand which—subject to capacity growing as planned—budgetary and monetary policy aimed to produce.

There will inevitably be occasions when the long-term policy has to be modified in the light of unexpected developments. But there is now better reason to hope that, in the formulation of policy, long-run as well as short-run considerations will be taken into account; and the fact that it will now be formulated in the perspective of a long-term plan might be enough to work a quiet revolution in the practical conduct of fiscal and credit policy. Economic policy has already, as compared with pre-war, revolutionized social conditions and the climate in which business has to operate. The improvements in the management of the economy that may be made in the next decade could bring benefits as important again.

APPENDIX

CALENDAR OF EVENTS, 1945–60

1945

May 7	War with Germany ends
July 5	General election: results July 26, Lab. 393; Cons. 203
August 15	New government: Mr Attlee, Prime Minister; Dr Dalton, Chancellor of Exchequer; Mr Morrison, Lord President of Council with responsibility for economic co-ordination; Sir Stafford Cripps, President of Board of Trade
August 15	War with Japan ends
August 21	End of lend-lease
October 23–31	Autumn budget debate
December 12–13	Debate on United States Loan

1946

March 1	Bank of England nationalized (vesting date)
April 9–17	Budget debate
July 13	United States Loan Agreement ratified by United States Congress

1947

January 1	Coal industry nationalized (vesting date)
February 10	Fuel crisis: use of electricity by industry restricted (till March 3)
February 22	First *Economic Survey* published
March 10–12	Economic debate
April 15–23	Budget debate
June 5	General Marshall's Harvard speech on European recovery
July 15	Sterling made convertible (till August 20)
August 6–7	Economic debate ('State of the nation')
August 15	Independence of India
August 20	Convertibility of sterling withdrawn
September 29	Sir Stafford Cripps, Minister for Economic Affairs
November 12–19	Autumn budget debate
November 13	Dr Dalton resigns: Sir Stafford Cripps, Chancellor of Exchequer

1948

January 1	Railways nationalized (vesting date)
February	White Paper on *Personal Incomes, Costs and Prices* (Cmd. 7321)
April 6–15	Budget debate
April 16	OEEC formally established
June 24	Russian blockade of Berlin (till May 1949)
October 11–22	Commonwealth Prime Ministers' conference in London
November 4	Mr Wilson's 'bonfire of controls'

1949

March 1	Lord Catto retires: Mr Cobbold, Governor of Bank of England
April 4	North Atlantic Treaty signed
April 6–13	Budget debate
July 14–18	Economic debate
July 13–18	Commonwealth finance ministers' conference in London
September 18	Devaluation of the pound
September 27–29	Debate on sterling exchange rate
October 26–27	Debate on government measures

1950
February 23	General election: Lab. 315; Cons. 297
	New government: Mr Attlee, Prime Minister; Sir Stafford Cripps, Chancellor of Exchequer; Mr Gaitskell, Minister of State for Economic Affairs
April 18–26	Budget debate
June 27	Korea: United States assistance to South Korean government
August 3	New British defence programme
September 19	European Payments Union established (with retroactive effect from July)
October 19	Sir Stafford Cripps resigns: Mr Gaitskell, Chancellor of Exchequer

1951
February 15	Steel nationalization (vesting day)
February 26	International Materials Conference commences operations in Washington
March 9	Mr Morrison, Foreign Secretary: Mr Bevin resigns (died 14 April)
March 19	European Iron and Steel Community ('Schuman Plan') agreement initialled
April 10–18	Budget debate
June 27	Ministry of Materials set up
July 9	Stoppage of oil exports from Abadan
October 25	General election: Cons. 321; Lab. 295
	New government: Mr Churchill, Prime Minister; Mr Butler, Chancellor of Exchequer; Sir Arthur Salter, Minister of State for Economic Affairs
November 7	Import cuts: Bank rate, 2½ per cent

1952
January 15–21	Commonwealth finance ministers' conference in London
January 29	Further import cuts: hire-purchase restrictions
February 6	Elizabeth II, Queen
March 11–20	Budget debate: Bank rate, 4 per cent
July 29–30	Economic debate
November 27–	
December 9	Commonwealth Economic Conference in London

1953
January 20	United States: Eisenhower administration takes office
February 3	Debate on Commonwealth Economic Conference
March 4	Mr Eden, Mr Butler visit Washington
March 23–24	OEEC discussion of British 'convertibility plan'
April 14–22	Budget debate
June 2	Coronation (economic discussion with Commonwealth ministers)

1954
January 8–15	Commonwealth finance ministers' conference in Sydney
April 6–14	Budget debate
July 3	Food rationing ends
July 15–16	OEEC ministerial meeting in London on convertibility

1955
February 24–25	Bank rate, 4½ per cent: hire-purchase controls reintroduced
April 5	Sir Winston Churchill retires: Sir Anthony Eden, Prime Minister; Mr Butler remains Chancellor of Exchequer; Sir Edward Boyle, Economic Secretary to Treasury
April 19–22	Budget debate

1955 contd.

May 26	General election: Cons. 344; Lab. 277
June 9–10	Ministerial discussion in OEEC on convertibility
July 25–26	Economic debate
October 26–31	Autumn budget
December 14	Mr Attlee resigns as Leader of Labour Party; Mr Gaitskell, Leader of Opposition
December 20	Mr Butler transferred to Home Office: Mr Macmillan, Chancellor of Exchequer

1956

February 16–18	Bank rate, $5\frac{1}{2}$ per cent; hire-purchase controls tightened; investment allowances withdrawn; restrictions on public investment
February 22–23	Economic debate
April 17–25	Budget debate
June 28–July 6	Commonwealth Prime Ministers' conference in London
July 17–19	OEEC ministerial meeting: Mr Macmillan proposes investigation of 'free trade zone'
July 26	Egypt seizes Suez canal
September 29	Meeting between Mr Macmillan and Mr Thorneycroft with Commonwealth finance ministers in Washington
October 31–	
November 6	Franco-British armed intervention in Egypt
December 17	Petrol rationing (till 14 May 1957)

1957

January 9	Sir Anthony Eden resigns: Mr Macmillan, Prime Minister; Mr Thorneycroft, Chancellor of Exchequer; Mr Eccles, President of Board of Trade; Mr Birch, Economic Secretary to Treasury
March 25	European Economic Community treaty signed in Rome
April 9–15	Budget debate: Committee on the Working of Monetary System (Radcliffe Committee) announced
July 6	Rent Act comes in force
July 25	Economic debate
August 12	Council on Prices, Productivity and Incomes appointed
September 19	New economic measures: Bank rate, 7 per cent

1958

January 6	Mr Thorneycroft resigns: Mr Heathcoat Amory, Chancellor of Exchequer
January 23	Economic debate
April 15–23	Budget debate
July 3	Restraint of bank advances removed: 'special deposit' scheme announced
September 15–22	Commonwealth Economic Conference in Montreal
October 29	Hire-purchase controls removed
November 3	Economic debate
December 15	Free trade area negotiations in OEEC break down
December 29	Convertibility for external sterling: European Monetary Agreement replaces European Payments Union

1959

January 28	Debate on convertibility (European Monetary Agreement Bill)
February 5	Control of capital issues withdrawn (except overseas issues)
April 7–13	Budget debate
August 20	Report of Committee on Working of Monetary System (*Radcliffe Report*), Cmnd. 827

1959 contd.

October 8	General election: Cons. 366; Lab. 258
November 20	European Free Trade Area: treaty agreed
November 26	Debate on *Radcliffe Report*

1960

April 4–7	Budget debate
April 28	Hire-purchase restrictions reimposed: first call for special deposits
June 23	Bank rate, 6 per cent: further call for special deposits
July 27	Mr Heathcoat Amory resigns: Mr Selwyn Lloyd, Chancellor of Exchequer
November 8	Mr Kennedy, President of the United States of America

LIST OF WORKS CITED

I. BOOKS, ARTICLES AND SERIAL PUBLICATIONS

ABRAMOVITZ, M. [1950] *Inventories and Business Cycles, with special reference to Manufacturers' Inventories*, Studies in Business Cycles 4 (New York, National Bureau of Economic Research).

ALFORD, R. F. G. and ROSE, H. B. [1959] 'The Radcliffe Report and Domestic Monetary Policy', *London and Cambridge Economic Bulletin*, N.S. no. 32, December 1959, p. ii.

ANDREWS, P. W. S. [1940] 'A Further Inquiry into the Effects of Rates of Interest', in *Oxford Studies in the Price Mechanism*, ed. T. Wilson and P. W. S. Andrews (Oxford, Clarendon Press, 1951).

AUKRUST, O. [1959] 'Investment and Economic Growth', *Productivity Measurement Review*, no. 16, February 1959, p. 35.

BALOGH, T. [1947] 'The Problem of the British Balance of Payments', *Bulletin of the Oxford Institute of Statistics*, vol. 9, no. 7, July 1947, p. 211.

BARNA, T. [1962] *Investment and Growth Policies in British Industrial Firms*, National Institute of Economic and Social Research, Occasional Paper 20 (Cambridge, University Press).

BASSIE, V. L. [1951] 'Recent Developments in Short-term Forecasting', in *Short-term Economic Forecasting*, National Bureau of Economic Research, Studies in Income and Wealth 17 (Princeton (N.J.), University Press, 1955).

BATES, J. A. [1957] 'Hire Purchase in Small Manufacturing Business', *Bankers' Magazine*, vol. 184, nos. 1362 and 1363, September and October 1957, pp. 171 and 275.

BAUMOL, W. J. [1952] 'The Transactions Demand for Cash: An Inventory Theoretic Approach', *Quarterly Journal of Economics*, vol. 66, no. 4, November 1952, p. 545.

BAUMOL, W. J. [1959] *Business Behavior, Value and Growth* (New York, Macmillan).

BIRKENHEAD, LORD [1961] *The Prof in Two Worlds: The Official Life of Professor F. A. Lindemann, Viscount Cherwell* (London, Collins).

BRETHERTON, R. F., BURCHARDT, F. A. and RUTHERFORD, R. S. G. [1941] *Public Investment and the Trade Cycle in Great Britain* (Oxford, Clarendon Press).

BRIDGES, LORD (Edward Bridges) [1950] *Treasury Control*, Stamp Memorial Lecture, 1950 (London, Athlone Press).

BRITISH BANKERS' ASSOCIATION. *Quarterly Analysis of Advances* (London).

BRITTAIN, SIR HERBERT [1959] *The British Budgetary System* (London, Allen and Unwin).

BROWN, A. J. [1939] 'Interest, Prices, and the Demand Schedule for Idle Money', in *Oxford Studies in the Price Mechanism*, ed. T. Wilson and P. W. S. Andrews (Oxford, Clarendon Press, 1951).

BROWN, A. J. [1955] *The Great Inflation, 1939–1951* (London, Oxford University Press).

BROWN, E. H. PHELPS and BROWNE, M. H. [1962] 'Earnings in Industries of the United Kingdom, 1948–59', *Economic Journal*, vol. 72, no. 287, September 1962, p. 517.

BRUNNER, E. [1952] 'Competition and the Theory of the Firm', *Economia internazionale*, vol. 5, nos. 3 and 4, August and November 1952, pp. 509 and 727.

CAGAN, P. [1956] 'The Monetary Dynamics of Hyperinflation', in *Studies in the Quantity Theory of Money*, ed. M. Friedman (Chicago (Ill.), University of Chicago Press).

CARTER, C. F. and WILLIAMS, B. R. [1957] *Industry and Technical Progress: Factors Governing the Speed of Application of Science* (London, Oxford University Press).

CHESTER, D. N. [1951] 'The Central Machinery for Economic Policy', in *Lessons of the British War Economy*, ed. D. N. Chester, National Institute of Economic and Social Research, Economic and Social Studies 10 (Cambridge, University Press).

CHESTER, D. N. [1952] 'Machinery of Government and Planning', in *The British Economy, 1945–1950*, ed. G. D. N. Worswick and P. H. Ady (Oxford, Clarendon Press).

CLAY, SIR HENRY [1957] *Lord Norman* (London, Macmillan).

COLE, G. D. H. [1935] *Principles of Economic Planning* (London, Macmillan).

COOKE, C. [1957] *The Life of Richard Stafford Cripps* (London, Hodder and Stoughton).

CORDEN, W. M. [1958] 'The Control of Imports: A Case Study—The United Kingdom Import Restrictions of 1951–2', *Manchester School of Economic and Social Studies*, vol. 26, no. 3, September 1958, p. 181.

CRIPPS, SIR STAFFORD [1934] *Why this Socialism?* (London, Gollancz).

CUTHBERTSON, J. R. [1961] 'Hire Purchase Controls and Fluctuations in the Car Market', *Economica*, N.S. vol. 28, no. 110, May 1961, p. 125.

DALTON, LORD (Hugh Dalton) [1922] *Principles of Public Finance* (London, Routledge).

DALTON, LORD (Hugh Dalton) [1935] *Practical Socialism for Britain* (London, Routledge).

DALTON, LORD (Hugh Dalton) [1962] *High Tide and After: Memoirs, 1945–1960* (London, Muller).

DAY, A. C. L. [1957] *Outline of Monetary Economics* (Oxford, Clarendon Press).

DENISON, E. F. [1962] *The Sources of Economic Growth in the United States and the Alternatives before us*, Supplementary Paper 13, (New York, Committee for Economic Development).

DEVONS, E. [1950] *Planning in Practice: Essays in Aircraft Planning in War-time* (Cambridge, University Press).

DICKS-MIREAUX, L. A. and DOW, J. C. R. [1959] 'The Determinants of Wage Inflation: United Kingdom, 1946–56', *Journal of the Royal Statistical Society, Series A*, vol. 122, part 2, p. 145.

DICKS-MIREAUX, L. A. [1961] 'The Interrelationship between Cost and Price Changes, 1946–1959: A Study of Inflation in Post-war Britain', *Oxford Economic Papers*, N.S. vol. 13, no. 3, October 1961, p. 267.

DICKS-MIREAUX, L. A. and SHEPHERD, J. R. [1962] 'The Wages Structure and Some Implications for Incomes Policy', *National Institute Economic Review*, no. 22, November 1962, p. 38.

DICKS-MIREAUX, L. A. [forthcoming] *Studies in Cost and Price Behaviour*, National Institute of Economic and Social Research.

DICKS-MIREAUX, L. A. and ELKAN, P. G. [forthcoming] 'The Extent of Supplementary Payments', in *Studies in Cost and Price Behaviour*, by L. A. Dicks-Mireaux, National Institute of Economic and Social Research.

DICKS-MIREAUX, L. A. and SHEPHERD, J. R. [forthcoming] 'The Dynamics of Wage Drift', in *Studies in Cost and Price Behaviour*, by L. A. Dicks-Mireaux, National Institute of Economic and Social Research.

DOMAR, E. D. [1961] 'On the Measurement of Technological Change', *Economic Journal*, vol. 71, no. 284, December 1961, p. 709.

DOW, J. C. R. [1956] 'Analysis of the Generation of Price Inflation: A Study of Cost and Price Changes in the United Kingdom, 1946–54, *Oxford Economic Papers*, N.S. vol. 8, no. 3, October 1956, p. 252.

DOW, J. C. R. [1958] 'The Economic Effect of Monetary Policy, 1945–57', *Committee on the Working of the Monetary System: Principal Memoranda of Evidence*, part XIII, no. 9, p. 76 (London, H.M. Stationery Office, 1960).

DOW, J. C. R. and DICKS-MIREAUX, L. A. [1958] 'The Excess Demand for Labour: A Study of Conditions in Great Britain, 1946–56', *Oxford Economic Papers*, N.S. vol. 10, no. 1, February 1958, p. 1.

DOW, J. C. R. [1959] 'Internal Factors Causing and Propagating Inflation', in *Inflation: Proceedings of a Conference held by the International Economic Association*, ed. D. C. Hague (London, Macmillan, 1962).

DOW, J. C. R. [1960] 'Fiscal Policy and Monetary Policy as Instruments of Economic Control' *Westminster Bank Review*, May, August and November 1960, pp. 7, 3 and 2.

Dow, J. C. R. [1961] 'Forecasting and Budgetary Policy in the United Kingdom since the War', in *Les Prévisions budgétaires dans le Cadre des Prévisions économiques et leurs Adaptations*, Travaux de l'Institut International des Finances Publiques, Warsaw Conference, 1961 (Brussels, Emil Bruylant, 1963).

Dow, J. C. R. [1962] 'L'expérience britannique en matière de prévisions économiques officielles, 1946–1960', *Bulletin d'Information et de Documentation de la Banque Nationale de Belgique*, 37th year, vol. 1, no. 3, March 1962.

DUESENBERRY, J. S. [1949] *Income, Saving and the Theory of Consumer Behavior*, Harvard Economic Studies 87 (Cambridge (Mass.), Harvard University Press).

DUESENBERRY, J. S. [1958] *Business Cycles and Economic Growth* (New York, McGraw-Hill).

DURBIN, E. F. M. [1949] *Problems of Economic Planning: Papers on Planning and Economics* (London, Routledge and Kegan Paul).

EARLE, E. M. [1951] 'The American Stake in Europe: Retrospect and Prospect', *International Affairs*, vol. 27, no. 4, October 1951, p. 423.

EBERSOLE, J. F. [1938] 'The Influence of Interest Rates upon Entrepreneurial Decisions in Business: A Case Study', *Harvard Business Review*, vol. 17, no. 1, Autumn 1938, p. 35.

ECKSTEIN, O. and WILSON, T. A. [1962] 'The Determination of Money Wages in American Industry', *Quarterly Journal of Economics*, vol. 76, no. 3, August 1962, p. 379.

EDWARDS, R. S. and TOWNSEND, H. [1958] *Business Enterprise: its Growth and Organisation* (London, Macmillan).

EISNER, R. [1957] 'Interview and Other Survey Techniques and the Study of Investment', in *Problems of Capital Formation: Concepts, Measurement, and Controlling Factors*, National Bureau of Economic Research, Studies in Income and Wealth 19 (Princeton (N.J.), University Press).

EISNER, R. [1960] 'A Distributed Lag Investment Function', *Econometrica*, vol. 28, no. 1, January 1960, p. 1.

FARRELL, M. J. [1959] 'The New Theories of the Consumption Function', *Economic Journal*, vol. 69, no. 276, December 1959, p. 678.

FRANKS, LORD (Oliver Franks) [1947] *Central Planning and Control in War and Peace* (London, Longmans, Green).

FRIEDMAN, M. [1956] 'The Quantity Theory of Money: A Restatement', in *Studies in the Quantity Theory of Money*, ed. M. Friedman (Chicago (Ill.), University of Chicago Press).

FRIEDMAN, M. [1957] *A Theory of the Consumption Function*, National Bureau of Economic Research, General Series 63 (Princeton (N.J.), University Press).

FRIEDMAN, M. [1959] 'The Demand for Money: Some Theoretical and Empirical Results', *Journal of Political Economy*, vol. 67, no. 4, August 1959, p. 327.

GAITSKELL, H. [1952] 'The Sterling Area', *International Affairs*, vol. 28, no. 2, April 1952, p. 170.

GALBRAITH, J. K. [1952] *A Theory of Price Control* (Cambridge (Mass.), Harvard University Press).

GARDNER, R. N. [1956] *Sterling-Dollar Diplomacy: Anglo-American Collaboration in the Reconstruction of Multilateral Trade* (Oxford, Clarendon Press).

GASKIN, M. [1960] 'Liquidity and the Monetary Mechanism', *Oxford Economic Papers*, N.S. vol. 12, no. 3, October 1960, p. 274.

GRUNFELD, Y. [1960] 'The Determinants of Corporate Investment', in *The Demand for Durable Goods*, ed. A. C. Harberger (Chicago (Ill.), University of Chicago Press).

GURLEY, J. G. and SHAW, E. S. [1960] *Money in a Theory of Finance* (Washington, Brookings Institution).

HALL, SIR ROBERT [1959] 'Reflections on the Practical Application of Economics', *Economic Journal*, vol. 69, no. 276, December 1959, p. 639.

HAMMOND, R. J. [1951] *Food. Vol. I. The Growth of Policy*, History of the Second World War, U.K. Civil Series (London, H.M. Stationery Office and Longmans, Green).

HANCOCK, W. K. and GOWING, M. M. [1949] *British War Economy*, History of the Second World War, U.K. Civil Series (London, H.M. Stationery Office).

HANSEN, B. [1951] *A Study in the Theory of Inflation* (London, Allen and Unwin).

HANSEN, B. and REHN, G. [1956] 'On Wage Drift: A Problem of Money-wage Dynamics', in *25 Economic Essays . . . in Honour of Eric Lindahl* (Stockholm, Ekonomisk Tidskrift).

HARGREAVES, E. L. [1947] 'Price Control of (Non-food) Consumer Goods', *Oxford Economic Papers*, no. 8, November 1947, p. 1.

HARGREAVES, E. L. and GOWING, M. M. [1952] *Civil Industry and Trade*, History of the Second World War, U.K. Civil Series (London, H.M. Stationery Office and Longmans, Green).

HARRIS, R., NAYLOR, M. and SELDON, A. [1961] *Hire Purchase in a Free Society, 3rd ed.* (London, Hutchinson, for the Institute of Economic Affairs).

HARROD, SIR ROY [1936] *The Trade Cycle: An Essay* (Oxford, Clarendon Press).

HARROD, SIR ROY [1948] *Towards a Dynamic Economics: Some Recent Developments of Economic Theory and their Application to Policy* (London, Macmillan).

HARROD, SIR ROY [1951] *The Life of John Maynard Keynes* (London, Macmillan).

HAWTREY, SIR RALPH [1932] *The Art of Central Banking* (London, Longmans, Green).

HAWTREY, SIR RALPH [1960] 'Stocks of Commodities, Fixed Capital and the Interest Rate', *Bankers' Magazine*, vol. 189, no. 1394, May 1960, p. 410.

HAZLEWOOD, A. and VANDOME, P. [1961] 'A Post Mortem on Econometric Forecasts for 1959', *Bulletin of the Oxford University Institute of Statistics*, vol. 23, no. 1, February 1961, p. 67.

HELLER, W. W. [1951] 'The Anatomy of Investment Decisions', *Harvard Business Review*, vol. 29, no. 2, March 1951, p. 95.

HEMMING, M. F. W. and CORDEN, W. M. [1958] 'Import Restriction as an Instrument of Balance-of-payments Policy', *Economic Journal*, vol. 68, no. 271, September 1958, p. 483.

HEMMING, M. F. W., MILES, C. M. and RAY, G. F. [1958] 'A Statistical Summary of the Extent of Import Control in the United Kingdom since the War', *Review of Economic Studies*, vol. 26, no. 70, February 1959, p. 75.

HENDERSON, SIR HUBERT [1938] 'The Significance of the Rate of Interest', in *Oxford Studies in the Price Mechanism*, ed. T. Wilson and P. W. S. Andrews (Oxford, Clarendon Press, 1951).

HENDERSON, SIR HUBERT [1946] 'The Anglo-American Financial Agreement', *Bulletin of the Oxford Institute of Statistics*, vol. 8, no. 1, January 1946, p. 1.

HENDERSON, SIR HUBERT [1955] *The Inter-war Years and Other Papers: A Selection from the Writings of Hubert Douglas Henderson*, ed. H. Clay (Oxford, Clarendon Press).

HENDERSON, P. D. [1952] 'Development Councils: An Industrial Experiment', in *The British Economy, 1945–1950*, ed. G. D. N. Worswick and P. H. Ady (Oxford, Clarendon Press).

HICKS, J. R. [1948] *The Problem of Budgetary Reform* (Oxford, Clarendon Press).

HICKS, J. R. [1950] *A Contribution to the Theory of the Trade Cycle* (Oxford, Clarendon Press).

HICKS, J. R. [1960] 'Thoughts on the Theory of Capital: The Corfu Conference', *Oxford Economic Papers*, N.S. vol. 12, no. 2, June 1960, p. 123.

HURSTFIELD, J. [1953] *The Control of Raw Materials*, History of the Second World War, U.K. Civil Series (London, H.M. Stationery Office and Longmans, Green).

JACKSON, E. F. [1949] 'The Recent Use of Social Accounting in the United Kingdom', in *Income and Wealth, Series 1*, ed. E. Lundberg, International Association for Research in Income and Wealth (Cambridge, Bowes and Bowes, 1951).

JASAY, A. E. [1960] 'The Working of the Radcliffe Monetary System', *Oxford Economic Papers*, N.S. vol. 12, no. 2, June 1960, p. 170.

JAY, D. [1938] *The Socialist Case* (London, Faber and Faber).

JEWKES, J. [1948] *Ordeal by Planning* (London, Macmillan).

JOHNSON, H. G. [1961] 'The *General Theory* after Twenty-five Years', *American Economic Review*, vol. 51, no. 2, May 1961, p. 1.

JOHNSON, H. G. [1962] 'Monetary Theory and Policy', *American Economic Review*, vol. 52, no. 3, June 1962, p. 335.

KALACHEK, E. and WESTEBBE, R. [1961] 'Rates of Unemployment in Great Britain and the United States, 1950–1960', *Review of Economics and Statistics*, vol. 43, no. 4, November 1961, p. 340.

KALDOR, N. [1955] *An Expenditure Tax* (London, Allen and Unwin).

KALDOR, N. [1958] 'Monetary Policy, Economic Stability and Growth', *Committee on the Working of the Monetary System: Principal Memoranda of Evidence*, part XIII, no. 20, p. 146 (London, H.M. Stationery Office, 1960).

KALECKI, M. [1937] 'The Principle of Increasing Risk', *Economica*, N.S. vol. 4, no. 16, November 1937, p. 440.

KALECKI, M. [1943] *Studies in Economic Dynamics* (London, Allen and Unwin).

KALECKI, M. [1944] 'Employment in the United Kingdom during and after the Transition Period', *Bulletin of the Oxford Institute of Statistics*, vol. 6, no. 16–17, 4 December 1944, p. 265.

KATONA, G. [1945] *Price Control and Business: Field Studies among Producers and Distributors of Consumer Goods in the Chicago Area, 1942–44*, Cowles Commission for Research in Economics, Monograph 9 (Bloomington (Ind.), Principia Press).

KENEN, P. B. [1960] *British Monetary Policy and the Balance of Payments, 1951–1957*, Harvard Economic Studies 116 (Cambridge (Mass.), Harvard University Press).

KENNEDY, C. [1960] 'Inflation and the Bond Rate', *Oxford Economic Papers*, N.S. vol. 12, no. 3, October 1960, p. 269.

KEYNES, LORD (J. M. Keynes) [1923] *A Tract on Monetary Reform* (London, Macmillan).

KEYNES, LORD (J. M. Keynes) [1930] *A Treatise on Money* (London, Macmillan).

KEYNES, LORD (J. M. Keynes) [1936] *The General Theory of Employment, Interest and Money* (London, Macmillan).

KEYNES, LORD (J. M. Keynes) [1940] *How to Pay for the War: A Radical Plan for the Chancellor of the Exchequer* (London, Macmillan).

KHUSRO, A. M. [1952] 'An Investigation of Liquidity Preference', *Yorkshire Bulletin of Economic and Social Research*, vol. 4, no. 1, January 1952, p. 1.

KING, W. T. C. [1946] 'Gilt-edged and the Volume of Money', *Banker*, vol. 80, no. 249, October 1946, p. 7.

KISSELGOFF, A. [1952] *Factors affecting the Demand for Consumer Instalment Sales Credit*, Technical Paper 7 (New York, National Bureau of Economic Research).

KLEIN, L. R. [1947] *The Keynesian Revolution* (New York, Macmillan).

KLEIN, L. R. [1950] *Economic Fluctuations in the United States, 1921–1941*, Cowles Commission for Research in Economics, Monograph 11 (New York, Wiley).

KLEIN, L. R. [1951] 'Studies in Investment Behavior', in *Conference on Business Cycles*, Special Conference Series 2 (New York, National Bureau of Economic Research).

KLEIN, L. R. [1955] 'Patterns of Savings: The Surveys of 1953 and 1954', *Bulletin of the Oxford Institute of Statistics*, vol. 17, no. 2, May 1955, p. 173.

KLEIN, L. R. and GOLDBERGER, A. S. [1955] *An Econometric Model of the United States, 1929–1952*, Contributions to Economic Analysis 9 (Amsterdam, North-Holland Publishing Company).

KLEIN, L. R., STRAW, K. H. and VANDOME, P. [1956] 'Savings and Finances of the Upper Income Classes', *Bulletin of the Oxford University Institute of Statistics*, vol. 18, no. 4, November 1956, p. 293.

KLEIN, L. R. [1958] 'The British Propensity to Save', *Journal of the Royal Statistical Society, Series A*, vol. 121, part 1, p. 60.

KLEIN, L. R. and BALL, R. J. [1959] 'Some Econometrics of the Determination of Absolute Prices and Wages', *Economic Journal*, vol. 69, no. 275, September 1959, p. 465.

KLEIN, L. R., BALL, R. J., HAZLEWOOD, A. and VANDOME, P. [1961] *An Econometric Model of the United Kingdom* (Oxford, Blackwell).

KRAGH, B. [1955] 'The Meaning and Use of Liquidity Curves in Keynesian Interest Theory', *International Economic Papers*, no. 5, p. 155.

KUZNETS, S. [1952] 'Proportion of Capital Formation to National Product', *American Economic Review*, vol. 42, no. 2, May 1952, p. 507.

LABOUR PARTY [1945] *Let us Face the Future: A Declaration of Labour Policy for the Consideration of the Nation* (London).

LAVINGTON, F. [1921] *The English Capital Market* (London, Methuen).

LEYSHON, A. M. [1957] 'Import Restrictions in Post-war Britain', *Scottish Journal of Political Economy*, vol. 4, no. 3, October 1957, p. 177.

LIPSEY, R. G. [1960] 'The Relation between Unemployment and the Rate of Change of Money Wage Rates in the United Kingdom, 1862–1957: A Further Analysis', *Economica*, N.S. vol. 27, no. 105, February 1960, p. 1.

LIPSEY, R. G. and STEUER, M. D. [1961] 'The Relation between Profits and Wage Rates', *Economica*, N.S. vol. 28, no. 110, May 1961, p. 137.

LITTLE, I. M. D. [1952] 'Fiscal Policy', in *The British Economy, 1945–1950*, ed. G. D. N. Worswick and P. H. Ady (Oxford, Clarendon Press).

LITTLE, I. M. D. [1962] 'Fiscal Policy', in *The British Economy in the nineteen-fifties*, ed. G. D. N. Worswick and P. H. Ady (Oxford, Clarendon Press).

LOMAX, K. S. [1959] 'Production and Productivity Movements in the United Kingdom since 1900', *Journal of the Royal Statistical Society, Series A*, vol. 122, part 2, p. 185.

LOVELL, M. [1961] 'Manufacturers' Inventories, Sales Expectations, and the Acceleration Principle', *Econometrica*, vol. 29, no. 3, July 1961, p. 293.

LUBOFF, A. [1956] 'Some Aspects of Post-war Company Finance: An Analysis of Tabulations of Company Accounts published in *The Economist*', *Accounting Research*, vol. 7, no. 2, April 1956, p. 154.

LUNDBERG, E. [1937] *Studies in the Theory of Economic Expansion*, Stockholm Economic Studies 6 (London, King).

LUNDBERG, E. [1953] *Business Cycles and Economic Policy*, translated by J. Potter (London, Allen and Unwin, 1957).

LUNDBERG, E. [1959] 'The Profitability of Investment', *Economic Journal*, vol. 69, no. 276, December 1959, p. 653.

LUTZ, F. A. [1945] 'The Interest Rate and Investment in a Dynamic Economy', *American Economic Review*, vol. 35, no. 5, December 1945, p. 811.

LYDALL, H. F. [1955] *British Incomes and Savings* (Oxford, Blackwell).

LYDALL, H. F. [1957] 'The Impact of the Credit Squeeze on Small and Medium-sized Manufacturing Firms', *Economic Journal*, vol. 67, no. 267, September 1957, p. 415.

MCCALLUM, R. B. and READMAN, A. [1947] *The British General Election of 1945* (London, Oxford University Press).

MACDOUGALL, SIR DONALD (G. D. A. MacDougall) [1951] 'British and American Exports: A Study suggested by the Theory of Comparative Costs. Part 1', *Economic Journal*, vol. 61, no. 244, December 1951, p. 697.

MACKINTOSH, A. S. [1963] *The Development of Firms: An Empirical Study with special reference to the Economic Effects of Taxation* (Cambridge, University Press).

MADDISON, A. [1959] 'Economic Growth in Western Europe, 1870–1957', *Banca nazionale del Lavoro Quarterly Review*, no. 48, March 1959, p. 58.

MARQUAND, J. [1960] 'Earnings-drift in the United Kingdom, 1948–57', *Oxford Economic Papers*, N.S. vol. 12, no. 1, February 1960, p. 77.

MARRIS, R. L. [1954] 'The Position of Economics and Economists in the Government Machine: A Comparative Critique of the United Kingdom and the Netherlands', *Economic Journal*, vol. 64, no. 256, December 1954, p. 759.

MARRIS, S. [1961] 'Wage Determination in Selected Countries', appendix 4 to *The Problem of Rising Prices*, Organisation for European Economic Co-operation (Paris).

MARSHALL, A. [1920] *Principles of Economics: An Introductory Volume, 8th ed.* (London, Macmillan, 1938).

MEADE, J. E. [1936] *An Introduction to Economic Analysis and Policy* (London, Oxford University Press).

MEADE, J. E. and ANDREWS, P. W. S. [1938] 'Summary of Replies to Questions on Effects of Interest Rates', in *Oxford Studies in the Price Mechanism*, ed. T. Wilson and P. W. S. Andrews (Oxford, Clarendon Press, 1951).

MEADE, J. E. [1948] *Planning and the Price Mechanism: The Liberal-Socialist Solution* (London, Allen and Unwin).

METZLER, L. A. [1941] 'The Nature and Stability of Inventory Cycles', *Review of Economic Statistics*, vol. 23, no. 3, August 1941, p. 113.

METZLER, L. A. [1947] 'Factors Governing the Length of Inventory Cycles', *Review of Economic Statistics*, vol. 29, no. 1, February 1947, p. 1.

MEYER, J. R. and KUH, E. [1957] *The Investment Decision: An Empirical Study*, Harvard Economic Studies 102 (Cambridge (Mass.), Harvard University Press).

MITCHELL, J. [1956] *Economic Planning and the Long-term Programme* (thesis submitted to the University of Nottingham).

MODIGLIANI, F. and BRUMBERG, R. [1954] 'Utility Analysis and the Consumption Function: An Interpretation of Cross-section Data', in *Post-Keynesian Economics*, ed. K. K. Kurihara (London, Allen and Unwin, 1955).

MODIGLIANI, F. [1957] 'Business Reasons for Holding Inventories and their Macro-economic Implications', in *Problems of Capital Formation: Concepts, Measurement, and Controlling Factors*, National Bureau of Economic Research, Studies in Income and Wealth 19 (Princeton (N.J.), University Press).

MORGAN, E. V. [1960] *The Structure of Property Ownership in Great Britain* (Oxford, Clarendon Press).

MORRISON, LORD (Herbert Morrison) [1954] *Government and Parliament: A Survey from the Inside* (London, Oxford University Press).

MORRISON, LORD (Herbert Morrison) [1960] 'The Great Health Service Row', 5th and last of a series of extracts from *Herbert Morrison: An Autobiography* (London, Odhams Press, 1960), *Sunday Times*, 3 April 1960, p. 14.

MORTON, W. A. [1950] 'Trade Unionism, Full Employment and Inflation', *American Economic Review*, vol. 40, no. 1, March 1950, p. 13.

MUSGRAVE, R. A. and MILLER, M. H. [1948] 'Built-in Flexibility', *American Economic Review*, vol. 38, no. 1, March 1948, p. 122.

MUSGRAVE, R. A. [1951] 'Money, Liquidity and the Valuation of Assets', in *Money, Trade, and Economic Growth: in honor of John Henry Williams* (New York, Macmillan).

MUSGRAVE, R. A. [1959] *The Theory of Public Finance: A Study in Public Economy* (New York, McGraw-Hill).

NATIONAL INSTITUTE OF ECONOMIC AND SOCIAL RESEARCH [1956] *Company Income and Finance, 1949–53* (London).

NEEDLEMAN, L. [1960] 'The Demand for Domestic Appliances', *National Institute Economic Review*, no. 12, November 1960, p. 24.

NEILD, R. R. and SHIRLEY, E. A. [1961] 'Economic Review: An Assessment of Forecasts, 1959–1960', *National Institute Economic Review*, no. 15, May 1961, p. 12.

NEUMARK, F. [1959] 'Fiscal Policy as a Weapon to Control Inflation', in *Inflation: Proceedings of a Conference held by the International Economic Association*, ed. D. C. Hague (London, Macmillan, 1962).

NURKSE, R. [1952] 'The Cyclical Pattern of Inventory Investment', *Quarterly Journal of Economics*, vol. 66, no. 3, August 1952, p. 385.

OLIVER, F. R. [1961] *The Control of Hire-Purchase* (London, Allen and Unwin).

PAIGE, D. C. [1961] 'Economic Growth: The Last Hundred Years', *National Institute Economic Review*, no. 16, July 1961, p. 24.

PAISH, F. W. [1959] 'Gilt-edged and the Money Supply', *Banker*, vol. 109, no. 396, January 1959, p. 17.

PAISH, F. W. [1962] *Studies in an Inflationary Economy: The United Kingdom, 1948–1961* (London, Macmillan).

PATINKIN, D. [1948] 'Price Flexibility and Full Employment', *American Economic Review*, vol. 38, no. 4, September 1948, p. 543.

PATINKIN, D. [1956] *Money, Interest and Prices: An Integration of Monetary and Value Theory* (Evanston (Ill.), Row, Peterson).

PEARSE, P. H. [1962] 'Automatic Stabilization and the British Taxes on Income', *Review of Economic Studies*, vol. 29, no. 79, February 1962, p. 124.

PEP (Political and Economic Planning) [1952] *Government and Industry: A Survey of the Relations between the Government and Privately-owned Industry* (London).

PEP (Political and Economic Planning) [1961] 'Economic Planning in France', *Planning*, vol. 27, no. 454, April 1961.

PHILLIPS, A. W. [1958] 'The Relation between Unemployment and the Rate of Change of Money Wage Rates in the United Kingdom, 1861–1957', *Economica*, N.S. vol. 25, no. 100, November 1958, p. 283.

PHILLIPS, A. W. [1962] 'Employment, Inflation and Growth', *Economica*, N.S. vol. 29, no. 113, February 1962, p. 1.

PIGOU, A. C. [1945] *Lapses from Full Employment* (London, Macmillan).

PLEASE, S. [1959] 'The Counter-cyclical Behaviour of Public Investment in the United Kingdom since the War', *Public Finance*, vol. 14, no. 3–4, p. 269.

PREST, A. R. [1962] 'The Sensitivity of the Yield of Personal Income Tax in the United Kingdom', *Economic Journal*, vol. 72, no. 287, September 1962, p. 576.

RAY, G. F. [1960] 'British Imports of Manufactured Goods', *National Institute Economic Review*, no. 8, March 1960, p. 12.

RAY, G. F. [1961] 'British Imports of Manufactures', *National Institute Economic Review*, no. 15, May 1961, p. 36.

REDDAWAY, W. B. and SMITH, A. D. [1960] 'Progress in British Manufacturing Industries in the Period 1948–54', *Economic Journal*, vol. 70, no. 277, March 1960, p. 17.

ROBBINS, LORD (Lionel Robbins) [1947] *The Economic Problem in Peace and War : Some Reflections on Objectives and Mechanisms*, Marshall Lecture (London, Macmillan).

ROBBINS, LORD (Lionel Robbins) [1947] 'Inquest on the Crisis', *Lloyds Bank Review*, N.S. no. 6, October 1947, p. 1.

ROBBINS, LORD (Lionel Robbins) [1951] *The Balance of Payments*, Stamp Memorial Lecture, 1951 (London, Athlone Press).

ROBBINS, LORD (Lionel Robbins) [1957] 'A "Monarch" in the City', *Listener*, vol. 57, no. 1471, 6 June 1957, p. 913.

ROBBINS, LORD (Lionel Robbins) [1958] 'Thoughts on the Crisis', *Lloyds Bank Review*, N.S. no. 48, April 1958, p. 1.

ROBBINS, LORD (Lionel Robbins) [1960] 'Monetary Theory and the Radcliffe Report', in *Politics and Economics: Papers in Political Economy*, by Lord Robbins (London, Macmillan, 1963).

ROBERTSON, SIR DENNIS [1954] 'The Path of Progress towards Currency Convertibility', *Optima*, vol. 4, no. 1, March 1954, p. 1.

ROBINSON, J. [1952] *The Rate of Interest and Other Essays* (London, Macmillan).

ROSA, R. V. [1951] 'Interest Rates and the Central Bank', in *Money, Trade, and Economic Growth: in honor of John Henry Williams* (New York, Macmillan).

ROSE, H. B. [1960] 'Financial Institutions and Monetary Policy', *Bankers' Magazine*, vol. 190, no. 1396, July 1960, p. 14.

ROSENBERG, N. [1960] *Economic Planning in the British Building Industry, 1945–49* (Philadelphia (Pa.), University of Pennsylvania Press).

ROWAN, D. C. [1961] 'Radcliffe Monetary Theory', *Economic Record*, vol. 37, no. 80, December 1961, p. 420.

SAHNI, I. M. [1951] 'A Study of Share Prices, 1918–1947', *Yorkshire Bulletin of Economic and Social Research*, vol. 3, no. 1, February 1951, p. 57.

SAYERS, R. S. [1940] 'Business Men and the Terms of Borrowing', in *Oxford Studies in the Price Mechanism*, ed. T. Wilson and P. W. S. Andrews (Oxford, Clarendon Press, 1951).

SAYERS, R. S. [1951] 'The Rate of Interest as a Weapon of Economic Policy', in *Oxford Studies in the Price Mechanism*, ed. T. Wilson and P. W. S. Andrews (Oxford, Clarendon Press).

SAYERS, R. S. [1956] *Financial Policy, 1939–45*, History of the Second World War, U.K. Civil Series (London, H.M. Stationery Office and Longmans, Green).

SCOTT, M. FG. [1958] 'Changes in Stocks of Mainly Imported Goods in the United Kingdom', *Bulletin of the Oxford University Institute of Statistics*, vol. 20, no. 1, February 1958, p. 53.

SCOTT, M. FG. [1959] 'What should be done about the Sterling Area?', *Bulletin of the Oxford University Institute of Statistics*, vol. 21, no. 4, November 1959, p. 213.

SCOTT, M. FG. [1963] *A Study of United Kingdom Imports*, National Institute of Economic and Social Research, Economic and Social Studies 20 (Cambridge, University Press).

SHACKLE, G. L. S. [1946] 'Interest-rates and the Pace of Investment', *Economic Journal*, vol. 56, no. 221, March 1946, p. 1.

SHACKLE, G. L. S. [1961] 'Recent Theories concerning the Nature and Role of Interest', *Economic Journal*, vol. 71, no. 282, June 1961, p. 209.

SHONFIELD, A. [1958] *British Economic Policy since the War* (Harmondsworth (Mx.), Penguin Books).

SOLOW, R. M. [1957] 'Technical Change and the Aggregate Production Function', *Review of Economics and Statistics*, vol. 39, no. 3, August 1957, p. 312.

STONE, J. R. N. [1951] 'The Use and Development of National Income and Expenditure Estimates', in *Lessons of the British War Economy*, ed. D. N. Chester, National Institute of Economic and Social Research, Economic and Social Studies 10 (Cambridge, University Press).

STONE, J. R. N. and ROWE, D. A. [1956] 'Aggregate Consumption and Investment Functions for the Household Sector considered in the Light of British Experience', *Nationaløkonomisk Tidsskrift*, vol. 94, no. 1–2, p. 1.

STONE, J. R. N. and ROWE, D. A. [1958] 'Dynamic Demand Functions: Some Econometric Results', *Economic Journal*, vol. 68, no. 270, June 1958, p. 256.

STRAW, K. H. [1956] 'Consumers' Net Worth: the 1953 Savings Survey', *Bulletin of the Oxford University Institute of Statistics*, vol. 18, no. 1, February 1956, p. 1.

TEW, B. [1952] 'The Finance of Investment', *Oxford Economic Papers*, N.S. vol. 4, no. 2, July 1952, p. 108.

TEW, B. [1952] *International Monetary Co-operation, 1945–52* (London, Hutchinson's University Library).

TEW, B. and HENDERSON, R. F., editors [1959] *Studies in Company Finance: A Symposium on the Economic Analysis and Interpretation of British Company Accounts*, National Institute of Economic and Social Research, Economic and Social Studies 17 (Cambridge, University Press).

THEIL, H. [1955] 'Who forecasts best?', *International Economic Papers*, no. 5, p. 194.

THEIL, H. [1958] *Economic forecasts and policy*, Contributions to Economic Analysis 15 (Amsterdam, North-Holland Publishing Company).

THORNEYCROFT, P. [1960] 'Policy in Practice', in *Not Unanimous: A Rival Verdict to Radcliffe's on Money*, ed. A. Seldon (London, Institute of Economic Affairs).

TINBERGEN, J. [1939] *Statistical Testing of Business-Cycle Theories. Vol. I. A Method and its Application to Investment Activity. Vol. II. Business Cycles in the United States of America, 1919–1932*, Economic and Financial Series, 1938.II.A.23 and 1939.II.A.16 (Geneva, League of Nations).

TINBERGEN, J. and POLAK, J. J. [1950] *The Dynamics of Business Cycles: A Study in Economic Fluctuations* (London, Routledge and Kegan Paul).

TINBERGEN, J. [1951] *Business Cycles in the United Kingdom, 1871–1914*, Verhandelingen der K. Nederlandse Akademie van Wetenschapen, afd. Letterkunde, N.S. vol. 57, no. 4 (Amsterdam, North-Holland Publishing Company).

TINBERGEN, J. [1956] *Economic Policy: Principles and Design*, Contributions to Economic Analysis (Amsterdam, North-Holland Publishing Company).

TOBIN, J. [1947] 'Liquidity Preference and Monetary Policy', *Review of Economic Statistics*, vol. 29, no. 2, May 1947, p. 124.

TOBIN, J. [1956] 'The Interest-Elasticity of Transactions Demand for Cash', *Review of Economics and Statistics*, vol. 38, no. 3, August 1956, p. 241.

TOBIN, J. [1958] 'Liquidity Preference as Behavior towards Risk', *Review of Economic Studies*, vol. 25, no. 67, February 1958, p. 65.

TOBIN, J. [1961] 'Money, Capital, and other Stores of Value', *American Economic Review*, vol. 51, no. 2, May 1961, p. 26.

TRESS, R. C. [1953–7 [Various titles] *London and Cambridge Economic Bulletin*, N.S. no. 6, June 1953, p. ii, no. 10, June 1954, p. iv, no. 14, June 1955, p. ii, no. 18, June 1956, p. ii and no. 22, June 1957, p. ii.

TRESS, R. C. [1959] 'The Contribution of Economic Theory to Economic Prognostication', *Economica*, N.S. vol. 26, no. 103, August 1959, p. 194.

TRIFFIN, R. [1957] *Europe and the Money Muddle: From Bilateralism to Near-Convertibility, 1947–1956*, Yale Studies in Economics 7 (New Haven (Conn.), Yale University Press).

TURNER, H. A. [1959] 'Employment Fluctuations, Labour Supply and Bargaining Power', *Manchester School of Economic and Social Studies*, vol. 27, no. 2, May 1959, p. 175.

TURVEY, R. [1949] 'A Further Note on the Inflationary Gap', *Ekonomisk Tidskrift*, vol. 51, no. 2, June 1949, p. 92.

TURVEY, R. [1960] *Interest Rates and Asset Prices* (London, Allen and Unwin).

WEMELSFELDER, J. [1960] 'The Short-term Effect of the Lowering of Import Duties in Germany', *Economic Journal*, vol. 70, no. 277, March 1960, p. 94.

WHITE, W. H. [1956] 'Interest Inelasticity of Investment Demand: The Case from Business Attitude Surveys Re-examined', *American Economic Review*, vol. 46, no. 4, September 1956, p. 565.

WHITIN, T. M. [1952] 'Inventory Control in Theory and Practice', *Quarterly Journal of Economics*, vol. 66, no. 4, November 1952, p. 502.

WICKSELL, K. [1898] *Interest and Prices: A Study of the Causes Regulating the Value of Money*, translated by R. F. Kahn (London, Macmillan, 1936).

WILLIAMS, F. (Lord Francis-Williams) [1952] *Ernest Bevin: Portrait of a Great Englishman* (London, Hutchinson).

WOOTTON, LADY (Barbara Wootton) [1934] *Plan or No Plan* (London, Gollancz).

II.   OFFICIAL PUBLICATIONS

(1) UNITED KINGDOM

1952, Cmd. 8717] Cabinet Office. *Commonwealth Economic Conference: Final Communiqué* (London, H.M. Stationery Office).

[—] Central Statistical Office. *Annual Abstract of Statistics* (London, H.M. Stationery Office).

[—] Central Statistical Office. *Economic Trends* (London, H.M. Stationery Office, monthly).

[—] Central Statistical Office. *Monthly Digest of Statistics* (London, H.M. Stationery Office).

[—] Central Statistical Office. *National Income and Expenditure* (London, H.M. Stationery Office, annual).

[1951] Central Statistical Office. *Statistical Digest of the War*, History of the Second World War, U.K. Civil Series (London, H.M. Stationery Office and Longmans, Green).

[1956] Central Statistical Office. *National Income Statistics: Sources and Methods* (London, H.M. Stationery Office).

—] H.M. Customs and Excise. *Annual Statement of the Trade of the United Kingdom with Commonwealth Countries and Foreign Countries* (London, H.M. Stationery Office).

1945, Cmd. 6709] Foreign Office. *Proposals for Consideration by an International Conference on Trade and Employment*, Miscellaneous No. 15 (1945) (London, H.M. Stationery Office).

[1948, Cmd. 7572] Foreign Office. *European Co-operation: Memoranda submitted to the Organisation for European Economic Co-operation relating to Economic Affairs in the period 1949 to 1953* (London, H.M. Stationery Office).

[1958] Home Office. *Proceedings of the Tribunal appointed to Inquire into Allegations that Information about the Raising of Bank Rate was improperly disclosed, with the Minutes of Evidence taken before the Tribunal, December 1957* (London, H.M. Stationery Office).

[1958, Cmnd. 350] Home Office. *Report of the Tribunal appointed to Inquire into Allegations of Improper Disclosure of Information relating to the Raising of the Bank Rate* (London, H.M. Stationery Office).

[—] *House of Commons: Parliamentary Debates* (London, H.M. Stationery Office, daily or weekly).

[—] *House of Lords: Parliamentary Debates* (London, H.M. Stationery Office, daily or weekly).

[1962, Cmnd. 1598] H.M. Inland Revenue. *Report of the Commissioners of H.M. Inland Revenue for the year ended 31st March 1961: 104th Report* (London, H.M. Stationery Office).

[—] Ministry of Agriculture, Fisheries and Food. *Domestic Food Consumption and Expenditure: Annual Report of the National Food Survey Committee* (London, H.M. Stationery Office).

[1958, Cmnd. 571] Ministry of Housing and Local Government, Minister for Welsh Affairs and Secretary of State for Scotland. *House Purchase: Proposed Government Scheme* (London, H.M. Stationery Office).

[1960, Cmnd. 1027] Ministry of Housing and Local Government. *Report* (London, H.M. Stationery Office).

[—] Ministry of Labour. *Gazette* (London, H.M. Stationery Office, monthly).

[—] Ministry of Labour. *Statistics on Incomes, Prices, Employment and Production* (London, H.M. Stationery Office, quarterly).

[1957, Cmnd. 159] Ministry of Labour and National Service. *Report of a Court of Inquiry into a Dispute between Employers who are Members of the Engineering and Allied Employers' National Federation and Workmen who are Members of Trade Unions affiliated to the Confederation of Shipbuilding and Engineering Unions* (London, H.M. Stationery Office).

[1944, Cmd. 6527] Ministry of Reconstruction. *Employment Policy* (London, H.M. Stationery Office).

[1948, Cmd. 7321] Prime Minister. *Statement on Personal Incomes, Costs and Prices* (London, H.M. Stationery Office).

[1955, Cmd. 9474] Royal Commission on the Taxation of Profits and Income. *Final Report* (London, H.M. Stationery Office).

[—] Treasury. *Economic Survey* (London, H.M. Stationery Office, annual 1947–1962).

[—] Treasury. *Financial Statement* (London, H.M. Stationery Office, annual).

[—] Treasury. *National Income and Expenditure of the United Kingdom* (later *Preliminary Estimates of National Income and Expenditure*) (London, H.M. Stationery Office, annual).

[—] Treasury. *Public Investment in Great Britain* (London, H.M. Stationery Office, annual).

[—] Treasury. *United Kingdom Balance of Payments* (London, H.M. Stationery Office, twice yearly).

[1931, Cmd. 3897] Treasury. *Committee on Finance and Industry: Report* (Macmillan Report) (London, H.M. Stationery Office).

[1941, Cmd. 6261] Treasury. *An Analysis of the Sources of War Finance and an Estimate of the National Income and Expenditure in 1938 and 1940* (London, H.M. Stationery Office).

[1944, Cmd. 6546] Treasury. *United Nations Monetary and Financial Conference, Bretton Woods, New Hampshire, U.S.A., July 1 to 22, 1944: Final Act* (London, H.M. Stationery Office).

[1945, Cmd. 6645] Treasury. *Capital Issues Control: Memorandum of Guidance to the Capital Issues Committee* (London, H.M. Stationery Office).

[1945, Cmd. 6707] Treasury. *Statistical Material presented during the Washington Negotiations* (London, H.M. Stationery Office).

[1945, Cmd. 6708] Treasury. *Financial Agreement between the Governments of the United States and the United Kingdom dated 6th December 1945, together with a Joint Statement regarding Settlement for Lend-Lease, Reciprocal Aid, Surplus War Property and Claims* (London, H.M. Stationery Office).

[1947, Cmd. 7268] Treasury. *Capital Investment in 1948* (London, H.M. Stationery Office).

[1950, Cmd. 7969] Treasury. *Final Report of the [Crick] Committee on the Form of the Government Accounts* (London, H.M. Stationery Office).

[1951, Cmd. 8318] Treasury. *Control of Dividends* (London, H.M. Stationery Office).

[1959, Cmnd. 827] Treasury. *Committee on the Working of the Monetary System: Report* (Radcliffe Report) (London, H.M. Stationery Office.)

[1959] Treasury. *United Kingdom Balance of Payments, 1946–1957* (London, H.M. Stationery Office).

[1960] Treasury. *Committee on the Working of the Monetary System: Minutes of Evidence* (London, H.M. Stationery Office).

[1960] Treasury. *Committee on the Working of the Monetary System: Principal Memoranda of Evidence* (London, H.M. Stationery Office).

[1962, H.C. 142 of 1961–62] Treasury. *Estimates, 1962–63 . . . Memorandum by the Financial Secretary to the Treasury* (London, H.M. Stationery Office).

(2) UNITED STATES OF AMERICA

[1957] Federal Reserve System. *Consumer Instalment Credit* (Washington, Government Printing Office).

(3) INTERNATIONAL

COMMITTEE OF EUROPEAN ECONOMIC CO-OPERATION [1947] *July–September 1947. Vol. I. General Report* (London, H.M. Stationery Office).

ORGANISATION FOR EUROPEAN ECONOMIC CO-OPERATION (*later* ORGANISATION FOR ECONOMIC CO-OPERATION AND DEVELOPMENT). *Statistical Bulletins: General Statistics* (Paris, 6 times yearly).

[1950] *Internal Financial Stability in Member Countries* (Paris).

[1951] *Economic Progress and Problems of Western Europe*, Third Report of the O.E.E.C. (Paris).

[1958] *A Decade of Co-operation: achievements and perspectives*, Ninth Report of the O.E.E.C. (Paris).

[1961] *The Problem of Rising Prices; by William Fellner, Milton Gilbert, Bent Hansen, Richard Kahn, Friedrich Lutz, Pieter de Wolff* (Paris).

UNITED NATIONS. Economic Commission for Europe. *Economic Survey of Europe* (Geneva, annual).

Statistical Office. *Monthly Bulletin of Statistics* (New York).

[1961] Statistical Office. *Standard International Trade Classification, revised*, Statistical Papers M 34 (New York).

INDEX

n. = footnote

Full employment output, *see* Capacity of the economy

Gaitskell, H. T. N.: Minister of State for Economic Affairs, 34; concern with devaluation, 43 n.; and negotiations for the European Payments Union, 52; Chancellor of the Exchequer, 54–65; on cost inflation, 58; budget, 58–9, 198–201, 205; and monetary policy, 59–60, 238; on Mr Butler's metaphors, 71 n.; on Lord Cherwell and convertibility, 82 n.

Galbraith, J. K., on price control, 167 n., 172

Gardner, R. N.: on loan negotiations, 17 n., 19 n.; on convertibility in 1947, 23 n., 25 n.

Gaskin, M., on *Radcliffe Report*, 323 n., 324 n.

Gilbert, M., part author, *The Problem of Rising Prices*, 353 n., 366 n., 395 n., 402 n.

Goldberger, A. S., 127, 289 n.

Government (current) expenditure: fluctuations in, 15, 39, 74, 93, 382–3; attempts to cut, 45–6, 101–2; defence expenditure in 1951, 56–7, 60–1 n.; strategic stockpiling, 57, 64 n., 157; small role in stabilization policy, 180–1; *see also* Food subsidies

Gowing, M. M., 9 n., 144 n., 149 n., 153 n., 163 n.

Grunfeld, Y., on determinants of investment, 291

Gurley, J. G., 300 n., 322 n.

Hall, R. L. (Sir Robert): on use of economics in government, 123 n.; on monetary policy and magic, 258 n.

Hammond, R. J., on wartime control of food prices, 163 n.

Hancock, W. K. (Sir Keith): on wartime economic policy, 9 n.; on direct controls during war, 144 n., 153 n., 163 n.

Hansen, B.: on the inflationary gap, 335 n.; on wage drift, 352; part author, *The Problem of Rising Prices*, 353 n., 366 n., 395 n., 402 n.

Hargreaves, E. L.: on machinery licensing, 149 n.; on price control, 162 n., 163 n.

Harris, R., 246 n., 276 n.

Harrod, R. F. (Sir Roy): on the end of lend-lease, 17 n.; on interest rates and stockbuilding, 292 n.; on economic growth, 395 n.

Hawtrey, R. G. (Sir Ralph): on post-war transition, 13 n.; on interest rates and stockbuilding, 292 n., 294 n.

Hazlewood, A., 127 n., 272 n., 274 n., 278 n., 289 n., 355 n.; post mortem on Klein's model for United Kingdom, 127 n.

Heller, W. W., on investment decisions, 287–8 n.

Hemming, M. F. W., on import controls, 50 n., 153 n., 156 n., 174

Henderson, H. D. (Sir Hubert): in Treasury in war, 14 n.; on planning, 16 n.; on United States Loan Agreement, 25–6 n.; on contra-cyclical variation of public investment, 214 n., 215; on interest rates and investment, 287; on interest rates and stockbuilding, 292 n.

Henderson, P. D., on development councils, 35 n.

Henderson, R. F.: on new issues, 244 n.; ed. *Studies in Company Finance*, 244 n., 288 n., 295 n.

Hicks, J. R.: on reform of exchequer accounts, 183; on stock cycles, 293 n.; on theory of capital, 316 n., 317 n.

Hinchingbrooke, Viscount, on Keynesian budgeting, 67 n.

Hire-purchase controls: changes in prescribed terms, 247–8, 278–82; *Radcliffe Report* on, 259–60; effect of changes on final demand, 370–1; future role for, 408–9; *see also* Consumer credit

Hours worked, as indicator of pressure of demand, 114–15, 367–8; *see also* Multiplier effects

House Purchase and Housing Act, 1959, 249

Hurstfield, J., on materials control, 160 n.

Import controls: extent of, 153–8; effect of, 170–1; general disadvantages of, 401 n.

Imports: cuts in 1947, 26; cuts in 1949, 42; 'liberalization' in 1949–50, 50; cuts in 1951–2, 71, 75, 156–8; forecasts of, 138–41; fluctuations in, 385–90; and changes in stocks of imported materials, 387–90; *see also* Balance of payments fluctuations, Import controls

Income tax: effect (£m.) of changes in, 198–200; level of standard rate, 199 n.

PUBLICATIONS OF THE

NATIONAL INSTITUTE OF ECONOMIC

AND SOCIAL RESEARCH

published by

THE CAMBRIDGE UNIVERSITY PRESS

Books published for the Institute by the Cambridge University Press are available through the ordinary booksellers. They appear in the three series below.

ECONOMIC & SOCIAL STUDIES

*At present out of print.

OCCASIONAL PAPERS

*At present out of print.

STUDIES IN THE NATIONAL INCOME AND EXPENDITURE OF THE UNITED KINGDOM

Published under the joint auspices of the National Institute and the Department of Applied Economics, Cambridge.

1 *The Measurement of Consumers' Expenditure and Behaviour in the United Kingdom, 1920–1938*, vol. 1
By RICHARD STONE, assisted by D. A. ROWE and by W. J. CORLETT, RENEE HURSTFIELD, MURIEL POTTER. 1954. pp. 448. £7 10s. net.

3 *Consumers' Expenditure in the United Kingdom, 1900–1919*
By A. R. PREST, assisted by A. A. ADAMS. 1954. pp. 196. 55s. net.

5 *Wages and Salaries in the United Kingdom, 1920–1938*
By AGATHA CHAPMAN, assisted by ROSE KNIGHT. 1953. pp. 254. 75s. net.

THE NATIONAL INSTITUTE OF ECONOMIC AND SOCIAL RESEARCH

publishes regularly

THE NATIONAL INSTITUTE ECONOMIC REVIEW

A quarterly Review of the economic situation and prospects.

Annual subscription £2; single issues 12s. 6d. each.

The Review is available directly from N.I.E.S.R.,
2, Dean Trench St., Smith Square, London, S.W.1.

The Institute has also published

FACTORY LOCATION AND INDUSTRIAL MOVEMENT: a Study of Recent Experience

in Britain, volumes I and II

By W. F. Luttrell

N.I.E.S.R. 1962. pp. 1,080. £5 5s. net the set.
This is also available directly from the Institute.